The World's Religions in Figures

The World's Religions in Figures

An Introduction to International Religious Demography

Todd M. Johnson and Brian J. Grim

With Gina A. Bellofatto

Foreword by Peter L. Berger

WILEY-BLACKWELL

A John Wiley & Sons, Ltd., Publication

This edition first published 2013
© 2013 John Wiley & Sons, Ltd

Wiley-Blackwell is an imprint of John Wiley & Sons, formed by the merger of Wiley's global
Scientific, Technical and Medical business with Blackwell Publishing.

Registered Office
John Wiley & Sons, Ltd, The Atrium, Southern Gate, Chichester, West Sussex, PO19 8SQ, UK

Editorial Offices
350 Main Street, Malden, MA 02148-5020, USA
9600 Garsington Road, Oxford, OX4 2DQ, UK
The Atrium, Southern Gate, Chichester, West Sussex, PO19 8SQ, UK

For details of our global editorial offices, for customer services, and for information about
how to apply for permission to reuse the copyright material in this book please see our
website at www.wiley.com/wiley-blackwell.

The right of Todd M. Johnson and Brian J. Grim to be identified as the authors of this work
has been asserted in accordance with the UK Copyright, Designs and Patents Act 1988.

Library of Congress Cataloging-in-Publication Data

Johnson, Todd M. (Todd Michael), 1958–
    The world's religions in figures : an introduction to international religious demography /
Todd M. Johnson, Brian J. Grim; editorial associate, Gina A. Bellofatto.
        pages   cm
    Includes bibliographical references and index.
    ISBN 978-0-470-67454-3 (cloth)
1. Religions–Statistics.   I. Bellofatto, Gina A.   II. Title.
    BL80.3.J65 2013
    200.2′1–dc23
                                                            2012047272

A catalogue record for this book is available from the British Library.

Cover image: Top: Praying with rosary beads © spxChrome. Detail from people praying on
a sajadah © Eray Haciosmanoglu. Priest in robe blessing wine for Communion © kokophoto.
Bottom: Sadhu Indian holyman sitting in the temple © Bartosz Hadyniak. Three Hasidic
Jews © Keith Reicher. Detail of bust of Buddha © Navin Khianey.
Cover design by www.simonlevyassociates.co.uk

Set in 10/12.5pt Galliard by SPi Publisher Services, Pondicherry, India
Printed and bound in Malaysia by Vivar Printing Sdn Bhd

1   2013

Brief Contents

Contents

List of Figures

List of Tables

Foreword

This book is a remarkable achievement. It is the result of many years of work by the two authors, who must be considered the deans of international religious demography, a discipline that now has as its primary location the two centers with which the authors are associated (Todd Johnson with the Center for the Study of Global Christianity, near Boston, and Brian Grim with the Pew Forum for Religion and Public Life, in Washington). It pleases me that they have deposited (if that is the right word in our electronic age) their database at our Institute on Culture, Religion and World Affairs at Boston University. The book, with its plenitude of numerical tables, is a wonderful companion to another recent publication, this one full of maps, by Todd Johnson and Kenneth Ross, *Atlas of Global Christianity* (2009). The two volumes together constitute an indispensable and enormously useful resource for anyone interested in the shape of religion in the contemporary world. These are not books to be read once and all from cover to cover, but rather to be kept close at hand for ready reference (my own case).

The present volume consists of three sections. The first section, the juiciest of the three, contains an overview of the findings. There follows an elaborate discussion of the methodology employed. This is obviously of most interest for any putative practitioners of religious demography, but it is also useful in allaying the skepticism about statistics felt with good reason by many scholars of religion: we know that people lie about their own religious activity or find it difficult to fit themselves into the categories of a survey questionnaire, that numbers declared by religious institutions and by governments are iffy, and that many believers meet in informal or even illegal gatherings which are difficult to count. Johnson and Grim are skeptical themselves, and they explain in great detail how they have developed methods which painstakingly cull credible findings from highly discrepant bodies of evidence. The third section of the volume consists of what they call "case studies" – two from very important areas, the Muslim world and China – to which is added the religious demography of the new nation of South Sudan and of what remains of Sudan after its southern parts seceded. Needless to say, this unhappy region is not very important on the contemporary scene, but the secession is the result of a violent conflict (not yet fully ended) between the Christian South and the Muslim North – an instructive case of what Samuel Huntington famously called "the bloody frontiers of Islam" (in *The Clash of Civilizations*, 1996).

It would be futile, indeed impossible, to summarize the rich contents of the present volume. It contains well over 150 numerical tables (I started to count, gave up before I got to the end). This is a formidable mountain to climb even for someone less numerophobic than me. (I have often explained that, every time arithmetic was taught in my elementary school in Vienna, I had the measles – like three times weekly.) I will not pretend to have studied every table (no one would believe me if I did). I have skimmed through the volume, especially the first section, and often stopped to read especially intriguing portions of the text. What I will do here is to comment briefly on what I think are key findings, some of which throw startling light on the global religious scene. Then I will, also briefly, point out significant political implications that should be of interest to people not particularly enamored of religious demography. Johnson and Grim are obviously fond of numbers. But they succeed in making the numbers speak. Often the numbers make us change the way we look at the world.

Perhaps the most startling findings come from a comparison of two dates – 1910 and 2010. The former date, not so incidentally, marks the international Protestant missionary conference in Edinburgh, which proclaimed the twentieth century as the era of world evangelization. That purpose was remarkably successful. However, in addition to spreading Christianity in general and Protestantism in particular, into previously "heathen" regions, the time span between the two dates saw an amazing demographic shift from the global North to the global South. In 1910 over 80% of Christians lived in Europe and North America; in 2010 that had shrunk to less than 40%. Today the majority of Christians live in Latin America, Africa, and Asia. This shift has many important implications. Possibly the most important is the fact that Christians in the global South (Protestant as well Catholic) are more robustly supernaturalist than their coreligionists in the North. Thus African Christians, for example, live in a world of spirits (divine as well as demonic), miracles, and exorcisms quite different from their Northern brethren – and much closer to the world of the New Testament. This theological fact is now beginning to sink in widely. It is vividly illustrated by developments in the Anglican communion, as dissident conservative Episcopalians in places like the parish in Falls Church, Virginia (where George Washington, no less, used to worship), put themselves under the care of African bishops, and as the Archbishop of York, the second-ranking cleric in the Church of England, is an African. But it is mostly through immigration that Southern Christianity is washing over into the Global North – for example, in the increasing presence of Latinos in the Catholic Church in the United States.

Despite the great successes of Evangelical and especially Pentecostal missionaries in many countries, notably in Latin America, there are now more Catholics than Protestants among Christians globally (51.5%) than there were in 1910 (47.6%). While Catholics may not match Protestants in missionary successes, they keep up demographically by way of fertility. But this comparison obscures an enormously important fact: the dramatic growth in both groupings of what the authors call "Renewalist" Christianity (a less than happy synonym, in my opinion, for what is conventionally called Pentecostal or Charismatic). This is, precisely, a robustly supernaturalist version of the faith, characterized by the "gifts of the spirit," notably miraculous healing and "speaking in tongues." "Renewalists" were 0.2% of all Christians in 1910, but had grown to 25.8% in 2010. Put simply, *at least* one fourth of today's Christians have a worldview much closer to the New Testament than that of most theology professors in Europe and the United States. This fact should be understood in the larger context that, in all likelihood, the majority of all Christians in the global South, not only the Charismatic ones, have a familiar relationship with the supernatural that is much rarer in the North. In other words, the "gifts of the spirit" are even washing up into the suburbs of Washington.

Islam has grown substantially in the relevant time span – from 12.6% of the world population to 22.5% in 2010. In some parts of the world the increase was due to missionary activity, especially in Africa, but mostly it was caused by high fertility. The future projections are interesting; I'll get to them presently. But today the geographical distribution of Muslims is very interesting indeed: The largest number is in Indonesia, followed by India, Pakistan, Bangladesh, and Iran. Egypt occupies the sixth place in this demographic hierarchy. The denizens of Cairo may be justified in thinking of themselves as being at the heart of the *Arab* world, but surely not of the *Muslim* world. In other words, the center of the Muslim world is *not* in the Middle East, as is widely assumed. Arabs can proudly recall that Islam originated in Arabia, that the language of the Qur'an is Arabic, and that the holiest cities for Muslims are indeed in the Middle East. But today most Muslims live in countries to the east of that region.

Those of us who have long pondered the questions raised by so-called secularization theory – the proposition that modernity means a decline of religion – can also derive useful lessons from the demographic data in this volume. If there was a process of secularization in the past, it reached its worldwide peak in 1970, when around 20% of the global population was self-described as "not religious." Needless to say, one might quibble about what this phrase actually means (probably very different things to different people), or for that matter about the categories of "agnostic" and "atheist" used by the authors. Be this as it may, the number of people who can be described as "nones" (having no allegiance to any religion, here arrived at by a combination of "agnostics" and "atheists") stands today at 11.8%. By contrast, there has been a steady increase since 1970 of people who describe themselves as religious. *That* category is projected to be 91% by 2050. Again, this may be due to differential fertility – the religious have more kids – not necessarily to greater religious fervor. In many countries there will be greater religious diversity. If I may beat my own drum in this connection, I have long argued that secularization theory should be replaced by pluralization theory. But that is another story.

I am much intrigued by the authors' projections of future demographics. Of course these are prefaced by the phrase "if present trends continue." The phrase reminds me of the one coined by Herman Kahn, sometimes called the father of futurology – "surprise-free future"; we know all too well how many surprises, many of them very unpleasant, the future may hold. Still, some present trends *will* continue, and it is instructive to imagine the ensuing demographic scenarios.

There is what the authors call "the continued resilience of world religions into the future." Christians in 2010 number 32.8% of the world population, and are projected to number 35.8% in 2050. The corresponding Muslim numbers are, respectively, 22.5% and 27.5%. In other words, there will probably be no great change in the global distribution of the two major religions. There is projected a significant decrease in the number of people under the age of 30 in Muslim-majority countries, from 60% to 50% – bad news for Jihadist recruiters (even worse news would be comparable or larger decreases of unemployed young men in this age bracket). The aforementioned decrease in the "agnostic/atheist" category will likely continue unabatedly, from 11.8% to 8.7%. In other words, the age of triumphant secularity, whether hoped for or feared, is becoming more implausible as we look into the future.

As an old joke has it: As the lady said to the insect specialist after sitting next to him at a dinner party, during which he told her endlessly about his beloved insects – "This is very interesting, if you are interested in it." There are important *political* reasons to be interested in demographic data about religion. This has become increasingly clear to people in international relations and in the policy community since the terrorist attacks of September 11, 2001. The first focus, logically enough, was on Islam. Then grew an understanding of the complexity of the Muslim world, and the insight that religious groups with no terrorist activists can be politically relevant. If the Muslim projection is broken down from the "resilient" total, things become very interesting indeed. The Muslim population in Europe is projected to go from 5.6% now to 6.9% in 2050 – a sizable increase, but hardly supporting the "Eurabia" dystopia evoked by anti-Muslim agitators. In the United States the Muslim population is projected to go from 2.6 millions now to 6.2 millions in 2050. The political implications of this become clear when one reflects that the increase will mean that there will be roughly equal numbers of Muslims and Jews in the country, with probable consequences for US Middle East policy. Demography is also likely to be significant for the domestic future of Israel. Palestinian fertility seems to be declining, while the fertility of Orthodox Jews in Israel (as in America) is expected to remain high. Consequently, demography suggests that there is no basis for the fear (by many Israelis) and the hope (by many Arabs) that there will be before long a Palestinian majority even within the 1967 borders of Israel (not to mention the entire territory "between the river and the sea," that is within the borders of historic Palestine).

China is another focus in this volume. Demography features highly in any speculation about its future. Overall is the much-discussed consequence of the one-child family policy. A shrinking workforce will have to take care of an expanding population of the non-working aged. No religious factors come immediately to mind (unless it be a decline in the Confucian virtue of filial piety). But there are two demographic developments involving religion. Ethnic minorities have been exempted from the one-child policy, thus making for a higher birthrate among ethnic Muslims than among Han Chinese. Also, there has been a big increase in the number of Christians, now estimated by Johnson and Grim to be about 67 millions, or 5% of the population. Given the great difficulties of counting Christians in China, because of the illegal or semi-legal status of many churches, I suspect that this estimate is too low. If present trends continue, the number of Christians is likely to grow considerably. Much of this growth is Protestant, not (as in many other regions) by upwardly mobile poor people, but through the conversion of people who are already middle class (some with the wonderful title of "boss Christians"). One can only speculate on the political effects of an assertive Protestant middle class in China, possibly similar to effects already visible in Latin America.

I think I have said enough on why this book is important and why it should be read by people who are not, and do not aspire to become, religious demographers. Todd Johnson and Brian Grim are to be warmly congratulated and thanked.

Peter L. Berger
Senior Research Fellow
Institute on Culture, Religion and World Affairs, Boston University

Acknowledgments

This book would not have been possible without the support of our two research projects: the Center for the Study of Global Christianity at Gordon-Conwell Theological Seminary in South Hamilton, MA, and Pew-Templeton Global Religious Futures Project at the Pew Research Center's Forum on Religion and Public Life in Washington, DC, funded by the Pew Charitable Trusts and the John Templeton Foundation.

We would not have been able to write this book without significant help from our Editorial Associate, Gina Bellofatto. Gina worked with us from the beginning of this project, organizing and editing the material, filling in the gaps, and keeping us moving in the midst of many other commitments.

At the Center for the Study of Global Christianity we are grateful for the work of our Data Analyst, Peter Crossing, who provided all the detailed tables extracted from the *World Religion Database*. We are also thankful to Research Associate Albert Hickman for copy-editing this text, making numerous suggestions and improvements throughout. Other researchers working at the Center include LouAnn Stropoli, Brad Coon, Shawn Woo, Joanne Yen, Elizabeth LeLievre, Chak Him Chow, Sam Rogers, and Katie Bethea.

At the Pew Research Center, we thank Conrad Hackett, Philip Connor, Juan Carlos Esparza Ochoa, Chris Gao, Noble Kuriakose, Anne Shi, Peter Henne (now at the University of Virginia), Becky Hsu (now at Georgetown University), and Mehtab Karim (now at George Mason University). Also, Vegard Skirbekk, Marcin Stonawski, Michaela Potančoková, and Anne Goujon, researchers at the Age and Cohort Change Project at the International Institute for Advanced Systems Analysis (IIASA), Laxenburg, Austria, contributed to the case studies on Muslim population growth.

We are also grateful to Peter Berger and Robert Hefner at the Institute on Culture, Religion and World Affairs at Boston University for hosting us as Visiting Research Fellows in the Study of International Religious Demography. The *World Religion Database*, on which much of this study is based, is housed there.

The opinions expressed in this book are those of the authors and do not necessarily reflect the views of the organizations with which they are affiliated.

Introduction

Censuses of people have been conducted for several centuries. The science of counting religionists around the world, however, is a relatively new field of study – the development of the academic discipline of international religious demography has taken place largely in the latter part of the twentieth century. In 1969, Hyman Alterman published *Counting People: The Census in History*,[1] one of the first comprehensive treatments of censuses. Our book, over 40 years later, is an attempt to compose an analogous volume on counting religionists around the world. We describe the emerging discipline of international religious demography by examining its methods and techniques in the context of national, regional, and global statistics on religious adherents. We define "religious demography" as the scientific and statistical study of the demographic characteristics of religious populations, primarily with respect to their size, age-sex structure, density, growth, distribution, development, migration, and vital statistics, including the change of religious identity within human populations and how these characteristics relate to other social and economic indicators. In this sense, we go beyond basic demographic features of religion (age, sex, fertility, mortality) and look at religion as a demographic characteristic of human populations deserving its own field of inquiry.

The increased prominence religion has assumed in academic fields including history, sociology, international relations, and a host of others is one of the unexpected developments of the early twenty-first century. In the latter part of the twentieth century, conventional wisdom held that religion was on the wane and, by implication, that the study of religion was of little importance to understanding the world. In particular, leading anthropologists and sociologists such as Anthony F. C. Wallace and Bryan Wilson predicted the demise or even disappearance of religion within a very short time. One of the first sociologists to recant this position was Peter Berger, who

The World's Religions in Figures: An Introduction to International Religious Demography,
First Edition. Todd M. Johnson and Brian J. Grim.
© 2013 John Wiley & Sons, Ltd. Published 2013 by John Wiley & Sons, Ltd.

founded the Institute on Culture, Religion and World Affairs (CURA) at Boston University and later published *The Desecularization of the World*.[2]

Recent books, such as John Micklethwait and Adrian Wooldridge's *God is Back*,[3] show that journalists' and scholars' treatments of religion as a passing fad were not simply minor oversights. *God's Century: Resurgent Religion and Global Politics* by Monica Duffy Toft, Daniel Philpott, and Timothy Samuel Shah[4] offers evidence that a lack of attention to religion has greatly hindered international relations and peacemaking.

In the meantime, the number of sources of religious data has greatly expanded (see chapter 7 for a detailed overview of major sources). Approximately half of the world's national censuses ask questions on religion. Religious communities continue to collect data on their members and publish annual reports of the results. Professional survey groups conduct polls and surveys, increasingly outside of the Western world. Scholars are writing monographs on religious communities, including their demographics. All of these data offer a rich repository of information for an assessment of religious demographics.

While the main purpose of this book is to describe in detail *how* one counts religionists around the world, we felt that it would be helpful to provide a summary of the number of people counted in each religion in the first chapter. While in other publications we have used maps to display these data,[5] in this volume the data are presented in sets of tables. Explanations of the methodology, sources, and techniques of analyses behind these figures follow in the remainder of the book. The documentation for these estimates resides in our databases and research centers: the *World Christian Database*,[6] the *World Religion Database*,[7] the Center for the Study of Global Christianity at Gordon-Conwell Theological Seminary (South Hamilton, MA), and the Pew Research Center's Forum on Religion and Public Life (Washington, DC).

This book is divided into three parts: (1) Overview; (2) Data and Methods; and (3) Case Studies. In addition, we offer a technical glossary and appendix with country-by-country statistics on religion. Each chapter also includes lists of references.

Part I: Overview

The overview offers results of our analysis of religious populations around the world. Detailed tables list the number of adherents in each of the world's major religions by United Nations continents and regions.[8] Religious diversity is also explored via three distinct measurement techniques, highlighting the reality that due to movement of the world's peoples (as well as conversions to and from religion), most countries are becoming more diverse in their religious composition. Next is a comprehensive treatment of the future of religion worldwide, with projections to 2050. The chapter explains the methodology undergirding these projections and makes suggestions for research on the future of religion.

Part I ends with a series of projections to 2050 for the future of the largest world religions, as well as agnostics and atheists. The overview addresses important issues about the status of religion in the beginning of the twenty-first century, issues that have critical implications for governments, non-governmental organizations, religious communities, and others.

Part II: Data and Methods

The chapters on data and methods offer the rationale, techniques, and specific problems associated with counting religionists. They begin by discussing differing definitions of religion, settling on one that allows the creation of a taxonomy of religions and their followers – essential for counting religionists. Also discussed are complexities related specifically to counting religionists, such as multiple religious belonging.

The academic study of religious demography is introduced by examining its context in the broader field of demography. Demography is not well integrated with other academic disciplines, yet at the same time, religious demography is increasingly recognized as impacting foreign policy, development, health, education, and a host of other fields.

The methodology chapters continue with an examination of sources of data on religion. While the three most significant are government censuses, commissioned surveys, and membership reports from the religious communities themselves, other sources of data are investigated and commented on. Part II also considers the limitations of each source of data on religion. We conclude by exploring the three sets of dynamics of religious change – births and deaths, conversions to and conversions from, immigration and emigration – that serve as the foundation for analyzing religious populations around the world.

Part III: Case Studies

The included case studies reproduce recent scholarship that provides the results of specific demographic inquiries. The most detailed of these case studies centers on counting Muslims, the world's second most populous religion. Other case studies include reflections on how to count religionists in the largest country in the world (China) as well as one way of interpreting the religious demographics of the world's newest country (South Sudan) and of the remainder of the former Sudan. Also included is perhaps the most detailed examination of the religious affiliations of migrants – highlighting especially the religious diasporas created around the world by the movement of peoples.

Recent History

This book emerges from two sources on religious demography that have developed over the past several decades. First, Anglican researcher David Barrett essentially pioneered this field with the award-winning *World Christian Encyclopedia*,[9] first produced in 1982. Barrett studied the demographics of Christianity in detail but also collected data on other religions. Thus, Barrett produced the first country-by-country comprehensive statistical assessment of religion. Todd Johnson joined Barrett in 1989 and helped him to produce the second edition of the *World Christian Encyclopedia*, published in 2001.[10] In 2003, Johnson moved the research center to Gordon-Conwell Theological Seminary near Boston, where he established the Center for the Study of

Global Christianity and launched the *World Christian Database* – an online database with detailed demographics on over 9,000 Christian denominations. In 2009, he co-edited the *Atlas of Global Christianity* with Kenneth R. Ross, offering the first comprehensive visual representation of international religious demographics.

Second, the Pew Research Center's Forum on Religion and Public Life in Washington, DC has given great priority to researching international religious demography. Thus, through the work of sociologist Brian Grim (and, more recently, including Conrad Hackett and Phillip Conner), the Pew Forum has released a series of reports on various aspects of religious demography. Some of these are reproduced with permission in the case studies in part III.

In 2008, we started the International Religious Demography project at Peter Berger's Institute on Culture, Religion and World Affairs at Boston University. This project has provided a place to work out specific challenges in the field of international religious demography. The first achievement was launching the *World Religion Database* in 2008, the source of most of the data in part I. The *World Religion Database* is updated every quarter, and new variables are added regularly.

A First Offering

Our hope is that this book will offer a starting place for a global conversation on the academic field of religious demography. We recognize the crucial nature of this field for understanding the world today and believe that these studies can have a direct impact on international relations, diplomacy, foreign policy, and a host of other practical considerations in how the world is governed. An additional hope is that a deeper understanding of religious demography will help inform debates that are often driven by anecdotes and conjecture instead of facts and figures.

Notes

1   Hyman Alterman, *Counting People: The Census in History* (New York: Houghton Mifflin, 1969).
2   Peter L. Berger, *The Desecularization of the World* (Grand Rapids, MI: Eerdmans, 1999).
3   John Micklethwait and Adrian Wooldridge, *God is Back: How the Global Revival of Faith is Changing the World* (New York: Penguin Press, 2009).
4   Monica Duffy Toft, Daniel Philpott, and Timothy Samuel Shah, *God's Century: Resurgent Religion and Global Politics* (New York: W. W. Norton, 2011).
5   Todd M. Johnson and Kenneth R. Ross, eds., *Atlas of Global Christianity* (Edinburgh: Edinburgh University Press, 2009).
6   Todd M. Johnson, ed., *World Christian Database* (Leiden/Boston: Brill, 2007).
7   Todd M. Johnson and Brian J. Grim, eds., *World Religion Database* (Leiden/Boston: Brill, 2008).
8   Since the data in this volume originate from two different sources (the *World Religion Database* and The Pew Forum on Religion and Public Life), some differences in nomenclature regarding names of world regions and some countries exist.
9   David B. Barrett, *World Christian Encyclopedia* (Nairobi: Oxford University Press, 1982).

10 David B. Barrett, George T. Kurian, and Todd M. Johnson, eds., *World Christian Encyclopedia: A Comparative Survey of Churches and Religions in the Modern World*, 2 vols., 2nd ed. (New York: Oxford University Press, 2001).

References

Alterman, Hyman. *Counting People: The Census in History.* New York: Houghton Mifflin, 1969.

Barrett, David B. *World Christian Encyclopedia.* Nairobi: Oxford University Press, 1982.

Barrett, David B., George T. Kurian, and Todd M. Johnson, eds. *World Christian Encyclopedia: A Comparative Survey of Churches and Religions in the Modern World*, 2 vols. 2nd ed. New York: Oxford University Press, 2001.

Berger, Peter L., ed. *The Desecularization of the World: Resurgent Religion and World Politics.* Grand Rapids, MI: Eerdmans, 1999.

Johnson, Todd M., ed. *World Christian Database.* Leiden/Boston: Brill, 2007.

Johnson, Todd M., and Brian J. Grim, eds. *World Religion Database.* Leiden/Boston: Brill, 2008.

Johnson, Todd M., and Kenneth R. Ross, eds. *Atlas of Global Christianity.* Edinburgh: Edinburgh University Press, 2009.

Micklethwait, John, and Adrian Wooldridge. *God is Back: How the Global Revival of Faith is Changing the World.* New York: Penguin Press, 2009.

Toft, Monica Duffy, Daniel Philpott, and Timothy Samuel Shah. *God's Century: Resurgent Religion and Global Politics.* New York: W. W. Norton, 2011.

Part I
Overview

Chapter 1

Global Religious Populations, 1910–2010

Religion is a fundamental characteristic of humankind. While it is possible to find commonalities in different religions across history, peoples, languages, and cultures, it is also true that "religion" encompasses a dizzying array of rituals, practices, doctrines, sacred spaces, and personalities. This diversity is found even *within* major religions. For the purposes of creating a taxonomy it is possible to refer to seven or eight major religions, and to approximately 10,000 total different religions.[1] At the same time, a significant minority of people claim no religion. Even in the past 100 years this "group" has waxed and waned as a percentage of the world's population. Any serious treatment of religious demography must take both religionists and non-religionists into account.

Viewing the world's religions on a global scale reveals a striking demographic reality.[2] Christians, Muslims, Hindus, Buddhists, and even agnostics live side-by-side in many countries, often showing diversity within a province or state.[3] These huge blocs represent to some extent cultural realities (for example, Arabs as Muslims, South Asians as Hindus), but each of these religions also has enormous cultural diversity (for example, most Muslims are not Arabs). This clustering gives rise to other seeming contradictions as well. For example, the Muslim world is perceived as stronger at its core than on the periphery (e.g., Muslims constitute a higher percentage of the population in Saudi Arabia than in Indonesia, the country with the largest Muslim population). Yet, at the same time, the majority of Muslims live in Asia, not the Middle East or North Africa.

Chinese folk-religionists are an absolute majority in no country or province, although they make up over 6% of the global population; most live in China (which is majority agnostic). Conversely, Sikhism and Judaism – although less than 0.3% of the global total each – have local majorities in the Indian state of Punjab and in Israel, respectively. India is also notable for having the highest number of different provincial majority religions (five) in a single country.

The World's Religions in Figures: An Introduction to International Religious Demography,
First Edition. Todd M. Johnson and Brian J. Grim.

Table 1.1 World religions by adherents, 1910–2010.

Religion	Adherents 1910	% 1910	Adherents 2010	% 2010	1910–2010 % p.a.	2000–10 % p.a.
Christians	611,810,000	34.8	2,260,440,000	32.8	1.32	1.31
Muslims	221,749,000	12.6	1,553,773,000	22.5	1.97	1.86
Hindus	223,383,000	12.7	948,575,000	13.8	1.46	1.41
Agnostics	3,369,000	0.2	676,944,000	9.8	5.45	0.32
Chinese folk-religionists	390,504,000	22.2	436,258,000	6.3	0.11	0.16
Buddhists	138,064,000	7.9	494,881,000	7.2	1.28	0.99
Ethnoreligionists	135,074,000	7.7	242,516,000	3.5	0.59	1.06
Atheists	243,000	0.0	136,652,000	2.0	6.54	0.05
New Religionists	6,865,000	0.4	63,004,000	0.9	2.24	0.29
Sikhs	3,232,000	0.2	23,927,000	0.3	2.02	1.54
Jews	13,193,000	0.8	14,761,000	0.2	0.11	0.72
Spiritists	324,000	0.0	13,700,000	0.2	3.82	0.94
Daoists	437,000	0.0	8,429,000	0.1	3.00	1.73
Baha'is	225,000	0.0	7,306,000	0.1	3.54	1.72
Confucianists	760,000	0.0	6,449,000	0.1	2.16	0.36
Jains	1,446,000	0.1	5,316,000	0.1	1.31	1.53
Shintoists	7,613,000	0.4	2,761,000	0.0	-1.01	0.09
Zoroastrians	119,000	0.0	197,000	0.0	0.51	0.74
Total population	**1,758,412,000**	**100.0**	**6,895,889,000**	**100.0**	**1.38**	**1.20**

Data source: Todd M. Johnson and Brian J. Grim, eds., *World Religion Database* (Leiden/Boston: Brill, accessed January 2012).

The activities of groups as diverse as missionaries, militaries, and migrants can lead to significant differences in religious demographics over time. As a result, one can see two profound changes when comparing the strengths of religions globally in 1910 with those of 2010. First, sub-Saharan Africa was predominantly ethnoreligionist in 1910; by 2010 ethnoreligionists had been displaced as a majority bloc, with either Christianity introduced from the south or Islam from the north now forming the majority in almost all provinces. Second, Eastern Asia has gone from a majority of Chinese folk-religionists to a majority of agnostics and atheists. The growth of agnostics and atheists globally is shown in table 1.1.

Table 1.1 is a quick-reference for comparing the global strength of each of 18 religions as a percentage of the world's population in 1910 and 2010, as well as a way to compare a religion's growth rate with those of other religions and of the world's population as a whole. In addition, one can compare growth rates over the century (1910–2010) or over the past 10 years (2000–10). Four trends for the 100-year period are immediately apparent. First, Christianity, as a percentage of the world's population, has declined slightly (from 34.8% to 32.8%). Second, Islam has grown from 12.6% to 22.5% of the world's population, the most significant change in proportion for any of the large religions. Third, Buddhists and Chinese folk-religionists have together shrunk from over 30% of the world's population to only about 13.5%. Fourth, agnostics and atheists grew from less than 1% of the world's population to well over 11%.

One-hundred-year growth rates (expressed as average annual growth rate[4]) in table 1.1 put these changes in context. World population grew at an average rate of about 1.38% per year from 1910–2010. Atheists (6.54% p.a.) and agnostics (5.45% p.a.) grew more than four times faster than the world's population while Confucianists grew at 2.16% p.a., nearly twice as fast as the world's population. A different situation is described by the 10-year growth rates from 2000–10. During that period, world population grew at an average rate of 1.20% p.a. Among the larger religions, Islam was the fastest growing during this period, at 1.86% p.a.; Christianity lagged somewhat, at 1.31% p.a.[5] Note that both agnostics (0.32% p.a.) and atheists (0.05% p.a.) are now growing much more slowly than the world's population. This is due largely to the resurgence of religion in China.

Religiously Affiliated and Unaffiliated

Despite attempts to depict the twentieth century as a "secular" century, most of the people who lived during that period were, in fact, affiliated with a religion. In 1910, well over 99% of the world's population was religiously affiliated. By 2010 the figure had fallen below 89%, but this 100-year trend hides the fact that the high point for the non-religious was around 1970, when almost 20% of the world's population was either agnostic or atheist (see table 1.2). The collapse of European Communism in the late twentieth century was accompanied by a resurgence of religion, making the world more religiously affiliated in 2010 than in 1970. While religious affiliation is not a direct indication of how religiously active people are, political scientists Pippa Norris and Ronald Inglehart point out, "The publics of virtually all advanced industrial

Table 1.2   Percentage of the world's population belonging to no religion or religion, 1910–2010.

	1910	*1950*	*1970*	*2000*	*2010*
No religion	0.2	6.7	19.2	12.9	11.8
Agnostics	0.2	5.1	14.7	10.7	9.8
Atheists	0.0	1.6	4.5	2.2	2.0
Religion	99.8	93.3	80.8	87.1	88.2
Christians	34.8	34.2	33.2	32.4	32.8
Muslims	12.6	13.6	15.6	21.1	22.5
Hindus	12.7	12.6	12.5	13.5	13.8
Buddhists	7.9	7.0	6.4	7.3	7.2
Other religionists	31.8	25.9	13.1	12.8	12.0

Data source: Todd M. Johnson and Brian J. Grim, eds., *World Religion Database* (Leiden/Boston: Brill, accessed January 2012).

societies have been moving towards more secular orientations during the past fifty years. Nevertheless, the world as a whole now has more people with traditional religious views than ever before – and they constitute a growing proportion of the world's population."[6]

This resurgence of religious affiliation continues in the present (even though the number of atheists and agnostics continues to rise in the Western world), and the current growth of religions of all kinds in China (where the vast majority of the non-religious live today) indicates that the religious future of the world is indeed one worth studying.

What follows is a statistical summary of religious adherents (ordered largest to smallest in 2010 from table 1.1), including agnostics and atheists as separate categories.

Christians

Christianity – the world's largest religion – traces its origins to a small group of Jewish disciples in first-century Palestine. Christians believe that Jesus Christ is divine, was crucified in Jerusalem, but rose from the dead. Jesus was seen as the fulfillment of messianic promises recorded in the Jewish scriptures. He is worshipped today in hundreds of languages around the world. The Bible is its foundational document, divided into Old and New Testaments.

As observed in table 1.1, Christians have constituted approximately one third of the world's population over the past 100 years.[7] Yet, over this same period, Christianity has experienced a profound shift in its ethnic and linguistic composition (examined more closely in table 1.3). In 1910 over 80% of all Christians lived in Europe and Northern America (the "global North").[8] By 2010 this had fallen to less than 40%, with the majority of Christians located in Africa, Asia, and Latin America. The global North was 95% Christian in 1910. Five regions in the global South,[9] all the recipients of intense Christian missionary activity over the preceding centuries, were also at least

Table 1.3 Christians (C) by United Nations continents and regions, 1910–2010.

Region	Population 1910	C 1910	% 1910	Population 2010	C 2010	% 2010	C 1910–2010	Pop 1910–2010	C 2000–10	Pop 2000–10
Africa	**124,541,000**	**11,636,000**	**9.3**	**1,022,234,000**	**494,053,000**	**48.3**	**3.82**	**2.13**	**2.56**	**2.34**
Eastern	33,012,000	5,266,000	16.0	324,044,000	214,013,000	66.0	3.77	2.31	2.72	2.56
Middle	19,445,000	207,000	1.1	126,689,000	104,579,000	82.5	6.42	1.89	2.91	2.79
Northern	31,968,000	3,081,000	9.6	209,459,000	16,761,000	8.0	1.71	1.90	1.79	1.75
Southern	6,819,000	2,526,000	37.0	57,780,000	47,598,000	82.4	2.98	2.16	1.18	1.17
Western	33,296,000	557,000	1.7	304,261,000	111,103,000	36.5	5.44	2.24	2.69	2.59
Asia	**1,026,693,000**	**25,086,000**	**2.4**	**4,164,252,000**	**342,012,000**	**8.2**	**2.65**	**1.41**	**2.23**	**1.14**
Eastern	554,135,000	2,251,000	0.4	1,573,970,000	127,573,000	8.1	4.12	1.05	2.97	0.51
South-central	345,718,000	5,182,000	1.5	1,764,872,000	69,990,000	4.0	2.64	1.64	2.09	1.53
South-eastern	93,859,000	10,124,000	10.8	593,415,000	130,271,000	22.0	2.59	1.86	1.78	1.26
Western	32,982,000	7,529,000	22.8	231,995,000	14,178,000	6.1	0.63	1.97	0.99	2.32
Europe	**427,044,000**	**403,546,000**	**94.5**	**738,199,000**	**580,116,000**	**78.6**	**0.36**	**0.55**	**0.27**	**0.16**
Eastern	178,184,000	159,695,000	89.6	294,771,000	247,550,000	84.0	0.44	0.50	0.35	-0.31
Northern	61,473,000	60,324,000	98.1	99,205,000	74,228,000	74.8	0.21	0.48	0.25	0.50
Southern	76,828,000	74,391,000	96.8	155,171,000	127,943,000	82.5	0.54	0.71	0.60	0.67
Western	110,558,000	109,136,000	98.7	189,052,000	130,395,000	69.0	0.18	0.54	-0.17	0.32
Latin America	**78,254,000**	**74,462,000**	**95.2**	**590,082,000**	**544,686,000**	**92.3**	**2.01**	**2.04**	**1.24**	**1.24**
Caribbean	8,172,000	7,986,000	97.7	41,646,000	34,774,000	83.5	1.48	1.64	1.08	0.80
Central	20,806,000	20,595,000	99.0	155,881,000	149,426,000	95.9	2.00	2.03	1.38	1.41
South	49,276,000	45,881,000	93.1	392,555,000	360,486,000	91.8	2.08	2.10	1.19	1.23
Northern America	**94,689,000**	**91,429,000**	**96.6**	**344,529,000**	**271,554,000**	**78.8**	**1.09**	**1.30**	**0.63**	**0.96**
Oceania	**7,192,000**	**5,651,000**	**78.6**	**36,593,000**	**28,019,000**	**76.6**	**1.61**	**1.64**	**1.27**	**1.63**
Australia/New Zealand	5,375,000	5,207,000	96.9	26,637,000	18,869,000	70.8	1.30	1.61	0.88	1.47
Melanesia	1,596,000	245,000	15.4	8,748,000	8,004,000	91.5	3.55	1.72	2.32	2.26
Micronesia	89,400	68,600	76.7	536,000	499,000	93.1	2.00	1.81	0.82	0.78
Polynesia	131,000	130,000	99.2	673,000	647,000	96.1	1.62	1.65	0.88	0.91
Global total	**1,758,412,000**	**611,810,000**	**34.8**	**6,895,889,000**	**2,260,440,000**	**32.8**	**1.32**	**1.38**	**1.31**	**1.20**

Data source: Todd M. Johnson and Brian J. Grim, eds., *World Religion Database* (Leiden/Boston: Brill, accessed January 2012).

90% Christian in 1910. The 21 United Nations regions listed in table 1.3 (and similar, subsequent tables) illustrate the North/South dichotomy.[10] This dichotomy is especially significant today for Christians because the term "Southern Christians" or "Christians of the global South" is increasingly replacing the synonymous term "non-Western Christians."[11] Christians were all Southerners[12] at the time of Christ, gradually becoming more Northern until 1500, when fully 92% of all Christians were Northerners (Europeans). This percentage began to decline gradually until 1900 when it was 83%. After 1900 the Northern percentage declined precipitously while the Southern rose meteorically. By 2100, over three fourths of all Christians will likely be living in the South.[13] This represents a return to the demographic makeup of Christianity at the time of Christ (predominantly Southern), but also depicts a vast expansion of Christianity into all countries as well as thousands of peoples, languages, and cultures.

Following what Kenneth Scott Latourette refers to as the Great Century for Christianity,[14] churches outside Europe and the Americas that took root in the nineteenth century grew rapidly in the twentieth century.[15] Africa, in particular, led this transformation, growing from only 11.6 million Christians in 1910 to 494 million by 2010. Given current trends, Africa could be home to more than 1 billion Christians by 2050.

By 2010 only three of the "most Christian" regions in 1910 (Central America, South America, and Polynesia) were still at least 90% Christian, and each one is in the global South. They have been joined by Micronesia and Melanesia (the latter seeing its Christian population rise from 15.4% in 1910 to 91.5% in 2010). An additional seven regions exceeded 80%, including Middle Africa, which also saw phenomenal growth in its Christian population (from 1.1% in 1910 to 82.5% in 2010). Africa as a continent grew from 9.3% Christian in 1910 to 48.3% in 2010. Both Australia/New Zealand and Western Europe, however, had fallen below 80% Christian by 2010. Although three of the five regions that were less than 10% Christian in 1910 remain below that level in 2010, the Christian percentages increased over the century, except in Northern Africa. Western Asia also saw its Christian percentage drop, to 6.1% in 2010 from 22.8% in 1910.

In 1910 nine of the 10 countries with the most Christians were in the North (see table 1.4). The shift of Christianity southward over the following century has left the United States, Russia, and Germany as the only Northern countries on the list. The percentage of Christians in all of 1910's "top 10" in Christian population also declined between 1910 and 2010 (see table 1.5). Of the countries with the fastest Christian growth between 1910 and 2010, seven were in Africa and three in Asia (see table 1.6). In the period 2000–10, the fastest growth is found in Asia (seven countries) and Africa (three countries).

Of the major traditions in Christianity, Roman Catholicism represents just over half of all Christians, growing from 47.6% of all Christians in 1910 to 51.5% in 2010. Catholics' percentage of the global population grew slightly, from 16.6% in 1910 to 16.9% in 2010. This rise, however, masks a steep decline in adherents in Europe accompanied by a simultaneous rise in Africa, Asia, and Latin America. Since 1910, the percentages of the population, both within Christianity and globally, that are Orthodox and Anglican have declined. Orthodoxy, decimated by the

Table 1.4   Countries with the most Christians, 1910 and 2010.

Country	Christians 1910	Country	Christians 2010
United States	84,800,000	United States	247,920,000
Russia	65,757,000	Brazil	177,304,000
Germany	45,755,000	Russia	116,147,000
France	40,895,000	Mexico	108,721,000
United Kingdom	39,298,000	China	106,035,000
Italy	35,219,000	Philippines	84,769,000
Ukraine	29,904,000	Nigeria	73,606,000
Poland	22,102,000	DR Congo	62,673,000
Brazil	21,576,000	Germany	57,617,000
Spain	20,354,000	India	57,265,000

Data source: Todd M. Johnson and Brian J. Grim, eds., *World Religion Database* (Leiden/Boston: Brill, accessed January 2012).

Table 1.5   Countries with the highest percentage of Christians, 1910 and 2010.

Country	% Christian 1910	Country	% Christian 2010
Finland	100.0	Samoa	98.8
Slovenia	100.0	Romania	98.5
Barbados	100.0	Malta	98.0
Netherlands Antilles	100.0	Guatemala	97.4
Samoa	100.0	Ecuador	97.1
United States Virgin Islands	100.0	Grenada	96.6
Tonga	100.0	El Salvador	96.5
Aruba	100.0	Martinique	96.5
Spain	100.0	Peru	96.5
Portugal	100.0	Aruba	96.4

Data source: Todd M. Johnson and Brian J. Grim, eds., *World Religion Database* (Leiden/Boston: Brill, accessed January 2012). Countries >100,000 population.

Table 1.6   Countries with the fastest annual growth of Christians, 1910–2010 and 2000–10.

Country	% 1910–2010 p.a.	Country	% 2000–10 p.a.
Chad	13.7	Afghanistan	17.8
Burkina Faso	13.7	United Arab Emirates	9.5
Nepal	12.1	Qatar	9.3
Rwanda	12.0	Cambodia	8.8
Burundi	11.7	Bahrain	6.1
Central African Republic	11.6	Burkina Faso	5.7
Saudi Arabia	10.6	Mali	5.5
United Arab Emirates	9.8	Western Sahara	5.1
South Sudan	9.6	Singapore	4.8
Cote d'Ivoire	9.5	Mongolia	4.7

Data source: Todd M. Johnson and Brian J. Grim, eds., *World Religion Database* (Leiden/Boston: Brill, accessed January 2012). Countries >100,000 population.

rise of the Communism in Europe, dropped from 20.4% of the global population in 1910 to 12.2% in 2010. At the same time, Orthodox fell from 7.1% of all Christians in 1910 to 4.0% in 2010. Anglicans, like Roman Catholics, lost many adherents in the global North while gaining in the global South. In 1910, Anglicans represented 1.9% of the global population, dropping to 1.3% in 2010. Over the 100-year period, Anglicans as a percentage of all Christians fell from 5.4% to 3.8%. Protestants also experienced slight losses, going from 18.8% to 18.6% of all Christians between 1910 and 2010. Their share of the global population also decreased from 6.5% to 6.1% in the same period. Independents and Marginals,[16] on the other hand, increased their shares of the total Christian community and of the global population. Independents, especially in Africa and Asia, represented only 1.5% of all Christians in 1910 but rose meteorically to 15.0% by 2010. Their share of the global population also increased from 0.5% to 4.9%. Marginals, especially Jehovah's Witnesses and Mormons, experienced significant growth over this century, growing from 0.2% to 1.5% of all Christians and from 0.1% to 0.5% of the global population from 1910 to 2010.

Movements within Christianity[17] (and across the traditions) also experienced changes in size and percentage over the 100-year period (see table 1.7). In 1910, Evangelicals, mainly Protestants in the global North, represented 13.1% of all Christians and 4.6% of the global population. By 2010, these had dropped to 12.6% and 4.1%, respectively. Renewalists (Pentecostals and Charismatics), on the other hand, grew rapidly from just 0.1% of the global population and 0.2% of all Christians in 1910 to 8.5% and 25.8%, respectively, by 2010.[18]

Another important aspect of Christian demographics, mother tongues spoken by Christians, is shown below in table 1.8. Note that Spanish is in the top position (and has been so since at least 1970). English is a distant second, followed by Portuguese and then Russian. The surprise is in the fifth position. With the recent growth of Christianity in China, Mandarin Chinese is now the fifth-largest Christian mother tongue, surpassing traditionally "Christian" languages such as French, German, Polish, and Ukrainian. Languages of the global South are moving up the list, with Tagalog, Amharic, Yoruba, Igbo, and Korean poised to push European languages out of the top 10.

Muslims

Islam was founded in the seventh century in the Arabian Peninsula where Muhammad (570–632 CE), honored by Muslims as the last and final messenger of God, brought a monotheistic message to Arab tribes. Within 100 years of the Prophet's death, Muslims could be found from Spain to China. Today, Muslims are found in nearly every country of the world.[19] (See chapters 10 and 11 for a separate case study looking at Muslim population trends from 1990 to 2010, including projections to 2030.)

The growth of Islam over the past century has been remarkable. Globally, Islam has grown almost 1.5 times faster than the general population.[20] While experiencing steady growth in both Africa and Asia, it has grown almost three times faster than the general population in Europe and almost five times faster in Northern America.[21]

Table 1.7 Christian (C) traditions and movements, 1910 and 2010.

	Name	Adherents 1910	% world 1910	% all Cs 1910	Adherents 2010	% world 2010	% all Cs 2010
Traditions	Anglicans	32,892,000	1.9	5.4	86,592,000	1.3	3.8
	Independents	9,269,000	0.5	1.5	339,933,000	4.9	15.0
	Marginals	1,070,000	0.1	0.2	34,884,000	0.5	1.5
	Orthodox	124,871,000	7.1	20.4	275,156,000	4.0	12.2
	Protestants	115,016,000	6.5	18.8	419,331,000	6.1	18.6
	Catholics	291,291,000	16.6	47.6	1,167,897,000	16.9	51.7
Movements	Evangelicals	80,196,000	4.6	13.1	285,479,000	4.1	12.6
	Renewalists	1,203,000	0.1	0.2	583,372,000	8.5	25.8

Data source: Todd M. Johnson and Brian J. Grim, eds., *World Religion Database* (Leiden/Boston: Brill, accessed January 2012).

Table 1.8 Christians by mother tongue, mid-2010.

Rank	Language	Main country	Total countries	Total speakers	Christians	% Christian
1	Spanish	Mexico	76	391,766,000	367,820,000	93.9
2	English	United States	193	323,850,000	252,323,000	77.9
3	Portuguese	Brazil	57	207,299,000	189,524,000	91.4
4	Russian	Russia	76	135,837,000	121,208,000	89.2
5	Chinese, Mandarin	China	116	880,662,000	89,103,000	10.1
6	French	France	139	60,740,000	42,790,000	70.4
7	German, Standard	Germany	91	59,074,000	41,809,000	70.8
8	Polish	Poland	46	41,137,000	38,694,000	94.1
9	Ukrainian	Ukraine	40	39,931,000	35,494,000	88.9
10	Tagalog	Philippines	54	34,222,000	33,560,000	98.1
11	Italian	Italy	64	29,661,000	24,340,000	82.1
12	Romanian	Romania	47	24,772,000	23,776,000	96.0
13	Amharic	Ethiopia	12	23,805,000	23,411,000	98.3
14	Yoruba	Nigeria	15	32,566,000	19,539,000	60.0
15	Igbo	Nigeria	5	19,316,000	19,079,000	98.8
16	Korean	South Korea	41	77,040,000	18,889,000	24.5
17	Cebuano	Philippines	1	18,462,000	18,175,000	98.4
18	Malayalam	India	18	45,264,000	15,429,000	34.1
19	Tamil	India	29	85,223,000	12,997,000	15.3
20	Catalan-Valencian-Balear	Spain	8	13,385,000	12,461,000	93.1
21	Greek	Greece	84	12,672,000	12,265,000	96.8
22	Dutch	Netherlands	28	17,070,000	11,306,000	66.2
23	Hungarian	Hungary	30	12,896,000	11,159,000	86.5
24	Haitian	Haiti	10	11,329,000	10,692,000	94.4
25	Bavarian	Austria	15	13,653,000	10,547,000	77.3

Data source: Todd M. Johnson and Brian J. Grim, eds., *World Religion Database* (Leiden/Boston: Brill, accessed January 2012).

Table 1.9 Muslims (M) by United Nations continents and regions, 1910–2010.

Region	Pop 1910	Muslims 1910	% 1910	Pop 2010	Muslims 2010	% 2010	M 1910–2010	Pop 1910–2010	M 2000–10	Pop 2000–10
Africa	**124,541,000**	**39,916,000**	**32.1**	**1,022,234,000**	**425,860,000**	**41.7**	**2.40**	**2.13**	**2.28**	**2.34**
Eastern	33,012,000	4,250,000	12.9	324,044,000	70,824,000	21.9	2.85	2.31	2.62	2.56
Middle	19,445,000	871,000	4.5	126,689,000	12,226,000	9.7	2.68	1.89	2.88	2.79
Northern	31,968,000	26,275,000	82.2	209,459,000	186,697,000	89.1	1.98	1.90	1.75	1.75
Southern	6,819,000	36,800	0.5	57,780,000	887,000	1.5	3.23	2.16	1.15	1.17
Western	33,296,000	8,482,000	25.5	304,261,000	155,227,000	51.0	2.95	2.24	2.74	2.59
Asia	**1,026,693,000**	**171,690,000**	**16.7**	**4,164,252,000**	**1,078,854,000**	**25.9**	**1.85**	**1.41**	**1.75**	**1.14**
Eastern	554,135,000	24,450,000	4.4	1,573,970,000	21,601,000	1.4	-0.12	1.05	0.64	0.51
South-central	345,718,000	102,025,000	29.5	1,764,872,000	632,333,000	35.8	1.84	1.64	1.76	1.53
South-eastern	93,859,000	20,234,000	21.6	593,415,000	218,910,000	36.9	2.41	1.86	1.26	1.26
Western	32,982,000	24,981,000	75.7	231,995,000	206,010,000	88.8	2.13	1.97	2.43	2.32
Europe	**427,044,000**	**10,048,000**	**2.4**	**738,199,000**	**41,492,000**	**5.6**	**1.43**	**0.55**	**0.60**	**0.16**
Eastern	178,184,000	7,920,000	4.4	294,771,000	16,776,000	5.7	0.75	0.50	0.07	-0.31
Northern	61,473,000	570	0.0	99,205,000	2,865,000	2.9	8.90	0.48	1.51	0.50
Southern	76,828,000	2,077,000	2.7	155,171,000	10,276,000	6.6	1.61	0.71	0.96	0.67
Western	110,558,000	51,000	0.0	189,052,000	11,576,000	6.1	5.57	0.54	0.88	0.32
Latin America	**78,254,000**	**67,800**	**0.1**	**590,082,000**	**1,527,000**	**0.3**	**3.16**	**2.04**	**1.01**	**1.24**
Caribbean	8,172,000	18,000	0.2	41,646,000	114,000	0.3	1.86	1.64	0.45	0.80
Central	20,806,000	2,500	0.0	155,881,000	148,000	0.1	4.17	2.03	1.38	1.41
South	49,276,000	47,300	0.1	392,555,000	1,265,000	0.3	3.34	2.10	1.02	1.23
Northern America	**94,689,000**	**11,700**	**0.0**	**344,529,000**	**5,492,000**	**1.6**	**6.34**	**1.30**	**1.86**	**0.96**
Oceania	**7,192,000**	**14,800**	**0.2**	**36,593,000**	**549,000**	**1.5**	**3.68**	**1.64**	**2.43**	**1.63**
Australia/New Zealand	5,375,000	11,800	0.2	26,637,000	484,000	1.8	3.78	1.61	2.69	1.47
Melanesia	1,596,000	3,100	0.2	8,748,000	63,800	0.7	3.07	1.72	0.58	2.26
Micronesia	89,400	0	0.0	536,000	950	0.2	4.66	1.81	-0.21	0.78
Polynesia	131,000	0	0.0	673,000	69	0.0	1.95	1.65	1.75	0.91
Global total	**1,758,412,000**	**221,749,000**	**12.6**	**6,895,889,000**	**1,553,773,000**	**22.5**	**1.97**	**1.38**	**1.86**	**1.20**

Data source: Todd M. Johnson and Brian J. Grim, eds., *World Religion Database* (Leiden/Boston: Brill, accessed January 2012).

Muslims constitute a greater share in 2010 than in 1910 of the population globally (22.5%, up from 12.6%) as well as in every region of the world except Eastern Asia (where they constitute a small portion of most countries) and Polynesia (with few reported Muslims). Interestingly, despite these increases Muslims are even more strongly concentrated in Asia and Africa than they were a century ago. From 95.4% in 1910, the proportion of the world's Muslims living on these two continents had increased to 96.8% by 2010. The effect is even more dramatic in the historic Muslim homelands. When Eastern Asia and Middle and Southern Africa are excluded, the share of the world's Muslims in the remainder of Africa and Asia increased from 83% in 1910 to over 92% in 2010. Asia continues to have the most Muslims in absolute terms – 69% of the world's Muslims in 2010. This figure is down from 77% in 1910 as a result of the migration of Muslims from their historic home countries. Africa, however, had the highest percentage of Muslims relative to the total population in both 1910 (32.1%) and 2010 (41.7%). The shift of the global center of gravity[22] of Islam toward the South and West reflects the increasing African presence of Islam; 18% of Muslims lived in Africa in 1910, compared with 27% in 2010.

The growth of the Muslim population in Europe has been remarkable. In Eastern Europe (including present-day Russia) the Muslim population has more than doubled from 1910 to 2010, from almost 8 million to almost 17 million. This represents an increase from 4.4% of the population to 5.7%. In Southern Europe (including the Balkans) over the same period, the Muslim population has increased from 2 million to over 10 million, or from 2.7% of the population to over 6.6%. These increases (in both regions) are because of high birthrates in indigenous Muslim populations. But it is in Northern and Western Europe where the greatest changes have been seen, and most of this can be attributed to immigration. In Northern Europe in 1910 there were fewer than 600 Muslims; in 2010 there were over 2.8 million. This represents a dramatic increase from 0.0% to 2.9% of the population. Western Europe had 51,000 Muslims in 1910, growing to 11.5 million, or from 0.0% of the population to 6.1%.

Northern America has experienced similar growth in its Muslim population. In 1910 fewer than 12,000 Muslims lived in the region, while in 2010 there were well over 5 million. Although much of this can be attributed to immigration, significant growth among the African American population occurred through conversion.

Nine of the 10 countries with the largest Muslim populations in 1910 (table 1.10) were in Asia or Northern Africa. Russia (ranked ninth), though classified as an Eastern European country, in reality lies mostly in Asia, and thus the majority of its Muslims (likely) lived in the Asiatic portion of the country as well. The situation was much the same in 2010. Each of the top six countries was also in the top 10 in 1910. The seventh, Nigeria, represents a demographic shift of Islam towards Africa. All countries in Western Africa have significant Muslim populations. In 1910 most of the countries with the highest percentages of Muslims in their total populations (table 1.11) were located on the Arabian Peninsula (five), the birthplace of Islam, or opposite it on the Horn of Africa (two). The remaining three were Indian Ocean island states near Madagascar. In 2010, Afghanistan has the second highest percentage of Muslims, and seven in the top 10 are found in Africa. Table 1.12 reveals that Muslim growth has been fastest in Europe over the 100-year period (largely through immigration). For fastest growth over the past 10 years, Gulf States (Qatar, United Arab Emirates, and

Table 1.10 Countries with the most Muslims, 1910 and 2010.

Country	Muslims 1910	Country	Muslims 2010
India	34,666,000	Indonesia	190,521,000
China	24,436,000	India	173,367,000
Pakistan	23,130,000	Pakistan	166,927,000
Bangladesh	20,542,000	Bangladesh	132,112,000
Indonesia	17,916,000	Iran	73,079,000
Turkey	11,909,000	Egypt	72,436,000
Iran	10,424,000	Nigeria	72,149,000
Egypt	9,822,000	Turkey	71,513,000
Russia	7,026,000	Algeria	34,937,000
Morocco	5,609,000	Morocco	31,840,000

Data source: Todd M. Johnson and Brian J. Grim, eds., *World Religion Database* (Leiden/Boston: Brill, accessed January 2012).

Table 1.11 Countries with the highest percentage of Muslims, 1910 and 2010.

Country	% Muslim 1910	Country	% Muslim 2010
Maldives	100.0	Somalia	99.8
Saudi Arabia	100.0	Afghanistan	99.7
Oman	100.0	Morocco	99.7
Somalia	99.9	Tunisia	99.5
Comoros	99.9	Western Sahara	99.4
United Arab Emirates	99.9	Mauritania	99.1
Mayotte	99.7	Yemen	99.1
Bahrain	99.7	Iran	98.8
Kuwait	99.7	Mayotte	98.6
Qatar	99.6	Algeria	98.5

Data source: Todd M. Johnson and Brian J. Grim, eds., *World Religion Database* (Leiden/Boston: Brill, accessed January 2012). Countries >100,000 population.

Table 1.12 Countries with the fastest annual growth of Muslims, 1910–2010 and 2000–10.

Country	% 1910–2010 p.a.	Country	% 2000–10 p.a.
Germany	13.7	Qatar	11.8
United Kingdom	13.0	United Arab Emirates	9.5
Belgium	11.6	Bahrain	7.2
Austria	11.2	Solomon Islands	6.4
Sweden	11.0	Norway	5.7
Denmark	10.5	Western Sahara	5.3
Angola	10.5	Rwanda	4.9
Japan	10.4	Benin	4.2
Gabon	10.1	Finland	3.9
Norway	10.0	Paraguay	3.7

Data source: Todd M. Johnson and Brian J. Grim, eds., *World Religion Database* (Leiden/Boston: Brill, accessed January 2012). Countries >100,000 population.

Table 1.13   Muslim traditions, 1910 and 2010.

Tradition	Adherents 1910	% world 1910	% all Muslims 1910	Adherents 2010	% world 2010	% all Muslims 2010
Sunnis	191,104,700	10.9	86.2	1,329,944,304	19.3	85.6
Sufis	88,400,000	5.0	39.9	309,700,000	4.5	19.9
Shi'as	28,700,000	1.6	12.9	200,000,000	2.9	12.9
Schismatic	1,090,000	0.1	0.5	19,500,000	0.3	1.3

Data source: Todd M. Johnson and Brian J. Grim, eds., *World Religion Database* (Leiden/Boston: Brill, accessed January 2012).

Table 1.14   Muslims by mother tongue, mid-2010.

Rank	Language	Country	Total countries	Total speakers	Muslims	% Muslim
1	Bengali	Bangladesh	23	202,156,000	125,123,000	61.9
2	Urdu	India	32	80,735,000	79,156,000	98.0
3	Panjabi, Western	Pakistan	5	76,810,000	71,717,000	93.4
4	Turkish	Turkey	50	64,703,000	63,984,000	98.9
5	Arabic, Egyptian	Egypt	30	57,782,000	52,180,000	90.3
6	Javanese	Indonesia	10	59,713,000	48,513,000	81.2
7	Hausa	Nigeria	18	44,495,000	43,702,000	98.2
8	Indonesian	Indonesia	10	39,473,000	34,332,000	87.0
9	Farsi, Western	Iran	39	31,997,000	31,317,000	97.9
10	Sunda	Indonesia	1	31,778,000	30,825,000	97.0
11	Arabic, Sudanese	Sudan	11	29,381,000	28,269,000	96.2
12	Pashto, Northern	Pakistan	19	28,112,000	28,049,000	99.8
13	Uzbek, Northern	Uzbekistan	18	25,304,000	24,512,000	96.9
14	Arabic, Najdi	Saudi Arabia	11	24,449,000	24,329,000	99.5
15	Arabic, Algerian	Algeria	8	24,723,000	24,252,000	98.1
16	Arabic, North Levantine	Syria	86	32,211,000	23,949,000	74.4
17	Sindhi	Pakistan	8	23,672,000	20,628,000	87.1
18	Arabic, Moroccan	Morocco	19	20,391,000	20,330,000	99.7
19	Arabic, Mesopotamian	Iraq	18	17,901,000	17,583,000	98.2
20	Seraiki	Pakistan	2	17,089,000	16,408,000	96.0
21	Arabic, Sa'idi	Egypt	3	19,643,000	16,253,000	82.7
22	Malay	Malaysia	25	15,834,000	15,824,000	99.9
23	Deccan	India	1	15,374,000	15,374,000	100.0
24	Somali	Somalia	21	15,350,000	15,344,000	100.0
25	Tajiki	Afghanistan	15	15,305,000	15,206,000	99.4

Data source: Todd M. Johnson and Brian J. Grim, eds., *World Religion Database* (Leiden/Boston: Brill, accessed January 2012).

Bahrain) are at the top of the list largely because of massive influxes of guest workers after the discovery of oil.

Over the twentieth century, most Muslims (86%) have considered themselves Sunni in tradition. The next largest group is the Shi'a, whose percentage remained the same from 1910 to 2010 at 12.9%. Gains were made by schismatic groups, especially the Ahmadiyya,[23] a fast-growing movement founded in India, who now claim over 10 million followers worldwide.

The largest mother tongues of the Muslim world contain several surprises (table 1.14).[24] The four largest languages are all in Asia. Bengali is by far the largest, followed by Urdu, Western Panjabi, and Turkish. The first Arabic language (Egyptian) appears at number five and no other Arabic languages are in the top 10. However, if all Arabic dialects were combined into a single language, then it would be the Muslim language with the most mother-tongue speakers.

Hindus

Hinduism, the oldest major religion still practiced today, is the world's third largest (after Christianity and Islam).[25] Hinduism is the most diverse of the world religions in terms of religious practice. Hindus have shared scriptures (such as the Upanishads, Vedas, and Bhagavad Gita), but they have no original founder or current leader for the religion as a whole (though many gurus act as spiritual leaders and teachers for smaller groups of followers). Neither do Hindus have any shared doctrine – it rather focuses on orthopraxy over orthodoxy – or modern mechanism for religious exclusion. Hinduism boasts millions of gods, but some Hindus focus their worship toward one god, while others revere many. From this perspective, Hinduism is essentially an umbrella term for millions of religionists practicing a dizzying array of "minireligions" in India and abroad.

Over the last century, the global growth rate of Hinduism exceeded the world population growth rate; Hinduism's share of the world's population increased from 12.7% in 1910 to 13.8% in 2010 (see table 1.15). In many ways, however, Hinduism remains tied to South-central Asia – the region of its origins – and to India in particular. Hindus were found in at least 40 present-day countries in 1910, but South-central Asia was home to 99.1% of the world's Hindu population, with 96.9% of the global total in British India (modern India, Pakistan, and Bangladesh). The overwhelming majority of the global total (90.6%) lived in modern India. Most of the rest (0.7% of global Hindus) lived in other parts of Asia. The remaining 0.2% were mostly former indentured servants from India and their descendants, living in other parts of the British Empire.

Reflecting this, eight of the 10 countries with the largest Hindu populations in 1910 (table 1.16) were in Asia: five in South-central Asia, and three in South-eastern Asia. The other two, Mauritius and Trinidad & Tobago, were recipients of Indian indentured servants. Similarly, the countries with the largest Hindu percentages (table 1.17), which included seven of the countries with the most Hindus, were either in South-central Asia (six) or recipients of Indian indentured servants (four, including modern Suriname, a Dutch colony at the time). The picture has changed only slightly in 2010.

Table 1.15 Hindus by United Nations continents and regions, 1910–2010.

Region	Population 1910	Hindus 1910	% 1910	Population 2010	Hindus 2010	% 2010	Hindu 1910–2010	Pop 1910–2010	Hindu 2000–10	Pop 2000–10
Africa	**124,541,000**	**303,000**	**0.2**	**1,022,234,000**	**2,930,000**	**0.3**	**2.29**	**2.13**	**1.68**	**2.34**
Eastern	33,012,000	242,000	0.7	324,044,000	1,612,000	0.5	1.91	2.31	2.02	2.56
Middle	19,445,000	0	0.0	126,689,000	99,300	0.1	9.64	1.89	2.89	2.79
Northern	31,968,000	0	0.0	209,459,000	7,400	0.0	6.83	1.90	1.95	1.75
Southern	6,819,000	61,400	0.9	57,780,000	1,201,000	2.1	3.02	2.16	1.13	1.17
Western	33,296,000	100	0.0	304,261,000	9,700	0.0	4.68	2.24	2.61	2.59
Asia	**1,026,693,000**	**222,876,000**	**21.7**	**4,164,252,000**	**941,481,000**	**22.6**	**1.45**	**1.41**	**1.41**	**1.14**
Eastern	554,135,000	8,000	0.0	1,573,970,000	61,800	0.0	2.07	1.05	0.31	0.51
South-central	345,718,000	221,364,000	64.0	1,764,872,000	933,161,000	52.9	1.45	1.64	1.40	1.53
South-eastern	93,859,000	1,501,000	1.6	593,415,000	6,918,000	1.2	1.54	1.86	1.47	1.26
Western	32,982,000	3,100	0.0	231,995,000	1,340,000	0.6	6.26	1.97	5.24	2.32
Europe	**427,044,000**	**65**	**0.0**	**738,199,000**	**1,052,000**	**0.1**	**10.18**	**0.55**	**1.27**	**0.16**
Eastern	178,184,000	0	0.0	294,771,000	47,700	0.0	8.84	0.50	0.50	-0.31
Northern	61,473,000	10	0.0	99,205,000	692,000	0.7	11.79	0.48	1.56	0.50
Southern	76,828,000	55	0.0	155,171,000	30,300	0.0	6.52	0.71	0.44	0.67
Western	110,558,000	0	0.0	189,052,000	282,000	0.1	10.79	0.54	0.82	0.32
Latin America	**78,254,000**	**186,000**	**0.2**	**590,082,000**	**765,000**	**0.1**	**1.42**	**2.04**	**0.59**	**1.24**
Caribbean	8,172,000	84,600	1.0	41,646,000	382,000	0.9	1.52	1.64	0.51	0.80
Central	20,806,000	0	0.0	155,881,000	18,000	0.0	7.78	2.03	1.64	1.41
South	49,276,000	102,000	0.2	392,555,000	365,000	0.1	1.28	2.10	0.65	1.23
Northern America	**94,689,000**	**1,200**	**0.0**	**344,529,000**	**1,835,000**	**0.5**	**7.61**	**1.30**	**1.76**	**0.96**
Oceania	**7,192,000**	**16,400**	**0.2**	**36,593,000**	**513,000**	**1.4**	**3.50**	**1.64**	**2.02**	**1.63**
Australia/New Zealand	5,375,000	0	0.0	26,637,000	274,000	1.0	10.76	1.61	3.84	1.47
Melanesia	1,596,000	16,400	1.0	8,748,000	239,000	2.7	2.72	1.72	0.30	2.26
Micronesia	89,400	0	0.0	536,000	26	0.0	3.31	1.81	0.80	0.78
Polynesia	131,000	0	0.0	673,000	100	0.0	2.33	1.65	0.00	0.91
Global total	**1,758,412,000**	**223,383,000**	**12.7**	**6,895,889,000**	**948,575,000**	**13.8**	**1.46**	**1.38**	**1.41**	**1.20**

Data source: Todd M. Johnson and Brian J. Grim, eds., *World Religion Database* (Leiden/Boston: Brill, accessed January 2012).

Table 1.16   Countries with the most Hindus, 1910 and 2010.

Country	Hindus 1910	Country	Hindus 2010
India	202,590,000	India	893,642,000
Bangladesh	10,104,000	Nepal	20,282,000
Pakistan	3,835,000	Bangladesh	14,096,000
Nepal	3,835,000	Indonesia	3,891,000
Sri Lanka	975,000	Sri Lanka	2,722,000
Indonesia	896,000	Pakistan	2,290,000
Myanmar	316,000	Malaysia	1,780,000
Malaysia	260,000	United States	1,445,000
Mauritius	217,000	South Africa	1,196,000
Trinidad & Tobago	81,200	Myanmar	818,000

Data source: Todd M. Johnson and Brian J. Grim, eds., *World Religion Database* (Leiden/ Boston: Brill, accessed January 2012).

Table 1.17   Countries with the highest percentage of Hindus, 1910 and 2010.

Country	% 1910	Country	% 2010
India	80.0	India	73.0
Nepal	76.7	Nepal	67.7
Mauritius	54.3	Mauritius	44.2
Bangladesh	32.4	Guyana	30.1
Suriname	26.4	Fiji	27.7
Trinidad & Tobago	25.1	Trinidad & Tobago	24.3
Guyana	25.0	Suriname	20.4
Sri Lanka	23.1	Sri Lanka	13.0
Bhutan	16.5	Bhutan	11.4
Pakistan	13.7	Bangladesh	9.5

Data source: Todd M. Johnson and Brian J. Grim, eds., *World Religion Database* (Leiden/ Boston: Brill, accessed January 2012). Countries >100,000 population.

South-central Asia is still home to 98.4% of global Hindus and the rest of Asia home to 0.9%. Although Hinduism has spread, that spread has come about mostly though emigration (from countries of the 1910 "diaspora" as well as from Asia) rather than conversion.[26] Today only about 1 million of the world's Hindus are *not* from ethnic groups who are either traditionally Hindu or descended from emigrant Hindu peoples (for example, emigrants from Guyana and Suriname to the rest of South America). That equates to about 0.1% of the global total. Table 1.18 illustrates a century of growth of Hindu communities around the world through immigration as well as recent growth through guest-worker programs in the Gulf States. In addition, nearly half the world's countries still lack statistically significant Hindu communities in 2010.

Nonetheless, the presence of Hindus in both Northern America and Europe is profoundly different in 2010 than in 1910. Hindus, now numbering over 1 million on both continents, are found in all the major cities and participate at all levels of society. This will likely continue well in the decades ahead.[27]

Table 1.18 Countries with the fastest annual growth of Hindus, 1910–2010 and 2000–2010.

Country	% p.a. 1910–2010	Country	% p.a. 2000–10
United Kingdom	11.7	Qatar	11.5
United Arab Emirates	11.4	United Arab Emirates	9.5
Canada	11.2	Bahrain	6.3
Saudi Arabia	10.9	Australia	5.1
Australia	10.3	Eritrea	4.2
Oman	10.1	Sierra Leone	3.6
Netherlands	9.7	French Guiana	3.6
DR Congo	9.6	Kuwait	3.5
Kuwait	9.6	Uganda	3.3
Germany	9.6	Saudi Arabia	3.2

Data source: Todd M. Johnson and Brian J. Grim, eds., *World Religion Database* (Leiden/Boston: Brill, accessed January 2012). Countries >100,000 population.

Table 1.19 Hindu traditions, 1910 and 2010.

Tradition	Adherents 1910	% world 1910	% all Hindus 1910	Adherents 2010	% world 2010	% all Hindus 2010
Vashnivism	157,529,217	9.0	70.5	640,806,845	9.3	67.6
Shaivism	58,100,000	3.3	26.0	252,200,000	3.7	26.6
Shaktism	7,400,000	0.4	3.3	30,000,000	0.4	3.2
Neo-Hinduism	110,000	0.0	0.0	20,300,000	0.3	2.1
Reform Hinduism	280,000	0.0	0.1	5,200,000	0.1	0.5

Data source: Todd M. Johnson and Brian J. Grim, eds., *World Religion Database* (Leiden/Boston: Brill, accessed January 2012).

Table 1.19 illustrates the major traditions within Hinduism, the largest of which are Vashnivism (followers of Vishnu, 67.6%) and Shaivism (followers of Shiva, 26.6%). In addition, Shaktists (followers of Shakti, 3.2%), Neo-Hinduism, and Reform Hinduism comprise smaller movements.

Not surprisingly, the top 25 Hindu mother tongues (table 1.20) are all found in India with the exception of Nepali at number 20. The number two language, Bengali, is also the number one Muslim mother tongue.

Agnostics

"Agnosticism" is an umbrella term that includes "classical" agnostics (who believe it is impossible to know for certain whether or not there is an ultimate reality or God), individuals who profess uncertainly as to the existence of ultimate reality/God, and other non-religious persons such as secularists, materialists, and humanists.[28] In an

Table 1.20 Hindus by mother tongue, mid-2010.

Rank	Language	Main country	Total countries	Total speakers	Hindus	% Hindu
1	Hindi	India	68	148,718,000	134,980,000	90.8
2	Bengali	India	21	202,156,000	74,035,000	36.6
3	Telugu	India	14	86,948,000	66,417,000	76.4
4	Tamil	India	29	85,223,000	64,724,000	75.9
5	Marathi	India	6	84,320,000	62,669,000	74.3
6	Gujarati	India	31	61,906,000	52,356,000	84.6
7	Kannada	India	4	47,473,000	41,971,000	88.4
8	Maithili	India	2	42,541,000	41,746,000	98.1
9	Oriya	India	3	41,058,000	39,234,000	95.6
10	Bhojpuri	India	6	44,508,000	36,956,000	83.0
11	Awadhi	India	2	25,166,000	22,875,000	90.9
12	Malayalam	India	17	45,264,000	22,051,000	48.7
13	Braj Bhasha	India	1	21,476,000	19,943,000	92.9
14	Panjabi, Eastern	India	36	37,403,000	16,703,000	44.7
15	Assamese	India	3	19,590,000	16,453,000	84.0
16	Chhattisgarhi	India	1	16,265,000	15,743,000	96.8
17	Magahi	India	1	15,099,000	14,767,000	97.8
18	Haryanvi	India	1	14,760,000	14,244,000	96.5
19	Bundeli	India	1	15,120,000	14,190,000	93.8
20	Nepali	Nepal	9	17,946,000	14,136,000	78.8
21	Kanauji	India	1	11,340,000	11,158,000	98.4
22	Malvi	India	1	11,384,000	10,137,000	89.0
23	Dhundari	India	1	10,458,000	9,203,000	88.0
24	Bagheli	India	2	8,703,000	8,531,000	98.0
25	Varhadi-Nagpuri	India	1	9,123,000	8,120,000	89.0

Data source: Todd M. Johnson and Brian J. Grim, eds., *World Religion Database* (Leiden/Boston: Brill, accessed January 2012).

attempt to describe his own relationship to religion, Thomas Henry Huxley, an English biologist and fierce advocate for Darwinian evolution, coined the term "agnostic" in 1869. He found that he could neither affirm nor deny many of the core tenets of religious faith, though he could not write them off entirely with no means of disproving them. The term "agnostic" came into greater usage to refer to a lack of religion or profession of unbelief in a religion. Interestingly, agnostics, while religiously unaffiliated, might still hold some religious beliefs and participate in religious groups and activities, as was found in a recent survey by the Pew Forum. For instance, the 2007 *US Religious Landscape Survey* by the Pew Forum found that 42% of unaffiliated pray at least monthly, and 41% consider religion at least somewhat important in their lives.

Though atheists are frequently classified together with agnostics, atheists are categorized separately in this text in that they explicitly do not accept the existence of a God or gods.

Table 1.21 Agnostics (A) by United Nations continents and regions, 1910–2010.

Region	Population 1910	A 1910	% 1910	Population 2010	A 2010	% 2010	A 1910–2010	Pop 1910–2010	A 2000–10	Pop 2000–10
Africa	**124,541,000**	**8,400**	**0.0**	**1,022,234,000**	**6,497,000**	**0.6**	**6.88**	**2.13**	**2.72**	**2.34**
Eastern	33,012,000	220	0.0	324,044,000	854,000	0.3	8.62	2.31	2.13	2.56
Middle	19,445,000	0	0.0	126,689,000	727,000	0.6	11.84	1.89	3.19	2.79
Northern	31,968,000	5,700	0.0	209,459,000	1,267,000	0.6	5.55	1.90	3.37	1.75
Southern	6,819,000	2,500	0.0	57,780,000	2,765,000	4.8	7.26	2.16	2.53	1.17
Western	33,296,000	0	0.0	304,261,000	884,000	0.3	12.06	2.24	2.64	2.59
Asia	**1,026,693,000**	**50,400**	**0.0**	**4,164,252,000**	**504,762,000**	**12.1**	**9.65**	**1.41**	**0.17**	**1.14**
Eastern	554,135,000	30,900	0.0	1,573,970,000	467,232,000	29.7	10.10	1.05	0.13	0.51
South-central	345,718,000	15,800	0.0	1,764,872,000	17,302,000	1.0	7.25	1.64	0.17	1.53
South-eastern	93,859,000	2,500	0.0	593,415,000	17,126,000	2.9	9.23	1.86	1.14	1.26
Western	32,982,000	1,200	0.0	231,995,000	3,102,000	1.3	8.17	1.97	1.30	2.32
Europe	**427,044,000**	**1,643,000**	**0.4**	**738,199,000**	**93,325,000**	**12.6**	**4.12**	**0.55**	**-0.51**	**0.16**
Eastern	178,184,000	306,000	0.2	294,771,000	23,612,000	8.0	4.44	0.50	-4.72	-0.31
Northern	61,473,000	836,000	1.4	99,205,000	17,568,000	17.7	3.09	0.48	1.35	0.50
Southern	76,828,000	179,000	0.2	155,171,000	13,262,000	8.5	4.40	0.71	1.04	0.67
Western	110,558,000	322,000	0.3	189,052,000	38,882,000	20.6	4.91	0.54	1.79	0.32
Latin America	**78,254,000**	**446,000**	**0.6**	**590,082,000**	**18,712,000**	**3.2**	**3.81**	**2.04**	**1.66**	**1.24**
Caribbean	8,172,000	2,500	0.0	41,646,000	2,804,000	6.7	7.27	1.64	-1.46	0.80
Central	20,806,000	11,700	0.1	155,881,000	3,772,000	2.4	5.95	2.03	2.46	1.41
South	49,276,000	432,000	0.9	392,555,000	12,136,000	3.1	3.39	2.10	2.31	1.23
Northern America	**94,689,000**	**1,169,000**	**1.2**	**344,529,000**	**48,119,000**	**14.0**	**3.79**	**1.30**	**2.91**	**0.96**
Oceania	**7,192,000**	**51,100**	**0.7**	**36,593,000**	**5,529,000**	**15.1**	**4.80**	**1.64**	**3.24**	**1.63**
Australia/New Zealand	5,375,000	50,100	0.9	26,637,000	5,433,000	20.4	4.80	1.61	3.24	1.47
Melanesia	1,596,000	1,000	0.1	8,748,000	74,600	0.9	4.41	1.72	4.31	2.26
Micronesia	89,400	0	0.0	536,000	6,600	1.2	6.71	1.81	2.41	0.78
Polynesia	131,000	0	0.0	673,000	14,800	2.2	7.57	1.65	1.62	0.91
Global total	**1,758,412,000**	**3,369,000**	**0.2**	**6,895,889,000**	**676,944,000**	**9.8**	**5.45**	**1.38**	**0.32**	**1.20**

Data source: Todd M. Johnson and Brian J. Grim, eds., *World Religion Database* (Leiden/Boston: Brill, accessed January 2012).

Table 1.22 Countries with the most agnostics, 1910 and 2010.

Country	Agnostics 1910	Country	Agnostics 2010
United States	1,157,000	China	437,155,000
United Kingdom	760,000	United States	41,922,000
Uruguay	407,000	Germany	18,288,000
Russia	118,000	India	14,194,000
Croatia	107,000	North Korea	13,648,000
France	92,400	Japan	12,873,000
Germany	88,100	United Kingdom	12,169,000
Netherlands	74,300	France	11,861,000
Ukraine	63,000	Viet Nam	11,109,000
Italy	53,700	Russia	8,653,000

Data source: Todd M. Johnson and Brian J. Grim, eds., *World Religion Database* (Leiden/ Boston: Brill, accessed January 2012).

Table 1.23 Countries with the highest percentage of agnostics, 1910 and 2010.

Country	% 1910	Country	% 2010
Uruguay	37.2	North Korea	56.1
Croatia	3.6	Estonia	50.9
United Kingdom	1.9	Czech Republic	39.4
New Caledonia	1.8	China	32.6
Kosovo	1.4	New Zealand	30.6
United States	1.3	Uruguay	28.0
Netherlands	1.3	Netherlands	26.4
Australia	1.0	Latvia	25.0
Sweden	1.0	Germany	22.2
Channel Islands	0.9	Belarus	22.2

Data source: Todd M. Johnson and Brian J. Grim, eds., *World Religion Database* (Leiden/Boston: Brill, accessed January 2012). Countries >100,000 population.

Agnosticism grew out of the eighteenth-century Enlightenment, though later, in the nineteenth century, the natural sciences and their associated rationalist thinking gained increased prominence. Its history over the past century was especially eventful. In 1910 agnostics numbered only 0.2% of the global population, and agnosticism was almost exclusively a Northern phenomenon (83% of all agnostics lived in the global North; see table 1.21). One notable exception was Uruguay (in the global South), which was home to another 12%; however, in 1910 Uruguay's population consisted mainly of nineteenth-century European immigrants and their descendants, and it was by far the most agnostic country in the world (37% of the country's population; see table 1.23). The early to mid-twentieth century saw dramatic growth of agnosticism for a number of reasons, including the expansion of scientific discovery and thinking. Additionally, the optimism of the twentieth century had greatly waned after World War I, with deleterious effects on Christian

Table 1.24 Countries with the fastest annual growth of agnostics, 1910–2010 and 2000–10.

Country	% 1910–2010 p.a.	Country	% 2000–10 p.a.
North Korea	15.2	Afghanistan	13.8
Japan	15.1	Qatar	11.3
Viet Nam	14.9	United Arab Emirates	9.5
Indonesia	13.5	Luxembourg	8.4
Hong Kong	12.5	Ireland	7.1
Thailand	12.4	Papua New Guinea	6.7
Venezuela	12.4	Bahrain	6.3
Taiwan	12.2	El Salvador	6.3
Finland	12.1	Saint Lucia	5.9
Turkey	11.9	Namibia	5.9

Data source: Todd M. Johnson and Brian J. Grim, eds., *World Religion Database* (Leiden/ Boston: Brill, accessed January 2012). Countries >100,000 population.

faith in Europe. Even more significant was the rise of Communism, with its associated Marxist denunciation of all religion, first in the global North (following the 1917 Russian Revolution) and then in the global South (following the 1949 Chinese Revolution). It is not surprising that some of the countries with the largest agnostic populations – China, North Korea, and Viet Nam – are countries with Communist governments (parts of Germany, with the third-largest number of agnostics, notably spent 40 years under Communist rule; see table 1.22). Likewise, two of the 10 countries with the highest percentages of agnostics (table 1.23) have current Communist governments, former Communists are the ruling party in another, and five more are former Communist countries.

The changes in percentages of agnostics (table 1.24) illustrate the growth of non-belief throughout the twentieth century. In 1910 agnostics represented relatively small proportions of the total population even in the countries (Uruguay excepted) with the largest percentages of agnostics (table 1.23). By 2010 most of the top 10 countries' populations are a quarter or more agnostic. This is quite drastic change in a relatively short period of time.

Chinese Folk-Religionists

Chinese folk-religion is deeply ingrained in Chinese history, with many of its beliefs, practices, and rituals traceable to tribal animism and shamanism.[29] As a result, the religion is a belief system that includes the worship of a myriad of gods, goddesses, and demi-gods in temple complexes scattered throughout the globe. Chinese folk-religion has no unified beliefs, though many practices and rituals serve as unifying activities for adherents, including ancestor veneration, magic, worship of household gods, and festivals (such as Chinese New Year). These practices are observed alongside Buddhist, Confucian, and Daoist traditions with no hint of competition or conflict between them; many Chinese folk-religionists practice and apply numerous religious rituals anywhere and at any time. Taiwanese philosopher Chung-Ying Cheng states that "the spirit of religion in China is basically the spirit of unity in variety and variety in unity with religion understood in both the narrow sense of explicit commitments and the broad sense of implicit beliefs."[30] The all-inclusive nature of Chinese folk-religion among Eastern religious beliefs decisively sets it apart from other world religions.

Adherence to Chinese folk-religion is typically greater among rural populations, while residents of urban centers generally focus on Daoist or Confucianist rites. In 1910 Chinese folk-religion was confined largely to Asian countries, and this reality persists into the twenty-first century (see table 1.25). Over 99% of the world's Chinese folk-religionists reside in Asia, with 93.7% of these in China and 2.3% in Taiwan (96.0% total). Growth rates indicate an increasing presence of Chinese folk-religionists in African and Western Asian countries.

The center of gravity for this religion has moved little over the past 100 years. In 2010 nine of the 10 countries with the most Chinese folk-religionists (table 1.26) were the same as in 1910. Canada, with 672,000 adherents, has replaced the United States as the only non-Asian country on the list. China continues to top the list, but massive conversions from Chinese folk-religion to atheism or agnosticism following the Communist revolution there drastically slowed global growth. Although Chinese folk-religionists remain heavily concentrated in China and Taiwan, they are present in every region of the world because of immigration from those countries. All of Europe and most of Latin America showed no Chinese folk-religionists in 1910, but by 2010 they have very small populations. The Han Chinese are the largest ethnic group in China (and the world) and a large minority adheres to Chinese folk-religion. Additionally, Han Chinese are found in nearly half of the countries of the world. Most of the world's countries (146), however, continue to report very few (under 1,000) or no Chinese folk-religionists. Recent survey research in China has shown an increase in interest in traditional Chinese religion. This could reverse a century-long decline in Chinese folk-religion, although the greatest interest has been in Buddhism. Table 1.27 shows that Chinese folk-religionists are concentrated in Asia with a few significant populations in diaspora communities such as French Guiana and Canada. Table 1.28 documents recent growth in Finland, Mozambique, Iran, and other countries.

Buddhists

Images of the Buddha, ancient and new, are ubiquitous around the globe.[31] The diversity and continuity of the images are astonishing – ranging from the Buddha's gaunt appearance in India to his portly image in the Far East. Hundreds of millions of Buddhists turn to these varying images as objects of religious devotion and as a sign of their affiliation. Thus, in today's world, one encounters "Buddhisms" as well as "Buddhism." This is consistent with the first meaning of *sāsana*, a term that can be rendered as the religion or tradition of a particular nation.[32] In this localized sense, Buddhism represents the practice and ritual of an ethnic, linguistic, or cultural community. At the same time, local Buddhists will be aware that they belong to a

Table 1.25 Chinese folk-religionists (CFR) by United Nations continents and regions, 1910–2010.

Region	Population 1910	CFR 1910	% 1910	Population 2010	CFR 2010	% 2010	CFR 1910–2010	Pop 1910–2010	CFR 2000–10	Pop 2000–10
Africa	**124,541,000**	**2,200**	**0.0**	**1,022,234,000**	**132,000**	**0.0**	**4.18**	**2.13**	**2.41**	**2.34**
Eastern	33,012,000	1,500	0.0	324,044,000	70,700	0.0	3.93	2.31	2.81	2.56
Middle	19,445,000	0	0.0	126,689,000	4,800	0.0	6.37	1.89	5.54	2.79
Northern	31,968,000	0	0.0	209,459,000	17,100	0.0	7.73	1.90	2.70	1.75
Southern	6,819,000	610	0.0	57,780,000	33,700	0.1	4.09	2.16	1.14	1.17
Western	33,296,000	0	0.0	304,261,000	5,800	0.0	6.57	2.24	2.80	2.59
Asia	**1,026,693,000**	**390,399,000**	**38.0**	**4,164,252,000**	**434,614,000**	**10.4**	**0.11**	**1.41**	**0.16**	**1.14**
Eastern	554,135,000	388,659,000	70.1	1,573,970,000	422,862,000	26.9	0.08	1.05	0.12	0.51
South-central	345,718,000	10,900	0.0	1,764,872,000	191,000	0.0	2.90	1.64	1.60	1.53
South-eastern	93,859,000	1,729,000	1.8	593,415,000	11,496,000	1.9	1.91	1.86	1.61	1.26
Western	32,982,000	0	0.0	231,995,000	65,500	0.0	9.18	1.97	2.35	2.32
Europe	**427,044,000**	**0**	**0.0**	**738,199,000**	**439,000**	**0.1**	**11.28**	**0.55**	**1.51**	**0.16**
Eastern	178,184,000	0	0.0	294,771,000	11,100	0.0	7.26	0.50	0.09	-0.31
Northern	61,473,000	0	0.0	99,205,000	80,800	0.1	9.41	0.48	1.10	0.50
Southern	76,828,000	0	0.0	155,171,000	103,000	0.1	9.68	0.71	1.31	0.67
Western	110,558,000	0	0.0	189,052,000	244,000	0.1	10.63	0.54	1.76	0.32
Latin America	**78,254,000**	**1,900**	**0.0**	**590,082,000**	**189,000**	**0.0**	**4.71**	**2.04**	**1.25**	**1.24**
Caribbean	8,172,000	350	0.0	41,646,000	39,800	0.1	4.85	1.64	0.46	0.80
Central	20,806,000	500	0.0	155,881,000	49,500	0.0	4.70	2.03	1.66	1.41
South	49,276,000	1,100	0.0	392,555,000	100,000	0.0	4.61	2.10	1.41	1.23
Northern America	**94,689,000**	**87,100**	**0.1**	**344,529,000**	**781,000**	**0.2**	**2.22**	**1.30**	**1.03**	**0.96**
Oceania	**7,192,000**	**14,300**	**0.2**	**36,593,000**	**103,000**	**0.3**	**1.99**	**1.64**	**1.95**	**1.63**
Australia/New Zealand	5,375,000	14,100	0.3	26,637,000	89,000	0.3	1.86	1.61	2.09	1.47
Melanesia	1,596,000	0	0.0	8,748,000	6,000	0.1	6.61	1.72	2.26	2.26
Micronesia	89,400	0	0.0	536,000	6,300	1.2	6.66	1.81	-0.16	0.78
Polynesia	131,000	220	0.2	673,000	1,400	0.2	1.87	1.65	1.55	0.91
Global total	**1,758,412,000**	**390,504,000**	**22.2**	**6,895,889,000**	**436,258,000**	**6.3**	**0.11**	**1.38**	**0.16**	**1.20**

Data source: Todd M. Johnson and Brian J. Grim, eds., *World Religion Database* (Leiden/Boston: Brill, accessed January 2012).

Table 1.26 Countries with the most Chinese folk-religionists (CFR), 1910 and 2010.

Country	CFR 1910	Country	CFR 2010
China	385,487,000	China	408,959,000
Taiwan	2,634,000	Taiwan	9,995,000
Malaysia	650,000	Malaysia	5,220,000
Hong Kong	467,000	Hong Kong	3,236,000
Thailand	304,000	Indonesia	2,126,000
Viet Nam	240,000	Singapore	1,987,000
Indonesia	225,000	Viet Nam	878,000
Singapore	164,000	Canada	672,000
Cambodia	112,000	Thailand	644,000
United States	81,000	Cambodia	417,000

Data source: Todd M. Johnson and Brian J. Grim, eds., *World Religion Database* (Leiden/ Boston: Brill, accessed January 2012).

Table 1.27 Countries with the highest percentage of Chinese folk-religionists, 1910 and 2010.

Country	% 1910	Country	% 2010
Hong Kong	88.5	Macau	58.9
Macau	81.2	Hong Kong	45.9
China	79.6	Taiwan	43.1
Taiwan	68.6	Singapore	39.1
Singapore	49.5	China	30.5
Malaysia	25.0	Malaysia	18.4
Brunei	6.1	Brunei	5.2
Cambodia	4.0	French Guiana	3.6
Thailand	3.9	Cambodia	2.9
Viet Nam	1.8	Canada	2.0

Data source: Todd M. Johnson and Brian J. Grim, eds., *World Religion Database* (Leiden/ Boston: Brill, accessed January 2012). Countries >100,000 population.

Table 1.28 Countries with the fastest annual growth of Chinese folk-religionists, 1910–2010 and 2000–10.

Country	% 1910–2010 p.a.	Country	% 2000–10 p.a.
France	10.5	Finland	11.9
United Kingdom	9.1	Mozambique	9.7
Italy	8.8	Iran	8.5
Brazil	8.7	Senegal	6.7
South Korea	8.5	Kenya	6.6
Israel	8.2	Cameroon	6.5
Saudi Arabia	8.1	Uganda	6.5
Spain	8.1	Chad	5.5
Tanzania	8.1	Kazakhstan	4.4
Portugal	8.0	Egypt	4.4

Data source: Todd M. Johnson and Brian J. Grim, eds., *World Religion Database* (Leiden/ Boston: Brill, accessed January 2012). Countries >100,000 population.

Table 1.29 Buddhists by United Nations continents and regions, 1910–2010.

Region	Population 1910	Buddhists 1910	% 1910	Population 2010	Buddhists 2010	% 2010	Buddhist 1910–2010	Pop 1910–2010	Buddhist 2000–10	Pop 2000–10
Africa	**124,541,000**	**3,600**	**0.0**	**1,022,234,000**	**254,000**	**0.0**	**4.35**	**2.13**	**1.63**	**2.34**
Eastern	33,012,000	3,500	0.0	324,044,000	29,600	0.0	2.16	2.31	3.11	2.56
Middle	19,445,000	0	0.0	126,689,000	7,600	0.0	6.86	1.89	3.67	2.79
Northern	31,968,000	0	0.0	209,459,000	27,400	0.0	8.24	1.90	2.17	1.75
Southern	6,819,000	120	0.0	57,780,000	160,000	0.3	7.46	2.16	1.13	1.17
Western	33,296,000	0	0.0	304,261,000	29,500	0.0	8.32	2.24	2.08	2.59
Asia	**1,026,693,000**	**137,570,000**	**13.4**	**4,164,252,000**	**487,038,000**	**11.7**	**1.27**	**1.41**	**0.99**	**1.14**
Eastern	554,135,000	103,665,000	18.7	1,573,970,000	299,334,000	19.0	1.07	1.05	0.97	0.51
South-central	345,718,000	4,010,000	1.2	1,764,872,000	28,326,000	1.6	1.97	1.64	1.47	1.53
South-eastern	93,859,000	29,895,000	31.9	593,415,000	158,923,000	26.8	1.68	1.86	0.95	1.26
Western	32,982,000	0	0.0	231,995,000	455,000	0.2	11.32	1.97	4.61	2.32
Europe	**427,044,000**	**428,000**	**0.1**	**738,199,000**	**1,789,000**	**0.2**	**1.44**	**0.55**	**0.49**	**0.16**
Eastern	178,184,000	428,000	0.2	294,771,000	578,000	0.2	0.30	0.50	-0.24	-0.31
Northern	61,473,000	100	0.0	99,205,000	299,000	0.3	8.33	0.48	0.99	0.50
Southern	76,828,000	0	0.0	155,171,000	88,400	0.1	9.51	0.71	0.83	0.67
Western	110,558,000	0	0.0	189,052,000	824,000	0.4	11.98	0.54	0.80	0.32
Latin America	**78,254,000**	**7,100**	**0.0**	**590,082,000**	**759,000**	**0.1**	**4.78**	**2.04**	**1.21**	**1.24**
Caribbean	8,172,000	210	0.0	41,646,000	14,400	0.0	4.32	1.64	0.43	0.80
Central	20,806,000	2,600	0.0	155,881,000	70,000	0.0	3.35	2.03	1.57	1.41
South	49,276,000	4,300	0.0	392,555,000	674,000	0.2	5.18	2.10	1.19	1.23
Northern America	**94,689,000**	**47,200**	**0.0**	**344,529,000**	**4,454,000**	**1.3**	**4.65**	**1.30**	**1.32**	**0.96**
Oceania	**7,192,000**	**7,600**	**0.1**	**36,593,000**	**587,000**	**1.6**	**4.44**	**1.64**	**2.72**	**1.63**
Australia/New Zealand	5,375,000	7,500	0.1	26,637,000	562,000	2.1	4.41	1.61	2.79	1.47
Melanesia	1,596,000	0	0.0	8,748,000	15,000	0.2	7.59	1.72	2.43	2.26
Micronesia	89,400	0	0.0	536,000	9,100	1.7	7.05	1.81	-0.53	0.78
Polynesia	131,000	110	0.1	673,000	610	0.1	1.73	1.65	1.23	0.91
Global total	**1,758,412,000**	**138,064,000**	**7.9**	**6,895,889,000**	**494,881,000**	**7.2**	**1.28**	**1.38**	**0.99**	**1.20**

Data source: Todd M. Johnson and Brian J. Grim, eds., *World Religion Database* (Leiden/Boston: Brill, accessed January 2012).

Table 1.30 Countries with the most Buddhists, 1910 and 2010.

Country	Buddhists 1910	Country	Buddhists 2010
China	61,200,000	China	206,898,000
Japan	40,304,000	Japan	71,307,000
Myanmar	9,987,000	Thailand	60,298,000
Viet Nam	9,148,000	Viet Nam	43,212,000
Thailand	7,021,000	Myanmar	35,823,000
Sri Lanka	2,508,000	Sri Lanka	14,378,000
Cambodia	2,387,000	Cambodia	12,007,000
Nepal	1,013,000	South Korea	11,954,000
South Korea	950,000	India	8,772,000
Laos	924,000	Taiwan	6,145,000

Data source: Todd M. Johnson and Brian J. Grim, eds., *World Religion Database* (Leiden/Boston: Brill, accessed January 2012).

Table 1.31 Countries with the highest percentage of Buddhists, 1910 and 2010.

Country	% 1910	Country	% 2010
Thailand	90.9	Thailand	87.2
Myanmar	86.6	Cambodia	84.9
Cambodia	85.5	Bhutan	84.0
Japan	79.5	Myanmar	74.7
Bhutan	77.6	Sri Lanka	68.9
Viet Nam	69.3	Japan	56.4
Laos	60.3	Mongolia	54.2
Sri Lanka	59.4	Laos	52.2
Mongolia	38.4	Viet Nam	49.2
Nepal	20.3	Taiwan	26.5

Data source: Todd M. Johnson and Brian J. Grim, eds., *World Religion Database* (Leiden/Boston: Brill, accessed January 2012). Countries >100,000 population.

wider religious community. It is this second meaning of *sāsana* that gives Buddhism its transcendental and universalizing vision. All local Buddhist communities (*sāsana*) are part of a larger global community of Buddhists (*sāsana*).

At the beginning of the twentieth century Buddhism was almost exclusively an Asian religion. In 1910, 99.6% of the world's Buddhists lived in Asia, particularly China and Japan (73.5% of the global population). After 100 years Asia is still home to 98.4% of the global total (table 1.29). The list of countries with the most Buddhists (table 1.30) has not changed much over the past 100 years, especially at the top of the list. Buddhists in these countries are growing at rates similar to those of the general population.

In 1910 the Buddhist center of gravity was in southern China. By 2010 the more rapidly growing Buddhist populations in South-eastern Asia had shifted it to the South

Table 1.32 Countries with the fastest annual growth of Buddhists, 1910–2010 and 2000–10.

Country	% p.a. 1910–2010	Country	% p.a. 2000–10
France	11.4	Qatar	11.5
Netherlands	10.4	United Arab Emirates	9.4
United Kingdom	10.4	Mozambique	9.3
United Arab Emirates	10.1	Iran	8.2
Pakistan	9.7	Bahrain	7.2
Saudi Arabia	9.5	Cameroon	6.3
Lebanon	9.5	Uganda	6.2
Germany	9.5	Kenya	5.7
Portugal	9.1	Chad	5.6
Sweden	8.6	Ireland	5.0

Data source: Todd M. Johnson and Brian J. Grim, eds., *World Religion Database* (Leiden/Boston: Brill, accessed January 2012). Countries >100,000 population.

Table 1.33 Buddhist traditions, 1910 and 2010.

Tradition	Adherents 1910	% world 1910	% all Buddhists 1910	Adherents 2010	% world 2010	% all Buddhists 2010
Mahayana	78,024,900	4.4	56.5	263,336,390	3.8	53.2
Theravada	52,000,000	3.0	37.7	177,400,000	2.6	35.8
Tibetan (Lamaist)	8,000,000	0.5	5.8	28,000,000	0.4	5.7

Data source: Todd M. Johnson and Brian J. Grim, eds., *World Religion Database* (Leiden/Boston: Brill, accessed January 2012).

and West. Many Latin American and European countries had no Buddhists in 1910 but now contain small populations. The shift to the West has been for various reasons, not the least being a Western interest in Eastern ideals and traditions.[33] In addition, Buddhists have taken a more deliberate "missionary" posture in many countries around the world.[34] Increased international travel also has brought large numbers of Westerners to predominantly Buddhist Asian countries. The global celebrity of the fourteenth Dalai Lama, who represents Tibetan Buddhism, has influenced Western interest in and growth of the religion as well.[35] In addition, immigration patterns to various Western countries have affected Buddhist populations outside Asia. The countries with the fastest Buddhist growth rates are all in atypical Buddhist lands, with Qatar, United Arab Emirates, and Mozambique the top three in the period 2000–10 (table 1.32).

The demographics of Buddhism can be considered in two ways: core Buddhism and wider Buddhism. Core Buddhism (table 1.33) includes the major schools of Buddhist thought: Theravada, Mahayana, and Tibetan. The concept of wider Buddhism includes all Buddhists of core Buddhism, plus all Chinese folk-religionists and most other Chinese. The Buddhist worldview and key rituals impact the whole of Chinese culture, including many Chinese who claim to be agnostic or atheist. In this "wider" definition it is appropriate to speak of 1 billion Buddhists.

Table 1.34 Buddhists by mother tongue, mid-2010.

Rank	Language	Main country	Total countries	Total speakers	Buddhists	% Buddhist
1	Chinese, Mandarin	China	90	880,662,000	155,821,000	17.7
2	Japanese	Japan	42	127,794,000	71,656,000	56.1
3	Vietnamese	Viet Nam	28	77,920,000	42,600,000	54.7
4	Thai	Thailand	23	28,864,000	27,310,000	94.6
5	Burmese	Myanmar	11	26,628,000	25,875,000	97.2
6	Thai, North-eastern	Thailand	2	18,327,000	18,162,000	99.1
7	Chinese, Yue	China	38	80,715,000	16,321,000	20.2
8	Sinhala	Sri Lanka	21	15,845,000	14,932,000	94.2
9	Korean	South Korea	37	77,040,000	13,221,000	17.2
10	Khmer, Central	Cambodia	10	14,021,000	12,917,000	92.1
11	Chinese, Wu	China	7	86,396,000	12,126,000	14.0
12	Chinese, Min Nan	Taiwan	15	65,696,000	10,233,000	15.6
13	Thai, Northern	Thailand	1	7,338,000	7,195,000	98.1
14	Tibetan, Central	China	7	5,650,000	5,499,000	97.3
15	Marathi	India	1	84,320,000	5,224,000	6.2
16	Thai, Southern	Thailand	1	5,433,000	4,982,000	91.7
17	Shan	Myanmar	2	4,152,000	4,108,000	98.9
18	Chinese, Hakka	China	18	40,104,000	3,976,000	9.9
19	Chinese, Jinyu	China	1	56,202,000	3,934,000	7.0
20	Lao	Laos	9	3,025,000	2,626,000	86.8
21	Chinese, Min Dong	China	4	9,550,000	1,811,000	19.0
22	Hindi	India	2	148,718,000	1,641,000	1.1
23	Nepali	Nepal	2	17,946,000	1,604,000	8.9
24	Rakhine	Myanmar	3	1,934,000	1,550,000	80.1
25	Mongolian, Halh	Mongolia	7	2,101,000	1,498,000	71.3

Data source: Todd M. Johnson and Brian J. Grim, eds., *World Religion Database* (Leiden/Boston: Brill, accessed January 2012).

Three major branches of Buddhism – Theravada, Mahayana, and Tibetan – are found worldwide (listed in table 1.33). Theravada Buddhism, the oldest and most conservative branch, is practiced by a majority of the population in countries such as Sri Lanka, Thailand, and Cambodia. Mahayana Buddhism emerged in reaction against Theravada and emphasizes the Bodhisattva ideal (forgoing Nirvana to teach others how to achieve it). Buddhists in China, Japan, Korea, and Singapore adhere primarily to the Mahayana school. Tibetan Buddhism, found mainly in Tibet and Mongolia, focuses more on spiritual and physical exercises to enhance the Buddhist experience.

The global mother tongues of Buddhism are clearly situated in Eastern and South-eastern Asia. However, several in the top 10, including first-ranked Mandarin Chinese, are spoken by Buddhist minorities in large populations (table 1.34). Most of these Buddhists are also Chinese folk-religionists (mixing Buddhism, Daoism, and Confucianism).

Ethnoreligionists

"Ethnoreligionists" is a collective term for animists, spirit-worshippers, shaman-ists, ancestor-venerators, polytheists, pantheists, and local or tribal folk-religionists. These religions are typically transmitted orally, with no unifying written text but many rich traditions, myths, and histories that are passed on throughout the gen-erations. Although ethnoreligions differ greatly from location to location, many characteristics bind them together. The primal worldview involves a free-flowing exchange between the spiritual and physical worlds in daily life, thus invoking individuals to attempt the ritual manipulation of power and of the spiritual realm, from which the answers to life's joys and sorrows can be found. Typically there is a hierarchy of spiritual power, with the main deity at the top of the ladder, followed by helper gods, diviners, elders, warriors and so on, in a kind of diffused monotheism.

In some instances, ethnoreligions are heavily blended with aspects of mis-sionary religions that arrived in a culture at a specific time. This is particularly true in sub-Saharan Africa, which saw great growth of both Islam and Christianity over the course of the twentieth century; many African ethnoreligions adapted beliefs from these monotheistic faiths and it is not uncommon, for example, to see a shaman use the Qur'an as part of a prophetic or healing session (this specific type of blending is also referred to as "folk Islam"). Individual ethnoreligions are usually confined to a single tribe or people and are thus uniquely tribal or local.

In 1910 a majority of Africans (58%) – as well as a significant minority of the population of Oceania (almost 20%) – were ethnoreligionists (see table 1.35). The highest global concentrations were in Middle Africa (94.5% of the regional population), Melanesia (83.3%), Western Africa (72.9%) and Eastern Africa (70.4%). The 10 coun-tries with the highest percentages of ethnoreligionists were in Africa (table 1.37). While Indonesia was the country with the most ethnoreligionists in 1910, China holds that position in 2010 (table 1.36), with 54 different ethnic minorities, perhaps half of which have a tradition of folk-religion. In 2010, as a result of twentieth-century migration, ethnoreligionists are found in 62% of the world's countries as opposed to 40% in 1910. Bahrain represents the fastest-growing population of ethnoreligionists, largely through the guest-worker program there (table 1.38). Although their absolute numbers increased in most regions during the twentieth century, the ethnoreligionist share of the global population declined by half (from 7.7% to 3.5%). Underlying this change have been the missionary efforts of Christians and Muslims in Africa, South-eastern Asia, and Oceania.

In Middle Africa, for example, ethnoreligionists now make up less than 7% of the population. Throughout the last century ethnoreligionists declined from 94.5% of the population to 6.7%, as Christians increased from 1.1% to 82.5% and Muslims from 4.5% to 9.7%. Africa, however, is still home to nine of the 10 countries with the high-est percentages of ethnoreligionists (table 1.37). Shamanism, one form of ethnoreli-gion, has shown resiliency – despite demographic decline – in both Mongolia and South Korea, where its practice has been on the rise.

Table 1.35 Ethnoreligionists (E) by United Nations continents and regions, 1910–2010.

Region	Population 1910	E 1910	% 1910	Population 2010	E 2010	% 2010	E 1910–2010	Pop 1910–2010	E 2000–10	Pop 2000–10
Africa	**124,541,000**	**72,210,000**	**58.0**	**1,022,234,000**	**89,354,000**	**8.7**	**0.21**	**2.13**	**1.48**	**2.34**
Eastern	33,012,000	23,230,000	70.4	324,044,000	35,208,000	10.9	0.42	2.31	1.59	2.56
Middle	19,445,000	18,367,000	94.5	126,689,000	8,430,000	6.7	−0.78	1.89	1.33	2.79
Northern	31,968,000	2,203,000	6.9	209,459,000	4,475,000	2.1	0.71	1.90	0.89	1.75
Southern	6,819,000	4,153,000	60.9	57,780,000	4,567,000	7.9	0.10	2.16	0.33	1.17
Western	33,296,000	24,257,000	72.9	304,261,000	36,674,000	12.1	0.41	2.24	1.64	2.59
Asia	**1,026,693,000**	**57,894,000**	**5.6**	**4,164,252,000**	**146,779,000**	**3.5**	**0.93**	**1.41**	**0.82**	**1.14**
Eastern	554,135,000	23,954,000	4.3	1,573,970,000	68,524,000	4.4	1.06	1.05	0.49	0.51
South-central	345,718,000	8,009,000	2.3	1,764,872,000	50,823,000	2.9	1.86	1.64	1.23	1.53
South-eastern	93,859,000	25,875,000	27.6	593,415,000	27,370,000	4.6	0.06	1.86	0.93	1.26
Western	32,982,000	54,800	0.2	231,995,000	62,500	0.0	0.13	1.97	2.83	2.32
Europe	**427,044,000**	**662,000**	**0.2**	**738,199,000**	**1,168,000**	**0.2**	**0.57**	**0.55**	**−0.15**	**0.16**
Eastern	178,184,000	662,000	0.4	294,771,000	1,005,000	0.3	0.42	0.50	−0.26	−0.31
Northern	61,473,000	0	0.0	99,205,000	35,400	0.0	8.52	0.48	0.32	0.50
Southern	76,828,000	0	0.0	155,171,000	5,300	0.0	6.47	0.71	0.00	0.67
Western	110,558,000	0	0.0	189,052,000	122,000	0.1	9.87	0.54	0.59	0.32
Latin America	**78,254,000**	**2,725,000**	**3.5**	**590,082,000**	**3,626,000**	**0.6**	**0.29**	**2.04**	**1.21**	**1.24**
Caribbean	8,172,000	0	0.0	41,646,000	420	0.0	3.81	1.64	0.00	0.80
Central	20,806,000	188,000	0.9	155,881,000	1,550,000	1.0	2.13	2.03	1.38	1.41
South	49,276,000	2,536,000	5.1	392,555,000	2,075,000	0.5	−0.20	2.10	1.09	1.23
Northern America	**94,689,000**	**170,000**	**0.2**	**344,529,000**	**1,221,000**	**0.4**	**1.99**	**1.30**	**1.12**	**0.96**
Oceania	**7,192,000**	**1,414,000**	**19.7**	**36,593,000**	**369,000**	**1.0**	**−1.33**	**1.64**	**2.30**	**1.63**
Australia/New Zealand	5,375,000	63,100	1.2	26,637,000	103,000	0.4	0.49	1.61	2.29	1.47
Melanesia	1,596,000	1,330,000	83.3	8,748,000	261,000	3.0	−1.62	1.72	2.35	2.26
Micronesia	89,400	20,800	23.3	536,000	4,400	0.8	−1.54	1.81	−0.22	0.78
Polynesia	131,000	0	0.0	673,000	420	0.1	3.81	1.65	0.49	0.91
Global total	**1,758,412,000**	**135,074,000**	**7.7**	**6,895,889,000**	**242,516,000**	**3.5**	**0.59**	**1.38**	**1.06**	**1.20**

Data source: Todd M. Johnson and Brian J. Grim, eds., *World Religion Database* (Leiden/Boston: Brill, accessed January 2012).

Table 1.36 Countries with the most ethnoreligionists (E), 1910 and 2010.

Country	E 1910	Country	E 2010
Indonesia	20,128,000	China	57,890,000
Nigeria	13,870,000	India	45,891,000
China	11,228,000	Nigeria	12,152,000
DR Congo	9,411,000	Viet Nam	9,104,000
South Korea	7,759,000	Madagascar	8,370,000
India	7,386,000	South Korea	7,062,000
North Korea	4,494,000	Mozambique	6,887,000
Tanzania	3,957,000	Indonesia	5,521,000
South Africa	3,430,000	Tanzania	5,312,000
Ethiopia	3,369,000	Ethiopia	5,017,000

Data source: Todd M. Johnson and Brian J. Grim, eds., *World Religion Database* (Leiden/Boston: Brill, accessed January 2012).

Table 1.37 Countries with the highest percentage of ethnoreligionists, 1910 and 2010.

Country	% 1910	Country	% 2010
Rwanda	99.8	Laos	42.8
Burundi	99.8	Guinea-Bissau	42.0
Zambia	99.7	Liberia	41.6
Central African Republic	99.6	Madagascar	40.4
Angola	99.4	Togo	33.9
Swaziland	99.0	South Sudan	32.9
DR Congo	98.1	Benin	30.4
Congo	97.5	Botswana	29.8
São Tomé & Príncipe	96.8	Mozambique	29.4
Mozambique	96.3	Cote d'Ivoire	24.5

Data source: Todd M. Johnson and Brian J. Grim, eds., *World Religion Database* (Leiden/Boston: Brill, accessed January 2012). Countries >100,000 population.

Table 1.38 Countries with the fastest annual growth of ethnoreligionists, 1910–2010 and 2000–10.

Country	% 1910–2010 p.a.	Country	% 2000–10 p.a.
France	9.8	Bahrain	7.2
Uzbekistan	9.0	Eritrea	3.7
Saudi Arabia	8.9	Afghanistan	3.3
United Kingdom	8.0	Mayotte	3.3
Japan	7.1	Saudi Arabia	3.2
Sweden	7.1	French Guiana	3.2
Comoros	6.8	Liberia	3.1
Somalia	6.7	Mali	3.1
Tajikistan	6.7	DR Congo	2.9
Ukraine	6.7	Singapore	2.9

Data source: Todd M. Johnson and Brian J. Grim, eds., *World Religion Database* (Leiden/Boston: Brill, accessed January 2012). Countries >100,000 population.

Atheists

Atheists, unlike agnostics, reject the idea of any deity.[36] This rejection often includes opposition to theism and all forms of organized religion. In sociological evaluation, the heading "atheist" also includes adherents of anti-religious groups such as Communists, materialists, Maoists, and Marxists. The term entered common usage during the eighteenth-century Enlightenment, akin to its fellow term, "agnostic." The French Revolution and ensuing Napoleonic era helped atheist scholars and thinkers in Europe rise in social rank and become prominent and constructive members of society. The twentieth century saw a heightened awareness of atheism around the world, largely because of Communist, anti-religious governments in the Soviet Union, Viet Nam, China, and other countries (including Albania, which was the first country in the world to become an officially atheistic state, although state atheism was repudiated in 1991). Several famous "new atheist" scholars have written bestselling books on the subject, including Sam Harris, Daniel Dennett, Richard Dawkins, and Christopher Hitchens.[37]

Agnostics and atheists have shared some similarities over the past 100 years. In 1910, more than 80% of both lived in the global North, while in 2010, at least 75% of each is found primarily in Asia (see table 1.39). Europe's share of the world's non-religious has dwindled to 10%, with China alone accounting for 70% of the global total. After experiencing dramatic growth in the early twentieth century, followed by significant declines later in the century, both agnostics and atheists are found in nearly every country today. Like agnostics, atheists are found in many countries with current or former Communist governments. Of countries with the largest populations of atheists (table 1.40), six have Communist influence; for countries with the largest percentages of atheists (table 1.41), eight fall into the same category.

Key differences, however, exist between the location of atheists and agnostics over the century. Agnostics in the global North were split between Europe (48.8% of the global total) and Northern America (34.7%) in 1910, but Northern atheism was nearly exclusively European (90.1% of the global total). Twice as many regions had no atheists in 1910 (nine) as no agnostics (four), and in 2010 atheists still constituted a smaller share of both the global population and individual countries' populations than did agnostics. Atheists' share of the global population also both increased more rapidly than agnostics' in the early and mid-twentieth century and declined more rapidly late in the century, a result of Communism's rise and fall.

New Religionists

New Religions are seldom actually "new"; rather, they are religions that include adherents of Hindu or Buddhist sects or offshoots, as well as syncretistic religions that combine Christianity with Eastern religions.[38] Although primarily an Asian phenomenon, some of the world's largest New Religions can be found in significant numbers outside of Asia. By definition, these religions generally were founded after 1800, and mostly since 1945, including the Japanese neo-Buddhist and neo-Shinto movements. There is a push by sociologists and scholars to adopt the terminology of "New Religions" as opposed to the pejorative term "cult."

Table 1.39 Atheists (a) by United Nations continents and regions, 1910–2010.

Region	Population 1910	Atheists 1910	% 1910	Population 2010	Atheists 2010	% 2010	a 1910–2010	Pop 1910–2010	a 2000–10	Pop 2000–10
Africa	**124,541,000**	**1,100**	**0.0**	**1,022,234,000**	**571,000**	**0.1**	**6.45**	**2.13**	**2.05**	**2.34**
Eastern	33,012,000	20	0.0	324,044,000	113,000	0.0	9.02	2.31	2.30	2.56
Middle	19,445,000	0	0.0	126,689,000	102,000	0.1	9.67	1.89	2.77	2.79
Northern	31,968,000	1,100	0.0	209,459,000	147,000	0.1	5.02	1.90	2.14	1.75
Southern	6,819,000	0	0.0	57,780,000	140,000	0.2	10.02	2.16	1.14	1.17
Western	33,296,000	0	0.0	304,261,000	69,000	0.0	9.24	2.24	2.41	2.59
Asia	**1,026,693,000**	**7,600**	**0.0**	**4,164,252,000**	**114,851,000**	**2.8**	**10.10**	**1.41**	**0.15**	**1.14**
Eastern	554,135,000	1,000	0.0	1,573,970,000	105,421,000	6.7	12.26	1.05	0.14	0.51
South-central	345,718,000	6,100	0.0	1,764,872,000	2,676,000	0.2	6.27	1.64	-0.92	1.53
South-eastern	93,859,000	0	0.0	593,415,000	6,408,000	1.1	14.31	1.86	0.79	1.26
Western	32,982,000	550	0.0	231,995,000	347,000	0.1	6.66	1.97	-0.26	2.32
Europe	**427,044,000**	**219,000**	**0.1**	**738,199,000**	**15,697,000**	**2.1**	**4.36**	**0.55**	**-1.19**	**0.16**
Eastern	178,184,000	84,100	0.0	294,771,000	4,593,000	1.6	4.08	0.50	-5.10	-0.31
Northern	61,473,000	20,800	0.0	99,205,000	2,423,000	2.4	4.87	0.48	0.61	0.50
Southern	76,828,000	14,300	0.0	155,171,000	3,263,000	2.1	5.58	0.71	1.00	0.67
Western	110,558,000	99,300	0.1	189,052,000	5,417,000	2.9	4.08	0.54	1.40	0.32
Latin America	**78,254,000**	**12,500**	**0.0**	**590,082,000**	**2,900,000**	**0.5**	**5.60**	**2.04**	**1.44**	**1.24**
Caribbean	8,172,000	0	0.0	41,646,000	645,000	1.5	11.71	1.64	-0.93	0.80
Central	20,806,000	0	0.0	155,881,000	240,000	0.2	10.61	2.03	1.84	1.41
South	49,276,000	12,500	0.0	392,555,000	2,014,000	0.5	5.21	2.10	2.29	1.23
Northern America	**94,689,000**	**2,400**	**0.0**	**344,529,000**	**2,156,000**	**0.6**	**7.04**	**1.30**	**2.18**	**0.96**
Oceania	**7,192,000**	**1,000**	**0.0**	**36,593,000**	**477,000**	**1.3**	**6.36**	**1.64**	**2.71**	**1.63**
Australia/New Zealand	5,375,000	1,000	0.0	26,637,000	470,000	1.8	6.35	1.61	2.73	1.47
Melanesia	1,596,000	0	0.0	8,748,000	5,200	0.1	6.45	1.72	2.16	2.26
Micronesia	89,400	0	0.0	536,000	230	0.0	3.19	1.81	0.91	0.78
Polynesia	131,000	0	0.0	673,000	1,600	0.2	5.21	1.65	1.34	0.91
Global total	**1,758,412,000**	**243,000**	**0.0**	**6,895,889,000**	**136,652,000**	**2.0**	**6.54**	**1.38**	**0.05**	**1.20**

Data source: Todd M. Johnson and Brian J. Grim, eds., *World Religion Database* (Leiden/Boston: Brill, accessed January 2012).

Table 1.40   Countries with the most atheists, 1910 and 2010.

Country	Atheists 1910	Country	Atheists 2010
Germany	44,100	China	97,643,000
Russia	42,700	Viet Nam	5,810,000
France	30,100	North Korea	3,793,000
Netherlands	11,400	Japan	3,630,000
Italy	10,700	France	2,596,000
United Kingdom	10,600	Italy	2,178,000
Hungary	10,600	Germany	2,056,000
Belgium	10,500	India	1,954,000
Czech Republic	8,200	Russia	1,512,000
Argentina	6,600	Ukraine	1,398,000

Data source: Todd M. Johnson and Brian J. Grim, eds., *World Religion Database* (Leiden/Boston: Brill, accessed January 2012).

Table 1.41   Countries with the highest percentage of atheists, 1910 and 2010.

Country	% 1910	Country	% 2010
Netherlands	0.2	North Korea	15.6
Belgium	0.1	Sweden	11.7
Hungary	0.1	China	7.3
Argentina	0.1	Viet Nam	6.6
Uruguay	0.1	Uruguay	6.5
Czech Republic	0.1	Latvia	5.4
Sweden	0.1	Cuba	5.1
Germany	0.1	Czech Republic	4.9
Serbia	0.1	Estonia	4.7
Denmark	0.1	Hungary	4.4

Data source: Todd M. Johnson and Brian J. Grim, eds., *World Religion Database* (Leiden/Boston: Brill, accessed January 2012). Countries >100,000 population.

Table 1.42   Countries with the fastest annual growth of atheists, 1910–2010 and 2000–10.

Country	% 1910–2010 p.a.	Country	% 2000–10 p.a.
Viet Nam	14.2	Afghanistan	19.5
North Korea	13.7	Qatar	11.2
Japan	13.7	United Arab Emirates	9.5
China	12.2	Bahrain	7.2
Spain	11.8	Austria	6.9
Cuba	11.6	Haiti	6.5
Indonesia	10.7	Ireland	5.9
Uzbekistan	10.7	Western Sahara	5.2
Philippines	10.3	New Zealand	4.5
Hong Kong	10.2	Chad	4.4

Data source: Todd M. Johnson and Brian J. Grim, eds., *World Religion Database* (Leiden/Boston: Brill, accessed January 2012). Countries >100,000 population.

Table 1.43 New Religionists (NR) by United Nations continents and regions, 1910–2010.

Region	Population 1910	NR 1910	% 1910	Population 2010	NR 2010	% 2010	NR 1910–2010	Pop 1910–2010	NR 2000–10	Pop 2000–10
Africa	**124,541,000**	**1,200**	**0.0**	**1,022,234,000**	**116,000**	**0.0**	**4.68**	**2.13**	**2.15**	**2.34**
Eastern	33,012,000	0	0.0	324,044,000	3,200	0.0	5.94	2.31	0.65	2.56
Middle	19,445,000	0	0.0	126,689,000	39,200	0.0	8.63	1.89	2.41	2.79
Northern	31,968,000	0	0.0	209,459,000	0	0.0	0.00	1.90	0.00	1.75
Southern	6,819,000	1,200	0.0	57,780,000	17,800	0.0	2.73	2.16	1.14	1.17
Western	33,296,000	0	0.0	304,261,000	56,100	0.0	9.02	2.24	2.46	2.59
Asia	**1,026,693,000**	**6,821,000**	**0.7**	**4,164,252,000**	**58,970,000**	**1.4**	**2.18**	**1.41**	**0.23**	**1.14**
Eastern	554,135,000	2,303,000	0.4	1,573,970,000	44,766,000	2.8	3.01	1.05	0.08	0.51
South-central	345,718,000	8,900	0.0	1,764,872,000	24,000	0.0	1.00	1.64	1.01	1.53
South-eastern	93,859,000	4,479,000	4.8	593,415,000	13,916,000	2.3	1.14	1.86	0.68	1.26
Western	32,982,000	30,000	0.1	231,995,000	265,000	0.1	2.20	1.97	1.70	2.32
Europe	**427,044,000**	**24,800**	**0.0**	**738,199,000**	**365,000**	**0.0**	**2.73**	**0.55**	**0.45**	**0.16**
Eastern	178,184,000	6,200	0.0	294,771,000	16,600	0.0	0.99	0.50	0.00	-0.31
Northern	61,473,000	1,000	0.0	99,205,000	93,300	0.1	4.64	0.48	0.52	0.50
Southern	76,828,000	1,100	0.0	155,171,000	22,700	0.0	3.07	0.71	0.41	0.67
Western	110,558,000	16,500	0.0	189,052,000	232,000	0.1	2.68	0.54	0.40	0.32
Latin America	**78,254,000**	**5,000**	**0.0**	**590,082,000**	**1,739,000**	**0.3**	**6.03**	**2.04**	**1.72**	**1.24**
Caribbean	8,172,000	1,300	0.0	41,646,000	16,100	0.0	2.55	1.64	0.85	0.80
Central	20,806,000	0	0.0	155,881,000	45,300	0.0	8.78	2.03	1.56	1.41
South	49,276,000	3,700	0.0	392,555,000	1,678,000	0.4	6.31	2.10	1.74	1.23
Northern America	**94,689,000**	**12,800**	**0.0**	**344,529,000**	**1,709,000**	**0.5**	**5.02**	**1.30**	**0.97**	**0.96**
Oceania	**7,192,000**	**360**	**0.0**	**36,593,000**	**104,000**	**0.3**	**5.83**	**1.64**	**2.07**	**1.63**
Australia/New Zealand	5,375,000	360	0.0	26,637,000	99,100	0.4	5.78	1.61	2.09	1.47
Melanesia	1,596,000	0	0.0	8,748,000	2,800	0.0	5.80	1.72	1.99	2.26
Micronesia	89,400	0	0.0	536,000	1,500	0.3	5.14	1.81	0.69	0.78
Polynesia	131,000	0	0.0	673,000	450	0.1	3.88	1.65	1.44	0.91
Global total	**1,758,412,000**	**6,865,000**	**0.4**	**6,895,889,000**	**63,004,000**	**0.9**	**2.24**	**1.38**	**0.29**	**1.20**

Data source: Todd M. Johnson and Brian J. Grim, eds., *World Religion Database* (Leiden/Boston: Brill, accessed January 2012).

Table 1.44   Largest New Religions, 2010.

New Religion	Adherents	% of New Religionists
Soka Gakkai International	18,537,000	29.4
Rissho Koseikai	5,149,000	8.2
Jilliwhoi	4,768,000	7.6
Society of Companions of the Spirits	4,387,000	7.0
As of Believers in One Supreme God	3,604,000	5.7
Cao Dai Missionary Church	3,295,000	5.2
International New Thought Alliance	3,089,000	4.9
I-kuan Tao	3,089,000	4.9
Religion of Heavenly Wisdom	3,079,000	4.9
House of Growth	2,487,000	3.9
Izumo-taishakyo	2,328,000	3.7
Hoa Hao	2,111,000	3.4
Oomoto	1,545,000	2.5
Church of Perfect Liberty	1,517,000	2.4
Religion of the Heavenly Way	1,236,000	2.0
Nusairis	1,133,000	1.8
True Nichiren School	1,030,000	1.6

Data source: Todd M. Johnson and Brian J. Grim, eds., *World Religion Database* (Leiden/Boston: Brill, accessed January 2012).

As seen in table 1.44, Soka Gakkai International (SGI) is today the largest of the New Religions, representing 29.4% of all New Religionists (18.5 million adherents in over 190 countries). Soka Gakkai was founded in Japan in 1930 as a lay movement within the Nichiren Shoshu priesthood of Buddhism. After much suffering and opposition during World War II, the movement experienced substantial growth and became one of Japan's most successful New Religions in the twentieth century. The movement expanded internationally when the third president of Soka Gakkai traveled to the United States, Brazil, and Canada in 1960. SGI was founded in 1975 as a global support system for members. The movement's popularity stems from Buddhist respect for all of life, leading to political activism for peace, respect for other religions, support of diversity, and the pursuit of peace and happiness. SGI is generally not a proselytizing religion, but rather reaches out to new members through active community involvement. Members are encouraged to contribute positively to the lives of others, rooted in the belief in the interconnectedness of all things.

Japan and Indonesia are home to a significant portion of the world's New Religionists (over 58% combined in 2010; table 1.45 shows 33 million in Japan alone), with Indonesia's New Religionists sharing many similarities with Japan's. Since 1970, however, many New Religionists in Indonesia have reconverted to Islam, although many syncretistic practices remain. South Korea (14.2% New Religionist) was heavily influenced by Japan under colonialism (1910–45), and a number of New Religions entered the country then. The first and most prominent of South Korea's New Religions is Cheondoism ("religion of the Heavenly Way"), a combination of Neo-Confucian, Buddhist, Shamanist, Daoist, and Catholic practices.

Table 1.45   Countries with the most New Religionists, 1910 and 2010.

Country	New Religionists 1910	Country	New Religionists 2010
Indonesia	4,479,000	Japan	32,809,000
Japan	2,266,000	Viet Nam	9,705,000
North Korea	24,400	South Korea	6,853,000
Turkey	21,700	Indonesia	3,993,000
South Korea	11,900	North Korea	3,135,000
United States	11,600	United States	1,625,000
France	10,000	Taiwan	1,567,000
Iraq	5,900	Brazil	1,456,000
Iran	5,600	China	215,000
Germany	5,500	Hong Kong	183,000

Data source: Todd M. Johnson and Brian J. Grim, eds., *World Religion Database* (Leiden/Boston: Brill, accessed January 2012).

Table 1.46   Countries with the highest percentage of New Religionists, 1910 and 2010.

Country	% 1910	Country	% 2010
Indonesia	10.1	Japan	25.9
Japan	4.5	South Korea	14.2
North Korea	0.5	North Korea	12.9
Armenia	0.3	Viet Nam	11.0
Iraq	0.2	Taiwan	6.7
Turkey	0.1	Hong Kong	2.6
South Korea	0.1	Indonesia	1.7
Kyrgyzstan	0.1	Singapore	1.5
Kazakhstan	0.1	Armenia	1.4
Cuba	0.1	Macau	0.9

Data source: Todd M. Johnson and Brian J. Grim, eds., *World Religion Database* (Leiden/ Boston: Brill, accessed January 2012). Countries >100,000 population.

New Religionists historically have been and continue to remain concentrated in Asia. As shown in table 1.45, only two of the top 10 countries with the most New Religionists – the United States and Brazil – are located outside Asia. Due to the large representation in Japan, South Korea, North Korea, and Viet Nam, today Eastern Asia and South-eastern Asia have the highest percentages of New Religionists in the world at 2.8% and 2.3%, respectively (see table 1.46). No other region of the world is more than 2% New Religionist. However, there is great growth of these religions in Africa, due largely to emigration. Eastern, Middle, and Western Africa all have 10-year New Religionist growth rates above 2% (2.6%, 2.8%, and 2.6%, respectively; see table 1.46). Although the home countries of the majority of adherents are largely the same in 1910 and 2010, their percentages have grown (with the exception of Indonesia); for example, in 1910 Japan was 4.5% New Religionist but is 25.9% in 2010 (see table 1.46). New Religionists likely will continue to disperse around the world through migration and, perhaps, expand through the founding of additional

Table 1.47 Countries with the fastest annual growth of New Religionists, 1910–2010 and 2000–10.

Country	% 1910–2010 p.a.	Country	% 2000–10 p.a.
Viet Nam	14.8	United Arab Emirates	9.7
Taiwan	12.7	Bahrain	7.2
Hong Kong	10.3	French Guiana	3.7
Australia	9.6	Sierra Leone	3.6
Peru	9.6	Timor-Leste	3.3
Singapore	9.3	DR Congo	3.2
United Kingdom	9.1	Saudi Arabia	3.2
Malaysia	9.1	Mali	3.1
Cambodia	8.7	Benin	3.1
Ghana	8.2	Iraq	3.0

Data source: Todd M. Johnson and Brian J. Grim, eds., *World Religion Database* (Leiden/Boston: Brill, accessed January 2012). Countries >100,000 population.

New Religions. The migration trend is observable in table 1.47, where the greatest growth of New Religions over the 10-year period is occurring in many African and Western Asian countries.

Sikhs

Sikhism is one of the lesser-known world religions, despite the fact that it is the fifth largest; there are currently more Sikhs in the world than Jews. Sikhism originated in the fifteenth century out of criticism of both Muslim and Buddhist religious rites in the Punjab on the Indian subcontinent.[39] The first of 10 gurus, Guru Nanak Dev, was born in 1469 and at the age of 30 had a vision of God's court where he was told the path to follow, thus founding Sikhism. Sikhism is built upon the foundation of equality of all humans and the rejection of caste and gender discrimination. Similar to Islam, Sikhism is a monotheistic and revealed religion, yet in line with Buddhism teaches that conflict and greed are barriers to salvation, continuing the cycle of life and death (reincarnation). The primary text of Sikhism is the Guru Granth Sahib, also known as the Adi Granth ("First Volume").

Sikh migration beginning in the nineteenth century led to the founding of small communities in other Asian countries, particularly Myanmar, Malaysia, Singapore, and Thailand. Migration to Britain had also begun in the nineteenth century under British India. The partition of the Punjab – the birthplace of Sikhism – by the British in 1947 precipitated larger-scale migration from the religion's historic homeland. Pakistan neglected to protect the Sikh community during the uproar of partition, and many areas saw widespread persecution and ethnic cleansing of Sikhs. By the 1960s many Sikhs had migrated to Western countries, in particular Britain, Canada, Italy, and the United States, in search of economic security. As a result of migration over the last century, Sikhs can now be found in most United Nations regions (see table 1.48). Nonetheless, the vast majority of Sikhs are still found in India (table 1.49) but even

Table 1.48 Sikhs by United Nations continents and regions, 1910–2010.

Region	Population 1910	Sikhs 1910	% 1910	Population 2010	Sikhs 2010	% 2010	Sikh 1910–2010	Pop 1910–2010	Sikh 2000–10	Pop 2000–10
Africa	**124,541,000**	**2,600**	**0.0**	**1,022,234,000**	**73,300**	**0.0**	**3.40**	**2.13**	**2.37**	**2.34**
Eastern	33,012,000	2,300	0.0	324,044,000	56,500	0.0	3.25	2.31	2.58	2.56
Middle	19,445,000	0	0.0	126,689,000	0	0.0	0.00	1.89	0.00	2.79
Northern	31,968,000	0	0.0	209,459,000	2,300	0.0	5.59	1.90	1.93	1.75
Southern	6,819,000	250	0.0	57,780,000	10,900	0.0	3.85	2.16	1.17	1.17
Western	33,296,000	0	0.0	304,261,000	3,700	0.0	6.09	2.24	3.59	2.59
Asia	**1,026,693,000**	**3,229,000**	**0.3**	**4,164,252,000**	**22,689,000**	**0.5**	**1.97**	**1.41**	**1.52**	**1.14**
Eastern	554,135,000	120	0.0	1,573,970,000	23,100	0.0	5.40	1.05	0.49	0.51
South-central	345,718,000	3,212,000	0.9	1,764,872,000	22,399,000	1.3	1.96	1.64	1.51	1.53
South-eastern	93,859,000	16,900	0.0	593,415,000	157,000	0.0	2.25	1.86	1.60	1.26
Western	32,982,000	450	0.0	231,995,000	109,000	0.0	5.64	1.97	3.58	2.32
Europe	**427,044,000**	**0**	**0.0**	**738,199,000**	**501,000**	**0.1**	**11.43**	**0.55**	**2.12**	**0.16**
Eastern	178,184,000	0	0.0	294,771,000	10,800	0.0	7.23	0.50	-0.18	-0.31
Northern	61,473,000	0	0.0	99,205,000	414,000	0.4	11.22	0.48	2.58	0.50
Southern	76,828,000	0	0.0	155,171,000	31,700	0.0	8.40	0.71	0.59	0.67
Western	110,558,000	0	0.0	189,052,000	44,500	0.0	8.76	0.54	0.20	0.32
Latin America	**78,254,000**	**0**	**0.0**	**590,082,000**	**7,100**	**0.0**	**6.79**	**2.04**	**1.20**	**1.24**
Caribbean	8,172,000	0	0.0	41,646,000	0	0.0	0.00	1.64	0.00	0.80
Central	20,806,000	0	0.0	155,881,000	5,900	0.0	6.59	2.03	1.27	1.41
South	49,276,000	0	0.0	392,555,000	1,200	0.0	4.90	2.10	0.87	1.23
Northern America	**94,689,000**	**0**	**0.0**	**344,529,000**	**607,000**	**0.2**	**11.64**	**1.30**	**1.42**	**0.96**
Oceania	**7,192,000**	**250**	**0.0**	**36,593,000**	**49,600**	**0.1**	**5.43**	**1.64**	**3.73**	**1.63**
Australia/New Zealand	5,375,000	0	0.0	26,637,000	45,300	0.2	8.78	1.61	4.14	1.47
Melanesia	1,596,000	250	0.0	8,748,000	4,400	0.1	2.91	1.72	0.47	2.26
Micronesia	89,400	0	0.0	536,000	0	0.0	0.00	1.81	0.00	0.78
Polynesia	131,000	0	0.0	673,000	0	0.0	0.00	1.65	0.00	0.91
Global total	**1,758,412,000**	**3,232,000**	**0.2**	**6,895,889,000**	**23,927,000**	**0.3**	**2.02**	**1.38**	**1.54**	**1.20**

Data source: Todd M. Johnson and Brian J. Grim, eds., *World Religion Database* (Leiden/Boston: Brill, accessed January 2012).

Table 1.49 Countries with the most Sikhs, 1910 and 2010.

Country	Sikhs 1910	Country	Sikhs 2010
India	2,387,000	India	22,303,000
Pakistan	819,000	United Kingdom	412,000
Myanmar	7,300	Canada	328,000
Malaysia	5,000	United States	279,000
Sri Lanka	4,700	Thailand	56,000
Singapore	3,300	Saudi Arabia	52,700
Kenya	2,300	Malaysia	47,100
Thailand	1,300	Pakistan	44,600
Bangladesh	1,100	Kenya	37,100
Yemen	450	Australia	36,500

Data source: Todd M. Johnson and Brian J. Grim, eds., *World Religion Database* (Leiden/ Boston: Brill, accessed January 2012).

Table 1.50 Countries with the highest percentage of Sikhs, 1910 and 2010.

Country	% 1910	Country	% 2010
Pakistan	2.9	India	1.8
Singapore	1.0	Canada	1.0
India	0.9	Cyprus	0.9
Malaysia	0.2	United Kingdom	0.7
Fiji	0.2	Oman	0.7
Sri Lanka	0.1	Fiji	0.5
Kenya	0.1	Singapore	0.4
Myanmar	0.1	United Arab Emirates	0.2
Hong Kong	0.0	Mauritius	0.2
Thailand	0.0	New Zealand	0.2

Data source: Todd M. Johnson and Brian J. Grim, eds., *World Religion Database* (Leiden/ Boston: Brill, accessed January 2012). Countries >100,000 population.

there represent less than 2% of the population (table 1.50). The countries where Sikhs are growing the fastest are where there are guest-worker programs or immigration (table 1.51).

Sikh communities worldwide endured trouble throughout the twentieth century and into the twenty-first. Tensions between Hindus and Sikhs were high in the 1960s and 1970s, with major outbreaks of violence in 1984 after Sikh bodyguards assassinated Indian Prime Minister Indira Gandhi following prolonged religious disturbances there. Since the terrorist attacks of September 11, 2001, Sikhs in the United States have been wrongly identified as Taliban supporters or Muslims, largely because they wear turbans. In France, Sikhs are prohibited from wearing turbans in public schools as part of the larger legislation banning Muslim headscarves. Sikhs have traditionally been involved in agro-business and have carried this vocation to the countries to which they have migrated. Sikh gurdwaras (places of worship) can be found across Europe, Northern America, Australia, and Asia.

Table 1.51   Countries with the fastest annual growth of Sikhs, 1910–2010
and 2000–10.

Country	% 1910–2010 p.a.	Country	% 2000–10 p.a.
United Kingdom	11.2	United Arab Emirates	9.4
Canada	11.0	Australia	5.0
United States	10.8	Niger	3.6
Saudi Arabia	8.9	Uganda	3.5
Australia	8.5	Kuwait	3.5
Germany	8.1	Saudi Arabia	3.2
Italy	8.1	Tanzania	2.8
Philippines	8.1	Malawi	2.8
China	7.8	Iraq	2.8
Oman	7.8	Yemen	2.7

Data source: Todd M. Johnson and Brian J. Grim, eds., *World Religion Database* (Leiden/
Boston: Brill, accessed January 2012). Countries >100,000 population.

The growth of Sikhism outside India over the 100-year period has been fastest in
Northern America, Northern Europe, Australia/New Zealand, and Western Europe
(table 1.51). As noted earlier, however, these patterns changed in the early part of the
twenty-first century. It is now expected that growth, largely through immigration,
will be stronger in other regions, such as Southern Europe and South-eastern Asia.

Jews

Judaism has been described, among other designations, as a religion, an ethnicity, a
culture, and a nation.[40] Each of these descriptions has validity, and the question "Who
is a Jew?" continues in both Jewish and non-Jewish dialogue. The discussion has great
significance for the sociological study of the religion and the tracking of Jewish demographics over the past century. Scholar Harvey Goldberg writes, "Judaism is perhaps
the most global of religious traditions, since for most of its history it has existed in
myriad diaspora communities throughout the Middle East, Europe, and eventually
the Americas and elsewhere."[41]

Historically, the Jewish people have been a moving community, from the time of
Moses and throughout the twentieth century. In 1910 the hub of religious Judaism
was Eastern Europe, in particular Russia, Poland, and Ukraine (table 1.53). The
United States was also home to well over 1 million Jews, largely Ashkenazim from
Germany who had emigrated en masse beginning in the 1820s. The rise of Hitler in
the 1930s and the Holocaust (*Shoah*) led to a demographic shift in the global Jewish
population from mid-century to 2010. Almost 6 million Jews perished in the
Holocaust, shrinking the total world Jewish population from over 16 million in 1933
to less than 11 million in 1945. Extreme persecution widened the Jewish Diaspora to
a truly global level. Emigration to Israel following its establishment in 1948 under the
Law of Return, however, reduced the Diaspora population in many countries. Most
countries still have relatively small populations of Jews, constituting less than 2% of
total country populations (see table 1.54).

Table 1.52 Jews by United Nations continents and regions, 1910–2010.

Region	Population 1910	Jews 1910	% 1910	Population 2010	Jews 2010	% 2010	Jews 1910–2010	Pop 1910–2010	Jews 2000–10	Pop 2000–10
Africa	**124,541,000**	**451,000**	**0.4**	**1,022,234,000**	**132,000**	**0.0**	**-1.22**	**2.13**	**0.96**	**2.34**
Eastern	33,012,000	12,500	0.0	324,044,000	36,100	0.0	1.07	2.31	1.67	2.56
Middle	19,445,000	0	0.0	126,689,000	400	0.0	3.76	1.89	-0.95	2.79
Northern	31,968,000	401,000	1.3	209,459,000	9,400	0.0	-3.68	1.90	1.01	1.75
Southern	6,819,000	36,800	0.5	57,780,000	84,900	0.1	0.84	2.16	0.61	1.17
Western	33,296,000	0	0.0	304,261,000	1,200	0.0	4.90	2.24	2.36	2.59
Asia	**1,026,693,000**	**476,000**	**0.0**	**4,164,252,000**	**6,030,000**	**0.1**	**2.57**	**1.41**	**2.06**	**1.14**
Eastern	554,135,000	930	0.0	1,573,970,000	5,100	0.0	1.72	1.05	0.40	0.51
South-central	345,718,000	94,200	0.0	1,764,872,000	97,500	0.0	0.03	1.64	0.37	1.53
South-eastern	93,859,000	760	0.0	593,415,000	2,500	0.0	1.20	1.86	2.26	1.26
Western	32,982,000	380,000	1.2	231,995,000	5,925,000	2.6	2.78	1.97	2.09	2.32
Europe	**427,044,000**	**10,462,000**	**2.4**	**738,199,000**	**1,918,000**	**0.3**	**-1.68**	**0.55**	**-0.02**	**0.16**
Eastern	178,184,000	9,082,000	5.1	294,771,000	537,000	0.2	-2.79	0.50	-1.20	-0.31
Northern	61,473,000	279,000	0.5	99,205,000	335,000	0.3	0.18	0.48	0.30	0.50
Southern	76,828,000	167,000	0.2	155,171,000	111,000	0.1	-0.41	0.71	1.31	0.67
Western	110,558,000	934,000	0.8	189,052,000	935,000	0.5	0.00	0.54	0.46	0.32
Latin America	**78,254,000**	**29,300**	**0.0**	**590,082,000**	**962,000**	**0.2**	**3.55**	**2.04**	**0.58**	**1.24**
Caribbean	8,172,000	12,000	0.1	41,646,000	8,100	0.0	-0.39	1.64	0.64	0.80
Central	20,806,000	630	0.0	155,881,000	153,000	0.1	5.65	2.03	1.33	1.41
South	49,276,000	16,700	0.0	392,555,000	801,000	0.2	3.95	2.10	0.45	1.23
Northern America	**94,689,000**	**1,756,000**	**1.9**	**344,529,000**	**5,602,000**	**1.6**	**1.17**	**1.30**	**-0.30**	**0.96**
Oceania	**7,192,000**	**19,800**	**0.3**	**36,593,000**	**117,000**	**0.3**	**1.79**	**1.64**	**1.48**	**1.63**
Australia/New Zealand	5,375,000	19,700	0.4	26,637,000	116,000	0.4	1.79	1.61	1.53	1.47
Melanesia	1,596,000	100	0.0	8,748,000	1,000	0.0	2.33	1.72	1.76	2.26
Micronesia	89,400	0	0.0	536,000	0	0.0	0.00	1.81	0.00	0.78
Polynesia	131,000	0	0.0	673,000	160	0.0	2.81	1.65	0.65	0.91
Global total	**1,758,412,000**	**13,193,000**	**0.8**	**6,895,889,000**	**14,761,000**	**0.2**	**0.11**	**1.38**	**0.72**	**1.20**

Data source: Todd M. Johnson and Brian J. Grim, eds., *World Religion Database* (Leiden/Boston: Brill, accessed January 2012).

Table 1.53   Countries with the most Jews, 1910 and 2010.

Country	Jews 1910	Country	Jews 2010
Russia	4,776,000	Israel	5,379,000
Poland	2,191,000	United States	5,122,000
United States	1,736,000	France	628,000
Ukraine	755,000	Argentina	501,000
Romania	537,000	Canada	480,000
Germany	529,000	Palestine	477,000
Hungary	436,000	United Kingdom	291,000
United Kingdom	248,000	Germany	224,000
Czech Republic	222,000	Russia	187,000
Morocco	174,000	Ukraine	177,000

Data source: Todd M. Johnson and Brian J. Grim, eds., *World Religion Database* (Leiden/Boston: Brill, accessed January 2012).

Table 1.54   Countries with the highest percentage of Jews, 1910 and 2010.

Country	% 1910	Country	% 2010
Poland	9.0	Israel	72.5
Palestine	8.8	Palestine	11.8
Israel	8.6	United States	1.7
Russia	6.1	Canada	1.4
Hungary	6.0	Argentina	1.2
Tunisia	5.0	Uruguay	1.2
Libya	5.0	Belize	1.1
Romania	4.5	France	1.0
Iraq	3.9	Hungary	0.9
Morocco	3.0	Moldova	0.8

Data source: Todd M. Johnson and Brian J. Grim, eds., *World Religion Database* (Leiden/Boston: Brill, accessed January 2012). Countries >100,000 population.

Judaism has experienced not only significant changes in demographics, but also in religious observance. Reform Judaism (which was founded in Germany and strongly influenced the practice of Judaism in the United States beginning in the mid-nineteenth century) was born out of a desire for "Jewish" to no longer refer solely to a nation, but instead to a religious community. The American Jewish synagogue came to resemble a Protestant church, jettisoning the prayer shawl and gender-separate seating while adopting services conducted by rabbis, complete with sermons and mixed choirs. With the wave of immigration of traditional Eastern European Jews to the United States between 1880 and 1914, many more-progressive Jews longed for the conservatism and traditions of the past, thus establishing Conservative (or Traditional) Judaism, which promoted Jewishness as an ethnocultural identity as well as a religious one. Orthodox Judaism is known for its strict adherence to the 613 *mitzvot* (commandments) and its attempt to maintain the Jewish unity of the past. However, in the twenty-first century, a significant percentage of Jews worldwide self-identify as agnostic or atheist.

Table 1.55 Countries with the fastest annual growth of Jews, 1910–2010 and 2000–10.

Country	% 1910–2010 p.a.	Country	% 2000–10 p.a.
Colombia	7.3	Bahrain	3.4
Peru	7.2	Uganda	3.2
Mexico	6.9	Malawi	3.0
Uruguay	6.6	French Guiana	3.0
Panama	6.3	Madagascar	3.0
Ecuador	6.3	Tanzania	2.8
Bolivia	6.1	Singapore	2.7
Uganda	6.0	Zambia	2.7
Paraguay	5.9	Guatemala	2.7
Namibia	5.7	Libya	2.7

Data source: Todd M. Johnson and Brian J. Grim, eds., *World Religion Database* (Leiden/Boston: Brill, accessed January 2012). Countries >100,000 population.

Concerning the Jewish population in Israel, many Jewish sources combine the states of Israel and Palestine, but here they are represented as two different countries in line with United Nations designations. Using this demarcation, the Jewish population in the United States was recently surpassed by that in Israel. If current trends (such as higher birthrates among Orthodox Jews in Israel[42]) continue it is likely that the gap between the two will grow larger throughout the twenty-first century. In addition, table 1.55 illustrates that over the 100-year period, Jewish populations were growing largely in Latin American countries, but growth over the 10-year period is occurring more in Asia and Africa, though these communities are still quite small.

Spiritists

Spiritism was born out of the mixing of African religious traditions, brought to the Caribbean by slaves with local, traditional beliefs.[43] Spiritism is popularly known through various indigenous Afro-Caribbean religions, particularly in Latin America (though with significant populations in Britain and the United States). Forms of low Spiritism typically syncretize Catholicism with African and Amerindian animistic religions, and include the strong communities of Candomblé and Umbanda in Brazil,[44] Voodoo in Haiti and the Dominican Republic, and the Rastafari movement in Jamaica. These differ from high forms of Spiritism that do *not* draw on Christian theology or practices, and thus rely more so on the institution of the medium. Despite many overarching commonalities between them, each of these religions is completely unique, with its own rituals, festivals, beliefs, and cultural significance.

Since being introduced to Brazil toward the middle of the eighteenth century, Spiritism has evidenced consistent growth there, despite some prognostication that the religion would gradually fade away in the twentieth century. For example, in 1910 Spiritists represented 0.8% of Brazil's population; in 1970, 2.7%; in 2000, 4.9%; and in 2010, 4.8%. In addition, Spiritists have had a disproportionate impact on the followers of other religions, especially Christianity (both Protestant and Roman

Table 1.56 Spiritists (Sp) by United Nations continents and regions, 1910–2010.

Region	Population 1910	Spiritists 1910	% 1910	Population 2010	Spiritists 2010	% 2010	Sp 1910–2010	Pop 1910–2010	Sp 2000–10	Pop 2000–10
Africa	**124,541,000**	**1,200**	**0.0**	**1,022,234,000**	**2,900**	**0.0**	**0.89**	**2.13**	**1.10**	**2.34**
Eastern	33,012,000	0	0.0	324,044,000	570	0.0	4.13	2.31	0.00	2.56
Middle	19,445,000	0	0.0	126,689,000	0	0.0	0.00	1.89	0.00	2.79
Northern	31,968,000	0	0.0	209,459,000	0	0.0	0.00	1.90	0.00	1.75
Southern	6,819,000	1,200	0.0	57,780,000	2,300	0.0	0.65	2.16	1.41	1.17
Western	33,296,000	0	0.0	304,261,000	0	0.0	0.00	2.24	0.00	2.59
Asia	**1,026,693,000**	**0**	**0.0**	**4,164,252,000**	**2,100**	**0.0**	**5.49**	**1.41**	**0.49**	**1.14**
Eastern	554,135,000	0	0.0	1,573,970,000	2,100	0.0	5.49	1.05	0.49	0.51
South-central	345,718,000	0	0.0	1,764,872,000	0	0.0	0.00	1.64	0.00	1.53
South-eastern	93,859,000	0	0.0	593,415,000	0	0.0	0.00	1.86	0.00	1.26
Western	32,982,000	0	0.0	231,995,000	0	0.0	0.00	1.97	0.00	2.32
Europe	**427,044,000**	**10,600**	**0.0**	**738,199,000**	**144,000**	**0.0**	**2.64**	**0.55**	**0.57**	**0.16**
Eastern	178,184,000	0	0.0	294,771,000	7,300	0.0	6.82	0.50	0.00	-0.31
Northern	61,473,000	10,600	0.0	99,205,000	78,300	0.1	2.02	0.48	0.58	0.50
Southern	76,828,000	0	0.0	155,171,000	4,700	0.0	6.35	0.71	0.44	0.67
Western	110,558,000	0	0.0	189,052,000	53,300	0.0	8.96	0.54	0.54	0.32
Latin America	**78,254,000**	**312,000**	**0.4**	**590,082,000**	**13,302,000**	**2.3**	**3.82**	**2.04**	**0.94**	**1.24**
Caribbean	8,172,000	67,800	0.8	41,646,000	2,779,000	6.7	3.78	1.64	0.48	0.80
Central	20,806,000	5,200	0.0	155,881,000	205,000	0.1	3.74	2.03	1.77	1.41
South	49,276,000	239,000	0.5	392,555,000	10,318,000	2.6	3.84	2.10	1.05	1.23
Northern America	**94,689,000**	**0**	**0.0**	**344,529,000**	**242,000**	**0.1**	**10.62**	**1.30**	**1.53**	**0.96**
Oceania	**7,192,000**	**590**	**0.0**	**36,593,000**	**7,800**	**0.0**	**2.62**	**1.64**	**1.53**	**1.63**
Australia/New Zealand	5,375,000	590	0.0	26,637,000	7,800	0.0	2.62	1.61	1.53	1.47
Melanesia	1,596,000	0	0.0	8,748,000	0	0.0	0.00	1.72	0.00	2.26
Micronesia	89,400	0	0.0	536,000	0	0.0	0.00	1.81	0.00	0.78
Polynesia	131,000	0	0.0	673,000	0	0.0	0.00	1.65	0.00	0.91
Global total	**1,758,412,000**	**324,000**	**0.0**	**6,895,889,000**	**13,700,000**	**0.2**	**3.82**	**1.38**	**0.94**	**1.20**

Data source: Todd M. Johnson and Brian J. Grim, eds., *World Religion Database* (Leiden/Boston: Brill, accessed January 2012).

Table 1.57   Countries with the most Spiritists, 1910 and 2010.

Country	Spiritists 1910	Country	Spiritists 2010
Brazil	171,000	Brazil	9,421,000
Venezuela	56,600	Cuba	1,934,000
Jamaica	41,200	Colombia	461,000
Dominican Republic	15,800	Venezuela	305,000
United Kingdom	10,600	Jamaica	278,000
Cuba	6,300	Haiti	271,000
Guyana	6,200	United States	225,000
Guatemala	1,900	Dominican Republic	217,000
Suriname	1,800	Argentina	93,300
Colombia	1,300	Nicaragua	84,000

Data source: Todd M. Johnson and Brian J. Grim, eds., *World Religion Database* (Leiden/ Boston: Brill, accessed January 2012).

Table 1.58   Countries with the highest percentage of Spiritists, 1910 and 2010.

Country	% 1910	Country	% 2010
Jamaica	5.0	Cuba	17.2
Belize	2.0	Jamaica	10.1
Guyana	2.0	Brazil	4.8
Dominican Republic	2.0	French Guiana	3.3
Venezuela	2.0	Suriname	3.0
French Guiana	1.9	Haiti	2.7
Suriname	1.9	Dominican Republic	2.2
Bahamas	1.9	Bahamas	1.9
Saint Vincent	1.1	Saint Vincent	1.8
Brazil	0.8	Saint Lucia	1.7

Data source: Todd M. Johnson and Brian J. Grim, eds., *World Religion Database* (Leiden/Boston: Brill, accessed January 2012). Countries >100,000 population.

Catholic). Candomblé and Umbanda practices, for instance, influence large numbers of Roman Catholics in Brazil. In fact, the majority of Brazilian Roman Catholics, over 60 million, incorporate some type of Spiritist beliefs and practices into their faith.

Today, Spiritists make up approximately 17% of the population of Cuba (traditionally a Catholic county) – the second largest Spiritist population and the highest percentage of any country in 2010 (see tables 1.57 and 1.58). After Christians and agnostics, Spiritists are the third-largest religious group in Cuba. Many of them hold to the syncretistic beliefs of Santería, a religion similar to Brazilian Umbanda, originating from a combination of West African and Caribbean beliefs. The change has been significant since 1910, when Spiritism represented less than 1% of Cuba's population. In 2010 over half of all black and mulatto peoples in Cuba adhered to some type of Spiritism, whereas little more than 2% of white Cubans were Spiritists.

Spiritists have begun to make inroads into Europe and Northern America as well, primarily through immigration, with Ireland as the fastest-growing Spiritist population

Table 1.59   Countries with the fastest annual growth of Spiritists, 1910–2010 and 2000–10.

Country	% 1910–2010 p.a.	Country	% 2000–10 p.a.
United States	10.5	Ireland	5.7
France	8.1	French Guiana	3.5
Netherlands	8.1	Guatemala	2.5
Panama	7.7	Belize	2.3
Canada	7.6	Haiti	2.2
Poland	6.8	Honduras	2.0
Australia	6.7	Aruba	1.8
Uruguay	6.3	Panama	1.8
Haiti	6.3	Costa Rica	1.7
Costa Rica	6.1	Bolivia	1.7

Data source: Todd M. Johnson and Brian J. Grim, eds., *World Religion Database* (Leiden/Boston: Brill, accessed January 2012). Countries >100,000 population.

in the world (table 1.59). In fact, in addition to Latin America, Europe and Northern America had the fastest rates of growth of all the UN continental areas over the last century (table 1.56). In Northern America (where growth has been the fastest), however, Spiritists still represent only about 0.1% of the total population in 2010.

Daoists

Rather than constituting one well-defined religion, Daoism (Taoism) can be viewed historically as more of an amalgam of similar religious and philosophical beliefs.[45] The primary aim of the religion is to establish harmony with the *Dao*, a Chinese word meaning "way" or "path," but also sometimes roughly translated as "principle." Daoism arguably can be seen in prehistoric Chinese religions, though the modern form as it is known today began with the composition of the *Dao De Jing* (translated "The Classic of the Way and its Virtue/Power"), composed in the third or fourth century BCE by Chinese philosopher Laozi, who is revered as a deity in most forms of the religion today, as well as the *Zhuangzi* (traditionally attributed to a fourth-century Chinese philosopher of the same name). Daoism's third major text, the *Daozang*, is a compilation by monks of nearly 5,000 Daoist writings. Its compilation began around 400 CE in an effort to bring together the entire corpus of Daoist teaching, including commentary and expositions of the texts. *Daozang* literally means "canon of Daoism" or "treasury of Dao." During China's Qing Dynasty (1644–1912) scholars advocated a return to classic Confucian philosophies, resulting in a wholesale rejection of Daoism. By the end of this dynastic period, and specifically during the Japanese occupation beginning in 1895, Daoism had fallen so out of favor in China that locating copies of the religion's texts became exceptionally difficult.

Estimating the number of adherents to Daoism is difficult because of the complexities of religious life in Asia. Daoism has highly influenced the practice of Chinese folk-religion both in China and abroad; likewise, other religions, especially Buddhism,

Table 1.60 Daoists (D) by United Nations continents, 1910–2010.

Region	Population 1910	Daoists 1910	% 1910	Population 2010	Daoists 2010	% 2010	D 1910–2010	Pop 1910–2010	D 2000–10	Pop 2000–10
Africa	124,541,000	0	0.0	1,022,234,000	0	0.0	0.00	2.13	0.00	2.34
Asia	1,026,693,000	437,000	0.0	4,164,252,000	8,412,000	0.2	3.00	1.41	1.74	1.14
Europe	427,044,000	0	0.0	738,199,000	0	0.0	0.00	0.55	0.00	0.16
Latin America	78,254,000	0	0.0	590,082,000	0	0.0	0.00	2.04	0.00	1.24
Northern America	94,689,000	0	0.0	344,529,000	12,400	0.0	7.38	1.30	0.93	0.96
Oceania	7,192,000	0	0.0	36,593,000	4,600	0.0	6.32	1.64	1.41	1.63
Global total	**1,758,412,000**	**437,000**	**0.0**	**6,895,889,000**	**8,429,000**	**0.1**	**3.00**	**1.38**	**1.73**	**1.20**

Data source: Todd M. Johnson and Brian J. Grim, eds., *World Religion Database* (Leiden/Boston: Brill, accessed January 2012).

have played a significant role in influencing and changing Daoist practice. Many Asians see no conflict in practicing Daoism and Buddhism, Confucianism, or any other Asian religion simultaneously. The highly spiritual nature of many Asian societies makes it easy to pick and choose religious rituals according to circumstance, necessity, and personal preference.

Like other religionists in China, Daoists faced severe persecution and oppression during the Cultural Revolution, causing the number of adherents to dwindle. Today, Daoists are a small community living mostly in Taiwan, where a fragmented form of Daoism arrived during the eighteenth century. In addition, some Daoists took refuge in Taiwan after the mid-century turmoil in China. The religion continues to play a significant role in the lives of most Chinese folk-religionists and Buddhists in the region. Daoism typically has a more prevalent presence in societies with communities of immigrant Chinese, such as Malaysia and Singapore. In addition, Western interest in Eastern religion has resulted in growing numbers of non-Chinese Daoists, mostly in Northern America. This is seen in the listing of countries with the most Daoists (table 1.61): the United States ranks third, after China and Taiwan (notably, the United States had no Daoists in 1910). The countries with the fastest Daoist growth (table 1.63) continue to be primarily in Asia, though notably, Australia and the United States hold the numbers three and five spots, respectively. Table 1.62 illustrates the reality of very small Daoist populations outside of mainland China and Taiwan, less than 1% across the rest of Asia and the West.

Table 1.61   Countries with the most Daoists, 1910 and 2010.

Country	Daoists 1910	Country	Daoists 2010
Taiwan	360,000	China	5,483,000
China	77,300	Taiwan	2,929,000
		United States	12,400
		Australia	4,600

Data source: Todd M. Johnson and Brian J. Grim, eds., *World Religion Database* (Leiden/Boston: Brill, accessed January 2012). Daoists >1,000.

Table 1.62   Countries with the highest percentage of Daoists, 1910 and 2010.

Country	% 1910	Country	% 2010
Taiwan	9.4	Taiwan	12.6
China	0.0	China	0.4
United States	<0.1	Australia	<0.1
Viet Nam	<0.1	Laos	<0.1
Australia	<0.1	United States	<0.1
Hong Kong	<0.1	Viet Nam	<0.1
Laos	<0.1	Hong Kong	<0.1
Macau	<0.1	Macau	<0.1

Data source: Todd M. Johnson and Brian J. Grim, eds., *World Religion Database* (Leiden/Boston: Brill, accessed January 2012). Countries >100,000 population.

Table 1.63 Countries with the fastest annual growth of Daoists, 1910–2010 and 2000–10.

Country	% 1910–2010 p.a.	Country	% 2000–10 p.a.
United States	7.4	China	2.2
Australia	6.3	Laos	1.6
China	4.4	Australia	1.4
Laos	3.4	Viet Nam	1.3
Viet Nam	2.8	United States	0.9
Taiwan	2.1	Taiwan	0.9

Data source: Todd M. Johnson and Brian J. Grim, eds., *World Religion Database* (Leiden/Boston: Brill, accessed January 2012). Countries >100,000 population.

Baha'is

Adherents of the youngest of the major world religions (with the exception of some New Religions), Baha'is follow Mirza Husayn Ali Nuri (who later designated himself as Baha'u'llah), born in Tehran, Iran, in 1817.[46] He claimed to be the messianic figure that the Bab, Siyyid Ali-Muhammad, had prophesied would come. Baha'is believe the Bab (who was executed in 1850) to be a forerunner to their own faith, and his tomb, located in Haifa, Israel, remains a pilgrimage site for Baha'is today. Baha'u'llah is revered as the latest in the line of messengers that includes Abraham, Moses, Buddha, Krishna, Zoroaster, Jesus Christ, and Muhammad. Baha'is see the emergence of their religion from Islam as similar to the relationship first-century Christianity had with Judaism.

The Baha'i faith is, among other things, centered on themes of social justice, the equality of humankind, and the relativity of religious truth. Only the writings of the Bab and Baha'u'llah are considered divine revelation from God; other writings by prominent Baha'i figures are deemed as authoritative interpretation, legislation, and explanations. Sacred texts by the Baha'u'llah include the *Kitab-I-Aqdad* (the "Most Holy Book") and the *Kitab-I-Iqan* (the "Book of Certitude"). The Baha'i community worldwide is united through the study of and adherence to these revelations, along with the administrative order of the "two pillars" of the Guardianship and the Universal House of Justice.

At the beginning of their history in the mid-nineteenth century, Baha'is were found in Iran only. Within a decade, persecution resulted in emigration to many other countries, most notably India. In addition, Baha'is have promoted their message of unity in more countries than any other smaller, independent, religion. The tenets of the Baha'i faith cut across ethnic, gender, and socio-economic barriers, making it a highly accessible and desirable religious way of life, particularly in countries with disadvantageous class distinctions and wide wealth gaps. The Baha'i faith is the only religion to have grown faster in every United Nations region over the past 100 years than the general population; Baha'i was thus the fastest-growing religion between 1910 and 2010, growing at least twice as fast as the population of almost every UN region (see table 1.64).

Table 1.64 Baha'is (Ba) by United Nations continents and regions, 1910–2010.

Region	Population 1910	Baha'i 1910	% 1910	Population 2010	Baha'i 2010	% 2010	Ba 1910–2010	Pop 1910–2010	Ba 2000–10	Pop 2000–10
Africa	**124,541,000**	**240**	**0.0**	**1,022,234,000**	**2,143,000**	**0.2**	**9.52**	**2.13**	**2.39**	**2.34**
Eastern	33,012,000	0	0.0	324,044,000	1,131,000	0.3	12.34	2.31	2.54	2.56
Middle	19,445,000	0	0.0	126,689,000	474,000	0.4	11.37	1.89	2.82	2.79
Northern	31,968,000	240	0.0	209,459,000	48,500	0.0	5.45	1.90	1.28	1.75
Southern	6,819,000	0	0.0	57,780,000	291,000	0.5	10.83	2.16	1.17	1.17
Western	33,296,000	0	0.0	304,261,000	199,000	0.1	10.40	2.24	2.73	2.59
Asia	**1,026,693,000**	**221,000**	**0.0**	**4,164,252,000**	**3,440,000**	**0.1**	**2.78**	**1.41**	**1.38**	**1.14**
Eastern	554,135,000	100	0.0	1,573,970,000	72,300	0.0	6.80	1.05	0.42	0.51
South-central	345,718,000	220,000	0.1	1,764,872,000	2,294,000	0.1	2.37	1.64	1.33	1.53
South-eastern	93,859,000	110	0.0	593,415,000	939,000	0.2	9.47	1.86	1.28	1.26
Western	32,982,000	600	0.0	231,995,000	134,000	0.1	5.56	1.97	3.92	2.32
Europe	**427,044,000**	**220**	**0.0**	**738,199,000**	**153,000**	**0.0**	**6.76**	**0.55**	**0.68**	**0.16**
Eastern	178,184,000	210	0.0	294,771,000	25,400	0.0	4.91	0.50	-0.23	-0.31
Northern	61,473,000	10	0.0	99,205,000	63,900	0.1	9.16	0.48	1.11	0.50
Southern	76,828,000	0	0.0	155,171,000	30,400	0.0	8.35	0.71	0.75	0.67
Western	110,558,000	0	0.0	189,052,000	33,600	0.0	8.46	0.54	0.55	0.32
Latin America	**78,254,000**	**0**	**0.0**	**590,082,000**	**898,000**	**0.2**	**12.08**	**2.04**	**1.64**	**1.24**
Caribbean	8,172,000	0	0.0	41,646,000	69,700	0.2	9.25	1.64	1.14	0.80
Central	20,806,000	0	0.0	155,881,000	197,000	0.1	10.39	2.03	1.54	1.41
South	49,276,000	0	0.0	392,555,000	632,000	0.2	11.69	2.10	1.74	1.23
Northern America	**94,689,000**	**3,200**	**0.0**	**344,529,000**	**561,000**	**0.2**	**5.30**	**1.30**	**1.70**	**0.96**
Oceania	**7,192,000**	**520**	**0.0**	**36,593,000**	**111,000**	**0.3**	**5.51**	**1.64**	**2.13**	**1.63**
Australia/New Zealand	5,375,000	0	0.0	26,637,000	26,900	0.1	8.22	1.61	1.85	1.47
Melanesia	1,596,000	0	0.0	8,748,000	69,700	0.8	9.25	1.72	2.45	2.26
Micronesia	89,400	0	0.0	536,000	8,000	1.5	6.91	1.81	0.92	0.78
Polynesia	131,000	520	0.4	673,000	6,100	0.9	2.49	1.65	1.04	0.91
Global total	**1,758,412,000**	**225,000**	**0.0**	**6,895,889,000**	**7,306,000**	**0.1**	**3.54**	**1.38**	**1.72**	**1.20**

Data source: Todd M. Johnson and Brian J. Grim, eds., *World Religion Database* (Leiden/Boston: Brill, accessed January 2012).

Baha'is have suffered persecution in their home country of Iran and elsewhere, partially because they located their world headquarters, the Baha'i World Centre, in Haifa, Israel. After the creation of the Islamic Republic, Baha'is began to experience increased persecution in Iran, including denial of civil rights and some executions. The Baha'i religion still remains the largest minority religion in Iran; with over 250,000 adherents, it represents approximately 0.3% of the population.

Today, the largest Baha'i population is in India (1.9 million, see table 1.65), where efforts by Shoghi Effendi, the appointed head of the Baha'i faith from 1921 to 1957, encouraged rural work, attracting many lower-caste Hindus. The faith has also attracted many Hindus through recognition of Krishna as a Messenger of God, as well as making inroads among Muslims and tribal peoples in India. However, Baha'is still represent only 0.2% of India's population. The global spread of the Baha'i faith since 1910 is apparent in the list of countries with the most Baha'is by percentage (table 1.66); none of the top 10 are located in Asia, the home region of the religion. Over the past century, Baha'is in Africa have grown so fast that today over 29% of all adherents can be found there (though 47% of Baha'is worldwide are still found in Asia).

Table 1.65 Countries with the most Baha'is, 1910 and 2010.

Country	Baha'is 1910	Country	Baha'is 2010
Iran	220,000	India	1,896,000
United States	3,200	United States	513,000
Russia	210	Kenya	423,000
Sudan	140	Viet Nam	389,000
Israel	130	DR Congo	283,000
Lebanon	130	Philippines	275,000
Iraq	120	Iran	251,000
Pakistan	110	Zambia	241,000
Turkey	110	South Africa	239,000
Myanmar	110	Bolivia	215,000

Data source: Todd M. Johnson and Brian J. Grim, eds., *World Religion Database* (Leiden/Boston: Brill, accessed January 2012).

Table 1.66 Countries with the highest percentage of Baha'is, 1910 and 2010.

Country	% 1910	Country	% 2010
Iran	2.0	Tonga	3.5
Israel	0.0	Belize	2.5
Lebanon	0.0	São Tomé & Príncipe	2.4
Channel Islands	0.0	Bolivia	2.2
Syria	0.0	Zambia	1.8
Iraq	0.0	Mauritius	1.8
United States	0.0	Guyana	1.6
Sudan	0.0	Saint Vincent	1.5
Myanmar	0.0	Vanuatu	1.4
Egypt	0.0	Barbados	1.2

Data source: Todd M. Johnson and Brian J. Grim, eds., *World Religion Database* (Leiden/Boston: Brill, accessed January 2012). Countries >100,000 population.

Table 1.67   Countries with the fastest annual growth of Baha'is, 1910–2010 and 2000–10.

Country	% 1910–2010 p.a.	Country	% 2000–10 p.a.
Kenya	11.2	Qatar	11.9
Viet Nam	11.1	United Arab Emirates	9.5
DR Congo	10.8	Bahrain	7.2
Philippines	10.8	Kazakhstan	5.5
Zambia	10.6	Western Sahara	5.4
South Africa	10.6	Kyrgyzstan	3.8
Bolivia	10.5	Laos	3.6
Tanzania	10.4	Sierra Leone	3.6
India	10.4	Niger	3.5
Venezuela	10.2	Liberia	3.4

Data source: Todd M. Johnson and Brian J. Grim, eds., *World Religion Database* (Leiden/Boston: Brill, accessed January 2012). Countries >100,000 population.

Confucianists

Confucianism is often defined as a philosophy rather than a religion, yet it is almost always included in sociological and theological studies of religious systems worldwide because of its highly developed rituals and comprehensive worldview.[47] The ethical system was developed by Confucius (551–479 BCE), a Chinese thinker born in Qufu during the Zhou Dynasty. The core of Confucianism revolves around humanity, where ritual and filial piety control one's actions and attitudes toward others in everyday life. Largely absent from Confucianism is the concept of divinity, with "ritual" defined as secular ceremonial behaviors, not religious rites. Nonetheless, as in many other Asian religions, ancestor worship, ritual, and sacrifice are important aspects of the Confucian philosophy, including reverence for Heaven and Earth as powers that control nature. The primary text of Confucianism is the *Analects*, likely compiled by the second generation of Confucius's disciples. It captures both the oral and written transmissions of the great teacher, and holds significant influence on not only Confucianism itself, but also Chinese folk-religion as a whole.

Confucianism survived for hundreds of years in China and finally was made the official state philosophy during the Han Dynasty (206 BCE–220 CE) under the rule of Emperor Wu. Neo-Confucianism began with the inauguration of the Sung Dynasty (960–1279), which attempted to promote a more rationalistic philosophy without the superstitious trappings that had crept into Confucius thought from Daoism and Buddhism during the reign of the Han Dynasty. Metaphysics became the foundation of the system to promote ethics and spiritual development.

Only after the establishment of the Republic of China in 1912 was Confucianism/Neo-Confucianism seriously resisted. The Cultural Revolution brought criticism against traditional Chinese life, which was permeated with Confucian thought and practice. Although the authorities attempted to purge the nation of these teachings by 1976, in the twenty-first century Confucian philosophy is experiencing a surge of interest among the Chinese and restoration by the government. Confucianism also

Table 1.68 Confucianists (Co) by United Nations continents, 1910–2010.

Region	Population 1910	Co 1910	% 1910	Population 2010	Co 2010	% 2010	Co 1910–2010	Pop 1910–2010	Co 2000–10	Pop 2000–10
Africa	124,541,000	0	0.0	1,022,234,000	20,100	0.0	7.90	2.13	1.17	2.34
Asia	1,026,693,000	760,000	0.1	4,164,252,000	6,363,000	0.2	2.15	1.41	0.34	1.14
Europe	427,044,000	0	0.0	738,199,000	15,600	0.0	7.63	0.55	0.46	0.16
Latin America	78,254,000	0	0.0	590,082,000	480	0.0	3.95	2.04	0.87	1.24
Northern America	94,689,000	0	0.0	344,529,000	0	0.0	0.00	1.30	0.00	0.96
Oceania	7,192,000	0	0.0	36,593,000	49,200	0.1	8.87	1.64	2.12	1.63
Global total	1,758,412,000	760,000	0.0	6,895,889,000	6,449,000	0.1	2.16	1.38	0.36	1.20

Data source: Todd M. Johnson and Brian J. Grim, eds., *World Religion Database* (Leiden/Boston: Brill, accessed January 2012).

Table 1.69 Countries with the most Confucianists, 1910 and 2010.

Country	Confucianists 1910	Country	Confucianists 2010
South Korea	760,000	South Korea	5,270,000
		Myanmar	711,000
		Thailand	251,000
		Japan	121,000
		Australia	49,000
		South Africa	20,100
		Brunei	7,500
		Sweden	6,100
		Belgium	6,000
		Philippines	2,200

Data source: Todd M. Johnson and Brian J. Grim, eds., *World Religion Database* (Leiden/Boston: Brill, accessed January 2012). Confucianists >1,000.

Table 1.70 Countries with the highest percentage of Confucianists, 1910 and 2010.

Country	% 1910	Country	% 2010
South Korea	8.0	South Korea	10.9
		Brunei	1.9
		Myanmar	1.5
		Thailand	0.4
		Australia	0.2
		Guam	0.1
		Japan	0.1
		Sweden	0.1
		Belgium	0.1
		South Africa	<0.1

Data source: Todd M. Johnson and Brian J. Grim, eds., *World Religion Database* (Leiden/ Boston: Brill, accessed January 2012). Countries >100,000 population.

has a long history in Japan. The first evidence of the belief system there can be found as early as the third century BCE. This was solely through the efforts of Chinese emigrants working in Japan.

The vast majority of Confucianists also identify with other religions, primarily Chinese folk-religion and Buddhism. Statistically, Confucianists might seem small in number – only 0.1% of the global population (table 1.68) – but given the overlapping nature of religion in Asia, their fundamental beliefs and way of life are quite strong across the continent. Confucianism is especially prominent in South Korea, a legacy of China's historical cultural influence on the country. Numbering over 5 million adherents in South Korea, Confucianists make up approximately 11% of the country's population (table 1.70). The Choson/Yi Dynasty (1392–1910) established Confucianism as a dominant system of thought in the country. Today, approximately 82% of all Confucianists are found in South Korea. Thus, the movement of the religion around the world today is related to the movement of Koreans through business,

Table 1.71 Countries with the fastest annual growth of Confucianists, 1910–2010 and 2000–10.

Country	% 1910–2010 p.a.	Country	% 2000–10 p.a.
Myanmar	11.8	Australia	2.1
Thailand	10.7	Brunei	1.9
Japan	9.9	Guam	1.8
Australia	8.9	Philippines	1.5
South Africa	7.9	South Africa	1.2
Brunei	6.8	Thailand	1.0
Sweden	6.6	Argentina	0.9
Belgium	6.6	Austria	0.7
Philippines	5.5	Myanmar	0.6
Germany	5.4	Belgium	0.5

Data source: Todd M. Johnson and Brian J. Grim, eds., *World Religion Database* (Leiden/Boston: Brill, accessed January 2012). Countries >100,000 population.

trade, and migration. Despite such migration, however, the vast majority of Confucianists are still found in Asia, with small populations growing in Australia and some European countries (see table 1.71).

Jains

Jainism originated in India as early as the ninth century BCE, making it one of the world's oldest religions.[48] Some, however, believe the religion originated in the Indus Valley civilization, making the Indo-Aryan migration into India along with Hinduism (Jainism, like Buddhism, was considered a movement against Hinduism). The spiritual aim of Jainism, like other Indian religions, is to achieve liberation (*moksha*) from the transmigration of souls (*samsara*). Fundamental to achieving this goal is living a life of non-violence; hence Jains are renowned for their compassion for all life, both human and non-human (including strict vegetarianism). Other principles include truthfulness, monogamy, and detachment from material wealth.

Although less than 1% of the Indian population, Jains have contributed greatly to Indian culture, including the push for India's independence through the non-violent movement (which Mahatma Gandhi adopted from Jainism). Jains are some of the more literate in the country and have given much to the development of Indian literature. They also place great importance on obtaining higher education, and many of the nation's oldest libraries are preserved by Jains. Ironically, Jainism only recently received constitutional status in India in 2006 as a religion separate from Hinduism.

Jains belong to two major schools, Digambara and Svetambara, and the differences between the two are not severe. Monks in the Digambara school do not wear clothes (out of a complete renunciation of material wealth), whereas monks in the Svetambara school wear white, seamless clothes. The two schools also differ in their attitudes about whether one can achieve *moksha* as a woman. The two schools split in the third century BCE, though likely this schism took time to fully materialize.

Table 1.72 Jains by United Nations continents, 1910–2010.

Region	Population 1910	Jain 1910	% 1910	Population 2010	Jain 2010	% 2010	Jain 1910–2010	Pop 1910–2010	Jain 2000–10	Pop 2000–10
Africa	124,541,000	3,700	0.0	1,022,234,000	94,400	0.0	3.29	2.13	2.62	2.34
Asia	1,026,693,000	1,443,000	0.1	4,164,252,000	5,098,000	0.1	1.27	1.41	1.51	1.14
Europe	427,044,000	0	0.0	738,199,000	18,800	0.0	7.83	0.55	1.56	0.16
Latin America	78,254,000	0	0.0	590,082,000	1,400	0.0	5.07	2.04	0.74	1.24
Northern America	94,689,000	0	0.0	344,529,000	99,700	0.0	9.64	1.30	1.69	0.96
Oceania	7,192,000	0	0.0	36,593,000	3,000	0.0	5.87	1.64	3.15	1.63
Global total	1,758,412,000	1,446,000	0.1	6,895,889,000	5,316,000	0.1	1.31	1.38	1.53	1.20

Data source: Todd M. Johnson and Brian J. Grim, eds., *World Religion Database* (Leiden/Boston: Brill, accessed January 2012).

Throughout their history, Jains lived almost exclusively in India. Table 1.60 shows that Kenya was one of the few places in the world outside India with a Jain population in 1910 (3,500 adherents). By the twenty-first century, however, Jains had migrated around the world, with significant communities appearing in East Africa (Kenya, Tanzania, and Uganda; see growth in Eastern Africa in table 1.59); local Gujarati constructed the first Jain temple outside of India in Mombasa, Kenya, in the 1960s. Emigration to Western countries began in the 1970s and 1980s, with strong communities in Britain, Canada, and the United States. The most significant Jain growth over the past 100 years has been in Northern America, with zero adherents in 1910 and nearly 100,000 in 2010 (see table 1.73). The largest Jain temple outside of India was constructed in 2010 in Belgium. Jain communities are typically highly organized, and many organize pilgrimages to sites in India.

Despite the spread of the religion in the twentieth century, however, approximately 96% of all Jains are still found in India (although India itself is only 0.4% Jain in 2010; see table 1.74). Within India, the largest populations of Jains are found in Maharashtra,

Table 1.73 Countries with the most Jains, 1910 and 2010.

Country	Jains 1910	Country	Jains 2010
India	1,442,000	India	5,085,000
Kenya	3,500	United States	85,400
		Kenya	78,400
		United Kingdom	18,000
		Canada	14,300
		Tanzania	9,800
		Nepal	7,500
		Uganda	3,100
		Myanmar	2,400
		Malaysia	2,300

Data source: Todd M. Johnson and Brian J. Grim, eds., *World Religion Database* (Leiden/Boston: Brill, accessed January 2012). Jains >1,000.

Table 1.74 Countries with the highest percentage of Jains, 1910 and 2010.

Country	% 1910	Country	% 2010
India	0.6	India	0.4
Kenya	0.1	Suriname	0.3
Malaysia	<0.1	Kenya	0.2
Tanzania	<0.1	Fiji	0.2
Myanmar	<0.1	Reunion	0.1
United States	<0.1	Canada	<0.1
Japan	<0.1	United Kingdom	<0.1
United Kingdom	<0.1	United States	<0.1
South Africa	<0.1	Nepal	<0.1
Canada	<0.1	Tanzania	<0.1

Data source: Todd M. Johnson and Brian J. Grim, eds., *World Religion Database* (Leiden/Boston: Brill, accessed January 2012). Countries >100,000 population.

Table 1.75   Countries with the fastest annual growth of Jains, 1910–2010 and 2000–10.

Country	% 1910–2010 p.a.	Country	% 2000–10 p.a.
United States	9.5	Australia	7.0
United Kingdom	7.8	Uganda	3.5
Canada	7.5	Yemen	3.2
Nepal	6.8	Canada	2.8
Uganda	5.9	Tanzania	2.7
South Africa	5.4	Kenya	2.6
Australia	5.2	Nepal	2.1
Japan	5.1	Malaysia	1.9
Suriname	5.1	Reunion	1.8
Fiji	5.1	United Kingdom	1.6

Data source: Todd M. Johnson and Brian J. Grim, eds., *World Religion Database* (Leiden/ Boston: Brill, accessed January 2012). Countries >100,000 population.

Rajasthan, and Gujarat. Jains were found in large numbers in Lahore, Pakistan, before the 1947 partition. Most of these fled to India and are now found in the Punjab. In fact, Punjabi emigrants, along with the Gujarati, make up a significant portion of Jains in nations other than India.

Shintoists

Shinto ("way of the spirits") is the ancestral religion of Japan.[49] Unlike many other world religions, Shinto practice does not revolve around the worship of a God or gods, but rather devotion to and communication with *kami*. *Kami* are spirits that take the form of recognizable objects and concepts, such as wind, mountains, and fertility; they include even objects of worship in other religions, such as the Christian God or Muslim Allah. These spirits care about the state of humans and desire their happiness and success, which are granted when humans give the spirits proper respect and devotion. *Kami* reside in all things and are worshipped in various shrines, including shrines inside the home, making Shinto a very localized religion. The most revered *kami* is the sun goddess Amaterasu. Shinto has no founder, no canon of sacred scriptures, and no concept of a transcendental world beyond this one.

Shinto was made the state religion of Japan in 1868 during the Meiji Restoration (the return of imperial rule) in an effort to bring unity to the country. State Shinto included increased emperor worship, believing him to be divine. Shinto remained the state religion until the end of World War II, when its ties with the government were severed under order of the occupying military government led by the United States. Following this separation of religion and the state, religiosity in Japan decreased and many New Religions were formed, some loosely based on Shinto beliefs.

Today Shinto generally can be divided into three types: Shrine Shinto, Sect Shinto, and Folk Shinto. The more than 100,000 Shinto shrines in Japan play a central role in the oldest and most prevalent type, Shrine Shinto. Sect Shinto was a legal designation

Table 1.76 Shintoists by United Nations continents, 1910–2010.

Region	Population 1910	Shinto 1910	% 1910	Population 2010	Shinto 2010	% 2010	Shinto 1910–2010	Pop 1910–2010	Shinto 2000–10	Pop 2000–10
Africa	124,541,000	0	0.0	1,022,234,000	0	0.0	0.00	2.13	0.00	2.34
Asia	1,026,693,000	7,613,000	0.7	4,164,252,000	2,690,000	0.1	-1.03	1.41	0.07	1.14
Europe	427,044,000	0	0.0	738,199,000	0	0.0	0.00	0.55	0.00	0.16
Latin America	78,254,000	0	0.0	590,082,000	7,800	0.0	6.89	2.04	1.09	1.24
Northern America	94,689,000	0	0.0	344,529,000	62,700	0.0	9.14	1.30	0.94	0.96
Oceania	7,192,000	0	0.0	36,593,000	0	0.0	0.00	1.64	0.00	1.63
Global total	1,758,412,000	7,613,000	0.4	6,895,889,000	2,761,000	0.0	-1.01	1.38	0.09	1.20

Data source: Todd M. Johnson and Brian J. Grim, eds., *World Religion Database* (Leiden/Boston: Brill, accessed January 2012).

Table 1.77   Countries with the most Shintoists, 1910 and 2010.

Country	Shintoist 1910	Country	Shintoist 2010
Japan	7,613,000	Japan	2,660,000
		United States	62,700
		South Korea	28,900
		Brazil	7,800
		Singapore	1,200

Data source: Todd M. Johnson and Brian J. Grim, eds., *World Religion Database* (Leiden/Boston: Brill, accessed January 2012). Shinto >1,000.

Table 1.78   Countries with the highest percentage of Shintoists, 1910 and 2010.

Country	% 1910	Country	% 2010
Japan	15.0	Japan	2.1
		South Korea	0.1
		Singapore	<0.1
		United States	<0.1
		Brazil	<0.1
		Sri Lanka	<0.1
		Thailand	<0.1
		Viet Nam	<0.1

Data source: Todd M. Johnson and Brian J. Grim, eds., *World Religion Database* (Leiden/Boston: Brill, accessed January 2012). Countries >100,000 population.

created in the 1890s to identify non-Buddhist religious movements that, while distinct from State Shinto, nonetheless supported its broad aims. Folk Shinto is similar to Chinese folk-religion in that it includes practices from Daoism, Buddhism, and Confucianism, mixed with practices of divination and healing.

Shinto experienced a significant decline in Japan in the twentieth century. Whereas the religion represented 15% of the population in 1910, it had declined to little more than 2% in 2010 (see table 1.78). After 1945 the number of adherents in Japan plummeted. For example, in 1970 there were 4.2 million Shintoists in Japan (4% of the population). This number dropped to fewer than 3 million in 1990 (2.4% of the population). However, note that many who considered themselves Shintoists prior to World War II later adopted the New Religions that arose during the second half of the century; many of these religions share characteristics with Shinto.

Outside Japan, large communities of Shintoists can be found in Brazil, the United States, and South Korea (see table 1.78). Much of the growth of Shinto beyond Japan has been a result of emigration during the twentieth century. Growth in Korea, however, was largely because of Japanese colonial rule from 1910–45, during which State Shinto was imposed on Korean society. This was especially true in the nation's education system, where children were required to worship at the Shinto shrine regardless

Table 1.79 Countries with the fastest annual growth of Shintoists, 1910–2010 and 2000–10.

Country	% 1910–2010 p.a.	Country	% 2000–10 p.a.
United States	9.1	Singapore	2.4
South Korea	8.3	Sri Lanka	1.3
Brazil	6.9	Viet Nam	1.2
Singapore	4.9	Brazil	1.1
Thailand	3.8	Thailand	1.0
Viet Nam	2.9	United States	0.9
Sri Lanka	2.9	South Korea	0.5
Japan	–1.0	Japan	0.1

Data source: Todd M. Johnson and Brian J. Grim, eds., *World Religion Database* (Leiden/Boston: Brill, accessed January 2012). Countries >100,000 population.

of religious belief. Shinto's highest growth rate during the past century can be seen in Northern America at over 9% per year (see table 1.76). Table 1.79 shows that in South Korea, the Shintoist growth rate over the century was 8.3%, in Brazil 6.9%, and in Singapore 4.9%.

Zoroastrians

Zoroastrianism is a monotheistic religion founded in Iran by Zoroaster (or Zarathustra), whom scholars estimate to have lived between 1500 and 1200 BCE.[50] Zoroaster is said to have received direct revelation from the supreme being Ahura Mazda and his archangels, thus authoring the primary sacred scripture, the Avesta (of which much has been lost). Fundamental to Zoroastrianism is the cosmic struggle between good and evil, or between Ahura Mazda and the evil Angra Mainya. The religion is apocalyptic, awaiting a final cosmic battle that will occur at (and signify the end of) time, complete with a savior-figure who will initiate the resurrection of the dead. Some believe these doctrines had direct influence on the development of other monotheistic religions, specifically Christianity and Islam. Peculiar to Zoroastrianism is the special place fire holds in worship and prayer (representing the light or wisdom of God).

Zoroastrians have a long and illustrious history stretching back to ancient Persia, where they had a close relationship with the Sassanid Empire, under which Zoroastrianism was declared the state religion. After the Arabs overthrew the empire in the seventh century, Zoroastrians were protected as *dhimmis* under Islamic law, but not without social and economic pressure to convert. Arab hostility prompted many Iranian Zoroastrians to immigrate in the tenth century to India, where they became known as Parsis ("Persians"). The Safavid dynasty (1501–1722), in an attempt to establish Shi'a Islam as the official religion of Persia, executed hundreds of thousands of religious minorities, including Zoroastrians, Jews, and Sunnis. Following this period – and especially after the further persecution of the Qajar dynasty – most

Table 1.80 Zoroastrians (Z) by United Nations continents, 1910–2010.

Region	Population 1910	Z 1910	% 1910	Population 2010	Z 2010	% 2010	Z 1910–2010	Pop 1910–2010	Z 2000–10	Pop 2000–10
Africa	124,541,000	230	0.0	1,022,234,000	960	0.0	1.44	2.13	0.99	2.34
Asia	1,026,693,000	119,000	0.0	4,164,252,000	167,000	0.0	0.34	1.41	0.68	1.14
Europe	427,044,000	0	0.0	738,199,000	5,700	0.0	6.55	0.55	0.54	0.16
Latin America	78,254,000	0	0.0	590,082,000	0	0.0	0.00	2.04	0.00	1.24
Northern America	94,689,000	0	0.0	344,529,000	21,000	0.0	7.95	1.30	0.95	0.96
Oceania	7,192,000	0	0.0	36,593,000	2,600	0.0	5.72	1.64	3.19	1.63
Global total	**1,758,412,000**	**119,000**	**0.0**	**6,895,889,000**	**197,000**	**0.0**	**0.51**	**1.38**	**0.74**	**1.20**

Data source: Todd M. Johnson and Brian J. Grim, eds., *World Religion Database* (Leiden/Boston: Brill, accessed January 2012).

Table 1.81 Countries with the most Zoroastrians, 1910 and 2010.

Country	Zoroastrians 1910	Country	Zoroastrians 2010
India	102,000	India	73,400
Iran	11,200	Iran	68,400
Pakistan	4,300	United States	17,600
Sri Lanka	580	Pakistan	8,700
Yemen	390	United Kingdom	4,800
Myanmar	270	Afghanistan	4,300
Kenya	230	Canada	3,400
China	210	Australia	2,600
Hong Kong	130	Sri Lanka	2,500
		Tajikistan	2,500

Data source: Todd M. Johnson and Brian J. Grim, eds., *World Religion Database* (Leiden/ Boston: Brill, accessed January 2012).

Table 1.82 Countries with the highest percentage of Zoroastrians, 1910 and 2010.

Country	% 1910	Country	% 2010
Iran	0.1	Iran	0.1
India	<0.1	Tajikistan	<0.1
Hong Kong	<0.1	Kazakhstan	<0.1
Pakistan	<0.1	Kyrgyzstan	<0.1
Yemen	<0.1	Afghanistan	<0.1
Sri Lanka	<0.1	Sri Lanka	<0.1
Kenya	<0.1	Australia	<0.1
Myanmar	<0.1	Canada	<0.1
China	<0.1	United Kingdom	<0.1
United States	<0.1	India	<0.1

Data source: Todd M. Johnson and Brian J. Grim, eds., *World Religion Database* (Leiden/ Boston: Brill, accessed January 2012). Countries >100,000 population.

remaining Zoroastrians fled to India. The two groups in Iran and India continue to be the most prominent Zoroastrian communities today, although these groups are still less than 0.1% of the general populations (see table 1.80). The number of Parsis declined throughout the twentieth century, however, because of low birthrates and no way to receive converts, as Zoroastrianism is not typically a proselytizing religion (with the notable exception of the earliest periods in its history).

The Iranian Revolution of 1979 pushed many Zoroastrians to emigrate to the United States, Canada, Australia, and the United Kingdom. This is illustrated in table 1.80, with increases of 21,000 adherents in Northern America and 5,700 in Europe (growth rates of 8% and 6.5%, respectively). The United States has the third-largest community of Zoroastrians worldwide (see table 1.81), and during the past century Zoroastrian scholarship has elaborated the religion's history and

Table 1.83 Countries with the fastest annual growth of Zoroastrians, 1910–2010 and 2000–10.

Country	% 1910–2010 p.a.	Country	% 2000–10 p.a.
United States	7.8	Tanzania	3.4
United Kingdom	6.4	Australia	3.2
Afghanistan	6.3	Yemen	2.3
Canada	6.0	Singapore	2.3
Australia	5.7	Syria	2.1
Tajikistan	5.7	Pakistan	1.9
Kazakhstan	5.6	Netherlands	1.8
Uzbekistan	4.7	Macau	1.8
Kyrgyzstan	4.5	Sri Lanka	1.3
France	4.2	Tajikistan	1.3

Data source: Todd M. Johnson and Brian J. Grim, eds., *World Religion Database* (Leiden/Boston: Brill, accessed January 2012). Countries >100,000 population.

philosophy. Approximately 15% of Zoroastrians can be found in Europe, Northern America, and Oceania. This growth is due primarily to emigration by peoples of Persian descent. Growth rates over the 10-year period indicate a widening of the Zoroastrian diaspora around the world, with presence of the religion growing in Europe, Asia, Oceania, and Africa (see table 1.83). Nonetheless, the Zoroastrian community worldwide is focused on survival. Table 1.82 reveals that in no country do Zoroastrians represent more than 0.1% of the population. The religion supports opportunities for women, who, like most other female professionals, tend to have fewer (or no) children.

Notes

1   The seven religions considered "major religions" in this book are Christianity, Islam, Hinduism, Buddhism, Chinese folk-religion, Judaism, and ethnoreligions (tribal religions). For an accessible and engaging overview of the world's religions see Stephen Prothero, *God is Not One: The Eight Rival Religions That Run the World – and Why Their Differences Matter* (New York: HarperOne, 2010). Prothero lists the following as major religions: Islam, Christianity, Confucianism, Hinduism, Buddhism, Yoruba religion, Judaism, and Daoism. A collection of excellent scholarly articles on world religions is found in Mark Juergensmeyer, ed., *The Oxford Handbook of Global Religions* (Oxford: Oxford University Press, 2006). See also an earlier condensed version by Juergensmeyer, *Global Religions: An Introduction* (Oxford: Oxford University Press, 2003).

2   For a full-color map of the world's religions by the religion with the most adherents in each of the world's 3,000 major civil divisions, see Todd M. Johnson and Kenneth R. Ross, *Atlas of Global Christianity* (Edinburgh: Edinburgh University Press, 2009), 6–7.

3   See chapter 3 in this volume for an analysis of religious diversity. There are very few places in the world where true religious diversity exists (that is, with no single religion more than 30% of the population).

4   Calculated with the formula $[(\text{Adherents } 2010/\text{Adherents } 1910)0.01 - 1] \times 100$.

5   Note that although Christian growth has slowed slightly (1.32% p.a. to 1.31% p.a.), it is now outpacing world population growth and is therefore gaining a small percentage of the world's population every year.

6   Pippa Norris and Ronald Inglehart, *Sacred and Secular: Religion and Politics Worldwide* (Cambridge: Cambridge University Press, 2004), 5.

7   For a detailed enumeration of Christians past, present, and future in every country of the world, see David B. Barrett, George T. Kurian, and Todd M. Johnson, eds., *World Christian Encyclopedia: A Comparative Survey of Churches and Religions in the Modern World*, vol. 1, *The World by Countries, Religionists, Churches, Ministries*, 2nd ed. (New York: Oxford University Press, 2001).

8   Here, "North" is defined in geopolitical terms by five current United Nations (UN) regions (comprising 53 countries): Eastern Europe (including all of Russia), Northern Europe, Southern Europe, Western Europe, and Northern America (Australia and New Zealand, also included in the North by the United Nations, are considered part of the South in this volume).

9   "South" is defined as the remaining 16 current UN regions (comprising 185 countries): Eastern Africa, Middle Africa, Northern Africa, Southern Africa, Western Africa, Eastern Asia, South-central Asia, South-eastern Asia, Western Asia, Caribbean, Central America, South America, Australia/New Zealand, Melanesia, Micronesia, and Polynesia. Three geographic alternatives could be proposed. First, one could consider the dividing line between North and South as the equator (Northern and Southern Hemisphere). Second, one could move the line north to the Tropic of Cancer (23° 26′ north latitude), thus capturing most of Latin America, Africa, and Asia in the South. Third, one could consider Jerusalem's parallel of latitude (31.8° north) as the dividing line. Each of these alternatives has advantages and disadvantages. For the purposes of this study, the geopolitical model based on current UN regions is the most practical because statistics on demography and religious affiliation are most readily available for these regions.

10 A United Nations Development Programme document, "Forging a Global South" (New York: May 2003), states, "The use of the term 'South' to refer to developing countries collectively has been part of the shorthand of international relations since the 1970s. It rests on the fact that all of the world's industrially developed countries (with the exception of Australia and New Zealand) lie to the north of its developing countries."

11 For example, Anglicans in the global South spoke out under the leadership of Nigerian Primate Akinola in the document, "Statement of the Primates of the Global South in the Anglican Communion in Response to the Consecration of Gene Robinson on 2 November 2003," www.anglican-nig.org/glbsouthst.htm.

12 Ancient Palestine is located in the present-day UN region of Western Asia, defined above as part of the South.

13 Increasingly, "Northern" Christians are Southern Christians who have immigrated to the North. For example, some of the largest single congregations in Europe are led by and composed of Africans.

14 Defined as between 1815 and 1914 in Kenneth Scott Latourette, *A History of Christianity*, vol. 2, *Reformation to the Present* (New York: Harper & Row, 1975), 1,063.

15 Note that Latin America was already 95% Christian (overwhelmingly Roman Catholic) in 1900. The changes in Latin American Christianity since then refer to the growth of Protestantism and Pentecostalism.

16 Members affiliated to churches and denominations with doctrines deviant from mainstream Christianity (primarily concerning the nature of Christ and the existence of the Trinity), usually claiming another source of divine revelation in addition to the Bible.

17 Unlike traditions, these movements are not mutually exclusive categories. For example, some Renewalists are Evangelicals and some are not. Evangelicals and Renewalists are made up of individuals from the six traditions listed above.

18 Renewalists are church members involved in the Pentecostal renewal in the Holy Spirit expressed by three different types. The first type is Pentecostals, individuals who are members of Pentecostal denominations. The second type is Charismatics, members of non-Pentecostal churches (Catholic, Anglican, Protestant, etc.) who have been filled with the Holy Spirit. Thus, individuals do not have to leave their denomination or Christian tradition to embrace the Charismatic experience. Lastly, the third type is Independent Charismatics, usually found in Independent churches, experiencing the same gifts of the Holy Spirit but without accepting the same terminology or polity.

19 Recent historical and descriptive works on global Islam include Akbar Ahmed, *Journey into Islam: The Crisis of Globalization* (Washington, DC: Brookings Institute Press, 2007); Olivier Roy, *Globalized Islam: The Search for a New Ummah* (New York: Columbia University Press, 2004); John Esposito, ed., *The Oxford History of Islam* (Oxford: Oxford University Press, 2000); and Francis Robinson, ed., *The Cambridge Illustrated History of the Islamic World* (Cambridge: Cambridge University Press, 1996).

20 For detailed Muslim demographics and analysis see The Pew Forum on Religion and Public Life, *Mapping the Global Muslim Population: A Report on the Size and Distribution of the World's Muslim Population*, October 7, 2009, http://www.pewforum.org/Mapping-the-Global-Muslim-Population.aspx; and The Pew Forum on Religion and Public Life, *The Future of the Global Muslim Population: Projections for 2010–2030*, January 27, 2011, http://pewresearch.org/pubs/1872/muslim-population-projections-worldwide-fast-growth.

21 This is primarily due to immigration of Muslims followed by high birthrates among immigrants. In addition, large numbers of conversions to Islam have occurred among the African American population in the United States.

22 The conceptual statistical center of gravity is a geographical point in which an equal number of followers of a particular religion live to the north, south, east, and west. The statistical center of gravity is calculated by assigning all followers to a single point for each of the countries of the world and then determining the center of all those weighted points. For a more detailed explanation, see Johnson and Ross, *Atlas of Global Christianity*, 325.

23 See Simon Ross Valentine, *Islam and the Ahmadiyya Jama'at: History, Belief, Practice* (New York: Columbia University Press, 2008).

24 For a detailed analysis of Muslim languages and ethnic groups see Richard V. Weekes, *Muslim Peoples: A World Ethnographic Survey*, 2nd ed. (Westport, CT: Greenwood Press, 1984).

25 For recent overviews of Hinduism see Wendy Doniger, *The Hindus: An Alternative History* (New York: Penguin Press, 2009); Hillary Rodrigues, *Introducing Hinduism* (New York: Routledge, 2006); and Gavin Flood, *An Introduction to Hinduism* (Cambridge: Cambridge University Press, 1996).

26 See Rajesh Rai and Peter Reeves, eds., *The South Asian Diaspora: Transnational Networks and Changing Identities* (London: Routledge, 2008); Gijsbert Oonk, *Global Indian Diasporas: Exploring Trajectories of Migration and Theory* (Amsterdam: Amsterdam University Press, 2008); Judith M. Brown, *South Asians Abroad: Introducing the Modern Diaspora* (Cambridge: Cambridge University Press, 2006); and Colin Clarke, Ceri Peach, and Steven Vertovec, eds., *South Asians Overseas: Migration and Ethnicity* (Cambridge: Cambridge University Press, 1990).

27 See Harold Coward, John R. Hinnells, and Raymond Brady Williams, eds., *The South Asian Religious Diaspora in Britain, Canada, and the United States* (Albany: State

University of New York, 2000), and Sandhya Shukla, *India Abroad: Diasporic Cultures of Postwar America and England* (Princeton: Princeton University Press, 2003).

28 A recent moral defense of the agnostic position is found in Greg M. Epstein, *Good Without God: What a Billion Nonreligious People Do Believe* (New York: Harper, 2009). For a recent report on demographic details regarding the religiously unaffiliated in the United States, see Pew Forum on Religion and Public Life, *"Nones" on the Rise*, October 9, 2012, http://www.pewforum.org/Unaffiliated/nones-on-the-rise.aspx.

29 A classic survey of Chinese folk-religion is D. Howard Smith, *Chinese Religions* (New York: Holt, Rinehart, and Winston, 1968). A more recent treatment is Mario Poceski, *Introducing Chinese Religions* (London: Routledge, 2009).

30 Chung-Ying Cheng, "A Chinese Religious Perspective," in *The Oxford Handbook of Religious Diversity*, ed. Chad Meister (Oxford: Oxford University Press, 2011), 356.

31 For recent overviews of Buddhism see Charles S. Prebish and Damien Keown, *Introducing Buddhism* (New York: Routledge, 2006), and Steven Heine and Charles S. Prebish, eds., *Buddhism in the Modern World: Adaptations of an Ancient Tradition* (Oxford: Oxford University Press, 2003).

32 This concept is summarized in Gananath Obeyesekere, "Buddhism," in *Global Religions*, ed. Mark Juergensmeyer (New York: Oxford University Press, 2003), 63–77.

33 For a comprehensive survey of the history of Buddhism and its encounter with the West, see Lawrence Sutin, *All is Change: The Two-Thousand-Year Journey of Buddhism to the West* (New York: Little, Brown, and Company, 2008).

34 Documented in Linda Learman, ed., *Buddhist Missionaries in the Era of Globalization* (Honolulu: University of Hawaii Press, 2005).

35 See Melvyn C. Goldstein and Matthew T. Kapstein, eds., *Buddhism in Contemporary Tibet: Religious Revival and Cultural Identity* (Berkeley: University of California Press, 1998).

36 For a recent overview of atheism, see Michael Martin, ed., *The Cambridge Companion to Atheism* (Cambridge: Cambridge University Press, 2007).

37 See Sam Harris, *The End of Faith: Religion, Terror, and the Future of Reason* (New York: W. W. Norton & Company, 2004); Daniel C. Dennett, *Breaking the Spell: Religion as a Natural Phenomenon* (New York: Penguin Group, 2007); Richard Dawkins, *The God Delusion* (Boston: Houghton Mifflin Company, 2006); and Christopher Hitchens, *God is Not Great: How Religion Poisons Everything* (New York: Hachette Book Group, 2007).

38 Helpful overviews include Peter Clarke, *New Religions in Global Perspective* (London: Routledge, 2005); Dareck Daschke and W. Michael Ashcraft, eds., *New Religious Movements: A Documentary Reader* (New York: New York University Press, 2005); and James R. Lewis, ed., *The Oxford Handbook of New Religious Movements* (Oxford: Oxford University Press, 2004).

39 For more information on Sikhism, see W. H. McLeod, *Exploring Sikhism: Aspects of Sikh Identity, Culture, and Thought* (New Delhi: Oxford University Press, 2000).

40 For major recent works on Judaism, see Leora Batnitzky, *How Judaism Became a Religion: An Introduction to Modern Jewish Thought* (Princeton: Princeton University Press, 2011); Jacob Neusner, *The Transformation of Judaism: From Philosophy to Religion (Studies in Judaism)*, 2nd ed. (Lanham, MD: University Press of America, 2011); Fred Skolnik, Shmeul Himselstein, and Geoffrey Wigoder, eds., *The New Encyclopedia of Judaism* (New York: New York University Press, 2002); Sergio DellaPergola, *World Jewish Population, 2010* (Storrs, CT: Mandell L. Berman Institute, 2010).

41 Harvey E. Goldberg, "Judaism," in *Global Religions: An Introduction*, ed. Mark Juergensmeyer (Oxford: Oxford University Press, 2003), 40.

42 An ultra-Orthodox Jewish woman in Israel will produce nearly three times as many children as her secular counterpart. See John Micklethwait and Adrian Wooldridge, *God is Back: How the Global Revival of Faith is Changing the World* (New York: Penguin Press, 2009), 17–18.

43 On Afro-Caribbean religion, see Nathaniel Samuel Murrell, *Afro-Caribbean Religions: An Introduction to Their Historical, Cultural, and Sacred Traditions* (Philadelphia: Temple University Press, 2009). On African spirituality, see Adama and Naomi Doumbia, *The Way of the Elders: West African Spirituality and Tradition* (St. Paul, MN: Llewellyn Publications, 2004).

44 On Candomblé, see Mikelle Smith Omari-Tunkara, *Manipulating the Sacred: Yoruba Art, Ritual, and Resistance in Brazilian Candomblé* (Detroit: Wayne State University Press, 2006). On Umbanda, see Diana DeGroats Brown, *Umbanda: Religion and Politics in Urban Brazil* (New York: Columbia University Press, 1994).

45 See Livia Kohn, *Introducing Daoism* (London: Routledge, 2009).

46 See William S. Hatcher and J. Douglas Martin, *The Baha'i Faith: The Emerging Global Religion* (Wilmette, IL: Baha'i Publications, 2002).

47 This case is made in Xinzhong Yao, *An Introduction to Confucianism* (Cambridge: Cambridge University Press, 2000). See also John H. and Evelyn Nagai Berthrong, *Confucianism: A Short Introduction* (Oxford: Oneworld Publications, 2000).

48 See Paul Dundas, *The Jains* (London: Routledge, 2002).

49 See Robert Ellwood, *Introducing Japanese Religion* (New York: Routledge, 2008).

50 See John R. Hinnells, *The Zoroastrian Diaspora: Religion and Migration* (Oxford: Oxford University Press, 2005).

References

Ahmed, Akbar. *Journey into Islam: The Crisis of Globalization*. Washington, DC: Brookings Institute Press, 2007.

Barrett, David B., George T. Kurian, and Todd M. Johnson, eds. *World Christian Encyclopedia: A Comparative Survey of Churches and Religions in the Modern World*. Vol. 1, *The World by Countries, Religionists, Churches, Ministries*, 2nd ed. New York: Oxford University Press, 2001.

Batnitzky, Leora. *How Judaism Became a Religion: An Introduction to Modern Jewish Thought*. Princeton: Princeton University Press, 2011.

Berthrong, John H., and Evelyn Nagai Berthrong. *Confucianism: A Short Introduction*. Oxford: Oneworld Publications, 2000.

Brown, Diana DeGroats. *Umbanda: Religion and Politics in Urban Brazil*. New York: Columbia University Press, 1994.

Brown, Judith M. *South Asians Abroad: Introducing the Modern Diaspora*. Cambridge: Cambridge University Press, 2006.

Cheng, Chung-Ying. "A Chinese Religious Perspective." In *The Oxford Handbook of Religious Diversity*, edited by Chad Meister, 351–64. Oxford: Oxford University Press, 2011.

Church of Nigeria Anglican Communion, The. "Statement of the Primates of the Global South in the Anglican Communion in Response to the Consecration of Gene Robinson on 2 November 2003." November 2, 2003. http://www.anglican-nig.org/glbsouthst.htm.

Clarke, Colin, Ceri Peach, and Steven Vertovec, eds. *South Asians Overseas: Migration and Ethnicity*. Cambridge: Cambridge University Press, 1990.

Clarke, Peter. *New Religions in Global Perspective*. London: Routledge, 2005.

Coward, Harold, John R. Hinnells, and Raymond Brady Williams, eds. *The South Asian Religious Diaspora in Britain, Canada, and the United States.* Albany: State University of New York, 2000.

Daschke, Dareck, and W. Michael Ashcraft, eds. *New Religious Movements: A Documentary Reader.* New York: New York University Press, 2005.

Dawkins, Richard. *The God Delusion.* Boston: Houghton Mifflin Company, 2006.

DellaPergola, Sergio. *World Jewish Population, 2010.* Storrs, CT: Mandell L. Berman Institute, 2010.

Dennett, Daniel C. *Breaking the Spell: Religion as a Natural Phenomenon.* New York: Penguin Group, 2007.

Doniger, Wendy. *The Hindus: An Alternative History.* New York: Penguin Press, 2009.

Doumbia, Adama, and Naomi Doumbia. *The Way of the Elders: West African Spirituality and Tradition.* St. Paul, MN: Llewellyn Publications, 2004.

Dundas, Paul. *The Jains.* London: Routledge, 2002.

Ellwood, Robert. *Introducing Japanese Religion.* New York: Routledge, 2008.

Epstein, Greg M. *Good Without God: What a Billion Nonreligious People Do Believe.* New York: Harper, 2009.

Esposito, John, ed. *The Oxford History of Islam.* Oxford: Oxford University Press, 2000.

Flood, Gavin. *An Introduction to Hinduism.* Cambridge: Cambridge University Press, 1996.

Goldberg, Harvey E. "Judaism." In *Global Religions: An Introduction*, edited by Mark Juergensmeyer, 40–52. Oxford: Oxford University Press, 2003.

Goldstein, Melvyn C., and Matthew T. Kapstein, eds. *Buddhism in Contemporary Tibet: Religious Revival and Cultural Identity.* Berkeley: University of California Press, 1998.

Harris, Sam. *The End of Faith: Religion, Terror, and the Future of Reason.* New York: W. W. Norton & Company, 2004.

Hatcher, William S., and J. Douglas Martin, *The Baha'i Faith: The Emerging Global Religion.* Wilmette, IL: Baha'i Publications, 2002.

Heine, Steven, and Charles S. Prebish, eds. *Buddhism in the Modern World: Adaptations of an Ancient Tradition.* Oxford: Oxford University Press, 2003.

Hinnells, John R. *The Zoroastrian Diaspora: Religion and Migration.* Oxford: Oxford University Press, 2005.

Hitchens, Christopher. *God is Not Great: How Religion Poisons Everything.* New York: Hachette Book Group, 2007.

Johnson, Todd M., and Brian J. Grim, eds. *World Religion Database.* Leiden/Boston: Brill, 2008.

Johnson, Todd M., and Kenneth R. Ross, *Atlas of Global Christianity.* Edinburgh: Edinburgh University Press, 2009.

Juergensmeyer, Mark. *Global Religions: An Introduction.* Oxford: Oxford University Press, 2003.

Juergensmeyer, Mark, ed. *The Oxford Handbook of Global Religions.* Oxford: Oxford University Press, 2006.

Kohn, Livia. *Introducing Daoism.* London: Routledge, 2009.

Latourette, Kenneth Scott. *A History of Christianity.* Vol. 2, *Reformation to the Present.* New York: Harper & Row, 1975.

Learman, Linda, ed. *Buddhist Missionaries in the Era of Globalization.* Honolulu: University of Hawaii Press, 2005.

Lewis, James R., ed. *The Oxford Handbook of New Religious Movements.* Oxford: Oxford University Press, 2004.

Martin, Michael, ed., *The Cambridge Companion to Atheism.* Cambridge: Cambridge University Press, 2007.

McLeod, W. H. *Exploring Sikhism: Aspects of Sikh Identity, Culture, and Thought.* New Delhi: Oxford University Press, 2000.

Micklethwait, John, and Adrian Wooldridge, *God is Back: How the Global Revival of Faith is Changing the World*. New York: Penguin Press, 2009.

Murrell, Nathaniel Samuel. *Afro-Caribbean Religions: An Introduction to Their Historical, Cultural, and Sacred Traditions*. Philadelphia: Temple University Press, 2009.

Neusner, Jacob. *The Transformation of Judaism: From Philosophy to Religion. Studies in Judaism.* 2nd ed. Lanham, MD: University Press of America, 2011.

Norris, Pippa, and Ronald Inglehart. *Sacred and Secular: Religion and Politics Worldwide*. Cambridge: Cambridge University Press, 2004.

Obeyesekere, Gananath. "Buddhism." In *Global Religions*, edited by Mark Juergensmeyer, 63–77. New York: Oxford University Press, 2003.

Omari-Tunkara, Mikelle Smith. *Manipulating the Sacred: Yoruba Art, Ritual, and Resistance in Brazilian Candomblé*. Detroit: Wayne State University Press, 2006.

Oonk, Gijsbert. *Global Indian Diasporas: Exploring Trajectories of Migration and Theory*. Amsterdam: Amsterdam University Press, 2008.

Pew Forum on Religion and Public Life. *Mapping the Global Muslim Population: A Report on the Size and Distribution of the World's Muslim Population. October 7, 2009.* http://www.pewforum.org/Mapping-the-Global-Muslim-Population.aspx.

Pew Forum on Religion and Public Life. *"Nones" on the Rise*. October 9, 2012. http://www.pewforum.org/Unaffiliated/nones-on-the-rise.aspx.

Pew Forum on Religion and Public Life. *The Future of the Global Muslim Population: Projections for 2010–2030.* January 27, 2011. http://pewresearch.org/pubs/1872/muslim-population-projections-worldwide-fast-growth.

Poceski, Mario. *Introducing Chinese Religions*. London: Routledge, 2009.

Prebish Charles S., and Damien Keown. *Introducing Buddhism*. New York: Routledge, 2006.

Prothero, Stephen. *God is Not One: The Eight Rival Religions That Run the World – and Why Their Differences Matter*. New York: HarperOne, 2010.

Rai, Rajesh, and Peter Reeves, eds. *The South Asian Diaspora: Transnational Networks and Changing Identities*. London: Routledge, 2008.

Robinson, Francis, ed. *The Cambridge Illustrated History of the Islamic World*. Cambridge: Cambridge University Press, 1996.

Rodrigues, Hillary. *Introducing Hinduism*. New York: Routledge, 2006.

Roy, Olivier. *Globalized Islam: The Search for a New Ummah*. New York: Columbia University Press, 2004.

Shukla, Sandhya. *India Abroad: Diasporic Cultures of Postwar America and England*. Princeton: Princeton University Press, 2003.

Skolnik, Fred, Shmeul Himselstein, and Geoffrey Wigoder, eds. *The New Encyclopedia of Judaism*. New York: New York University Press, 2002.

Smith, D. Howard. *Chinese Religions*. New York: Holt, Rinehart, and Winston, 1968.

Sutin, Lawrence. *All is Change: The Two-Thousand-Year Journey of Buddhism to the West*. New York: Little, Brown, and Company, 2008.

United Nations Development Programme. "Forging a Global South." New York: United Nations Development Programme, 2003.

Valentine, Simon Ross. *Islam and the Ahmadiyya Jama'at: History, Belief, Practice*. New York: Columbia University Press, 2008.

Weekes, Richard V. *Muslim Peoples: A World Ethnographic Survey*. 2nd ed. Westport, CT: Greenwood Press, 1984.

Yao, Xinzhong. *An Introduction to Confucianism*. Cambridge: Cambridge University Press, 2000.

Chapter 2

Regional Religious Populations, 1910–2010

This chapter presents a profile of religious affiliation by United Nations continental areas. These include Africa, Asia, Europe, Latin America, Northern America, and Oceania. Each of these can be divided further into regions, then countries.[1] Country-by-country statistics on religious affiliation are presented in the appendix, World Religions by Country. The tables that follow offer estimates for 18 religious categories for both 1910 and 2010, with growth rates calculated for 1910–2010 and 2000–10.[2]

Africa

Over the past 100 years Africa has experienced the most profound transformation in religious populations of any continent.[3] The most dramatic numerical increase of Christians in the world occurred on the continent in the twentieth century, growing from 11 million (9.3%) in 1910 to 494 million (48.3%) by 2010 (see table 2.1). This represents an average 100-year growth rate of 3.8% per year, almost twice that of the African population as a whole. Fewer than 2% of the world's Christians lived in Africa in 1910; this had changed to 22% by 2010. When considering just sub-Saharan Africa, over 70% are Christian. Muslims in Africa also grew from nearly 40 million in 1910 (32%) to 426 million (41.7%) by 2010. Ethnoreligionists (tribal religionists) increased from 72 million to 89 million over the 100 years but declined as a percentage of Africa's population, from 58.0% in 1910 to only 8.7% by 2010. The continuing presence of ethnoreligionists was a surprise to many demographers and sociologists; these religions had been predicted to disappear with the arrival and growth of Christianity and Islam. Another surprising trend has been the rise of agnostics, who are found largely in urban centers and number over 6 million.

The World's Religions in Figures: An Introduction to International Religious Demography,
First Edition. Todd M. Johnson and Brian J. Grim.

Table 2.1 Religious affiliation and growth in Africa, 1910–2010.

Religion	Adherents 1910	% 1910	Adherents 2010	% 2010	1910–2010 % p.a.	2000–10 % p.a.
Christians	11,636,000	9.3	494,053,000	48.3	3.82	2.56
Muslims	39,916,000	32.1	425,860,000	41.7	2.40	2.28
Ethnoreligionists	72,210,000	58.0	89,354,000	8.7	0.21	1.48
Agnostics	8,400	0.0	6,497,000	0.6	6.88	2.72
Hindus	303,000	0.2	2,930,000	0.3	2.29	1.68
Baha'is	240	0.0	2,143,000	0.2	9.52	2.39
Atheists	1,100	0.0	571,000	0.1	6.45	2.05
Buddhists	3,600	0.0	254,000	0.0	4.35	1.63
Chinese folk-religionists	2,200	0.0	132,000	0.0	4.18	2.41
Jews	451,000	0.4	132,000	0.0	-1.22	0.96
New Religionists	1,200	0.0	116,000	0.0	4.68	2.15
Jains	3,700	0.0	94,400	0.0	3.29	2.62
Sikhs	2,600	0.0	73,300	0.0	3.40	2.37
Confucianists	0	0.0	20,100	0.0	7.90	1.17
Spiritists	1,200	0.0	2,900	0.0	0.89	1.10
Zoroastrians	230	0.0	960	0.0	1.44	0.99
Total population	**124,541,000**	**100.0**	**1,022,234,000**	**100.0**	**2.13**	**2.34**

Data source: Todd M. Johnson and Brian J. Grim, eds., *World Religion Database* (Leiden/Boston: Brill, accessed January 2012).

Asia

Asia has also experienced significant religious change over the past century.[4] As seen in table 2.2, in 1910 over 50% of Asia's population was Chinese folk-religionist or Buddhist; this percentage fell to only 22% by 2010. As in Africa, ethnoreligionists fell steadily over the century as a percentage of Asia's population, from 5.6% in 1910 to 3.5% in 2010. These changes resulted in part from increases in the percentages of Muslims (from 16.7% to 25.9%) and Christians (2.4% to 8.2%). The increased share of Asia's population claimed by agnostics (from 0.0% in 1910 to 12.1% in 2010) and atheists (0.0% to 2.8%) resulted mainly from their gains in China after the Communist revolution there. The expansion of religiously unaffiliated populations was truly unprecedented, with both agnostics and atheists growing an average of around 10% annually over the entire century, making Asia the most religiously unaffiliated continent in 2010. This is due largely to the spread of Communist regimes whose policies prohibited religions in order to propagate atheistic ideology. Significantly, Muslims have displaced Chinese folk-religionists as Asia's most numerous religious adherents (largely through growth in Western and Southeast Asia). Asia is also the world's most religiously diverse continent. In six countries, five or more religions each claim more than 5% of the population as adherents: Viet Nam, China, South Korea, Malaysia, Taiwan, and Brunei. The greatest religious diversity is found in Southeast Asia and Korea. South Korea has five religions with over 10% of the population each, and Viet Nam, North Korea, and Singapore each have four. (See chapter 3 of this volume for more on religious diversity.)

Europe

Over the past 100 years Europe[5] has become more diverse in its religious demographics.[6] The most drastic changes can be seen in the Christian and religiously unaffiliated populations on the continent. Europe has for centuries been the heartland of Christianity, not only in terms of demographics, but also in global influence in theology and mission. In 1910, 66% of the world's Christians lived in Europe, but this had fallen substantially to around 25% a century later. In 1910 Europe was nearly 95% Christian and the religiously unaffiliated represented only 0.5% of the population. By 2010 the Christian percentage had fallen to 78.6%; Christian switching to atheism and agnosticism had raised the religiously unaffiliated combined share of the European population to 14.7% (see table 2.3). The Muslim percentage also rose over the century, from 2.4% in 1910 to 5.6% in 2010. The European Muslim population today consists of a mix of immigrants from North Africa and Western Asia in the West while Southern Europe has indigenous populations of Muslims who have lived there for centuries in countries such as Bosnia, Albania, and Kosovo. At the same time, Jews declined from 2.4% to 0.3% in Europe as a result of the Holocaust and emigration (including to the newly created state of Israel). Surprisingly, however, the number of Jews is on the rise in Western Europe because of recent immigration of Eastern European Jews to Germany. The numbers of Hindus and Buddhists are on the rise in Europe as well.

Table 2.2 Religious affiliation and growth in Asia, 1910–2010.

Religion	Adherents 1910	% 1910	Adherents 2010	% 2010	1910–2010 % p.a.	2000–10 % p.a.
Muslims	171,690,000	16.7	1,078,854,000	25.9	1.85	1.75
Hindus	222,876,000	21.7	941,481,000	22.6	1.45	1.41
Agnostics	50,400	0.0	504,762,000	12.1	9.65	0.17
Buddhists	137,570,000	13.4	487,038,000	11.7	1.27	0.99
Chinese folk-religionists	390,399,000	38.0	434,614,000	10.4	0.11	0.16
Christians	25,086,000	2.4	342,012,000	8.2	2.65	2.23
Ethnoreligionists	57,894,000	5.6	146,779,000	3.5	0.93	0.82
Atheists	7,600	0.0	114,851,000	2.8	10.10	0.15
New Religionists	6,821,000	0.7	58,970,000	1.4	2.18	0.23
Sikhs	3,229,000	0.3	22,689,000	0.5	1.97	1.52
Daoists	437,000	0.0	8,412,000	0.2	3.00	1.74
Confucianists	760,000	0.1	6,363,000	0.2	2.15	0.34
Jews	476,000	0.0	6,030,000	0.1	2.57	2.06
Jains	1,443,000	0.1	5,098,000	0.1	1.27	1.51
Baha'is	221,000	0.0	3,440,000	0.1	2.78	1.38
Shintoists	7,613,000	0.7	2,690,000	0.1	-1.03	0.07
Zoroastrians	119,000	0.0	167,000	0.0	0.34	0.68
Spiritists	0	0.0	2,100	0.0	5.49	0.49
Total population	**1,026,693,000**	**100.0**	**4,164,252,000**	**100.0**	**1.41**	**1.14**

Data source: Todd M. Johnson and Brian J. Grim, eds., *World Religion Database* (Leiden/Boston: Brill, accessed January 2012).

Table 2.3 Religious affiliation and growth in Europe, 1910–2010.

Religion	Adherents 1910	% 1910	Adherents 2010	% 2010	1910–2010 % p.a.	2000–10 % p.a.
Christians	403,546,000	94.5	580,116,000	78.6	0.36	0.27
Agnostics	1,643,000	0.4	93,325,000	12.6	4.12	-0.51
Muslims	10,048,000	2.4	41,492,000	5.6	1.43	0.60
Atheists	219,000	0.1	15,697,000	2.1	4.36	-1.19
Jews	10,462,000	2.4	1,918,000	0.3	-1.68	-0.02
Buddhists	428,000	0.1	1,789,000	0.2	1.44	0.49
Ethnoreligionists	662,000	0.2	1,168,000	0.2	0.57	-0.15
Hindus	65	0.0	1,052,000	0.1	10.18	1.27
Sikhs	0	0.0	501,000	0.1	11.43	2.12
Chinese folk-religionists	0	0.0	439,000	0.1	11.28	1.51
New Religionists	24,800	0.0	365,000	0.0	2.73	0.45
Baha'is	220	0.0	153,000	0.0	6.76	0.68
Spiritists	10,600	0.0	144,000	0.0	2.64	0.57
Jains	0	0.0	18,800	0.0	7.83	1.56
Confucianists	0	0.0	15,600	0.0	7.63	0.46
Zoroastrians	0	0.0	5,700	0.0	6.55	0.54
Total population	**427,044,000**	**100.0**	**738,199,000**	**100.0**	**0.55**	**0.16**

Data source: Todd M. Johnson and Brian J. Grim, eds., *World Religion Database* (Leiden/Boston: Brill, accessed January 2012).

Latin America

At first glance, table 2.4 appears to indicate that the religious populations of Latin America[7] have changed very little over the past 100 years.[8] In 1910 the population was 95.2% Christian; by 2010 it had dropped only slightly to 92.3% Christian. There has been, however, growth in other religions on the continent that affect the life and culture of communities there. As on other continents during the twentieth century, religiously unaffiliated communities grew significantly. In 1910 atheists and agnostics totaled only 0.6% of the population; by 2010 this percentage had grown to 3.7%, with agnostics (who now constitute the second largest "religious" group on the continent, by percentage) accounting for most of the growth. Spiritists are the third largest religious group in Latin America (2.3% in 2010), rising significantly from 0.4% in 1910. As a result of unanticipated, massive emigration mid-century from Europe in the wake of the Holocaust, Latin American countries accepted many Jewish refugees, resulting in the percentage of Jews to rise from 0.0% in 1910 to 0.2% in 2010 (this despite many Jews emigrating recently back to their European homelands or to Israel). Some 962,000 Jews lived in Latin America in 2010, mostly in Argentina, Mexico, and Brazil, although even small islands in the Caribbean had fledging Jewish communities. Also through immigration, between 1910 and 2010, increases occurred in the shares of Muslims (from 0.1% to 0.3%) and Baha'is (0.0% to 0.2%) on the continent. Baha'is have also seen growth through as a result of conversions as well, a factor contributing to a growth rate of over 12% per annum over the 100-year period. Only ethnoreligionists declined as a percentage of the population between 1910 and 2010, losing adherents to both Roman Catholic and Protestant Christianity and dropping from 3.5% in 1910 to 0.6% in 2010.

Northern America

The religious populations of Northern America[9] have changed dramatically over the past 100 years.[10] As seen in table 2.5, the region was 96.6% Christian in 1910 but fell to 78.8% in 2010. This change is due mainly to the impact of secularization and the effects of immigration. A large number of Christians have switched to agnosticism, claiming no religious affiliation; over 48.1 million agnostics lived on the continent in 2010, compared to 1.2 million in 1910. Canada was especially affected by secularization, with its Christian percentage dropping nearly 30 percentage points in 100 years (from 98% to 69%). Agnostics also had the highest 10-year growth rate (2000–10) for the continent, at 2.9%. With respect to immigration, large numbers of Muslims, Buddhists, and Hindus have moved to Northern America, especially in the latter half the twentieth century. Muslims grew to 5.5 million, Buddhists to 4.5 million, and Hindus to 1.8 million. These three religions were statistically insignificant on the continent 100 years ago but now rank fourth, fifth, and seventh, respectively, in total population. A number of smaller religious communities have also appeared, including New Religionists, Baha'is, Spiritists, and Jains. Many of these smaller religions grew at annual rates of 9% or more over the period 1910–2010, though growth slowed over the 10-year period 2000–10.

Table 2.4 Religious affiliation and growth in Latin America, 1910–2010.

Religion	Adherents 1910	% 1910	Adherents 2010	% 2010	1910–2010 % p.a.	2000–10 % p.a.
Christians	74,462,000	95.2	544,686,000	92.3	2.01	1.24
Agnostics	446,000	0.6	18,712,000	3.2	3.81	1.66
Spiritists	312,000	0.4	13,302,000	2.3	3.82	0.94
Ethnoreligionists	2,725,000	3.5	3,626,000	0.6	0.29	1.21
Atheists	12,500	0.0	2,900,000	0.5	5.60	1.44
New Religionists	5,000	0.0	1,739,000	0.3	6.03	1.72
Muslims	67,800	0.1	1,527,000	0.3	3.16	1.01
Jews	29,300	0.0	962,000	0.2	3.55	0.58
Baha'is	0	0.0	898,000	0.2	12.08	1.64
Hindus	186,000	0.2	765,000	0.1	1.42	0.59
Buddhists	7,100	0.0	759,000	0.1	4.78	1.21
Chinese folk-religionists	1,900	0.0	189,000	0.0	4.71	1.25
Shintoists	0	0.0	7,800	0.0	6.89	1.09
Sikhs	0	0.0	7,100	0.0	6.79	1.20
Jains	0	0.0	1,400	0.0	5.07	0.74
Confucianists	0	0.0	480	0.0	3.95	0.87
Total population	**78,254,000**	**100.0**	**590,082,000**	**100.0**	**2.04**	**1.24**

Data source: Todd M. Johnson and Brian J. Grim, eds., *World Religion Database* (Leiden/Boston: Brill, accessed January 2012).

Table 2.5 Religious affiliation and growth in Northern America, 1910–2010.

Religion	Adherents 1910	% 1910	Adherents 2010	% 2010	1910–2010 % p.a.	2000–10 % p.a.
Christians	91,429,000	96.6	271,554,000	78.8	1.09	0.63
Agnostics	1,169,000	1.2	48,119,000	14.0	3.79	2.91
Jews	1,756,000	1.9	5,602,000	1.6	1.17	-0.30
Muslims	11,700	0.0	5,492,000	1.6	6.34	1.86
Buddhists	47,200	0.0	4,454,000	1.3	4.65	1.32
Atheists	2,400	0.0	2,156,000	0.6	7.04	2.18
Hindus	1,200	0.0	1,835,000	0.5	7.61	1.76
New Religionists	12,800	0.0	1,709,000	0.5	5.02	0.97
Ethnoreligionists	170,000	0.2	1,221,000	0.4	1.99	1.12
Chinese folk-religionists	87,100	0.1	781,000	0.2	2.22	1.03
Sikhs	0	0.0	607,000	0.2	11.64	1.42
Baha'is	3,200	0.0	561,000	0.2	5.30	1.70
Spiritists	0	0.0	242,000	0.1	10.62	1.53
Jains	0	0.0	99,700	0.0	9.64	1.69
Shintoists	0	0.0	62,700	0.0	9.14	0.94
Zoroastrians	0	0.0	21,000	0.0	7.95	0.95
Daoists	0	0.0	12,400	0.0	7.38	0.93
Total population	**94,689,000**	**100.0**	**344,529,000**	**100.0**	**1.30**	**0.96**

Data source: Todd M. Johnson and Brian J. Grim, eds., *World Religion Database* (Leiden/Boston: Brill, accessed January 2012).

Table 2.6 Religious affiliation and growth in Oceania, 1910–2010.

Religion	Adherents 1910	% 1910	Adherents 2010	% 2010	1910–2010 % p.a.	2000–10 % p.a.
Christians	5,651,000	78.6	28,019,000	76.6	1.61	1.27
Agnostics	51,100	0.7	5,529,000	15.1	4.80	3.24
Buddhists	7,600	0.1	587,000	1.6	4.44	2.72
Muslims	14,800	0.2	549,000	1.5	3.68	2.43
Hindus	16,400	0.2	513,000	1.4	3.50	2.02
Atheists	1,000	0.0	477,000	1.3	6.36	2.71
Ethnoreligionists	1,414,000	19.7	369,000	1.0	-1.33	2.30
Jews	19,800	0.3	117,000	0.3	1.79	1.48
Baha'is	520	0.0	111,000	0.3	5.51	2.13
New Religionists	360	0.0	104,000	0.3	5.83	2.07
Chinese folk-religionists	14,300	0.2	103,000	0.3	1.99	1.95
Sikhs	250	0.0	49,600	0.1	5.43	3.73
Confucianists	0	0.0	49,200	0.1	8.87	2.12
Spiritists	590	0.0	7,800	0.0	2.62	1.53
Daoists	0	0.0	4,600	0.0	6.32	1.41
Jains	0	0.0	3,000	0.0	5.87	3.15
Zoroastrians	0	0.0	2,600	0.0	5.72	3.19
Total population	**7,192,000**	**100.0**	**36,593,000**	**100.0**	**1.64**	**1.63**

Data source: Todd M. Johnson and Brian J. Grim, eds., *World Religion Database* (Leiden/Boston: Brill, accessed January 2012).

Oceania

Table 2.6 indicates that nearly every major world religion present in Oceania[11] experienced significant growth over the twentieth century.[12] The only exception to this was ethnoreligions, which dropped from 19.7% of the region's population in 1910 to 1.0% in 2010. The growth of Christianity and associated decline in ethnoreligions in several of Oceania's regions was quite dramatic over the century. Melanesia, only 15% Christian in 1910, was over 91% Christian in 2010. In particular, Papua New Guinea rose from 4.0% Christian in 1910 to 95.0% in 2010, though many adherents tend to combine traditional indigenous beliefs with Christian practices. Much of this growth occurred after the country declared independence from Australia in 1975. Similar to the global North, Australia and New Zealand fell from almost 97% Christian in 1910 to 70.8% Christian in 2010, as the numbers of agnostics and atheists in the region increased. Numerous religionists have immigrated to Oceania, primarily Asian immigrants to Australia. Buddhists, Muslims, and Hindus combined were only 0.5% of the continent's population in 1910 but now total 4.5%. As in Northern America, many pockets of minor religionists have settled in Oceania, including Daoists, Jains, Zoroastrians, Sikhs, and Confucianists.

Notes

1 Regional tables can be generated in Todd M. Johnson and Brian J. Grim, eds., *World Religion Database* (Leiden/Boston: Brill, 2008).

2 Year 2000 estimates for all religions are found in Johnson and Grim, *World Religion Database*. Calculations for the 2000–10 growth rates are produced from these.

3 Helpful works on the subject include Thomas D. Blakely, Dennis L. Thomson, and Walter E. A. van Beek, *Religion in Africa: Experience and Expression* (Portsmouth, NH: Heinemann, 1994); Elizabeth Isichei, *The Religious Traditions of Africa: A History* (Westport, CT: Greenwood, 2004); Laurenti Magesa, *African Religion: The Moral Traditions of Abundant Life* (Maryknoll, NY: Orbis, 1997); and Benjamin C. Ray, *African Religions: Symbol, Ritual, and Community*, 2nd ed. (Upper Saddle River, NJ: Prentice-Hall, 1999).

4 See, for example, John L. Esposito, Darrell J. Fasching, and Todd Lewis, *Religions of Asia Today*, 2nd ed. (Oxford: Oxford University Press, 2011); John Y. Fenton, Norvin Hein, Frank E. Reynolds, Alan L. Miller, Niels C. Nielsen, Grace G. Burford, and Robert K. C. Forman, *Religions of Asia* (New York: St Martin's Press, 1993); and Donald S. Lopez, *Religions of Asia in Practice: An Anthology* (Princeton: Princeton University Press, 2002).

5 The United Nations continental area of Europe includes all of Russia (both European and Asian).

6 See Kaspar von Greyerz, *Religion and Culture in Early Modern Europe, 1500–1800* (Oxford: Oxford University Press, 2007); Grace Davie, *Religion in Modern Europe: A Memory Mutates* (Oxford: Oxford University Press, 2001); Hugh McLeod, *Religion and the People of Western Europe 1789–1989*, 2nd ed. (Oxford: Oxford University Press, 1998); and René Rémond and Antonia Nevill, *Religion and Society in Modern Europe (Making of Europe)* (Oxford: Blackwell Publishers, 1999).

7 The United Nations continental area of Latin America includes Central America, South America, and the Caribbean.

8   For more information, see Lee M. Penyak and Walter J. Petry, *Religion in Latin America: A Documentary History* (Maryknoll, NY: Orbis, 2006); Lee M. Penyak and Walter J. Petry, *Religion and Society in Latin America: Interpretive Essays from Conquest to Present* (Maryknoll, NY: Orbis, 2009); Anna Peterson and Manuel Vasquez, *Latin American Religions: Histories and Documents in Context* (New York: New York University Press, 2008); and R. Andrew Chesnut, *Competitive Spirits: Latin America's New Religious Economy* (Oxford: Oxford University Press, 2007).

9   The United Nations defines Northern America as the United States, Canada, Bermuda, Greenland, and St Pierre & Miquelon. The overwhelming majority of the population lives in the first two countries.

10 For an overview of religious change in the United States, see Diana Eck, *A New Religious America: How a "Christian County" Has Become the World's Most Religiously Diverse Nation* (New York: HarperSanFrancisco, 2001), and Julia Corbett Hemeyer, *Religion in America*, 6th ed. (Upper Saddle River, NJ: Prentice-Hall, 2009). For Canada, see Paul Bramadat and David Seljak, eds., *Religion and Ethnicity in Canada* (Toronto: University of Toronto Press, 2009) and Robert Choquette, *Canada's Religions: An Historical Introduction* (Ottawa: University of Ottawa Press, 2004).

11 Australia and New Zealand were home to 53% of Oceania's total population in 2010 (down from 72% in 1910). Papua New Guinea's population constituted another 17% of Oceania's total in 2010 (up from only 0.7% in 1910).

12 See Tony Swain and Garry Trompf, *The Religions of Oceania* (London: Routledge, 1995); G. W. Trompf, *Melanesian Religion* (Cambridge: Cambridge University Press, 2004); and Gary D. Bouma, Rodney Ling, and Douglas Pratt, eds., *Religious Diversity in Southeast Asia and the Pacific: National Case Studies* (Dordrecht, Netherlands: Springer, 2010).

References

Blakely, Thomas D., Dennis L. Thomson, and Walter E. A. van Beek. *Religion in Africa: Experience and Expression.* Portsmouth, NH: Heinemann, 1994.

Bouma, Gary D., Rodney Ling, and Douglas Pratt, eds. *Religious Diversity in Southeast Asia and the Pacific: National Case Studies.* Dordrecht, Netherlands: Springer, 2010.

Bramadat, Paul, and David Seljak, eds. *Religion and Ethnicity in Canada.* Toronto: University of Toronto Press, 2009.

Chesnut, R. Andrew. *Competitive Spirits: Latin America's New Religious Economy.* Oxford: Oxford University Press, 2007.

Choquette, Robert. *Canada's Religions: An Historical Introduction.* Ottawa: University of Ottawa Press, 2004.

Davie, Grace. *Religion in Modern Europe: A Memory Mutates.* Oxford: Oxford University Press, 2001.

Eck, Diana L. *A New Religious America: How a "Christian County" Has Become the World's Most Religiously Diverse Nation.* New York: HarperSanFrancisco, 2001.

Esposito, John L., Darrell J. Fasching, and Todd Lewis. *Religions of Asia Today.* 2nd ed. Oxford: Oxford University Press, 2011.

Fenton, John Y., Norvin Hein, Frank E. Reynolds, Alan L. Miller, Niels C. Nielsen, Grace G. Burford, and Robert K. C. Forman. *Religions of Asia.* New York: St Martin's Press, 1993.

Greyerz, Kaspar von. *Religion and Culture in Early Modern Europe, 1500–1800.* Oxford: Oxford University Press, 2007.

Hemeyer, Julia Corbett. *Religion in America.* 6th ed. Upper Saddle River, NJ: Prentice-Hall, 2009.

Isichei, Elizabeth. *The Religious Traditions of Africa: A History*. Westport, CT: Greenwood, 2004.

Johnson, Todd M., and Brian J. Grim, eds. *World Religion Database*. Leiden/Boston: Brill, 2008.

Lopez, Donald S. *Religions of Asia in Practice: An Anthology*. Princeton: Princeton University Press, 2002.

Magesa, Laurenti. *African Religion: The Moral Traditions of Abundant Life*. Maryknoll, NY: Orbis, 1997.

McLeod, Hugh. *Religion and the People of Western Europe 1789–1989*. 2nd ed. Oxford: Oxford University Press, 1998.

Penyak, Lee M., and Walter J. Petry. *Religion and Society in Latin America: Interpretive Essays from Conquest to Present*. Maryknoll, NY: Orbis, 2009.

Penyak, Lee M., and Walter J. Petry. *Religion in Latin America: A Documentary History*. Maryknoll, NY: Orbis, 2006.

Peterson, Anna, and Manuel Vasquez. *Latin American Religions: Histories and Documents in Context*. New York: New York University Press, 2008.

Ray, Benjamin C. *African Religions: Symbol, Ritual, and Community*. 2nd ed. Upper Saddle River, NJ: Prentice-Hall, 1999.

Rémond, René, and Antonia Nevill. *Religion and Society in Modern Europe (Making of Europe)*. Oxford: Blackwell Publishers, 1999.

Swain, Tony, and Garry Trompf. *The Religions of Oceania*. London: Routledge, 1995.

Trompf, G. W. *Melanesian Religion*. Cambridge: Cambridge University Press, 2004.

Chapter 3
Religious Diversity

Underlying the reality of a changing global religious landscape is increasing religious diversity. Religious diversity can be measured for any population grouping, but in this chapter it is expressed primarily in national terms. "Religious diversity" is present at two levels: intra-religious and inter-religious diversity. Intra-religious diversity encompasses the diversity found within a given world religion (for example, traditions such as Roman Catholicism, Orthodoxy, and Protestantism within Christianity), whereas inter-religious diversity describes the degree of overall diversity of world religions (Islam, Hinduism, Judaism, and so on) in a given population or geographical area. This chapter focuses primarily on levels of inter-religious diversity.[1] It is important to note that, within a particular country, inter-religious diversity can vary greatly from one locale to another, because religious adherents often cluster in local communities. Such is often the case for countries receiving significant numbers of immigrants or refugees, many of whom settle in major metropolitan areas.[2]

Diversity versus Pluralism

The fields of religious diversity and pluralism have been the objects of a great deal of scholarship. In popular use, these two terms are sometimes considered interchangeable. This volume, however, treats diversity as a demographic characteristic that is distinct from pluralism, which scholars often treat as a relational characteristic.[3] Scholars such as Diana Eck, director of the Pluralism Project at Harvard University, conceptualize religious pluralism along the lines of the Latin saying on the Great Seal of the United States, *E pluribus unum*: "Out of many One."[4] For instance, a religiously *diverse* town in the United States might have a Christian church, a Native American spiritual center, a humanist society, a Jewish synagogue, a Muslim mosque,

The World's Religions in Figures: An Introduction to International Religious Demography,
First Edition. Todd M. Johnson and Brian J. Grim.
© 2013 John Wiley & Sons, Ltd. Published 2013 by John Wiley & Sons, Ltd.

and Buddhist, Hindu, and Sikh temples. But the town would be considered to have religious *pluralism* only if these diverse groups contribute to a common civil society, accept one another, and approach differences respectfully. While measuring religious pluralism is interesting and valuable, this chapter focuses on a simpler but still challenging task – measuring the demographics of diversity.[5]

Changes in Religious Diversity from 1910 to 2010

The twentieth century was a transformative period for religion. As outlined in chapter 1, the world in 2010 was less religious in general than it was in 1910. In 1910, nearly the entire world claimed adherence to some form of religious belief. By 2010, however, 11.8% of the world's population was either atheist or agnostic. The reasons for this are twofold: the rise of Communism worldwide, and the phenomenon of secularization, particularly in the global North.[6] Individual secularization, which involves personal conversion from a religion, is one significant way by which a population becomes more diverse (since both agnosticism and atheism are considered "religious" categories). Another way is conversion from one religion to another. In Africa, for example, this typically involved conversion from ethnoreligions to either Christianity or Islam. A third way is the migration of religionists from one location to another. By virtue of these three dynamics, the countries of the world are becoming more diverse in their religious makeup.

Indexes used to measure diversity are of five main types: (1) fractionalization/ fragmentation; (2) polarization; (3) dominance; (4) minority size; and (5) cleavages. "Fractionalization" indexes capture the degree to which a society is split into distinct groups, defined as the probability that two randomly chosen individuals belong to different faiths. The number of religious groups and their relative sizes play a role here. A higher probability of belonging to different religions gives rise to a higher index value. "Polarization" indexes are similar, reaching a maximum when there are only two religious groups of equal size. Polarization is not strictly an indication of diversity, but rather an indication of the degree to which society is split down the middle between two religious groups. "Dominance" indexes are based on the size of the largest group, while "minority size" indexes refer to the percentage in the second-largest group (the largest minority). Having a religious "cleavage" means that the population includes one large group (45–90%) and at least one other group with a significant minority of the total population (8% or more).[7]

This chapter describes three ways in which religious diversity can be measured. First, we develop a Religious Diversity Index (RDI) based on the Herfindahl Index used in economics. Second, we look at the number of religions above a certain percentage in each country. Third, we measure religious diversity by taking into account both the absolute and relative sizes of eight major religious groups.

Method 1: Religious Diversity Index (RDI)

The Religious Diversity Index, based upon the Herfindahl Index (used by economists studying market competition), describes the inter-religious diversity of a particular country's or region's population using a scale from 0.00 (no diversity) to 1.00 (most diverse).[8] The Herfindahl Index (also called the Herfindahl-Hirschman Index, HHI), which measures the concentration of competitors within a market or industry, is calculated as the sum of the squares of the market share of each competitor.[9] For example, the maximum HHI score (100^2, or 10,000) occurs when a country has a single religious group. To translate this into a diversity measure, its inverse (HHI_{max} − HHI) is used; if only one religious groups is present, HHI_{max} − HHI=10,000 − 10,000=0, indicating no religious diversity. For a country in which four religious groups are present with shares of 40%, 30%, 20%, and 10%, the HHI is 3,000 (1,600 +900+400+100=3,000), and its inverse is 10,000 − 3,000=7,000. In a country with eight religious groups of 12.5% each, for instance, the inverse HHI represents high religious diversity ($12.5^2 \times 8 = 1,250$; inverse=8,750). For ease of comparison with other indexes, these figures are converted into a scale ranging from 0.0 (no diversity) to 1.00 (greatest possible diversity).

Calculating measurements on both the country and world regional levels provides a "local" perspective of diversity (country-level) as well as a cross-national view of diversity (world regional-level). Table 3.1 reports on diversity at the regional level, showing that between 1910 and 2010, all but six regions in the world experienced increases in both country and regional RDI levels.[10] Some of the greatest regional increases, primarily due to migration, were found in Australia/New Zealand (+0.42), Eastern Asia, (+0.34), Northern America (+0.31), and Western Europe (+0.27).[11]

Despite significant changes since 1910, Asia has remained the most religiously diverse continent in the world. In 1910 over 50% of Asia's population was Chinese folk-religionist or Buddhist; today, these two religions together total only 22%. Ethnoreligions declined from 5.6% of the population in 1910 to 3.7% in 2010. These declines were the result of gains by Muslims (from 16.6% to 26.0%) and Christians (2.4% to 8.5%). However, greater proportional gains were made by agnostics (0.0% to 11.8%) and atheists (0.0% to 2.8%), especially in China.

These religious changes in Asia are not entirely surprising, considering the inherently pluralistic nature of Asian culture; in a sense, to be Asian is to be inter-religious.[12] It is also common for Asians to cross national boundaries in search of employment, such as the large Indian and Filipino migrant worker communities in various Persian Gulf countries. The World Bank estimates that 3 million Indonesian women work abroad, primarily in Malaysia and Saudi Arabia, and mostly in domestic work.[13] Increases in religious diversity are particularly apparent in the global North, where secularization and immigration continue to transform the religious landscape (see sections below).

The countries with the highest Religious Diversity Index values using the method described above are outlined in table 3.2. Note that the top five countries are found in Asia.

Method 2: Religious Diversity by Number of Religions

Another way of viewing religious diversity is by examining the number of religions representing more than a given percentage (for example, 0.5%, 5%, or 10%) of the population of a country. Table 3.3 puts Canada and Suriname at the top of the list, with nine religions over 0.5% of the population. As the criterion becomes stricter

Table 3.1 Religious Diversity Index (RDI), 1910 and 2010.

Region	Population 1910	RDI 1910	Majority adherents 1910	Population 2010	RDI 2010	Majority adherents 2010
Africa	**124,541,000**	**0.58**	**Ethnoreligionists**	**1,022,234,000**	**0.62**	**Christians**
Eastern Africa	33,012,000	0.49	Ethnoreligionists	324,044,000	0.53	Christians
Middle Africa	19,445,000	0.11	Ethnoreligionists	126,689,000	0.32	Christians
Northern Africa	31,968,000	0.33	Muslims	209,459,000	0.21	Muslims
Southern Africa	6,819,000	0.52	Ethnoreligionists	57,780,000	0.33	Christians
Western Africa	33,296,000	0.43	Ethnoreligionists	304,261,000	0.63	Muslims
Asia	**1,026,693,000**	**0.80**	**Chinese folk**	**4,164,252,000**	**0.88**	**Muslims**
Eastern Asia	554,135,000	0.50	Chinese folk	1,573,970,000	0.84	Agnostics
South-central Asia	345,718,000	0.53	Hindu	1,764,872,000	0.62	Hindu
South-eastern Asia	93,859,000	0.81	Buddhists	593,415,000	0.78	Muslims
Western Asia	32,982,000	0.40	Muslims	231,995,000	0.22	Muslims
Europe	**427,044,000**	**0.11**	**Christians**	**738,199,000**	**0.38**	**Christians**
Eastern Europe	178,184,000	0.20	Christians	294,771,000	0.30	Christians
Northern Europe	61,473,000	0.04	Christians	99,205,000	0.43	Christians
Southern Europe	76,828,000	0.07	Christians	155,171,000	0.33	Christians
Western Europe	110,558,000	0.03	Christians	189,052,000	0.51	Christians
Latin America	**78,254,000**	**0.10**	**Christians**	**590,082,000**	**0.15**	**Christians**
Caribbean	8,172,000	0.05	Christians	41,646,000	0.31	Christians
Central America	20,806,000	0.02	Christians	155,881,000	0.09	Christians
South America	49,276,000	0.14	Christians	392,555,000	0.16	Christians
Northern America	**94,689,000**	**0.07**	**Christians**	**344,529,000**	**0.38**	**Christians**
Oceania	**7,192,000**	**0.36**	**Christians**	**36,593,000**	**0.41**	**Christians**
Australia/New Zealand	5,375,000	0.06	Christians	26,637,000	0.48	Christians
Melanesia	1,596,000	0.30	Ethnoreligionists	8,748,000	0.17	Christians
Micronesia	89,400	0.38	Christians	536,000	0.14	Christians
Polynesia	131,000	0.01	Christians	673,000	0.08	Christians
Global total	**1,758,412,000**	**0.83**	**Christians**	**6,895,889,000**	**0.85**	**Christians**

Data source: Todd M. Johnson and Brian J. Grim, eds., *World Religion Database* (Leiden/Boston: Brill, accessed January 2012). Religions included in the analysis: agnostics, atheists, Baha'is, Buddhists, Chinese folk-religionists, Christians, Confucianists, Daoists, Ethnoreligionists, Hindus, Jains, Jews, Muslims, New Religionists, Sikhs, Spiritists, Shintoists, and Zoroastrians.

Table 3.2 Countries with highest Religious Diversity Index (RDI) values, 2010.

Country	RDI value
China	0.84
South Korea	0.84
Singapore	0.82
Taiwan	0.79
Viet Nam	0.79
Liberia	0.76
Hong Kong	0.76
Benin	0.76
Cote d'Ivoire	0.74
Togo	0.74

Data source: Todd M. Johnson and Brian J. Grim, eds., *World Religion Database* (Leiden/Boston: Brill, accessed January 2012).

Table 3.3 Countries with the most religions over 0.5% of the population, 2010.

Rank	Country	Number of religions
1	Canada	9
1	Suriname	9
3	Belize	8
3	Brunei	8
3	Guyana	8
3	Indonesia	8
3	Panama	8
8	China	7
8	French Guiana	7
8	Hong Kong	7

Data source: Todd M. Johnson and Brian J. Grim, eds., *World Religion Database* (Leiden/Boston: Brill, accessed January 2012).

Table 3.4 Countries with the most religions over 5% of the population, 2010.

Rank	Country	Number of religions
1	Viet Nam	6
2	Brunei	5
2	China	5
2	Malaysia	5
2	Singapore	5
2	South Korea	5
2	Taiwan	5
8	Cuba	4
8	Hong Kong	4
8	Macau	4

Data source: Todd M. Johnson and Brian J. Grim, eds., *World Religion Database* (Leiden/Boston: Brill, accessed January 2012).

Table 3.5 Countries with the most religions over 10% of the population, 2010.

Rank	Country	Number of religions
1	South Korea	5
2	Hong Kong	4
2	North Korea	4
2	Singapore	4
2	Viet Nam	4
6	Benin	3
6	Brunei	3
6	Burkina Faso	3
6	Cameroon	3
6	Central African Republic	3

Data source: Todd M. Johnson and Brian J. Grim, eds., *World Religion Database* (Leiden/Boston: Brill, accessed January 2012).

(a higher percentage cutoff), however, Eastern and South-eastern Asia claim the most diversity, as indicated by table 3.4 (the top seven countries) and table 3.5 (the top five). Only Viet Nam has six religions over 5%,[14] while only South Korea has five different religions numbering over 10% of the population (Buddhism, Christianity, Confucianism, ethnoreligions, and New Religions).[15]

Method 3: Religious Diversity by Size of Population

Most diversity indexes come from ecology or business studies and focus on *market shares* within a population. In addition to market share, *market size* is also an important indication of diversity, though is not typically measured by diversity indexes.[16] This chapter looks at ways to measure diversity taking into account both share and size.[17] In looking at share, only proportion matters. Having a large share of adherents in multiple religious groups increases diversity. However, if one group is overwhelmingly dominant, the experience of religious diversity by religious minorities becomes less. For instance, Jews and Muslims in the United States are likely to feel themselves to be a religious minority on a daily basis. In contrast, size matters in the sense that having a large number of adherents in multiple groups increases visible diversity. For instance, Jews and Muslims are a small share of the US population, but because each group numbers in the millions, they can organize in ways that increase their visibility yielding greater perceived diversity. Measuring population size allows a better understanding than measuring only population share.[18]

This third method of measuring diversity begins by grouping the 18 major religious categories in the *World Religion Database*[19] into eight major religious groups tracked by the Pew Research Center's Forum on Religion and Public Life: (1) Buddhists; (2) Christians; (3) folk/traditional religionists (including Confucianists, ethnoreligionists, Spiritists, and Chinese folk-religionists); (4) Hindus; (5) Jews; (6) Muslims; (7) others (Baha'is, Daoists, New Religionists, Jains, Shinto, Sikhs, and Zoroastrians) and (8) unaffiliated (agnostics and atheists).[20] This regrouping makes it more likely that numerous members of each of the eight groups are present in a country than when all 18 religions are considered separately.

Considering raw sizes of religious groups is a new contribution to the study of religious diversity – most previous diversity measures calculated diversity based on shares, using some variation of the Herfindahl-Hirschman Index (HHI) described above. However, the HHI does not adequately account for the impact of group size on diversity. Size matters when religious groups are present in numbers large enough to influence society, although their percentage shares are not large enough to impact the HHI, which is the case for Jews and Muslims in the United States, as illustrated by a recent Pew Forum study.

The study by the Pew Forum examined a total of 212 religion-related advocacy groups operating in the US capital.[21] It reported that Muslim and Jewish advocacy organizations account for a much larger share of the advocacy organizations in the study than they do of the general population. Specifically, there are 17 Muslim advocacy organizations in Washington, DC (8% of the total) and 25 Jewish advocacy organizations (12%), while Muslims make up 0.8% of US adults and Jews make up 1.7%. Such disproportionate visibility might not increase a religion's share of the population, but it contributes to a country's "visible diversity" – the active presence of multiple religions in the public life of a country. Visible diversity might be an indirect measure of pluralism if the groups contribute to a common civil society, accept one another, and approach differences respectfully. Having enough size to engage in the public life of a country, however, does not necessarily result in pluralism.

Measuring the impact of size on diversity

There are a number of mathematical ways to measure the impact of size on diversity. For instance, the country with the greatest number of people in each of the eight categories could be considered the most religiously diverse. This approach, however, would unreasonably disadvantage countries with small populations. Alternatively, countries with at least some members of each of the eight groups might be considered diverse.[22] But this approach would over-represent extremely small populations. So, what population thresholds are reasonable? The answer requires addressing two other questions.

Threshold question 1: What size populations are needed for the majority to experience religious diversity?

One possibility is to use as thresholds 1,000, 10,000, and 100,000 adherents of a religious group.[23] A group with 1,000 adherents is sizeable enough to be present. In some circumstances this becomes an important threshold. For instance, they may be among the first representatives of a religious group in a country, such as the 1,000 Jews in South Korea, or the last remaining representatives of a religious group, such as the approximately 500 Yemeni Jews remaining in Yemen (most of whom have emigrated to Israel). A group with 10,000 becomes large enough to have critical mass, or staying power, and to develop networks and small institutions that might impact others in society.[24] Populations of 100,000 or more might be able to develop more complex institutions that have broader and more noticeable impacts on society.[25]

Consider the following hypothetical and illustrative real examples of these three thresholds.

Hypothetical example   In a country with a population of 10.07 million, where one group numbers 10 million (approximately 99.3%) and seven groups each number 10,000 (approximately 0.1% each), the HHI would be 9,861.5 $[99.3^2+(0.1^2\times7)]$. This score is only slightly larger than if the largest group numbered 1.063 million and the seven other groups numbered 1,000, in which case the HHI would be 9,986. Arguably, however, seven minority groups of 10,000 might yield greater visible diversity than would seven groups of 1,000.

Illustrative real examples   A comparison of Switzerland's Jewish population of about 20,000 out of 46 million with Kenya's of about 2,000 out of 42 million illustrates that greater visible diversity accompanies numerical size. In Switzerland, 20 cities and towns have organized Jewish communities including traditional, ultra-Orthodox, Reform, and Conservative. Nine Jewish schools operate in five cities (Zurich, Lausanne, Lucerne, Basel, and Kriens-Obernau), and an Orthodox seminary operates in Basel. Switzerland has four Jewish newspapers, three in German and one in French. The Swiss Federation of Jewish Communities (SIG), Switzerland's main Jewish organization, organizes the importation of kosher food for the country, operates a Jewish cemetery in Davos and produces a sophisticated tri-lingual website.[26] Additionally, Chabad (Orthodox) Houses operate in six cities.[27]

By contrast, Judaism adds much less to the visible diversity in Kenya. Though Jews settled and have been living in Kenya for nearly a century, only one synagogue serves the entire community.[28] The Nairobi Hebrew Congregation is located in the capital, Nairobi, and operates a basic English and Hebrew website.[29]

When religious groups number more than 100,000, they can engage in many more activities that help to religiously diversify the public sphere. For instance, Muslims in Switzerland number nearly 400,000 and are ethnically diverse, coming from Turkey, Eastern Europe, and North Africa. As these linguistically divided Muslim communities grew through immigration and natural population growth, they began to organize umbrella organizations to serve the general community. For instance, the Federation of Islamic Organizations in Switzerland (FIDS) is an association of 13 separate Islamic organizations representing some 170 Islamic centers, making it the largest Islamic organization in the country.[30] In addition to political lobbying, the organization has programs for youth and connections with multiple religious organizations abroad, such as Turkey's Diyanet (authority for religious affairs). Swiss Muslim websites are numerous and multifaceted, and a web television station with multifaceted and original programming is planned.[31] The growth of the Swiss Muslim population has not been without negative reaction, however. As Muslims have become a more visible community, the native, non-Muslim Swiss population has reacted by, for example, passing a national referendum forbidding the building of minarets on mosques.[32]

Threshold question 2: To determine what population thresholds
are reasonable, how much size bias is tolerable?

Of course, thresholds could be set at any levels. However, if the logic for using the
1,000, 10,000, and 100,000 thresholds outlined above holds, this might not overly
bias the results in favor of large population countries. As shown in table 3.6, the vast
majority of countries (86%) have populations of at least 100,000, and a substantial
majority (70%) have 800,000 or more. Theoretically, the majority of countries could
attain the highest score on this measure by having eight world religious groups
of 100,000 members each.

Table 3.7 provides an example of computing a religious diversity score based on
the sizes of the eight aggregated world religious groups. The five countries
presented – one from each major world region monitored in the Pew Forum
studies – were selected to illustrate different patterns of religious affiliation. Based
on the absolute sizes of the religious groups, the United States has the highest level
of diversity of the five countries, scoring 24 on the total calculation (the maximum
possible value) because all eight world religious groups are present and each
numbers more than 100,000 adherents. To set the religious diversity by size index
on the same scale as the RDI score (described above), the size-index score is converted to a scale of 0–1.0. (See notes below table 3.7 for explanations of these
calculations.)

Table 3.8 shows the results of using this measure to estimate the amount of
religious diversity by size in the top 25 countries and territories. By contrast, table 3.9
lists the bottom 16 countries that are the least diverse by size.

Finally, it is useful to note that size can sometimes be an indicator of the
geographic spread of religions.[33] For instance, in countries with small land areas
such as Singapore, larger shares and sizes of particular groups are more noticeable,
since all groups share already limited space. Size can also transcend location in a
more technologically connected world. For example, less than three decades ago
there were no high-speed train lines, easy airline connections, or instant telecommu-
nications linking most of China with the northwest Xinjiang-Uyghur Autonomous
Region. Approximately half of all China's Muslims are concentrated in that region,
and until these advances, the diversity they brought to China was seen mostly in
government propaganda extolling the virtues of China's 54 officially recognized
minorities. Today, however, many thousands of Uyghur have spread throughout
China in search of economic opportunities, thus diversifying China in fact (rather

Table 3.6 Number of countries with total populations
crossing population thresholds, 2012.

Total population	Countries	
800,000+	162	70%
100,000–799,999	38	16%
10,000–99,999	24	10%
1,000–9,999	8	3%

Source: United Nations Population Division.

Table 3.7 Religious diversity by size (example of a country from each major region), 2012.

Region	Americas		Asia–Pacific		Middle East–North Africa		Sub-Saharan Africa		Europe	
	United States		South Korea		Syria		Kenya		Switzerland	
Country	Population	Score*	Population	Score	Population	Score	Population	Score	Population	Score
Buddhists	2,152,000	3	11,213,000	3	<1,000	0	1,000	1	23,000	2
Christians	251,084,000	3	14,215,000	3	1,097,000	3	36,238,000	3	6,409,000	3
Folk/Traditional	1,443,000	3	393,000	3	<1,000	0	727,000	3	<1,000	0
Hindus	1,155,000	3	1,000	1	<1,000	0	61,000	2	31,000	2
Jews	5,497,000	3	1,000	1	<1,000	0	2,000	1	20,000	2
Muslims	2,463,000	3	71,000	2	19,590,000	3	4,138,000	3	345,000	3
Others	2,356,000	3	110,000	3	<1,000	0	530,000	3	7,000	1
Unaffiliated	49,640,000	3	22,584,000	3	430,000	3	1,052,000	3	898,000	3
Total	315,791,000	24	48,588,000	19	21,118,000	9	42,749,000	19	7,734,000	16
Index Value**		1.00		0.79		0.38		0.79		0.67

*Countries are scored as follows: "3" = 100,000 or more adherents in a group; "2" = 10,000 – 99,999; "1" = 1,000 – 9,999; "0" <1,000. Data are from Pew Research Center's Forum on Religion & Public Life.

**The Religious Diversity by Size index value is a recalculation of the total score, which has a maximum of 24 points, to an index value with a maximum value of 1.00 point For example, 24 = 1.00, 12 = 5.0, and 0 = 0.

Populations may not sum to total due to rounding; populations are for 2012.

Source: Author's analysis of data from the Pew Forum on Religion and Public Life, Global Religious Landsape, December 2012.

Table 3.8 Most religious diversity by size, 2012.

Country	Score	Country	Score
Australia	1.00	Brazil	.83
Canada	1.00	Myanmar	.83
United Kingdom	1.00	Germany	.83
United States	1.00	Malaysia	.83
India	.96	Bangladesh	.79
South Africa	.96	Hong Kong	.79
France	.92	Kenya	.79
Argentina	.88	Nepal	.79
China	.88	Netherlands	.79
Indonesia	.88	South Korea	.79
Japan	.88	Sweden	.79
Russia	.88	Viet Nam	.79
Singapore	.88		

Source: Author's analysis of data from the Pew Forum on Religion and Public Life, *Global Religious Landscape*, December 2012.

Table 3.9 Least religious diversity by size, 2012.

Country	Score	Country	Score
Holy See	0	Falkland Islands (Malvinas)	.04
Tuvalu	.04	Wallis & Futuna	.08
Tokelau	.04	St Kitts & Nevis	.08
St Pierre & Miquelon	.04	Marshall Islands	.08
St Helena	.04	Faeroe Islands	.08
Niue	.04	Cook Islands	.08
Nauru	.04	Anguilla	.08
Montserrat	.04	American Samoa	.08

Source: Author's analysis of data from the Pew Forum on Religion and Public Life, *Global Religious Landscape*, December 2012.

than simply in theory). At the same time, millions of Chinese from outside of Xinjiang have been encouraged by the government to migrate to the region, diversifying Xinjiang.

Religious Diversity in the United States

One significant example of religious diversity in the global North is the United States, where immigrant communities have visibly changed the religious and cultural landscape of the country.[34] Table 3.1 reports that Northern America (which includes Bermuda, Canada, Greenland, St Pierre & Miquelon, and the United States) had a religious diversity index of only 0.07 in 1910, rising to 0.38 in 2010 (and size index from 0.79 to 1.0). Protestantism remains the largest religious group, but it is not monolithic, encompassing over 2,400 different denominations with different beliefs and practices. A 2007 public opinion survey by the Pew Forum on Religion and Public Life found that the United States "is on the verge of becoming a minority Protestant country for the first time in its history."[35] Nearly 30% of all Christians in the United States are Roman Catholic, and it is largely the growing Hispanic communities who maintain the Christian percentage of the population (around 78%), while changing the ethnic makeup of the Roman Catholic Church in America.

Sociologist Peggy Levitt states that the United States should be moving toward a situation in which American religious pluralism is "an integral piece of the global religious puzzle," meaning that religion must be viewed from a transnational perspective.[36] While the United States has a history of demanding assimilation and acceptance of "American values," it at the same time is an intensely *religious* (not just Christian) country. According to Levitt, migrants to America "belong to religious communities that simultaneously promote their integration into the United States, keep them connected to their ancestral homes, and link them to religious movements around the world." American religious diversity, she states, "is sometimes shaped as much by forces at work outside our borders as within them."[37] An equally important observation about religious diversity in the United States is its lack of dogmatism. Researchers Brian Grim and David Masci state that "The lack of dogmatism in American religion, combined with the legal protections afforded to all religious groups, means that religious minorities are likely to continue to find a welcoming home in the United States."[38] It remains to be seen how churches in the United States (and Europe as well, with its swelling immigrant population[39]) will deal with the challenges posed by religious diversity. A sociological framework posed by Roger Finke and Rodney Stark argues that "religious diversity nurtures religious competition."[40]

Globalization

One factor driving religious diversity in the twenty-first century is a strong trend toward globalization. Globalization involves the development of a certain sector of society (for example, economic, political, cultural, or technological) to the point where international influence and operation are gained with relative ease. Studies of this phenomenon are multifaceted, complex, and not without criticism.[41] With respect to religion, globalization not only facilitates the presence of multiple religions in a particular geographic area, but it also hastens such a plurality[42] as the movement of peoples, ideas, and cultures across new boundaries becomes the new normal. Religious diversity owes much to globalization, which has made historical religious monopolies (such as Orthodox churches in Europe, the Roman Catholic Church in Latin America, and Hinduism in India) more difficult to sustain.[43] One salient feature of pluralistic societies is the greater possibility of religious choice: an individual is no longer tied to the religion of his parents or country of birth if adherents of the world's religions surround him in his own backyard.

Conclusion

All three of the methods of measuring religious diversity described in this chapter – the Religious Diversity Index, religious diversity by number of religions, and religious diversity by size of population – point to a world that is more religiously diverse today than it was 100 years ago. At the same time, the underlying trends that drive increasing diversity (secularization, conversion,[44] and migration) seem to point to a world in the future that is more religiously diverse than the present.

Globally, the relationships between religious diversity, on the one hand, and government restrictions and social hostilities related to religion, on the other, differ depending on the perspective from which they are examined (i.e., the relative *share* of the total population claimed by adherents of a given religion versus their *size* in absolute terms). Notably: (1) countries with higher "share diversity" (that is, in which several religions each represent a sizeable portion of the population, as opposed to one religion having a monopoly on adherence) tend to have *lower* levels of social hostilities involving religion; and (2) countries with higher "size diversity" (that is, in which several religions have the "critical mass" of adherents necessary to influence society, even if their share of the total population is low) tend to have *higher* levels of social hostilities involving religion and government restrictions on religion. This paradox suggests that the challenge of pluralism discussed at the beginning of the chapter differs depending on the type of diversity present in a society. These challenges also are likely to provide fruitful ground for further examination by ambitious students of demography.

Notes

1 For a complete survey of intra-religious diversity of Christianity, see Todd M. Johnson and Kenneth R. Ross, eds., *Atlas of Global Christianity* (Edinburgh: Edinburgh University Press, 2009), parts II and III.

2 Ibid., 32.

3 See Mark Silk, "Defining Religious Pluralism in America: A Regional Analysis," *The ANNALS of the American Academy of Political and Social Science* 612:1 (July 2007): 62–81.

4 See Diana L. Eck, "The Challenge of Pluralism," Nieman Reports "God in the Newsroom" Issue, 17:2 (Summer 1993).

5 One important, measurable aspect of religious pluralism is how populations react to the presence of "outgroups" in their communities. See Richard Wike and Brian J. Grim, "Western Views Towards Muslims: Evidence from a 2006 Cross-National Survey," *International Journal of Public Opinion Research* 22:1 (2010): 4–25.

6 Johnson and Ross, *Atlas of Global Christianity*, 6. But note that the percentage of atheists and agnostics has declined since the collapse of Communism in the former Soviet Union. Here, "global North" is defined in geopolitical terms by five current United Nations regions (comprising 53 countries): Eastern Europe (including Russia), Northern Europe, Southern Europe, Western Europe, and Northern America. The United Nations definition also includes Australia and New Zealand, which are part of the "global South" in this chapter.

7   For further discussion, see Ragnhild Nordås, "How Religious Diversity Matters (Or Not) for Intrastate Armed Conflict," paper presented at the Population Association of America annual meeting, Washington, DC, March 9, 2011.

8   The Herfindahl-Hirschman Index (HHI), sometimes called the Simpsons Ecological Diversity Index, is named for economists Orris C. Herfindahl and Albert O. Hirschman, who were the first to use it to measure industry concentration (that is, the extent to which a small number of companies account for the majority of a given market). See Charles R. Laine, "The Herfindahl-Hirschman Index: A Concentration Measure Taking the Consumer's Point of View," *Antitrust Bulletin* (June 22, 1995). Numerous researchers have used the HHI to measure religious concentration, including Rachel M. McCleary and Robert J. Barro, "Religion and Political Economy in an International Panel," *Journal for the Scientific Study of Religion* 45:2 (June 2006): 149–75; Michael McBride, "Religious Pluralism and Religious Participation: Game Theoretic Analysis," *American Journal of Sociology* 114:1 (July 2008): 77–108; Johnson and Ross, *Atlas of Global Christianity*, 32–3, 352; and Brian J. Grim and Roger Finke, "Religious Persecution in Cross-National Context: Clashing Civilizations or Regulated Economies?" *American Sociological Review* 72:4 (2007): 633–58. The 2010 Religious Congregations and Membership Study (RCMS: http://www.rcms2010.org/) also uses the HHI to measure religious diversity in the United States. The RCMS is a county-by-county enumeration of religious bodies in the United States. It is an update of the 1952, 1971, 1980, 1990, and 2000 studies originally done by the National Council of Churches and the Glenmary Research Center. Since 1990, the Association of Statisticians of American Religious Bodies (ASARB) has sponsored the studies.

9   That is, $HHI = s_1^2 + s_2^2 + \ldots + s_N^2$, where $s_1, s_2, \ldots s_N$ represent the percentage shares of each competitor and N is the total number of competitors. The RDI is calculated as $1 - [(\rho - 1/N) / (1 - 1/N)]$, where $\rho = [(r_1/100)^2 + (r_2/100)^2 + \ldots + (r_N/100)^2]$ and r_1, $r_2, \ldots r_N$ represent the percentages of a country's total population that profess adherence to each of N different religions (in this analysis, $N = 18$); each r_i value is divided by 100 to change it from a percentage to a fraction. Thus, when a population exhibits the maximum possible religious diversity (each religion claims an equal percentage of adherents), then $r_i = 100/N$ for each religion, $\rho = 1/N$ and $RDI = 1$. Conversely, if there is no religious diversity (that is, 100% of a country's population adheres to a single religion), then $r_1 = 100$, all other r_i values $= 0$, $\rho = 1$, and $RDI = 0$.

10 The six regions *not* experiencing an increase in religious diversity in this time period were Northern Africa, Southern Africa, South-eastern Asia, Western Asia, Melanesia, and Micronesia. For more on measuring religious diversity, see Pippa Norris and Ronald Inglehart, *Sacred and Secular: Religion and Politics Worldwide* (Cambridge: Cambridge University Press, 2004), 100.

11 Johnson and Ross, *Atlas of Global Christianity*, 33.

12 Peter Phan, *Being Religious Interreligiously: Asian Perspectives on Interreligious Dialogue* (Maryknoll: Orbis Books, 2004), 117, 127.

13 Nisha Varia, "Asia's Migrant Workers Need Better Protection," *Human Rights Watch*, September 2, 2004, http://www.hrw.org/news/2004/08/31/asias-migrant-workers-need-better-protection.

14 Viet Nam's six religions over 5% of the population are agnostics, atheists, Buddhists, Christians, ethnoreligionists, and New Religionists.

15 Johnson and Ross, *Atlas of Global Christianity*, 32.

16 Ecology literature also considers critical mass to be important. Maintaining an adequately sized population entails saving seed from enough plants to retain your variety's genetic

variability. See Organic Seed Alliance, "A Seed Saving Guide," at http://www.seedalliance. org/uploads/publications/Seed_Saving_Guide.pdf.

17 Geographic spread is also an indication of diversity. Having a wide geographic spread of adherents in multiple religious groups increases diversity. Mormons, for instance, have numerous churches in every state of the United States, not just in Utah where they are concentrated. As a result, a wide range of people in society experience greater religious diversity.

18 The use of multiple indexes of diversity produces a better picture of diversity than just one. See Barney Warf and Mort Winsberg, "The Geography of Religious Diversity in the United States," *The Professional Geographer* 60:3 (2008): 413–24. Warf and Winsberg employed four empirical measures of religious diversity drawn from different disciplines: (1) the simple number of denominations present in each county, n. It represents the number of religious choices available to individuals without regard to their size; (2) total adherents who belong to the county's largest denomination (nmax) as a proportion of the total (i.e., nmax/N, where N=total number of adherents). This measure assesses the relative dominance of one faith in particular areas; (3) Shannon's index (H), a widely used entropy maximizing measure that quantifies diversity based on the number of denominations and their proportional areal distribution. It is calculated by adding for each denomination the product of the proportion of adherents and its natural logarithm, $H=-(p \times \ln pi)$ (1) in which p is the proportion of a county's adherents found in denomination i. The maximum value is attained when all denominations have the same distribution; (4) Simpson's index (D), which assesses the probability that two individuals drawn at random will fall in the same denomination. It is defined as $D=p2 i$ (2) in which p is the proportion of a county's adherents found in denomination i. It ranges from zero to one.

19 Todd M. Johnson and Brian J. Grim, eds., *World Religion Database* (Leiden/Boston: Brill, 2008).

20 The data for this section are from the Pew Forum.

21 Pew Forum on Religion and Public Life, *Lobbying for the Faithful: Religious Advocacy Groups in Washington, DC,* November 21, 2011, http://www.pewforum.org/Government/ Lobbying-for-the-faithful--exec.aspx.

22 Some studies count the number of groups a person has contact with. For instance, the Social Capital Community Benchmark Survey (2000) uses a Diversity of Friendships Index formed by counting how many different kinds of personal friendship the respondents has from the possible 11 types of people. See http://www.hks.harvard.edu/ saguaro/communitysurvey/docs/exec_summ.pdf.

23 An alternative to using set cut-points is to use the log of the eight world religious group populations. Doing this, however, produces results that are more highly correlated with total population size.

24 Critical mass is a concept borrowed from nuclear physics where it refers to the smallest amount of fissionable material needed for a sustained nuclear chain reaction. In social dynamics it refers to the existence of a sufficient number of adopters of an innovation to spark its diffusion through society. Critical mass is also a concept discussed in diversifying educational institutions and executive bodies. See Lissa L. Broome, John M. Conley, and Kimberly D. Krawiec, "Does Critical Mass Matter? Views from the Boardroom," *Seattle University Law Review* (forthcoming).

25 All three thresholds might be meaningless if group members are isolated individuals scattered widely throughout a country. It is often the case, however, that smaller groups are geographically clustered. For instance, Yemeni Jews live in only one town, and the Jews in South Korea are expatriates predominantly living in Seoul.

26 Information obtained from the websites of the Swiss Federation of Jewish Communities (SIG) (http://www.swissjews.ch/en/index.php) and the European Jewish Congress (EJC) (http://www.eurojewcong.org/ejc/news.php?id_article=121).

27 Information obtained from the Nairobi Hebrew Congregation website, http://www.nhc.co.ke/welcome.html.

28 According to JTA, the global news service for the Jewish people (http://www.jta.org/news/article/2008/04/08/107966/litzmanchabadseoul).

29 http://www.nhc.co.ke/index.html

30 http://www.fids.ch/

31 Swiss Muslim websites range from countrywide to canton-specific. They also have specific websites dedicated to issues as wide-ranging as political lobbying to dating, diet, and devotions.

32 See US Department of State, "Switzerland: International Religious Freedom Report," November 17, 2010, http://www.state.gov/j/drl/rls/irf/2010/148989.htm.

33 Social scientists use a variety of geographic proximity indexes to study several different topics, one of which is racial segregation. For instance, Douglas Massey and Nancy Denton identified 20 different indexes of segregation that focus on five separate dimensions: evenness (differential distribution of the population), exposure (potential contact), concentration (relative amount of physical space occupied), centralization (degree to which a group is located near the center of an urban area), and clustering (degree to which minority group members live disproportionately in contiguous areas). See Douglas S. Massey and Nancy A. Denton, "The Dimensions of Residential Segregation," *Social Forces* 67 (1988): 281–315. Also see Michael J. White, "The Measurement of Spatial Segregation," *American Journal of Sociology* 88:5 (March 1983): 1,008–18.

34 See Diana L. Eck, *A New Religious America: How A "Christian Country" has become the World's Most Religiously Diverse Nation* (New York: HarperCollins, 2001).

35 Brian J. Grim and David Masci, "The Demographics of Faith," August 2008, http://www.america.gov/st/peopleplace-english/2008/August/20080819121858cmretrop0.5310633.html.

36 Peggy Levitt, *God Needs No Passport: Immigrants and the Changing American Religious Landscape* (New York: The New Press, 2007), 11, 202.

37 Ibid.

38 Grim and Masci, "The Demographics of Faith."

39 See Darrell Jackson and Alessia Passarelli, *Mapping Migration: Mapping Churches' Responses: Europe Study* (Brussels: Churches' Commission for Migrants in Europe, 2008), 25–7 for an analysis of European church response to growing migrant communities in the European Union. Research results from the 2001 European Values Survey and World Values Survey reported that individuals who attended religious services with higher frequently were more likely to show concern for the living conditions of migrants. This leads the authors to conclude that religious communities in Europe can "become a bridging tool for integration, avoiding marginalisation, and overcoming the frustrations felt by migrant faith communities which may lead to radicalisation of the religious community or individuals within it." In addition, faith communities themselves have much to gain from migrant communities, such as intercultural experiences.

40 Roger Finke and Rodney Stark, *The Churching of America: Winners and Losers in the Religious Economy* (New Brunswick, NJ: Rutgers University Press, 1992), cited in Michele Dillon, "A Sociological Approach to Questions about Religious Diversity," in *The Oxford Handbook of Religious Diversity*, ed. Chad Meister (Oxford: Oxford University Press, 2011), 49.

41 This is expressed by Stanley Fischer in "Globalization and Its Challenges," paper presented at the American Economic Association meetings in Washington, DC, January 3, 2003.

42 Ole Riis, "Modes of Religious Pluralism under Conditions of Globalization," in *Democracy and Human Rights in Multicultural Societies,* ed. Matthias Koenig and Paul de Guchteneire (Aldershot: Ashgate Publishing Limited, 2007), 251.

43 Scott M. Thomas, "A Globalized God: Religion's Growing Influence in International Politics," *Foreign Affairs* 89:6 (Nov/Dec 2010): 98.

44 For instance, see chapter 12 on China.

References

Broome, Lissa L., John M. Conley, and Kimberly D. Krawiec. "Does Critical Mass Matter? Views from the Boardroom." *Seattle University Law Review* (forthcoming).

Dillon, Michele. "A Sociological Approach to Questions about Religious Diversity." In *The Oxford Handbook of Religious Diversity*, edited by Chad Meister, 42–60. Oxford: Oxford University Press, 2011.

Eck, Diana L. *A New Religious America: How a "Christian County" Has Become the World's Most Religiously Diverse Nation.* New York: HarperSanFrancisco, 2001.

Eck, Diana L. "The Challenge of Pluralism." Nieman Reports "God in the Newsroom" Issue, 17:2 (Summer 1993).

Finke, Roger, and Rodney Stark. *The Churching of America: Winners and Losers in the Religious Economy.* New Brunswick, NJ: Rutgers University Press, 1992.

Fischer, Stanley. "Globalization and Its Challenges." Paper presented at the American Economic Association meetings, Washington, DC, January 3, 2003.

Grim, Brian J., and Roger Finke. "Religious Persecution in Cross-National Context: Clashing Civilizations or Regulated Economies?" *American Sociological Review* 72:4 (2007): 633–58.

Grim, Brian J., and David Masci. "The Demographics of Faith." August 2008. http://www.america.gov/st/peopleplace-english/2008/August/20080819121858cmretrop0.5310633.html.

Jackson, Darrell, and Alessia Passarelli. *Mapping Migration: Mapping Churches' Responses: Europe Study.* Brussels: Churches' Commission for Migrants in Europe, 2008.

Johnson, Todd M., and Brian J. Grim, eds. *World Religion Database.* Leiden/Boston: Brill, 2008.

Johnson, Todd M., and Kenneth R. Ross, eds. *Atlas of Global Christianity.* Edinburgh: Edinburgh University Press, 2009.

Laine, Charles R. "The Herfindahl-Hirschman Index: A Concentration Measure Taking the Consumer's Point of View." *Antitrust Bulletin* (June 22, 1995).

Levitt, Peggy. *God Needs No Passport: Immigrants and the Changing American Religious Landscape.* New York: The New Press, 2007.

Massey, Douglas S., and Nancy A. Denton. "The Dimensions of Residential Segregation." *Social Forces* 67 (1988): 281–315.

McBride, Michael. "Religious Pluralism and Religious Participation: Game Theoretic Analysis." *American Journal of Sociology* 114:1 (July 2008): 77–108.

McCleary, Rachel M., and Robert J. Barro. "Religion and Political Economy in an International Panel." *Journal for the Scientific Study of Religion* 45:2 (June 2006): 149–75.

Nordås, Ragnhild. "How Religious Diversity Matters (Or Not) for Intrastate Armed Conflict." Paper presented at the Population Association of America annual meeting, Washington, DC, March 9, 2011.

Norris, Pippa, and Ronald Inglehart. *Sacred and Secular: Religion and Politics Worldwide*
Cambridge: Cambridge University Press, 2004.

Pew Forum on Religion and Public Life. *The Global Religious Landscape: A Report on the Size
and Distribution of the World's Major Religious Groups as of 2010*. December 2012. http://
www.pewforum.org/global-religious-landscape-about.aspx.

Pew Forum on Religion and Public Life, *Lobbying the Faithful: Religious Advocacy Groups
in Washington, DC.* November 21, 2011. http://www.pewforum.org/government/
lobbying-for-the-faithful--exec.aspx.

Phan, Peter. *Being Religious Interreligiously: Asian Perspectives on Interreligious Dialogue.*
Maryknoll, NY: Orbis Books, 2004.

Riis, Ole. "Modes of Religious Pluralism under Conditions of Globalization." In *Democracy
and Human Rights in Multicultural Societies*, edited by Matthias Koenig and Paul de
Guchteneire, 251–65. Aldershot: Ashgate Publishing Limited, 2007.

Silk, Mark. "Defining Religious Pluralism in America: A Regional Analysis." *The ANNALS of
the American Academy of Political and Social Science* 612:1 (July 2007): 62–81.

Thomas, Scott M. "A Globalized God: Religion's Growing Influence in International Politics."
Foreign Affairs 89:6 (Nov/Dec 2010): 93–101.

US Department of State. "Switzerland: International Religious Freedom Report." November
17, 2010. http://www.state.gov/j/drl/rls/irf/2010/148989.htm.

Varia, Nisha. "Asia's Migrant Workers Need Better Protection." *Human Rights Watch*,
September 2, 2004. http://www.hrw.org/news/2004/08/31/asias-migrant-workers-
need-better-protection.

Warf, Barney, and Mort Winsberg. "The Geography of Religious Diversity in the United
States." *The Professional Geographer* 60:3 (2008): 413–24.

White, Michael J. "The Measurement of Spatial Segregation." *American Journal of Sociology*
88:5 (March 1983): 1,008–18.

Wike, Richard, and Brian J. Grim. "Western Views Towards Muslims: Evidence from a
2006 Cross-National Survey." *International Journal of Public Opinion Research* 22:1
(2010): 4–25.

Chapter 4

Projecting Religious Populations, 2010–50

For many, the most surprising finding of the tables and graphs in this chapter will be the projected continued resiliency of world religions into the future. In the mid-twentieth century the demise of religion was a near-accepted fact inside and outside the academic community. Several decades on, however, the strongest evidence shows that the global trend of religious resurgence is likely to continue into the near and, perhaps, distant future. In documenting that resurgence, this chapter focuses on presenting and commenting on the findings of future projections for the world's religions. Following will be a brief reflection on needed improvements in projection methodology, although much of this is described in detail in part II, especially chapters 7 and 9.

In examining the future of religion, a natural place to begin is with the question of whether there has been or currently is a global resurgence of religion. Comparing today's situation to that of 100 years ago, the answer has to be a resounding "no." In 1910 the world was home to very few atheists and agnostics. By 2010, they numbered in the hundreds of millions and represented 11.8% of the world's population. Thus, over the twentieth century, religionists' share of the global population declined steadily in the context of the expansion of Communism and its ardent promotion of atheism, as well as secularization in much of the West. In 1910 virtually 100% of the world's population was religious, but by 2010 this had fallen to 88.2%. However, hidden in this 100-year trend is a profound turn-around in the religious composition of the world's population.

Examining the data more closely, one can see that the raw percentage of non-religious people peaked around 1970 at approximately 19.2% (80.8% being religious). Since then the percentage of religionists has risen steadily and is expected to exceed 91% by 2050. The early part of this shift (between 1970 and 1990 in the larger context of 1970–2010) is due largely to the collapse of Communism in the former Soviet Union,

The World's Religions in Figures: An Introduction to International Religious Demography,
First Edition. Todd M. Johnson and Brian J. Grim.
© 2013 John Wiley & Sons, Ltd. Published 2013 by John Wiley & Sons, Ltd.

Table 4.1   Major world religions, 2010–50.

Religion	Adherents 2010	% 2010	Adherents 2050	% 2050	Gr % 2010–50
Christians	2,260,440,000	32.8	3,327,384,000	35.8	0.97
Muslims	1,553,773,000	22.5	2,554,874,000	27.5	1.25
Hindus	948,575,000	13.8	1,264,863,000	13.6	0.72
Agnostics	676,944,000	9.8	674,949,000	7.3	−0.01
Buddhists	494,881,000	7.2	556,286,000	6.0	0.29
Chinese folk-religionists	436,258,000	6.3	379,459,000	4.1	−0.35
Ethnoreligionists	242,516,000	3.5	240,408,000	2.6	−0.02
Atheists	136,652,000	2.0	132,613,000	1.4	−0.07
New Religionists	63,004,000	0.9	59,964,000	0.6	−0.12
Sikhs	23,927,000	0.3	34,267,000	0.4	0.90
Jews	14,761,000	0.2	18,338,000	0.2	0.54
Spiritists	13,700,000	0.2	15,883,000	0.2	0.37
Baha'is	7,306,000	0.1	15,343,000	0.2	1.87
Daoists	8,429,000	0.1	15,018,000	0.2	1.45
Jains	5,316,000	0.1	7,943,000	0.1	1.01
Confucianists	6,449,000	0.1	6,015,000	0.1	−0.17
Shintoists	2,761,000	0.0	2,355,000	0.0	−0.40
Zoroastrians	197,000	0.0	168,000	0.0	−0.40
Total population	**6,895,889,000**	**100.0**	**9,306,949,000**	**100.0**	**0.75**

Data source: Todd M. Johnson and Brian J. Grim, eds., *World Religion Database* (Leiden/Boston: Brill, accessed January 2012).

which was accompanied by the (re-)legalization of, and return of many people to, religious bodies of many kinds. Although the number of atheists and agnostics continues to rise in the Western world, the current growth of a variety of religions in China, in particular (where the vast majority of the non-religious live today), suggests continued future demographic growth of religion. Thus, from this second point of view (1970–present), there has been a global religious resurgence in recent years, and it seems likely to continue into the future.

Two religions – Christianity and Islam – dominate religious demographics at present and seem poised to continue that dominance in the future. In 1910 these two religions represented less than 50% of the world's population; it appears that by 2050 they will claim over 63% (table 4.1). Islam will likely see the greatest growth, doubling its share of the world's population in 140 years (from 13% in 1910 to a projected 27.5% in 2050). Christianity will likely make modest gains, from 34.8% in 1910 to 35.8% by 2050, having passed through a low point of around 32% in 2000.

While both Christianity and Islam are flourishing in sub-Saharan Africa, present data suggest that neither faith is likely to expand as rapidly in this region in the years ahead as it did in the twentieth century, except possibly through natural population growth. There are two primary reasons for this conclusion. First, most people in the region have already committed to either Christianity or Islam, which means that in terms of percentage, the pool of potential converts from outside these two faiths has decreased dramatically. In most of the countries of sub-Saharan Africa, 90% or more of the population describe themselves as either Christian or Muslim; fewer than one in 10 identify as adherents of other faiths (including African traditional religions) or no faith.

Second, there is little evidence that either Christianity or Islam is growing in sub-Saharan Africa at the expense of the other. Although a relatively small percentage of Muslims have become Christians, and a relatively small percentage of Christians have become Muslims, over all there is no substantial shift in either direction. One notable exception is Uganda, where surveys show that roughly one third of those who were raised Muslim now describe themselves as Christian, while far fewer Ugandans who were raised Christian now describe themselves as Muslim.[1]

On the other hand, Chinese folk-religion is projected to see the greatest 140-year decline in adherents as a global percentage, falling from 22.2% of the world's population in 1910 to only 4.1% by 2050.[2] The projected decline of non-religionists' (agnostics' and atheists') share of the global population through 2050 seems equally surprising in light of past trends. From only 0.2% in 1910, together non-religionists accounted for over 20% of the world's population in 1970. By 2010, however, their share had fallen to about 11.8%, and it is projected to fall to only 8.7% by 2050.

Table 4.1 also allows for comparisons of projected religious growth rates from 2010–50. Only three religions are projected to have substantial growth (in percentage terms) over this period. Both Muslims and Daoists will likely grow at approximately 1.5 times the world population growth rate (1.25% and 1.45%, respectively).[3] Even more impressively, Baha'is, with a robust global program of sharing their message, are expected to grow at more than twice the world population growth rate (1.87% p.a.). Zoroastrians, Shintoists, Confucianists, agnostics, atheists, Chinese folk-religionists, ethnoreligionists, and New Religionists are projected to experience net *losses* in their numbers of adherents over the same period.[4] The worldwide Jewish community is expected to grow from 14.8 million in 2010 to about 17.5 million in 2050, though its 40-year growth rate of 0.54% p.a. is slower than that of the global population (0.75% p.a. over the same period). Fortunately, Jewish demography and the future of the world Jewish population is studied in great detail.[5]

South-central Asia is an area of particular interest looking forward to 2050. Significantly, this region includes the countries (Pakistan, Bangladesh, and India) forecast to have the largest populations globally of both Muslims and Hindus in 2050. The addition of over a half-billion people (from a population of 1.7 billion in 2010 to 2.4 billion in 2050)[6] is likely to compound social, economic, and religious pressures in a region already simmering from longstanding inter-communal tensions. A new generation of peacemakers at local, national, and regional levels will be challenged to bridge the divide between these religious communities.

Foundational to the reality of a changing religious landscape are the increases and decreases in religious diversity in the world's countries and regions (examined in detail in chapter 3). In 2050, most countries will be more religiously plural than they were in 2010; that is, they will be home to adherents of a greater number of religions. In 1910 Suriname was the world's most religiously diverse country, with five major religious traditions having sizeable populations of adherents there (2% or more of the population). By 2050 it is likely that China will be the most religiously diverse as a result of the religious resurgence explained above. An increase in religious diversity also will be particularly apparent in the global North, where secularization and immigration will continue to transform the religious landscape. In the global South, how-ever, many countries will continue to see growth mainly in one religion, most likely Christianity or Islam, thus decreasing overall diversity.

Methodology

As described in more detail in chapter 9, the starting point of future studies is natural growth of the total population of the country or region of interest, utilizing demographic projections as a baseline.[7] Three major areas beyond natural growth were then utilized to improve the projections. First, birth and death rates vary among religious communities within a particular country. Second, increasing numbers of people are likely to change their religious affiliations in the future. Third, immigration and emigration trends will impact a country's population over time. The results of incorporating all three of these dynamics can be applied to any religious tradition and are presented in tables 4.2–4.13.

The highest-quality projections for religious communities are built on cohort-component projections – ones that use differential rates for each religion: age-specific fertility rates by religion, age structure in 5-year age-and-sex cohorts by religion, migration rates by religion, and mortality by religion. For instance, cohort-component projections are used for the projections in chapters 10 and 11 that Brian Grim did with colleagues at the Pew Research Center's Forum on Religion and Public Life and at the Age and Cohort Change Project of the International Institute for Applied Systems Analysis (IIASA).

Unfortunately, this kind of detail is not yet available for many countries (half of censuses do not ask a question about religion). Fortunately, the process of filling in missing data using demographic and smaller-scale general population surveys is underway at the Pew Forum (see chapter 8). As these data become available through the Pew-Templeton Global Religious Futures Project, researchers will have access to these data through the *World Religion Database*, where they will be archived in full, with summary results available at the Pew Forum's website.

In the meantime, the projections presented in this chapter cannot solely rely on the cohort-component method. Instead, they use a hybrid projection method. First, the 2010 religious composition of each country is established as the baseline (see chapters 1–2 and chapter 7 for sources). Then, utilizing the United Nations medium variant cohort-component projections of populations for five-year periods up to 2050,[8] future religious shares are modestly adjusted from the 2010 baseline. Adjustments are based on analysis of past differential growth rates of religious groups, factoring in historical patterns of religious switching and possible future attenuation of past trends. Finally, these projections take into account how immigrants might alter the future religious composition of country populations (see chapter 14). This method is built on the dynamics of religious change formula found in chapter 9.

These projections are calculated one religion at a time utilizing assumptions about the impact of the six dynamics on each over a given time period. For example, the Christian population in China is estimated to be currently growing at 2.7% per year with the following gains (births, 1.3%; converts in, 2.5%; immigrants, 0.0%) and losses (deaths, 0.7%; converts out, 0.3%; emigrants, 0.1%). For the 2010–50 period we assume that total losses will continue at 1.1% per year but that gains will slow, with birthrates falling to 1.0% and converts in to 1.9%. This places the overall growth rate for that 40-year period at 1.8% per year. In the *World Religion Database*, each of these assumptions will appear as annotations on particular projections.

In other cases a more cautious approach may be taken when data are poor or missing. In Nigeria, for example, with a number of demographic and health surveys giving contradictory information and no reliable census, we have estimated that the number of Christians and Muslims is approximately equal. The *World Religion Database* reports both at around 46% in 2010, with Christians slightly higher. Over the twentieth century, generally, ethnoreligionists in the south became Christians while those in the north became Muslims. For example, ethnoreligionists were thought to be 73% of the population in 1900, with Christians at only 1% while Muslims were estimated at 26%. Ethnoreligionists numbered nearly 20% as recently as 1970. Our analysis assumes that in 2010 over 7% of the country's population still adhered to ethnoreligions (as a primary identification). Thus, ethnoreligionists have continued to convert to one of the two largest religions in Nigeria. In our projections for 2050, we expect this to continue. Looking carefully at an ethnolinguistic map of Nigeria, we have determined that slightly more ethnoreligionists live in proximity to Muslims than Christians. Therefore, if there were little else in demographic changes over the next 40 years, we would project the Muslim population to be slightly higher than the Christian population by then. Other factors – including differential fertility, mortality, migration, and conversion (for instance, to agnosticism or atheism) – will impact the future size of the Christian and Muslim populations. As shown in chapter 10, taking these factors into account, the Pew Forum projects Nigeria to have a slight Muslim majority by 2030.

It is important to point out that the existing data for China and Nigeria are sufficiently deficient that any projections are tentative at best.

Findings for the Larger World Religions

Christians

Projections concerning the future of global Christianity can be made based on detailed information on Christian denominations available for mid-2010, taking account of growth since mid-2000. The well-known demographic shift of Christianity to the global South is expected to continue into the future, with declining church member-ship projected for Europe (especially Western and Northern) and growth (through birthrates and conversion) of Christianity in Africa, Asia, and Latin America. By 2050 only 26% of all Christians will be found in Europe and Northern America[9] (down from 38% in 2010 and over 80% in 1910).

Indeed, the share of Christians who reside in Africa in 2050 could be as high as 34% (over 1.1 billion Christians). The fastest-growing regional Christian population in the world from 2010 to 2050 is expected to be that of West Africa[10] (2.38% p.a.), almost five times faster than that of Christians in Northern America (table 4.2).

Table 4.2 Christians (C) by United Nations continents and regions, 2010–50.

Region	Population 2010	Christians 2010	% 2010	Population 2050	Christians 2050	% 2050	Pop gr % 2010–50	C gr % 2010–50
Africa	**1,022,234,000**	**494,053,000**	**48.3**	**2,191,597,000**	**1,152,653,000**	**52.6**	**1.92**	**2.14**
Eastern Africa	324,044,000	214,013,000	66.0	779,613,000	548,030,000	70.3	2.22	2.38
Middle Africa	126,689,000	104,579,000	82.5	278,350,000	234,514,000	84.3	1.99	2.04
Northern Africa	209,459,000	16,761,000	8.0	322,459,000	30,557,000	9.5	1.08	1.51
Southern Africa	57,780,000	47,598,000	82.4	67,326,000	54,794,000	81.4	0.38	0.35
Western Africa	304,261,000	111,103,000	36.5	743,849,000	284,757,000	38.3	2.26	2.38
Asia	**4,164,252,000**	**342,012,000**	**8.2**	**5,142,223,000**	**604,749,000**	**11.8**	**0.53**	**1.44**
Eastern Asia	1,573,970,000	127,573,000	8.1	1,511,963,000	247,301,000	16.4	-0.10	1.67
South-central Asia	1,764,872,000	69,990,000	4.0	2,475,685,000	131,024,000	5.3	0.85	1.58
South-eastern Asia	593,415,000	130,271,000	22.0	759,208,000	209,872,000	27.6	0.62	1.20
Western Asia	231,995,000	14,178,000	6.1	395,367,000	16,552,000	4.2	1.34	0.39
Europe	**738,199,000**	**580,116,000**	**78.6**	**719,258,000**	**535,501,000**	**74.5**	**-0.06**	**-0.20**
Eastern Europe	294,771,000	247,550,000	84.0	256,946,000	226,416,000	88.1	-0.34	-0.22
Northern Europe	99,205,000	74,228,000	74.8	114,036,000	76,350,000	67.0	0.35	0.07
Southern Europe	155,171,000	127,943,000	82.5	155,229,000	121,531,000	78.3	0.00	-0.13
Western Europe	189,052,000	130,395,000	69.0	193,047,000	111,203,000	57.6	0.05	-0.40
Latin America	**590,082,000**	**544,686,000**	**92.3**	**750,954,000**	**672,648,000**	**89.6**	**0.60**	**0.53**
Caribbean	41,646,000	34,774,000	83.5	47,312,000	39,876,000	84.3	0.32	0.34
Central America	155,881,000	149,426,000	95.9	215,570,000	202,183,000	93.8	0.81	0.76
South America	392,555,000	360,486,000	91.8	488,072,000	430,588,000	88.2	0.55	0.45
Northern America	**344,529,000**	**271,554,000**	**78.8**	**446,864,000**	**322,822,000**	**72.2**	**0.65**	**0.43**
Oceania	**36,593,000**	**28,019,000**	**76.6**	**55,234,000**	**39,011,000**	**70.6**	**1.03**	**0.83**
Australia/New Zealand	26,637,000	18,869,000	70.8	37,063,000	22,048,000	59.5	0.83	0.39
Melanesia	8,748,000	8,004,000	91.5	16,586,000	15,507,000	93.5	1.61	1.67
Micronesia	536,000	499,000	93.1	726,000	654,000	90.1	0.76	0.68
Polynesia	673,000	647,000	96.1	859,000	802,000	93.3	0.61	0.54
Global	**6,895,889,000**	**2,260,440,000**	**32.8**	**9,306,130,000**	**3,327,384,000**	**35.8**	**0.75**	**0.97**

Data source: Todd M. Johnson and Brian J. Grim, eds., *World Religion Database* (Leiden/Boston: Brill, accessed January 2012).

Table 4.3 Countries with the most Christians, 2010–50.

	Country	Christians 2010	Country	Christians 2025	Country	Christians 2050
1	United States	247,920,000	United States	266,990,000	United States	297,648,000
2	Brazil	177,304,000	Brazil	191,363,000	China	219,380,000
3	Russia	116,147,000	China	172,920,000	Brazil	192,427,000
4	Mexico	108,721,000	Mexico	124,194,000	Nigeria	189,000,000
5	China	106,035,000	Russia	116,978,000	DR Congo	140,618,000
6	Philippines	84,769,000	Nigeria	109,170,000	Philippines	140,525,000
7	Nigeria	73,606,000	Philippines	107,098,000	Mexico	134,857,000
8	DR Congo	62,673,000	DR Congo	90,414,000	India	113,800,000
9	Germany	57,617,000	India	86,790,000	Russia	106,473,000
10	India	57,265,000	Ethiopia	67,775,000	Ethiopia	90,929,000

Data source: Todd M. Johnson and Brian J. Grim, eds., *World Religion Database* (Leiden/Boston: Brill, accessed January 2012).

The percentage of the world's Christians who live in Asia is predicted to rise between 2010 and 2050, from 8.2% to 11.8%. Christian communities in China and the Philippines are expected to experience continued growth, such that in 2050 the two countries rank second and sixth globally in total Christian population, with 219 million and 140 million Christians, respectively. Note, however, that while Christianity is the majority religion in the Philippines, the Christian community in China, although demographically significant, is a comparatively small minority.

Notably, the only European country among the "top 10" in Christian population in 2050 is predominately Orthodox Russia, ranking ninth. This would have been unexpected from the vantage point of 1970 or 1980, when Communism dominated Eastern Europe and especially the Soviet Union. The number of Christians is expected to decrease in three of Europe's four regions between 2010 and 2050 (the exception being Northern Europe, projected to grow at only 0.07% p.a.). Even the steady stream of Christian migrants from the global South into Europe appears unable to stem the tide of conversion, mainly from the state churches.

By 2050 eight of the 10 countries with the most Christians globally will be in the global South; the list in 1910 included only Brazil from the global South (table 4.3). Note also that the 298 million Christians projected for the United States in 2050 includes large numbers of Christians who have emigrated from the global South.

Muslims

The world's Muslim population is expected to increase by about 64% between 2010 and 2050, rising from 1.53 billion to 2.5 billion.[11] Globally, the Muslim population is forecast to grow at about twice the rate of the non-Muslim population over that period – an average annual growth rate of 1.3% for Muslims, compared with 0.7% for non-Muslims.[12]

If current trends continue, Muslims will make up 27.5% of the world's total projected population of 9.3 billion in 2050, up from 22.5% of the estimated 2010 global

Table 4.4 Muslims (M) by United Nations continents and regions, 2010–50.

Region	Population 2010	Muslims 2010	% 2010	Population 2050	Muslims 2050	% 2050	Pop.gr % 2010–50	M.gr % 2010–50
Africa	**1,022,234,000**	**425,860,000**	**41.7**	**2,191,597,000**	**902,770,000**	**41.2**	**1.92**	**1.90**
Eastern Africa	324,044,000	70,824,000	21.9	779,613,000	172,008,000	22.1	2.22	2.24
Middle Africa	126,689,000	12,226,000	9.7	278,350,000	29,210,000	10.5	1.99	2.20
Northern Africa	209,459,000	186,697,000	89.1	322,459,000	285,253,000	88.5	1.08	1.07
Southern Africa	57,780,000	887,000	1.5	67,326,000	1,342,000	2.0	0.38	1.04
Western Africa	304,261,000	155,227,000	51.0	743,849,000	414,957,000	55.8	2.26	2.49
Asia	**4,164,252,000**	**1,078,854,000**	**25.9**	**5,142,223,000**	**1,586,528,000**	**30.9**	**0.53**	**0.97**
Eastern Asia	1,573,970,000	21,601,000	1.4	1,511,963,000	24,872,000	1.6	-0.10	0.35
South-central Asia	1,764,872,000	632,333,000	35.8	2,475,685,000	931,271,000	37.6	0.85	0.97
South-eastern Asia	593,415,000	218,910,000	36.9	759,208,000	273,233,000	36.0	0.62	0.56
Western Asia	231,995,000	206,010,000	88.8	395,367,000	357,153,000	90.3	1.34	1.39
Europe	**738,199,000**	**41,492,000**	**5.6**	**719,258,000**	**49,973,000**	**6.9**	**-0.06**	**0.47**
Eastern Europe	294,771,000	16,776,000	5.7	256,946,000	15,910,000	6.2	-0.34	-0.13
Northern Europe	99,205,000	2,865,000	2.9	114,036,000	4,339,000	3.8	0.35	1.04
Southern Europe	155,171,000	10,276,000	6.6	155,229,000	11,483,000	7.4	0.00	0.28
Western Europe	189,052,000	11,576,000	6.1	193,047,000	18,242,000	9.4	0.05	1.14
Latin America	**590,082,000**	**1,527,000**	**0.3**	**750,954,000**	**2,668,000**	**0.4**	**0.60**	**1.40**
Caribbean	41,646,000	114,000	0.3	47,312,000	143,000	0.3	0.32	0.57
Central America	155,881,000	148,000	0.1	215,570,000	279,000	0.1	0.81	1.60
South America	392,555,000	1,265,000	0.3	488,072,000	2,246,000	0.5	0.55	1.45
Northern America	**344,529,000**	**5,492,000**	**1.6**	**446,864,000**	**11,551,000**	**2.6**	**0.65**	**1.88**
Oceania	**36,593,000**	**549,000**	**1.5**	**55,234,000**	**1,384,000**	**2.5**	**1.03**	**2.34**
Australia/New Zealand	26,637,000	484,000	1.8	37,063,000	1,300,000	3.5	0.83	2.50
Melanesia	8,748,000	63,800	0.7	16,586,000	81,000	0.5	1.61	0.60
Micronesia	536,000	950	0.2	726,000	2,300	0.3	0.76	2.24
Polynesia	673,000	69	0.0	859,000	230	0.0	0.61	3.06
Global	**6,895,889,000**	**1,553,773,000**	**22.5**	**9,306,130,000**	**2,554,874,000**	**27.5**	**0.75**	**1.25**

Data source: Todd M. Johnson and Brian J. Grim, eds., *World Religion Database* (Leiden/Boston: Brill, accessed January 2012).

Table 4.5   Countries with the most Muslims, 2010–50.

	Country	Muslims 2010	Country	Muslims 2025	Country	Muslims 2050
1	Indonesia	190,521,000	India	215,000,000	Pakistan	264,872,000
2	India	173,367,000	Indonesia	214,197,000	India	255,000,000
3	Pakistan	166,927,000	Pakistan	212,518,000	Indonesia	228,209,000
4	Bangladesh	132,112,000	Bangladesh	155,236,000	Nigeria	189,000,000
5	Iran	73,079,000	Nigeria	109,170,000	Bangladesh	171,546,000
6	Egypt	72,436,000	Egypt	90,984,000	Egypt	111,937,000
7	Nigeria	72,149,000	Iran	81,885,000	Turkey	88,698,000
8	Turkey	71,513,000	Turkey	81,846,000	Iran	83,809,000
9	Algeria	34,937,000	Iraq	47,927,000	Iraq	82,077,000
10	Morocco	31,840,000	Afghanistan	47,535,000	Afghanistan	76,158,000

Data source: Todd M. Johnson and Brian J. Grim, eds., *World Religion Database* (Leiden/Boston: Brill, accessed January 2012).

population of 6.9 billion (table 4.4). Despite growing more rapidly than the non-Muslim population, however, the Muslim population is expected to grow more slowly between 2010 and 2050 than it did in the previous decade, as fertility rates decline around the world. From 2000 to 2010, the global Muslim population increased at an average annual rate of 1.9%, compared with a projected rate of 1.3% for the period 2010–50.

Islam will continue to experience a shift in distribution by continent. In 2010, 27% of all Muslims lived in Africa, and this is expected to grow to over 35% by 2050. Interestingly, the percentage of Africa that is Muslim is not expected to change much over the same period (table 4.4). Consequently, the growth can be attributed largely to higher population growth rates in Africa compared with the rest of the world. At the same time, the percentage of the world's Muslims in Western Asia and Northern Africa (the traditional "Middle East") will level off, holding at about 25% for both 2010 and 2050 (up from just over 23% in 1910).

The majority of the world's Muslims (62%) will continue to live in the Asia–Pacific region. If current trends continue, however, 79 countries will have 1 million or more Muslims in 2030,[13] up from 72 countries in 2010. Notably, Pakistan is expected to surpass Indonesia as the country with the single largest Muslim population in the world (table 4.5). India is also expected to pass Indonesia and be ranked second. The portion of the world's Muslims living in sub-Saharan Africa is projected to rise as a result of high fertility rates; by 2030, for example, more Muslims are likely to live in Nigeria than in Egypt.

In Europe as a whole, the Muslim share of the population is expected to increase slightly, from 5.6% in 2010 to 6.9% in 2050, reflecting a 40-year growth rate of only 0.5% per year. In absolute numbers, Europe's Muslim population is projected to grow from 41.5 million in 2010 to 50.0 million in 2050.[14] Others have offered projections of more robust Muslim growth in Europe. For example, Eric Kaufmann offers higher estimates of Muslim populations in Europe for 2050 and 2100, but his predictions include several assumptions: resistance to secularization by Muslims,

Table 4.6 Hindus (H) by United Nations continents and regions, 2010–50.

Region	Population 2010	Hindus 2010	% 2010	Population 2050	Hindus 2050	% 2050	Pop.gr % 2010–50	H.gr % 2010–50
Africa	**1,022,234,000**	**2,930,000**	**0.3**	**2,191,597,000**	**5,234,000**	**0.2**	**1.92**	**1.46**
Eastern Africa	324,044,000	1,612,000	0.5	779,613,000	2,972,000	0.4	2.22	1.54
Middle Africa	126,689,000	99,300	0.1	278,350,000	401,000	0.1	1.99	3.55
Northern Africa	209,459,000	7,400	0.0	322,459,000	18,100	0.0	1.08	2.26
Southern Africa	57,780,000	1,201,000	2.1	67,326,000	1,808,000	2.7	0.38	1.03
Western Africa	304,261,000	9,700	0.0	743,849,000	34,800	0.0	2.26	3.25
Asia	**4,164,252,000**	**941,481,000**	**22.6**	**5,142,223,000**	**1,252,762,000**	**24.4**	**0.53**	**0.72**
Eastern Asia	1,573,970,000	61,800	0.0	1,511,963,000	90,000	0.0	-0.10	0.94
South-central Asia	1,764,872,000	933,161,000	52.9	2,475,685,000	1,241,384,000	50.1	0.85	0.72
South-eastern Asia	593,415,000	6,918,000	1.2	759,208,000	8,934,000	1.2	0.62	0.64
Western Asia	231,995,000	1,340,000	0.6	395,367,000	2,354,000	0.6	1.34	1.42
Europe	**738,199,000**	**1,052,000**	**0.1**	**719,258,000**	**1,575,000**	**0.2**	**-0.06**	**1.01**
Eastern Europe	294,771,000	47,700	0.0	256,946,000	87,000	0.0	-0.34	1.51
Northern Europe	99,205,000	692,000	0.7	114,036,000	994,000	0.9	0.35	0.91
Southern Europe	155,171,000	30,300	0.0	155,229,000	56,400	0.0	0.00	1.57
Western Europe	189,052,000	282,000	0.1	193,047,000	437,000	0.2	0.05	1.10
Latin America	**590,082,000**	**765,000**	**0.1**	**750,954,000**	**857,000**	**0.1**	**0.60**	**0.28**
Caribbean	41,646,000	382,000	0.9	47,312,000	399,000	0.8	0.32	0.11
Central America	155,881,000	18,000	0.0	215,570,000	35,500	0.0	0.81	1.71
South America	392,555,000	365,000	0.1	488,072,000	423,000	0.1	0.55	0.37
Northern America	**344,529,000**	**1,835,000**	**0.5**	**446,864,000**	**3,720,000**	**0.8**	**0.65**	**1.78**
Oceania	**36,593,000**	**513,000**	**1.4**	**55,234,000**	**715,000**	**1.3**	**1.03**	**0.83**
Australia/New Zealand	26,637,000	274,000	1.0	37,063,000	445,000	1.2	0.83	1.22
Melanesia	8,748,000	239,000	2.7	16,586,000	270,000	1.6	1.61	0.31
Micronesia	536,000	26	0.0	726,000	100	0.0	0.76	3.43
Polynesia	673,000	100	0.0	859,000	200	0.0	0.61	1.75
Global	**6,895,889,000**	**948,575,000**	**13.8**	**9,306,130,000**	**1,264,863,000**	**13.6**	**0.75**	**0.72**

Data source: Todd M. Johnson and Brian J. Grim, eds., *World Religion Database* (Leiden/Boston: Brill, accessed January 2012).

maintenance of current rates of Muslim immigration, and convergence of Muslim fertility rates with those of native populations by 2050.[15] With these caveats he projects that most large Western European countries will be 10–15% Muslim in 2050, though Sweden might approach 20–25%. In contrast, the estimates put forward in this chapter assume that Muslims will remain relatively small minorities in Europe (and the Americas) but will be expected to constitute a growing share of the total population in these regions.

Several factors account for the faster projected growth among Muslims than non-Muslims worldwide. Generally, Muslim populations tend to have higher fertility rates (more children per woman) than non-Muslim populations. In addition, a larger share of the Muslim population is in, or soon will enter, the prime childbearing years (ages 15–29). In the past few decades, improved health and economic conditions in Muslim-majority countries have led to greater-than-average declines in infant and child mortality rates, and life expectancy is rising even faster in Muslim-majority countries than in other less-developed countries.

At the same time, however, the rate of growth among Muslims has been falling. The declining growth rate is due primarily to falling fertility rates in many Muslim-majority countries, including such populous nations as Indonesia and Bangladesh. Fertility is dropping as more women in these countries obtain a secondary education, living standards rise, and people move from rural areas to cities and towns.[16]

The slowdown in Muslim population growth is most pronounced in the Asia–Pacific region, the Middle East–North Africa region, and Europe, and less sharp in sub-Saharan Africa. The only region in which Muslim population growth is expected to accelerate through 2020 is the Americas (both Northern and Latin America), largely because of immigration. Falling birthrates eventually will lead to significant shifts in the age structure of Muslim populations. While the worldwide Muslim population today is relatively young, the so-called Muslim "youth bulge" – the high percentage of Muslims in their teens and 20s – peaked around the year 2000 and is now declining.[17]

Hindus

While the global population is expected to grow at 0.75% per annum from 2010–50, the Hindu population is expected to grow slightly more slowly, at 0.72% per annum. Hindus represented about 950 million adherents (or 13.8% of the world's population) in 2010 and will grow to 1.26 billion by 2050, although their global share will decline slightly, to 13.6%. This drop is a function mainly of slowing population growth in India but also of the expected growth in India of minority religions, such as Islam and Christianity. Hindus make up 80% of India's population in 2010 but this is likely to fall to only 70% by 2050. Also, despite continued growth of the Hindu diaspora around the world, fully 98% of Hindus will likely still be resident in South-central Asia in 2050 (table 4.6). At the same time, growth in the Hindu diaspora is expected in Africa, Europe, Northern America, and Oceania. Not surprisingly, the list of countries with the largest Hindu populations (table 4.7) is expected to change very little.

Table 4.7   Countries with the most Hindus, 2010–50.

	Country	Hindus 2010	Country	Hindus 2025	Country	Hindus 2050
1	India	893,642,000	India	1,036,868,000	India	1,186,068,000
2	Nepal	20,282,000	Nepal	25,224,000	Nepal	30,458,000
3	Bangladesh	14,096,000	Bangladesh	16,300,000	Bangladesh	18,000,000
4	Indonesia	3,891,000	Indonesia	4,500,000	Indonesia	4,900,000
5	Sri Lanka	2,722,000	Sri Lanka	3,000,000	Pakistan	3,600,000
6	Pakistan	2,290,000	Pakistan	2,900,000	Sri Lanka	3,050,000
7	Malaysia	1,780,000	United States	2,100,000	United States	3,000,000
8	United States	1,445,000	Malaysia	2,100,000	Malaysia	2,450,000
9	South Africa	1,196,000	South Africa	1,500,000	South Africa	1,800,000
10	Myanmar	818,000	Myanmar	940,000	Myanmar	1,000,000

Data source: Todd M. Johnson and Brian J. Grim, eds., *World Religion Database* (Leiden/Boston: Brill, accessed January 2012).

Buddhists

Buddhists are also expected to decline as a percentage of the world's population, from 7.2% in 2010 to 6.0% in 2050 (table 4.8). This is also true of the related population of Chinese folk-religionists, who are expected to fall from 6.3% of the global population in 2010 to 4.1% in 2050. Nonetheless, these two religious communities together will represent 935 million people in 2050, up from 929 million in 2010. Including Confucianists, Daoists, and non-religious Chinese who nonetheless practice Chinese religions in their daily lives, the wider Buddhist/Chinese religion community[18] could exceed 1.3 billion by 2050.[19] Table 4.8 also illustrates the continued spread of Buddhists across the world; growth rates in most regions in Africa, Europe, Latin America, and Northern America exceed the rates in Asia.

The list of countries with the most Buddhists (table 4.9) has few changes from 2010 to 2050. Notably, the United States displaces Taiwan at the bottom of the list in 2050, due mainly to the continued immigration of Buddhist Asians to Northern America.

Agnostics/atheists

Agnostics are expected to decline from 9.8% of the world's population in 2010 to only 7.3% in 2050 (table 4.10). Atheists are also expected to decline from 2.0% in 2010 to 1.4% in 2050 (table 4.12). Both table 4.10 and table 4.12 show that the decreases are driven by decline in East Asia. Elsewhere, both groups are expected to grow rapidly in Africa, Latin America, and Oceania, while maintaining modest growth in Europe and Northern America. Nonetheless, little change is expected in the list of countries with the most agnostics or atheists (tables 4.11 and 4.13). Notably, China will continue to have the largest populations of agnostics and atheists despite significant declines in both (and particularly agnostics). Also, because of the resurgence of Christianity in Russia and religion in Viet Nam, both of these countries are expected to lose large numbers of agnostics in the future.

Table 4.8 Buddhists (B) by United Nations continents and regions, 2010–50.

Region	Population 2010	Buddhists 2010	% 2010	Population 2050	Buddhists 2050	% 2050	Pop gr % 2010–50	B gr % 2010–50
Africa	**1,022,234,000**	**254,000**	**0.0**	**2,191,597,000**	**458,000**	**0.0**	**1.92**	**1.48**
Eastern Africa	324,044,000	29,600	0.0	779,613,000	78,000	0.0	2.22	2.45
Middle Africa	126,689,000	7,600	0.0	278,350,000	28,000	0.0	1.99	3.31
Northern Africa	209,459,000	27,400	0.0	322,459,000	67,000	0.0	1.08	2.26
Southern Africa	57,780,000	160,000	0.3	67,326,000	202,000	0.3	0.38	0.58
Western Africa	304,261,000	29,500	0.0	743,849,000	82,500	0.0	2.26	2.60
Asia	**4,164,252,000**	**487,038,000**	**11.7**	**5,142,223,000**	**541,265,000**	**10.5**	**0.53**	**0.26**
Eastern Asia	1,573,970,000	299,334,000	19.0	1,511,963,000	326,928,000	21.6	-0.10	0.22
South-central Asia	1,764,872,000	28,326,000	1.6	2,475,685,000	38,950,000	1.6	0.85	0.80
South-eastern Asia	593,415,000	158,923,000	26.8	759,208,000	174,588,000	23.0	0.62	0.24
Western Asia	231,995,000	455,000	0.2	395,367,000	799,000	0.2	1.34	1.42
Europe	**738,199,000**	**1,789,000**	**0.2**	**719,258,000**	**2,855,000**	**0.4**	**-0.06**	**1.18**
Eastern Europe	294,771,000	578,000	0.2	256,946,000	708,000	0.3	-0.34	0.51
Northern Europe	99,205,000	299,000	0.3	114,036,000	464,000	0.4	0.35	1.10
Southern Europe	155,171,000	88,400	0.1	155,229,000	158,000	0.1	0.00	1.46
Western Europe	189,052,000	824,000	0.4	193,047,000	1,524,000	0.8	0.05	1.55
Latin America	**590,082,000**	**759,000**	**0.1**	**750,954,000**	**1,658,000**	**0.2**	**0.60**	**1.97**
Caribbean	41,646,000	14,400	0.0	47,312,000	25,000	0.1	0.32	1.39
Central America	155,881,000	70,000	0.0	215,570,000	152,000	0.1	0.81	1.96
South America	392,555,000	674,000	0.2	488,072,000	1,481,000	0.3	0.55	1.99
Northern America	**344,529,000**	**4,454,000**	**1.3**	**446,864,000**	**8,851,000**	**2.0**	**0.65**	**1.73**
Oceania	**36,593,000**	**587,000**	**1.6**	**55,234,000**	**1,200,000**	**2.2**	**1.03**	**1.80**
Australia/New Zealand	26,637,000	562,000	2.1	37,063,000	1,155,000	3.1	0.83	1.82
Melanesia	8,748,000	15,000	0.2	16,586,000	28,400	0.2	1.61	1.61
Micronesia	536,000	9,100	1.7	726,000	15,200	2.1	0.76	1.29
Polynesia	673,000	610	0.1	859,000	1,800	0.2	0.61	2.74
Global	**6,895,889,000**	**494,881,000**	**7.2**	**9,306,130,000**	**556,286,000**	**6.0**	**0.75**	**0.29**

Data source: Todd M. Johnson and Brian J. Grim, eds., *World Religion Database* (Leiden/Boston: Brill, accessed January 2012).

Table 4.9 Countries with the most Buddhists, 2010–50.

	Country	Buddhists 2010	Country	Buddhists 2025	Country	Buddhists 2050
1	China	206,898,000	China	246,000,000	China	247,000,000
2	Japan	71,307,000	Japan	66,508,000	Thailand	61,178,000
3	Thailand	60,298,000	Thailand	63,337,000	Japan	58,040,000
4	Viet Nam	43,212,000	Viet Nam	47,905,000	Viet Nam	48,290,000
5	Myanmar	35,823,000	Myanmar	39,099,000	Myanmar	40,239,000
6	Sri Lanka	14,378,000	Sri Lanka	15,568,000	Sri Lanka	15,751,000
7	Cambodia	12,007,000	Cambodia	13,794,000	Cambodia	15,080,000
8	South Korea	11,954,000	India	12,500,000	India	14,800,000
9	India	8,772,000	South Korea	11,708,000	South Korea	11,290,000
10	Taiwan	6,145,000	Taiwan	6,400,000	United States	8,000,000

Data source: Todd M. Johnson and Brian J. Grim, eds., *World Religion Database* (Leiden/Boston: Brill, accessed January 2012).

The expected decline (in global percentage) of agnostics and atheists by 2050 provides evidence for the quantitative resiliency of religion over the next 40 years. Purely demographic changes do not show a precipitous decline in religious adherence. Religionists generally have higher birthrates than the non-religious and death rates for both are similar. The author's current understanding of the impact of secularization does not seem to indicate widespread conversions from the world's religions in the years to come. The burden of proof, then, falls to observers who state that massive conversions from religious adherence are expected or likely. At present, the best quantitative tools for projecting the religious future of mankind forecast the perseverance and even flourishing of religion.[20] By these estimates, religionists would make up 91.3% of the world's population in 2050, up from 80.8% in 1970 (when the percentage of non-religious peaked worldwide in the twentieth century). Early gains after 1970 in the percentage of religionists were as a result of the collapse of Communism in the Soviet Union, while future gains are likely to come from the resurgence of religion in China. These numbers, however, mask the fact that secularization will likely continue to deepen in Western countries such as Sweden, where over 35% of the population is expected to be either agnostic or atheist by 2050.[21]

Research on the Future of Religion

Based on the advances made in both data collection and analytical techniques described in part II (Data and Methods), there are several pressing topics related to research on the future of religion. First, how will the global trend toward overall lower fertility affect the religious composition of nations and communities? For instance, as birthrates have plummeted in Western Europe, the demand for laborers has been filled in part through the immigration of large numbers of Muslims. Though fertility levels are dropping in most countries with Muslim majorities, the effects of past high fertility have created "youth bulges" that potentially will result in Muslim youth continuing to look outside their home countries for employment. Will the fertility levels of these

Table 4.10 Agnostics (A) by United Nations continents and regions, 2010–50.

Region	Population 2010	Agnostics 2010	% 2010	Population 2050	Agnostics 2050	% 2050	Pop.gr % 2010–50	A.gr % 2010–50
Africa	**1,022,234,000**	**6,497,000**	**0.6**	**2,191,597,000**	**16,530,000**	**0.8**	**1.92**	**2.36**
Eastern Africa	324,044,000	854,000	0.3	779,613,000	3,064,000	0.4	2.22	3.25
Middle Africa	126,689,000	727,000	0.6	278,350,000	2,915,000	1.0	1.99	3.53
Northern Africa	209,459,000	1,267,000	0.6	322,459,000	2,420,000	0.8	1.08	1.63
Southern Africa	57,780,000	2,765,000	4.8	67,326,000	4,967,000	7.4	0.38	1.48
Western Africa	304,261,000	884,000	0.3	743,849,000	3,163,000	0.4	2.26	3.24
Asia	**4,164,252,000**	**504,762,000**	**12.1**	**5,142,223,000**	**413,421,000**	**8.0**	**0.53**	**-0.50**
Eastern Asia	1,573,970,000	467,232,000	29.7	1,511,963,000	346,778,000	22.9	-0.10	-0.74
South-central Asia	1,764,872,000	17,302,000	1.0	2,475,685,000	35,001,000	1.4	0.85	1.78
South-eastern Asia	593,415,000	17,126,000	2.9	759,208,000	24,738,000	3.3	0.62	0.92
Western Asia	231,995,000	3,102,000	1.3	395,367,000	6,904,000	1.7	1.34	2.02
Europe	**738,199,000**	**93,325,000**	**12.6**	**719,258,000**	**107,167,000**	**14.9**	**-0.06**	**0.35**
Eastern Europe	294,771,000	23,612,000	8.0	256,946,000	11,326,000	4.4	-0.34	-1.82
Northern Europe	99,205,000	17,568,000	17.7	114,036,000	26,884,000	23.6	0.35	1.07
Southern Europe	155,171,000	13,262,000	8.5	155,229,000	17,431,000	11.2	0.00	0.69
Western Europe	189,052,000	38,882,000	20.6	193,047,000	51,525,000	26.7	0.05	0.71
Latin America	**590,082,000**	**18,712,000**	**3.2**	**750,954,000**	**44,208,000**	**5.9**	**0.60**	**2.17**
Caribbean	41,646,000	2,804,000	6.7	47,312,000	3,288,000	7.0	0.32	0.40
Central America	155,881,000	3,772,000	2.4	215,570,000	9,608,000	4.5	0.81	2.37
South America	392,555,000	12,136,000	3.1	488,072,000	31,312,000	6.4	0.55	2.40
Northern America	**344,529,000**	**48,119,000**	**14.0**	**446,864,000**	**83,072,000**	**18.6**	**0.65**	**1.37**
Oceania	**36,593,000**	**5,529,000**	**15.1**	**55,234,000**	**10,551,000**	**19.1**	**1.03**	**1.63**
Australia/New Zealand	26,637,000	5,433,000	20.4	37,063,000	10,298,000	27.8	0.83	1.61
Melanesia	8,748,000	74,600	0.9	16,586,000	198,000	1.2	1.61	2.47
Micronesia	536,000	6,600	1.2	726,000	20,700	2.9	0.76	2.90
Polynesia	673,000	14,800	2.2	859,000	34,600	4.0	0.61	2.15
Global	**6,895,889,000**	**676,944,000**	**9.8**	**9,306,130,000**	**674,949,000**	**7.3**	**0.75**	**-0.01**

Data source: Todd M. Johnson and Brian J. Grim, eds., *World Religion Database* (Leiden/Boston: Brill, accessed January 2012).

Table 4.11 Countries with the most agnostics, 2010–50.

Country	Agnostics 2010	Country	Agnostics 2025	Country	Agnostics 2050
1 China	437,155,000	China	400,000,000	China	315,283,000
2 United States	41,922,000	United States	56,150,000	United States	71,400,000
3 Germany	18,288,000	India	24,000,000	India	32,000,000
4 India	14,194,000	Germany	20,950,000	Germany	21,500,000
5 North Korea	13,648,000	UK	16,379,000	UK	19,750,000
6 Japan	12,873,000	France	15,000,000	France	17,500,000
7 UK	12,169,000	North Korea	14,183,000	Brazil	14,000,000
8 France	11,861,000	Japan	14,150,000	Japan	13,650,000
9 Viet Nam	11,109,000	Viet Nam	12,000,000	North Korea	13,285,000
10 Russia	8,653,000	Brazil	10,000,000	Nepal	4,700,000

Data source: Todd M. Johnson and Brian J. Grim, eds., *World Religion Database* (Leiden/Boston: Brill, accessed January 2012).

new, younger Muslim immigrants correspond to the generally lower fertility levels of their newfound homelands (the usual scenario), or will the newcomers persist in having family sizes more similar to those in their countries of origin? More generally, will new Muslim immigrants successfully integrate with largely non-Muslim societies, and how will that affect the religious outlook of the new arrivals, existing Muslim communities, and non-Muslims?

Second, will the religious future of the world be determined by Asia and sub-Saharan Africa, where, combined, seven in 10 people live today? This is important for assessing the strength of agnostic and atheist communities (China) and Christianity (sub-Saharan Africa). Also noteworthy is that not only Muslims immigrate to Western Europe – Hindus, Christians, and others of all faiths do so as well. How might emigrants to the more secularized lands of Europe from countries with high degrees of religiosity change the religious character of Europe?

Third, how can more accurate religious demographic measures be developed for religious populations? As noted earlier, the highest-quality projections for religious communities are built on cohort-component projections, but detailed data on cohorts are not available for most religious communities around the world. One obvious way to improve projections is to obtain more complete data for cohort-component projections. It is also particularly difficult to estimate the size of subgroups in other world religions; most figures for even basic religious identities such as Sunnis and Shi'as within Islam are tied not to census or survey data but primarily to ethnographic and historical analyses.[22] One way in which to obtain more accurate data on religious subgroups would be to develop better and more layered religious affiliation questions for future surveys. Interdisciplinary work is crucial for this process because, for instance, simply estimating how many people are associated with the four major schools of Islamic jurisprudence would require the cooperation of specialists in Islam, historians, anthropologists, ethnographers, and sociologists. (Obtaining detailed data via

Table 4.12 Atheists (a) by United Nations continents and regions, 2010–50.

Region	Population 2010	Atheists 2010	% 2010	Population 2050	Atheists 2050	% 2050	Pop gr % 2010–50	a.gr % 2010–50
Africa	**1,022,234,000**	**571,000**	**0.1**	**2,191,597,000**	**1,482,000**	**0.1**	**1.92**	**2.41**
Eastern Africa	324,044,000	113,000	0.0	779,613,000	316,000	0.0	2.22	2.60
Middle Africa	126,689,000	102,000	0.1	278,350,000	292,000	0.1	1.99	2.66
Northern Africa	209,459,000	147,000	0.1	322,459,000	275,000	0.1	1.08	1.58
Southern Africa	57,780,000	140,000	0.2	67,326,000	305,000	0.5	0.38	1.97
Western Africa	304,261,000	69,000	0.0	743,849,000	295,000	0.0	2.26	3.70
Asia	**4,164,252,000**	**114,851,000**	**2.8**	**5,142,223,000**	**106,123,000**	**2.1**	**0.53**	**-0.20**
Eastern Asia	1,573,970,000	105,421,000	6.7	1,511,963,000	94,062,000	6.2	-0.10	-0.28
South-central Asia	1,764,872,000	2,676,000	0.2	2,475,685,000	3,647,000	0.1	0.85	0.78
South-eastern Asia	593,415,000	6,408,000	1.1	759,208,000	7,774,000	1.0	0.62	0.48
Western Asia	231,995,000	347,000	0.1	395,367,000	640,000	0.2	1.34	1.54
Europe	**738,199,000**	**15,697,000**	**2.1**	**719,258,000**	**16,791,000**	**2.3**	**-0.06**	**0.17**
Eastern Europe	294,771,000	4,593,000	1.6	256,946,000	1,246,000	0.5	-0.34	-3.21
Northern Europe	99,205,000	2,423,000	2.4	114,036,000	3,438,000	3.0	0.35	0.88
Southern Europe	155,171,000	3,263,000	2.1	155,229,000	4,087,000	2.6	0.00	0.56
Western Europe	189,052,000	5,417,000	2.9	193,047,000	8,021,000	4.2	0.05	0.99
Latin America	**590,082,000**	**2,900,000**	**0.5**	**750,954,000**	**4,361,000**	**0.6**	**0.60**	**1.03**
Caribbean	41,646,000	645,000	1.5	47,312,000	549,000	1.2	0.32	-0.40
Central America	155,881,000	240,000	0.2	215,570,000	625,000	0.3	0.81	2.42
South America	392,555,000	2,014,000	0.5	488,072,000	3,187,000	0.7	0.55	1.15
Northern America	**344,529,000**	**2,156,000**	**0.6**	**446,864,000**	**2,951,000**	**0.7**	**0.65**	**0.79**
Oceania	**36,593,000**	**477,000**	**1.3**	**55,234,000**	**906,000**	**1.6**	**1.03**	**1.62**
Australia/New Zealand	26,637,000	470,000	1.8	37,063,000	890,000	2.4	0.83	1.61
Melanesia	8,748,000	5,200	0.1	16,586,000	11,600	0.1	1.61	2.03
Micronesia	536,000	230	0.0	726,000	950	0.1	0.76	3.61
Polynesia	673,000	1,600	0.2	859,000	3,100	0.4	0.61	1.67
Global	**6,895,889,000**	**136,652,000**	**2.0**	**9,306,130,000**	**132,613,000**	**1.4**	**0.75**	**-0.07**

Data source: Todd M. Johnson and Brian J. Grim, eds., *World Religion Database* (Leiden/Boston: Brill, accessed January 2012).

Table 4.13   Countries with the most atheists, 2010–50.

	Country	Atheists 2010	Country	Atheists 2025	Country	Atheists 2050
1	China	97,643,000	China	90,000,000	China	85,000,000
2	Viet Nam	5,810,000	Viet Nam	6,000,000	Viet Nam	6,400,000
3	North Korea	3,793,000	Japan	4,500,000	Japan	4,562,000
4	Japan	3,630,000	North Korea	3,950,000	France	4,400,000
5	France	2,596,000	France	3,300,000	North Korea	4,000,000
6	Italy	2,178,000	India	2,600,000	India	3,300,000
7	Germany	2,056,000	Italy	2,500,000	Italy	2,750,000
8	India	1,954,000	Germany	2,274,000	Germany	2,350,000
9	Russia	1,512,000	United States	1,500,000	United States	1,800,000
10	Ukraine	1,398,000	Sweden	1,365,000	Sweden	1,600,000

Data source: Todd M. Johnson and Brian J. Grim, eds., *World Religion Database* (Leiden/Boston: Brill, accessed January 2012).

censuses or other methods would require collaboration among even more groups – including governments – some of whom are likely to see cooperation as a threat to their vested interests.) Along these lines, tracking conversion rates is a pressing and underdeveloped demographic issue. Future work should aim to develop better estimations of how many people exit religious communities, convert to different religions, and revert to previous religious affiliations at later stages of life.

Fourth, does increasing religious diversity lead to less social solidarity and more conflict (the "clash of civilizations" theory)?[23] To answer this, religious demographers need to present data on religious diversity in ways that can be related to statistics on conflicts so that such a proposition can be tested. Some initial empirical tests have been done,[24] but much more work remains before the full picture of how religious plurality, and different configurations of religious plurality, relate to social solidarity and conflict.

Going forward, it is important to consider that the limits of demographic projection methodologies are real. For instance, traditional demographic analysis focusing on fertility, age structure, and life expectancy to project the religious composition of Africa over the twentieth century, had it been done around 1900, would never have predicted the dramatic growth of Christianity from less than 10% in 1900 to approximately 60% in 2000/2010, because most of the growth was a result of conversion. Likewise, global migration patterns of today would have been difficult to predict during the time of the Cold War (1950s–80s). Given such limits, in what ways can future projections construct various scenarios that take into account religion-specific processes of the future – that truly consider economic and environmental impacts?

The most important challenge for international religious demography remains the development of more accurate systems for measuring and analyzing both the present and the past, which form the basis of any future projections. These improved systems will allow future researchers to answer, or at least answer more accurately, many of the hotly debated issues of the current generation of social scientists, such as the role of modernization in the level of secularization. Perhaps futurist Warren Wagar phrased it best: "As futurists, we are really out of our depth in trying to chart the far future of religion."[25]

Notes

1   Pew Forum on Religion and Public Life, *Tolerance and Tension: Islam and Christianity in Sub-Saharan Africa*, April 15, 2010, http://www.pewforum.org/executive-summary-islam-and-christianity-in-sub-saharan-africa.aspx.

2   The current resurgence of religion in China is mainly limited to Buddhism, Daoism, Confucianism, Christianity, and Islam. If Chinese folk-religions experience an eventual resurgence, then this projection will be too conservative.

3   Muslims continue to experience higher than average worldwide fertility rates, whereas Daoists are growing because of a religious resurgence in China.

4   The result of losing demographic momentum through low fertility or losing members to majority world religions such as Islam, Christianity, Hinduism, or Buddhism.

5   On Jewish demography, see Sergio DellaPergola, *World Jewish Population, 2010* (Storrs, CT: Mandell L. Berman Institute, 2010). On wider trends, see Michael Brown and Bernard Lightman, eds., *Creating the Jewish Future* (Walnut Creek, CA: Altamira Press, 1999).

6   This includes an increase of Hindus from 933 million in 2010 to 1.2 billion in 2050; Muslims from 632 million in 2010 to 931 million in 2050.

7   Data for this section were obtained by using the year 2010 as a base from which to project all future figures, first using only demographic tools. Future country and regional total populations reflect United Nations projections, with all religious percentages within a country or region initially remaining unchanged. By varying only the rates of natural growth or decline, an observer can then examine their effects within a particular country or region on populations of religious adherents. This yields remarkable insights into what one might expect from the most consistent sources of growth and decline in religious and non-religious adherence – births and deaths.

8   Data are from United Nations, *World Population Prospects: The 2010 Revision* (Blue Ridge Summit, PA: United Nations Publications, 2012). Note that if a religious population is near 100% of a country's population, then the United Nations cohort data is applicable to the whole religious population. The challenge is estimating any variation from this in minority populations. If birth or death rates vary dramatically from the majority religious community, then the future share of that minority population can be very different from its present share.

9   Bermuda, Canada, Greenland, St Pierre & Miquelon, and the United States.

10   Includes Benin, Burkina Faso, Cape Verde, Gambia, Ghana, Guinea-Bissau, Ivory Coast, Liberia, Mali, Mauritania, Niger, Nigeria, St Helena, Senegal, Sierra Leone, and Togo.

11   See chapters 10 and 11 for an in-depth analysis of the world's Muslim population, both current and future.

12   These projections are based both on past demographic trends and on assumptions about how these trends will play out in future years. Making these projections inevitably entails a host of uncertainties, including significant political ones. Changes in the political climate in North America or Europe, for example, could dramatically affect the patterns of Muslim migration.

13   Future projections to 2050 for all religions are from data presented in Todd M. Johnson and Brian J. Grim, eds., *World Religion Database* (Leiden/Boston: Brill, 2008). Projections for the world's Muslim population to 2030 are data from the Pew Forum on Religion and

Public Life, *The Future of the Global Muslim Population, Projections for 2010–2030*, January 27, 2011, http://pewresearch.org/pubs/1872/muslim-population-projections-worldwide-fast-growth.

14 The greatest increases – driven primarily by continued migration – are likely to occur in Western and Northern Europe, where Muslims will be approaching double-digit percentages of the population in several countries. In the United Kingdom, for example, Muslims are expected to comprise 8.2% of the population in 2030, up from an estimated 4.6% in 2010. In Austria, Muslims are projected to reach 9.3% of the population in 2030, up from 5.7% in 2010; in Sweden, 9.9% (up from 4.9% in 2010); in Belgium, 10.2% (up from 6% in 2010); and in France, 10.3% (up from 7.5% in 2010).

15 Eric Kaufmann, *Shall the Religious Inherit the Earth? Demography and Politics in the Twenty-first Century* (London: Profile Books Ltd, 2010), 158–211.

16 See chapter 10 for more details regarding factors driving Muslim population growth.

17 Pew Forum on Religion and Public Life, *The Future of the Global Muslim Population*.

18 It is well known that popular religion in China draws on the "Three Teachings," one of which is Buddhism. This understanding of Chinese popular religion raises the suggestion that the religious group known as "Chinese folk-religionists" could be considered "Buddhists." Such enumeration may better reflect the broader influence and inclusion of Buddhism among the Chinese. Additionally, in practice, even the non-religious in China are seriously impacted by Buddhism in both worldview and key rituals. The concept of wider Buddhism, then, would include all professing Buddhists plus all Chinese folk-religionists and Chinese non-religious.

19 Figures for 2050 for Chinese folk-religionists, Confucianists, and Daoists are available online in Johnson and Grim, *World Religion Database*.

20 Todd M. Johnson and David B. Barrett, "Quantifying Alternate Futures of Religion and Religions," *Futures* 36:9 (November 2004): 960.

21 Johnson and Grim, *World Religion Database*.

22 See Pew Forum on Religion and Public Life, *Mapping the Global Muslim Population: A Report on the Size and Distribution of the World's Muslim Population*, October 7, 2009, http://www.pewforum.org/Mapping-the-Global-Muslim-Population.aspx, 38.

23 Samuel P. Huntington, *The Clash of Civilizations and the Remaking of World Order* (New York: Simon & Schuster, 1996).

24 Brian J. Grim and Roger Finke, "Religious Persecution in Cross-National Context: Clashing Civilizations or Regulated Economies?" *American Sociological Review* 72:4 (2007): 633–58.

25 Warren Wagar, *The Next Three Futures: Paradigms of Things to Come* (Santa Barbara: Praeger, 1991), 40.

References

Brown, Michael, and Bernard Lightman, eds. *Creating the Jewish Future*. Walnut Creek, CA: Altamira Press, 1999.

DellaPergola, Sergio. *World Jewish Population, 2010*. Storrs, CT: Mandell L. Berman Institute, 2010.

Grim, Brian J., and Roger Finke. "Religious Persecution in Cross-National Context: Clashing Civilizations or Regulated Economies?" *American Sociological Review* 72:4 (2007): 633–58.

Huntington, Samuel P. *The Clash of Civilizations and the Remaking of World Order*. New York: Simon & Schuster, 1996.

Johnson, Todd M., and David B. Barrett. "Quantifying Alternate Futures of Religion and Religions." *Futures* 36:9 (2004): 947–60.

Johnson, Todd M., and Brian J. Grim, eds. *World Religion Database*. Leiden/Boston: Brill, 2008.

Kaufmann, Eric. *Shall the Religious Inherit the Earth? Demography and Politics in the Twenty-First Century*. London: Profile Books Ltd, 2010.

Pew Forum on Religion and Public Life. *Mapping the Global Muslim Population: A Report on the Size and Distribution of the World's Muslim Population*. October 7, 2009. http://www.pewforum.org/Mapping-the-Global-Muslim-Population.aspx.

Pew Forum on Religion and Public Life. *The Future of the Global Muslim Population: Projections for 2010–2030*. January 27, 2011. http://pewresearch.org/pubs/1872/muslim-population-projections-worldwide-fast-growth.

Pew Forum on Religion and Public Life. *Tolerance and Tension: Islam and Christianity in Sub-Saharan Africa*. April 15, 2010. http://www.pewforum.org/executive-summary-islam-and-christianity-in-sub-saharan-africa.aspx.

United Nations. *World Population Prospects: The 2010 Revision*. Blue Ridge Summit, PA: United Nations Publications, 2012.

Wagar, Warren. *The Next Three Futures: Paradigms of Things to Come*. Santa Barbara: Praeger, 1991.

Part II
Data and Methods

Chapter 5
Defining Religion and Religious Identity

A starting point in pursuing religious demography is defining what is meant by "religion." While an entire field of study has been dedicated to this subject, a few observations here will at the very least set the subject in its wider context. In one sense, the answer is simple and straightforward, with helpful definitions offered by luminaries such as Émile Durkheim, who stated in his most popular definition of religion, "A religion is a unified system of beliefs and practices relative to sacred things, that is to say, things set apart and forbidden – beliefs and practices which unite into one single moral community called a Church, all those who adhere to them."[1] More recent scholarship has admitted that definitions are not set forth without context or perspective. In fact, the Durkheimian definition of religion, while important as a historical foundation, has been almost universally set aside because it seems not to fit modern circumstances. Organized religion simply does not function according to Durkheim's imagined dichotomy of sacred and profane.[2] Scholars of religion ask the question about who is demanding a definition of religion, why, and with what consequences. As sociologist Alan Aldridge has observed, "Defining religion involves an exercise of power."[3] Taking this notion a step further, scholars of religion such as Jonathan Smith posit, "there is [sic] no data for religion. Religion is solely the creation of the scholar's study."[4] With this in mind it is easy to see that efforts to define religion ultimately will be fraught with limitations, thus making explicit statements of underlying assumptions critical.

For religious demographers, the main challenge is to generate a definition of religion and to build a taxonomy based on that definition that allows for a comparative quantitative analysis of categories. Given the uncertainties accompanying foundational definitions of religion, however, it is easy to agree with scholars such as Aldridge that "It is doubtful that we shall ever arrive at a universally agreed classification of religious movements that will stand for all time."[5] His conclusion is predicated on the same

The World's Religions in Figures: An Introduction to International Religious Demography,
First Edition. Todd M. Johnson and Brian J. Grim.
© 2013 John Wiley & Sons, Ltd. Published 2013 by John Wiley & Sons, Ltd.

reason that there cannot be a universal definition of society and culture – they are constantly changing, and religion changes with them. Religion scholar Catherine Albanese observes that everyone knows what religion is until they try to define it. "Religion cannot be defined very easily because it thrives both within and outside of boundaries," she states, and it encompasses all of human life.[6] Albanese suggests that trying to describe religion might be better than attempting to define it. Defining religion would involve identifying territorial boundaries, temporal boundaries, and language boundaries, among others. She also observes that included in most definitions of religion are the "4 C's": creed (explanations of human life), code (rules that govern everyday behavior), cultus (rituals for acting out insights gleaned from creeds and codes), and community (groups of people formally or informally bound together by creed, code, and cultus).

Knowing how to differentiate among elements that distinguish populations is critical for identifying religious groups that can be enumerated. Religious identity is established early in life and often reinforced throughout adulthood.[7] It provides a comprehensive worldview that allows individuals to make sense of daily life. In doing so, individuals develop a cultural framework and boundaries for right and wrong, which ultimately play an important role in shaping societal attitudes.[8] Sociologist Clifford Geertz also claimed that religion demarcates group boundaries that define who is "in" and who is not.[9] Furthermore, religious identity can become intertwined with national and/or social identity, making it even more difficult to establish boundaries. All of these points are important for religious demographers as they attempt to define their own boundaries for what religion is and is not.

Nonetheless, even with all of these caveats, it is necessary to go forward in establishing a definition of religion in order to utilize the thousands of sources of quantitative information on religion. It is also important to recognize that the challenge of defining religious categories is faced first by those who produce source material on a national or regional basis. For example, the Australian government admits that it is difficult, if not impossible, to give a precise definition for "religion" in preparing religious categories for the decennial census. Nonetheless, they conclude that "generally, a religion is regarded as a set of beliefs and practices, usually involving acknowledgment of a divine or higher being or power, by which people order the conduct of their lives both practically and in a moral sense."[10] Under this kind of pragmatic definition, Buddhism is universally accepted as a religion despite its lack of a personal God, and Confucianism is regarded as religion despite its lack of teaching on the supernatural (it provides a moral code for adherents). In contrast, political philosophies are excluded from the definition of religion not only in the Australian census but also in most discussions of religion in general.

Knowing that no single definition of religion is sufficient, we use the following as our operational definition. Our definition requires that religion be more than just a single person's idiosyncratic beliefs: religion is defined as an organized group of committed individuals that adhere to and propagate a specific interpretation of explanations of existence based on supernatural assumptions through statements about the nature and workings of the supernatural and about ultimate meaning.[11] In this volume, religion as used in a demographic sense includes the unaffiliated (i.e., agnostics and atheists).

How Many Religions, and What Religions, Are World Religions?

Defining world religions

Social scientists usually describe the world of religions numerically by listing the seven or eight largest or best-known world religions,[12] along with the number of followers for each. This is valuable as a succinct global summary, but if it is not expanded further, such listings become gross oversimplifications of what is in fact a vast global complex of thousands of distinct and different religions. Accurately portraying the world's religious landscape really requires a comprehensive global investigation, description, typology, and classification of all religions. With this in mind, defining, describing, and classifying religions can be accomplished in a myriad of ways. Typically, definitions are based on beliefs, systems of belief, dogmas, doctrines, philosophies, origins, histories, founders, and current personalities. Such a comparative approach is intensely interesting and valuable for the understanding of religion that it provides. Unfortunately, this approach often ignores statistical enumeration as of little value in understanding religious issues.

Size, however, is not the only consideration when determining what makes a religion a "world" religion. Religious movements that define themselves as world religions are very likely to become world religions, more so than religious movements that do *not* make such claims about themselves.[13] A case in point is the Baha'i faith: although normally considered a world religion by religious scholars, it currently has only around 7 million adherents globally. Despite its comparatively small size, however, the Baha'i faith is more widespread than any other religion except Christianity. The Baha'i faith fulfills the self-identifying "world religion" claim quite well, as a religion that is "emically and normatively defined and portrayed through the doctrine of progressive revelation not only as *a* world religion but as *the* world religion."[14] In a sense, then, the making of a "world" religion can be something of a self-fulfilling prophecy.

Defining new religions

Another challenge relates to the difficulty in defining new religions. How does one differentiate between a "new" religion and "old" or established ones? Curiously, even publically available data that might be useful in answering this question have gone largely unanalyzed. James Lewis, a scholar specializing in new religious movements, notes, for example, that no one has attempted a taxonomical analysis of the four censuses of English-speaking countries (New Zealand, Australia, Canada, and the United Kingdom) that collected information on religious membership, including select new religions.[15] Further complicating the picture is the perennial problem of classifying movements. For example, scholars tend to classify Soka Gakkai, a movement dating from 1930 within Nichiren Buddhism, as New Religionist rather than Buddhist. At the same time, however, they classify many newer churches, such as the Church of Jesus Christ of Latter-day Saints or the Brazilian Igreja Universal do Reino de Deus, as Christian rather than New Religionist.

Defining folk religion

Defining and enumerating popular or folk religion can be difficult as well. Scholars have offered definitions such as "religion of ordinary folk, [lying] to some extent outside the realms of institutional, established beliefs and practices."[16] Another, more detailed, definition states, "The religious life of ordinary people who are not primarily oriented toward their religion as it is presented by its formal history, but who know and practice it as it is communicated and performed on family, village, or popular levels."[17]

In theory, the definitions above are fairly straightforward. The difficulty lies in the reality that so much folk-religious practice is intertwined with practices and beliefs of other world religions. An example of this is Daoism and folk religion in Taiwan. Daoists could in theory be defined according to historical rituals, theology, and organizational structure, but under this definition there would technically be no Daoists in Taiwan. Such a definition helps delineate between Daoists and folk religionists but does not give an adequate picture of religious practice in Taiwan.[18] China is an interesting example in this regard. The country experienced fierce anti-religious reforms in the twentieth century, and as a consequence the majority of the population identifies as non-religious (atheist or agnostic). However, China is actually a religious country "by virtue of its rich and widespread traditions of religious practice (when and where allowed), beliefs, and religious life, especially in rural areas and among ethnic minorities throughout the country."[19] Many of China's non-religious actually recognize beliefs and practices of many of the world's religions.

Doubly affiliated religionists

Finally, one must confront the issue of mutually exclusive categories in any taxonomy of religion. A burgeoning literature already is available on people who specifically identify themselves as adherents of more than one religion, a phenomenon known as multiple religious belonging or double belonging.[20] According to Catherine Cornille, a preeminent scholar on the subject, this religious phenomenon may be understood in three primary ways.[21] The first works off the assumption of unity among all the world's religions, making all religions expressions of the same reality and same experience. A second view requires, as she states, "remaining faithful to the symbolic framework of one tradition while adopting the hermeneutical frame of another."[22] Paul Knitter's double affiliation to Buddhism and Roman Catholicism, described in his 2009 book *Without Buddha I Could not be a Christian*, exemplifies this second view. The third approach is a general acknowledgment of the complementarity of religions; that is, all religions existing alongside one another, equally authentic and containing truth.[23] This last view generally aligns with religious life in an Asian context. To be Asian is in many ways to be inter-religious.[24] Some scholars hold that monotheistic religions are outside the scope of multiple religious belonging, claiming that the beliefs of each are mutually exclusive.[25] Others, however, have made claims of Muslim–Christian double belonging,[26] not to mention the issue of Messianic Jews sharing traditions, beliefs, and theology from both Judaism and Christianity.[27]

The best statistical approach to the question of multiple religious belonging would be to allow double counting in the numbers (that is, allow people to self-identify as both Buddhist and Christian, for example) and then utilize a negative number to reconcile totals back to 100%.[28] However, the data on these categories are not complete enough to allow for such a comprehensive picture at this time.

Defining not "Religion" but "a Religion"

One's area of interest will determine whether the object of study is the abstract category "religion" or the more specific category "a religion." For any scientific study of the latter, concrete aspects such as size, language, race, ethnicity, location, age, and relation to other religions are as important as the more philosophical considerations. This section of this chapter therefore attempts to present a taxonomy in which all religions can be listed with comparable variables that can be contrasted, listed, ranked, added, and totaled to give the overall global situation. For this purpose, a religion is compared and analyzed here *not* by its dogmas, beliefs, or practices, but primarily by its followers or believers or *adherents*, also termed here *religionists*.

A religion therefore is defined here as a religious community of believers, followers, or adherents who hold there to be something distinctive in their beliefs, and who give their primary religious allegiance and loyalty to that religion. What this means is that the basic unit of study and analysis here is a specific religion with its religionists, with a short list of features that can be described and measured. Note also that although our preferred terms for those belonging to a religion are (in this order) followers, believers, or adherents, these terms are used here as exact synonyms, with wide use of "adherents" as a slightly more technical sociological term. A distinct religion is defined here by its adherents' loyalty to it. They accept it as in some sense unique (and, sometimes, superior) to all other religions, even those closely related to it. In practice, adherents ignore other religions, not necessarily willfully or deliberately. In practice they can get along without depending on the existence of any or all other religions or their adherents. They do not need each other's existence, and get along well without it. In this definition, therefore, they are all distinct religions – however, this does not necessitate poor relations to exist between them all.[29]

The largest single specific family of religions in the world today is "ethnoreligions" (also called elsewhere "tribal religions").[30] These are religions each confined to members of one single ethnolinguistic people, tribe, or culture. No persons outside the tribe may join; no members may leave (although in this present analysis members who have joined another religion, for example Christianity or Islam, are no longer enumerated in an ethnoreligion's demographic totals). In most cases an ethnoreligion has a unique name for God or the Creator, or a complex of names for God or the gods. An ethnoreligion is also likely to have unique creation and/or flood and related stories, unique ethics and practices, and usually its own unique language, all of which function to exclude aliens from other tribes or people groups.

Thus, in our quest to find a practical way to measure religionists, we settle on an instrumental view of religion, in which followers or adherents are not only the main focus, but the starting place for definitions and dividing lines, both between religions (such as Christianity and Islam) and within religions (such as the Buddhist schools of Theravada and Mahayana). This approach aligns most closely with our major sources: government censuses, surveys, and reports from the religious communities themselves. In taking this approach we do not in any way minimize the important discussions taking place among scholars about definitions and classification in religion. We simply look for a way that is practical and makes good use of an ongoing international collection of data.

Notes

1 Émile Durkheim, *Les formes élémentaires de la vie religieuse* [The Elementary Forms of Religious Life] (London: G. Allen & Unwin, 1915), 47.

2 Kevin J. Christiano, William H. Swatos, and Peter Kivisto, *Sociology of Religion: Contemporary Developments* (Lanham, MD: Rowman & Littlefield Publishers, Inc., 2008), 36.

3 Alan Aldridge, *Religion in the Contemporary World: A Sociological Introduction* (Cambridge: Polity Press, 2007), 23.

4 Jonathan Z. Smith, *Imagining Religion: From Babylon to Jonestown* (Chicago: University of Chicago Press, 1982), xi.

5 Ibid., 55.

6 Catherine L. Albanese, *America: Religions and Religion*, 2nd ed. (Belmont, CA: Wadsworth Publishing Company, 1992), 2–16.

7 Jack Citrin, Beth A. Reingold, and Donald Philip Green, *American Identity and the Politics of Ethnic Change* (Berkeley: University of California Press, 1990).

8 Eric Leon McDaniel, Irfan Nooruddin, and Allyson Faith Shortle, "Divine Boundaries: How Religion Shapes Citizens' Attitudes Toward Immigrants," *American Politics Research* 39:1 (January 2011): 211–12.

9 Clifford Geertz, *The Interpretation of Cultures: Selected Essays* (New York: Basic Books, 1993).

10 Australia Bureau of Statistics, "1266.0 – Australian Standard Classification of Religious Groups (ASCRG), 1996," http://www.abs.gov.au/ausstats/abs@.nsf/0/775012EF005 8A77DCA25697E00184BDC?opendocument.

11 A similar definition is offered by Brian J. Grim in "The Defacto and Dejure Regulation of Religion," PhD dissertation, Pennsylvania State University, 2005.

12 Christianity, Islam, Hinduism, Buddhism, Judaism, agnosticism, atheism, and sometimes ethnoreligions. Religious scholar George Chryssides notes that Sikhism has been added to the list, and some scholars advocate for Baha'i faith to be added as well as an "emergent global religion." See George Chryssides, "The Concept of a World Religion," in *The Study of Religion: An Introduction to Key Ideas and Methods*, ed. George D. Chryssides and Ron Geaves (London: Continuum, 2007), 66.

13 Moshe Sharon, "New Religions and Religious Movements: The Common Heritage," in *Studies in Modern Religions, Religious Movements and the Bābī-Bahā'ī Faiths*, ed. Moshe Sharon (Leiden: Brill, 2004), 313.

14 Ibid., 314.

15 James R. Lewis, "New Religion Adherents: An Overview of Anglophone Census and Survey Data," *Marburg Journal of Religion* 9:1 (September 2004): 1–17.

16 Jeaneane Fowler and Merv Fowler, *Chinese Religions: Beliefs and Practices* (Eastbourne: Sussex Academic Press, 2008), 224.

17 Robert S. Ellwood and Gregory D. Alles, *The Encyclopedia of World Religions*, rev. ed. (New York: Facts on File Inc., 2007), 153.

18 Chenng-Tian Kuo, *Religion and Democracy in Taiwan* (Albany: State University of New York Press, 2008), 56–7.

19 Zhibin Xie, *Religious Diversity and Public Religion in China* (Aldershot: Ashgate Publishing Limited, 2006), 71.

20 See, for example, Sylvia Boorstein, *That's Funny, You Don't Look Buddhist: On Being a Faithful Jew and a Passionate Buddhist* (New York: HarperOne, 1998); Paul F. Knitter, *Without Buddha I Could not be a Christian* (Oxford: OneWorld Publications, 2009).

21 Catherine Cornille, ed., *Many Mansions: Multiple Religious Belonging and Christian Identity* (Maryknoll, NY: Orbis Books, 2002).

22 Ibid., 5.

23 Catherine Cornille, "Introduction," in Cornille, ed., *Many Mansions? Multiple Religious Belonging and Christian Identity*, 1–6.

24 Peter Phan, *Being Religious Interreligiously: Asian Perspectives on Interreligious Dialogue* (Maryknoll, NY: Orbis Books, 2004), 127.

25 John Cobb, "Multiple Religious Belonging and Reconciliation," in Cornille, ed., *Many Mansions? Multiple Religious Belonging and Christian Identity*, 23.

26 See Miroslav Volf, Ghazi bin Muhammad, and Melissa Yarrington, eds, *A Common Word: Muslims and Christians on Loving God and Neighbor* (Grand Rapids, MI: Wm. B. Eerdmans Publishing Co., 2010).

27 See Richard Harvey, *Mapping Messianic Jewish Theology: A Constructive Approach* (Milton Keynes, UK: Paternoster, 2009).

28 For example, if, in a population of 1,000 people, 400 identified as Buddhist, 400 as Christian, and 200 as Buddhist and Christian, then one might report that there are 600 Buddhists and 600 Christians. In a column of figures such an approach would require a –200 to arrive back at 1,000 people. One would still have the choice of reporting the population as 60% Buddhist and 60% Christian, or 50% Buddhist and 50% Christian.

29 David B. Barrett, Todd M. Johnson, Christopher Guidry, and Peter Crossing, *World Christian Trends, AD 30–AD 2200: Interpreting the Annual Christian Megacensus* (Pasadena, CA: William Carey Library Publication, 2003), 551–6.

30 Tribal religion or traditional religion has been recently rehabilitated in the study of religion. Religious scholar Ezra Chitando notes that "generations of European writers had dismissed African Traditional Religions as superstition, magic, idolatry, and a host of other condescending labels. African scholars have repositioned the study of African Traditional Religions as viable academic undertaking ... it was Africans such as John Mbiti and E. Bolaji Idowu who proceeded to formulate principles for the study of African Traditional Religions. They provided a more balanced perspective and illustrated the centrality of religion to African life." Ezra Chitando, "Sub-Saharan Africa," in *Religious Studies: A Global View*, ed. Gregory D. Alles (London: Routledge, 2008), 109.

References

Albanese, Catherine L. *America: Religions and Religion*. 2nd ed. Belmont, CA: Wadsworth Publishing Company, 1992.

Aldridge, Alan. *Religion in the Contemporary World: A Sociological Introduction*. Cambridge: Polity Press, 2007.

Australia Bureau of Statistics. "1266.0 – Australian Standard Classification of Religious Groups (ASCRG), 1996." http://www.abs.gov.au/ausstats/abs@.nsf/0/775012EF0058A77DC A25697E00184BDC?opendocument.

Barrett, David B., Todd M. Johnson, Christopher Guidry, and Peter Crossing. *World Christian Trends, AD 30–AD 2200: Interpreting the Annual Christian Megacensus*. Pasadena, CA: William Carey Library Publication, 2003.

Boorstein, Sylvia. *That's Funny, You Don't Look Buddhist: On Being a Faithful Jew and a Passionate Buddhist*. New York: HarperOne, 1998.

Chitando, Ezra. "Sub-Saharan Africa." In *Religious Studies: A Global View*, edited by Gregory D. Alles, 102–25. London: Routledge, 2008.

Christiano, Kevin J., William H. Swatos, and Peter Kivisto. *Sociology of Religion: Contemporary Developments*. Lanham, MD: Rowman & Littlefield Publishers, Inc., 2008.

Chryssides, George. "The Concept of a World Religion." In *The Study of Religion: An Introduction to Key Ideas and Methods*, edited by George D. Chryssides and Ron Geaves, 65–109. London: Continuum, 2007.

Citrin, Jack, Beth A. Reingold, and Donald Philip Green. *American Identity and the Politics of Ethnic Change*. Berkeley: University of California Press, 1990.

Cobb, John. "Multiple Religious Belonging and Reconciliation." In *Many Mansions? Multiple Religious Belonging and Christian Identity*, edited by Catherine Cornille, 20–28. Maryknoll, NY: Orbis Books, 2002.

Cornille, Catherine, ed. *Many Mansions: Multiple Religious Belonging and Christian Identity*. Maryknoll, NY: Orbis Books, 2002.

Durkheim, Émile. *Les formes élémentaires de la vie religieuse* [The Elementary Forms of Religious Life]. London: G. Allen & Unwin, 1915.

Ellwood, Robert S., and Gregory D. Alles. *The Encyclopedia of World Religions*. Rev. ed. New York: Facts on File Inc., 2007.

Fowler, Jeaneane, and Merv Fowler. *Chinese Religions: Beliefs and Practices*. Eastbourne: Sussex Academic Press, 2008.

Geertz, Clifford. *The Interpretation of Cultures: Selected Essays*. New York: Basic Books, 1993.

Grim, Brian J. "The Defacto and Dejure Regulation of Religion." PhD diss., Pennsylvania State University, 2005.

Harvey, Richard. *Mapping Messianic Jewish Theology: A Constructive Approach*. Milton Keynes, UK: Paternoster, 2009.

Knitter, Paul F. *Without Buddha I Could not be a Christian*. Oxford: OneWorld Publications, 2009.

Kuo, Chenng-Tian. *Religion and Democracy in Taiwan*. Albany: State University of New York Press, 2008.

Lewis, James R. "New Religion Adherents: An Overview of Anglophone Census and Survey Data." *Marburg Journal of Religion* 9:1 (September 2004): 1–17.

McDaniel, Eric Leon, Irfan Nooruddin, and Allyson Faith Shortle. "Divine Boundaries: How Religion Shapes Citizens' Attitudes Toward Immigrants." *American Politics Research* 39: 1 (January 2011): 205–33.

Phan, Peter. *Being Religious Interreligiously: Asian Perspectives on Interreligious Dialogue*. Maryknoll, NY: Orbis Books, 2004.

Sharon, Moshe. "New Religions and Religious Movements: The Common Heritage." In *Studies in Modern Religions, Religious Movements and the Bābī-Bahā'ī Faiths*, edited by Moshe Sharon, 3–40. Leiden: Brill, 2004.

Smith, Jonathan Z. *Imagining Religion: From Babylon to Jonestown*. Chicago: University of Chicago Press, 1982.

Volf, Miroslav, Ghazi bin Muhammad, and Melissa Yarrington, eds. *A Common Word: Muslims and Christians on Loving God and Neighbor*. Grand Rapids, MI: Wm. B. Eerdmans Publishing Co., 2010.

Xie, Zhibin. *Religious Diversity and Public Religion in China*. Aldershot: Ashgate Publishing Limited, 2006.

Chapter 6

Religious Demography as an Emerging Discipline

Demography is the statistical study of human population characteristics, such as size, fertility, mortality, migration, net growth, and location. Social demography focuses on a broader array of human characteristics related to populations, ranging from health and economic indicators to language and religion. Religious demography is the scientific and statistical study of the demographic characteristics of religious populations, primarily with respect to their size, age–sex structure, density, growth, distribution, development, migration, and vital statistics, including the change of religious identity within human populations and how these characteristics relate to other social and economic indicators. Since the middle of the twentieth century, all of these aspects of demography have been burgeoning fields of study.

Demography as a Growing Field of Study

Social scientists generally recognize that demography is essential to understanding the human condition, especially for policy makers. Understanding changes in human populations (and the reasons for such changes) includes taking into consideration factors such as births, deaths, fertility, migration, population density, male-to-female ratios, and other issues that aid social scientists in understanding how society as a whole functions, on both the individual and institutional levels. The importance of demography also extends beyond the scientific community, to people who are simply interested in how these factors affect their daily lives as local and global citizens.[1]

Although census data have been collected since ancient times (for example, in Egypt, Babylon, Persia, India, and China[2]), only with the rise of the nation state in nineteenth-century Europe, and subsequently, the United States, have more

The World's Religions in Figures: An Introduction to International Religious Demography,
First Edition. Todd M. Johnson and Brian J. Grim.
© 2013 John Wiley & Sons, Ltd. Published 2013 by John Wiley & Sons, Ltd.

comprehensive censuses emerged.[3] More recently, in the past 50 years, demographers (largely in the Western world) have analyzed an enormous body of data out of concern regarding worldwide population explosion.[4] John Caldwell states that, "The remarkable expansion of demography in the second half of the twentieth century was largely the product of concern about 'population explosion' in the developing world during a period of unprecedented international technical assistance."[5] This includes the monumental United Nations work on tracking changes in population, which results in a comprehensive survey of human populations published every two years as *World Population Prospects*. The work of the United Nations, a pioneer in the field, was largely Eurocentric and heavily influenced by Western ideas upon its founding in 1945. However, it has since helped to establish demographic research centers in Africa, Asia, and Latin America, a significant shift in the study of demography.[6]

By the end of World War II, demography had matured as an institutionalized, scientific field of inquiry. It did so by taking pieces of other fields (such as fertility studies from biology and sociology, migration studies from economics and geography, and mortality studies from health sciences) and relating them directly to demographic trends.[7] Demographers accurately foresaw the huge population changes that occurred in the twentieth century (high fertility rates in the non-Western world and lower mortality rates around the world), which in a way legitimized the field among scholars and academics.[8]

Historically, the field of demography was not without its critics, even from within. Some demographers argued that the term "demography" should be limited to purely quantitative (mathematical) measurements of population, such as fertility, mortality, and migration. In addition, these internal critics advocated using the term "population studies" in reference to social, economic, and cultural consequences of demographic change,[9] as opposed to including both the quantitative measures and "population studies" together. Today, however, a broader definition of demography generally is accepted by demographers and social scientists – demography is assumed to include both parts.[10]

Changes in methodology

Newer to the study of demography is an interest in how demographic indicators change over time. This generally requires at least two points of data, and preferably three or more. With such information, it is possible to track trends and analyze changes over various time periods. Today, it is common to find demographic indicators presented in comparison to or contrast with earlier or later data. For example, it is widely understood, due to comparison of data points, that birthrates in much of Europe are profoundly lower today than they were in the mid-twentieth century. This data can be used to forecast what kinds of societal changes might occur, such as shifting attitudes towards childbearing and household dynamics.[11]

In addition, demographic data are now collected on various kinds of population groupings. In a geographic sense this can include countries, counties, or states. But it can also include gender, ethnicities, languages, age sets, and religions, to name a few. Once again, with these data, it is possible to provide comparisons between groups, such as the growth of the elderly population in many modern societies (such as Japan[12]) or disparities in the female/male sex ratio in India.[13]

Challenges, strengths, and weaknesses

A consistent challenge of contemporary demography is the struggle to maintain scientific objectivity. While demography addresses topics that are of interest to policy makers and the general public, it does so without being influenced by other forces, whether political or ideological.[14] Studies have shown, however, that demographers do not have the ability to wholly isolate their research from outside influences, despite claims that they can.[15]

The strengths of demography are easy to identify. The core of the discipline is mathematical, invoking an accepted, rigorous, academic field that seeks to establish and prove patterns. The field of demography is well funded, mainly by governments who also sponsor (along with private corporations) robust training programs. Many of the world's best institutions of higher learning (such as Princeton University and Brown University) have centers that focus on statistical population research and offer corresponding academic degrees. The field has strong boundaries in terms of what it studies, making it a narrow discipline, but has many interdisciplinary connections. Demography provides information that is vital to governments, policy makers, and developers, therefore making its research in high demand by individuals and institutions alike. Perhaps most importantly, demography adapts to address current issues.[16] An example of this is the use of data on population change (most notably, growth) in addressing issues of potential food and resource scarcity, a realm historically outside of the field but that has recently been seriously considered in light of demographic realities.

It is important, however, to acknowledge weaknesses of demographic approaches. Chief among these is that demography as a science is essentially limited in its ability to explain human behavior. Although demography is useful for tracking changes in populations, the field has a limited scope of concepts, methods, and tools for understanding those changes. For example, demographic methods are useful for detecting a decline in fertility in a population, but not necessarily for explaining the decline, which may be due to later marriages as women attain higher education and begin careers.[17] Demography is most effective when brought as a partner into an interdisciplinary team of sciences.

Other weaknesses to the field of demography include its ambiguous role in policy making. Organizations dictate what data are required for addressing a particular social reality, thus often limiting the scope of demography to problems that need solving. Funding agencies can therefore influence the direction of the field as a whole, again limiting the range of topics addressed. Demography as a whole also often reflects an ethnocentric attitude toward third-world situations, in light of the fact that the modern academic discipline was largely born in a colonial context. While demography's mathematical core is important for bolstering confidence in statistical reports, its heavy reliance on quantitative measures and data limitations imposes methodological constraints. An example of this is the risk that demographers can be too invested in, and therefore reluctant to move away from, standard surveys as an investigational technique.[18]

Religious Demography

The origins of the field of religious demography lie in the church censuses conducted in most European societies. For many years and in many countries, churches produced the most complete censuses of the population.[19] They achieved this largely by recording baptisms and funerals. These data, however, were seen not as referring to specific religious communities, but rather to the larger homogenous societies. With the decline of national churches in Europe beginning in the nineteenth and continuing into the twentieth century, secular governments began tracking births and deaths, eventually replacing churches as the main bodies collecting detailed information on human populations.

Although thousands of sources for international religious demography are available, ranging from censuses and demographic surveys to statistics collected and reported by religious groups themselves, little has been done by scholars in religion, sociology, or other disciplines to collect, collate, and analyze these data over the past decades. A simple search of the WorldCat and American Theological Library Association (ATLA) databases[20] on the phrase "religious demography" demonstrates this: in each case there are few results relating to the overall study of religious populations.

As a consequence, there is much confusion over the status of religion and its adherents around the world.[21] Secondary sources for religious demographics, such as Wikipedia or the *CIA Factbook*, are woefully inadequate and riddled with contradictions and errors. For instance, the *CIA Factbook*, using 30-year-old census data, inaccurately reported the population of Afghanistan to be millions more than the best estimates from the United Nations Population Division until the *Factbook* was updated in the fall of 2009.[22]

The lack of emphasis on religious demography also negatively impacts the ability of the media to provide accurate figures when reporting news. For example, in November 2007 the BBC reported on denials by Kenyan Muslims that introducing shari'a was one of their political goals. As part of the story, the BBC stated, "roughly one-third of Kenya's population of 34 million is Muslim."[23] The correct figure is only approximately 8%, significantly changing the importance of the story.[24]

Popular writing on the future of religion

Thus, despite an abundance of religious demographic material, writings about religion often have the appearance of sheer guesswork. This is especially apparent in writings on the future of religion. Those brave enough to venture into this realm seem inexorably drawn to two extreme visions. At one pole are the writings of devout religionists who predict the onset of religious paradises, ranging from pseudo-humanistic utopias (still based on religion), to Christian, Muslim, or Buddhist eschatological visions (such as Aum Shinrikyo[25]), to New Age cosmic consciousness sans organized religion.[26] In a Christian context, these works range from Edward Bellamy's 1887 novel *Looking Backward, 2000–1887*, a long-term future scenario of utopia as the result of humankind's obedience to Christian ethics, to the bestselling *Left Behind* series,[27] with 65 million copies sold.

At the other extreme are the writings of those who predict the inexorable decline and collapse of religion, as in Lorie and Murray-Clark's *History of the Future: A Chronology*, which predicted the collapse of organized religion.[28] Stark and Bainbridge begin their book, *The Future of Religion*, with the following observation: "The most illustrious figures in sociology, anthropology, and psychology have unanimously expressed confidence that their children, or surely their grandchildren, would live to see the dawn of a new era in which, to paraphrase Freud, the infantile illusions of religion would be outgrown."[29] In some cases, the bias against religion is explicit. For example, authors Joseph Coates and Jennifer Jarratt write, "Religion. It's hard to kill."[30]

The consistent bias in predictions against the staying power of religion demonstrates that most of these writers either did not take religion seriously or were interested in only its aberrations or extremes (for example, fanaticism and fundamentalism). Notwithstanding differences in philosophical perspectives, however, what these two camps – those who foresee a glowing future for religion and those who predict its demise – have shared is the deficiency of quantitative evidence to support their views.

Positive developments in religious demography

Three recent efforts in religious demography deserve consideration. One, the Association of Religion Data Archives (ARDA), was founded in 1997 as the American Religion Data Archive and has as one of its goals providing broad access to the best data on religion available. The initial audience for the archive was researchers interested in American religion. Since going online in 1998, however, both the targeted audience and the data collection have greatly expanded. The ARDA now includes international as well as American collections and incorporates data submitted by scholars of religion and research centers from around the world. In addition to researchers, the audience now includes educators, journalists, and religious congregations, and new features have been developed especially for the expanding user base.[31]

The second, the Pew Forum on Religion and Public Life, has been active in analyzing religious data from around the world. Launched by the Pew Research Center in 2001, the Pew Forum utilizes surveys, demographic analyses, and other social science research on important aspects of religion and public life, both in the United States and around the world, in order to promote a deeper understanding of issues that bear upon both religion and public affairs. The Pew Forum also seeks to provide a neutral space for briefings, roundtables, and other discussions of contemporary issues. Among the fields of interest to the Pew Forum are religion and its role in American society (such as the changing religious composition of the United States and the influence of religion on politics), policy issues with a religious component (abortion, gay marriage, stem cell research, church–state controversies), and the role of religion in global affairs. A wide range of research products, many of them available online, includes both large public opinion surveys (for example, on religion and society) and in-depth demographic analyses (such as of the current distribution and future growth trajectory of major religious groups). Research conducted by the Pew Forum also documents the extent of restrictions on religion, both governmental and social, around the world.[32]

Third, the pioneering demographic work of David Barrett in Africa resulted, in 1982, in the publication of the *World Christian Encyclopedia* (*WCE*) which was immediately praised as the authoritative, definitive work in the field of international religious demography.[33] Its oversized 1,000 pages embodied the most extensive empirical investigation of Christianity and world religions attempted up to that time. In emphasizing its significance, *Time* magazine devoted a full two-page spread to its review, claiming it to be "a benchmark for our understanding of the true religious state of the planet." The heart of the *WCE* is a series of 223 chapters on the status of religion and Christianity in every country in the world, with statistical tables showing, in great detail, the religious and denominational breakdown of each country's population. In 2001, the authors produced a second edition of the work, updating every data point to the year 2000 and adding new areas of scholarship, such as the status of Christianity and evangelization in the world's people groups, cities, provinces, and languages.

In 2003 the data on Christian denominations underlying the *WCE* were updated from 1995 to 2000 and put online in the *World Christian Database* (*WCD*).[34] This first version included data on all religions for every country, with data on all Christians for every language, people, city, and province. In 2007 the Christian data were updated to 2005 and Brill Online became the publisher. The *WCD* brings together an updated and cohesive religious data set with robust database architecture. Information is readily available on religious activities, growth rates, religious literature, and worker activity. The online *WCD* includes detailed information on thousands of Christian denominations and on religions in every country of the world. In addition, extensive data are available on 239 countries and 13,000 ethnolinguistic peoples, as well as information on 7,000 cities and 3,000 provinces. The accuracy of the *WCD* was recently assessed by a team of researchers at Princeton University, who tested the reliability of the *WCD* by comparing its religious composition estimates to four other data sources (World Values Survey, Pew Global Assessment Project, *CIA World Factbook*, and the US Department of State), finding that estimates are highly correlated.[35]

In late 2008, a separate project was launched, the *World Religion Database* (*WRD*).[36] The *WRD* specifically includes data on world religions from the first two sets of major sources on religious demography already described – censuses and surveys. The *WRD* is substantively distinct from the *WCD*, as it focuses on sourcing estimates for all religions (not primarily Christianity, as is the focus of the *WCD*) and providing a clear methodology for reconciling differences between religious organization and social scientific estimates. The *WRD* also makes estimates of religious affiliation over time, available from censuses and surveys. It also provides its own estimates for religious change for all countries from 1900 through the present, with projections to 2050. The *WRD* aims to provide the academic community with the most comprehensive and current information on religious demography on all major religions.

Scholarly reflections on religious data

Robin Gill reveals his own surprise at the availability of data on religion in the introduction to his book on church membership:

In this book I examine a great deal of data, much from local censuses and most previously uncollated. It is astonishing that so many generalizations about church decline and secularization were made without anyone surveying this evidence before. To be honest, I had little concept myself of its extent until I started this research in the late 1980s. I had assumed for years that longitudinal statistics about regular churchgoing patterns were largely unattainable. Certainly I had assumed that little was available outside the three nationwide censuses of church attendances [sic].[37]

Gill's experience is typical within the study of religious data – that is, large amounts of data on religion often remain unexamined.

International coverage in religious demography

National, regional, and global religious demographics provide an essential backdrop to almost every kind of quantitative or qualitative study done on other aspects of religion. Virtually every article and book on religion makes some allusion to demographics. Yet the researcher interested in the social scientific study of international religion is confronted by two immediate challenges. First, survey data on societal attitudes about religion in countries outside the developed world are comparatively limited in scope and of varying quality, in spite of some good international social surveys such as the World Values Survey (WVS). While the WVS has many strong points, its methodology across 53 nations is not rigorously controlled. It is a confederated project of "equal partners," with each national research center carrying out the survey among a representative national sample in their own country. As a consequence, this "strategy of striving for inclusiveness" has led to noticeable variability in the quality of fieldwork among participating nations.[38] It is important to note that the WVS, one of the most highly used sources of international social science survey data, is limited to only a convenience sampling of nations (meaning, a sample is chosen because it is readily available, not because of probability) and does not have the same level of methodological control as do major US surveys, such as the General Social Survey (GSS).

Second, social science survey data are affected by culture. For example, in a recent national survey of Iraqi citizens,[39] 46.9% of the respondents indicated that issues of freedom are an important component of democracy. When choosing from a list of 20 countries offered as potential models for a future Iraq, however, the United Arab Emirates (a confederation of royal sheikdoms officially favoring and promoting Islam) was preferred by 21.1%, much more than the 6.5% who selected the United States. Even Saudi Arabia was favored by more people as a model than was the United Kingdom (3.6% versus 2.3%). These results indicate that an Iraqi citizen might have something very different in mind when he or she thinks of "freedom and democracy" than does an average Briton or American.

Even when survey instruments have been well translated, using questionnaires and other self-reporting measures in non-Western, non-industrialized cultures can be "risky business"[40] because of differences that can alter response in ways that bias the data. A growing body of literature has begun to examine differences between countries,[41] as well as cultural differences that are between and within countries.[42] This research builds on a larger literature on cultural differences related to survey nonresponse in the United States.[43]

One way around the unsolved problem of response bias is to use non-reactive measures, meaning, observations gained without the awareness of respondents.[44] These are often considered useful because they observe naturalness of behavior, though ethically they might be called into question. Another commonly used alternative is a "survey" of experts, such as is done by Freedom House, the leading source of information on political, civil, and religious freedom.[45] The use of the term "survey" is confusing here, however, since social scientists generally regard a survey to be "a systematic method for gathering information from (a sample of) entities for the purposes of constructing quantitative descriptors of the larger population of which the entities are members."[46] A survey of experts does not meet the usual under-standing either of a sample or of normal members of the larger population. A combination of these two ways of generating non-biased data is the coding of expert qualitative analysis.[47] This last method is used by social scientists at Freedom House to generate measures on international religious freedom for 225 different countries and territories.[48]

Innumeracy and religious demography

Policy makers and other users of religious demographic data face the formidable challenge of correctly handling numbers. Without some sort of quantitative guidance, leaders will continue to set agendas blindly and to produce plans that cannot be evaluated. As John Allen Paulos writes:

> In an increasingly complex world full of senseless coincidence, what's required in many situations is not more facts – we're inundated already – but a better command of known facts, and for this a course in probability is invaluable. … Probability, like logic, is not just for mathematicians anymore. It permeates our lives.[49]

Two conclusions can be made about the newly emerging discipline of religious demography. First, the vast annual output of new statistics on the religious context of the world is a veritable goldmine of new data unparalleled in the long history of human enumeration. However, second, few are analyzing these data with any sophis-tication beyond occasional simple sums. For example, the 10 million or so statistical questionnaires returned to church headquarters every year are read selectively for good quotes, illustrations, and sermon material, before being moved permanently to the archives, there to remain unavailable to researchers until the 20- or 50- or even 100-year rules eventually permit.[50]

The academic disciplines of theology, church history, comparative religion, religious studies, and the like have all been pursued without serious attention to the sciences of religious demography. Over 85% of the world's population is religionists, and descrip-tive demographic and numerical analyses of their welfare and their activities are long overdue.[51] In light of the lack of analysis of religious data and the widespread use of prognostication in its place, the goal of religious demography is to provide both data and a methodology for the quantitative analysis of religion. Students of religion will then possess a tool for evaluating the subjective statements of anyone venturing an opinion on the rise or fall of religion.[52]

Religious Demography and Other Disciplines

The field of religious demography has profound intersections with virtually all disciplines concerned with the study of human populations. Both the results of and the methodology behind religious demography can, and indeed should, influence how one understands the wider world. Eric Kaufmann illustrates this in his book *Shall the Religious Inherit the Earth?* – in which he concludes that from a demographic perspective, they will – as he carefully examines the impact of demographics on society and politics around the world.[53] It might come as something of a surprise, then, to learn that religious demography is not well connected to related fields of study such as anthropology, sociology, and political science.

Demography as a Disconnected Field of Study

Religious demography's relationship to neighboring fields of study is a product of the relatively poor relationship that demography in general has with other fields. Although demography is a mature, disciplinary field, it has little contact with neighboring and related fields, perhaps with the exception of economics. For example, demographers make little use of scholarship from fields like anthropology, history, and sociology and issues such as postmodernism, feminism, postcolonial theory, and social biology. At the same time, scholars in these fields do not cite demographers in their work. As Nancy Riley and James McCarthy note, "for a social science, demography is poorly connected to the major social scientific changes and discussions in focus today."[54]

One of the chief reasons for this disconnect is the difference in approaches taken by demography and other social scientific fields. In fact, many of the basic tenets of demography contradict those of sociology, putting the two disciplines at odds. The ahistorical and acultural approach of demographic research is connected to an overwhelming focus on behavior at the individual level – a focus that, according to sociologist Frank Furedi, distorts social science work.[55] Anthropology also remains mostly peripheral to demography, in the sense that the two fields do not fully acknowledge each other's principles and methods. What demography does borrow from anthropology, however, are field-based techniques – such as ethnographic interviewing – that are most applicable to demography's relatively unchanging methodology and epistemology, not areas of demography that are more prone to change.[56] In particular, demographers have paid little attention to foundational anthropological theory, such as the latter's insistence that the whole society be considered above simply the characteristics of individuals. As mentioned previously, economics is the social scientific field that has interacted most with demography. Riley and McCarthy observe, "one of the most compelling reasons for the dominance of economic modeling and theories in demography is that the [quantitative] epistemology and methodology of economics is in line with much of the thinking and priorities of demography."[57] Among the areas of intersection is the "rational actor" model in economics, which says that individuals with preferences are central to the analysis of trends, including fertility rates and other distinctly demographic variables.

Riley and McCarthy conclude that demography is "less rich" because of its lack of contact with other academic fields. They state, "It is thus doubly difficult for demographers to contribute to debates and discussions occurring in neighboring fields, because the methodological differences between them reflect important episte-mological divides as well."[58] In short, demography has not undergone the same deconstruction of underlying assumptions that other fields of inquiry have. Consequently, demographers often focus so much on quantitative methods that they tend to think that simply more and better data will allow them to produce higher-quality scholarship. This uncritical "positivist" approach to data gathering and analysis hinders demographers from deeper cooperation with social scientists and others who are more cautious in their use of quantitative methods.

Religious Demography Is Also Disconnected

Unfortunately, demography's lack of connection with other fields is even more pronounced for religious demography. As a field of study, religious demography has been separate from sociology and anthropology and only marginally connected to economics. Robert Barro and Rachel McCleary's excellent work on economics and religion is a notable exception.[59]

Even when religious demography and other fields do intersect, however, the result can be conflict. In anthropology, for example, religious identity and cultural identity are closely related. Thus, a study of a culture in a particular location always has an associated religious demographic context (whether or not it is acknowledged as such, or even at all). One such example is found in the Marshall Islands, where clashing identities give rise to paradoxical belief systems – traditional Marshallese religion versus the intrusion of Western Christian religion. Historically, Marshall Islanders consider themselves authentically Marshallese in culture and devoutly Christian in religion, causing a schism of belief and identity that is most starkly visible in historical narratives. This results in conflicting interpretations by anthro-pologists and church leaders of what pre-Christian Marshall Island culture was like. Was it a utopia of peace or a dystopia of heathen barbarianism?[60] In either case, the changing religious demographics – as reflected in who identifies in censuses as Christian and who identifies with traditional Marshallese religion – are an important part of the historical narrative.

As another example, the connections between religious demography and political science are closer than is often appreciated.[61] For instance, since the 1980s Latin America's rapidly expanding Pentecostal community has exercised an increasingly important role in public life. Guatemala has inaugurated two Pentecostal presidents. Brazil has witnessed the formation of an Evangelical congressional caucus that con-sists largely of Pentecostals and includes about 10% of the country's parliamentar-ians. Chile's Pentecostals host an annual Independence Day celebration attended by the president. Nicaragua's Pentecostals founded a political party that has fielded presidential candidates and won seats in congress. As Pentecostals have grown to constitute as much as one quarter to one third of the population in some Latin American countries, they have sought a greater share of public influence and political representation.[62] Understanding the modern politics of Latin America, then, is impossible apart from an appreciation of the changing religious demographics of that region.

Pentecostalism's growing presence in Latin American society and politics is attracting the attention of some of the region's most prominent politicians. Brazilian President Luiz Inácio Lula da Silva openly courted Pentecostal and other Evangelical voters in the runoffs of the October 2002 elections. For the October 2006 elections, Lula's Workers Party forged an alliance with the Brazilian Republican Party, organized in part by the Universal Church of the Kingdom of God, one of Brazil's largest Pentecostal churches. Responding to the concerns of Pentecostals and other Protestants, Chilean President Michelle Bachelet, in office from March 2006 to March 2010, established a new religious affairs office to equalize government treatment of the country's diverse religious groups.[63]

The demographics of religion can have a profound political impact on a local level as well, leading, in some cases, to greater-than-expected national influence for religious minorities. Kaufmann makes this association in relation to Europe's Muslims, who are " heavily concentrated in important urban areas."[64] He explains that such concentrations of immigrant groups can have a serious effect on local politics. Examples of this include Cubans in Miami and the Irish in Boston, two minority groups that have held disproportionate power at the national level. He points out that Turkish Germans had such an outsized role in the re-election of chancellor Gerhard Schröder in German elections in 2002.

The interaction between religion and politics is played out across the world and faced by democratic and non-democratic societies alike. Scott Thomas identifies the struggle that Chinese authorities face with young Chinese Muslims studying across the Middle East, especially Saudi Arabia.[65] Those in government fear the influence of Wahhabi ideology in the already-explosive context of Uyghur Muslims and Han Chinese clashes in the western province of Xinjiang. China's leaders are adamant about preventing a separate Islamic enclave from gaining autonomy in the western half of the country. Thomas states, "The rise of Christianity and Islam in China, then, will color discussions about political stability, democracy, human rights, and foreign policy there for years to come."[66]

Religious Demography and International Relations

Global religious demography has perhaps its most obvious connection to international relations and world affairs. In their book *God is Back*, editors John Micklethwait and Adrian Wooldridge of *The Economist* state,

> the greatest change in foreign policy in the recent past has been the revival of religion. It is impossible to understand international affairs today without taking faith into account. The most important single political act of the twenty-first century so far – the terrorist attacks of September 11 – was an act of religious war. The hijackers prepared for battle by performing intricate religious rituals; they went to their deaths shouting, "Allahu Akbar!"; they regarded their monstrous deeds as an act of faith.[67]

Beyond this perhaps obvious global case, scholars have been working since the 1980s in the field of human rights and religious freedom, showing how attention to religious rights has a profound impact on the relations between countries.[68] Religionists are helping to shape laws related to religious freedom and are seeing these freedoms reduce conflict and increase security around the world.[69]

The role of religion in the study and practice of international relations has not been significantly recognized because the role of religion in human societies has not been well understood. According to Scott Thomas, the study of international relations has been dominated by realism, neorealism, or structural realism, where religion is mere superstition.[70] In addition, the secularization thesis held sway across many disciplines as late as the early years of the twenty-first century. It is now recognized that the demographics of religion have a direct impact on world affairs. K. R. Dark, for instance, has noted that major religious changes at work on the global level – such as the decline of atheism, the decline of state secularism, the growth of Christianity and Islam, and the increase in religious diversity – are likely to have "profound implications for world politics."[71] In 2011, Monica Duffy Toft, Daniel Philpott, and Timothy Samuel Shah provided the first comprehensive look at the role of religion in the study of world affairs. The authors found that instead of declining in influence, "religion has come to exert its influence in parliaments, presidential palaces, lobbyists' offices, campaigns, militant training camps, negotiation rooms, protest rallies, city squares, and dissident jail cells."[72] As a consequence, their book attempts to reposition the role of religion in international relations.

The authors observe,

> religion has resurged in its political influence … with the help, rather than the opposition, of the very same forces that secularization theorists thought would spell its demise: democracy and open debate, rapid progress in communication and technology, and the historically unprecedented flow of people, ideas, and commerce around the globe.[73]

In addition, they note that "religion is enjoying a political ascendancy fundamentally because religious actors enjoy a qualitatively greater level of independence from political authorities than they enjoyed in the past – indeed, greater than they typically enjoyed in virtually any previous era of human history."[74] This is seen both in the case of Christianity in Europe, with the gradual disestablishment of religion by most states, and in Muslim societies where despots have recently been deposed, leading, in some cases, to more democratic political systems.

In addition, political scientist Elizabeth Shakman Hurd points out that religion creates a problem for international relations on two levels. First, religious fundamentalism and religious difference emerged as two factors in international conflict, national security, and foreign policy. Second, the power of religious resurgence in world politics does not fit into existing categories of thought in academic international relations. Hurd posits that these two problems lead to the "unquestioned acceptance of the secularist division between religion and politics." She further sees that "secularist division between religion and politics is not fixed but rather socially and historically constructed." The failure to recognize this explains why students of international relations have been unable to properly recognize the power of religion in world politics.[75]

The fortunes of religious demography as an area of study seem to be tied to the role that religion is assigned in many related academic fields. At the time of this writing, religion appears to be experiencing a renaissance in its perceived importance in the study of humanity. In other words, if Muslim beliefs are important in a society, then the questions "How many Muslims are in the population?" and "How is that population changing – or not – demographically?" are also important. Consequently, both the significance of and breadth of religious demography as an academic field of study and practice will likely increase in the coming years.

Notes

1   Nancy E. Riley and James McCarthy, *Demography in the Age of the Postmodern* (Cambridge: Cambridge University Press, 2003), 3.
2   In pre-Ptolemaic Egypt (304 BCE), censuses were taken largely in order to gain data for further exploitation of the labor force in improving irrigation systems and performing other public work projects. See Willy Clarysse and Dorothy J. Thompson, *Counting the People in Hellenistic Egypt,* vol. 2, *Historical Studies* (Cambridge: Cambridge University Press, 2006), 10. China's first known nationwide census was conducted in 2 CE, reporting a population of about 58 million individuals in 12 million households. See Nishijima Sadao, "The Economic and Social History of Former Han," in *The Cambridge History of China,* vol. 1, *The Ch'in and Han Empires: 221 BC–AD 220,* ed. Denis C. Twitchett and Michael Loewe (New York: Cambridge University Press, 1986), 595–6.
3   Such as the constitutionally mandated decennial census of the United States of America, first conducted in 1790. The primary purpose of the United States census was to measure the strength and size of the population in different parts of the country so as to ensure appropriate allocation of power. See Margo J. Anderson, *The American Census: A Social History* (New Haven, CT: Yale University Press, 1988), 8–9.
4   For example, in February 2011 the UN Population Division stated that in order to stabilize the world population and avoid overpopulation, fertility must drop below replacement level, even in countries with intermediate levels of fertility. See "World Demographic Trends," Report of the Secretary-General, http://www.un.org/esa/population/cpd/cpd2011/ecn92011-6buettner-presentation.pdf. Factors in this report include number of children per woman and life expectancy at birth, at intervals between 1950 and 2010.
5   John C. Caldwell, "History of Demography," in *Encyclopedia of Population,* ed. Paul Demeny and Geoffrey McNicoll (New York: Macmillan Reference USA, 2003), 217.
6   The story of United Nations involvement in population studies is recounted and critiqued in Michael Ward, *Quantifying the World: UN Ideas and Statistics* (Bloomington: Indiana University Press, 2004), 44. The UN Statistical Office maintains partnerships with some statistical training centers around the world, most notably the Statistical Institute for Asia and the Pacific (SIAP) in Tokyo, founded in 1970.
7   These and other connections allow demography to be a truly interdisciplinary field. See J. Mayone Stycos, "Introduction," in *Demography as an Interdiscipline,* ed. J. Mayone Stycos (New Brunswick, NJ: Transaction Publishers, 1989), vii.
8   Riley and McCarthy, *Age of the Postmodern,* 66. See also Joseph J. Spengler, "Population Prediction in Nineteenth Century America," *American Sociological Review* 1:6 (December 1936): 905–21. According to Spengler, population forecasting pre-World War I ("the World War") was only common in the United States, and to an extent, in France. It is only since then that population forecasting has become scientific commonplace.

9   See Philip Morris Hauser and Otis Dudley Duncan, *The Study of Population: An Inventory and Appraisal* (Chicago: University of Chicago Press, 1959); William Petersen, "Thoughts on Writing a Dictionary of Demography," *Population and Development Review* 9:4 (1983): 677–87.

10 Riley and McCarthy, *Age of the Postmodern*, 36.

11 Hans-Peter Kohler, Francesco C. Billari, and José A. Ortega, "Low Fertility in Europe: Causes, Implications and Policy Options," in *The Baby Bust: Who Will Do the Work? Who Will Pay the Taxes?* ed. Fred R. Harris (Lanham, MD: Rowman & Littlefield Publishers, 2006), 48–109.

12 See Tetsuo Fukawa, "Health and Long-Term Care Expenditures of the Elderly in Japan Using a Micro-Simulation Model," *The Japanese Journal of Social Security Policy* 6:2 (November 2007): 199–206.

13 According to the 2001 census, the female-to-male ratio in Kerala is 1,058 to 1,000, and in Haryana, 861 to 1,000, highlighting the challenge of female infanticide in the latter. See http://censusindia.gov.in/Census_Data_2001/India_at_glance/fsex.aspx.

14 Riley and McCarthy, *Age of the Postmodern*, 41.

15 Ibid.

16 Ibid., 74–7.

17 See Charles Hirschman, "Why Fertility Changes," *Annual Review of Sociology* 20 (1994): 203–33; John C. Caldwell, "The Global Fertility Transition: The Need for a Unifying Theory," *Population and Development Review* 23:4 (1997): 803–12, quoted in Riley and McCarthy, *Age of the Postmodern*, 56.

18 Ibid., 77–80.

19 According to John C. Caldwell, "Toledo in Spain made parish registration compulsory in 1497, and the Council of Trent in 1563 did the same for baptisms and marriages in the whole Catholic world. In England in 1538 Thomas Cromwell ordered the church to register all baptisms, marriages and burials; in the following year France did the same thing for baptisms and burials." See Caldwell, "History of Demography," 217.

20 WorldCat (www.worldcat.org) is the world's largest online network of library content and services. ATLA is an online index of religious journal articles, book reviews, and essay collections (www.atla.com).

21 Diana Eck recounts a speaking tour in the summer of 2001 where many attenders were surprised and reluctant to learn of the increasing religious diversity in their own country, the United States; all of which changed after September 11, 2001. Diana L. Eck, *A New Religious America: How a "Christian Country" Has Become the World's Most Religiously Diverse Nation* (New York: HarperCollins Publishers Inc., 2001). Religious leaders, government officials, and the general public alike still have a long way to go in conceptualizing a complete picture of the status of religion worldwide.

22 Al Kamen, "In the Loop: Afghanistan's Sudden Population Drop," *The Washington Post*, November 2, 2009, http://www.washingtonpost.com/wp-dyn/content/article/2009/11/01/AR2009110101904.html.

23 "Kenyan Muslims Deny Sharia Claims," *BBC News*, November 27, 2007, http://news.bbc.co.uk/2/hi/africa/7115387.stm.

24 Todd M. Johnson and Brian J. Grim, eds., *World Religion Database* (Leiden/Boston: Brill, 2012), reports that Kenya's population is approximately 8% Muslim.

25 Joseph Kitagawa, *Religion in Japanese History* (New York: Columbia University Press, 1966); Daniel Metraux, "Religious Terrorism in Japan: The Fatal Appeal of Aum Shinrikyo," *Asian Survey* 35:12 (1995): 1,140–54.

26 An example of this is the supposed advent of the Age of Aquarius in 2006.

27 The *Left Behind* series has produced 16 bestselling novels, published between 1995 and 2007, as well as 40 children's novels; "military" and "political" series; graphic novels; audio books and audio dramatizations for both children and adults; and Bible studies.

28 Peter Lorie and Sidd Murray-Clark, *History of the Future: A Chronology* (New York: Doubleday, 1989).

29 Rodney Stark and William Bainbridge, eds., *The Future of Religion: Secularization, Revival and Cult Formation* (Berkeley: University of California Press, 1985), 1.

30 Joseph F. Coates and Jennifer Jarratt, *What Futurists Believe* (Mt Airy, MD: Lomond, 1989), 25.

31 Currently housed in the Social Science Research Institute, the College of Liberal Arts, and the Department of Sociology at the Pennsylvania State University, the ARDA is funded by the Lilly Endowment, the John Templeton Foundation, Chapman University, and Pennsylvania State University.

32 The Pew Forum is one of seven projects that make up the Pew Research Center, a non-partisan "fact tank" that provides information on the issues, attitudes and trends shaping America and the world. The Pew Research Center does this by conducting public opinion polling and social science research, by analyzing news coverage, and by holding forums and briefings. It does not take positions on policy issues.

33 David B. Barrett, *World Christian Encyclopedia* (Nairobi: Oxford University Press, 1982).

34 Todd M Johnson, ed., *World Christian Database* (Leiden/Boston: Brill, 2007). The *WCD* is an initiative of the Center for the Study of Global Christianity at Gordon-Conwell Theological Seminary in South Hamilton, MA.

35 Becky Hsu, Amy Reynolds, Conrad Hackett, and James Gibbon, "Estimating the Religious Composition of All Nations: An Empirical Assessment of the World Christian Database," *Journal for the Scientific Study of Religion* 47:4 (2008): 678–93.

36 Johnson and Grim, *World Religion Database*. The *WRD* is an initiative of the Institute on Culture, Religion and World Affairs (CURA) at Boston University.

37 Robin Gill, *The "Empty" Church Revisited* (Burlington, VT: Ashgate, 2003), 14–15.

38 See Ronald Inglehart et al., *World Values Surveys and European Values Surveys, 1981–1984, 1990–1993, and 1995–1997* (Ann Arbor: MI: Institute for Social Research, 2000), 6.

39 Oxford Research International, Ltd., "National Survey of Iraq: February 2004, Frequency Tables," http://news.bbc.co.uk/nol/shared/bsp/hi/pdfs/15_03_04_iraqsurvey.pdf.

40 Orlando Behling and Kenneth S. Law, *Translating Questionnaires and Other Research Instruments: Problems and Solutions* (Thousand Oaks, CA: Sage Publications, 2000), 51.

41 See, for example Edith de Leeuw and Wim de Heer, "Trends in Household Survey Nonresponse: A Longitudinal and International Comparison," in *Survey Nonresponse*, ed. Robert M. Groves, Don A. Dillman, John L. Eltinge, and Roderick J. A. Little (New York: John Wiley & Sons, Inc., 2002), 41–54.

42 For example, Timothy P. Johnson, Diane O'Rourke, Jane Burris, and Linda Owens, "Culture and Survey Nonresponse," in *Survey Nonresponse*, ed. Robert M. Groves, Don A. Dillman, John L. Eltinge, and Roderick J. A. Little (New York: John Wiley & Sons, Inc., 2002), 55–70.

43 For example, Robert M. Groves, Robert B. Cialdini, and Mick P. Couper, "Understanding The Decision to Participate in a Survey," *Public Opinion Quarterly* 56 (1998): 475–95.

44 Eugene J. Webb, Donald T. Campbell, Richard D. Schwartz, Lee Sechrest, and Janet Belew Grove, *Nonreactive Measures in the Social Sciences*, 2nd ed. (Boston: Houghton Mifflin, 1981).

45   Adrian Karatnycky, Aili Piano, and Arch Puddington, *Freedom in the World: The Annual Survey of Political Rights and Civil Liberties* (New York: Freedom House, 2003); Paul Marshall, *Religious Freedom in the World: Global Report on Freedom and Persecution* (Nashville, TN: Broadman and Holdman, 2000).

46   Robert M. Groves, Floyd J. Fowler, Jr., Mick P. Couper, James M. Lepkowski, Eleanor Singer, and Roger Tourangeau, *Survey Methodology* (New York: Wiley-Interscience, 2004), 2.

47   Charles M. North and Carl R. Gwin, "Religious Freedom and the Unintended Consequences of the Establishment of Religion," *Southern Economic Journal* 71 (2004): 103–17. In the social sciences, "coding" is the process by which qualitative or quantitative data are categorized for analysis.

48   Brian J. Grim, "The Cities of God Versus the Countries of Earth: The Restriction of Religious Freedom (RRF) Index," Master's thesis, Pennsylvania State University, 5–6.

49   John Allen Paulos, *Innumeracy: Mathematical Illiteracy and its Consequences* (New York: Macmillian, 2001), 178.

50   David B. Barrett, Todd M. Johnson, Christopher Guidry, and Peter Crossing, *World Christian Trends, AD 30–AD 2200: Interpreting the Annual Christian Megacensus* (Pasadena, CA: William Carey Library Publication, 2003), 438.

51   Ibid., 550.

52   Todd M. Johnson and David B. Barrett, "Quantifying Alternate Futures of Religion and Religions," *Futures* 36:9 (November 2004): 948.

53   Eric Kaufmann, *Shall the Religious Inherit the Earth? Demography and Politics in the Twenty-First Century* (London: Profile Books Ltd, 2010).

54   Riley and McCarthy, *Age of the Postmodern*, 84.

55   Frank Furedi, *Population and Development: A Critical Introduction* (New York: St Martin's Press, 1997), 47.

56   Riley and McCarthy, *Age of the Postmodern*, 92.

57   Ibid., 85.

58   Ibid., 97.

59   Robert J. Barro and Rachel M. McCleary, "Religion and Economic Growth," *Milken Institute Review* (April 2004): 38–45.

60   Peter Rudiak-Gould, "Being Marshallese and Christian: A Case of Multiple Identities and Contradictory Beliefs," *Culture and Religion* 11:1 (March 2010): 69–87.

61   A recent book illustrating this connection is Jack A. Goldstone, Eric Kaufmann, and Monica Duffy Toft, *Political Demography: How Population Changes are Reshaping International Security and National Politics* (Boulder, CO: Paradigm Publishers, 2012).

62   Pew Forum on Religion and Public Life, *Spirit and Power: A 10-country Survey of Pentecostals*, October 2006, http://pewforum.org/Christian/Evangelical-Protestant-Churches/Overview-Pentecostalism-in-Latin-America.aspx.

63   Because of the great varieties of Latin American Pentecostalism, its political activism and impact defy simple categorization. Some observers and analysts argue that Pentecostal politics follows a clear and essentially monolithic pattern. They claim that Latin American Pentecostals exhibit a tendency either toward political quiescence and passivity or toward right-wing and authoritarian politics. But Latin America's Pentecostals have had very different growth patterns and theological emphases, and have also experienced very different political contexts. The result has been a great diversity of Pentecostal political styles and forms of activism. This diversity continues to evolve in ways that have important long-term consequences for Latin American society and politics.

64   Kaufmann, *Shall the Religious Inherit the Earth?*, 201.

65 Scott M. Thomas, "A Globalized God: Religion's Growing Influence in International Politics," *Foreign Affairs* 89:6 (Nov/Dec 2010): 93–101.

66 Ibid., 95.

67 John Micklethwait and Adrian Wooldridge, *God is Back: How the Global Revival of Faith is Changing the World* (New York: Penguin Press, 2009), 299.

68 See, especially, Douglas Johnston and Cynthia Sampson, *Religion: The Missing Dimension of Statecraft* (Oxford: Oxford University Press, 1995); and Madeleine Albright, *The Mighty and the Almighty: Reflections on America, God, and World Affairs* (New York: Harper Perennial, 2007). More recently, see Thomas F. Farr, *World of Faith and Freedom: Why International Religious Liberty Is Vital to American National Security* (Oxford: Oxford University Press, 2008); and Timothy S. Shah and Matthew J. Franck, *Religious Freedom: Why Now? Defending an Embattled Human Right* (Princeton: Witherspoon Institute, 2012).

69 The Pew Forum on Religion and Public Life has released a series of reports documenting religious freedom and restrictions around the world. See Pew Forum on Religion and Public Life, *Global Restrictions on Religion*, December 17, 2009, http://www.pewforum.org/Government/Global-Restrictions-on-Religion.aspx; *Rising Restrictions on Religion*, August 9, 2011, http://www.pewforum.org/Government/Rising-Restrictions-on-Religion.aspx; and *Rising Tide of Restrictions on Religion*, September 20, 2012, http://www.pewforum.org/Government/Rising-Tide-of-Restrictions-on-Religion.aspx.

70 Scott M. Thomas, *The Global Resurgence of Religion and the Transformation of International Relations: The Struggle for the Soul of the Twenty-First Century* (New York: Palgrave Macmillan, 2005), 55–6.

71 K. R. Dark, "Large-Scale Religious Change and World Politics," in *Religion and International Relations*, ed. K. R. Dark (Hampshire: Palgrave, 2000).

72 Monica Duffy Toft, Daniel Philpott, and Timothy Samuel Shah, *God's Century: Resurgent Religion and Global Politics* (New York: W. W. Norton, 2011), 3.

73 Ibid., 7.

74 Ibid., 81.

75 Elizabeth Shakman Hurd, *The Politics of Secularism in International Relations* (Princeton: Princeton University Press, 2008), 1.

References

Albright, Madeleine. *The Mighty and the Almighty: Reflections on America, God, and World Affairs.* New York: Harper Perennial, 2007.

Anderson, Margo J. *The American Census: A Social History.* New Haven, CT: Yale University Press, 1988.

Barrett, David B. *World Christian Encyclopedia.* Nairobi: Oxford University Press, 1982.

Barrett, David B., Todd M. Johnson, Christopher Guidry, and Peter Crossing. *World Christian Trends, AD 30–AD 2200: Interpreting the Annual Christian Megacensus.* Pasadena, CA: William Carey Library Publication, 2003.

Barro, Robert J., and Rachel M. McCleary. "Religion and Economic Growth." *Milken Institute Review* (April 2004): 38–45.

Behling, Orlando, and Kenneth S. Law. *Translating Questionnaires and Other Research Instruments: Problems and Solutions.* Thousand Oaks, CA: Sage Publications, 2000.

Caldwell, John C. "History of Demography." In *Encyclopedia of Population*, edited by Paul Demeny and Geoffrey McNicoll, 216–21 New York: Macmillan Reference USA, 2003.

Caldwell, John C. "The Global Fertility Transition: The Need for a Unifying Theory." *Population and Development Review* 23:4 (1997): 803–12.

Clarysse, Willy, and Dorothy J. Thompson. *Counting the People in Hellenistic Egypt.* Vol. 2, *Historical Studies.* Cambridge: Cambridge University Press, 2006.

Coates, Joseph F., and Jennifer Jarratt. *What Futurists Believe.* Mt Airy, MD: Lomond, 1989.

Dark, K. R. "Large-Scale Religious Change and World Politics." In *Religion and International Relations,* edited by K. R. Dark, 50–82. Hampshire: Palgrave, 2000.

Eck, Diana L. *A New Religious America: How a "Christian County" Has Become the World's Most Religiously Diverse Nation.* New York: HarperCollins Publishers Inc., 2001.

Farr, Thomas F. *World of Faith and Freedom: Why International Religious Liberty Is Vital to American National Security.* Oxford: Oxford University Press, 2008.

Fukawa, Tetsuo. "Health and Long-Term Care Expenditures of the Elderly in Japan Using a Micro-Simulation Model." *The Japanese Journal of Social Security Policy* 6:2 (November 2007): 199–206.

Furedi, Frank. *Population and Development: A Critical Introduction.* New York: St Martin's Press, 1997.

Gill, Robin. *The "Empty" Church Revisited.* Burlington, VT: Ashgate, 2003.

Goldstone, Jack A., Eric Kaufmann, and Monica Duffy Toft. *Political Demography: How Population Changes are Reshaping International Security and National Politics.* Boulder, CO: Paradigm Publishers, 2012.

Grim, Brian J. "The Cities of God Versus the Countries of Earth: The Restriction of Religious Freedom (RRF) Index." Master's thesis, Pennsylvania State University, 2004.

Groves, Robert M., Robert B. Cialdini, and Mick P. Couper. "Understanding The Decision to Participate in a Survey." *Public Opinion Quarterly* 56 (1998): 475–95.

Groves, Robert M., Floyd J. Fowler, Jr., Mick P. Couper, James M. Lepowski, Eleanor Singer, and Roger Tourangeau. *Survey Methodology.* Hoboken, NJ: Wiley-Interscience, 2004.

Hauser, Philip Morris, and Otis Dudley Duncan. *The Study of Population: An Inventory and Appraisal.* Chicago: University of Chicago Press, 1959.

Hirschman, Charles. "Why Fertility Changes." *Annual Review of Sociology* 20 (1994): 203–33.

Hsu, Becky, Amy Reynolds, Conrad Hackett, and James Gibbon. "Estimating the Religious Composition of All Nations: An Empirical Assessment of the World Christian Database." *Journal for the Scientific Study of Religion* 47:4 (2008): 678–93.

Hurd, Elizabeth Shakman. *The Politics of Secularism in International Relations.* Princeton: Princeton University Press, 2008.

Inglehart, Ronald, et al. *World Values Surveys and European Values Surveys, 1981–1984, 1990–1993, and 1995–1997.* Ann Arbor: MI: Institute for Social Research, 2000.

Johnson, Timothy P., Diane O'Rourke, Jane Burris, and Linda Owens. "Culture and Survey Nonresponse." In *Survey Nonresponse,* edited by Robert M. Groves, Don A. Dillman, John L. Eltinge, Roderick J. A. Little, 55–70. New York: John Wiley & Sons, Inc., 2002.

Johnson, Todd M., ed. *World Christian Database.* Leiden/Boston: Brill, 2007.

Johnson, Todd M., and David B. Barrett. "Quantifying Alternate Futures of Religion and Religions." *Futures* 36:9 (November 2004): 947–60.

Johnson, Todd M., and Brian J. Grim, eds. *World Religion Database.* Leiden/Boston: Brill, 2008.

Johnston, Douglas, and Cynthia Sampson. *Religion: The Missing Dimension of Statecraft.* Oxford: Oxford University Press, 1995.

Kamen, Al. "In the Loop: Afghanistan's Sudden Population Drop." *The Washington Post,* November 2, 2009. http://www.washingtonpost.com/wp-dyn/content/article/2009/11/01/AR2009110101904.html.

Karatnycky, Adrian, Aili Piano, and Arch Puddington. *Freedom in the World: The Annual Survey of Political Rights and Civil Liberties.* New York: Freedom House, 2003.

Kaufmann, Eric. *Shall the Religious Inherit the Earth? Demography and Politics in the Twenty-First Century.* London: Profile Books Ltd, 2010.

"Kenyan Muslims Deny Sharia Claims." *BBC News,* November 27, 2007. http://news.bbc.co.uk/2/hi/africa/7115387.stm.

Kitagawa, Joseph. *Religion in Japanese History.* New York: Columbia University Press, 1966.

Kohler, Hans-Peter, Francesco C. Billari, and José A. Ortega. "Low Fertility in Europe: Causes, Implications and Policy Options." In *The Baby Bust: Who will do the Work? Who Will Pay the Taxes?* edited by Fred R. Harris, 48–109. Lanham, MD: Rowman & Littlefield Publishers, 2006.

Leeuw, Edith de, and Wim de Heer. "Trends in Household Survey Nonresponse: A Longitudinal and International Comparison." In *Survey Nonresponse,* edited by Robert M. Groves, Don A. Dillman, John L. Eltinge, Roderick J. A. Little, 41–54. New York: John Wiley & Sons, Inc., 2002.

Lorie, Peter, and Sidd Murray-Clark. *History of the Future: A Chronology.* New York: Doubleday, 1989.

Marshall, Paul. *Religious Freedom in the World: Global Report on Freedom and Persecution.* Nashville, TN: Broadman and Holdman, 2000.

Metraux, Daniel. "Religious Terrorism in Japan: The Fatal Appeal of Aum Shinrikyo." *Asian Survey* 35:12 (1995): 1,140–54.

Micklethwait, John, and Adrian Wooldridge. *God is Back: How the Global Revival of Faith is Changing the World.* New York: Penguin Press, 2009.

North, Charles M., and Carl R. Gwin. "Religious Freedom and the Unintended Consequences of the Establishment of Religion." *Southern Economic Journal* 71 (2004): 103–17.

Oxford Research International, Ltd. "National Survey of Iraq: February 2004, Frequency Tables." http://news.bbc.co.uk/nol/shared/bsp/hi/pdfs/15_03_04_iraqsurvey.pdf.

Paulos, John Allen. *Innumeracy: Mathematical Illiteracy and its Consequences.* New York: Macmillian, 2001.

Petersen, William. "Thoughts on Writing a Dictionary of Demography." *Population and Development Review* 9:4 (1983): 677–87.

Pew Forum on Religion and Public Life. *Global Restrictions on Religion.* December 17, 2009. http://www.pewforum.org/Government/Global-Restrictions-on-Religion.aspx.

Pew Forum on Religion and Public Life. *Rising Restrictions on Religion.* August 9, 2011. http://www.pewforum.org/Government/Rising-Restrictions-on-Religion(2).aspx.

Pew Forum on Religion and Public Life. *Rising Tide of Restrictions on Religion.* September 20, 2012. http://www.pewforum.org/Government/Rising-Tide-of-Restrictions-on-Religion.aspx.

Pew Forum on Religion and Public Life. *Spirit and Power: A 10-Country Survey of Pentecostals.* October 5, 2006. http://www.pewforum.org/Christian/Evangelical-Protestant-Churches/Spirit-and-Power.aspx.

Riley, Nancy E., and James McCarthy. *Demography in the Age of the Postmodern.* Cambridge: Cambridge University Press, 2003.

Rudiak-Gould, Peter. "Being Marshallese and Christian: A Case of Multiple Identities and Contradictory Beliefs." *Culture and Religion* 11:1 (March 2010): 69–87.

Sadao, Nishijima. "The Economic and Social History of Former Han." In *The Cambridge History of China.* Vol. 1, *The Ch'in and Han Empires: 221 BC–AD 220,* edited by Denis C. Twitchett and Michael Loewe. New York: Cambridge University Press, 1986.

Shah, Timothy S., and Matthew J. Franck. *Religious Freedom: Why Now? Defending an Embattled Human Right.* Princeton: Witherspoon Institute, 2012.

Spengler, Joseph J. "Population Prediction in Nineteenth Century America." *American Socio-logical Review* 1:6 (December 1936): 905–21.

Stark, Rodney, and William Bainbridge, eds. *The Future of Religion: Secularization, Revival and Cult Formation*. Berkeley: University of California Press, 1985.

Stycos, J. Mayone. "Introduction." In *Demography as an Interdiscipline*, edited by J. Mayone Stycos. New Brunswick, NJ: Transaction Publishers, 1989.

Thomas, Scott M. "A Globalized God: Religion's Growing Influence in International Politics." *Foreign Affairs* 89:6 (Nov/Dec 2010): 93–101.

Thomas, Scott M. *The Global Resurgence of Religion and the Transformation of International Relations: The Struggle for the Soul of the Twenty-First Century*. New York: Palgrave Macmillan, 2005.

Toft, Monica Duffy, Daniel Philpott, and Timothy Samuel Shah. *God's Century: Resurgent Religion and Global Politics*. New York: W. W. Norton, 2011.

United Nations. "World Demographic Trends." Report of the Secretary-General. http://www.un.org/esa/population/cpd/cpd2011/ecn92011-6buettner-presentation.pdf.

Ward, Michael. *Quantifying the World: UN Ideas and Statistics*. Bloomington: Indiana University Press, 2004.

Webb, Eugene J., Donald T. Campbell, Richard D. Schwartz, Lee Sechrest, and Janet Belew Grove. *Nonreactive Measures in the Social Sciences*. 2nd ed. Boston: Houghton Mifflin, 1981.

Chapter 7

Major Sources and Collections of Data

Vast efforts are put into the collection of statistics relating to religion in today's world. The process of doing so is uncoordinated between scholars and uneven across religious traditions, but nonetheless a wealth of data is available for religious demographic analysis. The data fall broadly under 13 headings, with six under the heading "primary sources" and seven under "secondary sources":

Primary sources

- Censuses in which a religious question is asked
- Censuses in which an ethnicity or language question is asked
- Surveys and polls
- Scholarly monographs
- Religion statistics in yearbooks and handbooks
- Governmental statistical reports

Secondary sources

- Questionnaires and reports from collaborators
- Field surveys and interviews
- Correspondence with national informants
- Unpublished documentation
- Encyclopedias, dictionaries, and directories of religions
- Print and web-based contemporary descriptions of religions
- Dissertations and theses on religion

The World's Religions in Figures: An Introduction to International Religious Demography,
First Edition. Todd M. Johnson and Brian J. Grim.
© 2013 John Wiley & Sons, Ltd. Published 2013 by John Wiley & Sons, Ltd.

The strengths and limitations of each of these sources of data on religion are examined below. While each has its place in the constellation of data on religious demography, ideally all or most of these would be used in calculating the best estimate for the number of religionists in a particular country or other geographic area.

Censuses in Which a Religion Question Is Asked

Since the twelfth century, many governments around the world have collected information on religious populations and their practices. In the twentieth century, approximately half the world's countries asked a question related to religion in their official national population censuses. Since 1990, however, this number has been declining as developing countries have dropped the question, deeming it too expensive (in many countries each question in a census costs well over 1 million US dollars[1]), uninteresting, or controversial. As a result, some countries that historically included a religion question have not included the question in their censuses since 1990. In several countries, such as Nigeria and Sudan, the decision was for political expediency, to avoid offending particular religious constituencies. In other countries, such as Malta or Turkey, governments simply assume that the population is essentially 100% of a single religion (Roman Catholic and Muslim, respectively) and therefore justify the question's removal. France rejected the use of a religion question as early as the 1872 census. Instead its "efforts centered on clarifying 'national membership,' particularly on the basis of the distinctions formulated for foreigners recorded in the census."[2] By the twenty-first century, however, this trend had begun to reverse itself somewhat. For instance, Britain – which produced the world's first national census of religious affiliation (the Compton Census in 1676), and later had a religion question in the national census of 1851 (though none thereafter) – reintroduced the question in their 2001 census as the best way to obtain firm data on all religious minorities. Whether to include a question on a census can be a heavily politicized decision, as illustrated by India's choice to add questions on caste to its 2011 census. This was the first time such questions had been asked since the 1931 Indian census.[3] Even so, answering the questions on caste was optional. Pragmatists argued that the goal was to improve affirmative action among India's most socially disadvantaged peoples, but modernists saw it as regressive, exacerbating divisions in Indian society.

Censuses are one of the most comprehensive ways in which people are counted. From its historical usage with regard to population counting, the term "census" is implicitly reserved for total or complete analysis of a population, although several governments now include partial surveys through various sampling procedures. The term always uniquely refers to an official government population census. In a number of cases, religion data collected from these censuses were never published.[4] A major problem has been the use of non-standardized terms and categories, which makes comparison between censuses (whether within a single country or among multiple countries) difficult or impossible. Thus, many censuses omit certain minorities, such as tribal peoples, nomads, aliens, refugees, or military personnel. A classic example is the legally defined statistical "population of Australia," which comprised only non-Aboriginal peoples until 1967.

National censuses are the best starting point for the identification of religious adherents, because they generally cover the entire population. Some censuses, such as South Africa's, even provide information on subgroups of major religious traditions (such as Protestant/Catholic or Shi'a/Sunni). Governments typically take major population censuses around the end of every decade and then require three to five years to publish the complete data. In addition to the complete results from a single census date, obtaining these data every ten years enable the calculation of relatively accurate growth rates.[5]

Limitations of census religion questions

Whether respondents feel free to be completely truthful in answering census questions can be affected by methodological decisions, political biases, and social concerns over how the data will be managed. In addition, problems with comparability of census data can arise when the methods of collection vary (even – and perhaps especially – within a single census). Seemingly mundane issues, like the time of the year when the census is taken, are not irrelevant, because the associated environmental and social factors (such as the weather on enumeration days) can influence the results.

As observed previously, the primary drawback of relying on census data for data on religion is that approximately half of recent country censuses do not include a question on religious affiliation. Taking, for example, the specific case of the European Union (EU), only 14 of 27 EU recent country censuses included a religious affiliation question whose results were reported to the United Nations Statistics Division. The 14 countries in the European Union that included a religious identification question on their censuses are the Netherlands, 2013; Romania, 2012; Slovenia, 2012; Estonia, 2011; Finland, 2010; Austria, 2011; Bulgaria, 2011; Czech Republic, 2011; Hungary, 2011; Lithuania, 2011; Portugal, 2011; Slovakia, 2011; United Kingdom, 2011; and Ireland, 2011.

There are many other issues involved in counting individuals in censuses, one of which primarily revolves around who is and is not considered a legitimate resident of the state. Sociologist Calvin Goldscheider raises questions about how non-legal residents and temporary workers are treated in government statistics, and what exactly "residence" means in this context (limited to *de facto* residents, or also includes those temporarily living abroad?). He states that such inquiries "appear on the surface to be straightforward questions, but are at the center of some of the most complex and politically torturous issues facing old and new states."[6] In any analysis of religious demography, it is crucial that the entire population is accounted for. This is especially important when "official" statistics leave out an "undocumented" religious minority, which would be the case with Muslim immigrants in several European countries.[7]

Another shortcoming of censuses is that they sometimes force people to select their religion or their ethnicity from among a set list.[8] This can result in overestimates, when everyone picks a religion regardless of whether they actually practice it. It also has the potential to miss religions that are not recognized by the government, such as the Baha'i faith in Egypt, or that are considered illegal, as is the case with atheism in Indonesia. Yet, even asking a straightforward question about religion can be hazardous. According to Alan Aldridge, terms such as "religion" and "religious" are contentious;

as he states, "asking people such questions as 'are you religious?' is not only hopelessly imprecise but also likely to provoke unfavourable reactions and a negative response even from some of the most committed and active churchgoers."[9]

Issues related to religious self-identification can be particularly challenging in the West. For example, critics of the 2001 and 2011 United Kingdom censuses charge that even people who in other circumstances would not identify themselves as religious will select "Christian" (because they were baptized as children) when presented with that choice on a list.[10] On the other hand, pollsters note that making absolute measurements of religious adherence is difficult, because for many people religious identity and religious practice are separate matters. The question is not without economic consequence. If more of the population identifies as Christian, more money goes to Christian groups (schools, for example) and needs of non-religious groups aren't taken into account because they appear statistically fewer.

The UK's 2001 census was the first time since 1851 that a religious question was asked outside of Northern Ireland.[11] Unfortunately (for demographers), the question was not asked consistently across the countries of the United Kingdom. The censuses in Northern Ireland and Scotland included options for response relating to various Christian denominations, but this was not the case in England and Wales, making comparisons difficult. Furthermore, in an effort to addresses criticisms of the 2001 questions on religion, the formats have been changed for 2011,[12] thus complicating comparisons between the two.

The previous discussion reveals yet another problem: censuses are not free from political and social bias and controversy. David Abramson writes, "Censuses are somewhat like opinion polls in that they create public opinion, except that in the case of the census, its results also shape public constructions of the state."[13] In addition, Abramson agrees with political scientist Dominique Colas that the opinion poll – and in Abramson's opinion, the census as well – is "a universalizing process of abstraction that metamorphoses ethical questions into political ones, fabricating a reality that doesn't exist and which in turn legitimates the existing order, for is not what characterizes power relations precisely what gives them their 'power' in the first place?"[14] In 2008, for example, Nigerian officials removed the religious affiliation question from the census questionnaire in response to violent and deadly social protests before the census had even started. The country is nearly equally divided between Christians and Muslims, and various constituencies felt that the census results would be biased and show that one or the other religion predominated.[15] Another challenge is distinguishing between the religion of one's birth and one's political or social outlook later in life. This is the case in Egypt, where many "secularists" are Muslims who are expressing a particular political point of view that is "decidedly secular."[16]

In addition, official census and survey figures often are in need of revision (or at least qualification). For example, Georgia's 2003 population census showed that 83% of the population were Orthodox Christians, but analyst Ziza Piralishvili writes, "I doubt, however, that the census figures accounted for the high level of labor migration, primarily Azeris and Armenians, therefore I compared these figures with expert assessments."[17] In this case, large numbers of Azeris would raise the Muslim population, while immigrant Armenians would introduce a different variety of Orthodox Christians.

The wording of questions related to religion in censuses is not neutral. For example, much controversy has surrounded the 2011 Irish census and its question on religion. The question asks, "What is your religion?" and provides options for Roman Catholic, Church of Ireland (Anglican), Islam, Presbyterian, Orthodox, two rows for "other" (write-in) and then "no religion." The Humanist Association of Ireland (following an invitation by the Central Statistics Office) suggested replacing that question with "Do you have a religion?" This suggestion was rejected "on the basis it would make historical comparisons difficult."[18] Using the substitute question, however, would maximize the unaffiliated and non-religious count. Census respondents tend to fill in the religion box according to the religion into which they were born (as advised by census enumerators), not the one they actually practice (or don't practice). On the other hand, asking "What is your religion?" makes data more comparable cross-nationally and has the advantage of picking up "weak ties"[19] that have some significance, while other measures (such as surveys) can better pick up the strength of those weak ties.

Assessing the sizes of religious communities in newly independent countries is also a challenge for demographers. Kosovo declared independence on February 17, 2008, and while Muslim Kosovo Albanians are the vast majority, significant religious minorities are found there as well. These include both Muslim (Egyptians, Turks, and Kosovo Serbs) and Christian minorities (such as Bosniacs, Croats, Gorani, Roma, and Ashkali). In this particular case, assessing both the sizes of these communities and the shares of the current total population are difficult because ethnic Albanians largely boycotted the last census of Kosovo (in 1991, when it was part of Serbia). In addition, many Christians (especially Serbs) were displaced in the 1998–9 war, and have found it difficult to return to their homes.[20] As a result, current demographics for the Kosovo population can only be estimated. As a general estimate, approximately 90% of the 2 million people in Kosovo are ethnic Albanian Muslims, while 5–6% are Orthodox Christian Serbs.[21] Only a few hundred Croats remain, most of whom maintain a strong Catholic identity. According to the 1991 census, about 43,000 identified as Roma, although some consider this an underestimate.[22]

In some tragic cases, censuses have been used to discriminate by deliberately undercounting certain populations within a country. Historical examples include discrimination against Blacks and Native Americans in the United States, following the "one-drop rule," and similarly against Jews in Nazi Germany.[23] In addition, early censuses around the world did not seek so much to enumerate populations as to "register the part of most direct interest to state authorities" (that is, the household unit and not the individual per se).[24] This can be the case for ethnicity, language, social status, and religion as well. The first enumeration of population in the Ottoman Empire in the fifteenth and sixteenth centuries, for example, included only religious orders, the military, and judges (that is, only those exempted from taxation, which included relatively few, if any, non-Muslims).[25] In the twentieth century, Belgian colonial authorities in Rwanda legitimized ethnic Tutsi dominance by creating a racial distinction in the census, making Tutsis superior Africans due to an alleged "Hamitic" origin, while Hutus were relegated to the bottom of the racial scale.[26] In other cases authorities of one ethnic background refuse to count certain groups, such as Tutsis in Burundi and Kewri in Mauritania, for fear of having their majority status diminished (or even being shown to be in the minority) and thus losing political power. Even in the well-organized and massive colonial censuses in British India, the British government entreated people to make particular choices in the census.[27]

Who does the enumerating also greatly affects the outcome of censuses. In Macedonia at the end of the twentieth century, four different ethnic groups conducted four different surveys identifying ethnicities in the country, with four different results.[28] In 2000, the Greek government decided to omit the "religion" line from the country's identity cards, causing uproar from the Greek Orthodox Church, who argued that the move would "imperil Greek identity" as the only (at that time) Orthodox state in the European Union.[29] The Russian census of 1897 (in an officially and culturally Orthodox country) did not provide the option of selecting "nonbeliever" on the religion question; later Soviet censuses forced participants to answer a question on nationality but did not allow for belonging to more than one.[30]

In Uzbekistan (as in many other Central Asian nations), nationality and religion are bound together under the assumption that to be Uzbek is to be Muslim, thus providing no need for a census question on religion. The reverse, however ("to be Muslim is to be Uzbek"), is acknowledged not necessarily to be true. This raises the issue of whether, and how, to design census questions to reflect other nationalities in the country that are also Muslim (such as Tajiks, Kazakhs, and Turks). The outcome of the debate is likely to influence Uzbek attitudes on the relationship of Islam to both Uzbek nationalism and national culture. Some also postulate that the lack of a religion question on Uzbekistan's census indicates the government's desire to keep Muslim and Uzbek identity intertwined (that is, a person who identifies as Uzbek must then, by definition, be Muslim also).[31]

The issue of who does the enumerating for censuses is really one of power and legitimacy. This was certainly the case in much of colonized Africa in the twentieth century. Both Burundi and Rwanda in the 1950s, for example, had relatively well-functioning civil registration systems. Originally managed by the Catholic Church, after independence the systems were brought under the control of the state. This transfer – from the colonial religious hierarchy to the new civil authorities – involved more than simply responsibilities for certain bureaucratic functions. According to Peter Uvin, this illustrates "the enterprise of the powers-that-be – missionaries and colonial administrators first, the independent government and the development enterprise later – to count and categorize in order to control, to extend power, but also to obtain legitimacy."[32]

Censuses in Which an Ethnicity or Language Question Is Asked

In the absence of a question on religion, another helpful piece of information from a census is ethnicity or language. This is especially true when a particular ethnic group can be equated with a particular religion. For example, over 99% of Somalis are Muslim, so the number of Somalis in, say, Sweden is an indication of a part of the Muslim community there. Similarly, a question that asks for country of birth can use useful. If the answer is "Nepal" there is a significant chance that the individual or community is Hindu. In each of these cases the assumption is made (if there is no further information) that the religion of the transplanted ethnic or linguistic community is the same as that in the home country.

Limitations of census ethnicity and language questions

Using ethnic or language data as surrogates for religion can be helpful when such information is lacking, but it can also be risky. The most common problem, of course, is that the underlying assumption – that people abroad adhere to a particular religion in the same proportion as those their home country – is not always true. For example, the Palestinian Arab population, now less than 2% Christian in Palestine, offers considerable variety in the global diaspora. In neighboring Jordan, they are also 2% Christian, but in the United States they are about 30% Christian and in Australia, 70% Christian.[33]

Surveys and Polls

In the absence of census data on religion, large-scale demographic surveys, such as the MEASURE (Monitoring and Evaluation to Assess and Use Results) Demographic and Health Surveys (DHS), often include a question about the respondent's religious affiliation. In some instances, demographic surveys by groups such as UNICEF (United Nations Children's Fund) include a religious affiliation question, as did UNICEF's 2005 Multiple Indicator Cluster Survey in Albania.[34] Demographic surveys, though less comprehensive than a national census, have several advantages over other types of general population surveys and polls. As with most reputable general surveys, a demographic survey bases its sample on population parameters from the most recent census. In contrast to other general surveys, a demographic survey completes sufficient household interviews to produce an accurate demographic profile not only of the country as a whole but also of its major states, provinces, and/or regions. To provide this coverage, demographic surveys have larger sample sizes and choose more random locations for samples. Sample sizes for demographic surveys range from more than 5,000 to 100,000, depending on the population and complexity of the country. Early demographic surveys, however, generally included women (and later also men) only in the reproductive ages (15–49 for women and 15–59 for men).

DHS are highly-regarded by demographers and social scientists, and provide valuable nationally representative data on religion. The surveys target people ages 15–49 and usually sample at least 7,000 households, at multiple time points; these surveys often oversample (and sometimes only sample) women. This sampling strategy is, however, a limitation, because religious adherence differs, albeit slightly, by sex and age.

General population surveys also provide valuable information on the percentage of the population belonging to major religious groups. Such surveys include the Pew Global Attitudes Project,[35] the World Values Survey,[36] the Gallup World Poll,[37] the European Social Survey,[38] the International Social Survey Programme,[39] the Afrobarometer[40] as well as other regional Barometer surveys,[41] and occasional cross-national surveys by the Pew Forum on Religion and Public Life,[42] as well as single-nation surveys such as the Pew Forum's *US Religious Landscape Survey*.[43] However, because general population surveys typically involve only 1,000 to 2,000 respondents, they cannot provide accurate detail on the sizes of smaller religious groups.[44]

Surveys can also be commissioned in light of a dearth of data on a particular subject. For example, few quantitative studies have been conducted on the religious, political, and civic views of Pentecostal Christians. To address this shortcoming, the Pew Forum on Religion and Public Life, with generous support from the Templeton Foundation, conducted surveys in 10 countries with sizeable Pentecostal populations: the United States; Brazil, Chile, and Guatemala in Latin America; Kenya, Nigeria, and South Africa in Africa; and India, the Philippines, and South Korea in Asia. In each country, surveys were conducted among a random sample of the public at large, as well as among oversamples of Pentecostals (which included Charismatics).[45]

Survey results can be used to search for correlations between different variables. For example, Eric Kaufmann discovered an interesting link between Islamism and fertility in his study of World Values Survey data. He states:

> The proportion of Muslims favoring sharia was an impressive two-thirds, ranging from over 80 per cent in Egypt and Jordan to around half in Indonesia, Nigeria and Bangladesh. Mapping people's attitudes to sharia on to their fertility patterns, I discovered a strong association between Islamism and fertility, which is statistically significant even when controlling for age, education and income. On the other hand, the small minority who claimed not to be religious had markedly lower fertility.[46]

Much care, however, is required in interpreting such results, particularly in light of the well-known aphorism, "Correlation is not causation!"

Limitations of surveys and polls

As stated earlier, because general population surveys typically involve only 1,000 to 2,000 respondents, they cannot provide accurate detail on the sizes of smaller religious populations that might number too few to be picked up in a general survey.[47] Also, such surveys are sometimes conducted only in urban areas or areas that are easily accessible to pollsters, and therefore they might present a distorted picture of the country's religious composition. Because religious adherence can differ by age and gender, this is another potential limitation of such data.

While survey research is a widely accepted method for assessing public attitudes on religion and other topics, the validity of poll findings has been questioned by a variety of commentators who argue that the limitations of polls are given short shrift.[48] State-of-the-art survey methodology in the United States perennially wrestles with a host of challenges[49] ranging from satisficing and social desirability response bias,[50] to non-response,[51] to a growing population who use only cellular telephones.[52] Cross-national survey work has its own set of serious challenges (see chapter 8 of this volume for more details).[53] Moreover, less is known about the shortcomings of cross-national polling because less research has been done in this area.[54] Given these criticisms and uncertainties, the limitations of polling must be taken seriously[55] and poll results measured against other data sources when possible.[56]

The United States produces no official government statistics on the numbers of religionists because the census does not ask a religion question. Instead estimates are made mostly by national polls, which, as already discussed, tend to be inaccurate for small religious communities. For example, the "soundest approach" for identifying the number of Hindus in the United States has been equating that population with people in America of Indian origin. Some say – without evidence – that a large number of emigrants from India to the United States are Christians. As India's population is only 2.3% Christians (also a disputed figure), however, even doubling that percentage would make only a slight difference.[57] A more thorough assessment, including monographs, informants, and other studies, suggests that there are 1.4 million Hindus out of 2.8 million people of Indian origin in the United States.[58]

Scholarly Monographs

Every year, scholars publish hundreds of monographs on particular religions or religions in particular countries or regions. One example is *Globalization and the Re-Shaping of Christianity in the Pacific Islands*, edited by Manfred Ernst,[59] director for Projects and Research at the Pacific Theological College in Suva, Fiji. This massive, nearly-900-page tome contains details on all religions in Oceania, drawn from a wide variety of sources, including recent censuses. Such monographs differ from other sources in that they attempt to provide an overall profile of religion in an area or country, bringing to light local quantitative data sources as well as qualitative information that provides layers of context and background. In that sense, the *World Christian Encyclopedia*[60] is the largest such monograph produced on Christianity, combining quantitative data with qualitative description and background on the expressions of Christianity in each country of the world. The unique contribution of such monographs to scholars of religion is their provision of quantitative data in relevant contexts with meaningful analysis.

Books on country-based analysis of a particular religion or of religion in general can also be useful. Examples include *A History of Christianity in Indonesia*,[61] *Religious Demography in Southeast Asia and the Pacific*,[62] and *Zoroastrians in Britain*.[63]

Limitations of scholarly monographs

The perspective of an author can potentially bias a scholarly monograph. In religious studies, the conventional wisdom held that non-objectivity in the field was limited to members of religious communities, who might exhibit a bias toward either a particular religion or religion in general. More extensive examination, however, has found that the so-called "objective" position of the non-religious or anti-religious scholar has in fact been a major area of bias.[64] In his 1989 presidential address to the American Academy of Religion, Robert Wilken defended the position of the scholar from the religious community when he stated that to dismiss the great religious thinkers of the past is "not only a loss of depth but also a sacrifice of memory."[65]

Religion Statistics in Yearbooks and Handbooks

Religious communities keep track of their members, using everything from simple lists to elaborate membership reports. The most detailed data collection and analysis is undertaken each year by some 43,000 Christian denominations and their 4.7 million constituent churches and congregations of believers.[66] The latter invest over 1.1 billion US dollars annually for a massive, decentralized, and largely uncoordinated global census of Christians. In sum, they send out around 10 million printed questionnaires in 3,000 different languages, covering 180 major religious subjects reporting on 2,000 socio-religious variables. This collection of data provides a year-by-year snapshot of the progress or decline of Christianity's diverse movements, offering an enormous body of data from which researchers can track trends and make projections.[67]

The Roman Catholic Church does the most extensive of these inquiries. Parallel to the obligation of many other religious leaders, all Roman Catholic bishops are required to answer, by a fixed date every year, a 21-page schedule in Latin and one other language asking 140 precise statistical questions concerning their work in the previous 12 months. Results are then published the following January.[68] Other kinds of handbooks focus on a particular country, such as J. N. Amanze's (1996) *Botswana Handbook of Churches*, which carries the subtitle *A Handbook of Churches, Ecumenical Organisations, Theological Institutions, and Other World Religions in Botswana.* This handbook is well organized, with data sources clearly displayed, and offers the reader a large amount of information on most of the Christian denominations and other religions in Botswana. Another example is the more wide-ranging *Guía de Entidades Religiosas de España (Iglesias, Confesiones y Comunidades Minoritarias)* published by the Ministry of Justice in Spain.[69] This book covers all the religious minorities besides the majority Roman Catholic Church, with entries on Hinduism, Buddhism, and Islam.

At least seven varieties of religious statistics are compiled and kept by religious communities, mainly at the national level. These are: (1) demographic and sociographic statistics on religious populations in particular areas and among particular peoples; (2) statistics of religious behavior and practice; (3) statistics of religious and ecclesiastical jurisdiction and structures; (4) statistics of personnel and lay workers; (5) statistics of social and cultural institutions (such as schools and hospitals); (6) statistics of prosperity and finance; and (7) statistics of religious psychology, beliefs, motivation, and attitudes.

Statistics collected by religious communities often enable researchers to distinguish between two categories of religionists – practicing and non-practicing – based on whether or not they take part in the ongoing organized life of the religion. In relation to Islam, especially in Europe, much of the focus is on Islamic identity as it is both promoted and developed by Muslim youth organizations.[70] In relation to Christianity, practicing Christians are affiliated Christians who are involved in or active in or participate in the institutional life of the churches they are affiliated to (or members of); or who are regarded by their churches as practicing members because they fulfill their churches' minimum annual attendance obligations or other membership requirements; or who in some way take a recognized part in the churches' ongoing practice of Christianity. Thus in the Church of Scotland, for example, "active communicants" are defined as persons who communicate (receive communion) at least once a year. In 1939 this was 76.8% of all communicants on the rolls, 56.7% in 1943, 72.0% in 1946, and 71.3% in 1959.[71] In the Coptic Orthodox Church (Egypt), a "practicing Copt" is one who receives communion at least once every 40 days. Sometimes there is a financial connotation as well; some denominations count as practicing adult members only those who contribute each year to local or central church funds. Certain denominations publish detailed definitions: the Christian Church (Disciples of Christ) in the United

States explains, "A 'participating' member is one who exercises a continuing interest in one or more of the following ways: attendance, giving, activity, spiritual concern for the fellowship of the congregation regardless of the place of residence."[72]

Limitations of yearbooks and handbooks

Membership figures for major Japanese religious bodies are presented in the Heisei 17 (2006) *Shukyo Nenkan* (Religion Annual) assembled by the Japanese Government Bunkacho (Agency for Cultural Affairs) from figures provided by the organizations themselves. These figures should be used carefully, especially in comparison with Western religious statistics, because many are based on different understandings of membership. Some of the discrepancies arise because many Japanese count themselves adherents to two or more religions (see chapter 5 of this volume for a discussion of the doubly affiliated, or multiple religious belonging). In addition, Japanese count membership by household or families; as a result, the number of individual "members" includes many who are inactive or who might even deny any connect to that particular religion (as, for example, a Christian living in a Shintoist household). Additionally, despite the high membership figures reported for some major world religions, many Japanese would say they have no religion at all. For example, many Japanese view a Buddhist temple only as a place to perform religious and lifecycle ceremonies; thus, temple membership is more an "entry pass" to the site of ritual duties than a sign of religious devotion. Note as well that various studies can produce differing results for the same religion, depending on how they are conducted. One study reports 1 million Christians in Japan, for example, while independent surveys give as many as 4.5 million Christians.[73]

Such differences in adherent numbers contribute to the popular misperception that religious communities tend to exaggerate their membership figures. For example, Leslie Allen Paul stated that clergy reports of parish populations in the twentieth century were "notoriously exaggerated,"[74] but this is not necessarily the case. Perhaps the most convincing evidence comes from two of the most aggressively evangelistic groups in Christianity. The Church of Jesus Christ of Latter-day Saints (Mormons) is diligent in assembling accurate statistics of membership, an indication of its efficiency as a thoroughly modern organization.[75] The same is true for the Watch Tower Society (Jehovah's Witnesses). Aldridge states that there is "no reason to doubt that these [Watch Tower statistics] are accurate. They are in line with estimates produced by government agencies and independent scholars. The society reports poor results as well as good ones, which may well be a sign of honesty."[76] In addition, no organization (religious or otherwise) can realistically sustain the reporting of inflated numbers. Eventually, there will either be a ceasing of "growth" or the fraud will be exposed as the numbers reach obviously impossible levels.

Governmental Statistical Reports

Governments often collect statistics on religion beyond those collected in censuses. For example, every year the *Statistical Yearbook of Norway*[77] publishes figures collected by the Church of Norway as well as from all other religious communities, including groups such as Buddhists and Baha'is. The added value of this type of publication is the greater granularity on religion when compared to censuses, such as marriages within churches, financial data, and worship service participation, all of which are reported in the *Statistical Yearbook of Norway*.

Different departments within governments also issue reports on religion. One extensive example is the United States State Department's reports on religious freedom around the world. The State Department reports are comprehensive and draw upon the extensive country-specific knowledge of department personnel. In fulfillment of US law, each US embassy prepares an annual report on its host country.[78] Embassy staff are trained to investigate the state of religious freedom and to prepare the reports according to a common set of guidelines. Expert analysis by trained staff resident in each country in which the United States has an embassy can be a definite strength. Following completion, each report is vetted by State Department offices with expertise in the affairs of that country and in universal human rights. The reports incorporate information from other human rights reports (such as from non-governmental organizations) as well. As such, the data reflect a positive balance between nearness and remoteness.

The US Commission on Religious Freedom assists the State Department by conducting research that feeds into the religious freedom reports; research and data from both the commission and the embassy are then arranged and critically examined under the supervision of the special US ambassador for international religious freedom. Theoretically, having observers culturally separate from the society being studied has merit. The reports cover the following standard reporting fields for each country: religious demography, legal/policy issues, restrictions of religious freedom, abuses of religious freedom, forced conversions, improvements in respect for religious freedom, societal attitudes, and the United States government's actions concerning that particular country. The resulting reports contain loosely structured, retrospective, qualitative analyses of most countries of the world, with embedded quantitative data.

The US State Department has been compiling such annual reports since 1997, taking on the reporting format described above in 2001. Though the reports are bounded (for example, July 1, 2002, to June 30, 2003), they include retrospective information on events that have been systematically monitored since 1997. Therefore, the data in these reports approximate a trend study, which captures both recurring and specific problems that occurred during the reporting period. The reports do not have a systematic interview or survey component, but some multi-modality is approximated in that, for example, embassies are directly involved in inter-faith dialogues in various countries. At times, the reports draw on local survey data unavailable to Western researchers.

Limitations of governmental statistical reports

Problems such as bias in the responses,[79] and non-response[80] are serious issues for data collected and presented in government reports. For international surveys that include data from several nations, these problems might have special and/or unidentified dimensions. For example, both the number and truthfulness of survey responses are likely to be higher in countries where trust of strangers is generally high, like the United States, than in countries where trust of strangers is lower, like Japan.[81] A serious problem facing international survey research is the lack of statistically proven methods to account for such cultural differences within and between countries. Trust, or lack of trust, in a government can also impact survey results, though it has not been studied as a measurable phenomenon.[82]

In the case of the US State Department's religious freedom reports, although they seek to be comprehensive, they are produced primarily by embassy officials in country capitals and other cities with US consulates, which limits their scope and can be a potential source of error. Reliance upon (or catering to) groups with the loudest national voices might also bias the reports. However, the practice of incorporating multiple sources of information (as mentioned above) can help attenuate these problems. The varying length of country reports should also be noted. For example, the 2003 report for Indonesia is 14 pages long (single-spaced, with 10-point font) when printed from the State Department's website,[83] while the reports for many countries in the Caribbean are less than three pages long when printed in the same format.[84] Rather than view the shorter reports as a problem of missing data, a more helpful assumption might be that if abuses or restrictions were not reported, then they were negligible or nonexistent.[85]

Another source of bias might be the over-reporting of problems in countries where information is readily accessible. For example, firm statistics on anti-Semitism are more likely to be available in countries with active Jewish human rights groups than in countries without such organizations. Therefore, it is possible that freer countries will appear worse than they really are (in comparison to less-free countries) because abuses are freely reported. Finally, while analysis can benefit from scholars with considerable knowledge, in many cases, expert opinion has been shown to be notoriously inaccurate.[86]

Questionnaires and Reports from Collaborators

Researchers sometimes initiate queries related to religious demography that result in brief reports. Most of these are never published but are available in the headquarters or national study centers of many religious groups or denominations. One example is a special questionnaire that was designed to verify Pentecostal[87] and Charismatic[88] demographics for a major report prepared on global Christianity by the Pew Forum on Religion and Public Life. The questionnaire asked about the size of Pentecostal denominations, but it also asked three questions to determine whether or not the denomination was actually Pentecostal.[89] A series of additional questions were asked to ascertain with which tradition within Pentecostalism each denomination was affiliated.[90] Finally, three further questions were asked about Pentecostal practices within the denomination.[91]

Another example of this kind of report is the self-assessment performed by the Jain community in the United Kingdom after the 2001 census. The census does not include "Jain" as one of the official religions but requires Jains to write in the name of their religion. As a result, the Jain community claims that their community was vastly undercounted (7,000 instead of 35,000), with most ticking the "Hindu" box or professing "no religion." Leading up to the 2011 census, the Institute of Jainology launched a campaign to get Jains to write in their religion, in part to break the 10,000 barrier that would allow them "minority religion" status, giving them access to jobs and other benefits.[92]

Limitations of questionnaires and reports from collaborators

Assessing the quality of data obtained through informal questionnaires can be difficult because information about the source(s) is often very limited. If one is dependent on these answers as primary data, there is often no additional source to corroborate them. Thus, this type of data is more useful for verifying other results, or at least in giving an impression as to whether one's first source can be corroborated.

Field Surveys and Interviews

For the past 50 years, scholars have visited virtually every country in the world to conduct interviews with religionists. Most of these are never published but, once again, are available in private collections[93] in many countries of the world. In the Pentecostal project mentioned above, investigators conducted a series of interviews at the Third Lausanne Congress on World Evangelization, held in Cape Town, South Africa, in October 2010. Researchers identified Pentecostal attendees from around the world who were invited to the congress and made appointments with them. In most interviews, the researchers presented existing data on the demographics of Pentecostalism in the interviewee's home country and asked for comments and corrections. In some cases, such as that of house churches in China, important adjustments to the data were made based on the interviews.[94]

Limitations of field surveys and interviews

As with questionnaires, the accuracy of the data collected in these interviews can be difficult to assess. Sometimes the information on the interviewees is limited (for example, are there known biases?). Nonetheless, information obtained through interviews can be critical in determining the context or accuracy of other sources. For example, survey data might not register the existence of a small group of religionists, whereas an interviewee might have first-hand knowledge of the community. Asking for a rough approximation of the community's size is an important step along the way in documenting its existence.

Correspondence with National Informants

Scholars and others who have extensive knowledge of a particular religious community can be a source of critical information on religious demographics. Correspondence with informants is often most helpful when trying to clear up discrepancies in existing data, such as when figures reported by government entities and those of religious communities disagree significantly; when no recent data have been collected, for example, as a result of ongoing political or economic instability; or when political or social pressures inhibit collection or publication of data on religions, especially minority religions. Informants have been used to supply missing data or to enable reconciliation of conflicting figures in some of the most difficult assessments of religious demographics, such as the number of Christians in China, the number of Muslims in the United States, and the number of religious minorities in Saudi Arabia.

Limitations of correspondence with national informants

As with other types of information collected in interviews, it is difficult to assess the reliability of individual informants. Outsiders (usually the case with researchers collecting data) cannot easily discern how an informant might be biased. Consequently, this kind of information needs to be correlated with other sources. It is also common for multiple respondents to give contradictory answers to the same question. For example, in assessing the number of Muslims in the United States, there is a broad range of opinions (from informants and from more robust surveys and methodologies) from 1 million to over 10 million.[95]

Unpublished Documentation (or Published Items with Limited Distribution)

These documents are collected in the field and include reports, memoranda, facsimiles, photocopies, photographs, maps, statistical summaries, and historical documents. For example, in 2000 the Christian Research Association published and distributed a limited-edition CD-ROM titled *Australia's Religious Communities*.[96] Updated in 2004 and again in 2010, the multimedia disc contains information on all of Australia's Christian denominations as well as other religions, including history, beliefs and practices, and current statistics.

Limitations of unpublished documentation

The quality of the data in these documents is highly variable and often difficult to assess. In the example of *Australia's Religious Communities* above, professional researchers produced the report with a high level of accuracy and methodological transparency. In other cases, however, the sources of data (never mind the reliability) can be hard to ascertain or verify. Less robust reports can still be used as markers, such as for verifying the existence of a religious community. More in-depth investigations can then lead to better documentation.

Encyclopedias, Dictionaries, and Directories of Religions

Numerous encyclopedias, dictionaries, and directories describing religions in different countries are available as secondary sources. Unlike yearbooks, these compilations are not normally the products of a single religious community or church. Two of the most comprehensive multi-volume encyclopedias are *The Encyclopedia of Religion*[97] and *The Religions of the World*;[98] *The HarperCollins Dictionary of Religion*[99] is also quite comprehensive as a single-volume dictionary.

Directories often focus on contact information but often contain data as well. One of the most comprehensive related to Christianity is the *Handbook of Churches and Councils: Profiles of Ecumenical Relationships*, which reports on churches related to the World Council of Churches, covering nearly 150 countries with summary data on hundreds of thousands of local congregations and the nearly 590 million people affiliated with those churches.[100]

Limitations of encyclopedias, dictionaries, and directories

These works do not reference original source material directly but usually rely on existing sources, especially in citing statistics. For example, an article on religion in a particular country will cite census or survey figures when reporting on the size of the religious community. On the other hand, because individual scholars often author these entries, they often contain original insights related to the demography of a religious community (for example, whether or not the community is growing or shrinking over time). In addition, one might encounter the world's expert on a particular religious community via an encyclopedia entry, with references to more expansive works.[101]

Print and Web-Based Contemporary Descriptions of Religions

There are numerous descriptions of religious communities around the world that are produced for a particular purpose (often a conference or meeting) that are circulated but never published. In more recent years, websites related to religion have proliferated. Scholar Rosalind Hackett has performed a study of the websites of major Nigerian megachurches.[102] Her work highlights how quickly the sites change and how they tend to have a high level of sophistication. Most of these websites contain detailed histories of the churches and often make reference to the size of the community, sometimes offering comparative statistics of change over time.

Limitations of print and web-based contemporary descriptions

These kinds of print materials are difficult to assess in part because most of the authors are not identified. For example, does a rival Sunni community produce a particular "fact sheet" describing a Shi'a group or is it promotional material created by the Shi'a group itself? In addition, websites range widely in their reliability and accuracy and almost always must be evaluated by other sources. In addition, websites are not permanent and are constantly changing. Consequently, most research centers have a specific policy for printing web source material.

Dissertations and Theses on Religion

Unpublished theses and dissertations often contain tables, charts, and graphs on religious demographics, either from primary sources listed above or from original research done for the dissertation itself. These can be searched by subject and (in cases where they have been scanned) by keywords. Often such searches can be performed via the Internet. Yale Divinity School Library, for example, has compiled a database of over 6,000 dissertations related to Christianity outside the Western World.[103] Yale University Library has a more expansive portal to dissertations on religion.[104]

Limitations of dissertations and theses

Dissertations have their greatest value for very focused or specific descriptions of religious communities. For general statistics of national religious demography, dissertations tend to be too narrow, limited to a particular village or city or on only one tradition within a religion (for example, Sunnis in a Shi'a majority in one village in Iraq).

Physical and Electronic Collections of Data

While information on religious demography is found in various government offices, in survey companies, at religious headquarters, and in the offices and homes of scholars, there are a few collections of data on religion that have recently emerged. As a general source of census material, the most complete international collections of census data are found at the United Nations in New York and at the US Census Bureau in Washington, DC. In addition, most governments around the world have physical collections in their administrative centers as well as an online presence.[105] A more comprehensive collection of data on religion is found in the library at the headquarters of *Encyclopedia Britannica* in Chicago. As mentioned in chapter 6, specific data on religion is found in three major collections, (1) the *World Christian Database* and the *World Religion Database*, (2) The Pew Forum on Religion and Public Life, and (3) The Association of Religion Data Archives (ARDA).

This chapter has offered evidence that, for the researcher on religious demography, a vast global collection of data has been built up over many decades by governments, religious communities, scholars, and others. While much of this information cannot be found either on the Internet or in a single convenient location, researchers have more opportunities to obtain and analyze data than ever before. The best strategy for determining the size of religious populations around the world continues to be utilizing as many sources as possible and maintaining a robust global network of scholars and informants.

Notes

1 For example, the 29 questions asked in the 2011 Indian Census cost approximately 440 million US dollars, or 15 million US dollars per question. See C. Chandramouli, "Census of India 2011 – A Story of Innovations," Press Information Bureau, Government of India, http://pib.nic.in/newsite/efeatures.aspx?relid=74556.
2 Alain Blum, "Resistance to Identity Categorization in France," in *Census and Identity: The Politics of Race, Ethnicity, and Language in National Censuses*, ed. David I. Kertzer and Dominique Arel (Cambridge: Cambridge University Press, 2002), 128. See Catherine Gousseff, "L'élaboration des catégories des nationales dans les recensements: décalages entre législation et outils de mesure," *Revue française des affaires sociales* 2 (1997): 53–70.

3   "Indian Cabinet Approves Caste-Based Census for 2011," *BBC News*, September 9, 2010, http://www.bbc.co.uk/news/world-south-asia-11241916.

4   For example, in the United States, the Census of Religious Bodies was conducted every 10 years until 1946. The US Congress failed to appropriate money either to tabulate or to publish the information collected in the 1946 census. See Pew Forum on Religion and Public Life, *A Brief History of Religion and the US Census*, January 26, 2010, http://www.pewforum.org/Government/A-Brief-History-of-Religion-and-the-U-S--Census.aspx.

5   It should be noted that there are many countries where a proper census has not been conducted for many years. Examples include Afghanistan (1979), Lebanon (1932), and Somalia (1987).

6   For a detailed critique of the Australian religious questions see the Atheist Foundation of Australia's "No Religion" campaign website, http://www.censusnoreligion.org/, which objects to the religion question on the census for the following reasons:

First and foremost, the question on the Census form is what is known as a "leading question." That is, it is formulated is such a way as to elicit a desired answer. A survey company using such a method would very quickly be dismissed as not worth hiring. The question reads, "What is the person's religion?" Firstly, the phrasing of the question suggests the person has a religious belief. The Atheist Foundation of Australia believes this is a false assumption. Second, the response options presented allows the person to write their religion of baptism, or the religion they were introduced to as a child, even though the individual may not hold any religious beliefs anymore. Furthermore, the question lists the common religions at the top and places the "No religion" box at the bottom.

On the ethnicity question, see Calvin Goldscheider, "Ethnic Categorizations in Censuses: Comparative Observations from Israel, Canada, and the United States," in *Census and Identity: The Politics of Race, Ethnicity, and Language in National Censuses*, ed. David I. Kertzer and Dominique Arel (Cambridge: Cambridge University Press, 2002), 71.

7   See Amikam Nachmani, *Europe and Its Muslim Minorities: Aspects of Conflict, Attempts at Accord* (Brighton: Sussex Academic Press, 2009), 17.

8   For a discussion of religious classification problems in the United States, see Roger Finke and Christopher D. Bader, "Data and Directions for Research in the Economics of Religion," in *The Oxford Handbook of The Economics of Religion*, ed. Rachel M. McCleary (Oxford: Oxford University Press, 2011), 343–64.

9   Alan Aldridge, *Religion in the Contemporary World: A Sociological Introduction*, 2nd ed. (Cambridge: Polity Press, 2007), 21.

10 "Census: How religious is the UK?" *BBC News Magazine*, February 21, 2011, http://www.bbc.co.uk/news/magazine-12507319.

11 Paul Weller, "Identity, Politics, and the Future(s) of Religion in the UK: The Case of the Religion Questions in the 2001 Decennial Census," *Journal of Contemporary Religion* 19:1 (2004): 3–21.

12 "Census," *BBC News Magazine*.

13 David Abramson, "Identity Counts: The Soviet Legacy and the Census in Uzbekistan," in *Census and Identity: The Politics of Race, Ethnicity, and Language in National Censuses*, ed. David I. Kertzer and Dominique Arel (Cambridge: Cambridge University Press, 2002), 178.

14 Dominique Colas, *Civil Society and Fanaticism: Conjoined Histories*, trans. Amy Jacobs (Stanford: Stanford University Press, 1997), xxix. Cited in Abramson, "Identity Counts," 178.

15 For a detailed examination of these problems see Abraham Okolo, "The Nigerian Census: Problems and Prospects," *The American Statistician* 53:4 (November 1999): 321–5.

16 Bret Stephens, "Egypt–The Hangover," *The Wall Street Journal*, March 29, 2011, http://online.wsj.com/article/SB10001424052748704471904576228473270290208.html.

17 Zaza Piralishvili, "Religion," *Central Eurasia 2005 Analytical Annual: Georgia* (Sweden: CA&CC Press, 2006), 152.

18 Brian Whiteside, "Opinion: Think Carefully Before Answering Census Question on Religion," *The Irish Times*, March 3, 2011, http://www.irishtimes.com/newspaper/opinion/2011/0329/1224293298294.html.

19 Such as those who self-identify with a religion but who are not active in that religion.

20 See Ian Bancroft, "Kosovo's Serbs Must Return," *The Guardian*, May 5, 2009, http://www.guardian.co.uk/commentisfree/2009/may/05/kosovo-serbs-return.

21 Georgina Stevens, *Filling the Vacuum: Ensuring Protection and Legal Remedies for Minorities in Kosovo* (London: Minority Rights Group International, 2009), 8.

22 Clive Baldwin, *Minority Rights in Kosovo under International Rule* (London, Minority Rights Group International, 2006).

23 David I. Kertzer and Dominique Arel, "Censuses, Identity Formation, and the Struggle for Political Power," in *Census and Identity: The Politics of Race, Ethnicity, and Language in National Censuses*, ed. David I. Kertzer and Dominique Arel (Cambridge: Cambridge University Press, 2002), 4.

24 Ibid., 7.

25 Ibid.

26 Ibid., 11.

27 Ibid., 28. A flyer was distributed by British officials in Lahore before the 1931 census telling people the correct responses for religion, sect, caste, race, and language.

28 Kertzer and Arel, "Censuses, Identity Formation," 21–3.

29 Ibid., 36. See Helena Smith, "Greece Tackles Identity Issue," *Dawn* (May 2000).

30 Abramson, "Identity Counts," 177.

31 Ibid., 194–5. See paragraph for religious tolerance and ethnic pluralism in Uzbekistan.

32 Peter Uvin, "On Counting, Categorizing, and Violence in Burundi and Rwanda," in *Census and Identity: The Politics of Race, Ethnicity, and Language in National Censuses*, ed. David I. Kertzer and Dominique Arel (Cambridge: Cambridge University Press, *2002*), 170.

33 See Todd M. Johnson and Brian J. Grim, eds., *World Religion Database* (Leiden/Boston: Brill, accessed January 2012). Ethnolinguistic queries filtered for "Palestinian Arabs."

34 United Nations Children's Fund, Childinfo: Monitoring the Situation of Children and Women, "Multiple Indicator Cluster Surveys/MICS3," March 2012, http://www.childinfo.org/mics3_surveys.html.

35 Pew Forum on Religion and Public Life, *17-Nation Pew Global Attitudes Survey*, November 17, 2011, http://pewglobal.org.

36 http://www.worldvaluessurvey.org

37 http://www.gallup.com/consulting/worldpoll/24046/About.aspx

38 http://www.europeansocialsurvey.org

39 http://www.issp.org

40 http://www.afrobarometer.org/. "The Afrobarometer is an independent, nonpartisan research project that measures the social, political, and economic atmosphere in Africa."

41 http://www.globalbarometer.net

42 http://pewforum.org

43 Pew Forum on Religion and Public Life, *US Religious Landscape Survey*, 2007, http://religions.pewforum.org/.

44   Pew Forum on Religion and Public Life, *Tolerance and Tension: Islam and Christianity in Sub-Saharan Africa*, April 15, 2010, http://www.pewforum.org/executive-summary-islam-and-christianity-in-sub-saharan-africa.aspx.

45   Pew Forum on Religion and Public Life, *Spirit and Power: A 10-country Survey of Pentecostals*, October 2006, http://pewforum.org/Christian/Evangelical-Protestant-Churches/Overview-Pentecostalism-in-Latin-America.aspx.

46   Eric Kaufmann, *Shall the Religious Inherit the Earth? Demography and Politics in the Twenty-First Century* (London: Profile Books Ltd, 2010), 130.

47   General population surveys typically have smaller sample sizes than demographic surveys and are not designed to measure the sizes of small minority populations. This can lead to undercounts of religionists in countries where they represent a small minority of the population and to overcounts where they represent the vast majority of the population. See The Pew Forum on Religion and Public Life, *The Future of the Global Muslim Population: Projections for 2010–2030*, January 27, 2011, Appendix A, http://pewforum.org/future-of-the-global-muslim-population-appendix-a.aspx.

48   Arianna Huffington, "Hang It Up," May 21, 2008, http://ariannaonline.huffingtonpost.com/columns/column.php?id=445; Kurt Lang, "What Polls Can and Cannot Tell us About Public Opinion: Keynote Speech at the 60th Annual Conference of WAPOR," *International Journal of Public Opinion Research* 20 (2008): 3–22; Gladys Engel Lang and Kurt Lang, comments in "The Future Study of Public Opinion: A Symposium," *Public Opinion Quarterly* 51 (1987): S181–2.

49   Robert M. Groves, Floyd J. Fowler, Jr., Mick P. Couper, James M. Lepowski, Eleanor Singer, and Roger Tourangeau, *Survey Methodology* (Hoboken, NJ: John Wiley & Sons, 2004).

50   Allyson L. Holbrook, Melanie C. Green, and Jon A. Krosnick, "Telephone Versus Face-to-Face Interviewing of National Probability Samples with Long Questionnaires: Comparisons of Respondent Satisficing and Social Desirability Response Bias," *Public Opinion Quarterly* 67 (2003): 79–125.

51   See Richard Curtin, Stanley Presser, and Eleanor Singer, "The Effect of Response Rate Changes on the Index of Consumer Sentiment," *Public Opinion Quarterly* 64 (2000): 413–28; Groves, Cialdini, and Couper, *Survey Methodology*; Scott Keeter, Carolyn Miller, Andrew Kohut, Robert M. Groves, and Stanley Presser, "Consequences of Reducing Nonresponse in a National Telephone Survey," *Public Opinion Quarterly* 64 (2000): 125–48; I-Fen Lin and Nora Cate Schaeffer, "Using Survey Participants to Estimate the Impact of Nonparticipation," *Public Opinion Quarterly* 59 (1995): 236–58; Julien O. Teitler, Nancy E. Reichman, and Susan Sprachman, "Costs and Benefits of Improving Response Rates for a Hard-to-Reach Population," *Public Opinion Quarterly* 67 (2003): 126–38.

52   Scott Keeter, Courtney Kennedy, April Clark, Trevor Tompson, and Mike Mokrzycki, "What's Missing from National Landline RDD Surveys? The Impact of The Growing Cell-Only Population," *Public Opinion Quarterly* 71 (2007): 772–92. The article is one of eight on cell-phone numbers and telephone surveying in the US published in a special issue of the *Public Opinion Quarterly*.

53   T. Yamagishi and M. Yamagishi, "Trust and Commitment in the United States and Japan," *Motivation and Emotion* 18 (1994): 129–66.

54   For a summary of basic research see Janet A. Harkness, Fons J. R. van de Vijver, and Peter Ph. Mohler, *Cross-Cultural Survey Methods* (Hoboken, NJ: Wiley-Interscience, 2002); and Anthony Health, Stephen Fisher, and Shawna Smith, "The Globalization of Public Opinion," *Annual Review of Political Science* 8 (2005): 297–333; as well as the proceeding from the International Conference on Survey Methods in Multicultural, Multinational, and Multiregional Contexts, June 25–9, 2008, Berlin, Germany.

55 Kathleen A. Frankovic, "Reporting 'the Polls' in 2004," *Public Opinion Quarterly* 69 (2005): 682–97; Sahar Igo, *The Averaged American: Surveys, Citizens, and the Making of a Mass Public* (Cambridge, MA: Harvard University Press, 2007).

56 Robert P. Daves and Frank Newport, "Pollsters Under Attack: 2004 Election Incivility and Its Consequences," *Public Opinion Quarterly* 69 (2005): 670–81.

57 "So, How Many Hindus are there in the US?" *Hinduism Today*, January/February/March 2008, http://www.hinduismtoday.com/archives/2008/1-3/61_swadhyay%20pariwar.shtml.

58 According to the 2010 US Census, results reported at: http://factfinder2.census.gov/faces/tableservices/jsf/pages/productview.xhtml?pid=DEC_10_DP_DPDP1&prodType=table.

59 Manfred Ernst, ed., *Globalization and the Re-Shaping of Christianity in the Pacific Islands* (Suva, Fiji: Pacific Theological College, 2006).

60 David B. Barrett, George T. Kurian, and Todd M. Johnson, eds., *World Christian Encyclopedia: A Comparative Survey of Churches and Religions in the Modern World*, 2 vols, 2nd ed. (New York: Oxford University Press, 2001).

61 Jan Sihar Aritonang and Karel Steenbrink, eds., *A History of Christianity in Indonesia* (Leiden, Netherlands: Brill, 2008).

62 Gary D. Bouma, Rodney Ling, and Douglas Pratt, eds., *Religious Diversity in Southeast Asia and the Pacific: National Case Studies* (Dordrecht: Springer, 2010).

63 John R. Hinnells, *Zoroastrians in Britain* (Oxford: Oxford University Press, 1996).

64 Rodney Starke and Roger Finke, *Acts of Faith: Explaining the Human Side of Religion* (Berkeley: University of California Press, 2000), 57–79.

65 Robert Louis Wilken, *Remembering the Christian Past* (Grand Rapids, MI: William B. Eerdmans Publishing Company, 1995), 13.

66 David B. Barrett, Todd M. Johnson, Christopher Guidry, and Peter Crossing, *World Christian Trends, AD 30–AD 2200: Interpreting the Annual Christian Megacensus*, (Pasadena, CA: William Carey Library Publication, 2003), xiii.

67 One attempt to organize a variety of source material for researchers is the website www.adherents.com, which offers thousands of figures for adherents of hundreds of religions. However, there is no attempt by its organizers to reconcile the numerous contradictions in the source material. Nonetheless, it offers an invaluable look at the amount of data researchers have at their disposal.

68 See *Annuario Pontificio* (Citta del Vaticano: Tipografia Poliglotta Vaticana).

69 Ministerio de Justicia, Secretaría General Técnica, *Guía de Entidades Religiosas de España (Iglesias, Confesiones y Comunidades Minoritarias)* [Guide to Religious Entities in Spain: Churches, Confessions and Minority Communities] (Madrid: Ministerio de Justicia, 1998).

70 See, for example, Pia Karlsson Minganti, "Becoming a 'Practising' Muslim – Reflections on Gender, Racism and Religious Identity among Women in a Swedish Muslim Youth Organisation," *Elore* 15:1 (2008): 1–16.

71 David B. Barrett, ed., World Christian *Encyclopedia* (Nairobi: Oxford University Press, 1981), xxx.

72 "Classification of church membership," General Assembly Resolution No. 57, Detroit 1964.

73 Robert Ellwood, *Introducing Japanese Religion* (New York: Routledge, 2008), 236–7.

74 Leslie Allen Paul, *The Deployment and Payment of the Clergy: A Report* (Westminster: Church Information Office for the Central Advisory Council for the Ministry, 1964).

75 Aldridge, *Religion in the Contemporary World*, 107.

76 Ibid., 118.

77 http://www.ssb.no/en/yearbook/

78   Ironically – and presumably inadvertently – the assignment of this responsibility to the State Department means that no report is produced for the United States (which, of course, does not have a US Embassy within its borders).

79   Holbrook, Green, and Krosnick, "Telephone Versus Face-to-Face Interviewing."

80   Curtin, Presser, and Singer, "Effect of Response Rate Changes"; Robert M. Groves, Robert B. Cialdini, and Mick P. Couper, "Understanding The Decision to Participate in a Survey," *Public Opinion Quarterly* 56 (1992): 475–95. Keeter et al., "Consequences of Reducing Nonresponse"; Lin and Schaeffer, "Impact of Nonparticipation"; Teitler, Reichman, and Sprachman, "Costs and Benefits of Improving Response Rates."

81   Yamagishi and Yamagishi, "Trust and Commitment."

82   On the general measurement of trust in government see Timothy E. Cook and Paul Gronke, "The Skeptical American: Revisiting the Meanings of Trust in Government and Confidence in Institutions," *Journal of Politics* 67 (2005): 784–803.

83   http://www.state.gov/j/drl/rls/irf/2003/23829.htm

84   For example, Antigua and Barbuda (http://www.state.gov/j/drl/rls/irf/2003/24475. htm), Dominican Republic (http://www.state.gov/j/drl/rls/irf/2003/24488.htm), and the Bahamas (http://www.state.gov/j/drl/rls/irf/2003/24477.htm).

85   The notable exceptions to this approach to missing data are the reports on North Korea, Libya, and Bhutan, where the US State Department did not have an official presence during the reporting period (July 1, 2002, to June 30, 2003). In the case of North Korea, the data for that country couldn't be considered reliable due to a lack of verifiable data from any international source. The situation may be worse (or better) in North Korea than the limited information reveals.

86   See, for example, Tetlock's 2005 study of expert predictions. Philip Tetlock, *Expert Political Judgment: How Good Is It? How Can We Know?* (Princeton: Princeton University Press, 2006).

87   Defined by Pew as "members of distinct Protestant denominations or independent churches that hold the teaching that all Christians should seek a post-conversion religious experience called the baptism of the Holy Spirit."

88   Defined by Pew as "members of non-pentecostal denominations – including Catholic, Orthodox and some Protestant denominations – who hold at least some pentecostal beliefs and engage in at least some spiritual practices associated with pentecostalism, including divine healing, prophecy and speaking in tongues."

89   The three questions were: (1) Does your church believe in a second and/or third experience subsequent to conversion, which is understood to be the baptism or filling of the Holy Spirit?; (2) Does your church recognize and practice speaking in tongues as a personal prayer language?; and (3) Does your church recognize and practice the spiritual gifts such as speaking in and interpretation of tongues, healing power, word of wisdom/ knowledge, prophecy, and deliverance?

90   The additional questions were: (1) Is your church an Apostolic Church?; (2) Is your church a Full Gospel Church?; (3) Is your church a Oneness Church?; (4) Is your church a Word-Faith/Prosperity Gospel Church?; and (5) Is your church a Zionist Church?

91   These were: (1) Does your church view speaking in tongues to be the required evidence of the filling or baptism of the Holy Spirit?; (2) Does your church acknowledge and receive messages from present-day prophets?; and (3) Does your church acknowledge and practice "healing prayer"?

92   See Institute of Jainology, "UK's General Census 2011," September 13, 2010, http:// www.jainology.org/1068/general-census-2011/.

93   These range from formal university research centers where the correspondence of a community of scholars can be accessed to the private offices of most religion scholars, nearly

all of whom have collected information from their sources that is used for their own monographs but never circulated or published.

94 Before these interviews it was widely believed by scholars that most house churches in China were Pentecostal in practice (especially experiencing miracles and healings). The interviews revealed that as rural house church members migrate to the cities, they become less Pentecostal in their practices. The "house church movement" in China thus has a diversity of practices that previously was unappreciated by outside scholars.

95 See, for example, Tom Smith, "Review: The Muslim Population of the United States: The Methodology of Estimates," *Public Opinion Quarterly* 66:3 (Autumn 2002): 404–17.

96 See http://www.cra.org.au/pages/00000082.cgi.

97 Mircea Eliade, ed., *The Encyclopedia of Religion*, 16 vols. (New York: Macmillan Library Reference, 1986).

98 Gordon Melton, ed., *Religions of the World: A Comprehensive Encyclopedia of Beliefs and Practices*, 6 vols. 2nd ed. (Santa Barbara, CA: ABC-CLIO, 2010).

99 Jonathan Z. Smith, ed., *The HarperCollins Dictionary of Religion* (San Francisco, CA: HarperSanFrancisco, 1995).

100 Huibert van Beek, ed., *Handbook of Churches and Councils: Profiles of Ecumenical Relationships* (Geneva: World Council of Churches, 2006).

101 For example, John R. Hinnells has written many of the general encyclopedia entries on Zoroastrianism. Searching for publications by Hinnells would lead an investigator to his extensive work on the religion, such as his magisterial *The Zoroastrian Diaspora: Religion and Migration* (Oxford: Oxford University Press, 2005).

102 See Rosalind Hackett, "The New Virtual (Inter)Face of African Pentecostalism," *Society* 46:6 (2009): 496–503.

103 See http://resources.library.yale.edu/dissertations/.

104 See http://www.library.yale.edu/rsc/religion/diss.html.

105 The United Nations maintains an update of the status of the world's censuses at http://unstats.un.org/unsd/demographic/sources/census/censusdates.htm.

References

Abramson, David. "Identity Counts: The Soviet Legacy and the Census in Uzbekistan." In *Census and Identity: The Politics of Race, Ethnicity, and Language in National Censuses*, edited by David I. Kertzer and Dominique Arel, 176–201. Cambridge: Cambridge University Press, 2002.

Aldridge, Alan. *Religion in the Contemporary World: A Sociological Introduction*. Cambridge: Polity Press, 2007.

Annuario Pontificio. Citta del Vaticano: Tipografia Poliglotta Vaticana.

Aritonang, Jan Sihar, and Karel Steenbrink, eds. *A History of Christianity in Indonesia*. Leiden: Brill, 2008.

Baldwin, Clive. *Minority Rights in Kosovo under International Rule*. London: Minority Rights Group International, 2006.

Bancroft, Ian. "Kosovo's Serbs Must Return." *The Guardian*, May 5, 2009. http://www.guardian.co.uk/commentisfree/2009/may/05/kosovo-serbs-return.

Barrett, David B. *World Christian Encyclopedia*. Nairobi: Oxford University Press, 1981.

Barrett, David B., Todd M. Johnson, Christopher Guidry, and Peter Crossing. *World Christian Trends, AD 30–AD 2200: Interpreting the Annual Christian Megacensus*. Pasadena, CA: William Carey Library Publication, 2003.

Barrett, David B., George T. Kurian, and Todd M. Johnson, eds. *World Christian Encyclopedia: A Comparative Survey of Churches and Religions in the Modern World.* 2 vols. 2nd ed. New York: Oxford University Press, 2001.

Beek, Huibert van, ed. *Handbook of Churches and Councils: Profiles of Ecumenical Relationships.* Geneva: World Council of Churches, 2006.

Blum, Alain. "Resistance to Identity Categorization in France." In *Census and Identity: The Politics of Race, Ethnicity, and Language in National Censuses,* edited by David I. Kertzer and Dominique Arel, 121–47. Cambridge: Cambridge University Press, 2002.

Bouma, Gary D., Rodney Ling, and Douglas Pratt, eds. *Religious Diversity in Southeast Asia and the Pacific: National Case Studies.* Dordrecht: Springer, 2010.

"Census: How religious is the UK?" *BBC News Magazine,* February 21, 2011. http://www.bbc.co.uk/news/magazine-12507319.

Chandramouli, C. "Census of India 2011 – A Story of Innovations." Press Information Bureau, Government of India. http://pib.nic.in/newsite/efeatures.aspx?relid=74556.

Christian Church (Disciples of Christ) in the USA. "Classification of Church Membership." General Assembly Resolution No. 57. Detroit: 1964.

Colas, Dominique. *Civil Society and Fanaticism: Conjoined Histories.* Translated by Amy Jacobs. Stanford: Stanford University Press, 1997.

Cook, Timothy E., and Paul Gronke. "The Skeptical American: Revisiting the Meanings of Trust in Government and Confidence in Institutions." *Journal of Politics* 67 (2005): 784–803.

Curtin, Richard, Stanley Presser, and Eleanor Singer. "The Effect of Response Rate Changes on the Index of Consumer Sentiment." *Public Opinion Quarterly* 64 (2000): 413–28.

Daves, Robert P., and Frank Newport. "Pollsters Under Attack: 2004 Election Incivility and Its Consequences." *Public Opinion Quarterly* 69 (2005): 670–81.

Eliade, Mircea, ed. *The Encyclopedia of Religion.* 16 vols. New York: Macmillan Library Reference, 1986.

Ellwood, Robert. *Introducing Japanese Religion.* New York: Routledge, 2008.

Ernst, Manfred, ed. *Globalization and the Re-Shaping of Christianity in the Pacific Islands.* Suva, Fiji: Pacific Theological College, 2006.

Finke, Roger, and Christopher D. Bader. "Data and Directions for Research in the Economics of Religion." In *The Oxford Handbook of The Economics of Religion,* edited by Rachel M. McCleary, 343–64. Oxford: Oxford University Press, 2011.

Frankovic, Kathleen A. "Reporting 'the Polls' in 2004." *Public Opinion Quarterly* 69 (2005): 682–97.

Goldscheider, Calvin. "Ethnic Categorizations in Censuses: Comparative Observations from Israel, Canada, and the United States." In *Census and Identity: The Politics of Race, Ethnicity, and Language in National Censuses,* edited by David I. Kertzer and Dominique Arel, 71–91. Cambridge: Cambridge University Press, 2002.

Gousseff, Catherine. "L'élaboration des catégories des nationales dans les recensements: décalages entre législation et outils de mesure." *Revue française des affaires sociales* 2 (1997): 53–70.

Groves, Robert M., Robert B. Cialdini, and Mick P. Couper. "Understanding The Decision to Participate in a Survey." *Public Opinion Quarterly* 56 (1992): 475–95.

Groves, Robert M., Floyd J. Fowler, Jr., Mick P. Couper, James M. Lepowski, Eleanor Singer, and Roger Tourangeau. *Survey Methodology.* Hoboken, NJ: John Wiley & Sons, 2004.

Hackett, Rosalind. "The New Virtual (Inter)Face of African Pentecostalism." *Society* 46:6 (2009): 496–503.

Harkness, Janet A., Fons J. R. van de Vijver, and Peter Ph. Mohler. *Cross-Cultural Survey Methods.* Hoboken, NJ: Wiley-Interscience, 2002.

Health, Anthony, Stephen Fisher, and Shawna Smith. "The Globalization of Public Opinion." *Annual Review of Political Science* 8 (2005): 297–333.

Hinnells, John R. *The Zoroastrian Diaspora: Religion and Migration*. Oxford: Oxford University Press, 2005.

Hinnells, John R. *Zoroastrians in Britain*. Oxford: Oxford University Press, 1996.

Holbrook, Allyson L., Melanie C. Green, and Jon A. Krosnick. "Telephone Versus Face-to-Face Interviewing of National Probability Samples with Long Questionnaires: Comparisons of Respondent Satisficing and Social Desirability Response Bias." *Public Opinion Quarterly* 67 (2003): 79–125.

Huffington, Arianna. "Hang It Up." May 21, 2008. http://ariannaonline.huffingtonpost.com/columns/column.php?id=445.

Igo, Sahar. *The Averaged American: Surveys, Citizens, and the Making of a Mass Public*. Cambridge, MA: Harvard University Press, 2007.

"Indian Cabinet Approves Caste-Based Census for 2011." *BBC News*, September 9, 2010. http://www.bbc.co.uk/news/world-south-asia-11241916.

Institute of Jainology. "UK's General Census 2011." September 13, 2010. http://www.jainology.org/1068/general-census-2011/.

International Conference on Survey Methods in Multicultural, Multinational, and Multi-regional Contexts, conference proceedings. Berlin, Germany, June 25–9, 2008.

Johnson, Todd M., and Brian J. Grim, eds. *World Religion Database*. Leiden/Boston: Brill, 2008.

Kaufmann, Eric. *Shall the Religious Inherit the Earth? Demography and Politics in the Twenty-First Century*. London: Profile Books Ltd, 2010.

Keeter, Scott, Courtney Kennedy, April Clark, Trevor Tompson, and Mike Mokrzycki. "What's Missing from National Landline RDD Surveys? The Impact of The Growing Cell-Only Population." *Public Opinion Quarterly* 71 (2007): 772–92.

Keeter, Scott, Carolyn Miller, Andrew Kohut, Robert M. Groves, and Stanley Presser. "Consequences of Reducing Nonresponse in a National Telephone Survey." *Public Opinion Quarterly* 64 (2000): 125–48.

Kertzer, David I., and Dominique Arel, "Censuses, Identity Formation, and the Struggle for Political Power." In *Census and Identity: The Politics of Race, Ethnicity, and Language in National Censuses*, edited by David I. Kertzer and Dominique Arel, 1–42. Cambridge: Cambridge University Press, 2002.

Lang, Gladys Engel, and Kurt Lang. Comments in "The Future Study of Public Opinion: A Symposium." *Public Opinion Quarterly* 51 (1987): S181–2.

Lang, Kurt. "What Polls Can and Cannot Tell us About Public Opinion: Keynote Speech at the 60th Annual Conference of WAPOR." *International Journal of Public Opinion Research* 20 (2008): 3–22.

Lin, I-Fen, and Nora Cate Schaeffer. "Using Survey Participants to Estimate the Impact of Nonparticipation." *Public Opinion Quarterly* 59 (1995): 236–58.

Melton, Gordon, ed. *Religions of the World: A Comprehensive Encyclopedia of Beliefs and Practices*. 6 vols. 2nd ed. Santa Barbara, CA: ABC-CLIO, 2010.

Minganti, Pia Karlsson. "Becoming a 'Practising' Muslim – Reflections on Gender, Racism and Religious Identity among Women in a Swedish Muslim Youth Organisation." *Elore* 15: 1 (2008): 1–16.

Ministerio de Justicia, Secretaría General Técnica. *Guía de Entidades Religiosas de España (Iglesias, Confesiones y Comunidades Minoritarias)* [Guide to Religious Entities in Spain: Churches, Confessions and Minority Communities]. Madrid: Ministerio de Justicia, 1998.

Nachmani, Amikam. *Europe and Its Muslim Minorities: Aspects of Conflict, Attempts at Accord*. Brighton: Sussex Academic Press, 2009.

Okolo, Abraham. "The Nigerian Census: Problems and Prospects." *The American Statistician* 53:4 (1999): 321–5.

Paul, Leslie Allen. *The Deployment and Payment of the Clergy: A Report.* Westminster: Church Information Office for the Central Advisory Council for the Ministry, 1964.

Pew Forum on Religion and Public Life. *17-Nation Pew Global Attitudes Survey.* November 17, 2011. http://pewglobal.org.

Pew Forum on Religion and Public Life. *A Brief History of Religion and the US Census.* January 26, 2010. http://www.pewforum.org/Government/A-Brief-History-of-Religion-and-the-U-S--Census.aspx.

Pew Forum on Religion and Public Life. *The Future of the Global Muslim Population: Projections for 2010–2030.* January 27, 2011. http://pewresearch.org/pubs/1872/muslim-population-projections-worldwide-fast-growth.

Pew Forum on Religion and Public Life. *Spirit and Power: A 10-Country Survey of Pentecostals.* October 5, 2006. http://www.pewforum.org/Christian/Evangelical-Protestant-Churches/Spirit-and-Power.aspx.

Pew Forum on Religion and Public Life. *Tolerance and Tension: Islam and Christianity in Sub-Saharan Africa.* April 15, 2010. http://www.pewforum.org/executive-summary-islam-and-christianity-in-sub-saharan-africa.aspx.

Pew Forum on Religion and Public Life. *US Religious Landscape Survey.* 2007. http://religions.pewforum.org/.

Piralishvili, Zaza. "Religion." *Central Eurasia 2005 Analytical Annual: Georgia.* Sweden: CA&CC Press, 2006.

Smith, Helena. "Greece Tackles Identity Issue." *Dawn* (May 2000).

Smith, Jonathan Z., ed. *The HarperCollins Dictionary of Religion.* San Francisco, CA: HarperSanFrancisco, 1995.

Smith, Tom. "Review: The Muslim Population of the United States: The Methodology of Estimates." *Public Opinion Quarterly* 66:3 (2002): 404–17.

"So, How Many Hindus are there in the US?" *Hinduism Today*, January/February/March 2008. http://www.hinduismtoday.com/archives/2008/1-3/61_swadhyay%20pariwar.shtml.

Stark, Rodney, and Roger Finke. *Acts of Faith: Explaining the Human Side of Religion.* Berkeley: University of California, 2000.

Stephens, Bret. "Egypt – The Hangover." *The Wall Street Journal*, March 29, 2011. http://online.wsj.com/article/SB10001424052748704471904576228473270290208.html.

Stevens, Georgina. *Filling the Vacuum: Ensuring Protection and Legal Remedies for Minorities in Kosovo.* London: Minority Rights Group International, 2009.

Teitler, Julien O., Nancy E. Reichman, and Susan Sprachman. "Costs and Benefits of Improving Response Rates for a Hard-to-Reach Population." *Public Opinion Quarterly* 67 (2003): 126–38.

Tetlock, Philip. *Expert Political Judgment: How Good Is It? How Can We Know?* Princeton: Princeton University Press, 2006.

United Nations Children's Fund (UNICEF). Childinfo: Monitoring the Situation of Children and Women, "Multiple Indicator Cluster Surveys/MICS3." March 2012. http://www.childinfo.org/mics3_surveys.html.

Uvin, Peter. "On Counting, Categorizing, and Violence in Burundi and Rwanda." In *Census and Identity: The Politics of Race, Ethnicity, and Language in National Censuses*, edited by David I. Kertzer and Dominique Arel, 148–175. Cambridge: Cambridge University Press, 2002.

Weller, Paul. "Identity, Politics, and the Future(s) of Religion in the UK: The Case of the Religion Questions in the 2001 Decennial Census." *Journal of Contemporary Religion* 19:1 (2004): 3–21.

Whiteside, Brian. "Opinion: Think Carefully Before Answering Census Question on Religion." *The Irish Times*, March 3, 2011. http://www.irishtimes.com/newspaper/opinion/2011/0329/1224293298294.html.

Wilken, Robert Louis. *Remembering the Christian Past*. Grand Rapids, MI: William B. Eerdmans Publishing Company, 1995.

Yamagishi, T., and M. Yamagishi. "Trust and Commitment in the United States and Japan." *Motivation and Emotion* 18 (1994): 129–66.

Chapter 8

Analyzing Data on Religion

Many of the statistics on religious membership presented throughout this volume come from censuses and general population surveys of individuals. These data are collected in ways that permit estimation of summary characteristics of the general population, such as the share of the population that adheres to a particular faith or the average number of children who are likely to be born to women of different religious groups. For instance, many of the statistics presented in the case studies on Muslim population growth in chapters 10 and 11 rely on censuses and a variety of general population surveys with differing levels of quality. This chapter provides an explanation of the strengths and weaknesses of different types of general population surveys and census data and focuses on reconciling discrepancies between data.

International Religious Demography
Data Quality Index[1]

As chapter 6 of this volume details, the field of religious demography is still developing. Amassing any large collection of data for tracking religious demographics poses two practical challenges. First, no data source includes every country in the world, which means researchers must use multiple sources to cover the entire globe. Second, the ways religion is categorized in different data sources that are available are often incompatible, and some reconciliation is required to make them suitable to be combined. For instance, some general population surveys might only estimate religious affiliation for the country's adult population, requiring inferences to be made about the religious affiliation of children. Other surveys may only have data on women, requiring inferences to be made about men. Still others may miss certain parts of a country or be representative only of the primary urban centers. In order to

The World's Religions in Figures: An Introduction to International Religious Demography,
First Edition. Todd M. Johnson and Brian J. Grim.
© 2013 John Wiley & Sons, Ltd. Published 2013 by John Wiley & Sons, Ltd.

assess the relative quality of common census and general population survey sources of religious demographic data, Brian J. Grim and Becky Hsu created an International Religious Demography Data Quality Index (DDQI).[2] The index score indicates the degree to which the information given by each source represents a country's religious composition accurately, ranging between 0 (not reliable) and 100 (highly reliable). Each census and general population survey data source was scored on the basis of four components: geographic representation (how well the survey covers all regions of the country), response rate (how many people who were randomly chosen to participate in the survey completed the survey), sampling quality (how well the people interviewed are likely to be representative of the overall population), and questionnaire design (how well the questions measure the item of interest). In addition, two components not included in the index but that are necessary for making population projections using the cohort-component method are (1) age structure by religion in five-year cohorts (0–4, 5–9, 10–14, and upwards), and (2) age-specific fertility rates (number of children born to women in different groups). Individual scores for each component were combined into one overall score that reflected how reliable each data source was for estimates of a specific country's religious composition (see table 8.1 for an example using data from Kenya.) Also indicated is whether the information for making population projections was also available in the data source.

The first component, geographic representation of the country, is measured with two indicators: (1) the number of provinces surveyed divided by total number of provinces,[3] and (2) the percentage of provinces with at least 100 cases (that is, at least 100 individuals interviewed using a random method of selection in which each person in the total population ideally has an equal probability of being selected for inclusion in the survey). The threshold of 100 cases is often considered the minimum need for statistically significant analysis because it has a sampling margin of error of about +/− 10 percentage points; in comparison, samples of 1,000 or more have a sampling margin of error of about +/− 3 percentage points (see formula below). These margins of error apply to any randomly chosen sample regardless of the county's population size as long as segments of the population are not clustered, in which case more complex samples are required. Indeed, the DDQI includes the number of provinces with at least 100 cases because religious groups do tend to be clustered in certain regions of countries (see chapters 12 and 13 on China and the Sudans).

The second component of the index is the response rate, which denotes the percentage of people who answer the questions out of those who are chosen randomly for the survey. For example, if 100 people are sent a mail survey and 41 of those people return the filled-out survey, the survey has a 41% response rate. Higher response rates generally produce results that more accurately represent the general population,[4] assuming the sample of people selected for participation from the general population is random.

Two measures of sampling quality make up the third component of the index: (1) a margin of error (to quantify uncertainty about the survey results), using $M = 1/SQRT(N)$, where M refers to margin of error and $SQRT(N)$ refers to the square root of the valid sample size (the actual number of people who could have been included in the survey), and (2) whether both males and females are included in the sample (some high-quality demographic surveys sometimes only interview women). Based

Table 8.1 International Religious Demography Data Quality Index.

Country: Kenya

Source		Kenya census 1999	DHS 2003	DHS 1998	Afrobarometer 2003	DHS 1993	GAP 2005
Geographic representation	% provinces covered	100	100	100	88	88	63
	% provinces with at least 100 cases	100	100	100	1	1	25
	Score	100	100	100	44	44	44
Response	Response rate	98	96	86	60	82	37
	Score	98	96	86	60	82	37
Sampling	Valid sample size	28,485,803	11,773	11,288	2,398	9,876	1,000
	Margin of error	0.0%	0.9%	0.9%	2.0%	1.0%	3.2%
	Male and female	1	1	1	1	0	1
	Score	100	100	100	99	49	98
Questionnaire design	Number of religious categories	30	5	5	25	5	10
	Multiple languages	1	1	1	1	1	1
	Score	100	58	58	92	58	67
Overall score		99	89	86	74	71	61
Five-year age-structure data		Yes	Yes	Yes	No	Limited	No
Fertility data		Yes	Yes	Yes	No	Limited	No

DHS: Demographic and Health Survey; **GAP**: Pew Global Attitudes Project. **% provinces covered**: number of provinces surveyed divided by total number of provinces; **response rate**: percentage of those who participate out of those chosen randomly for the survey; **margin of error**: a number that quantifies uncertainty about the survey results (here, M=1/SQRT(N). N refers to the valid sample size); **male and female**: whether both are represented in the data (1=female and male both represented, 0=only one sex represented); **number of religious categories**: number of religious categories given to respondents (for example, if the survey asks "Are you Muslim, Christian, or Other?" the value is 3); **multiple languages**: whether more than one language was offered for the survey respondents (1=multiple languages available, 0=only one language available).

Source: Brian J. Grim and Becky Hsu, "Estimating the Global Muslim Population: Size and Distribution of the World's Muslim Population," *Interdisciplinary Journal of Research on Religion* 7:2 (2011).

on the formula above, sample size is the basis of the margin of error, and although it is not considered independently as a component in the index, it is included in table 8.1 because it is more easily understandable to the naked eye. The index considered the valid sample size for the Kenyan Demographic and Health Survey (DHS) to include only women of childbearing age (even if men were included in the survey) because the sampling design did not sample women and men independently. That is, the sampling frame (all those initially considered eligible to be selected for the survey) included only women. Then, any men in their households were interviewed. That means men not living in a household with women of childbearing age would not have been considered for the interview.

The fourth component of the Grim and Hsu index is questionnaire design, measuring data quality with reference to aspects of the survey format that facilitate accurate and detailed demographic information. Two indicators of good religious questionnaire design were included: (1) the number of religious categories available to respondents, which measures how limited the responses were by set categories (if the survey asks "Are you Muslim, Christian, or Other?," the value is 3), and (2) whether multiple languages common in the country were available to respondents (1=multiple languages available; 0=only one language available). The multiple languages indicator allows for more accuracy, as it is more likely that the respondent was surveyed using his or her native language (minority linguistic populations – including minority ethnic groups, immigrants, and expatriates – can be substantial in size).

Using Kenya as an example, table 8.1 illustrates how the Grim and Hsu index, with the added age structure and fertility criteria, assess data sources on religious demography. The sources analyzed include: the 1999 Kenya census;[5] the 1993, 1998, and 2003 Kenya DHS;[6] the 2003 Afrobarometer;[7] and the 2005 Pew Global Attitudes Project (GAP) survey.[8] The Kenya census scored highest on the index (99) and had both age-structure and fertility information, followed by the 2003 DHS (89), 1998 DHS (86), which had both age-structure and fertility information (albeit the age-structure information was contained in a separate file that has to be separately analyzed), 2003 Afrobarometer (74), 1993 DHS (71), and 2005 Pew GAP (61). For Kenya, as for other countries, the Afrobarometer and Pew GAP tended to have less extensive geographic coverage, resulting in lower scores on the index (and age-structure data is limited only to the adults who participated in the surveys).

Theoretically, one could take the average of all the recent estimates of religious affiliation in Kenya and then weight them by their data quality index score. However, Grim and Hsu point out two roadblocks to using this method for assessing all data sources. First, in numerous surveys, such as the World Values Survey, the question about religious affiliation is asked as a two-step question (Step 1: Do you belong to a religion?; Step 2: Which one?), which gives less religiously committed respondents the option to say initially that they have no affiliation. This reflects a degree of religiosity and not just basic religious identity, which is the aim of this particular kind of question. Combining data from this type of survey (which, in effect, often measures level of commitment to religion) with data from surveys that use the general census and the DHS approach (giving people a list of potential responses rather than an initial opt-out, which measures personal identification with a religion) muddies the picture by mixing data types. Of course, religiosity is a highly interesting – even important – question, but it is best understood through other questions, ranging from frequency of participation in religious activities to self-described importance of religion.

Second, sufficient "metadata" (information about the data and how they are collected) are often unavailable for some surveys. Concerning geographic coverage, some data sources (notably general population surveys) give little documentation on which areas are included; indeed, such surveys are not designed to be representative at the subnational level. Some general population surveys are done in urban areas only, and in other surveys it is unclear which provinces are included. Metadata about the second measure of data quality, response rates, are less well reported for many general population surveys than they are for national censuses and DHS. Although one could construct a data quality index using the other measures, trying to do this without measures of geographic representation would yield misleading scores for the various data sources. This is especially important because religious groups, particularly when they are minorities, can be geographically concentrated, as is the case in Kenya, where Muslims are clustered along the coast and near the border with Somalia (see chapter 12, "Estimating China's Religious Populations" for further discussion of this issue).

For these two reasons – the potential for introducing inaccuracies by mixing surveys reflecting religiosity only with those that reflect religious identification, and the lack of metadata for many surveys – Grim and Hsu argue against using their data quality index to weight each source and then averaging them together for an overall country score. Some researchers, however, have done this successfully with polling questions in the United States that are simple choices between candidates using general population surveys that are of equal quality to each other. For instance, statistician Nate Silver uses a data-averaging technique to combine results from US election polls because they are of equivalent quality.[9] Using general population surveys as part of national average with better-quality censuses and surveys becomes problematic because they include what is known to be poorer data that may only account for parts of a country or population. It becomes even more problematic when trying to use a weighted method to estimate the sizes of multiple religious groups from surveys that do not have the same number and categories of religious affiliation.

Census data

By this analysis, Grim and Hsu found that national censuses score highest for demographic data quality across countries, having the most comprehensive geographic coverage, high response rates, a high number of cases, and the inclusion of both males and females. Based on these parameters, researchers are generally safe treating censuses as the source with the best-quality data. These results extend to questions about religious affiliation from national censuses as well, because censuses generally cover the entire population and are conducted on a fairly regular basis.

The chief limitation in using census data, however, is that fewer than half of country censuses since the mid-1990s included a question about religious affiliation. In addition, censuses are generally conducted only once every 10 years, so the data might not be particularly current. Furthermore, censuses are not easy to use because acquiring the data, which are not always made public and appear in various printed and electronic forms, can be difficult. Some census data are housed as archived documents sent by other countries to the US Census Bureau during the past century and must be accessed physically. Some are available through websites such as the Integrated Public Use Microdata Series (IPUMS), International. A few countries provide easy access to detailed census data, such as the Fact Finder database of the US Census Bureau and the Australian Bureau of Statistics CDATA (character data) portal, which permits users to create customized tables based on the Australian census.

As an example, only 14 of the 27 European Union country censuses recently included a religious affiliation question that was then reported to the UN Statistical Division. The following European countries included questions about religion on their census forms between 1995 and 2004: Austria, Bulgaria, Croatia, Czech Republic, Estonia, Hungary, Ireland, Lithuania, Macedonia, Moldova, Montenegro, Portugal, Romania, Serbia, Slovakia, Slovenia, and the United Kingdom.

A further drawback comes from the fact that censuses sometimes force respondents to select their religion from a set list of religions. This can result in high-end estimates when respondents pick one of the listed religions (particularly if "other" and/or "none" is not one of the choices) when in fact they identify with or practice a religion that is not listed. Offering a limited or closed-ended list also has the potential to exclude religions that are considered illegal or are not recognized by the government, such as the Baha'i faith, which is illegal in Iran and not a recognized religion in Egypt. Additionally, census questions sometimes do not allow people to indicate that they are atheists in countries where non-adherence to religion is illegal, such as Indonesia.

Furthermore, census bureaus sometimes do not report data on all religious groups, especially smaller groups, despite having the data. For instance, the 2010 Mexican census asked whether people were Roman Catholic or something else. The "something else" category was left open-ended, thus requiring respondents to write in their answers.

Finally, because governments conduct censuses, political and social concerns can affect and bias the data. For example, the 1956 census for what is now Zimbabwe[10] was racially organized and did not include "Africans." The reported explained, "Owing to considerable practical difficulties, mainly an insufficient supply of persons qualified to undertake a satisfactory enumeration and the limited time available to prepare for the Census, no attempt was made to include the total African population in the 1956 enumeration."[11]

Demographic and health surveys

Based on the Grim and Hsu analysis, the next-best survey source of those reviewed for religious affiliation information is Macro International's Monitoring and Evaluation to Assess and Use Results (MEASURE) Demographic and Health Surveys (DHS).[12] These surveys are usually carried out by the same agency that conducts the census, but with expert guidance from Macro International staff, funded by the US Agency for International Development (USAID). The methodology behind these surveys is clear and the samples are large (usually over 7,000 people in each survey) and nationally representative. Though less comprehensive than censuses, demographic surveys complete sufficiently high numbers of household interviews to produce a generally accurate demographic profile of the country because they also collect data on all members of the household. However, the quality of DHS data suffers because the focus of the survey is on fertility and may miss population trends in households that do not have women of childbearing age. Also, some data sets include only females. Because females and males generally have different religious patterns (women tend to say they belong to a particular religion slightly more than men do), the omission of males from any sample introduces significant bias. Additionally, the DHS surveys include fewer religious categories, so the data only include a breakdown of the country's major religious groups and do not allow for detailed looks at religious groups where they are a small minority. Other surveys that provide information on religion of similar quality to DHS include the Multiple Indicator Cluster Surveys[13] and Generations and Gender Surveys.[14]

Other survey sources

In addition to census and demographic surveys, there exists an array of multi-country surveys such as Afrobarometer (2003, 2006, 2010), the Pew Global Attitudes Project (2005, 2010), InterMedia (2007), Latinobarometro (2007, 2010), European Social Survey (2008, 2010), and World Values Survey (2009, 2010), all of which vary by country and survey to survey in reliability. Multi-country surveys are valuable in that they tend to ask questions on religion in similar ways from country to country (such as one-step or two-step), allowing trends in religious affiliation to be tracked. Generally, these surveys sample around 1,000 to 2,000 people per country and are, depending on the country, limited to either an urban sample or a sample that does not include all provinces or states. Because general population surveys typically employ smaller samples, they might provide less accurate estimates. This is especially true where the size of a particular religious population is quite small or a religious group lives in concentrated locations that are not oversampled to ensure that the regions where they live in concentrations are included in the survey. Also available are a variety of country-specific general population surveys, some which focus on specific religious groups, such as Muslims in Germany (2006),[15] in Turkey,[16] and in the United States.[17]

However, data on religion obtained from such surveys have significant limitations. In Bulgaria, for instance, the estimate for "no religious affiliation" from the 1999 World Values Survey (30.4%) is much higher than that from the 2001 census (3.9%). It is unlikely that religious "nones" (as used here, the term refers to those who either say that they have no religion or decline to specify a religion) decreased by 26.5 percentage points in just two years. The large discrepancy is likely because of how the question was presented to respondents in each case. The 2001 census questionnaire offered the six choices shown in figure 8.1. The only way for a person to be counted as a religious "none" was either to say "None" in the "Other" category (coded "6" in figure 8.1) or to offer no response at all (coded "99" in figure 8.1), which was possible because answering this question was voluntary. The census's approach presumes that most people will choose one of the five specific religions listed.

The World Values Survey, by contrast, did not begin with this presupposition. Instead, it asked a two-part question.[18] The first part asked whether respondents belonged to a "religious denomination." Only those who answered "yes" were asked "Which one?" and shown a list of choices, as illustrated in figure 8.2.[19]

16. Вероизповедание*
1. Източноправославно
2. Католическо
3. Протестантско
4. Мюсюлманско сунитско
5. Мюсюлманско шиитско
6. Друго 🖉..........................
99. Не се самоопределя

Religion: 1. Eastern Orthodox; 2. Catholic; 3. Protestant; 4. Sunni Muslim;
5. Shi'a Muslim; 6. Other _____; 99. Not stated.

Figure 8.1 Bulgarian census, 2001. *Source*: Brian J. Grim and Becky Hsu, "Estimating the Global Muslim Population: Size and Distribution of the World's Muslim Population," *Interdisciplinary Journal of Research on Religion* 7:2 (2011).

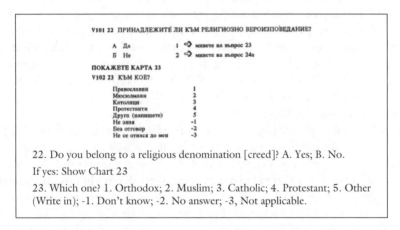

22. Do you belong to a religious denomination [creed]? A. Yes; B. No.

If yes: Show Chart 23

23. Which one? 1. Orthodox; 2. Muslim; 3. Catholic; 4. Protestant; 5. Other
(Write in); -1. Don't know; -2. No answer; -3, Not applicable.

Figure 8.2 World Values Survey religion question for Bulgaria (European Values Survey Edition), 1999. *Source*: Brian J. Grim and Becky Hsu, "Estimating the Global Muslim Population: Size and Distribution of the World's Muslim Population," *Interdisciplinary Journal of Research on Religion* 7:2 (2011).

There are several reasons why the World Values Survey approach will result in a lower estimate of people who are affiliated with religion. First, research has shown that some people who say that they do not belong to a religious group report later in the same survey that they attend worship services, sometimes regularly.[20] This might mean that they attend without being formally affiliated or that they did not understand or accurately answer the affiliation question. Other problems also arise in survey questions. For instance, the World Values Survey (European Values edition) does note for the 1999 Bulgarian survey that "[t]here were a couple of questions/concepts that caused problems as a result of translation. These were: q22, q24a. The term 'denomination' – not applicable to Muslims."[21] The results of the survey, however, seem to indicate that it was not Muslims, but Christians, who had difficulty with the question about denomination. The percentage of Muslims identified by the World Values Survey (11.0%) was comparable with the percentage shown by the census (12.2%), but there was a large difference between the percentage of Christians in the World Values Survey (58.6%) and that in the census (83.8%). This 25.2-percentage-point difference could account for the 26.5-point discrepancy seen in the "nones" category between the World Values Survey (30.4%) and the census (3.9%).

World Religion Database (WRD)

The launch of the *World Religion Database* (*WRD*)[22] in 2008 was significant, as it represented the first systematic effort to collect, collate, and analyze sources for international religious demography ranging from censuses and demographic surveys to statistics that are collected and reported by religious groups themselves. Before publication of the *World Religion Database*, the *World Christian Database*[23] and its predecessor, the *World Christian Encyclopedia* (1982 and 2001), collected information with a focus on measuring Christian populations, denominations, and movements. The *WRD*, however, provides a single place to access multiple census and survey estimates for the religious composition of countries. Compilation of the *WRD* involved collecting results from thousands of censuses and surveys into one database, including an analysis of religious affiliation data from Macro International's Demographic and Health Surveys (1998–2008) as well as cross-national general social surveys such as Afrobarometer (2006), the World Values Survey (2006–8), and the Pew Global Attitudes Project (2007).

The *WRD* also utilizes other sources of information on religious affiliation, including anthropological and ethnographic studies as well as statistical reports from religious groups themselves. Perhaps one of the most significant drawbacks of many censuses and surveys is that they do not measure Christian traditions, denominations, or movements adequately, due either to having insufficient sample sizes or to asking questions that do not allow a careful breakdown of Christians into their subgroups. This problem can be remedied somewhat by consulting the detailed membership and adherence statistics that many Christian and other religious groups collect, which can be cross-checked against census and survey sources. This problem is even more acute for other religious groups (such as Muslims) because few censuses, and historically only a limited number of surveys, ask about subgroup identity (such as Shi'a and Sunni Muslim). There is even less census and survey data on subgroups of Hindus, Buddhists, and Jews. Developing reliable measures for these subgroups is research that still needs to be accomplished.

The greatest strength of the *WRD* lies in its use of multiple sources of information to reach best estimates for a country's religious composition. For instance, when estimating the number of Hindus in the United States – where the census does not ask religious affiliation – the *WRD* takes into account survey evidence, such as the Pew Forum's 2007 *US Religious Landscape Survey*. The survey interviewed more than 35,000 American adults and found that approximately 0.4% of respondents indicated being Hindu. The *WRD* estimates a slightly larger number (0.47%, or 1.4 million people in 2010), which takes into account children and other sources of information, such as immigrant data found in another recent Pew Forum study.[24] The study found that outside of South Asia, the United States has by far the largest number of Hindu immigrants – 1.3 million first-generation (foreign-born) Hindus.

Since not all Hindus in the United States are foreign born, this justifies a slightly larger number than revealed by Pew's 2007 survey.[25]

This same methodology involving multiple sources of information is useful when estimating subgroups of major religions. For instance, the Pew Forum's 2009 estimate of Sunni and Shi'a Muslims around the world relied on multiple sources, and in a number of cases relied on *WRD* estimates.[26]

Unlike estimates for Muslim populations overall, almost no censuses and relatively few surveys ask Muslims about their Sunni or Shi'a affiliation. Accordingly, Pew Forum researchers relied on three primary sources to generate Sunni–Shi'a estimates:

- Analyses by more than 20 demographers and social scientists at universities and research centers around the world who acted as consultants on the project
- Ethnographic analyses included in the *WRD*
- A review of other published or frequently used estimates, including demographic summaries on some 200 countries in the annual International Religious Freedom reports published by the US State Department as well as estimates published in the *CIA World Factbook.*

For most countries with sizeable Muslim populations, one or more experts on Islam provided the Pew Forum with their best estimates of the Sunni–Shi'a breakdown based on their own reviews of the published sources and other expert analyses available to them.

Additionally, for all countries and territories in the 2009 Muslim population study, Pew Forum researchers consulted the *WRD* estimates of the proportions of Muslims who are Sunni and Shi'a in each country. These estimates are based in turn on the *WRD*'s ethnicity database of more than 4,300 ethnolinguistic groups. For instance, the *WRD* estimates that of the approximately 36,000 ethnically Persian refugees living in Yemen, 96% are Shi'a Muslims. Taking this into account adds to the overall Shi'a population of Yemen, which the *WRD* estimates to be 54% of the total population, a larger share than estimated by the expert consulted by the Pew Forum.

As a result, the Sunni–Shi'a estimates presented in the Pew Forum report are based primarily on data gathered via ethnographic and anthropological studies, necessitated by the fact that many Muslims either cannot (due to question wording) or will not identify themselves as Sunni or Shi'a. Therefore, Pew Forum staff were not able to estimate the possible margin of error associated with any particular estimate. Taking into account the three different sources (censuses, surveys, and the *WRD*), the study provided a likely range of the proportions of Muslims worldwide that are Sunni and Shi'a based on an analysis of each country. Some ranges are broader than others because the sources consulted provided different estimates or because the sources suggest a wider range due to the lack of more precise information for a particular country.

Examples of other WRD sources Much more scholarly attention has focused on the size and distribution of Christian communities around the globe than on those of adherents of other religions. As scholars collected data on Christian movements, however, they also collected information on other religious groups in order to provide the appropriate religious context. Several of the examples of other *WRD* sources described in this section embody this approach. These include scholarly monographs, church and religion yearbooks and handbooks, government statistical reports, field surveys and interviews, correspondence with national informants, unpublished documentation, directories of denominations and other religious bodies, print and web-based descriptions of religions, and computerized surveys of doctoral dissertations and master's theses on religion. All of these sources are explained in detail, including discussions of their limitations, in chapter 7 of this volume.

Reconciling Discrepancies Between Data

There are post-survey strategies that help general population surveys better reflect the actual composition of a particular country. For instance, if in a survey of 1,000 people, 60% were women and 40% were men, but we know that women and men are each 50% of the country's total population based on a recent census, then each woman's response on the general population survey would be weighted down by a factor of 500/600 and each man's response would be weighted up by a factor of 500/400. Such adjustments are called weighting.

Other adjustments made to general population surveys may require taking into account that they are meant to be representative of only adult populations. Therefore their results require adjustments, particularly if some religious groups have more children than others in the same country. This requires either a complete roster of members of each household or some other way to estimate of the number of children living in the household with the adults. When a complete roster is unavailable, most estimates of religious affiliation of children assume that they have the same religion as one of their parents (usually assumed by demographers to be the religion of the mother). Differences in fertility rates between religious groups are particularly useful in estimating religious differentials among children.[27]

At times the results from government censuses and information from religious communities can be strikingly different. For example, in Egypt, where the vast majority of the population is Muslim, government censuses taken every 10 years have shown consistently for the past 100 years that a declining share of the population declare themselves as or profess to be Christians. In the most recent census, some 5% identified as Christian. However, church estimates point to a percentage figure three times larger (15%). This discrepancy may be due to overestimates by the churches or attributed, at least in part, to social pressure on some Christians to record themselves as Muslims. Further, according to news reports, some Egyptian Christians have complained that they are listed on official identity cards as Muslims. It also might be that church reports include Egyptian Christians working as expatriates outside of Egypt, while the census does not, or that the churches simply overestimate their numbers.

Such a lack of clarity is compounded by media reports and even Egyptian government announcements repeatedly claiming that Christians make up 10% or more of the country's approximately 80 million people, despite the fact that the census repeatedly reports only 5%. The highest share of Christians found in an Egyptian census was in 1927 (8.3%). Figures for Egyptian Christians declined in each subsequent census, with Christians making up 5.7% of the Egyptian population in 1996. The report from the most recent census, conducted in 2006, does not, however, provide data on religious affiliation, but a sample of the 2006 census data is available through the Integrated Public Use Microdata Series, International (IPUMS).[28] The sample reports the same Christian share (about 5%) as the latest Egyptian DHS, with a sample size of 16,527 women ages 15 to 49.

Of course, as noted by Pew Forum demographer Conrad Hackett, "it is possible that Christians in Egypt have been undercounted in censuses and demographic surveys."[29] According to the Pew Forum's analysis of Global Restrictions on Religion,[30] Egypt has very high government restrictions on religion as well as high social hostilities involving religion. Hackett goes on to observe that "these factors may lead some Christians, particularly converts from Islam, to be cautious about revealing their identity."

Regardless of the actual number, it is very likely that Christians are declining as a proportion of Egypt's population, even if their absolute numbers are not falling. On the one hand, Christian fertility in Egypt has been lower than Muslim fertility. On the other, is possible that Christians have left the country, though a 2012 study by the Pew Forum on the religious affiliation of migrants around the world has not found evidence of an especially large Egyptian Christian diaspora.[31]

This chapter has discussed a variety of issues related to finding and choosing the best data sources of religious affiliation in countries. Censuses are generally accepted as the most reliable, but there are times when they fail to represent the full picture due to omitting certain regions of a country or because they do not offer clear and detailed questions about religion. General population surveys can often fill the gap, but, depending on their quality, they may also have some bias. At times, religious groups may have very different estimates of their sizes than are found by censuses and surveys, but for some types of data, such as denominations of Protestantism, estimates by the groups may be the best information available. And finally, for religions such as Islam, Hinduism, Buddhism, and Judaism, subgroup information is routinely missing from censuses and surveys. Estimates for the subgroups of these religions often rely on indirect measures, such as ethnic groups likely to adhere to a particular subgroup or expert analysis of multiple ethnological and anthropological sources.

Notes

1 This section is adapted from the article by Brian J. Grim and Becky Hsu, "Estimating the Global Muslim Population: Size and Distribution of the World's Muslim Population," *Interdisciplinary Journal of Research on Religion* 7:2 (2011).

2 Ibid.

3 While it is possible that a census or survey could have covered a large number of provinces but missed the largest ones, in practice this infrequently (if ever) happens. One reasonable alternative method that could improve the index would be to weight the provinces by their population sizes.

4 There is a large literature on the effect of response rates. For more information, see Robert M. Groves, Robert B. Cialdini, and Mick P. Couper, "Understanding The Decision to Participate in a Survey," *Public Opinion Quarterly* 56 (1998): 475–95.

5 Central Bureau of Statistics, *Kenya 1999 Population and Housing Census* (Nairobi: Central Bureau of Statistics, Ministry of Finance and Planning, 2002).

6   National Council for Population and Development, Central Bureau of Statistics, and Macro International, *Kenya Demographic and Health Survey 1993* (Nairobi: National Council for Population and Development, 1994); National Council for Population and Development, Central Bureau of Statistics, and Macro International, *Kenya Demographic and Health Survey 1998* (Nairobi: National Council for Population and Development, 1999); Central Bureau of Statistics, Ministry of Health, and ORC Macro, *Kenya Demographic and Health Survey 2003* (Nairobi: Central Bureau of Statistics, 2004).

7   Afrobarometer, *Round 2: Afrobarometer Survey in Kenya* (Nairobi: Institute for Democracy in South Africa, Ghana Centre for Democratic Development, and Michigan State University, 2003).

8   Pew Forum on Religion and Public Life, *17-Nation Pew Global Attitudes Survey*, November 17, 2011, http://pewglobal.org.

9   Nate Silver, "Methodology," *FiveThirtyEight: Nate Silver's Political Calculus*, http://fivethirtyeight.blogs.nytimes.com/methodology.

10 In 1956, the Federation of Rhodesia and Nyasaland included Northern Rhodesia (Zambia) and Nyasaland (Malawi) as well as Southern Rhodesia (Zimbabwe).

11 Federation of Rhodesia and Nyasaland Census Bureau, *Census of Population Report* (Salisbury, Rhodesia: Federation of Rhodesia and Nyasaland Census Bureau, 1956), 1.

12 See http://www.measuredhs.com for more information.

13 The United Nations Children's Fund (UNICEF), *Multiple Indicator Cluster Surveys 3* (New York/Geneva: United Nations, 2012), http://www.childinfo.org/mics3_surveys.html.

14 United Nations, *Generations and Gender Programme: Exploring Future Research and Data Collection Options* (New York/Geneva: United Nations, 2000).

15 Sonja Haug, Stephanie Müssig, and Anja Stichs, *Muslimisches Leben in Deutschland: im Auftrag der Deutschen Islam Konferenz* [Muslim Life in Germany: German Conference on Islam], Forschungsbericht 6 (Deutsche Islam Konferenz [German Islam Conference]).

16 Ali Çarkoğlu and Binnaz Toprak, *Religion, Society and Politics in a Changing Turkey* (Istanbul: Turkish Economic and Social Studies Foundation Publications, 2006).

17 Pew Research Center, *Muslim Americans: Middle Class and Mostly Mainstream*, May 22, 2007, http://pewresearch.org/assets/pdf/muslim-americans.pdf.

18 European Values Survey, "Documentation Report, European Values Survey, 1999, Bulgaria," available at http://www.wvsevsdb.com/wvs/WVSDocumentation.jsp.

19 The World Values Survey questionnaire is available at http://www.wvsevsdb.com/wvs/WVSDocumentation.jsp.

20 See Baylor Institute for Studies of Religion, *What Americans Really Believe: New Findings from the Baylor Surveys of Religion* (Waco, TX: Baylor University Press, 2008).

21 European Values Survey, "Documentation Report," 1.

22 Todd M. Johnson and Brian J. Grim, eds., *World Religion Database* (Leiden/Boston: Brill, 2008). Available at http://www.worldreligiondatabase.org.

23 Todd M. Johnson, ed., *World Christian Database* (Leiden/Boston: Brill, 2007).

24 Pew Forum on Religion and Public Life, *Faith on the Move: The Religious Affiliation of International Migrants*. March 8, 2012. See http://pewresearch.org/pubs/2214/religion-religious-migrants-christians-muslims-jews.

25 The Pew Forum's *Religious Landscape Survey* estimated that more than 80% of Hindus in the United States are foreign-born.

26 See Pew Forum on Religion and Public Life, "Mapping the Global Muslim Population," October 7, 2009, http://www.pewforum.org/Muslim/Mapping-the-Global-Muslim-Population%2820%29.aspx.

27 This is because demographic projections carry forward children born to women. It may introduce some bias to the degree that the father's religion is more likely to be the religion of the children than the mother.

28 https://international.ipums.org/international/sample_designs/sample_designs_eg.shtml

29 Pew Research Center, "Ask the Expert," May 11, 2011, http://pewresearch.org/pubs/1770/ask-the-expert-pew-research-center#christians-egypt.

30 Pew Forum on Religion and Public Life, *Global Restrictions on Religion*, December 17, 2009, http://www.pewforum.org/Government/Global-Restrictions-on-Religion.aspx.

31 See Pew Forum, "Faith on the Move." Additional sources of information include Fatma El-Zanaty and Ann Way, *Egyptian Demographic and Health Survey 2008* (Cairo: Ministry of Health, El-Zanaty and Associates, and Macro International, 2009); Juan E. Campo and John Iskander, "The Coptic Community," in *The Oxford Handbook of Global Religions*, ed. Mark Juergensmeyer (Oxford: Oxford University Press, 2006); Youssef Courbage and Philippe Fargues, *Christians and Jews under Islam*, trans. Judy Mabr (London: I. B. Tauris & Co., 1997); Elana Ambrosetti and Nahid Kamal, "The Relationship between Religion and Fertility: The Case of Bangladesh and Egypt," paper presented at the 2008 European Population Conference, Barcelona, Spain, July 9–12, 2008; Johnson and Grim, *World Religion Database*; Integrated Public Use Microdata Series International; 1996 Egyptian census data.

References

Afrobarometer. *Round 2: Afrobarometer Survey in Kenya*. Nairobi: Institute for Democracy in South Africa, Ghana Centre for Democratic Development, and Michigan State University, 2003.

Ambrosetti, Elana, and Nahid Kamal. "The Relationship between Religion and Fertility: The Case of Bangladesh and Egypt." Paper presented at the 2008 European Population Conference, Barcelona, Spain, July 9–12, 2008.

Baylor Institute for Studies of Religion. *What Americans Really Believe: New Findings from the Baylor Surveys of Religion*. Waco, TX: Baylor University Press, 2008.

Campo, Juan E., and John Iskander. "The Coptic Community." In *The Oxford Handbook of Global Religions*, edited by Mark Juergensmeyer, 315–24. Oxford: Oxford University Press, 2006.

Çarkoğlu, Ali, and Binnaz Toprak. *Religion, Society and Politics in a Changing Turkey*. Istanbul: Turkish Economic and Social Studies Foundation Publications, 2006.

Central Bureau of Statistics. *Kenya 1999 Population and Housing Census*. Nairobi: Central Bureau of Statistics, Ministry of Finance and Planning, 2002.

Central Bureau of Statistics, Ministry of Health, and ORC Macro. *Kenya Demographic and Health Survey 2003*. Nairobi: Central Bureau of Statistics, 2004.

Courbage, Youssef, and Philippe Fargues. *Christians and Jews under Islam*. Translated by Judy Mabr. London: I. B. Tauris & Co., 1997.

European Values Survey. "Documentation Report, European Values Survey, 1999, Bulgaria." http://www.wvsevsdb.com/wvs/WVSDocumentation.jsp.

Federation of Rhodesia and Nyasaland Census Bureau. *Census of Population Report*. Salisbury: Rhodesia: Federation of Rhodesia and Nyasaland Census Bureau, 1956.

Grim, Brian J., and Becky Hsu. "Estimating the Global Muslim Population: Size and Distribution of the World's Muslim Population." *Interdisciplinary Journal of Research on Religion* 7:2 (2011).

Groves, Robert M., Robert B. Cialdini, and Mick P. Couper. "Understanding The Decision to Participate in a Survey." *Public Opinion Quarterly* 56 (1998): 475–95.

Haug, Sonja, Stephanie Müssig, and Anja Stichs. *Muslimisches Leben in Deutschland: im Auftrag der Deutschen Islam Konferenz* [Muslim Life in Germany: German Conference on Islam] Forschungsbericht 6 [Research Report 6]. Deutsche Islam Konferenz [German Islam Conference].

Johnson, Todd M., ed. *World Christian Database*. Leiden/Boston: Brill, 2007.

Johnson, Todd M., and Brian J. Grim, eds. *World Religion Database*. Leiden/Boston: Brill, 2008.

National Council for Population and Development, Central Bureau of Statistics, and Macro International. *Kenya Demographic and Health Survey 1993*. Nairobi: National Council for Population and Development, 1994.

National Council for Population and Development, Central Bureau of Statistics, and Macro International. *Kenya Demographic and Health Survey 1998*. Nairobi: National Council for Population and Development, 1999.

Pew Forum on Religion and Public Life. *17-Nation Pew Global Attitudes Survey*. November 17, 2011. http://pewglobal.org.

Pew Forum on Religion and Public Life. *Faith on the Move: The Religious Affiliation of International Migrants*. March 8, 2012. http://pewresearch.org/pubs/2214/religion-religious-migrants-christians-muslims-jews.

Pew Forum on Religion and Public Life. *Global Restrictions on Religion*. December 17, 2009. http://www.pewforum.org/Government/Global-Restrictions-on-Religion.aspx.

Pew Forum on Religion and Public Life. *Mapping the Global Muslim Population: A Report on the Size and Distribution of the World's Muslim Population*. October 7, 2009. http://www.pewforum.org/Mapping-the-Global-Muslim-Population.aspx.

Pew Forum on Religion and Public Life. *US Religious Landscape Survey*. 2007. http://religions.pewforum.org/.

Pew Research Center. "Ask the Expert." May 11, 2011. http://pewresearch.org/pubs/1770/ask-the-expert-pew-research-center#christians-egypt.

Pew Research Center. *Muslim Americans: Middle Class and Mostly Mainstream*. May 22, 2007. http://pewresearch.org/assets/pdf/muslim-americans.pdf.

Silver, Nate. "Methodology." *FiveThirtyEight: Nate Silver's Political Calculus*. http://fivethirtyeight.blogs.nytimes.com/methodology.

United Nations. *Generations and Gender Programme: Exploring Future Research and Data Collection Options*. New York/Geneva: United Nations, 2000.

United Nations Children's Fund (UNICEF). *Multiple Indicator Cluster Surveys 3*. New York/Geneva: United Nations, 2012. http://www.childinfo.org/mics3_surveys.html.

Zanaty, Fatma El-, and Ann Way. *Egyptian Demographic and Health Survey 2008*. Cairo: Ministry of Health, El-Zanaty and Associates, and Macro International, 2009.

Chapter 9

Dynamics of Change in Religious Populations

The question of how and why the number of religious adherents changes over time is critical to the study of international religious demography. It is more complex than simply "counting heads" via births and deaths – a well-established area in quantitative sociological studies – but in addition involves the multifaceted areas of religious conversion and migration. The migration of religious people is only in the past few years become a more researched area of demographic study,[1] and issues surrounding religious conversion continue to be under-represented in the field.[2] Data on religion from a wide range of sources – including from the religious communities themselves, as well as governments and scholars – must be employed to understand the total scope of religious affiliation. Given data on a particular religion from two separate points in time, the question can be raised, "What are the dynamics by which the number of adherents changes over time?" The dynamics of change in religious affiliation can be reduced to three sets of empirical population data that together enable enumeration of the increase or decrease in adherents over time. To measure overall change, these three sets can be defined as follows: (1) births minus deaths; (2) converts to minus converts from; and (3) immigrants minus emigrants.[3] The first variable in each of these three sets (births, converts to, immigrants) measures increase, whereas the second (deaths, converts from, emigrants) measures decrease. All future (and current) projections of religious affiliation, within any subset of the global population (normally a country or region), will account for these dynamics, and the changes themselves are dependent on these dynamics.[4] This relationship is shown in figure 9.1.[5]

The World's Religions in Figures: An Introduction to International Religious Demography,
First Edition. Todd M. Johnson and Brian J. Grim.

Figure 9.1   Calculating net religious change. Based on Todd M. Johnson and Kenneth R. Ross, eds., *Atlas of Global Christianity* (Edinburgh: Edinburgh University Press, 2009).

Births

The primary mechanism of global religious demographic change is (live) births. Children are almost always counted as having the religion of their parents (as is the law in Norway, for example). In simple terms, if populations that are predominantly Muslim, for example, have more children on average than those that are predominantly Christian or Hindu, then over time (all other things being equal) Muslims will become an increasingly larger percentage of that population. This means that the relative size of a religious population has a close statistical relationship to birthrates. The two extremes are illustrated on the one side by Shakers, who practiced celibacy as preparation for the kingdom of God, and on the other side by Mormons, who place a high value on having large families. In general, it is important for the continuation of religion that children are raised in the faith. As Alan Aldridge has commented, "movements which fail to retain their own children in active membership will inevitably decline, since they will not be able to recruit enough committed new people to replace those they lost through the normal processes of attrition."[6] While this is true, it is also important to realize that raising children in the faith and *retaining* them in the faith arguably are, or at least seem to be, two different things.

Fertility rates can be compared across different religions or across different traditions within religions. The Indian census (1981, 1991, 2001) suggests that Muslims have higher fertility rates than Hindus, and that this may outweigh differences in mortality. Thus, the demographic transition (to replacement levels) started earlier for Hindus than Muslims and now Muslim women are bearing a larger number of children at earlier ages than either Hindu or Christian women.[7] One study of fertility among different Christian denominations in Australia compared data from the 1911 and 1921 censuses.[8] The results suggested that women immigrants born in England and Wales (Church of England, Methodists, Presbyterians) were the first to begin limiting family size. Later, Catholic women from Ireland and Lutheran women from Germany also began limiting their family sizes. In addition, the most rapid decline in fertility occurred between 1911 and 1966, largely among non-Catholics. Fertility rates often vary between religious and non-religious communities as well. Scott Thomas observes that, "religiosity is now one of the most accurate indicators of fertility, far more telling than denominational or ethnic identity, since religious people tend to have more children than their secular counterparts."[9]

One of the more profound differences in fertility found within a religious community is that of the ultra-Orthodox Jews in Israel. While the wider Jewish community has seen falling fertility rates, ultra-Orthodox Jews continue to have large families. Eric Kaufmann explains:

> Between 1950 and 1980, Jewish immigrants [to Israel] from high-fertility Muslim countries reduced their TFR [total fertility rate[10]] from over 6 to just over 3 children per woman, only slightly above the Jewish average. Israeli Arab TFR fell from 8.5 in 1950 to around 4 by the late 1980s. But Haredi [ultra-Orthodox] fertility remained stuck in a time warp, at 6.49 children per woman in 1980–82. This subsequently *rose* to 7.61 during 1990–96 and has remained at that level ever since. During the same period, the TFR of other Jews declined from 2.61 to 2.27.[11]

Relatively high birthrates are an important factor in the growth of the Muslim population (both native and immigrant) in Europe and continue to outstrip those of native (non-Muslim) Europeans. In Austria in 1981, for example, the Muslim total fertility rate was 3.09 children per woman, contrasted with a general population rate of 1.67. In 1991 and 2001 the ratios were 2.77 to 1.51, and 2.34 to 1.32, respectively.[12] A similar situation exists in many European countries, which has recently sparked concern about the "Islamization" of Europe.

Another important dynamic is how levels of religiosity impact fertility. Several studies have shown that increased religiosity correlates with higher fertility rates among women. This is true in Europe, where a woman's level of education traditionally has been considered the main determinant of her fertility. In Spain, for example, women who are practicing Catholics have more children than non-practicing Catholic women, across all income and education levels.[13] Religious Jewish women in Europe have twice the fertility rate of non-religious Jewish women, as was reported in the European Values Surveys of 1981, 1990, and 1997.[14] High fertility rates are often seen in small, isolated religious groups as well. The Old Order Amish in the United States, for example, have doubled in population roughly every 20 years: from only 5,000 in 1900, they have grown to over 200,000 today.[15] Other endogenous fundamentalist groups with high birthrates include the Laestadian Lutherans of Finland and Holland's Orthodox Calvinists.[16]

It is also important to realize that fertility rates within religious communities are not static, nor do they always continue without interruption. One example of their volatility is shown in Eric Kaufmann's analysis of Iran's family planning over a 50-year period. Kaufmann observes that in the 1960s and 70s, Iran's westernization policy focused on encouraging and enabling women to study or work outside the home. Contraception became available, resulting in a fertility decline. Following the Iranian Revolution of 1979, however, family planning clinics were seen as an imperialist plot against Islam. The government closed them, segregated the sexes, and discouraged women from working. At the same time, the minimum age for marriage was lowered from 14 years to 9 years. The loss of life in the Iran–Iraq war in 1980s added to the emphasis on higher fertility. Thus, fertility rates in Iran dropped from 7.7 to 6.3 children per woman between 1966 and 1976, and then rebounded to 7 children after the revolution. In another reversal, as the population approached 60 million, the younger generation challenged the state budget, and religion gave way to accommodate secular demands. By the late 1980s, family planning in Iran had gone full circle, from pregnancy prevention to pronatalism and back again.[17]

Examining groups with extremely low fertility rates, which continue to shrink (and many of which have disappeared altogether), is as important as studying those with high fertility. As Rodney Stark has observed, "Almost every day, somewhere in the world, a new religion appears."[18] Yet, almost all of these new religions fail, because they never gain enough demographic momentum to thrive. The Hutterites, for example, were the only group to have survived from the 83 American communes that formed in the nineteenth century (including 30 religious ones); a high fertility rate was the reason. Celibate groups like the Shakers withered when flows of converts failed to materialize. Today, three adherents living in Sabbathday Lake Shaker Village in New Gloucester, Maine, are all that remain of the Shakers.[19]

A larger, more ancient religious community suffering from demographic decline is the Zoroastrians. Their fertility rates have been well below replacement value for more than half a century in both Iran (where their numbers are also affected by emigration) and India. Endogamy and bans on conversion, combined with low birth-rates, have made it nearly impossible for Zoroastrians to maintain demographic momentum. Zoroastrians grew at less than one third of the world population growth rate from 1910–2010.[20] Christian Science also has seen a steady decline since 1926, a result of lower fertility among the wealthy demographic the group attracted.[21]

Globally, fertility rates have fallen in most Muslim-majority countries in recent decades. Among the many contributing factors are increasing education and economic well-being (especially of women), increased access to contraception and family planning, and urbanization. Yet Muslim fertility rates remain, on average, higher than in the rest of the developing world and considerably higher than in more-developed countries. This continued high fertility is one of the main reasons that the global Muslim population is projected to rise both in absolute numbers and as a share of all the people in the world. In addition, political scientists Pippa Norris and Ronald Inglehart document the fact that secularization and human development have powerful, negative impact on fertility rates. Almost all countries with more advanced secularization have fertility rates at or below replacement level while countries with traditional religious orientations are at two or three times the replacement rate. They conclude, "as a result of these two interlocking trends, rich nations are becoming more secular, but the world as a whole is becoming more religious."[22]

Moreover, high fertility rates in the past create a certain demographic momentum. As a result of previously high fertility, large numbers of Muslim youth and young adults are now in (or entering) their prime childbearing years, all but ensuring that relatively rapid population growth will continue in the next two decades, even if the number of births per woman goes down. These trends are examined in more detail in chapter 11 of this volume.

Despite its significant role, however, the total impact of religion on fertility rates is difficult to assess and remains a subject of debate.[23] One should not assume that because fertility tends to be higher in Muslim-majority countries than in other developing countries, Islamic teachings are the reason. Cultural, social, economic, political, histor-ical, and other factors may play equal or greater roles. For example, many Muslims live in countries with higher rates of poverty, less access to adequate health care, fewer educational opportunities, and populations that are more rural than the global averages. All of these conditions are generally associated with higher fertility rates.

As mentioned previously, there is also some evidence that, across a variety of religious traditions, women who are more religious have higher fertility rates than less religious women. This suggests that religiosity in general, rather than Islam in particular, may boost the number of children per woman. In short, while Islamic beliefs might directly or indirectly influence the size of Muslim families, religion does not operate in isolation from other forces; fertility rates appear to be driven by a complex mixture of cultural, social, economic, religious, and other factors.[24]

Deaths

Even as births increase their memberships, religious communities experience constant loss through the deaths of members. Though this often includes tragic, unanticipated deaths of younger members, it most frequently affects the elderly members. Thus, changes in health care and technology can positively impact religious communities if members live longer.

Just as differences in birthrates contribute to the growth or decline of religious communities, death rates also have a similar impact. One example is the 1,000 Nazarene Christians in Somalia, who represent less than 0.05% of the country's total population. During the first decade of the twenty-first century, some 500 Christians, including many Nazarenes, reportedly were killed in Somalia. With high deaths rates as the major determinant of their group's change in size, the dwindling Nazarene community might soon disappear.[25]

One of the most devastating combinations of factors for a religious group is a high death rate combined with a high emigration rate. This is the case for the Sabian Mandeans, an indigenous religious and ethnic community in Iraq, whose numbers have declined dramatically in recent years due to both of these factors.[26] In 2003, prior to the US-led coalition invasion, some 60,000 Sabian Mandeans lived in Iraq. Today, only about 5,000 remain in the country. Out of a national population of about 31 million, they represent less than 0.02%. Iraq's Sabian Mandean community is at risk of imminent extinction in the face of violence at the hands of Sunni and Shi'a extremists – unpunished by the country's central and provincial authorities – and of massive emigration to neighboring countries and across the globe.[27] The name of the group derives from elements of its distinctive Aramaic language, heritage, and beliefs. The Mandaic language itself appeared in UNESCO's *Atlas of the World's Languages in Danger of Disappearing*.[28] Fearing mistreatment if they call attention to themselves, members of the community now use the language for liturgical purposes only.

Births Minus Deaths/Total Fertility Rate

The change over time in any given population is most simply expressed as the number of births into the community minus the number of deaths out of it. Many religious communities around the world experience little else in the dynamics of their growth or decline. Detailed projections rely on a number of estimated measures, including life expectancy, population age structures, and the total fertility rate. This means that any attempt to understand the dynamics of religious affiliation must be based firmly on demographic projections of births and deaths.

The impact of births and deaths on religious affiliation can, of course, change over time. For example, the 2001 Northern Ireland census revealed a continued closing of the population gap between Protestants and Catholics over the previous three decades. Protestants made up over 62% of the population in 1971,[29] but by 2001 this had dropped to 53%.[30] Catholics, in the meantime, had grown from nearly 37% to almost 44% of the population. This shift is due primarily to the higher birthrate among Catholic women. One would expect that, given time, Catholics would eventually claim over 50% of the population of Northern Ireland, but the 2001 census also revealed two countertrends: (1) the death rate among Protestants is falling, and (2) the birthrate among Catholics is falling. Given these trends, forecasters believe that, barring unexpected changes from this pattern, Protestants will remain in the majority in the coming decades.[31]

Another possible population dynamic is a falling death rate combined with a low birthrate. This is the case for Muslims in Finland, specifically Turkish Tatars. A 1996 survey among members of the Tatar community showed that 30% were over 60 years old. The proportion of elderly in this group is twice that of the general population in Finland. At the same time, the share of those under 20 years old is 16%, significantly lower than the Finnish average. The percentage of Tatars in the youngest group had dropped by 10% since May 1994. The report concludes, "in light of the receding birth rate in the community, it was therefore estimated that, if the development proceeds at this rate, in 2050 there will be no members under twenty years in the community."[32]

Converts To

It is a common observation that individuals (or even whole villages or communities) change allegiance from one religion to another (or to no religion at all). Conversions in the twentieth century were most pronounced in one general area: large numbers of ethnoreligionists who converted to Christianity, Islam, Hinduism, and Buddhism. In the African Sahel (the semi-arid region south of the Sahara Desert), many countries continue to experience competition between Islam and Christianity for those individuals and communities still adhering to ethnoreligions. Early in the twentieth century it was assumed that within a generation all ethnoreligionists in Africa would become either Muslims or Christians.[33] Although many conversions took place, over 96 million had not converted by 2000.[34] In the twenty-first century, one might project continued conversions to Christianity and Islam but be more modest about overall losses among ethnoreligionists.

Conversion is not a simple phenomenon. As a scholar of psychology and religion, Lewis Rambo identifies five different types of conversion: (1) apostasy/defection: a rejection of religious tradition that leads people away from religion to non-religion; (2) intensification: a revitalized commitment to a particular religion (formal or informal); (3) affiliation: a movement from no or minimal commitment to full involvement with an institution or community; (4) institutional transition: change from one community or major tradition to another (e.g., Baptist to Presbyterian); and (5) tradition transition, movement from one religion to another (e.g., Christianity to Islam).[35] Rambo, above, states that "conversion" can take place within traditions, such as when Catholics become Protestants or when people shift allegiances among various Hindu traditions, castes, and sects. This definition of conversion would also apply to Muslim, Buddhist, Jain, and Sikh traditions as well as to shifting allegiances among tribal peoples.[36] An analysis of religious affiliation by major religions however, does not reflect such "internal" changes.

Conversion, then, plays a vital role in the growth of religious communities. But as Eric Kaufmann observes, conversion must be viewed in tandem with birth and death rates. He writes, "No religion can grow without first enlisting converts from the wider society. Later, the two strategies for fundamentalist expansion are external proselytisation and endogenous growth. External proselytisation is quicker, but rapid conversion is often accompanied by rapid exit. Endogenous growth is often more enduring."[37] Kaufmann then cites the growth of Mormonism as an example of conversion growth accompanied by strong demographic growth. In other words, Mormons work hard at spreading their message as well as having large families.

In a similar way, Rodney Stark argues that the rise of Christianity in the Roman Empire owed a great deal to both conversion and demographics. He documents how a tiny band of 40 Christians in 30 CE, the "Jesus movement," could grow to 6 million by 300 CE. Conversion was central, but birthrates of Christians helped to drive and maintain growth.[38] As identified by Stark, factors that fueled Christian growth included family-centered evangelism, more female converts leading to more Christian children, higher Christian birthrates, and Christians caring for the sick during plagues (reducing mortality).[39]

Unfortunately, one of the problems in studying conversion is the paucity of information on it. Reliable data on conversions are hard to obtain for a number of reasons. Although some national censuses ask people about their religion, they do not directly ask whether people have converted to their present faith. A few cross-national surveys do contain questions about religious switching, but even in those surveys it is difficult to assess whether more people leave a religion than enter it. In some countries, legal and social consequences make conversion difficult, and survey respondents might be reluctant to speak honestly about the topic. In particular, Hinduism is for many Hindus (as is Islam for many Muslims) not just a religion but also an ethnic or cultural identity that does not depend on whether a person actively practices the faith. Thus even non-practicing or secular Hindus may still consider themselves, and be viewed by their neighbors, as Hindus.

Statistical data on conversion to and from Islam are particularly scarce. What little information is available suggests that there is no substantial net gain or loss through conversion in the number of Muslims globally; the number of people who become Muslims through conversion seems to be roughly equal to the number of Muslims who leave the faith. The Pew Forum's survey of 19 nations in sub-Saharan Africa, conducted in 2009, found that neither Christianity nor Islam is growing significantly at the expense of the other through religious conversion in those countries. Uganda was the only country surveyed where the number of people who identified themselves as Muslim was significantly different than the number of people who said they were raised Muslim: 18% of Ugandans surveyed said they were raised Muslim, while 13%

now describe themselves as Muslim, a net loss of five percentage points. In every other sub-Saharan Africa country surveyed, the number of people who are currently Muslim is roughly equivalent to the number saying they were raised as Muslims. This does not mean that there is no religious switching taking place. Rather, it indicates that the number of people becoming Muslim roughly offsets the number of people leaving Islam.[40]

The Pew Forum's *US Religious Landscape Survey*, conducted in 2007, found a similar pattern in the United States.[41] In that survey, the number of respondents who described themselves as Muslim was roughly the same as the number who said they were raised as Muslims, and the portion of all US adults who have converted either to or from Islam was less than three tenths of one percent (<0.3%). As a result of the relatively small number of Muslims in the nationally representative survey sample, however, it was not possible to calculate a precise retention rate for the Islamic faith in the United States. An independent study published in 2010 that examined patterns of religious conversion among various faiths in 40 countries, mainly in Europe, also found that the number of people who were raised Muslim in those countries, as a whole, roughly equaled the number who currently are Muslim. But again, the sample sizes for Muslims were so small that the results cannot reliably predict Muslim conversion trends.[42]

Converts From

Conversion to a new religion, as mentioned above, also involves conversion from a previous one.[43] Thus, a convert to Islam is, at the same time, a convert from another religion. In the twentieth and twenty-first centuries, the most converts from Christianity were and continue to be found largely among those in the Western world who have decided to be agnostics or atheists.

Many case studies have examined why people leave religious communities. In particular, decline in the mainline Protestant churches in the United States has been vigorously studied. One such study identified five factors related to decline in mainline American Protestantism, including: (1) the high point of membership was between 1963 and 1967, but the rate of growth had actually begun to decrease in the early 1960s; (2) decline was caused by underlying social factors rather than specific changes in leadership or policy (disproving the theory that decline was largely caused by denominational conflicts in the 1960s and 1970s); (3) denominations with the greatest decline since the 1960s were the ones with the highest levels of affluence and education; (4) decline was largely a result of reduced flow of young adults into church membership rather than an exodus of older members; and (5) studies that start analysis in the 1960s are misleading, since the 1950s was an unusual period of church growth, and decline in 1960s and 1970s shows a return to normalcy.[44]

One should exercise caution when attempting to ascertain the statistical impact of conversion from religion. According to another study, "most apostasy does not represent a 'reversal' in the socialization process, but rather it might be characterized as a slight bend in the religious socialization line. That is, apostates tend to come from homes where religion was only weakly emphasized, if at all, and parental modeling of religion was not strong."[45] In one sense, this supports the insistence that children be counted in the religion of their parents until they make a choice to switch to a different religion or to no religion.

Likewise, other studies show that second-generation immigrants are not abandoning their faith. In 2001, 71.4% of British-born Muslims said their Muslim identity was important to them, considerably more than the 64.7% of foreign-born Muslims who answered likewise. Among Bengalis and Pakistanis in Britain, 97% of both native and foreign-born respondents identified themselves as Muslims.[46]

Converts To Minus Converts From

The net conversion rate in a population is calculated by subtracting the number of converts from from the number of converts to. The most significant movements of conversion to and from religion in the twentieth century were conversions of ethnoreligionists in Africa to Christianity or Islam and conversions from Christianity to agnosticism in the West. However, both of these trends had slowed considerably by the dawn of the twenty-first century. In fact, emerging trends predict that ethnoreligionist populations will remain relatively stable while world religions experience fewer conversions from, with corresponding decreases in the percentages of atheists and agnostics.[47]

Conversion to and conversion from will likely continue to play a role in changing religious demographics in the future. Numerous studies are available on the impact of secularization on the world's religious communities.[48] Of course, many of these studies are now infamous for overestimating the numerical impact of secularization, some foreseeing (or even encouraging) the imminent collapse of religion altogether.[49] Notably, a few researchers have changed their minds and are now more cautious in their predictions.[50] On the other hand, the resurgence of religions, the founding of new religions, and the continued rise of fundamentalism (all, in a sense, conversion factors) all seem to work in favor of a more religious future for mankind.

Immigrants

Equally important at the international level is how the movement of people across national borders impacts religious affiliation. For example, in the United States, the immigration of non-Christian Asians has resulted in accelerated growth in religions such as Islam, Hinduism, and Buddhism. In Europe, the spiritual influence of the large numbers of Muslim immigrants has extended into national political arenas, notably in France, Germany, Austria, and Italy, as well as into plans for European Union (EU) expansion. Turkey's desire for EU membership has brought out the interesting contrast of an EU that is mainly "Christian" with one that could extend to countries not predominantly Christian.[51]

Examples of how immigration impacts religious demography abound. A case in point is the increasing Muslim presence in Sweden. From no discernible presence at all in the early 1930s, Muslims have become a significant minority in Sweden. The first Muslim immigrants were Tatar refugees and migrants who came from Finland

and Estonia during World War II. In 1949 they formed an association in Stockholm, mainly for the purpose of Islamic religious education. The most significant changes have come beginning in the 1970s with large numbers of refugees and migrants from the Middle East, Somalia, Bosnia, and Iraq. Estimating the numbers of Muslims is fraught with difficulty because religious affiliation is not registered in Sweden and there is no official census of religion. As a result, figures vary widely, because they depend on how religious affiliation is defined (for example, on the basis of activity, membership, practice, ethnicity, and/or names). Estimates range from 60,000 (too low) to 500,000 (too high).[52] The analysis in the *World Religion Database*, based on estimates of the sizes of various ethnic groups, arrives at a figure of about 340,000 in mid-2010.

Immigration of Muslims to Finland and Ireland is the subject of a study by Tuula Sakaranaho.[53] In the past, both countries mainly sent off emigrants rather than received immigrants. After 1990, that changed; now both countries are receiving immigrants and refugees (especially from the Muslim world) in a way not anticipated in previous decades, and each is home to roughly 30,000 Muslims. Significantly, Sakaranaho points out the difficulty in utilizing data on country of origin when assessing the religion of immigrants. For example, one could easily, and wrongly, assume that all immigrants from Iraq are Muslims. Yet part of the immigration pattern from Iraq was the exodus of the Christian community, so that while Christians might number only 2–3% of the population in Iraq, more than 5% of Iraqi Arabs who fled to Finland were Christians. Although there are Iraqi Christians in Finland, however, it is impossible to know how many.[54]

The study of specifically Christian migrant communities is in its infancy. Klaus Hock sees it as "a field which is rapidly changing and undergoing all kind of diversifications and transformations."[55] Christian diaspora groups around the world today range from the large Hispanic Christian population in the United States, to Palestinian Christians outside of the Occupied Territories, to Korean Christian communities in Western and Central Asia. Diaspora communities face a series of common challenges in assimilation and differentiation with their host countries. In most cases they are not content to keep their religious beliefs in the private sphere. The study of religion in migrant communities is important because religion can strongly influence behaviors; everyone must strive to adapt to these new situations in order for the process of integration to be successful.[56]

One significant historical and ongoing emigration of a religious community is that of the thousands of middle-class Coptic Orthodox from Egypt who have moved to the United States, Canada, and Australia. Emigration rates were high in the 1950s and 1960s, though have experienced resurgence in recent years. In the 1980s, an estimated 90,000 Copts lived in North America and 20,000 in Australia, with smaller communities in Western Europe.[57] In September 2011, the Egyptian Organization for Human Rights released a report stating that nearly 93,000 Coptic Christians have left Egypt since March 2011, soon after the start of the political revolution the previous January. Around 32,000 of these went to the United States, 14,000 to Canada, and 20,000 to various European countries.[58]

The largest single migration of a religious community in the twentieth century was the movement of Jews from around the world to the newly founded state of Israel. These migrants are largely secular, not religious, with the exception of Oriental Jews migrating in the 1950s and 60s. Immigration to Israel began to decrease in the 1950s as the economic attractiveness of Israel began to wane; by the late 1980s Israeli emigrants began to outnumber immigrants.[59] Since then, three migration trends have been shifting the religious landscape in Israel in favor of Orthodox Judaism: (1) Jews with more marketable skills tend to leave Israel (and also tend to be secular); (2) secular Jews tend to marry non-Jews more than Orthodox Jews do; and (3) many Jews who chose to immigrate to Israel now do so for religious reasons. Kaufmann observes, "this dynamic is almost certain to deepen over time, accelerating the decline of secularism in Israel."[60]

Another large migration since the latter part of the twentieth century has been the movement of individuals from Africa and Asia into Europe. Roughly a million people a year have entered Western Europe since the 1980s. One third of these arrive illegally. As Kaufmann notes,

> in most West European countries, the intake is roughly half non-European, of whom perhaps half are estimated to be Muslim. This means that only about a quarter of the current immigrant inflow into the EU is Muslim. This proportion may, however, increase as the supply of Eastern European immigrants dries up because of rising prosperity and the demographic implosion of ex-communist lands.[61]

Thus, immigration brings with it new religious communities. As a result, the religious makeup of Europe will likely change over time, with the tide of (mostly religious) immigrants slowing or perhaps halting the rise of secularism. Kaufmann further comments,

> current projections suggest that up to a quarter of Western Europeans will be non-white in 2050, rising to 60 per cent – if we include those of mixed race – by 2100. Immigrants to Europe tend to be religious Christians or Muslims, while their host societies are mainly secular. Immigration therefore makes Europe both more colorful and more faithful.[62]

Once religious communities are established through immigration they often grow vigorously (for a time) via high birthrates. Joint research from the Pew Hispanic Center and the Pew Forum on Religion and Public Life presents one scenario concerning Hispanic Catholics in the United States. Standing at 68% in 2006, the percentage of Hispanics who are Catholic will decline to 61% by 2030. The proportion of US Catholics who are Hispanic will *increase* over the same period, however, from 33% to 41%. This is largely as a result of conversions among Hispanics to non-Catholic traditions within Christianity, yet Catholicism will continue to be the dominant faith among Hispanics in the United States. The combination of high immigration rates and high fertility with demographic decline of non-Hispanic populations ensures that Hispanics are on a trajectory to share an even greater proportion of US Catholics in years to come.[63]

Complexities surrounding immigrant religious communities are illustrated well by Martin Baumann's study of immigrant Hinduism in Germany. In 2005 there were around 100,000 Hindus in Germany, 90% of whom were immigrants who came as workers and refugees. In addition, there are small communities of Hindus found among refugees from Afghanistan (about 5,000 people), arriving from 1980 onwards.

Paralleling this immigration is the rising population of "western Hindus" – German converts to Neo-Hindu groupings such as the International Society for Krishna Consciousness (ISKCON), Ananda Marga, and Transcendental Meditation, estimated to number between 7,000 and 10,000 in 2005. Finally, there are Tamil Hindu immigrants from Sri Lanka, approximately 6,000 of whom came as asylum seekers during the 1980s.[64] This study illustrates how migrant communities within a particular country are in no way monolithic, justifying the call for more research of migration viewed through the lens of religion.

In their research on the global Muslim population, the Pew Forum found that, on average, more people are leaving Muslim-majority countries than migrating to them. Although the rate of emigration has declined significantly since 1990–95, Muslim-majority countries are still losing part of their populations to emigration, and that trend is projected to continue over the next 20 years. Nonetheless, if economic conditions in developing countries – including Muslim-majority countries – continue to improve, there will be less economic motivation, or "push" factors, encouraging emigration. Likewise, if economic conditions in more-developed countries worsen, there will be fewer "pull" factors attracting new immigrants, including temporary workers. Of course, not all people who immigrate to the more-developed world from Muslim-majority countries are Muslims (or do so for economic reasons alone). Religious minorities – such as Christians living in majority-Muslim countries in the Middle East – sometimes emigrate in larger proportions than religious majorities.[65]

Pew also found that immigration is a key driver of Muslim population growth in Europe and North America. Muslim immigration to countries in more-developed parts of the world has risen steadily for decades as a result of evolving labor markets, changes in immigration laws, growing connections of immigrant families to communities abroad and increased globalization. Muslim immigration has been an ongoing phenomenon for decades in a number of European countries. Pew's study assumed that Muslim populations in Europe are projected to increase less in the coming years.[66]

In North America, however, the number of new Muslim immigrants has risen steadily in recent years, even after accounting for a slight dip in immigration among both Muslims and non-Muslims following the September 11, 2001, terrorist attacks. As a result, Pew's projections for the US assume that overall annual immigration will increase slowly, by about 1% per year. Based on recent trends that show more Muslims leaving Muslim-majority countries and immigrating to the US, the Pew study assumed that Muslims will constitute a slightly larger share of all immigrants to the US each year over the period 2010–30.[67]

The issue of illegal immigration to the US has become highly contentious in recent years. However, there is no evidence that illegal immigration is a significant factor in Muslim population growth in the US, partly because the overwhelming majority of Muslim immigrants enter through airports rather than at land crossings, which are more difficult than airports to monitor.[68]

An important area of study is attitudes towards immigrants, religious or otherwise. Studies in the United States have shown that Evangelical Protestants evince more negative opinions about immigrants than do mainline Protestants or Catholics. This opposition is particularly pronounced with respect to cultural concerns, such as retaining "American" culture. Some of this cultural opposition to immigrants appears to be rooted in a particular understanding of America's origins as a Christian nation, most closely associated with Evangelical Protestants.[69] (Notably, the Catholic Church is generally strongly opposed to measures making illegal immigration a felony; Pope Benedict XVI spoke of protecting immigrant rights.[70]) At the same time, there are efforts to educate Protestants to "welcome the stranger" based on biblical admonitions.[71]

Emigrants

In a reversal of nineteenth-century European colonization of Africa, Asia, and parts of the Americas, the late twentieth century witnessed waves of emigration of people from these regions to the Western world. The impact on religious affiliation is significant. The earliest of these migrations was the movement of Arab-Berbers from Algeria to France in the 1960s and 1970s, including hundreds of thousands of North African Jews. By 1968, Sephardic North African Jews were the majority of Jews in France.[72] Another example are the Central Asian countries of the former Soviet Union, where Christianity has declined significantly every year since 1990 as a result of the emigration of ethnic Russians, Germans, and Ukrainians.

As mentioned previously, one of the largest emigration events of the twentieth century was the movement of Jews in the period immediately after the Holocaust and the establishment of the state of Israel. This was especially true for Jews living in Arab lands, where extensive anti-Semitism in the forms of persecution and violence caused many Jews to seek better opportunities elsewhere. The First Freedom Center reported that between 1948 and the early 1970s, some 800,000 to 1,000,000 Jews left Arab countries and resettled in Israel, Europe, the United States, and other countries, though movement has slowed since the early 1970s.[73] Looking at individual communities, the First Freedom Center's study showed that in 1948, Iraqi Jews numbered some 135,000 to 140,000, tracing that community's origins to the biblical Babylonian Captivity 2,500 years in the past. By 2010, there were fewer than 100 Jews to be found in Iraq. Some Iraqi Jews are reported to be living in hiding, unable to establish a properly functioning liturgical life. In North Africa, Jewish populations have shrunk from about 260,000 in Morocco (pre-1948) to only 4,000 in 2010; in Tunisia there were 100,000 Jews pre-1948 and in 2010 only slightly more than 1,000. Jewish communities in these two countries are likely to survive the next 10 years, but those in Egypt and Yemen might not have the same fortune.[74]

The Jewish population in Venezuela grew with German refugees arriving after World War II, and experienced even more growth after the 1967 Six-Day War with refugees arriving from Morocco. The community peaked at 45,000, with a Jewish population nearly evenly split between Ashkenazi (Eastern European) and Sephardic (Iberian Peninsula) Jews. Recent research on the Jews of Venezuela has shown significant decline there during the last decade, similar to realities in Arab countries. Many Venezuelan Jews believe that Hugo Chavez's harsh anti-Israel stance promotes anti-Semitic violence, including attacks on prominent synagogues. Many wealthier Jews have settled in Florida (USA), Spain, and Israel, and no longer maintain financial support for Venezuela.[75] The Jewish community in Venezuela has decreased by at least half in the past 10 years.

Another religious community impacted by emigration is the Masalit Muslims of Sudan. The Masalit people converted to Islam in the seventeenth century, but differ from the more traditional Shi'a and Sunni Muslims in that they retain most of the practices from their former African ethnoreligion, save attendance at Friday prayers. These non-Arab people reside in Darfur Province, and have suffered great violence and persecution by other Muslims. There are as many as 145,000 ethnic Masalit in Sudan (pre-partition of Sudan and South Sudan) who exist as a homeless people, surviving in refugee camps. The rest of the Sudanese Masalit (about 60,000) fled to refugee camps in neighboring Chad during the 2003–6 civil war, when all the Masalit villages of Sudan were destroyed.[76]

Immigrants Minus Emigrants

In the twenty-first century, international migration continues to have a significant impact on the religious composition of individual countries. One can try to anticipate the way in which expected immigration and emigration trends will affect a country's population over time. One profound change to be expected is the increase of religious pluralism in most every country of the world.[77] Increasing religious pluralism is not always welcomed and can be seen as a political, cultural, national, or religious threat. Current debates in Israel, for example, are examining the difference between religious and secular Jews as it relates to immigration, especially the return of over a million Russians and other citizens of the former Soviet Union. The ultra-Orthodox want to limit the "right of return" to religious Jews, whereas moderates want to welcome secular Jews to counter the rising numbers of Arabs (with their much higher birthrate).[78] In light of these, and other, migration realities, by 2100 it might be difficult to find any country in which 90% or more of its population belong to any one single religion.[79]

Immigration clearly has important political ramifications for the host country. In the United States, the total population of each state, including illegal immigrants and other non-citizens, determines the distribution of seats in the House of Representatives. In 2000, the presence of illegal aliens caused Indiana, Michigan, and Mississippi to each lose one seat in the House.[80] Such political consequences directly affect the functioning of society as a whole, including religious bodies. Emigration also impacts ecclesiology. While at one time as many as 100,000 Greek Orthodox lived in Turkey, today, because of steady emigration, the population stands at less than 3,000. The First Freedom Center observes,

> According to Turkish law, the members of the Ecumenical Patriarchate's Holy Synod must be Turkish citizens in order to participate or stand as candidates in elections to the church's hierarchy. With fewer than 3,000 members in the country, the community may soon provide too small a pool of Turkish citizens to fulfill either purpose and thereby become unsustainable. Ecumenical Patriarch Bartholomew, therefore, may well have no successor drawn from the ranks of the Patriarchate's own clergy.[81]

Many declining religious communities around the world face similar challenges, such as Tibetan Buddhists in both China and India and Zoroastrians in Iran.

The six dynamics discussed above determine changes in religious demographics. Gains are the result of three positive dynamics: births, conversions to, and immigration. Losses are the result of three negative dynamics: deaths, conversions from, and emigration. The net change in religious demographics is the result of gains minus losses. The balance of dynamics can be reflected in any proportions (for example, mainly births for gains, mainly conversions from for losses) but can also be represented by pairing the gains and losses by type: births versus deaths, converts to versus converts from, and immigrants versus emigrants. In each case, the net change (either positive or negative) will be the difference between the two. This means that any attempt to understand religious affiliation in the past, present, or future must be firmly based on demographic dynamics.[82] A proper awareness of these dynamics and their significance is thus vital both for undertaking and for interpreting studies of the future of religion.

Notes

1 For an excellent treatment of religious migration, see Pew Forum on Religion and Public Life, *Faith on the Move: The Religious Affiliation of International Migrants*, March 8, 2012, http://www.pewforum.org/Geography/Religious-Migration-exec.aspx. Also see chapter 14 of this volume for a case study of migration and religious diasporas.

2 Some relevant texts on religious conversion include H. Newton Malony and Samuel Southard, eds, *Handbook of Religious Conversion* (Birmingham, AL: Religious Education Press, 1992); Lewis R. Rambo, *Understanding Religious Conversion* (New Haven: Yale University Press, 1993); and Andrew Bruckser and Stephen D. Glazier, eds., *The Anthropology of Religious Conversion* (Lanham, MD: Rowman & Littlefield Publishers, Inc., 2003).

3 On a global scale, immigrants and emigrants are the same; that is, when one immigrates *to* a host country, he is also emigrating *from* a home country. In essence, the difference here is zero.

4 As mentioned in chapter 4, the highest-quality projections for religious communities are built on cohort-component projections – ones that use differential rates for each religion: age-specific fertility rates by religion, age structure in 5-year cohorts by religion, migration rates by religion and mortality by religion. Unfortunately, this kind of detail is not available for religious communities from censuses or surveys for many countries (half do not ask a question about religion). Thus, the cohort data related to religious communities has to be obtained elsewhere or estimated, often as a rough estimate of its variation from the United Nations figures for the whole country. Examples of fertility variation among different religious groups are presented in this chapter.

5 These dynamics are examined in detail in Todd M. Johnson and Kenneth R. Ross, eds., *Atlas of Global Christianity* (Edinburgh: Edinburgh University Press, 2009), 60–1.

6 Alan Aldridge, *Religion in the Contemporary World: A Sociological Introduction*, 2nd ed. (Cambridge: Polity Press, 2007), 108.

7 Sriya Iyer, *Demography and Religion in India* (Oxford: Oxford University Press, 2002), 2–3.

8 Lareen Newman, "Demographic Fertility Research: A Question of Disciplinary Beliefs and Methods," in Basia Spalek and Alia Imtoual, eds., *Religion, Spirituality and the Social Sciences: Challenging Marginalisation* (Bristol: The Policy Press, 2008), 93–4. See L. T. Ruzicka and J. C. Caldwell, "Fertility," in United Nations, *Population of Australia*, Country Monograph Series No. 9 (Bangkok: Economic and Social Commission for Asia and the Pacific, 1982), 214.

9   Scott M. Thomas, "A Globalized God: Religion's Growing Influence in International Politics," *Foreign Affairs* 89:6 (Nov/Dec 2010): 93.

10 The standard measure of fertility is the total fertility rate (TFR), defined as the total number of children an average woman would have in her lifetime if fertility patterns did not change. More specifically, the TFR is calculated by adding up all the age-specific fertility rates for women in a particular country (or region) during a given year (or other time period). Total fertility rate is defined as a basic indicator of the level of fertility, calculated by summing age-specific birthrates over all reproductive ages. It may be interpreted as the expected number of children a women who survives to the end of the reproductive age span will have during her lifetime if she experiences the given age-specific rates. United Nations Statistical Division, *Handbook on the Collection of Fertility and Mortality Data* (New York: United Nations, 2003).

11 Eric Kaufmann, *Shall the Religious Inherit the Earth? Demography and Politics in the Twenty-First Century* (London: Profile Books, Ltd., 2010), 226.

12 Ibid., 172.

13 Ibid., 159–60.

14 Ibid., 160.

15 Ibid., xi–xii.

16 Ibid., 161–2.

17 Ibid., 123–4.

18 Rodney Stark, "How New Religions Succeed: A Theoretical Model," in *The Future of New Religious Movements*, ed. D. G. Bromley and P. E. Hammond (Macon, GA: Mercer University Press, 1987), 11.

19 At the height of the movement around the time of the Civil War, there were nearly 6,000 Shakers in the United States. The community in New Gloucester, ME – once with 200 members – maintains working farms as well as a library and museum on Shaker history. See http://www.shaker.lib.me.us/ for more information.

20 Zoroastrians, 0.42% p.a. versus world population, 1.38% p.a. Todd M. Johnson and Brian J. Grim, eds., *World Religion Database*, (Leiden/Boston: Brill, accessed January 2012), www.worldreligiondatabase.org.

21 Kaufmann, *Shall the Religious Inherit the Earth?*, 40.

22 Pippa Norris and Ronald Inglehart, *Sacred and Secular: Religion and Politics Worldwide* (Cambridge: Cambridge University Press, 2004), 6, 22–3.

23 Kevin McQuillan states that religion plays an influential role in determining demographic behavior under three circumstances: (1) religion "articulates behavioral norms with a bearing on fertility behavior"; (2) religion "holds the means to communicate these values and promote compliance"; and (3) religion "forms a central component of the social identity of its followers." See Kevin McQuillan, "When Does Religion Influence Fertility?" *Population and Development Review* 30:1 (March 2004): 25–56. Scholars agree that religion does have an impact on fertility, but do not always agree on what this impact looks like. For example, Tim Heaton concludes that socio-economic status does not necessarily have a negative impact on Mormon fertility, as is generally the case with other religious groups. See Tim B. Heaton, "How Does Religion Influence Fertility? The Case of Mormons," *Journal for the Scientific Study of Religion* 25:2 (June 1986): 248–58.

24 Pew Forum on Religion and Public Life, *The Future of the Global Muslim Population, Projections for 2010–2030*, January 2011, http://pewresearch.org/pubs/1872/muslim-population-projections-worldwide-fast-growth

25 First Freedom Center, *Minority Communities at Risk*, January 2011, 15.

26 The Sabian Mandeans' faith combines elements of Islam, Judaism, Christianity, and Gnosticism. See Edmondo Lupieri, *The Mandaeans: The Last Gnostics* (Grand Rapids, MI: Eerdmans, 2002).

27 First Freedom Center, *Minority Communities*, 16.

28 Stephen Adolphe Wum and Ian Heyward, *Atlas of the World's Languages in Danger of Disappearing*, rev. ed. (Paris: UNESCO, 2001).

29 For 1971, 1981, and 1991 statistics, see Paul Compton, "Catholic/Non-Catholic Demographic Differentials in Northern Ireland," in *The Demographic Characteristics of National Minorities in Certain European States*, vol. 1, ed. Werner Haug, Youssef Courbage, and Paul Compton (Strasbourg: Council of Europe Publishing, 1998), 82.

30 For 2001 statistics, see Northern Ireland Statistics and Research Agency, *Northern Ireland Census 2001 Key Statistics* (Belfast: NIRSA, 2002), 22. The results are available online at the Northern Ireland Statistics and Research Agency's (NIRSA) website, at http://www.nisranew.nisra.gov.uk/census/Census2001Output/KeyStatistics/keystats.html

31 Ibid.

32 Tuula Sakaranaho, *Religious Freedom, Multiculturalism Islam: Cross-reading Finland and Ireland* (Leiden: Brill, 2006), 238.

33 For example, the now infamous statement from the reports of the World Missionary Conference in Edinburgh, Scotland, in 1910 that averred, "Most of these peoples will have lost their ancient faiths within a generation, and will accept that culture-religion with which they first came in contact." *World Missionary Conference, 1910. Report of Commission I: Carrying the Gospel to all the Non-Christian World* (Edinburgh: Oliphant, Anderson, and Ferrier, 1910), 365.

34 David B. Barrett, George T. Kurian, and Todd M. Johnson, eds., *World Christian Encyclopedia: A Comparative Survey of Churches and Religions in the Modern World*, vol. 1, *The World by Countries, Religionists, Churches, Ministries*, 2nd ed. (New York: Oxford University Press, 2001).

35 Lewis R. Rambo, *Understanding Religious Conversion* (New Haven: Yale University Press, 1993), 12–14.

36 Sarah Claerhout and Jakob De Roover, "Conversion of the World: Proselytization in India and the Universalization of Christianity," in *Proselytization Revisited: Rights Talk, Free Markets and Culture Wars*, ed. Rosalind I. J. Hackett (London: Equinox Publishing Ltd, 2008), 57.

37 Kaufmann, *Shall the Religious Inherit the Earth?*, 30–1. For a discussion of conversion in relation to birth and death rates, see Todd M. Johnson, "The Demographics of Religious Change," in *The Oxford Handbook on Conversion*, ed. Lewis Rambo and Charles Farhadian (Oxford: Oxford University Press, forthcoming).

38 Rodney Stark, *The Rise of Christianity: A Sociologist Reconsiders History* (Princeton: Princeton University Press, 1996), 4–7.

39 Ibid., 3–28.

40 Pew Forum on Religion and Public Life, *Mapping the Global Muslim Population: A Report on the Size and Distribution of the World's Muslim Population*, October 7, 2009, http://www.pewforum.org/Mapping-the-Global-Muslim-Population.aspx

41 Pew Forum on Religion and Public Life. *US Religious Landscape Survey: Religious Affiliation: Diverse and Dynamic*. February 2008. http://religions.pewforum.org/

42 Pew Forum on Religion and Public Life, *Mapping the Global Muslim Population*.

43 In the literature on conversion, individuals who leave religion or non-religion are referred to as "defectors" or "apostates." Such language in this volume is avoided because these terms can be pejorative.

44 Dean Hoge, Benton Johnson, and Donald A. Luidens, "Religious Views of Mainline Protestant Baby Boomers in the United States," in *Religion in a Changing World: Comparative Studies in Sociology*, ed. Madeleine Cousineau (Westport, CT: Praeger Publishers, 1998), 39–40.

45 Bruce Hunsberger, "Swimming Against the Current: Exceptional Cases of Apostates and Converts," in *Joining and Leaving Religion: Research Perspectives*, ed. Leslie J. Francis and Yaacov J. Katz (Leominster: Gracewing Publishing, 2000), 234.

46 Kaufmann, *Shall the Religious Inherit the Earth?*, 174.

47 Ethnoreligionist growth rates for the 1910–2010 period were 0.66% p.a., compared to a global population growth rate of 1.38% p.a. In the 2000–10 period this gap has shrunk to 1.21% p.a. for both ethnoreligionists and the global population. Johnson and Ross, *Atlas of Global Christianity*, 19.

48 See Aldridge, *Religion in the Contemporary World*; K. R. Dark, "Large-Scale Religious Change and World Politics," in *Religion and International Relations*, ed. K. R. Dark (Hampshire: Palgrave, 2000); Rodney Starke and Roger Finke, *Acts of Faith: Explaining the Human Side of Religion* (Berkeley and Los Angeles: University of California Press, 2000); Peter L. Berger, ed., *The Desecularization of the World: Resurgent Religion and World Politics* (Washington, DC: Ethics and Public Policy Center, 1999); John Micklethwait and Adrian Wooldridge, *God is Back: How the Global Revival of Faith is Changing the World* (New York: Penguin Press, 2009); and Charles Taylor, *A Secular Age* (Cambridge, MA: Harvard University Press, 2007).

49 See David Martin, *On Secularization: Towards a Revised General Theory* (Aldershot: Ashgate Publishing Limited, 2005). See also John G. Stackhouse, Jr., "Religious Diversity, Secularization, and Postmodernity," in *The Oxford Handbook of Religious Diversity*, ed. Chad Meister (Oxford: Oxford University Press, 2011), 239–49.

50 See especially Berger, *The Desecularization of the World*.

51 See Yannis A. Stivachtis and Meltem Müftüler-Baç, eds, *Turkey–European Union Relations: Dilemmas, Opportunities, and Constraints* (Lanham, MD: Lexington Books, 2008).

52 Jan Hjärpe, "Political Islam in Sweden: Integration and Deterrence," in *Transnational Political Islam: Religion, Ideology, and Power*, ed. Azza Karam (Sterling, VT: Pluto Press, 2004), 62–3.

53 Sakaranaho, *Religious Freedom, Multiculturalism Islam*.

54 Ibid., 249.

55 Klaus Hock, "Mainline Churches, Christian Diaspora, and Secularity in Europe," in *Religion and Society: Crossdisciplinary European Perspectives*, ed. Viggo Mortensen (Højbjerg, Denmark: Forlaget Univers, 2006), 29.

56 Marco Ricceri, "Italians and the Church: Faith and Disobedience," in *Religion and Society: Crossdisciplinary European Perspectives*, ed. Viggo Mortensen (Højbjerg, Denmark: Forlaget Univers, 2006), 75.

57 J. D. Pennington, "The Copts in Modern Egypt," *Middle Eastern Studies* 18:2 (April 1982): 158–79.

58 Emad Khalil, "NGO Report: 93,000 Copts Left Egypt Since March," *Egypt Independent*, September 25, 2011, http://www.egyptindependent.com/node/499187

59 Kaufmann, *Shall the Religious Inherit the Earth?*, 226.

60 Ibid., 227.

61 Ibid., 171.

62 Ibid., 163.

63 Pew Hispanic Center and Pew Forum on Religion and Public Life, *Changing Faiths: Latinos and the Transformation of American Religion*, April 25, 2007, http://www.pewforum.org/Changing-Faiths-Latinos-and-the-Transformation-of-American-Religion.aspx, 13.

64 Martin Baumann, "Immigrant Hinduism in Germany: Tamils from Sri Lanka and Their Temples," The Pluralism Project at Harvard University, http://pluralism.org/resources/slideshow/hindgerm/index.php

65 Pew Forum on Religion and Public Life, *Global Muslim Population*.

66 Projections for future immigration of Muslims to Europe were made in collaboration with the International Institute for Applied Systems Analysis (IIASA), primarily using immigration data provided by Eurostat.

67 These projections count only immigrants to the United States who receive permanent legal residency and do not include visiting family members, students, or others who are in the United States temporarily or illegally. Therefore, the report's projections on the number of Muslim immigrants can be considered conservative.

68 Pew Forum on Religion and Public Life, *Global Muslim Population*, Appendix A.

69 Eric Leon McDaniel, Irfan Nooruddin, and Allyson Faith Shortle, "Divine Boundaries: How Religion Shapes Citizens' Attitudes Toward Immigrants," *American Politics Research* 39:1 (January 2011): 226–7.

70 Ibid., 208.

71 See especially M. Daniel Carroll R., *Christians at the Border: Immigration, the Church, and the Bible* (Grand Rapids, MI: Baker Academic, 2008).

72 Esther Benbassa, *The Jews of France: A History from Antiquity to the Present* (Princeton: Princeton University Press, 1999), 194–6.

73 First Freedom Center, *Minority Communities*, 10.

74 Ibid., 10–11.

75 Ibid., 12.

76 Ibid., 14.

77 Todd M. Johnson and David B. Barrett, "Quantifying Alternate Futures of Religion and Religions," *Futures* 36:9 (November 2004): 10–11.

78 US Department of State, "International Religious Freedom Report: Israel and the Occupied Territories," September 13, 2011, http://www.state.gov/g/drl/rls/irf/2010_5/168266.htm.

79 Based on current projections in the *World Religion Database*.

80 Dudley L. Poston, Jr., Steven A. Camarota, and Amanda K. Baumle, "Remaking the Political Landscape: The Impact of Illegal and Legal Immigration on Congressional Apportionment," Center for Immigration Studies, *Backgrounder* (October 2003).

81 First Freedom Center, *Minority Communities*, 8.

82 Johnson and Barrett, "Alternate Futures," 6.

References

Aldridge, Alan. *Religion in the Contemporary World: A Sociological Introduction*. Cambridge: Polity Press, 2007.

Barrett, David B., George T. Kurian, and Todd M. Johnson, eds. *World Christian Encyclopedia: A Comparative Survey of Churches and Religions in the Modern World*. 2 vols. 2nd ed. New York: Oxford University Press, 2001.

Baumann, Martin. "Immigrant Hinduism in Germany: Tamils from Sri Lanka and Their Temples." The Pluralism Project at Harvard University. http://pluralism.org/resources/slideshow/hindgerm/index.php

Benbassa, Esther. *The Jews of France: A History from Antiquity to the Present*. Princeton: Princeton University Press, 1999.

Berger, Peter L., ed. *The Desecularization of the World: Resurgent Religion and World Politics*. Washington, DC: Ethics and Public Policy Center, 1999.

Bruckser, Andrew, and Stephen D. Glazier, eds. *The Anthropology of Religious Conversion*. Lanham, MD: Rowman & Littlefield Publishers, Inc., 2003.

Carroll R., M. Daniel. *Christians at the Border: Immigration, the Church, and the Bible*. Baker Academic, 2008.

Claerhout, Sarah, and Jakob De Roover. "Conversion of the World: Proselytization in India and the Universalization of Christianity." In *Proselytization Revisited: Rights Talk, Free*

Markets and Culture Wars, edited by Rosalind I. J. Hackett, 53–76. London: Equinox Publishing Ltd, 2008.

Compton, Paul. "Catholic/Non-Catholic Demographic Differentials in Northern Ireland." In *The Demographic Characteristics of National Minorities in Certain European States*. Vol. 1. Population Studies No. 30, edited by Werner Haug, Youssef Courbage, and Paul Compton. Strasbourg: Council of Europe Publishing, 1998.

Dark, K. R. "Large-Scale Religious Change and World Politics." In *Religion and International Relations*, edited by K. R. Dark, 50–82. Hampshire: Palgrave, 2000.

First Freedom Center. *Minority Communities at Risk*. January 2011.

Heaton, Tim B. "How Does Religion Influence Fertility? The Case of Mormons." *Journal for the Scientific Study of Religion* 25:2 (June 1986): 248–58.

Hjärpe, Jan. "Political Islam in Sweden: Integration and Deterrence." In *Transnational Political Islam: Religion, Ideology, and Power*, edited by Azza Karam, 58–78. Sterling, VT: Pluto Press, 2004.

Hock, Klaus. "Mainline Churches, Christian Diaspora, and Secularity in Europe." In *Religion and Society: Crossdisciplinary European Perspectives*, edited by Viggo Mortensen, 25–33. Højbjerg, Denmark: Forlaget Univers, 2006.

Hoge, Dean, Benton Johnson, and Donald A Luidens. "Religious Views of Mainline Protestant Baby Boomers in the United States." In *Religion in a Changing World: Comparative Studies in Sociology*, edited by Madeleine Cousineau, 39–48. Westport, CT: Praeger Publishers, 1998.

Hunsberger, Bruce. "Swimming Against the Current: Exceptional Cases of Apostates and Converts." In *Joining and Leaving Religion: Research Perspectives*, edited by Leslie J. Francis and Yaacov J. Katz, 233–48. Leominster: Gracewing, 2000.

Iyer, Sriya. *Demography and Religion in India*. Oxford: Oxford University Press, 2002.

Johnson, Todd M. "The Demographics of Religious Change." In *The Oxford Handbook on Conversion*, edited by Lewis Rambo and Charles Farhadian. Oxford: Oxford University Press, forthcoming.

Johnson, Todd M., and David B. Barrett. "Quantifying Alternate Futures of Religion and Religions." *Futures* 36:9 (November 2004): 947–60.

Johnson, Todd M., and Brian J. Grim, eds. *World Religion Database*. Leiden/Boston: Brill, 2008.

Johnson, Todd M., and Kenneth R. Ross, eds. *Atlas of Global Christianity*. Edinburgh: Edinburgh University Press, 2009.

Kaufmann, Eric. *Shall the Religious Inherit the Earth? Demography and Politics in the Twenty-First Century*. London: Profile Books Ltd, 2010.

Khalil, Emad. "NGO Report: 93,000 Copts Left Egypt Since March." *Egypt Independent*, September 25, 2011. http://www.egyptindependent.com/node/499187.

Lupieri, Edmondo. *The Mandaeans: The Last Gnostics*. Grand Rapids, MI: Eerdmans, 2002.

Malony, H. Newton, and Samuel Southard, eds. *Handbook of Religious Conversion*. Birmingham, AL: Religious Education Press, 1992.

Martin, David. *On Secularization: Towards a Revised General Theory*. Aldershot: Ashgate Publishing Limited, 2005.

McDaniel, Eric Leon, Irfan Nooruddin, and Allyson Faith Shortle. "Divine Boundaries: How Religion Shapes Citizens' Attitudes Toward Immigrants." *American Politics Research* 39:1 (January 2011): 205–33.

McQuillan, Kevin. "When Does Religion Influence Fertility?" *Population and Development Review* 30:1 (March 2004): 25–56.

Micklethwait, John, and Adrian Wooldridge. *God is Back: How the Global Revival of Faith is Changing the World*. New York: Penguin Press, 2009.

Newman, Lareen. "Demographic Fertility Research: A Question of Disciplinary Beliefs and Methods." In *Religion, Spirituality and the Social Sciences: Challenging Marginalisation*, edited by Basia Spalek and Alia Imtoual, 93–106. Bristol: The Policy Press, 2008.

Norris, Pippa, and Ronald Inglehart. *Sacred and Secular: Religion and Politics Worldwide* Cambridge: Cambridge University Press, 2004.

Northern Ireland Statistics and Research Agency. *Northern Ireland Census 2001 Key Statistics.* Belfast: NIRSA, 2002.

Pennington, J. D. "The Copts in Modern Egypt." *Middle Eastern Studies* 18:2 (April 1982): 158–79.

Pew Forum on Religion and Public Life. *Faith on the Move: The Religious Affiliation of International Migrants.* March 8, 2012. http://pewresearch.org/pubs/2214/religion-religious-migrants-christians-muslims-jews.

Pew Forum on Religion and Public Life. *The Future of the Global Muslim Population: Projections for 2010–2030.* January 27, 2011. http://pewresearch.org/pubs/1872/muslim-population-projections-worldwide-fast-growth.

Pew Forum on Religion and Public Life. *Mapping the Global Muslim Population: A Report on the Size and Distribution of the World's Muslim Population.* October 7, 2009. http://www.pewforum.org/Mapping-the-Global-Muslim-Population.aspx.

Pew Forum on Religion and Public Life. *US Religious Landscape Survey: Religious Affiliation: Diverse and Dynamic.* February 2008. http://religions.pewforum.org/.

Pew Hispanic Center and Pew Forum on Religion and Public Life. *Changing Faiths: Latinos and the Transformation of American Religion.* April 25, 2007. http://www.pewforum.org/Changing-Faiths-Latinos-and-the-Transformation-of-American-Religion.aspx.

Poston, Jr., Dudley L., Steven A. Camarota, and Amanda K. Baumle. "Remaking the Political Landscape: The Impact of Illegal and Legal Immigration on Congressional Apportionment." Center for Immigration Studies. *Backgrounder* (October 2003).

Rambo, Lewis R. *Understanding Religious Conversion.* New Haven: Yale University Press, 1993.

Ricceri, Marco. "Italians and the Church: Faith and Disobedience." In *Religion and Society: Crossdisciplinary European Perspectives*, edited by Viggo Mortensen, 59–80. Højbjerg, Denmark: Forlaget Univers, 2006.

Ruzicka, L. T., and J. C. Caldwell. "Fertility." In United Nations, *Population of Australia.* Country Monograph Series No 9. Bangkok: Economic and Social Commission for Asia and the Pacific (1982): 119–229.

Sakaranaho, Tuula. *Religious Freedom, Multiculturalism, Islam: Cross-reading Finland and Ireland.* Leiden: Brill, 2006.

Stackhouse, Jr., John G. "Religious Diversity, Secularization, and Postmodernity." In *The Oxford Handbook of Religious Diversity*, edited by Chad Meister, 239–49. Oxford: Oxford University Press, 2011.

Stark, Rodney. "How New Religions Succeed: A Theoretical Model." In *The Future of New Religious Movements*, edited by D. G. Bromley and P. E. Hammond, 11–29. Macon, GA: Mercer University Press, 1987.

Stark, Rodney. *The Rise of Christianity: A Sociologist Reconsiders History.* Princeton: Princeton University Press, 1996.

Stark, Rodney, and Roger Finke. *Acts of Faith: Explaining the Human Side of Religion.* Berkeley and Los Angeles: University of California Press, 2000.

Stivachtis, Yannis, and Meltem Müftüler-Baç, eds. *Turkey–European Union Relations: Dilemmas, Opportunities, and Constraints.* Lanham, MD: Lexington Books, 2008.

Taylor, Charles. *A Secular Age.* Cambridge, MA: Harvard University Press, 2007.

Thomas, Scott M. "A Globalized God: Religion's Growing Influence in International Politics."
     Foreign Affairs 89:6 (Nov/Dec 2010): 93–101.
United Nations Statistical Division. *Handbook on the Collection of Fertility and Mortality Data.*
     New York: United Nations, 2003.
US Department of State. "International Religious Freedom Report: Israel and the Occupied Ter-
     ritories." September 13, 2011. http://www.state.gov/g/drl/rls/irf/2010_5/168266.htm.
*World Missionary Conference, 1910. Report of Commission I: Carrying the Gospel to all the
     Non-Christian World.* Edinburgh: Oliphant, Anderson, and Ferrier, 1910.
Wum, Stephen Adolphe, and Ian Heyward. *Atlas of the World's Languages in Danger of Dis-
     appearing.* Rev. ed. Paris: UNESCO, 2001.

Part III
Case Studies

Chapter 10

Estimating Changes in the Global Muslim Population

The 2011 study by the Pew Research Center's Forum on Religion and Public Life, *The Future of the Global Muslim Population: Projections for 2010–2030*,[1] is one of the most ambitious attempts to estimate the current size of the global Muslim population and make projections about its growth. Chapters 10 and 11 of this volume describe numerous aspects of the Pew Forum's study. Chapter 10 discusses the methodology used by the study for estimating the global Muslim population and projecting its growth forward to 2030. It then presents a summary of the global findings, concluding with a demographic summary of Muslim-majority countries[2] and the projected breakdown of Sunni and Shi'a Muslim populations worldwide. Chapter 11 begins by investigating in greater depth the related factors that help explain why the global Muslim population is growing faster than the world population in general but also why the rate of Muslim growth is showing signs of slowing.

The primary researchers for the Pew Forum's study were Brian J. Grim and Mehtab S. Karim. Karim, a visiting senior research fellow at the Pew Center in 2008–10, came from the Aga Khan University in Karachi, Pakistan, where he was a professor of demography. They and numerous other Forum staff worked with consultants from around the globe, including experts from the International Institute for Applied Systems Analysis, one of the leading international organizations involved with population projections.[3]

The 2011 study followed a 2009 report by the Pew Forum, *Mapping the Global Muslim Population*, which estimated the global Muslim population (of all ages) to be 1.57 billion in 2009. The new report took the next step: using standard demographic methods to project – despite many uncertainties – how many Muslims were likely to be in each of the world's 232 countries and territories[4] by 2030.

The Muslim population projections presented in the Forum's 2011 report are based on the best available data on fertility, mortality, and migration rates, as well as

The World's Religions in Figures: An Introduction to International Religious Demography,
First Edition. Todd M. Johnson and Brian J. Grim.
© 2013 John Wiley & Sons, Ltd. Published 2013 by John Wiley & Sons, Ltd.

related factors such as education, economic well-being, and use of birth control. The following pages lay out the report's data sources, methodology, and assumptions so that readers can see how the study arrived at the population estimates described in chapter 11 and draw their own conclusions about the reliability of the projections. Because the figures for 2020 and 2030 are built in large part on measurable trends from 1990 to 2010, the Forum's study is an attempt both to look 20 years into the future and to provide a rich demographic portrait of Muslims around the world in 2010.

The study used the standard demographic method of making population projections. Called the cohort-component method, it takes the age and sex structure of a population into account when projecting the population forward in time. This has the advantage of recognizing that an initial, baseline population can be relatively "young," with a high proportion of people in younger age groups (such as Nigeria) or relatively "old," with a high proportion of older people (such as Japan). *Cohorts* are groups defined by age and sex, such as females ages 15–19 and males ages 15–19. *Components* are the three ways in which populations grow or shrink: new entrants via births, exits via deaths, and net changes from migration (both immigration and emigration). Each cohort of the population is projected into the future by adding likely gains year-by-year – births and people moving into the country (immigrants) – and subtracting likely losses – deaths and people moving out (emigrants). The very youngest cohorts, those ages 0–4, are created by applying age-specific birthrates to each female cohort in the childbearing years (ages 15–49).

The cohort-component method has been in existence for more than a century. First suggested by the English economist Edwin Cannan in 1895, then further improved by demographers in the 1930s and 40s, it has been adopted widely since World War II. It is used by the United Nations Population Division, the US Census Bureau, other national statistical offices and numerous academic and research institutions.[5]

For countries in which Muslim populations are large enough that fertility rates and other demographic data are available specifically for the Muslim portion of the population, the Forum's study's projections were made using the Demographic (DemProj) module of the Spectrum Policy Modeling System developed for the US Agency for International Development (USAID),[6] which is designed to integrate with data from the United Nations. However, projections for the United States and 25 European nations with significant Muslim populations were made by the Age and Cohort Change Project of the International Institute for Applied Systems Analysis (IIASA), following the same basic methodology but using IIASA's own software. IIASA, an independent research center supported by more than 15 countries and based in Laxenburg, Austria, is a recognized leader by scholars in population projections and is collaborating with the Pew Forum on demographic analyses of major religious groups around the world.[7]

For many countries with very small Muslim populations, data on the differences in fertility, mortality, and migration rates between Muslims and non-Muslims are not available. In such cases, the Muslim percentage in the baseline (2010) population is carried forward to future years and applied to the country's expected total population, which is projected using the cohort-component method. This assumes that the Muslim population in such countries is growing at the same rate as the country's overall population. Additionally, for a few countries, the study uses cohort-component projections made by demographic consultants for this project or independent estimates by national statistical agencies.

The projections of the Muslim populations for 2010, 2020, and 2030 are based on assumptions about patterns in births, deaths, migration, and age structures – the main factors driving population change – which are detailed below. There might, however, be political, environmental, or social events that affect fertility, mortality, migration, and age structures but that are not captured in these projections.

The Forum's study also considered conversion to or from Islam. Because recent survey data do not indicate that conversion is having any clear impact on the size of Muslim populations, the report assumes that future conversions into Islam will roughly equal conversions away from Islam, either to other faiths or to no particular faith. (See discussion in the Conversion section of chapter 11.)

Data

The Pew Forum's population projections take into account several types of data. In some cases, statistics are available specifically for Muslim populations. In other cases, however, they are available only for the general population. Inferences from data on the general population of Muslim-majority countries are more reliable than when the majority population is non-Muslim.

Baseline Muslim populations

To provide a current population baseline, the Pew Forum and its consultants used the best available sources to estimate the percentage of Muslims as a portion of each country's population in 2010. In some cases, the best source is a census from several years before, such as 2001 or 2005. However, the Forum's study does not simply carry the percentage of Muslims in 2001 or 2005 forward to 2010. Wherever sufficient data on the fertility and migration of Muslim populations in a particular country are available, they are used to project the earlier population forward to reach a 2010 estimate. This results in substantial differences, for some countries, between the 2010 Muslim population estimates contained in the study and the 2009 estimates published by the Pew Forum in its report *Mapping the Global Muslim Population*. (See the section below on "Differences Between this Study and the Pew Forum's 2009 Report.")

Fertility

The standard measure of fertility in the study is the total fertility rate (TFR), defined as the total number of children an average woman would have in her lifetime if fertility patterns did not change. More specifically, the TFR is calculated by adding all the age-specific fertility rates for women in a particular country (or region) during a given year (or other time period). The Forum's study includes estimates of TFRs for Muslim women in all countries in which Muslims make up a substantial portion of the population. For countries in which fertility rates for various religious groups are not available, the Forum's study assumes that the TFR of Muslims is the same as the TFR in the general population. This applies to some countries, for example, in which Muslims are an overwhelming majority (constituting approximately 90% or more of the country's population), such as Afghanistan and Morocco.

Fortunately, fertility rates specifically for Muslims (or for ethnic groups that are predominantly Muslim) are available for many countries with sizeable Muslim minorities, including India, Nigeria, Ethiopia, Russia, Tanzania, and many countries in Europe and North America. In such cases, the study has used those differential rates for projection purposes. In countries where Muslims are a minority, the Muslim TFR, in most instances, tends to be slightly higher than the rate among the general population. In addition, fertility rates of Muslims tend to be higher than average in countries where they are recent immigrants (though the Muslim TFRs are projected gradually to converge to the national level in those countries). Therefore, for countries that have small Muslim populations, and for which differential data are not available, the study's estimates of the Muslim population are believed to be conservative.

Age and sex structure

In countries for which demographic data specifically on Muslims are available, the age and sex structure of Muslim populations is incorporated into the projection models. In countries for which differential age and sex data for Muslims are not available (usually countries in which Muslims make up a very small portion of the overall population), Muslims are assumed to have demographic characteristics similar to the country's general population.

Life expectancy at birth

The study's projections use United Nations assumptions about life expectancy gains. The study assumes that life expectancy at birth will improve somewhat for all populations by 2030 and that the greatest gains will be made in less-developed countries (where the majority of Muslims live). The study also assumes that in countries where Muslims live as a minority, life expectancy at birth for Muslims is similar to the life expectancy of the general population and is reflective of national standards of living. In general, data on differences in life expectancy at birth among members of various religious groups within a country are not available.

Migration: Important primarily in Europe and North America

Immigration is a key driver of Muslim population growth in Europe and North America. Muslim immigration to countries in more-developed parts of the world has risen steadily for decades as a result of evolving labor markets, changes in immigration laws, growing connections of emigrant families to communities abroad, and increased globalization.

Projections for future immigration of Muslims to Europe were made in collaboration with IIASA, primarily using immigration data provided by Eurostat.[8] Muslim immigration has been an ongoing phenomenon for decades in a number of European countries. The Forum's study assumes that annual Muslim migrant flows to European countries will remain constant in absolute numbers or, in some cases, will decline in the years ahead.

In North America, however, the number of new Muslim immigrants has risen steadily since the 1990s, even after accounting for a slight dip in immigration for both Muslims and non-Muslims following the September 11, 2001, terrorist attacks. As a result, the projections for the US assume that overall annual immigration will increase slowly, by about 1% per year. Based on recent trends that show more Muslims are leaving Muslim-majority countries, the Forum's study assumes that Muslims will comprise a slightly larger share of all immigrants to the US each year. Canada has experienced a rapid increase in its immigration Muslim population in the latter half of the twentieth century as well, growing from 10,000 in the 1960s to almost 276,000 in the 1990s.

The study's projections count only immigrants to the United States who receive permanent legal residency and do not include visiting family members, students, or others who are in the US temporarily or illegally. Therefore, the report's projections on the number of Muslim immigrants can be considered conservative.[9]

Patterns of immigration to the US have varied from year to year, including a spike in 1998–2001, a sharp decline in 2002–04, and a subsequent return to average increases.[10] Despite these ups and downs, Muslim immigration to the US has grown steadily since the 1940s, contrasting with substantial long-term fluctuations during the nineteenth and early twentieth centuries. While short-term fluctuations seem likely to continue, the projections assume that those variations will be less important than the long-term trends.

The issue of illegal immigration to the United States has become highly contentious. However, there is no evidence that illegal immigration is a significant factor in Muslim population growth in the United States, partly because the overwhelming majority of Muslim immigrants enter through airports rather than at land crossings, which are more difficult than airports to monitor.

Projection Assumptions

The Forum's study made three alternative population projections – a high, medium, and low estimate – for Muslims in each country. The country estimates were then added to produce high, medium, and low projections for the entire world. The three estimates are based on different assumptions about fertility, life expectancy at birth, and migration of both Muslims and non-Muslims (where differential data are available). The results of the study summarized in the following chapter use figures from the medium scenario for 2020 and 2030 because it is considered to be the most likely indicator of future population growth.

Fertility assumptions

The assumptions about future changes in fertility used in the study largely follow those of the United Nations. The *medium fertility scenario* assumes that the Muslim total fertility rate in every country will eventually settle in the range of approximately 1.9 to

Table 10.1   Fertility scenarios: Examples from three Muslim-majority countries, 2005–35.

Country	Total fertility rates				Scenarios
	2005–10	2010–15	2020–5	2030–5	
Afghanistan	6.6				Beginning
		6.5	5.9	4.9	High
		6.3	5.4	4.4	Medium
		6.0	4.9	3.9	Low
Egypt	2.9				Beginning
		2.9	2.9	2.7	High
		2.7	2.4	2.2	Medium
		2.4	1.9	1.7	Low
Iran	1.8				Beginning
		2.0	2.3	2.4	High
		1.7	1.8	1.9	Medium
		1.5	1.3	1.4	Low

Data source: United Nations, Department of Economic and Social Affairs, Population Division, *World Population Prospects: The 2010 Revision* (New York, 2011). Based on Pew Forum on Religion and Public Life, *The Future of the Global Muslim Population: Projections for 2010–2030*, January 27, 2011, http://www.pewforum.org/the-future-of-the-global-muslim-population.aspx.

2.1 children per woman. Some countries are already in this range, and others are projected to reach this range by 2030–5. Accordingly, if a country has already dipped below 1.9, as Iran has, the medium projection assumes that it will eventually stabilize around 1.9. *The low fertility scenario* assumes 0.5 fewer children per woman in the decades ahead than the fertility rate in the medium scenario. *The high fertility scenario* assumes 0.5 more children per woman in the decades ahead than the fertility rate in the medium scenario. Projections for countries with Muslim-specific fertility data, including the United States and many European nations, used similar fertility assumptions.

Mortality assumptions

Based on United Nations estimates, the Forum's study projects that life expectancy at birth will increase gradually in all countries. There is no high, medium, or low assumption because each country, whatever its current economic condition, is assumed to be moving toward better living standards and, therefore, longer life expectancy at birth.

Migration assumptions

Based on United Nations estimates, the Forum's study assumes that in most countries the gap between the number of emigrants and the number of immigrants gradually will narrow. In Europe, for example, Muslim immigrant flows are projected to remain steady or decrease slightly. Based on historical patterns in US immigration, however, the study assumes that the most likely scenario is a modest increase in the flow of Muslim immigrants to the United States over the period 2010–30.

Table 10.2.1   Population projection scenarios outside of Europe and the US.

| | Assumptions for Muslim populations outside Europe and the US | | |
Projection scenario	Fertility	Life expectancy	Emigration
Low	Low	Gradually increasing	Some decline
Medium (main)	Medium	Gradually increasing	Some decline
High	High	Gradually increasing	Some decline

Based on Pew Forum on Religion and Public Life, *The Future of the Global Muslim Population: Projections for 2010–2030*, January 27, 2011, http://www.pewforum.org/the-future-of-the-global-muslim-population.aspx.

Table 10.2.2   European population projection scenario.

| | Assumptions for Muslim populations in Europe | | |
Projection scenario	Fertility	Life expectancy	Immigration
Low	Low	Gradually increasing	Substantial decline
Medium (main)	Medium	Gradually increasing	Some decline
High	High	Gradually increasing	No decline

Based on Pew Forum on Religion and Public Life, *The Future of the Global Muslim Population: Projections for 2010–2030*, January 27, 2011, http://www.pewforum.org/the-future-of-the-global-muslim-population.aspx.

Table 10.2.3   US population projection scenario.

| | Assumptions for Muslim populations in the U.S. | | |
Projection scenario	Fertility	Life expectancy	Immigration
Low	Low	Gradually increasing	No decline
Medium (main)	Medium	Gradually increasing	Some increase
High	High	Gradually increasing	Substantial increase

Based on Pew Forum on Religion and Public Life, *The Future of the Global Muslim Population: Projections for 2010–2030*, January 27, 2011, http://www.pewforum.org/the-future-of-the-global-muslim-population.aspx.

The Projected Global Muslim Population Scenarios

Unlike the projected number of Muslims, the proportion of Muslims in the world population is similar under all three growth scenarios. For example, the low scenario projects that Muslims will make up 26.27% of the world's population by 2030. The medium scenario projects 26.34% and the high scenario projects 26.42%.

Some regions also show little difference between the high, medium, and low scenarios. For example, the low scenario projects that Muslims will make up 7.9% of the European population in 2030. The medium scenario gives 8.0%, and the high estimate is 8.1%. Even if Russia – which has the largest number of Muslims of any European country but whose landmass extends into Asia – is not included in the

Table 10.3   World Muslim population growth scenarios, 2020 and 2030.

Scenario	Population	2020	2030
Low	Muslim % of world population	24.90%	26.29%
	Muslim population (billions)	1.87	2.07
	World population (billions)	7.50	7.86
Medium	Muslim % of world population	24.93%	26.36%
	Muslim population (billions)	1.91	2.19
	World population (billions)	7.67	8.31
High	Muslim % of world population	24.96%	26.43%
	Muslim population (billions)	1.96	2.32
	World population (billions)	7.85	8.76

Based on Pew Forum on Religion and Public Life, *The Future of the Global Muslim Population: Projections for 2010–2030*, January 27, 2011, http://www.pewforum.org/the-future-of-the-global-muslim-population.aspx. Population estimates are rounded to thousands. Percentages are calculated from unrounded numbers. Figures may not add exactly due to rounding.

Table 10.4   European Muslim population growth scenarios (includes Russia), 2020 and 2030.

Scenario	Population	2020	2030
Low	Muslim % of European population	7.0%	7.9%
	European Muslim population (millions)	50.3	54.5
	European population (millions)	721.6	691.5
Medium	Muslim % of European population	7.0%	8.0%
	European Muslim population (millions)	51.6	58.2
	European population (millions)	736.9	727.2
High	Muslim % of European population	7.0%	8.1%
	European Muslim population (millions)	52.9	61.9
	European population (millions)	752.1	762.1

Based on Pew Forum on Religion and Public Life, *The Future of the Global Muslim Population: Projections for 2010–2030*, January 27, 2011, http://www.pewforum.org/the-future-of-the-global-muslim-population.aspx, and International Institute for Applied Systems Analysis (IIASA). European Muslim share projections applied to Europe's population estimated by the United Nations Population Division. The low scenario assumes there will be a substantial decline in the number of Muslim immigrants and that fertility will converge to the national level by 2030. The medium scenario assumes more modest declines in both immigration and fertility. The high scenario assumes Muslim immigration numbers will remain constant through 2030 and no convergence in fertility rates. Population estimates are rounded to thousands. Percentages are calculated from unrounded numbers. Figures may not add exactly due to rounding.

European estimates, the overall difference (in percentage terms) between the high and low scenarios is still only 0.2 points.

While the three scenarios produce essentially the same projections at the global and regional levels, differences at the country level might be more noticeable, especially in countries with a large influx of Muslim immigrants, such as the United States. The low scenario projects that Muslims will make up 1.54% of the US population in 2030. The medium projection is 1.68% and the high projection is 1.89%. As in all cases throughout the study, the medium scenario is used as the best indicator of the future.

Table 10.5   US Muslim population growth scenarios, 2020 and 2030.

Scenario	Population	2020	2030
Low	Muslim % of US population	1.18%	1.54%
	US Muslim population (millions)	4.00	5.41
	US population (millions)	338.88	351.13
Medium	Muslim % of U.S. population	1.20%	1.68%
	US Muslim population (millions)	4.15	6.22
	US population (millions)	346.15	369.98
High	Muslim % of US population	1.24%	1.89%
	US Muslim population (millions)	4.38	7.35
	US population (millions)	353.44	388.81

Based on Pew Forum on Religion and Public Life, *The Future of the Global Muslim Population: Projections for 2010–2030*, January 27, 2011, http://www.pewforum.org/the-future-of-the-global-muslim-population.aspx. US Muslim share projections applied to US population estimated by the United Nations Population Division. The low scenario keeps the number of Muslim immigrants at the 2009 level through 2030 and assumes that fertility will converge to the national level by 2030. The medium variant assumes that Muslim immigration will continue at the current average annual rate of increase and that fertility will converge to average national levels for second-generation Muslim immigrants, with slightly higher fertility for foreign-born Muslims. The high scenario assumes that Muslim immigration will gradually increase 2.5% faster per year than the average trend line through 2030, with no convergence in fertility rates. Population estimates are rounded to thousands. Percentages are calculated from unrounded numbers. Figures may not add exactly due to rounding.

Definition of Muslims

The study seeks to provide the most up-to-date and comprehensive demographic esti-mates of the number of Muslims in the 232 countries and territories for which the United Nations Population Division provides general population estimates. Wherever possible, the Forum's study counts all groups and individuals who self-identify as Muslim in order to have statistics that are comparable across countries. This includes members of the Sunni and Shi'a sects as well as Sufi orders and various smaller groups, such as the Ahmadiyya movement and the Nation of Islam, which might be considered heterodox by some Muslim authorities. It also includes Muslims who might be secular or non-observant.

Differences between this study and the Pew Forum's 2009 report

The 2011 study builds on the findings from the Pew Forum's 2009 report *Mapping the Global Muslim Population*, which acquired and analyzed about 1,500 sources of data – including census reports, large-scale demographic studies, and general population surveys – to estimate the number of Muslims in every country. Some of those estimates have been revised to take into account new sources of data, such as the 2008 Nigerian Demographic and Health Survey, that were not available when the 2009 report was compiled.

In addition, the 2011 study improves on the methodology used to generate some of the 2009 estimates from older census and survey data. For the 2009 report, the number of Muslims in each country was calculated by multiplying the UN's 2009 total population estimate for that country by the single most-recent and most-reliable

estimate of the percentage of Muslims in the country's population, based on the conservative assumption that Muslim populations are growing at least as fast as the general population in each country. In contrast, the 2011 report uses estimates of the
differential growth rates of Muslim populations in many countries where Muslims are
a substantial minority, including India, China, Nigeria, the United States, Canada,
and numerous European nations. For instance, the United Kingdom's 2001 census
found that 2.7% of the UK's total population was Muslim, and that percentage was
reflected in the Pew Forum's 2009 report. The 2011 study, however, takes into
account higher-than-average fertility among Muslims in the UK as well as additional
Muslim immigration. Using the cohort-component method, it projects the UK's
2001 Muslim population forward to 2010, which results in a revised estimate that
Muslims comprise 4.6% of the country's current population.

Historical data

To illustrate trends, the study and its accompanying interactive maps provide Muslim
population estimates for 1990 and 2000 based on national censuses, demographic
and health surveys, and general population surveys and studies available for those
years. These data points have not been altered retrospectively; no attempt has been
made to correct or revise the historical figures in light of more recent data. However,
Forum staff did attempt to identify past overcounts or undercounts of Muslims. This
evaluation involved two steps. First, any country or territory whose Muslim population
size, as ranked in world order in 2010, was 15 or more places higher or lower than its
world ranking in 1990 or 2000 was marked for further analysis. Staff then assessed
whether the change likely was attributable to inconsistencies in the data sources rather
than to an actual change in the size of the Muslim population. For instance, a 1988
report published by the Population Reference Bureau[11] was identified as the best
available source for the 1990 Muslim population of France. That report, based on an
analysis of ethnicity data, estimated that slightly more than half a million Muslims
were living in France. In contrast, the 2010 estimate of 4.7 million Muslims in
France – more than an eightfold increase over the 1990 figure – is based on an analysis
of a 2008 nationally representative survey of the French population. Given the limitations of the source used for 1990, compared with the strengths of the 2010 source, it
seems more likely that the 1990 figure was an undercount than that the Muslim
population of France grew eightfold in 20 years.

All together, the sources for 1990 appear to have substantially *understated* the
actual numbers of Muslims in Angola, Cyprus, France, Gabon, Mozambique, and
Ukraine, while substantially *overstating* the numbers in Colombia, Georgia, Mongolia,
Panama, Taiwan, and Viet Nam. The 2000 estimates appear to have undercounted
Muslims in Cyprus, France, Guatemala, Hungary, Slovakia, and Viet Nam, while
overcounting the numbers in Laos, Lesotho, and Taiwan. These likely undercounts
and overcounts should be considered when looking at growth rates, particularly in
the affected countries. The number of Muslims in Viet Nam, for example, might not
have dropped from 1990 to 2000 and then climbed rapidly from 2000 to 2010;
rather, the 1990 figure was probably too high an estimate, and the 2000 figure might
have been too low.

Discussion of Sources

Sources for the study include United Nations data, national censuses, demographic and health surveys, and general population surveys and studies. The specific source used for the Muslim population in each country is listed in Appendix B of the Pew report.[12] Readers should note, however, that general population surveys typically have smaller sample sizes than demographic surveys and are not designed to measure the size of small minority populations. This can lead to undercounts of Muslims in countries where they represent a small minority of the population and overcounts where they represent the vast majority of the population. See sections below on data sources for more detail.

For all sources, results can be affected by methodological decisions with respect to how the data are collected and managed. Social, cultural, or political factors can also affect how answers to census and survey questions are provided and recorded. For instance, in some Muslim cultures it is unacceptable for men to interview women, and if they do, other men from the family will generally be present. Such a situation would likely produce different results than if the woman was interviewed by another woman.

United Nations and other international research agencies

Data on fertility rate, age structure, life expectancy, migration, and related factors come mainly from the United Nations Population Division. Differential demographic data on Muslims (for instance, different fertility rates for Muslims versus non-Muslims) are taken from censuses, demographic and health surveys, and national statistical offices. Specific data sources are identified in each chart and table throughout the report.

Censuses

For this study, Pew Forum researchers acquired and analyzed religious affiliation data from 81 censuses conducted since 1999, comparing more current non-census sources of data with older census data on religious affiliation for an additional 103 countries as a cross-check. Religious affiliation questions from national censuses are the best source for estimating the number of Muslims because they generally cover the entire population and are conducted on a fairly regular basis. The chief limitation in using census data is that fewer than half of recent country censuses include a religious affiliation question. In addition, censuses typically are conducted only once every 10 years.

Demographic surveys

Where recent census data on religion are not available, religious affiliation questions from large-scale demographic surveys, such as Macro International's MEASURE Demographic and Health Surveys (DHS),[13] are the second-best source because of their large sample sizes, large sampling frames, and representative results at the province level. Though many fewer people are interviewed in a demographic survey than in a census, demographic surveys complete sufficiently high numbers of interviews to produce a generally accurate demographic profile of the country. The chief limitation of demographic surveys, for purposes of the Forum's study, is that they assume that children in a household or older members of a household have the same religion as the people interviewed, who are women and men in their prime reproductive years (ages 15–49 for women and ages 15–54 for men).

For the study, DHS data were acquired and analyzed for more than 60 countries, or nearly two thirds of the countries for which census data are lacking or are older than 1999. For most of the DHS surveys, both women and men are interviewed and Macro International provides the data in separate male-female data sets. Pew Forum staff pooled the female and male data sets in consultation with sampling experts at Macro International so that the combined data set retains nationally representative results. In countries where only females are interviewed, Pew Forum staff used those data to make the overall Muslim population estimate for the country.

General population surveys

Pew Forum researchers acquired and analyzed religious affiliation data from general population surveys for about 100 countries. In more than 20 of these countries, these surveys provide religious affiliation data where a recent census or demographic survey is lacking. Because general population surveys typically involve only 1,000 to 2,000 respondents, however, they provide less accurate numbers. This is especially true where the size of the Muslim population is quite small or Muslims live in concentrated locations that are not oversampled.

World Religion Database

Pew Forum researchers also used estimates from the *World Religion Database* (*WRD*),[14] primarily for countries in which census and survey estimates are out of date, are unavailable, or lack sufficient coverage. Besides census and survey reports, *WRD* estimates also take into account other sources of information on religious affiliation, including anthropological and ethnographic studies as well as reputable statistical reports from religious groups themselves. The *WRD* is an outgrowth of the international religious demography project at Boston University's Institute on Culture, Religion and World Affairs.

A Note on Country and Territory Designation

The Forum's study provides population estimates for 232 countries and territories. The word "territories" is used as a general term for geographical entities that are not recognized as countries by the United Nations but that have separate population estimates reported by the UN Population Division. Territories in the study include entities such as Hong Kong and Macau (special administrative regions of China), Greenland (an autonomous constituent country within the Kingdom of Denmark) and the Commonwealth of Puerto Rico (an unincorporated territory of the United States). For convenience, "countries" is often used in charts, tables, and the text of the report as an umbrella term for countries and territories.

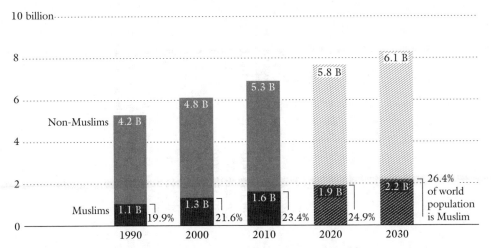

Percentages are calculated from unrounded numbers. Cross-hatching denotes projected figures.

Figure 10.1   Muslims as a share of world population, 1990–2030. *Source*: Reproduced by permission of Pew Research Center's Forum on Religion and Public Life, © 2011, Pew Research Center. Based on Pew Forum on Religion and Public Life, *The Future of the Global Muslim Population: Projections for 2010–2030*, January 27, 2011, http://www.pewforum.org/the-future-of-the-global-muslim-population.aspx.

Overview of the Findings

The projections by the Pew Forum on Religion and Public Life are based both on past demographic trends and on assumptions about how these trends will play out in future years. Making these projections inevitably entails a host of uncertainties, including political ones. Changes in the political climate in the United States or European nations, for example, could dramatically affect the patterns of Muslim migration and thus the rate of increase in the number of Muslims in these countries.

The world's Muslim population is expected to increase by about 35% between 2010 and 2030, rising from 1.6 billion to 2.2 billion, according to the 2011 population projections by the Pew Research Center's Forum on Religion and Public Life. Globally, the Muslim population is forecast to grow at about twice the rate of the non-Muslim population through 2030 – an average annual growth rate of 1.5% for Muslims, compared with 0.7% for non-Muslims. If current trends continue, Muslims will make up 26.4% of the world's total projected population of 8.3 billion in 2030, up from 23.4% of the estimated 2010 world population of 6.9 billion.

While the global Muslim population is expected to grow at a faster rate than the non-Muslim population, the Muslim population nevertheless is expected to grow at a slower pace in the period 2010–30 than it did in the previous two decades. From 1990 to 2010, the global Muslim population increased at an average annual rate of 2.3%, compared with the projected rate of 1.5% for the period from 2010 to 2030.

If current trends continue, however, the projections show that 79 countries will have a million or more Muslim inhabitants in 2030, up from 72 countries in 2010.[15] A majority of the world's Muslims (about 60%) will continue to live in the Asia–Pacific

Table 10.6 Muslim population by region, 2010 and 2030.

	2010		2030	
	Estimated Muslim population	*Percentage of global Muslim population*	*Projected Muslim population*	*Percentage of global Muslim population*
World	**1,619,314,000**	**100.0%**	**2,190,154,000**	**100.0%**
Asia–Pacific	1,005,507,000	62.1	1,295,625,000	59.2
Middle East–North Africa	321,869,000	19.9	439,453,000	20.1
Sub–Saharan Africa	242,544,000	15.0	385,939,000	17.6
Europe	44,138,000	2.7	58,209,000	2.7
Americas	5,256,000	0.3	10,927,000	0.5

Figures may not add exactly due to rounding; percentages are calculated from unrounded numbers. Population estimates are rounded to thousands.
Source: Reproduced by permission of Pew Research Center's Forum on Religion and Public Life, © 2011, Pew Research Center. Based on Pew Forum on Religion and Public Life, *The Future of the Global Muslim Population: Projections for 2010–2030*, January 27, 2011, http://www.pewforum.org/the-future-of-the-global-muslim-population.aspx.

region, while about 20% will live in the Middle East and North Africa, as was the case in 2010. Pakistan, however, is expected to surpass Indonesia as the country with the largest Muslim population. The portion of the world's Muslims living in sub-Saharan Africa is projected to rise; in 2030, for example, more Muslims are likely to live in Nigeria than in Egypt. Muslims will remain relatively small minorities in Europe and the Americas, but these regions are expected to have the fastest rates of growth in the sizes of their Muslim populations, primarily due to having a small base that initially increases rapidly through immigration. But in time as the base becomes larger, each new immigrant will add a proportionally smaller share to the overall population.

In the United States, for example, the population projections show the number of Muslims more than doubling, rising from 2.6 million in 2010 to 6.2 million in 2030, in large part because of immigration and higher-than-average US fertility among Muslims. The Muslim share of the US population (adults and children) is projected to grow from 0.8% in 2010 to 1.7% in 2030, making Muslims in 2030 roughly as numerous as Jews or Episcopalians are in the United States in 2010. Although several European countries will have substantially higher percentages of Muslims, the United States is projected to have a larger number of Muslims by 2030 than any European countries except Russia and France.

In Europe as a whole, the Muslim share of the population is expected to grow by more than a third by 2030, rising to 8% of the region's inhabitants from 6% in 2010. In absolute numbers, Europe's Muslim population is projected to grow from 44 million in 2010 to 58 million in 2030. The greatest increases – driven primarily by continued migration – are likely to occur in Western and Northern Europe, where Muslims will be approaching double-digit percentages of the population in several countries. In the United Kingdom, for example, Muslims are expected to constitute 8.2% of the population in 2030, up from an estimated 4.6% in 2010. In Austria, Muslims are projected to reach 9.3% of the population in 2030, up from 5.7% in 2010; in Sweden, 9.9% (up from 4.9%); in Belgium, 10.2% (up from 6%); and in France, 10.3% (up from 7.5%).

Several factors account for the faster projected growth among Muslims than non-Muslims worldwide. On average, Muslim populations have higher fertility rates (more children per woman) than non-Muslim populations. In addition, a larger share of the Muslim population is in, or soon will enter, their prime reproductive years (ages 15–29). Also, improved health and economic conditions in Muslim-majority countries have led to greater-than-average declines in infant and child mortality rates, and life expectancy is rising even faster in Muslim-majority countries than in other less-developed countries.

Growing, but at a Slower Rate

The growth of the global Muslim population, however, should not obscure another important demographic trend: the *rate* of growth among Muslims has been slowing in recent decades and is likely to continue to decline, as figure 10.3 shows. From 1990 to 2000, the global Muslim population grew at an average annual rate of 2.3%. The growth rate dipped to 2.1% from 2000 to 2010, and it is projected to drop to 1.7% from 2010 to 2020 and 1.4% from 2020 to 2030 (or 1.5% annually over the 20-year period from 2010 to 2030, as previously noted).

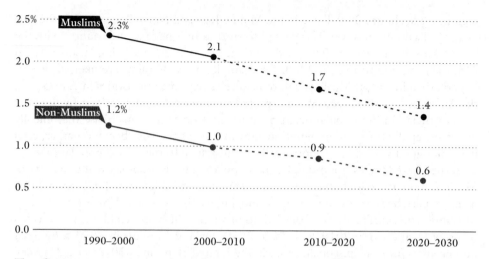

These figures are average compound annual growth rates over the 10-year periods shown.
Compounding takes into account that the population base for each year includes
growth from the previous year. Data points are plotted based on unrounded numbers.
Dotted lines denote projected figures. Percentages are calculated from unrounded numbers.

Figure 10.2   Annual population growth rates for Muslims and non-Muslims, 1990–2030.
Source: Reproduced by permission of Pew Research Center's Forum on Religion and Public
Life, © 2011, Pew Research Center. Based on Pew Forum on Religion and Public Life, *The
Future of the Global Muslim Population: Projections for 2010–2030,* January 27, 2011, http://
www.pewforum.org/the-future-of-the-global-muslim-population.aspx.

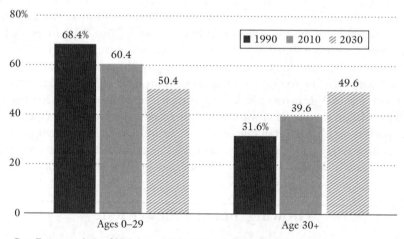

Pew Forum analysis of UN data, weighted by country populations so that
more populous countries affect the average more than smaller countries.
Percentages may not add to 100 due to rounding. Cross-hatching denotes
projected figures.

Figure 10.3   Percentage of population of Muslim-majority countries in selected age groups,
1990–2030. *Source*: Reproduced by permission of Pew Research Center's Forum on Religion
and Public Life, © 2011, Pew Research Center. Based on Pew Forum on Religion and Public
Life, *The Future of the Global Muslim Population: Projections for 2010–2030,* January 27, 2011,
http://www.pewforum.org/the-future-of-the-global-muslim-population.aspx.

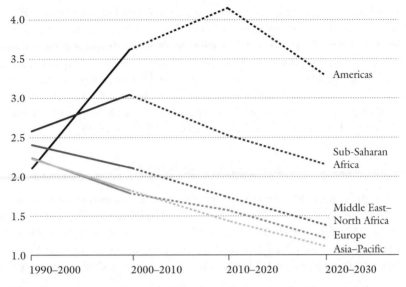

These figures are average compound annual growth rates over the 10-year periods shown. Compounding takes into account that the population base for each year includes growth from the previous year. Data points are plotted based on unrounded numbers. Dotted lines denote projected figures.

Figure 10.4 Annual population growth rates for Muslims by region, 1990–2030. *Source*: Reproduced by permission of Pew Research Center's Forum on Religion and Public Life, © 2011, Pew Research Center. Based on Pew Forum on Religion and Public Life, *The Future of the Global Muslim Population: Projections for 2010–2030*, January 27, 2011, http://www.pewforum.org/the-future-of-the-global-muslim-population.aspx.

The declining Muslim growth rate is due primarily to falling fertility rates in many Muslim-majority countries, including such populous nations as Indonesia and Bangladesh. Fertility is dropping as more women in these countries obtain a secondary education, living standards rise, and people move from rural areas to cities and towns.

The slowdown in Muslim population growth is most pronounced in the Asia–Pacific region, the Middle East–North Africa region, and Europe, and less sharp in sub-Saharan Africa. The only region in which Muslim population growth accelerates through 2020 is the Americas, largely because of immigration.

Falling birthrates eventually will lead to significant shifts in the age structures of Muslim populations. While the worldwide Muslim population was relatively young in 2010, the so-called Muslim "youth bulge" – the high percentage of Muslims in their teens and twenties – peaked around the year 2000 and began to decline. In 1990, more than two-thirds of the total population of Muslim-majority countries was under age 30. In 2010, people under 30 made up about 60% of the population of these countries, and by 2030 they are projected to fall to 50%.

At the same time, many Muslim-majority countries will have aging populations; between 2010 and 2030, the share of people age 30 and older in these countries is expected to rise from 40% to 50%, and the share of people age 60 and older is expected nearly to double, from 7% to 12%. Muslim-majority countries, however, are not the only ones with aging populations. As birthrates drop and people live longer all around the globe, the population of the entire world is aging, that is, the portion of people living to old age is increasing. As a result, the global Muslim population will remain *comparatively* youthful for decades to come. The median age in Muslim-majority countries, for example, rose from 19 in 1990 to 24 in 2010 and is expected to climb to 30 by 2030. Even so, it still will be about 14 years lower than the median age in North America, Europe, and other more-developed regions, which rose from 34 to 40 between 1990 and 2010 and is projected to be 44 in 2030. By that year, nearly three in 10 of the world's youth and young adults – 29% of people ages 15–29 – are projected to be Muslims, up from 26% in 2010 and 20% in 1990.

Muslim-Majority Countries

As of 2010, there were 49 countries in which Muslims comprised more than 50% of the population. A total of 1.2 billion Muslims lived in these nations, representing 74% of the global Muslim population of 1.6 billion. By 2030, Nigeria is projected to become the fiftieth Muslim-majority country. In that year, according to the projections in the Forum's study, a total of 1.7 billion Muslims will live in Muslim-majority nations,

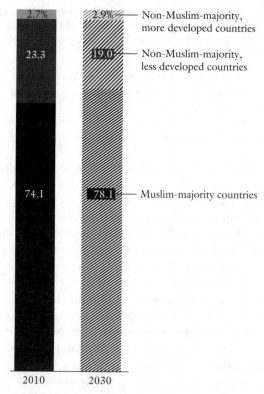

Percentages may not add to 100 due to rounding.
Cross hatching denotes projected figures.

Figure 10.5   Where Muslims live, 2010 and 2030. *Source*: Reproduced by permission of Pew Research Center's Forum on Religion and Public Life, © 2011, Pew Research Center. Based on Pew Forum on Religion and Public Life, *The Future of the Global Muslim Population: Projections for 2010–2030*, January 27, 2011, http://www.pewforum.org/the-future-of-the-global-muslim-population.aspx.

Table 10.7 Muslim population of Muslim-majority countries, 2010–30.

	2010			2030		
	Percent of population that is Muslim	*Estimated Muslim population*	*Percent of global Muslim population*	*Percent of population that is Muslim*	*Projected Muslim population*	*Percent of global Muslim population*
Afghanistan	99.8%	29,047,000	1.8%	99.8%	50,527,000	2.3%
Albania	82.1	2,601,000	0.2	83.2	2,841,000	0.1
Algeria	98.2	34,780,000	2.1	98.2	43,915,000	2.0
Azerbaijan	98.4	8,795,000	0.5	98.4	10,162,000	0.5
Bahrain	81.2	655,000	<0.1	81.2	881,000	<0.1
Bangladesh	90.4	148,607,000	9.2	92.3	187,506,000	8.6
Brunei	51.9	211,000	<0.1	51.9	284,000	<0.1
Burkina Faso	58.9	9,600,000	0.6	59.0	16,480,000	0.8
Chad	55.7	6,404,000	0.4	53.0	10,086,000	0.5
Comoros	98.3	679,000	<0.1	98.3	959,000	<0.1
Djibouti	97.0	853,000	0.1	97.0	1,157,000	0.1
Egypt	94.7	80,024,000	4.9	94.7	105,065,000	4.8
Gambia	95.3	1,669,000	0.1	95.3	2,607,000	0.1
Guinea	84.2	8,693,000	0.5	84.2	14,227,000	0.6
Indonesia	88.1	204,847,000	12.7	88.0	238,833,000	10.9
Iran	99.7	74,819,000	4.6	99.7	89,626,000	4.1
Iraq	98.9	31,108,000	1.9	98.9	48,350,000	2.2
Jordan	98.8	6,397,000	0.4	98.8	8,516,000	0.4
Kazakhstan	56.4	8,887,000	0.5	56.4	9,728,000	0.4
Kosovo	91.7	2,104,000	0.1	93.5	2,100,000	0.1

(Continued)

Table 10.7 (Cont'd).

	2010			2030		
	Percent of population that is Muslim	Estimated Muslim population	Percent of global Muslim population	Percent of population that is Muslim	Projected Muslim population	Percent of global Muslim population
Kuwait	86.4	2,636,000	0.2	86.4	3,692,000	0.2
Kyrgyzstan	88.8	4,927,00 0	0.3	93.8	6,140,000	0.3
Lebanon	59.7	2,542,000	0.2	59.7	2,902,000	0.1
Libya	96.6	6,325,000	0.4	96.6	8,232,000	0.4
Malaysia	61.4	17,139,000	1.1	64.5	22,752,000	1.0
Maldives	98.4	309,000	<0.1	98.4	396,000	<0.1
Mali	92.4	12,316,000	0.8	92.1	18,840,000	0.9
Mauritania	99.2%	3,338,000	0.2%	99.2%	4,750,000	0.2%
Mayotte	98.8	197,000	<0.1	98.8	298,000	<0.1
Morocco	99.9	32,381,000	2.0	99.9	39,259,000	1.8
Niger	98.3	15,627,000	1.0	98.3	32,022,000	1.5
Nigeria	**	**	**	51.5	116,832,000	5.3
Oman	87.7	2,547,000	0.2	87.7	3,549,000	0.2
Pakistan	96.4	178,097,000	11.0	96.4	256,117,000	11.7
Palestinian territories	97.5	4,298,000	0.3	97.5	7,136,000	0.3
Qatar	77.5	1,168,000	0.1	77.5	1,511,000	0.1
Saudi Arabia	97.1	25,493,000	1.6	97.1	35,497,000	1.6
Senegal	95.9	12,333,000	0.8	95.9	18,739,000	0.9
Sierra Leone	71.5	4,171,000	0.3	73.0	6,527,000	0.3
Somalia	98.6	9,231,000	0.6	98.6	15,529,000	0.7
Sudan	71.4	30,855,000	1.9	71.4	43,573,000	2.0

Syria	92.8	20,895,000	1.3	92.8	28,374,000	1.3
Tajikistan	99.0	7,006,000	0.4	99.0	9,525,000	0.4
Tunisia	99.8	10,349,000	0.6	99.8	12,097,000	0.6
Turkey	98.6	74,660,000	4.6	98.6	89,127,000	4.1
Turkmenistan	93.3	4,830,000	0.3	93.3	5,855,000	0.3
United Arab Emirates	76.0	3,577,000	0.2	76.0	4,981,000	0.2
Uzbekistan	96.5	26,833,000	1.7	96.5	32,760,000	1.5
Western Sahara	99.6	528,000	<0.1	99.6	816,000	<0.1
Yemen	99.0	24,023,000	1.5	99.0	38,973,000	1.8

**Not Muslim-majority in 2010.

Source: Reproduced by permission of Pew Research Center's Forum on Religion and Public Life, © 2011, Pew Research Center. Based on Pew Forum on Religion and Public Life, *The Future of the Global Muslim Population: Projections for 2010–2030,* January 27, 2011, http://www.pewforum.org/the-future-of-the-global-muslim-population.aspx.

representing 78% of the world's 2.2 billion Muslims. All Muslim-majority countries are in less-developed regions of the world, with the exception of Albania and Kosovo, which are in Europe (but still are among the least-developed countries in that region).

More than a fifth of the world's Muslims (23.3%) live in non-Muslim-majority, less-developed countries in 2010. These countries make up the rest of the "developing world"; they include all the non-Muslim-majority countries in sub-Saharan Africa, Asia–Pacific (excluding Japan), and Central and South America, including the Caribbean. These developing countries had a total of 376 million Muslim inhabitants in 2010. By 2030, they are projected to have 416 million Muslims, or 19% of all Muslims worldwide. The decline from 23% to 19% is due primarily to Nigeria (which accounts for about 5% of the world's Muslims) becoming a Muslim-majority country by 2030.

Less than 3% of the world's Muslims live in non-Muslim-majority, more-developed countries in 2010. This category is often described as the "developed world"; it includes all countries in Europe and North America, plus Australia, New Zealand, and Japan. These countries had a total of 42 million Muslim inhabitants in 2010. By 2030, they are projected to have 62 million Muslims, still about 3% of all Muslims worldwide.

Sunni and Shi'a Muslims

Sunni Muslims and Shi'a Muslims comprise the two main sects within Islam. Because data on the percentages of Sunni and Shi'a Muslims are rough estimates in many countries, this study presents them as ranges.[16]

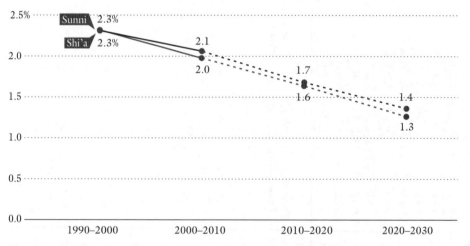

These figures are average compound annual growth rates over the 10-year periods shown. Compounding takes into account that the population base for each year includes growth from the previous year. Data points are plotted based on unrounded numbers. Dotted lines denote projected figures.

Figure 10.6 Annual population growth, Sunni and Shi'a Muslims, 1990–2030. *Source*: Reproduced by permission of Pew Research Center's Forum on Religion and Public Life, © 2011, Pew Research Center. Based on Pew Forum on Religion and Public Life, *The Future of the Global Muslim Population: Projections for 2010–2030*, January 27, 2011, http://www.pewforum.org/the-future-of-the-global-muslim-population.aspx.

Table 10.8 Shi'a Muslim population growth in the four largest Shi'a-majority countries and Sunni Muslim population growth in the four largest Sunni-majority countries, 2010–30.

Shi'a

Country	Estimated Shi'a population 2010	Projected Shi'a population 2030	Annual growth rate
Iraq	20,998,000	32,636,000	2.2%
Bahrain	459,000	617,000	1.5
Iran	69,208,000	82,904,330	0.9
Azerbaijan	6,156,000	7,113,000	0.7

Population estimates are calculated as ranges; figures listed are the mid-points of the ranges.

Sunni

Country	Estimated Sunni population 2010	Projected Sunni population 2030	Annual growth rate
Pakistan	155,834,000	224,103,000	1.8%
Egypt	79,624,000	104,539,000	1.4
Bangladesh	147,864,000	186,568,000	1.2
Indonesia	203,823,000	237,639,000	0.8

Population estimates are calculated as ranges; figures listed are the mid-points of the ranges.

Source: Reproduced by permission of Pew Research Center's Forum on Religion and Public Life, © 2011, Pew Research Center. Based on Pew Forum on Religion and Public Life, *The Future of the Global Muslim Population: Projections for 2010–2030*, January 27, 2011, http://www.pewforum.org/the-future-of-the-global-muslim-population.aspx.

Sunnis will continue to make up an overwhelming majority of Muslims in 2030. The number of Sunnis is projected to reach almost 2 billion by 2030 (between 1.91 billion and 1.97 billion), up from approximately 1.4 billion in 2010 (between 1.41 and 1.46 billion). The number of Shi'a Muslims is projected to be between 219 million and 285 million in 2030, up from between 162 million and 211 million in 2010. The percentages of the world's Muslims that are Sunni (87–90%) and Shi'a (10–13%), however, are expected to remain roughly the same in 2030 as they were in 2010.

Within these ranges, there might be a very slight increase in the percentage of Sunni Muslims and a very slight decline in the percentage of Shi'a Muslims. The annual rates of growth for the world's Sunni and Shi'a populations were identical from 1990 to 2000. The rate of growth of the Shi'a population, however, is expected to be slightly lower than the rate of growth for Sunnis for the period 2010–30, largely because of low fertility in Iran, where more than a third of the world's Shi'a Muslims live.

Four countries in the world have Shi'a-majority populations – Iran (where ~93% of Muslims are Shi'a), Azerbaijan (~70%), Bahrain (~70%), and Iraq (~67%). Of these, Iran has the most Shi'a Muslims. Iraq's Shi'a Muslim population is substantially smaller, but it is expected to grow at a faster rate than the Shi'a population in neighboring Iran.

The four countries with the largest Sunni-majority populations are Egypt (where >99% of Muslims are Sunni), Indonesia (~99%), Bangladesh (~99%), and Pakistan (~87%). Of these, Pakistan is expected to have the greatest annual growth in its number of Sunni Muslims. Indonesia's gains will be more modest.

Other Key Findings of the Study

Worldwide

- Fewer than half (48%) of married women ages 15–49 in Muslim-majority countries use some form of birth control. By comparison, in non-Muslim-majority, less-developed countries nearly two thirds (63%) of all married women in that age group use some form of birth control.

Asia–Pacific

- Nearly three in 10 people living in the Asia-Pacific region in 2030 (27.3%) will be Muslim, up from about a quarter in 2010 (24.8%) and roughly a fifth in 1990 (21.6%).
- Muslims make up only about 2% of the population in China, but because the country is so populous, its Muslim population is expected to be the nineteenth-largest in the world in 2030.

Middle East–North Africa

- The Middle East–North Africa region will continue to have the highest percentage of Muslim-majority countries. Of the 20 countries and territories in this region,

17 are expected to have populations that are more than 75% Muslim in 2030, with Israel, Lebanon, and Sudan (as demarcated in 2010 with Sudan and South Sudan combined) being the only exceptions.

- Nearly a quarter (23.2%) of Israel's population is expected to be Muslim in 2030, up from 17.7% in 2010 and 14.1% in 1990. Between 1990 and 2010, the Muslim population in Israel more than doubled, growing from 0.6 million to 1.3 million. The Muslim population in Israel (including all of Jerusalem but not the West Bank and Gaza) is expected to reach 2.1 million by 2030.
- Egypt, Algeria, and Morocco had the largest Muslim populations in the Middle East–North Africa region in 2010. By 2030, however, Iraq is expected to have the second-largest Muslim population in the region – exceeded only by Egypt – largely because Iraq has a higher fertility rate than Algeria or Morocco.

Sub-Saharan Africa

- The Muslim population in sub-Saharan Africa is projected to grow by nearly 60% between 2010 and 2030, from 243 million to 386 million. Because the region's non-Muslim population also is growing at a rapid pace, Muslims are expected to make up only a slightly larger share of the region's population in 2030 (31%) than they did in 2010 (29.6%).
- Various surveys give differing figures for the size of religious groups in Nigeria, which appeared to have roughly equal numbers of Muslims and Christians in 2010. By 2030, Nigeria is expected to have a slight Muslim majority (51.5%).

Europe

- In 2030, Muslims are projected to make up more than 10% of the total population in 10 European countries: Kosovo (93%), Albania (83.2%), Bosnia-Herzegovina (42.7%), Republic of Macedonia (40.3%), Montenegro (21.5%), Bulgaria (15.7%), Russia (14.4%), Georgia (11.5%), France (10.3%), and Belgium (10.2%).
- Russia will continue to have the largest Muslim population (in absolute numbers) in Europe in 2030. Its Muslim population is expected to rise from 16 million in 2010 to 19 million in 2030. The growth rate for the Muslim population in Russia is projected to be 0.6% annually over the two decades. By contrast, Russia's non-Muslim population is expected to shrink by 0.6% annually over the same period.
- More than 65,000 Muslims were expected to move to France, primarily from North Africa, representing about two thirds (68.5%) of all new immigrants to France. Spain was projected to have a larger number of Muslim immigrants (70,000), but they accounted for a much smaller portion of all immigrants to Spain (13.1%). The more than 63,000 Muslim immigrants predicted for the UK in 2010 accounted for more than a quarter (28.1%) of all the country's immigrants.

The Americas

- Canada's Muslim population is expected to roughly triple in 20 years, from about 940,000 in 2010 to nearly 2.7 million in 2030. Muslims are expected to constitute 6.6% of Canada's total population in 2030, up from 2.8% in 2010. Meanwhile, Argentina, whose Muslim population of about 1 million in 2010 ranked second in the Americas (behind the United States), is expected to drop to third (after the US and Canada).
- Children under age 15 made up a relatively small portion of the US Muslim population in 2010 (only 13% of Muslims were in the 0–14 age group). This reflects the fact that a large proportion of Muslims in the US are immigrants who arrived as adults. But by 2030, many of these immigrants are expected to have started families. The number of US Muslims under age 15 is projected to more than triple, from fewer than 500,000 in 2010 to 1.8 million in 2030. The number of Muslim children ages 0–4 living in the US is expected to increase from fewer than 200,000 in 2010 to more than 650,000 in 2030.
- About two thirds (64%) of the Muslims in the US in 2010 were first-generation immigrants (foreign-born), while slightly more than a third (36%) were born in the US. By 2030, however, nearly half (45%) of the Muslims in the US are expected to be native-born.
- The top countries of origin for Muslim immigrants to the US in 2009 were Pakistan, Bangladesh, Somalia, and Iran. They are expected to remain the top countries of origin for Muslim immigrants to the US in 2030.

The definition of Muslim in this report is very broad. The goal is to count all groups and individuals who *self-identify* as Muslims. This includes Muslims who might be secular or non-observant. No attempt is made in this report to measure how religious Muslims are or to forecast levels of religiosity (or secularism) in the decades ahead.[17]

The main factors, or inputs, in the population projections are:

- Births (fertility rates).
- Deaths (mortality rates).
- Migration (emigration and immigration).
- The age structure of the population (the numbers of people in various age groups).

Related factors – which are not direct inputs into the projections but which underlie vital assumptions about the way Muslim fertility rates are changing and Muslim populations are shifting – include:

- Education (particularly of women).
- Economic well-being (standards of living).
- Family planning (birth control and abortion).
- Urbanization (movement from rural areas into cities and towns).
- Religious conversion.

To understand the projections fully, one must understand these factors, which chapter 11 discusses in more detail.

Notes

1 This chapter is adapted from the Pew Research Center's Pew Forum on Religion and Public Life, *The Future of the Global Muslim Population: Projections for 2010–2030*, January 27, 2011,http://pewresearch.org/pubs/1872/muslim-population-projections-worldwide-fast-growth. In preparing this report, the Pew Forum consulted with numerous experts on Muslims in particular countries. In addition, the Forum is deeply indebted to researchers Vegard Skirbekk, K. C. Samir, Anne Valia Goujon, and Marcin Stonawski at the Age and Cohort Change Project of the International Institute for Applied Systems Analysis (IIASA) in Laxenburg, Austria, who collaborated with the Pew Forum on some of the most complex population projections. The Forum also received invaluable assistance and feedback on drafts of this report from Carl Haub, senior demographer, and Conrad Taeuber, Chair of Public Information at the Population Reference Bureau; Amaney Jamal, associate professor of politics at Princeton University and a Pew Forum consultant on global Islam; John Casterline, professor of sociology and director of the Initiative in Population Research at the Ohio State University; Charles F. Westoff, professor of demographic studies and sociology, emeritus, at Princeton University; Mohamed Ayad, regional coordinator of Demographic and Health Surveys at Macro International, Inc.; and our colleagues in the Pew Research Center's Social and Demographic Trends project, D'Vera Cohn and Jeffrey S. Passel. While the data collection and projection methodology were guided by numerous consultants and advisers, the Pew Forum is solely responsible for the interpretation and reporting of the data. In this chapter, "the study" or "the report," unless specified otherwise, are references to *The Future of the Global Muslim Population: Projections for 2010–2030*.

2 The Forum's study uses the term "Muslim-majority countries" rather than "Muslim countries" because many of them have secular rather than religious governments.

3 Additional discussion and evaluation of the sources can be found in Brian J. Grim and Becky Hsu, "Estimating the Global Muslim Population: Size and Distribution of the World's Muslim Population," *Interdisciplinary Journal of Research on Religion* 7:2 (2011).

4 In charts and tables throughout this chapter and the Pew report, the term "countries" is used loosely to refer both to sovereign nations and to a variety of territories and protectorates. No judgment on their legal status is intended.

5 For a detailed explanation of the cohort-component method as well as a discussion of the accuracy of population projections, see Brian O'Neill and Deborah Balk, "World Population Futures," *Population Bulletin* 56:3 (September 2001).

6 See John Stover and Sharon Kirmeyer, "DemProj Version 4: A Computer Program for Making Population Projections," March 2007, http://www.unaids.org/en/media/unaids/contentassets/dataimport/pub/manual/2007/demproj_2007_en.pdf.

7 Forthcoming global projections by the Pew Forum and IIASA will use multistate projection modeling, which goes beyond traditional cohort-component analysis by building projection scenarios that take into account not just fertility, mortality, and migration but also other predictors of demographic change – that is, other demographic "states" such as education levels. Multistate projection modeling was developed at IIASA by the American geographer Andrei Rogers in the 1970s. For further information on multi-state projection modeling, see Wolfgang Lutz and Anne Goujon, "The World's Changing Human Capital Stock: Multi-state Population Projections by Educational Attainment," *Population and Development Review* 27:2 (2001): 323–39.

8 Eurostat is the statistical office of the European Union. Situated in Luxembourg, its task is to provide the European Union with statistics that enable comparisons among countries and regions in Europe.

9   Data are not available on the number of permanent residents who move out of the US each year, including the number of Muslim permanent residents who leave. These losses may be partially offset by counting only legal, permanent residents as immigrants.

10 See Jeffrey S. Passel and Roberto Suro, *Rise, Peak and Decline: Trends in U.S. Immigration 1992–2004* (Washington, DC: Pew Hispanic Center, 2005). Available online at http://pewhispanic.org/reports/report.php?ReportID=53.

11 John R. Weeks, "The Demography of Islamic Nations," Population Reference Bureau, Inc. Population Bulletin 43:4 (December 1988).

12 See Pew Forum on Religion and Public Life, "Appendix B: Data Sources By Country," in *The Future of the Global Muslim Population: Projections for 2010–2030*, http://www.pewforum.org/future-of-the-global-muslim-population-appendix-b.aspx.

13 See MEASURE Demographic and Health Surveys (DHS) at http://www.measuredhs.com/.

14 Todd M. Johnson and Brian J. Grim, eds., *World Religion Database* (Leiden/Boston: Brill, 2008).

15 The seven countries projected to rise above 1 million Muslims by 2030 are Belgium, Canada, Congo, Djibouti, Guinea Bissau, Netherlands, and Togo.

16 For more information, see Pew Forum on Religion and Public Life, "Methodology for Sunni-Shia estimates," in *Mapping the Global Muslim Population*, 2009. Available online at http://www.pewforum.org/Muslim/Mapping-the-Global-Muslim-Population(20).aspx.

17 In other reports, the Pew Forum and the Pew Research Center have used large-scale public opinion surveys to measure the beliefs and practices of many religious groups, including Muslims in several countries. See, for example, *Tolerance and Tension: Islam and Christianity in Sub-Saharan Africa*, 2010, http://pewforum.org/executive-summary-islam-and-christianity-in-sub-saharan-africa.aspx, and *Muslim Americans: Middle Class and Mostly Mainstream*, 2007, http://pewforum.org/Muslim/Muslim-Americans-Middle-Class-and-Mostly-Mainstream%282%29.aspx.

References

Grim, Brian J., and Becky Hsu. "Estimating the Global Muslim Population: Size and Distribution of the World's Muslim Population." *Interdisciplinary Journal of Research on Religion* 7:2 (2011).

Johnson, Todd M., and Brian J. Grim, eds. *World Religion Database*. Leiden/Boston: Brill, 2008.

Lutz, Wolfgang, and Anne Goujon. "The World's Changing Human Capital Stock: Multi-state Population Projections by Educational Attainment." *Population and Development Review* 27:2 (2001): 323–39.

O'Neill, Brian, and Deborah Balk. "World Population Futures." *Population Bulletin* 56:3 (September 2001).

Passel, Jeffrey S., and Roberto Suro. *Rise, Peak and Decline: Trends in U.S. Immigration 1992–2004*. August 16, 2005. Washington, DC: Pew Hispanic Center, 2005. http://pewhispanic.org/reports/report.php?ReportID=53.

Pew Forum on Religion and Public Life. *Mapping the Global Muslim Population: A Report on the Size and Distribution of the World's Muslim Population*. October 7, 2009. http://www.pewforum.org/Mapping-the-Global-Muslim-Population.aspx.

Pew Forum on Religion and Public Life. *The Future of the Global Muslim Population: Projections for 2010–2030*. January 27, 2011. http://pewresearch.org/pubs/1872/muslim-population-projections-worldwide-fast-growth.

Pew Forum on Religion and Public Life. *Tolerance and Tension: Islam and Christianity in Sub-Saharan Africa*. April 15, 2010. http://www.pewforum.org/executive-summary-islam-and-christianity-in-sub-saharan-africa.aspx.

Stover, John, and Sharon Kirmeyer. "DemProj Version 4: A Computer Program for Making Population Projections." March 2007. http://www.unaids.org/en/media/unaids/contentassets/dataimport/pub/manual/2007/demproj_2007_en.pdf.

United Nations, Department of Economic and Social Affairs, Population Division. *World Population Prospects: The 2010 Revision* (New York, 2011).

Weeks, John R. "The Demography of Islamic Nations." Population Reference Bureau, Inc. *Population Bulletin* 43:4 (December 1988).

Chapter 11

Factors Driving Change in the Global Muslim Population

Main Factors Driving Population Growth

Fertility

Over the past four decades, fertility rates have fallen in most Muslim-majority countries.[1] Yet they remain, on average, higher than in the rest of the developing world and considerably higher than in more-developed countries. This is one of the main reasons that the global Muslim population is projected to rise both in absolute numbers and as a share of global total.[2]

Taken as a whole, the world's more-developed regions – including Europe, North America, Japan, and Australia – have total fertility rates (TFRs)[3] below the replacement level of about 2.1 children per woman, the minimum necessary to keep the population stable (absent other factors, such as immigration).[4] Fertility rates in these more-developed nations are projected to rise slightly between 2010–30 but remain, on average, well below replacement levels.

In non-Muslim-majority countries in less-developed regions – including all of Latin America, much of sub-Saharan Africa, and parts of Asia – fertility rates have dropped in recent decades. They are projected to continue to drop, reaching or even falling below replacement levels in these developing countries as a whole in 2030–35.

In many Muslim-majority countries – including Indonesia, Iran, the United Arab Emirates, Lebanon, Turkey, and Tunisia – fertility rates also have dropped substantially. The average TFR for all 49 Muslim-majority countries has fallen from 4.3 children per woman in 1990–95 to an estimated 2.9 children in 2010–15. Fertility rates in these Muslim-majority countries as a whole are expected to continue to decline, though not quite as steeply, dropping to 2.6 children per woman in 2020–25 and 2.3 children in 2030–35 – approaching and possibly reaching replacement levels.

The World's Religions in Figures: An Introduction to International Religious Demography,
First Edition. Todd M. Johnson and Brian J. Grim.
© 2013 John Wiley & Sons, Ltd. Published 2013 by John Wiley & Sons, Ltd.

Number of children an average woman is likely to have in her lifetime

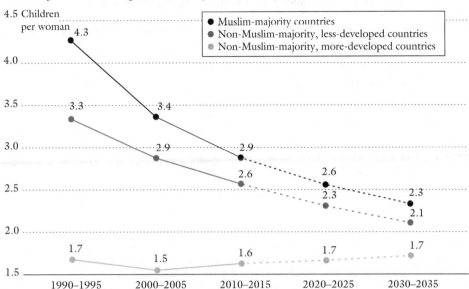

Pew Forum analysis of UN data, weighted by country populations so that more populous countries affect the average more than smaller countries. UN provides data as five-year averages. Data points are plotted based on unrounded numbers. Dotted lines denote projected figures.

Figure 11.1   Trends in fertility, 1990–2035. *Source*: Reproduced by permission of Pew Research Center's Forum on Religion and Public Life, © 2011, Pew Research Center. Based on Pew Forum on Religion and Public Life, *The Future of the Global Muslim Population: Projections for 2010–2030*, January 27, 2011, http://www.pewforum.org/the-future-of-the-global-muslim-population.aspx.

If current trends continue, fertility rates in Muslim-majority countries eventually might converge with fertility rates in other developing countries and in the world's more-developed regions. But complete convergence is not projected to occur for at least two decades, as figure 11.1 illustrates.

Moreover, high fertility rates in the past create a certain demographic momentum. Due to previously high fertility, large numbers of Muslim youth and young adults are now in (or entering) their prime childbearing years, all but ensuring that relatively rapid population growth will continue through 2030, even if the number of births *per woman* goes down.

Among the reasons for declining fertility rates in both Muslim-majority and non-Muslim-majority countries are economic development and improved living standards, higher levels of education, people waiting until they are older to get married, growing urbanization, and more extensive use of birth control. (See below for a discussion of how these factors affect the global Muslim population.) The overall trends in fertility, however, mask a considerable amount of variation from country to country. Among Muslim-majority countries, the highest TFRs for the period 2010–15 are found in Niger, Afghanistan, and Somalia, where the average woman has more than six children during her lifetime. The lowest TFRs are in Tunisia (1.8) and Iran (1.7), which are well below replacement levels.

A final, cautionary note: The impact of religion on fertility rates is difficult to assess and remains a subject of debate. One should not assume, simply because fertility tends to be higher in Muslim-majority countries than in other developing countries, that

Table 11.1   Most children per woman among Muslim-majority countries, 2010–15.

Country	2010–15	2030–35
Niger	6.9	5.3
Afghanistan	6.3	4.4
Somalia	6.2	4.3
Chad	5.8	3.8
Burkina Faso	5.6	3.6
Mali	5.2	3.5
Guinea	5.0	3.2
Sierra Leone	5.0	3.4
Yemen	4.7	2.8
Gambia	4.6	3.0
Senegal	4.5	2.9
Palestinian Territories	4.5	2.9

Data source: United Nations, Department of Economic and Social Affairs, Population Division, *World Population Prospects: The 2010 Revision* (New York, 2011). Based on Pew Forum on Religion and Public Life, *The Future of the Global Muslim Population: Projections for 2010–2030*, January 27, 2011, http://www.pewforum.org/the-future-of-the-global-muslim-population.aspx.

Table 11.2   Fewest children per woman among Muslim-majority countries, 2010–15.

Country	2010–15	2030–35
Iran	1.7	1.9
Tunisia	1.8	1.9
Albania	1.9	1.9
Lebanon	1.9	1.9
United Arab Emirates	1.9	1.9
Maldives	1.9	1.9
Brunei	2.0	1.9
Indonesia	2.0	1.9
Turkey	2.1	1.9
Kuwait	2.1	1.9
Bahrain	2.1	1.9
Azerbaijan	2.1	1.9

Data source: United Nations, Department of Economic and Social Affairs, Population Division, *World Population Prospects: The 2010 Revision* (New York, 2011). Based on Pew Forum on Religion and Public Life, *The Future of the Global Muslim Population: Projections for 2010–2030*, January 27, 2011, http://www.pewforum.org/the-future-of-the-global-muslim-population.aspx.

Islamic teachings are the reason. Cultural, social, economic, political, historical, and other factors can play equal or greater roles.[5] For example, many Muslims live in countries with higher-than-average rates of poverty, less-adequate health care, fewer educational opportunities, and more-rural populations. All of these conditions are associated with higher fertility rates.

Islamic authorities in some countries, such as Afghanistan and Saudi Arabia, reinforce cultural norms that limit women's autonomy by, for example, restricting their educational and career options or making it difficult for women to initiate a divorce. These restrictions might contribute to higher fertility because there is strong evidence that Muslim women, like other women around the world, tend to delay marriage – and consequently, childbirth – as they attain higher levels of education. (See the discussion of education below.) In Nigeria, for example, Muslim women generally have lower literacy levels and marry at younger ages; not surprisingly, Muslims also have higher fertility rates than non-Muslims in Nigeria. Recent studies, however, suggest that in a number of other countries, including India and Malaysia, measures of women's status cannot explain differences in fertility between Muslims and non-Muslims.[6]

Women in Muslim-majority countries tend to marry at much younger ages than women in more-developed countries, but there is little difference between the average age of marriage in Muslim-majority countries and in other less-developed countries. According to a Pew Forum analysis of UN data, women in Muslim-majority countries marry, on average, at 21.6 years, compared with 22 years in non-Muslim-majority, less-developed countries, and 26.2 years in more-developed countries.[7]

Family planning is another arena in which the role of religion is not as simple as it might seem. Islamic edicts generally have supported the use of birth control, and a number of Muslim-majority countries (including Pakistan, Bangladesh, Indonesia, Iran, Turkey, and Tunisia) have encouraged family-planning programs. Nonetheless, many Muslims either are uneasy about contraceptives or do not have access to them, and women in Muslim-majority countries report using birth control at lower rates than women in other developing countries. In addition, many Muslim-majority countries forbid or strictly limit abortions.

There is also some evidence that, across a variety of religious traditions, women who are more religious have higher fertility rates than less-religious women. This suggests that religiosity in general, rather than Islam in particular, might boost the number of children per woman.[8]

In short, Islamic beliefs might directly or indirectly influence the size of Muslim families, but religion does not operate in isolation from other forces; fertility rates appear to be driven by a complex mixture of cultural, social, economic, religious, and other factors.

Life expectancy at birth

Muslims are living much longer than they did just a generation ago. The average life expectancy at birth in Muslim-majority countries, which was 62 years in the five-year period 1990–95, is estimated to be 68 years in 2010–15.[9] By 2030–35, life expectancy at birth in Muslim-majority countries is projected to reach 73 years, equaling or slightly surpassing life expectancy in other (non-Muslim-majority) developing countries. This is another reason for the growth of the global Muslim population in both absolute and relative terms.

In more-developed countries, people tend to live considerably longer than in less-developed countries. In 2010–15, the average life expectancy in the world's more-developed countries is estimated by the United Nations Population Division to be a full decade longer than in developing countries (78 years vs. 68 years). Life expectancy,

Average number of years a newborn is expected to live

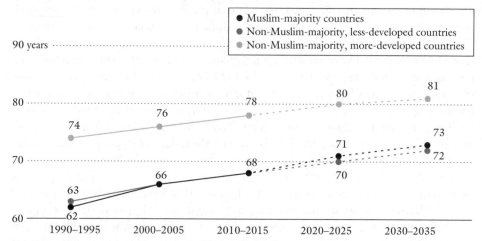

Pew Forum analysis of UN data, weighted by country populations so that more populous countries affect the average more than smaller countries. Dotted lines denote projected figures.

Figure 11.2   Trends in life expectancy at birth, 1990–2035. *Source*: Reproduced by permission of Pew Research Center's Forum on Religion and Public Life, © 2011, Pew Research Center. Based on Pew Forum on Religion and Public Life, *The Future of the Global Muslim Population: Projections for 2010–2030*, January 27, 2011, http://www.pewforum.org/the-future-of-the-global-muslim-population.aspx.

however, is rising in the developing world – including in countries with Muslim majorities – albeit from a lower base.

Between 1990–95 and 2010–15, the average gain in life expectancy in more-developed countries is estimated at four years (from 74 to 78). In less-developed countries where Muslims are in the minority, the gain is estimated to be five years (from 63 to 68). In Muslim-majority countries, it is estimated at six years (from 62 to 68).

A similar pattern is projected in the decades to come. Life expectancy in 2030–35 is projected to rise by three years over its 2010–15 value in more-developed countries (from 78 to 81), by four years in less-developed countries that do not have Muslim majorities (from 68 to 72), and by five years in Muslim-majority countries (from 68 to 73). The differences in the rate of improvement are small; the key point is that life expectancy at birth is rising across the board.

Behind the gains in longevity are numerous factors, including better health care, improved nutrition, rising incomes, and infrastructure development. One measure of health care quality, for example, is the percentage of births attended by skilled health professionals. This indicator has improved dramatically in Muslim-majority countries, rising from an average of 47% of all births in the 1990s to 63% of all births in 2000–08, a 16-percentage-point gain, according to the Pew Forum's analysis of data from the World Health Organization. In developing countries where Muslims are in the minority, by contrast, the percentage of births attended by skilled health professionals rose by five percentage points during this period, from 68% in the 1990s to 73% in 2000–08. Statistically speaking, virtually no improvement was possible in more-developed nations, where skilled health personnel already attended 99% of births in the 1990s.

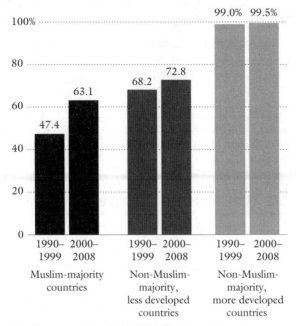

Pew Forum analysis of World Health Organization data, weighted by country populations so that more populous countries affect the average more than smaller countries.

Figure 11.3 Percentage of births attended by skilled health professionals, 1990–2008. *Source*: Reproduced by permission of Pew Research Center's Forum on Religion and Public Life, © 2011, Pew Research Center. Based on Pew Forum on Religion and Public Life, *The Future of the Global Muslim Population: Projections for 2010–2030,* January 27, 2011, http://www.pewforum.org/the-future-of-the-global-muslim-population.aspx.

To see how infrastructure development contributes to rising life expectancy in Muslim-majority countries, one might look, for example, at access to clean drinking water, which is less likely to carry diseases. Muslim-majority countries with better access to improved (that is, clean) drinking water have longer life expectancies. For instance, the average life expectancy in the five countries whose residents have the most access to improved drinking water is more than 70 years, compared with 60 years or less in the five Muslim-majority countries where access to clean drinking water is least common.

Improved health care and better access to clean drinking water, as well as many other gains in infrastructure development, living standards, and nutrition, have resulted in sharp declines in infant mortality rates in developing countries in general and Muslim-majority countries in particular. The decline in infant mortality, in turn, is one of the main factors driving up life expectancy at birth.

Between 1990–95 and 2010–15, the number of infant deaths per 1,000 live births is projected to drop by 30 in Muslim-majority countries, 17 in other less-developed countries, and five in more-developed countries. By 2020–25, Muslim-majority countries are expected to close the remaining gap and have infant mortality rates no higher than those in non-Muslim-majority developing countries.

Table 11.3 Most access to clean drinking water among Muslim-majority countries, 2006.

Country	Access to clean drinking water (%)	Life expectancy (years)
	2006	2010–15
Lebanon	100%	73
United Arab Emirates	100	78
Qatar	100	76
Malaysia	99	75
Jordan	98	74

Data source: World Health Organization, Global Health Observatory Data Repository; United Nations, Department of Economic and Social Affairs, Population Division, *World Population Prospects: The 2010 Revision* (New York, 2011).

Table 11.4 Least access to clean drinking water among Muslim-majority countries, 2006.

Country	Access to clean drinking water (%)	Life expectancy (years)
	2006	2010–15
Niger	42%	54
Mali	60	50
Mauritania	60	58
Sudan	70	60
Guinea	70	60

Data source: World Health Organization, Global Health Observatory Data Repository; United Nations, Department of Economic and Social Affairs, Population Division, *World Population Prospects: The 2010 Revision* (New York, 2011).

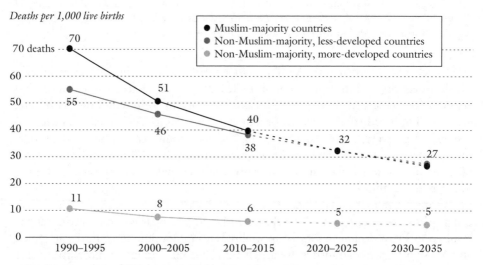

Deaths per 1,000 live births

Pew Forum analysis of UN data, weighted by country populations so that more populous countries affect the average more than smaller countries. Data points are plotted based on unrounded numbers. Dotted lines denote projected figures.

Figure 11.4 Trends in infant mortality, 1990–2035. *Source*: Reproduced by permission of Pew Research Center's Forum on Religion and Public Life, © 2011, Pew Research Center. Based on Pew Forum on Religion and Public Life, *The Future of the Global Muslim Population: Projections for 2010–2030*, January 27, 2011, http://www.pewforum.org/the-future-of-the-global-muslim-population.aspx.

Yet, despite such dramatic improvements, there is enormous variation among Muslim-majority countries in both infant mortality rates and life expectancy at birth. In Afghanistan, for example, the infant mortality rate is 147 deaths per 1,000 live births – the highest in the world and nearly four times the global average of 33 per 1,000, according to UN figures – while average life expectancy at birth is just 45 years.[10] By contrast, infant mortality rates in Bahrain, Kuwait, the United Arab Emirates, Brunei, and Malaysia are about the same as those in more-developed nations, and average life expectancy at birth is 75 years or more. Tables 11.5–11.8 highlight the wide range of infant mortality rates and life expectancies in Muslim-majority countries today and how they are projected to change in the decades to come.

Table 11.5 Highest projected infant mortality among Muslim-majority countries, ranked as of 2010–15.

Country	2010–15	2030–35
Afghanistan	147 deaths	106 deaths
Chad	123	93
Somalia	101	68
Mali	100	76
Sierra Leone	99	75
Guinea	88	56
Niger	81	59
Burkina Faso	76	60
Djibouti	75	44
Gambia	72	56

Data source: United Nations, Department of Economic and Social Affairs, Population Division, *World Population Prospects: The 2010 Revision* (New York, 2011). Based on Pew Forum on Religion and Public Life, *The Future of the Global Muslim Population: Projections for 2010–2030*, January 27, 2011, http://www.pewforum.org/the-future-of-the-global-muslim-population.aspx.

Table 11.6 Lowest projected infant mortality among Muslim-majority countries, ranked as of 2010–15.

Country	2010–15	2030–35
Brunei	5 deaths	5 deaths
Mayotte	6	5
Qatar	8	6
Malaysia	8	6
Kuwait	9	7
Bahrain	9	7
United Arab Emirates	9	7
Oman	11	8
Syria	14	9
Albania	14	10

Data source: United Nations, Department of Economic and Social Affairs, Population Division, *World Population Prospects: The 2010 Revision* (New York, 2011). Based on Pew Forum on Religion and Public Life, *The Future of the Global Muslim Population: Projections for 2010–2030*, January 27, 2011, http://www.pewforum.org/the-future-of-the-global-muslim-population.aspx.

Table 11.7 Highest projected life expectancies at birth among Muslim-majority countries, ranked as of 2010–15.

Country	2010–15	2030–35
Kuwait	78 years	80 years
United Arab Emirates	78	80
Brunei	78	80
Albania	77	80
Oman	77	79
Mayotte	76	79
Bahrain	76	79
Qatar	76	79
Malaysia	75	78
Syria	75	78
Libya	75	78
Tunisia	75	78

Data source: United Nations, Department of Economic and Social Affairs, Population Division, *World Population Prospects: The 2010 Revision* (New York, 2011). Based on Pew Forum on Religion and Public Life, *The Future of the Global Muslim Population: Projections for 2010–2030*, January 27, 2011, http://www.pewforum.org/the-future-of-the-global-muslim-population.aspx.

Table 11.8 Lowest projected life expectancies at birth among Muslim-majority countries, ranked as of 2010–15.

Country	2010–15	2030–35
Afghanistan	45 years	53 years
Sierra Leone	49	56
Chad	50	58
Mali	50	58
Somalia	51	59
Niger	54	63
Burkina Faso	55	61
Djibouti	57	64
Senegal	57	64
Gambia	57	64

Data source: United Nations, Department of Economic and Social Affairs, Population Division, *World Population Prospects: The 2010 Revision* (New York, 2011). Based on Pew Forum on Religion and Public Life, *The Future of the Global Muslim Population: Projections for 2010–2030*, January 27, 2011, http://www.pewforum.org/the-future-of-the-global-muslim-population.aspx.

Declining infant mortality rates and increased life expectancies mean that Muslim-majority countries will have more children surviving into adulthood as well as growing numbers of elderly people in the coming decades, as discussed in the section on age structure below.

Migration

On average, more people were leaving Muslim-majority countries than migrating to them. Although the rate has declined significantly since 1990, Muslim-majority countries are still losing part of their populations to emigration, and that trend is projected to continue through 2030, as figure 11.5 shows. Net migration from Muslim-majority countries to more-developed countries is one of the main reasons that both the numbers and the percentages of Muslims are projected to rise in Europe, North America, New Zealand, and Australia.

By 2030–35, average annual net migration (the difference between immigration into and emigration from a given area) in Muslim-majority countries, as a whole, is projected to be a loss of 47 per 100,000 people in the general population, down from a net loss of 81 per 100,000 people in the general population in 2010–15. As recently as 1990–95, Muslim-majority countries were losing many more people – an average of 160 annually per 100,000.

More-developed nations in Europe, North America, and elsewhere are likely to remain important destinations for immigrants from Muslim-majority countries (as well as from other less-developed countries) through 2030, and annual net migration

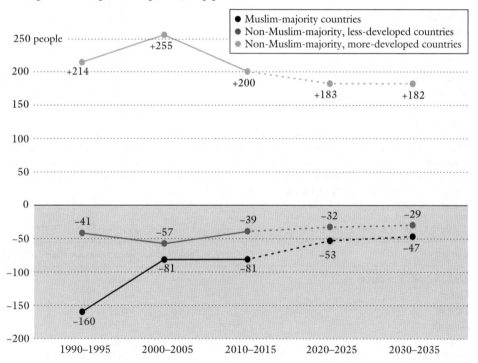

Average annual net gain or loss per 100,000 population

Net migration rate (net gain or loss per 100,000 people in the general population), Pew Forum analysis of UN data, weighted by country populations so that more populous countries affect the average more than smaller countries. The net migration rate is negative when the number of emigrants from a country exceeds the number of immigrants to the country. Afghanistan and Iraq are excluded from migration trends after 2005 because ongoing conflicts make projections for those countries unreliable. Dotted lines denote projected figures.

Figure 11.5   Trends in migration, 1990–2035. *Source*: Reproduced by permission of Pew Research Center's Forum on Religion and Public Life, © 2011, Pew Research Center. Based on Pew Forum on Religion and Public Life, *The Future of the Global Muslim Population: Projections for 2010–2030*, January 27, 2011, http://www.pewforum.org/the-future-of-the-global-muslim-population.aspx.

to more-developed nations is expected to be fairly stable. By 2030–35, more-developed countries are projected to have average annual gains of 182 people per 100,000 population, down from 200 per 100,000 in 2010–15.

If economic conditions in developing countries – including Muslim-majority countries – continue to improve, there will be less motivation, or "push" factors, encouraging emigration. Likewise, if economic conditions in more-developed countries worsen, there will be fewer "pull" factors attracting new immigrants, including temporary workers.

Of course, not all people who emigrate from Muslim-majority countries to the more-developed world are Muslims. Studies show that religious minorities – such as

Table 11.9 Largest losses from emigration among Muslim-majority countries, 2010–15.

Country	Projected net migration rate per 100,000
Jordan	−521
Syria	−508
Albania	−311
Mali	−283
Comoros	−274
Tajikistan	−270
Kyrgyzstan	−263
Morocco	−225
Uzbekistan	−210
Chad	−195

Data source: United Nations, Department of Economic and Social Affairs, Population Division, *World Population Prospects: The 2010 Revision* (New York, 2011). Based on Pew Forum on Religion and Public Life, *The Future of the Global Muslim Population: Projections for 2010–2030,* January 27, 2011, http://www.pewforum.org/the-future-of-the-global-muslim-population.aspx.

Table 11.10 Largest gains from immigration among Muslim-majority countries, 2010–15.

Country	Projected net migration rate per 100,000
United Arab Emirates	+808
Qatar	+637
Kuwait	+622
Bahrain	+355
Brunei	+165
Saudi Arabia	+109
Gambia	+85
Libya	+58
Malaysia	+41
Oman	+33

Data source: United Nations, Department of Economic and Social Affairs, Population Division, *World Population Prospects: The 2010 Revision* (New York, 2011). Countries with ongoing conflicts and territories with very small populations are excluded. Based on Pew Forum on Religion and Public Life, *The Future of the Global Muslim Population: Projections for 2010–2030,* January 27, 2011, http://www.pewforum.org/the-future-of-the-global-muslim-population.aspx.

Christians living in majority-Muslim countries in the Middle East – sometimes emigrate in larger proportions than religious majorities.[11] In addition, there is movement from one Muslim-majority country to another. Many immigrants to the Gulf region, for example, are from other Muslim-majority countries, and a substantial amount of internal migration occurs within the Middle East, as people move in search of employment and to escape conflicts.

In short, there is a net flow of migrants from Muslim-majority countries to countries in more-developed regions, such as Europe and North America, but Muslims also are moving in other directions, including into the Gulf States, which now have net inflows of migrants.

Age structure

Generally speaking, Muslim-majority countries have very youthful populations. As of 2010, people under age 30 made up 60% of the total population of Muslim-majority countries. By contrast, only about a third of all people living in the world's more-developed regions, such as Europe and North America, were under 30. The comparatively large number of Muslims who are in their prime childbearing years is another reason for the projected growth of the world's Muslim population.

When a country has a large percentage of people in their prime reproductive years, it gathers a kind of demographic momentum. Because many women are having babies, the population can grow rapidly even if the number of babies per woman (the fertility rate) is not especially high. Moreover, this momentum can last for generations, as the children born in one generation reach adulthood and begin having families of their own. Even when fertility rates are falling – as is the case in many Muslim-majority countries – the momentum can take more than one generation to dissipate.

As a result of high fertility in the past, Muslim-majority countries clearly have such demographic momentum today. Women between ages 15 and 29 – those who are in or soon will enter their prime procreative years – make up 14% of the total population in Muslim-majority countries, compared with 13% in non-Muslim-majority developing countries and 10% in more-developed countries.

More generally, 60% of the population in Muslim-majority countries is under age 30, compared with 54% in non-Muslim-majority developing countries and 35% in more-developed countries. In addition, Muslim-majority countries are projected to remain relatively youthful. In 2030, 50% of the population in Muslim-majority countries is expected to be under 30, compared with 46% in non-Muslim-majority developing countries, and 31% in countries in more-developed regions. Indeed, by 2030 the global population of Muslim youth and young adults (ages 15–29) will exceed 540 million, representing nearly one third (29%) of the projected total of 1.86 billion people in that age group, up from 26% in 2010 and 20% in 1990.

Yet, notwithstanding the high percentage of youth and young adults in Muslim-majority countries, the global Muslim population as a whole is aging as fertility rates drop (meaning that fewer babies are born per woman) and as life expectancy rises (meaning that more people are living into old age). This is reflected in the median age in Muslim-majority countries, which climbed from 19 in 1990 to 24 in 2010 and is projected to reach 30 in 2030.

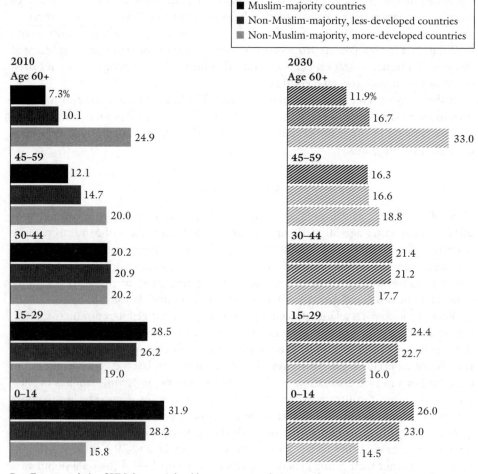

Pew Forum analysis of UN data, weighted by country populations so that more populous countries affect the average more than smaller ones. Percentages may not add to 100 due to rounding. Cross hatching denotes projected figures.

Figure 11.6 Percentage of population in selected age groups, 2010 and 2030. *Source*: Reproduced by permission of Pew Research Center's Forum on Religion and Public Life, © 2011, Pew Research Center. Based on Pew Forum on Religion and Public Life, *The Future of the Global Muslim Population: Projections for 2010–2030,* January 27, 2011, http://www. pewforum.org/the-future-of-the-global-muslim-population.aspx.

Figure 11.8 shows that the world population, as a whole, is aging. The median age – the point at which half the people in a given population are older and half are younger – is rising in Muslim-majority countries, but so are the median ages in non-Muslim-majority, less-developed countries and in more-developed countries. This explains how the world's Muslim population can be aging but, at the same time, remains very youthful compared with non-Muslim populations.

The so-called Muslim youth bulge – the high proportion of youth and young adults in many heavily Muslim societies – has attracted considerable attention from political scientists.[12] Less notice has been paid to the fact that the Muslim youth bulge peaked

People ages 15–29

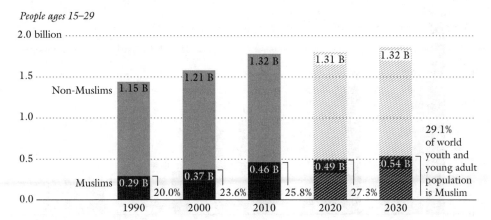

Percentages are calculated from unrounded numbers. Cross hatching denotes projected figures.

Figure 11.7   Muslims as a share of world youth and young adults, 1990–2030, people ages 15–29. *Source*: Reproduced by permission of Pew Research Center's Forum on Religion and Public Life, © 2011, Pew Research Center. Based on Pew Forum on Religion and Public Life, *The Future of the Global Muslim Population: Projections for 2010–2030*, January 27, 2011, http://www.pewforum.org/the-future-of-the-global-muslim-population.aspx.

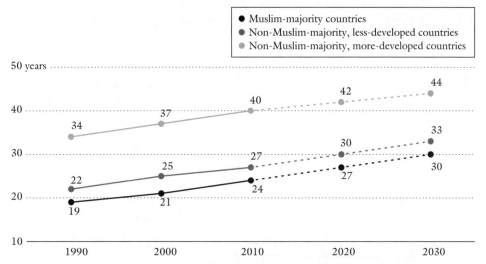

Pew Forum analysis of UN data, weighted by country populations so that more populous countries affect the average more than smaller countries. Dotted lines denote projected figures.

Figure 11.8   Trends in median age, 1990–2030. *Source*: Reproduced by permission of Pew Research Center's Forum on Religion and Public Life, © 2011, Pew Research Center. Based on Pew Forum on Religion and Public Life, *The Future of the Global Muslim Population: Projections for 2010–2030*, January 27, 2011, http://www.pewforum.org/the-future-of-the-global-muslim-population.aspx.

around the start of the twenty-first century and now is gradually declining as the Muslim population ages. The percentage of the population in Muslim-majority countries that is between 15 and 29 years old rose slightly between 1990 and 2000 (from 27% to 29%) but dipped to an estimated 28% in 2010 and is projected to continue to

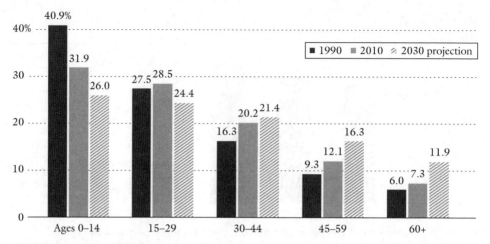

Pew Forum analysis of UN data, weighted by country populations so that more populous countries affect the average more than smaller countries. Percentages may not add to 100 due to rounding. Cross hatching denote projected figures.

Figure 11.9 Percentage of population of Muslim-majority countries in selected age groups, 1990–2030. *Source*: Reproduced by permission of Pew Research Center's Forum on Religion and Public Life, © 2011, Pew Research Center. Based on Pew Forum on Religion and Public Life, *The Future of the Global Muslim Population: Projections for 2010–2030*, January 27, 2011, http://www.pewforum.org/the-future-of-the-global-muslim-population.aspx.

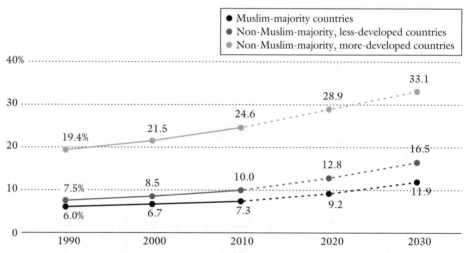

Pew Forum analysis of UN data, weighted by country populations so that more populous countries affect the average more than smaller countries. Data points are plotted based on unrounded numbers. Dotted lines denote projected figures.

Figure 11.10 Percentage of population age 60 and older, 1990–2030. *Source*: Reproduced by permission of Pew Research Center's Forum on Religion and Public Life, © 2011, Pew Research Center. Based on Pew Forum on Religion and Public Life, *The Future of the Global Muslim Population: Projections for 2010–2030*, January 27, 2011, http://www.pewforum.org/the-future-of-the-global-muslim-population.aspx.

decline, to 24% in 2030. While this is not a large drop, it does mean that the proportion of youth and young adults in many Muslim-majority countries has either reached a plateau or begun to fall.

As the generation represented by youth bulge ages, the proportion of the population between ages 30 and 44 in Muslim-majority countries is projected to remain fairly stable or rise slightly, from an estimated 20% in 2010 to 21% in 2030. The proportion aged 45–59 is expected to rise from 12% in 2010 to 16% in 2030. The fastest growth, in percentage terms, will be among people aged 60 and older, who are expected to make up 12% of the population in Muslim-majority countries as a whole in 2030, up from 7% in 2010. Yet the percentage of the population aged 60 and older will remain somewhat higher in non-Muslim-majority, less-developed countries and dramatically higher in more-developed countries, where a third of the population will be 60 or older in 2030.

Some Muslim-majority countries already have considerably older populations than others. The highest median ages in 2010 were in the United Arab Emirates, Kuwait, Qatar, and Albania. The lowest are in Niger, Burkina Faso, Afghanistan, and Chad.

In 2010, the Muslim-majority countries with the highest proportions of people aged 60 and older were Albania, Lebanon, Kazakhstan, and Tunisia. Albania will still be at the top of the list in 2030. By that year, nearly a quarter of Albania's population (24%) is expected to be age 60 or older, mirroring trends in Europe as a whole.

In 2030, the Muslim-majority countries with the highest proportion of youth and young adults (ages 15–29) will be Burkina Faso, Sierra Leone, Senegal, and Mali, where nearly a third of the population (30%) will be in that age group.

Table 11.11   Highest median age among Muslim-majority countries, 2010.

Country	Age
United Arab Emirates	32
Kuwait	31
Qatar	30
Albania	30
Kazakhstan	29
Lebanon	29
Tunisia	29
Azerbaijan	28
Turkey	28
Indonesia	28
Bahrain	28
Brunei	28

Data source: United Nations, Department of Economic and Social Affairs, Population Division, *World Population Prospects: The 2010 Revision* (New York, 2011). Based on Pew Forum on Religion and Public Life, *The Future of the Global Muslim Population: Projections for 2010–2030,* January 27, 2011, http://www.pewforum.org/the-future-of-the-global-muslim-population.aspx. Rankings are determined by unrounded numbers.

Table 11.12 Lowest median age among Muslim-majority countries, 2010.

Country	Age
Niger	15
Burkina Faso	17
Afghanistan	17
Chad	17
Somalia	18
Palestinian Territories	18
Mali	18
Yemen	18
Senegal	18
Sierra Leone	18

Data source: United Nations, Department of Economic and Social Affairs, Population Division, *World Population Prospects: The 2010 Revision* (New York, 2011). Based on Pew Forum on Religion and Public Life, *The Future of the Global Muslim Population: Projections for 2010–2030*, January 27, 2011, http://www.pewforum.org/the-future-of-the-global-muslim-population.aspx. Rankings are determined by unrounded numbers.

Table 11.13 Highest percentage of population age 60 and older among Muslim-majority countries, ranked as of 2030.

Country	% in 2010	Projected % in 2030
Albania	15	24
Lebanon	11	18
Kazakhstan	11	17
Tunisia	11	18
Turkey	10	17
Azerbaijan	10	19
Indonesia	10	17
Morocco	9	15
Malaysia	8	16
Kyrgyzstan	8	14

Data source: United Nations, Department of Economic and Social Affairs, Population Division, *World Population Prospects: The 2010 Revision* (New York, 2011). Based on Pew Forum on Religion and Public Life, *The Future of the Global Muslim Population: Projections for 2010–2030*, January 27, 2011, http://www.pewforum.org/the-future-of-the-global-muslim-population.aspx.

Related Factors

The following related factors are not direct inputs into the projections, but they underlie vital assumptions about the ways Muslim fertility rates are changing and Muslim populations are shifting.

Table 11.14 Highest percentage of population age 15–29 among Muslim-majority countries, ranked as of 2030.

Country	% in 2010	Projected % in 2030
Burkina Faso	27%	30%
Sierra Leone	27	30
Senegal	29	30
Mali	29	30
Chad	27	29
Gambia	26	29
Palestinian Territories	27	29
Yemen	30	29
Guinea	27	28
Afghanistan	27	28
Mauritania	28	28

Data source: United Nations, Department of Economic and Social Affairs, Population Division, *World Population Prospects: The 2010 Revision* (New York, 2011). Based on Pew Forum on Religion and Public Life, *The Future of the Global Muslim Population: Projections for 2010–2030*, January 27, 2011, http://www.pewforum.org/the-future-of-the-global-muslim-population.aspx.

Education

As in the rest of the world, fertility rates in countries with Muslim-majority populations are directly related to educational attainment. Women tend to delay childbearing when they attain higher levels of education. As Muslim women continue to receive more education, their fertility rates are projected to decline.

The relationship between educational attainment and fertility rates is shown in figure 11.11. Niger, for example, has an extremely high TFR (an average of 6.9 children per woman) for 2010–15, and a girl born can expect to receive an average of just four years of schooling in her lifetime. In Libya, by contrast, a girl born can expect to receive an average of 17 years of education; the country's fertility rate is just 2.5 children per woman in 2010–15.

The 10 Muslim-majority countries in which girls can expect to receive the fewest years of schooling have an average TFR of 5.0 children per woman. That is more than double the average TFR (2.3 children per woman) in the 10 Muslim-majority countries in which girls can expect to receive the most schooling. One exception is the Palestinian territories, which have a relatively high fertility rate (4.5 children per woman) although a girl born there can expect to receive 14 years of education, on average.[13]

Economic well-being

In Muslim-majority countries, as in many other countries, low economic standards of living are associated with rapid population growth. In general, in the 24 Muslim-majority countries for which data are available from the UN, the percentage of the population living in poverty correlates positively with the national fertility rate, as shown in figure 11.12. The reverse is also true: as living standards rise, fertility rates tend to drop.

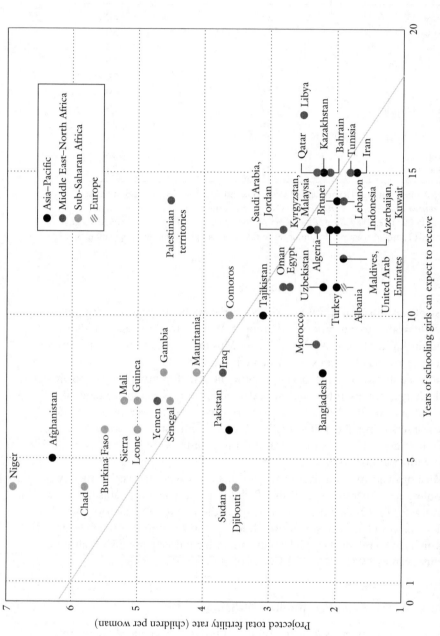

Figure 11.11 Education and fertility in Muslim-majority countries, 2011. *Source:* Reproduced by permission of Pew Research Center's Forum on Religion and Public Life, © 2011, Pew Research Center. Based on Pew Forum on Religion and Public Life, *The Future of the Global Muslim Population: Projections for 2010–2030*, January 27, 2011, http://www.pewforum.org/the-future-of-the-global-muslim-population.aspx.

Schooling, UN, 2010; Total Fertility Rate, UN, 2010–15. Expected years of schooling for Sudan includes boys and girls. Schooling data not available for Kosovo, Mayotte, Somalia, Syria, Turkmenistan and Western Sahara. $R^2 = .60$

The reasons for higher fertility rates in poor countries are numerous. In agricultural societies, high fertility might be related to the desire of families to have more workers. In countries with poor health-care infrastructures, families need to have more children to offset high child mortality rates. And in less-developed countries, parents might be more likely to see additional children as wealth-producing resources rather than as wealth-draining obligations.

The 10 Muslim-majority countries with the highest percentages of people living below the poverty line (as defined by each country) are projected to have an average TFR of 4.5 children per woman for 2010–15. This is nearly double the average projected rate (2.4 children per woman) in the 10 Muslim-majority countries with the lowest percentages of people living below the poverty line.

At present, Muslim-majority countries overall are among the poorest in the world, as measured by per capita gross domestic product (GDP) in US dollars adjusted for purchasing power parity (PPP).[14] Their median per capita GDP-PPP of $4,000 is substantially lower than the median for more-developed countries ($33,700) and somewhat lower than the median for less-developed countries where Muslims are in the minority ($6,600).

However, the median per capita GDP-PPP figure for all Muslim-majority countries masks an enormous amount of variation from country to country and region to region. For instance, the median per capita GDP-PPP in Muslim-majority countries in Central Asia is $11,200, compared with roughly $1,000 in Muslim-majority countries in sub-Saharan Africa. Some oil-rich countries with Muslim majorities, particularly the Gulf States, have median per capita GDP-PPP values higher than that of the United States.

Four of the 10 nations with the world's highest GDP-PPP per capita are Muslim-majority countries (Qatar, Kuwait, Brunei, and the United Arab Emirates), but three of the 10 countries with the world's lowest GDP-PPP per capita also are Muslim-majority countries (Afghanistan, Niger, and Somalia). Although fertility rates in the wealthiest Muslim-majority countries tend to be lower than in other Muslim-majority countries, they still are higher than in many of the world's wealthiest non-Muslim-majority countries.

Conversion

Statistical data on conversion to and from Islam are scarce. What little information is available suggests that there is no substantial net gain or loss globally in the number of Muslims through conversion; the number of people who become Muslims through conversion seems to be roughly equal to the number of Muslims who leave the faith. As a result, this chapter does not include any estimated future rate of conversions as a direct factor in the projections of Muslim population growth. Indirectly, however, conversions might affect the projections, because people who have converted to or from Islam are included – even if they are not counted separately – in numerous censuses and surveys used to estimate the size of the global Muslim population in 1990, 2000, and 2010.

Reliable data on conversions are hard to obtain for a number of reasons. Some national censuses ask people about their religion, but they do not ask whether people have converted to their present faith. A few cross-national surveys do contain questions about religious switching, but even in those surveys, it is difficult to assess whether more people leave Islam than enter the faith. In some countries, legal and social

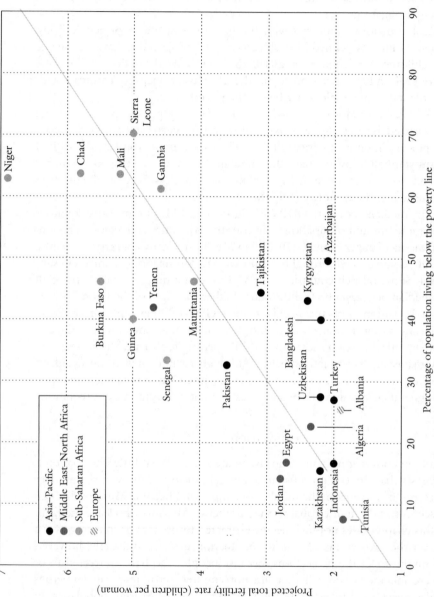

Poverty, UN, 2000–06, based on each country's definition of the poverty level in that country, for 24 Muslim-majority countries for which data are available; Total Fertility Rate, UN, 2010–15. R² = .57

Figure 11.12 Poverty and fertility in Muslim-majority countries, 2011. *Source:* Reproduced by permission of Pew Research Center's Forum on Religion and Public Life, © 2011, Pew Forum on Religion and Public Life, *The Future of the Global Muslim Population: Projections for 2010–2030*, January 27, 2011, http://www.pewforum.org/the-future-of-the-global-muslim-population.aspx.

Table 11.15   Where girls can expect to receive the most years of schooling among Muslim-majority countries, 2010.

Country	Expected years of school, 2010	Children per woman, 2010–15
Libya	17	2.5
Bahrain	15	2.1
Iran	15	1.7
Kazakhstan	15	2.2
Qatar	15	2.3
Tunisia	15	1.8
Brunei	14	2.0
Lebanon	14	1.9
Palestinian territories	14	4.5
Algeria	13	2.3
Average (unweighted)	**15**	**2.3**

Data source: United Nations, Department of Economic and Social Affairs, Population Division, *World Population Prospects: The 2010 Revision* (New York, 2011). Based on Pew Forum on Religion and Public Life, *The Future of the Global Muslim Population: Projections for 2010–2030*, January 27, 2011, http://www.pewforum.org/the-future-of-the-global-muslim-population.aspx. Rankings are determined by unrounded numbers. Averages are not weighted by country populations.

Table 11.16   Where girls can expect to receive the fewest years of schooling among Muslim-majority countries, 2010.

Country	Expected years of school, 2010	Children per woman, 2010–15
Sudan and South Sudan combined*	4	3.7
Niger	4	6.9
Djibouti	4	3.5
Chad	4	5.8
Afghanistan	5	6.3
Sierra Leone	6	5.0
Pakistan	6	3.6
Burkina Faso	6	5.5
Yemen	7	4.7
Senegal	7	4.5
Average (unweighted)	**5**	**5.0**

*National average, includes boys
Data source: United Nations, Department of Economic and Social Affairs, Population Division, *World Population Prospects: The 2010 Revision* (New York, 2011). Based on Pew Forum on Religion and Public Life, *The Future of the Global Muslim Population: Projections for 2010–2030*, January 27, 2011, http://www.pewforum.org/the-future-of-the-global-muslim-population.aspx. Rankings are determined by unrounded numbers. Averages are not weighted by country populations.

Table 11.17　Highest percentage of population below the poverty line among Muslim-majority countries, 2000–06.

Country	Percentage of population below poverty line, 2000–6*	TFR, 2010–15
Sierra Leone	70.2%	5.0
Chad	64.0	5.8
Mali	63.8	5.2
Niger	63.0	6.9
Gambia	61.3	4.6
Azerbaijan	49.6	2.1
Burkina Faso	46.4	5.5
Mauritania	46.3	4.1
Tajikistan	44.4	3.1
Kyrgyzstan	43.1	2.4
Average	**55.2**	**4.5**

*Most recent statistic available for the country between 2000 and 2006; the UN does not provide this statistic for countries in the Persian Gulf region. Averages are not weighted by country populations.

Data source: United Nations, Department of Economic and Social Affairs, Population Division, *World Population Prospects: The 2010 Revision* (New York, 2011). Based on Pew Forum on Religion and Public Life, *The Future of the Global Muslim Population: Projections for 2010–2030*, January 27, 2011, http://www.pewforum.org/the-future-of-the-global-muslim-population.aspx.

Table 11.18　Lowest percentage of population below the poverty line among Muslim-majority countries, 2000–06.

Country	Percentage of population below poverty line, 2000–6*	TFR, 2010–15
Tunisia	7.6%	1.8
Jordan	14.2	2.8
Kazakhstan	15.4	2.2
Egypt	16.7	2.7
Indonesia	16.7	2.0
Algeria	22.6	2.3
Albania	25.4	1.9
Turkey	27.0	2.0
Uzbekistan	27.5	2.2
Pakistan	32.6	3.6
Average	**20.6**	**2.4**

*Most recent statistic available for the country between 2000 and 2006; the UN does not provide this statistic for countries in the Persian Gulf. Averages are not weighted by country populations.

Data source: United Nations, Department of Economic and Social Affairs, Population Division, *World Population Prospects: The 2010 Revision* (New York, 2011). Based on Pew Forum on Religion and Public Life, *The Future of the Global Muslim Population: Projections for 2010–2030*, January 27, 2011, http://www.pewforum.org/the-future-of-the-global-muslim-population.aspx.

Table 11.19 Highest GDP-PPP per capita, 2010–15.

Country	GDP (US $ PPP)	TFR (2010–15)
Qatar*	121,700	2.27
Luxembourg	78,000	1.69
Norway	58,600	1.86
Kuwait*	54,100	2.09
Singapore	50,300	1.29
Brunei*	50,100	1.95
United States	46,400	2.02
Hong Kong	42,700	1.01
Ireland	42,200	1.92
United Arab Emirates*	42,000	1.88

*Muslim-majority. GDP in US dollars adjusted for purchasing power parity (PPP).
Data source: Central Intelligence Agency, *The World Factbook*; United Nations, Department of Economic and Social Affairs, Population Division, *World Population Prospects: The 2010 Revision* (New York, 2011). Based on Pew Forum on Religion and Public Life, *The Future of the Global Muslim Population: Projections for 2010–2030*, January 27, 2011, http://www.pewforum.org/the-future-of-the-global-muslim-population.aspx.

Table 11.20 Lowest GDP-PPP per capita, 2010–15.

Country	GDP (US $ PPP)	TFR (2010–15)
Zimbabwe	200	3.12
Congo	300	5.52
Burundi	300	4.03
Liberia	500	4.69
Somalia*	600	6.17
Guinea-Bissau	600	5.43
Niger*	700	6.86
Eritrea	700	4.17
Central African Republic	700	4.33
Afghanistan*	800	6.25

*Muslim-majority. GDP in US dollars adjusted for purchasing power parity (PPP).
Data source: Central Intelligence Agency, *The World Factbook*; United Nations, Department of Economic and Social Affairs, Population Division, *World Population Prospects: The 2010 Revision* (New York, 2011). Based on Pew Forum on Religion and Public Life, *The Future of the Global Muslim Population: Projections for 2010–2030*, January 27, 2011, http://www.pewforum.org/the-future-of-the-global-muslim-population.aspx.

consequences make conversion difficult, and survey respondents might be reluctant to speak honestly about the topic. Additionally, for many Muslims, Islam is not just a religion, but an ethnic or cultural identity that does not depend on whether a person actively practices the faith. This means that even non-practicing or secular Muslims might still consider themselves, and be viewed by their neighbors, as Muslims.

The limited information on conversion indicates that some movement both into and out of Islam occurs but that there is no major net gain or loss. For instance, the Pew Forum's 2009 survey of 19 nations in sub-Saharan Africa found that neither Christianity nor Islam was growing significantly at the expense of the other through religious conversion in those countries.[15] Uganda was the only country surveyed in which the number of people who identified themselves as Muslim was significantly different than the number of people who said they were raised Muslim: 18% of Ugandans surveyed said they were raised Muslim, while 13% now describe themselves as Muslim, a net loss of five percentage points. In every other sub-Saharan African country surveyed, the number of people who are currently Muslim is roughly equivalent to the number saying they were raised as Muslims. This does not mean that no religious switching is taking place. Rather, it indicates that the number of people leaving Islam roughly offsets the number of people becoming Muslim.

The Pew Forum's *US Religious Landscape Survey*, conducted in 2007, found a similar pattern in the United States.[16] In that survey, the number of respondents who described themselves as Muslim was roughly the same as the number who said they were raised as Muslims, and the portion of all US adults who have converted either to or from Islam was less than three tenths of 1 percent (<0.3%). Due to the relatively small number of Muslims in the nationally representative survey sample, however, calculating a precise retention rate for the Islamic faith in America was not possible.[17]

An independent study published in 2010 that examined patterns of religious conversion among various faiths in 40 countries, mainly in Europe, also found that the number of people who were raised Muslim in those countries, as a whole, roughly equaled the number who currently are Muslim. The sample sizes for Muslims, however, were so small that the results cannot reliably predict Muslim conversion trends.[18]

Notes

1   This chapter is adapted from Pew Research Center's Pew Forum on Religion and Public Life, *The Future of the Global Muslim Population: Projections for 2010–2030*, January 27, 2011, http://pewresearch.org/pubs/1872/muslim-population-projections-worldwide-fast-growth. Reprinted with permission of the Pew Research Center's Forum on Religion and Public Life. Unless otherwise indicated, references to "this report" and "this study" are to the 2011 Pew report. The full report contains additional material on contraception, abortion, and urbanization. For comparison purposes, this chapter provides demographic data on three types of countries: (1) *Muslim-majority countries.* As of 2010, there were 49 countries in which Muslims constituted more than 50% of the population. All Muslim-majority countries are in less-developed regions of the world, with the exception of Albania and Kosovo, which are in Europe; (2) *Non-Muslim-majority countries in less-developed regions.* These countries make up the rest of the "developing world"; they include all the non-Muslim-majority countries in Africa, Asia–Pacific (excluding Japan), and Central and South America (including the Caribbean); (3) *Non-Muslim-majority countries in more-developed regions.* This category often is described as the "developed world"; it includes all countries in Europe (excluding Albania and Kosovo) and North America, plus Australia, New Zealand, and Japan. The last two categories follow the United Nations definitions of "more-developed" and "less-developed," with the exception of Albania and Kosovo, which are included in the Muslim-majority category. (The UN puts Albania and Kosovo in the "more-developed" category because they are in Europe.) These UN categories – based on factors such as life

expectancy, education, and income – are used for statistical convenience and do not express a judgment about the political or social systems of particular countries or regions. As this chapter notes, there is great diversity among the countries in each category.

2 Data used in this chapter primarily come from the UN *World Population Prospects: The 2010 Revision*. It is available through "UNdata." UNdata is an internet-based data service that makes UN statistical databases available through a single entry point. http://data.un.org/.

3 The standard measure of fertility in this chapter is the total fertility rate (TFR), defined as the total number of children an average woman would have in her lifetime if fertility patterns did not change. The TFR is calculated by adding the birthrates among women in each age group in a particular country during a given period; in other words, it is a kind of snapshot of fertility patterns at one place and time.

4 The replacement level varies depending on mortality rates and sex ratios at birth. In countries with a normal sex ratio at birth and relatively low infant and child mortality, a fertility rate of about 2.1 children per woman is sufficient to replenish the population. In some developing countries with high infant and child mortality, the replacement fertility rate exceeds three children per woman. Based on 2001 UN data, Espenshade et al. estimated the average replacement rate in Africa at 2.7 and the worldwide average at 2.3. See Thomas J. Espenshade, Juan Carlos Guzman, and Charles F. Westoff, "The Surprising Global Variation in Replacement Fertility," *Population Research and Policy Review*, December 2003.

5 Jennifer Johnson-Hanks, for example, found that in West African countries in which Muslims are in the minority, they tend to have higher fertility than non-Muslims, while in countries in which Muslims are in the majority, they tend to have lower fertility than non-Muslims. "This reversal means that there is nothing about Islam per se that leads to specific demographic patterns," the author concludes. See Jennifer Johnson-Hanks, "On the Politics and Practice of Muslim Fertility: Comparative Evidence from West Africa," *Medical Anthropology Quarterly* 20:1 (2006): 12–30.

6 For instance, a study of Muslim and non-Muslim communities in India, Malaysia, Thailand, and the Philippines found that the Muslim communities had more children per woman even though they did not score any lower on measures of women's power or autonomy. See S. Philip Morgan, Sharon Stash, Herbert L. Smith, and Karen Oppenheim Mason, "Muslim and Non-Muslim Differences in Female Autonomy and Fertility: Evidence from Four Asian Countries," *Population and Development Review* 28:3 (2002): 515–37.

7 These figures are the average (mean) age of first marriage. They have been weighted by country populations so that more populous countries affect the average more than smaller countries.

8 A 2007 study, for example, found that Muslim women in Europe who are highly religious are significantly more likely than less-religious Muslim women to have at least two children. See Charles F. Westoff and Tomas Frejka, "Religiousness and Fertility Among European Muslims," *Population and Development Review* 33:4 (2007): 785–809. Other researchers have demonstrated the connection between fertility and religiosity in a variety of religious traditions. See, for example, Conrad Hackett, "Religion and Fertility in the United States: The Influence of Affiliation, Region, and Congregation," PhD dissertation, Department of Sociology and Office of Population Research, Princeton University, 2008; Sarah R. Hayford and S. Philip Morgan, "Religiosity and Fertility in the United States: The Role of Fertility Intentions," *Social Forces* 86:3 (2008): 1,163–88; Evelyn Lehrer, "Religion as a Determinant of Marital Fertility," *Journal of Population Economics* 9:2 (1996): 173–96; and William D. Mosher, Linda B. Williams, and David P. Johnson, "Religion and Fertility in the United States: New Patterns," *Demography* 29:2 (1992): 199–214.

9 Life expectancy at birth is the average number of years a newborn would be expected to live if health and living conditions at the time of his/her birth remained the same throughout his/her life.

10   United Nations, Department of Economic and Social Affairs, Population Division, *World Population Prospects: The 2010 Revision* (New York, 2011).

11   For example, the 2008 World Refugee Survey, conducted by the US Committee for Refugees and Immigrants, found that of the approximately 1.3 million refugees from the Iraq War living in Syria, fewer than 75% were Muslim, although Iraq is nearly 99% Muslim. For more information on the 2008 World Refugee Survey, see http://www.refugees.org/resources/ refugee-warehousing/archived-world-refugee-surveys/2008-world-refugee-survey.html. In addition, data from the 2003 New Immigrant Survey indicate that the proportion of Muslim immigrants to the United States from many Muslim-majority countries is lower than the proportion of Muslims in those countries. Immigrants to the US from Iran, for example, were about 50% Muslim, while Iran's population as a whole is 99.7% Muslim. For more information on the 2003 New Immigrant Survey, see http://nis.princeton.edu/.

12   See, for example, Graham E. Fuller, "The Youth Factor: The New Demographics of the Middle East and the Implications for US Policy," *The Brookings Project on US Policy Towards the Islamic World* 3 (June 2003): 1–42; and Jack A. Goldstone, "The New Population Bomb: The Four Megatrends That Will Change the World," *Foreign Affairs* (January/February 2010), available at http://www.foreignaffairs.com/articles/65735/ jack-a-goldstone/the-new-population-bomb.

13   The continuation of high fertility despite high education levels among Palestinians has been described as a demographic puzzle. The reasons for it are not entirely clear. Partly, it might reflect the persistence of traditional attitudes in Gaza; studies suggest that fertility has started to drop in the West Bank but not in Gaza. Some studies also find that highly educated Palestinian women are more likely than those who are less educated to remain single but that married Palestinians tend to have similar numbers of children regardless of their educational level. Some commentators have suggested that high Palestinian birth-rates might have a political basis as "weapons against occupation." Another study of fertility patterns among Palestinians in different political settings does not support this "political fertility" hypothesis, however. See Marwan Khawaja, "The Fertility of Palestinian Women in Gaza, the West Bank, Jordan and Lebanon," *Population* 58 (2003): 273–302.

14   Adjusting per capita GDP figures for purchasing power parity (PPP) shows the cost (in a given currency, such as US dollars) required to purchase equivalent amounts of goods and services in each country so that comparisons from country to country are more accurate.

15   Results from the survey are published in Pew Forum on Religion and Public Life, *Tolerance and Tension: Islam and Christianity in Sub-Saharan Africa*, April 15, 2010, http://www. pewforum.org/executive-summary-islam-and-christianity-in-sub-saharan-africa.aspx.

16   Pew Forum on Religion and Public Life, *US Religious Landscape Survey* (2007), http://religions.pewforum.org/.

17   Because Muslims currently constitute less than 1% of the adult US population, even such large studies as the *US Religious Landscape Survey* include relatively few Muslim respondents in their representative national samples. Of the more than 35,000 respondents in the *Landscape Survey*, only 90 said they were raised as Muslims. That number is too small to allow reliable conclusions about the percentage of Americans who leave Islam after being raised in the faith.

18   See Robert Barro, Jason Hwang, and Rachel McCleary, "Religious Conversion in 40 Countries," *Journal for the Scientific Study of Religion* 49 (2010): 15–36. This analysis of patterns of religious conversion among people age 30 and older found little evidence of a significant pattern of conversion to Islam in 40 countries where Islam is a minority religion. However, the country surveys were not designed specifically to study Muslim conversion and had too small a sample of Muslims in each country to draw firm conclusions. The most noticeable pattern of conversion across the 40 countries is movement from having some religious affiliation to having no reported religious affiliation. Using multivariate analysis, the study did find that Muslims tend to be less likely to convert to another religion than

people from other religious groups, which includes changes among Christian traditions. The cross-national surveys analyzed were conducted in 1991, 1998, and 2001. Overall, less than 1% of all the people surveyed identified as Muslim, according to the authors.

References

Barro, Robert, Jason Hwang, and Rachel McCleary. "Religious Conversion in 40 Countries." *Journal for the Scientific Study of Religion* 49 (2010): 15–36.

Central Intelligence Agency. *The World Factbook 2009*. Washington, DC: Central Intelligence Agency, 2009. https://cia.gov/library/publications/the-world-factbook/index.html.

Espenshade, Thomas J., Juan Carlos Guzman, and Charles F. Westoff. "The Surprising Global Variation in Replacement Fertility." *Population Research and Policy Review* (December 2003).

Fuller, Graham E. "The Youth Factor: The New Demographics of the Middle East and the Implications for US Policy." *The Brookings Project on US Policy Towards the Islamic World* 3 (June 2003): 1–42.

Goldstone, Jack A. "The New Population Bomb: The Four Megatrends That Will Change the World." *Foreign Affairs* (January/February 2010). http://www.foreignaffairs.com/articles/65735/jack-a-goldstone/the-new-population-bomb.

Hackett, Conrad. "Religion and Fertility in the United States: The Influence of Affiliation, Region, and Congregation." PhD diss., Princeton University, 2008.

Hayford, Sarah R., and S. Philip Morgan. "Religiosity and Fertility in the United States: The Role of Fertility Intentions." *Social Forces* 86:3 (2008): 1,163–88.

Jasso, Guillermina, Douglas S. Massey, Mark R. Rosenzweig, and James P. Smith. "New Immigrant Survey." Princeton: Princeton University, 2005. http://nis.princeton.edu.

Johnson-Hanks, Jennifer. "On the Politics and Practice of Muslim Fertility: Comparative Evidence from West Africa." *Medical Anthropology Quarterly* 20:1 (2006): 12–30.

Khawaja, Marwan. "The Fertility of Palestinian Women in Gaza, the West Bank, Jordan and Lebanon." *Population* 58 (2003): 273–302.

Lehrer, Evelyn. "Religion as a Determinant of Marital Fertility." *Journal of Population Economics* 9:2 (1996): 173–96.

Morgan, S. Philip, Sharon Stash, Herbert L. Smith, and Karen Oppenheim Mason. "Muslim and Non-Muslim Differences in Female Autonomy and Fertility: Evidence from Four Asian Countries." *Population and Development Review* 28:3 (2002): 515–37.

Mosher, William D., Linda B. Williams, and David P. Johnson. "Religion and Fertility in the United States: New Patterns." *Demography* 29:2 (1992): 199–214.

Pew Forum on Religion and Public Life. *The Future of the Global Muslim Population: Projections for 2010–2030*. January 27, 2011. http://pewresearch.org/pubs/1872/muslim-population-projections-worldwide-fast-growth.

Pew Forum on Religion and Public Life. *Tolerance and Tension: Islam and Christianity in Sub-Saharan Africa*. April 15, 2010. http://www.pewforum.org/executive-summary-islam-and-christianity-in-sub-saharan-africa.aspx.

Pew Forum on Religion and Public Life. *US Religious Landscape Survey*. 2007. http://religions.pewforum.org/.

United Nations. *World Population Prospects: The 2010 Revision*. Blue Ridge Summit, PA: United Nations Publications, 2012.

United States Committee for Refugees and Immigrants. *World Refugee Survey 2008*. June 2008. http://www.refugees.org/resources/refugee-warehousing/archived-world-refugee-surveys/2008-world-refugee-survey.html.

Westoff, Charles F., and Tomas Frejka. "Religiousness and Fertility Among European Muslims." *Population and Development Review* 33:4 (2007): 785–809.

Chapter 12

Estimating China's Religious Populations

Survey data, as well as Chinese government reports, have shown that relatively large percentages of the Chinese public consider religion to be important in their lives.[1] This is somewhat surprising given that China has adhered strictly to a secular and even atheistic national philosophy for over six decades. As China's influence on the world stage continues to grow, many people inside and outside China are watching to see whether Chinese Communism will adjust to religious market forces just as it has to economic market forces. Given the wide range of results from available public opinion surveys conducted between 2005 and 2007, indicating that religious affiliation ranges anywhere between 14% and 31% of the Chinese population and that between 31% and 56% consider religion at least somewhat important, these survey findings need further scrutiny in order to arrive at a more comprehensive picture of religious affiliation in China today. Taking into account multiple sources of data, this study estimates that while the majority of people in China have no religious attachments (53%), a substantial minority has some affiliation to religious faith or practice.

Overview

On August 8, 2008 – the eighth day of the eighth month of the year 2008 – at exactly 08:08:08 p.m., the Summer Olympics began in Beijing. The day and hour for the start of the opening ceremony was chosen for its good fortune – a widely held belief in Confucianism and Chinese folk-religions. In addition, the official English website of the 2008 Beijing Olympics highlighted officially approved Buddhist, Protestant, Catholic, and Muslim places of worship, complete with addresses and historical and architectural descriptions.[2] Compared with the early 1980s,[3] the growing presence and ambitions of religious groups in China are much more visible to a watching world.

The World's Religions in Figures: An Introduction to International Religious Demography,
First Edition. Todd M. Johnson and Brian J. Grim.
© 2013 John Wiley & Sons, Ltd. Published 2013 by John Wiley & Sons, Ltd.

Table 12.1   Importance of religion among Chinese public, 2006.

Response	Percentage
Very important	12
Somewhat important	19
Not too important	44
Not at all important	11
Don't know	13
Refused	1

Data source: Pew Research Center, "Publics of Asian Powers Hold Negative Views of One Another," Global Attitudes Project, September 21, 2006, http://www.pewglobal.org/2006/09/21/publics-of-asian-powers-hold-negative-views-of-one-another/. Total respondents 2,180; Sampling error±2.3; Question wording: How important is religion in your life – very important, somewhat important, not too important, or not at all important? (Horizon Research Consultancy Group survey reported by the Pew Global Attitudes Project.)

According to a 2006 survey by the Pew Global Attitudes Project, 31% of the Chinese public considers religion to be very or somewhat important in their lives, compared with only 11% who say religion is not at all important (see table 12.1). When asked a somewhat different question in a 2005 Pew poll, an even greater percentage of the Chinese public (56%) considered religion to be very or somewhat important in their lives.

One concrete indicator of religious importance is religious giving. More than one in five Chinese (21%) reported having donated money or goods to religious organizations such as Buddhist temples or Christian churches, according to the 2007 Spiritual Life Study of Chinese Residents. It should be noted, however, that the survey had an response rate of only 28.1%. The actual level of religious giving might be higher than indicated by these results if actively religious Chinese were less likely to have participated in the poll. (See the discussion in the section below on Christianity for a description of the challenge of measuring religious participation through public opinion surveys.)

Reported Religious Affiliation in China According to Surveys

While no fully nationally representative surveys of the religious affiliation of the Chinese public have been conducted, four surveys from the mid-2000s provide some sense of the number of people who acknowledged to researchers that they belong to one of China's five main recognized religious groups – Buddhism, Protestantism, Catholicism, Islam, and Taoism.

A Chinese public opinion polling firm, Horizon Research Consultancy Group, sponsored and carried out the surveys, which were reported in 2005[4] and 2006[5] by Pew, and in 2007 by the Association of Religion Data Archives (ARDA) as the Spiritual Life Study of Chinese Residents (SLSC)[6] and by the Committee of 100[7]

Table 12.2   Giving to religion among Chinese public, 2007.

Response	Percentage
Yes, I have made donations	21
No	78
Don't know	1
Refused	<1

Source: Association of Religion Data Archives, "Spiritual Life Study of Chinese
Residents." Horizon Research Consultancy Group survey reported by the Pew
Global Attitudes Project, 2007.
Total respondents 7,021; Sampling error±1.2.
Total made not add to 100 due to rounding.
Question wording: Have you donated any money or goods to religious organizations
(such as Protestant or Catholic churches, Buddhist temples, Daoist temples or
mosques) and/or religious individuals (such as Protestant ministers, Catholic priests,
Buddhist monks or nuns, Daoist priests, or imams) in the past 12 months?

Table 12.3   Reported formal religious affiliation from surveys in China.

	2007a %	2007b %	2006 %	2005 %
Total religious believers	**22**	**14**	**18**	**16**
Buddhist	18	12	16	11
Christian	3	2	1	4
Protestant	3	1	1	2
Catholic	<1	1	<1	2
Muslim	<1	<1	1	1
Taoist	<1	<1	<1	<1
Other	<1	–	<1	<1
None	77	81	77	77
Refused or didn't know	<1	5	5	7
Total respondents	7,021	4,104	2,180	2,191
Sampling error	±1.2	±1.6	±2.3	±2.3

Data sources: for 2007a, the Horizon Spiritual Life Study of Chinese Residents (SLSC), downloaded
from ARDA; for 2007b, the Horizon survey as reported by C100; for 2006 and 2005, the Horizon
survey as reported by the Pew Global Attitudes Project.
Question wording: "What is your religious faith?" (2005, 2006, 2007b) "Regardless of whether you have
been to churches or temples, do you believe in any of the following?" First mention 2007b.
Note: The differences in the four estimates might be due to sampling error and the cities sampled rather
than significant shifts in religious adherence among years.

(C100), a non-partisan organization composed of American citizens of Chinese
descent. The surveys are disproportionately urban and representative of slightly
more than half of China's adult population. Six cities and their surrounding areas
were surveyed in 2005 and 2006 (of the six cities in each survey, three were the
same), while seven cities and their surrounding areas were surveyed in 2007, again
with only some overlap.

The Pew Global Attitudes Project, the C100, and Baylor University purchased data
from the Horizon Research Consultancy Group's self-sponsored survey "Chinese

People View the World." The 2005 Pew Global Attitudes Project survey was a multi-stage random sample of 2,191 Chinese adults in six major cities and their surrounding rural areas (Beijing, Chengdu, Guangzhou, Shanghai, Shenyang, and Wuhan). This sample was disproportionately urban and not representative of the entire country. Interviews were conducted in person, in the appropriate Chinese dialect, with adults ages 18–60, with a sampling error of plus or minus 2.3%. The 2006 Pew Global Attitudes Project survey was also a multi-stage random sample of 2,180 Chinese adults in six cities and surrounding rural areas (Beijing, Guangzhou, Jinzhong, Luzhou, Shanghai, and Xinxiang). This sample was disproportionately urban and representative of 52% of the adult population, with a sampling error of plus or minus 2.3%. The C100 survey of 2007 was a multi-stage random sample of 4,104 Chinese adults ages 18–60 in seven cities, seven towns, and 10 villages, using a multi-stage random sample that was drawn to generally reflect the overall population. The survey had a sampling error of plus or minus 1.6%. The Spiritual Life Study of Chinese Residents (data archived at ARDA) was a multi-stage random survey of mainland China administered in three municipal cities (Beijing, Chongqing, Shanghai), six provincial capitals (Chengdu, Guangzhou, Hefei, Nanjing, Wuhan, Xi`an), 11 regional cities, 16 small towns, and 20 administrative villages. The study was conducted with face-to-face interviews of 7,021 Chinese adults aged 16 and older and had a response rate of 28.1%.

Three of the four surveys found that fewer than one in four Chinese adults (ranging from 14% to 22%) say they are religiously affiliated. This would make China one of the least religiously affiliated countries in the world. In the United States, by contrast, more than eight in 10 adults (83%) say they are religiously affiliated, according to the *US Religious Landscape Survey*[8] conducted by the Pew Forum on Religion and Public Life in 2007.

Although the total percentage of Chinese identifying as religiously affiliated might not be high, however, the sheer number of people who say they belong to any particular religion is quite large. If the findings from these surveys were applied to the national population, they would equal or surpass the estimated number of religiously affiliated adults in the United States.

A 2006 survey reported by researchers at Shanghai's East China Normal University, which was cited in the state-approved *China Daily*, found that "31.4% of Chinese aged 16 and above, or about 300 million, are religious."[9] While the actual survey data are not available, the fact that state-run media reported the figure is perhaps an indication of the large number of people the government believes might be religious (independent of whether these individuals actually consider themselves *affiliated* with a particular religion).

Toward a More Comprehensive Count of Religion

Given the wide range of findings from the public opinion surveys just discussed, indicating wide variation in the share of the religiously affiliated or who consider religion at least somewhat important, these survey findings need further scrutiny in order to arrive at a more comprehensive count of religious affiliation in China today.

Chinese Folk- or Traditional Religion

Somewhat distinct from the religious groups discussed thus far is a more diffuse category of religion that is widely practiced in China. Often it is referred to as Chinese folk- (or traditional) religion. Adherents in this category have perhaps the least recognized connection to religion because, by definition, they have no single institutional identity, but instead hold traditional religious beliefs and/or engage in various religious rituals without claiming adherence to any one of the five recognized religious groups. People associated with Chinese folk-religion do not overtly identify as Buddhist, Taoist, Protestant, Catholic, or Muslim, but instead engage in certain religious practices and hold a variety of religious beliefs ranging from ancestor worship to veneration of localized deities or spirits. Those who practice and hold such beliefs do not all share a systematic doctrine or authoritative scripture. Instead, they might pray at temples, offer incense, venerate their ancestors, and believe in powerful spirits and gods unique to a local area of China, or adherents might be centered on veneration of selected spirits or ancestors.

Such practices are widely recognized by scholars,[10] and there is even some high-level acknowledgement of such practices. The *Blue Book of Religions* (2010), a publication of the Chinese Academy of Social Sciences, suggests that observing the spring festival, Qingming holiday (also called Ancestors Day or Tomb Sweeping Day), or the Duanwu festival could be a folk-religious aspect of Confucianism. Additionally, the authors argue that folk beliefs are more than simply superstition and constitute a part of Chinese religious culture that should be held in the same regard by students of religion as Islam, Christianity, and Buddhism. Assessing the relative proportion of folk-religionists in China poses unique challenges, however. Since religious affiliation customarily is measured through survey instruments designed to capture adherence to an institutionalized religion *as reported by the respondent* and not based on practices or beliefs, survey research does not usually capture this diffused religious identity.

To provide a modest estimate of folk-religionists in China, a mix of various beliefs and practices from questions that were asked in the 2007 Spiritual Life Study of Chinese Residents (Horizon survey reported by ARDA) are used here. Respondents reporting a religious affiliation (as a Christian, Muslim, Hindu, Buddhist, or Taoist) were not counted in this analysis as traditional religionists regardless of answers to other questions. Table 12.4 details measures that could be used to indicate belief or practice. Only responses marked with an asterisk were included in the estimate for folk-religionists.

Based on strict criteria for being classified as an active practitioner of folk-religion – that is, the characteristics counted as folk-religion in table 12.4 – folk-religionists make up 22% of the Chinese population (this includes the < 1% of the population who self-identify as Confucianists). But beyond this stricter measure, traditional religion is widespread in China – more than four fifths of respondents affirmed belief in the supernatural or engaged in at least one of the practices that could be indicative of adherence to folk-religion. Of the 77% of respondents who did not report a religious identity when asked, more than one quarter were considered traditional religionists.

Table 12.4 Traditional/folk practices and beliefs in China, 2007.

Places of worship		%
Conventional religious sites (temples)	*	17
Gravesides or ancestral temples		54
Home	*	15
Traditional practices		
Workplace	*	<1
Venerate ancestral spirits		68
Attend formal temple services	*	1
Pray or burn incense in temples	*	16
Wear accessories for protection/fortune		9
Have statue of the God of Wealth		9
Have statues of Buddha, Laozi, or Confucius		10
Have ancestral tablets		12
Have statues of gods or spirits		9
Belief in the existence of:		
God		8
God of heaven	*	12
Evil forces/demons	*	2
Heaven	*	7
Hell/underworld	*	8
Soul		11
Buddha		18
Sages		8
Karma		21
Afterlife	*	6
Reincarnation	*	5
Gods and spirits	*	6
Fate/fortune		25
God of wealth	*	14
Ancestral spirits		20
At least one of the above		81
None of the above or don't know		19

*Used in analysis to estimate a folk-religion measure.
Source: Association of Religion Data Archives, "Spiritual Life Study of Chinese Residents."
Horizon Research Consultancy Group survey reported by the Pew Global Attitudes Project, 2007.
Question wordings: (1) Have you worshipped God or gods/spirits in the following settings in the past year?; (2) In the past year, which of the following activities did you participate in?; (3) Have you worn any of the following accessories in the past year?; (4) Do you have any of the following items at home?; (5) Here are some items I will ask you about one by one. Do you think any of them actually exists?
Total is greater than 100% because respondents could select all that apply.

Similarly, the 2005 Pew poll found that approximately three in five Chinese expressed a personal belief in the possible existence of one or more supernatural phenomena, religious figures, or supernatural beings that are often associated with Confucianism and popular forms of Chinese folk-religion. These beliefs range from fortune and fate, to the Jade Emperor (associated with Taoism) and Tathagata (a manifestation of Buddha), to immortal souls and ghosts. While this is not necessarily a measure of the extent to which Chinese self-consciously identify with folk or popular religion, it does suggest that popular religious beliefs might be more prevalent than is suggested by religious affiliation alone.

Buddhism and Taoism

In the four Horizon surveys, Buddhists represented the largest religious group in China, making up between 11% and 18% of the adult population. This seems a plausible range given that Xinhua, a state-approved news agency, recently put the total number of Chinese Buddhists at "approximately 100 million."[11] If the figure of 18%, from the Horizon survey with the largest sample size, is correct, then more than 240 million people in China are Buddhist (assuming children are affiliated in the same patterns as adults).

Ethnic Tibetans, who are predominantly Buddhist, make up only a small portion of China's overall population and thus only a small proportion of the overall number of Buddhists. The number of ethnic Tibetans, however, is growing. Between the 1990 and 2000 censuses, for instance, their numbers increased by nearly 18% to approximately 5.4 million, compared with China's overall population growth of almost 12% during those same years. One reason for the more rapid growth among the ethnic Tibetan population may be that, as one of 55 officially recognized ethnic minorities in China, they receive an exception from the government's strict one-child-per-family policy. Less than half of ethnic Tibetans live in the Tibet Autonomous Region, which helps explain why the unrest in 2008 was spread over several provinces.[12]

All four Horizon surveys also indicate that adherents of Taoism, an indigenous Chinese religion, make up less than 1% of the Chinese adult population. No government estimates are available to either corroborate or question this estimate.

Christianity

Published estimates of the Christian share of the Chinese population range from about 1% in some relatively small-sample public opinion surveys to about 8% in reviews of membership reports from churches and church leaders (including unregistered churches) within China. Given the size of China's population, a difference of a single percentage point represents more than 10 million people. In light of such a wide range of estimates, this study carefully considered multiple sources of data – including public opinion surveys, church membership reports, and Chinese government statistics – in an attempt to provide a reasonable estimate of the number of Christians in China.

This methodology builds on the 2008 Pew Forum analysis of religion in China.[13] Since its publication in May 2008, that analysis has been well received by scholars at numerous scientific and professional meetings in the United States and China.[14]

Table 12.5 Christians in China, 2010.

	Estimated population	Percentage of 2010 population in China
Protestant	58,040,000	4.3
Independent	35,040,000	2.6
Other Protestant	23,000,000	1.7
Anglican	<1,000	<0.1
Orthodox	20,000	<0.1
Catholic	9,000,000	0.7
Other Christian	<10,000	<0.1
Total Christian	**67,070,000**	**5.0**

Source: Reproduced by permission of Pew Research Center's Forum on Religion and Public Life, © 2011, Pew Research Center. Based on Pew Forum on Religion and Public Life, *Global Christianity: A Report on the Size and Distribution of the World's Christian Population*, December 19, 2011, http://www.pewforum.org/christian/global-christianity-exec.aspx.
Population estimates are rounded to ten thousands. Percentages are calculated from unrounded numbers. Figures may not add exactly due to rounding.

At these meetings, the Pew Forum received feedback on the initial analysis as well as helpful input on its current estimates.

There is general consensus among scholars of mainland China that its Christian population numbers somewhere in the tens of millions. Several efforts have been made to come up with more precise figures on the number of Christians in both state-approved associations and unregistered churches. Based on a review of these estimates, the Pew Forum's demographers think that the 2010 Christian share of China's population is likely in the neighborhood of 5% (or 67 million people of all ages), as shown in table 12.5. This figure includes non-adult children of Chinese believers and unbaptized persons who attend Christian worship services. It can be broken down as follows.

Catholics total roughly 9 million, or 0.7% of China's overall population. They include 5.7 million people affiliated with the state-approved Catholic Patriotic Association, as reported by the 2010 *Blue Book of Religions*, which is produced by the Chinese Academy of Social Sciences (CASS).[15] This study conservatively estimates that an additional 3.3 million people are affiliated solely with unregistered Catholic congregations.

Protestants total about 58 million, or 4.3% of China's overall population. They include members of churches aligned with the state-approved Protestant Three-Self Patriotic Movement Committee (TSPM), which has roughly 23 million adherents (1.7% of China's population), according to the China Christian Council (the TSPM's sister organization that oversees such matters as theological education, external relations, and Bible printing). In addition, this study estimates that China has some 35 million independent Christians (2.6% of the population), who are also classified in this study as Protestants. Many people in the independent Christian category meet without state approval in homes, rented facilities, and public spaces. As a result, they are sometimes called "house church" Christians.[16] Independent Christians also include unbaptized persons, often referred to as "seekers," attending either registered or unregistered churches.

Table 12.6 Range of existing Christian* population estimates for mainland China, 2010.

Source	Minimum percentage of total population that is Christian	Maximum percentage of total population that is Christian	Best estimate percentage of total population that is Christian	Best estimate of 2010 Christian population
Chinese Academy of Social Sciences' *Blue Book of Religions*, 2010	2.1%	>2.1%	>2.1%	29,000,000
Spiritual Life Study of Chinese Residents, 2007	3.2	5.9	5.0**	67,000,000
Meta Analysis by Global China Center's Carol Lee Hamrin, 2005	NA	NA	5.0	67,000,000
China Christian Council (2011) estimate of Protestants *plus* Chinese Catholic Patriotic Association estimate in *Blue Book plus* House Church estimate by Liu Peng, 2009	2.1	5.8	NA	79,000,000^
Asia Harvest, 2010	6.1	9.2	7.7	104,000,000
World Christian Database, 2010	NA	NA	8.0	108,000,000

*Chinese authorities sometimes use the term "Christian" to mean "Protestant." Here, "Christian" includes all Christian traditions.

**Best estimate takes into account nonresponse follow-up survey reported by Stark, Johnson, and Mencken (2011).

^Adds the estimates of Protestants and Catholics (28.7 million) to Liu Peng's estimate of unregistered house church members (50 million).

Source: Reproduced by permission of Pew Research Center's Forum on Religion and Public Life, © 2011, Pew Research Center. Based on Pew Forum on Religion and Public Life, *Global Christianity: A Report on the Size and Distribution of the World's Christian Population*, December 19, 2011, http://www.pewforum.org/christian/global-christianity-exec.aspx.

Orthodox Christians number about 20,000. Other Christians number fewer than 1,000. Among the members of these groups are some expatriates living in China. The Pew Forum's estimate of roughly 67 million Christians falls in the middle range of previous estimates, which vary from less than 30 million to more than 100 million.[17]

Background on the Chinese context

Because there are no truly nationally representative surveys of the religious affiliation of the Chinese public, only a rough estimate of the country's Christian population is possible. Also, because the number of religious adherents in China is a politically sensitive issue,[18] the national census does not ask questions about personal religious affiliation. Additionally, there might be underreporting by the registered churches and the State Religious Affairs Bureau (SARA). Part of the sensitivity is that followers of some of China's five officially recognized religious traditions – Buddhism, Protestantism, Catholicism, Islam, and Daoism – very likely outnumber members of the Chinese Communist Party. For instance, about 6% of Chinese are Party members, compared with more than 20% who are thought to be affiliated with the five recognized religions, combined.[19]

Despite the data limitations, a great deal of scholarship has been devoted to the study of China's religious populations and their growth since the late 1970s, when the nationwide prohibition of religion was lifted following the end of the Cultural Revolution.[20] This growing body of empirical research comes from a number of different sources, including reports sponsored by the Chinese government, reviews of membership reports from churches and church leaders within China, ethnographic case studies,[21] and surveys of the Chinese public.[22] Taken together, these studies have produced valuable insights into the nature of religion in China today.

Among scholars of China, there is a general consensus that religion and its influence have grown substantially during the past three decades. This includes growth in institutional forms of religion as well as more "diffused" forms of religious belief and practice expressed in family and community contexts, including house churches, rather than within an organized or institutional religious framework.[23] However, a consensus has not developed on the current size of the various religious communities in China. In addition to the lack of an authoritative census or survey, the absence of a consensus on numbers also stems from differences in defining who should be counted as a member of the various religious communities.

Although there are challenges with measuring other religious groups in China,[24] researchers face a particularly daunting measurement challenge regarding Christianity. Here, the central issue is not so much the diffuse nature of Christian identity and practice in China, though that is also an issue,[25] but also the large number of Christians who do not affiliate with either of the two state-approved denominations. Christians who decline to put themselves under the theological and administrative oversight of these two denominations operate in what Professor Yang Fenggang of Purdue University refers to as gray and black religious marketplaces.[26] Indeed, unregistered churches operate on the edges of the law – in the realm of administrative policies – because there are few laws that establish the limits of the government or the freedom of religious groups in society.[27] And because of the ambiguous, sometimes adversarial relationship between the government and Christian groups that are not willing to join state-approved denominations, attempts to measure these groups often are met with suspicion by all sides – the government, the state-approved churches, and the unregistered groups.

Indeed, government and academic researchers have found evidence that Christians in general, and members of unregistered Christian groups in particular, are less likely than Chinese as a whole to participate in public opinion surveys. For instance, a follow-up study[28] to the 2007 Spiritual Life Study of Chinese Residents found that independent Christians were less than half as likely to agree to participate than the average of all those surveyed in the main study. Separately, one of the authors of the 2010 *Blue Book of Religions* discussed reasons that public opinion surveys may yield somewhat lower estimates of Christians than actually exist in the population:

1. It is a sensitive subject for local officials, and they do not want to facilitate the poll or have large numbers reported (a potential sampling bias).
2. It is a sensitive subject for some Christians, and for churches that do not want to report their true numbers (a reliability issue).
3. Some "Christians" who have not yet been baptized do not want to say that they are Christian because, according to the churches, they are not[29] (a classification issue).

In addition to these issues, researchers also face the challenge of adequately representing regional variances in religious affiliation. Evidence suggests that religious groups are geographically concentrated; therefore, a reliable design for a survey to measure religious affiliation would need to include strategies for sampling across China's 33 provinces, regions, and municipalities – many of which individually surpass the population of entire countries.

One rough indication of the geographic concentration of religion is a 2004 Chinese government economic census that reports the number and location of economic institutions, including religious organizations officially registered with the government. In the analysis by Purdue University's Center on Religion and Chinese Society, directed by Professor Yang Fenggang, each Chinese county is color-coded to show the religion that has the largest number of registered places of worship or religious institutions. According to this mapping, Protestant institutions are domi-nant in the east, Muslim institutions in the west,[30] Catholic institutions in north and central regions of the country, and Buddhist institutions in the south.

The 2007 Spiritual Life Study of Chinese Residents survey[31] attempted to address this potential bias by interviewing in most Chinese provinces, but fewer than 150 people were interviewed in many provinces, and some provinces were not included at all. While this sampling strategy is not unusual for national surveys, it has the potential to miss religious groups that are geographically concentrated within provinces.

These are some of the reasons that any estimate of Chinese Christian numbers must draw on multiple sources of information rather than rely only on existing surveys of the public.

Chinese government estimates

Chinese government estimates can be considered a minimum figure for the number of Christians because they are based primarily on reports from the state-approved Three-Self Patriotic Movement Committee of the Protestant Churches of China (for

Protestants) and from the Chinese Catholic Patriotic Association (for Catholics). These estimates typically include only members of these two officially recognized associations. They generally do not include unbaptized persons attending Christian groups, non-adult children of Christian believers, or other persons under age 18. And, most importantly, they generally do not take into account unregistered Christian groups.

Despite these limitations, government reports do provide some useful data as well as some indication of recent trends. Most notably, they show dramatic growth among officially recognized Protestants and Catholics, as is seen by comparing the numbers reported in the government's 1997 White Paper[32] on religion with an updated 2006 Background Brief provided to the Pew Forum by the Chinese Embassy in Washington, DC. The officially reported number of Christians increased from 14 million to 21 million, or 50%, in approximately 10 years. During this time, government figures indicate that the number of Protestants rose from 10 million to 16 million – a 60% increase – while the number of Catholics went from 4 million to 5 million – a 25% increase. The 2006 Background Brief goes so far as to say that Protestantism, in particular, has increased "by more than 20 times" since it "was first brought to China in the early 19th century."

More recently, the 2010 *Blue Book of Religions* estimates Christians in China to number about 28.7 million (2.1% of the population), 37% more than were reported in the 2006 Background Brief. This includes 23 million Protestants, or 1.8% of the 2007 total population of 1.31 billion, based on a survey on Protestantism carried out by the government's Chinese Academy of Social Sciences (CASS) in 2008–9, which claimed to be a full population survey and not just a survey of Protestants in registered churches. The *Blue Book of Religions* separately estimates that China has 5.7 million Catholics, but it also acknowledges that this figure may be an undercount, possibly because it includes only Catholics who attend churches affiliated with the state-approved Catholic Patriotic Association.

There is some evidence that the growth in Protestant numbers, in particular, has occurred mainly through conversion rather than as a result of better reporting or the registration of previously unregistered groups, though both of those factors also may account for some of the increase.[33] Despite its limitations, the 2008–9 CASS study of Protestantism shows that a substantial portion of Protestants in mainland China are recent converts.[34] Of the Protestants interviewed in the study, 44.4% said they had converted to Christianity between the ages of 35 and 54. Though that figure seems high, it suggests that a substantial amount of conversion is occurring. Nevertheless, it is important to note that the results of the CASS survey are not possible to evaluate because there is no access to the individual survey data. Moreover, there are other unanswered questions about the survey. For instance, the *Blue Book* claims that of the 63,680 surveys distributed, all were completed, resulting in a 100% response rate. It is highly unlikely that out of such a large number of questionnaires, all would have been returned and completed. It is also difficult to understand why such a large survey would have been used to estimate only the number of Protestants and not the number of Catholics as well.

The China Christian Council reports that there are more than 23 million Protestants in China.[35] This number is similar to the number of Protestants reported in the 2010

Blue Book. How many more is difficult to determine, especially when unbaptized believers and members of unregistered groups are considered. One indirect indicator is the demand for Bibles, especially in a country where not every Christian has a Bible[36] and where, since most still live at a subsistence level, owning multiple copies of the Bible is a luxury.[37] Since its founding in 1988, the Amity Printing Company, the official printing arm of the China Christian Council, has printed nearly 90 million Bibles, reportedly including about 56 million for distribution in China and more than 33 million for overseas markets.[38] Moreover, the Amity presses now are printing more than 10 million additional Bibles per year,[39] with the capacity to "print more than 18 million Bibles a year."[40] Of course, more than just church members in China may read Bibles and not all will be distributed within China. At a minimum, however, this level of demand is an indication of the number of people with some interest in Christianity.

The 2006 Background Brief provided by the Chinese Embassy states that "There are no [government] data available on the number of 'house meetings' that exist." But even though the government has not released an official estimate of the number of Christians associated with unregistered groups, in December 2009, the *China Daily*, China's national English-language newspaper, published an interview with Chinese Academy of Social Sciences religion scholar Liu Peng, perhaps the government's leading expert on unregistered churches,[41] in which Professor Liu claimed that "'house churches' – praying facilities that do not register or report to the State Administration for Religious Affairs – have at least 50 million followers nationwide."[42] The basis for this ballpark estimate has not been made public. But the fact that an important state-run news organization would publish such a statement indicates that house-church believers may outnumber those affiliated with the official churches.

Membership-based estimates

As previously noted, attempts to count the number of unregistered (or "independent" or "house church") Christians can be met with suspicion by the government, the officially approved churches, and the independent groups themselves. Given these difficulties, it is not surprising that a range of estimates exist. The *World Christian Database* estimates that China has more than 100 million Christians, including more than 300 house church networks (among the Han majority alone) claiming to represent approximately 70 million people.[43] However, a separate review of estimates of Christians in China by Senior Researcher Carol Lee Hamrin at the Global China Center, an academic and research institution based in the US and devoted to the study of China and religion, suggests a smaller overall number. She estimated that "[a]s of 2005, Christians were approaching 5 percent of the population, four-fifths of them Protestants," and that "[u]nregistered Christians may be the largest autonomous social group in China."[44]

Asia Harvest, an inter-denominational Christian ministry working in Asia, recently carried out an ambitious assessment of the number of Chinese affiliated with all forms of Christianity in every county of China.[45] The study's numbers are based on secondary analysis of more than 2,000 published sources as well as interviews with leaders of unregistered churches who granted the research team access to statistics on their membership. The study estimates that there are 104 million Christians of all ages in mainland China (7.7% of the country's total population), including children as well as un-baptized adult believers. This includes an estimated 83.5 million Protestants (6.1%), of whom 29.5 million belong to the state-approved church and 54 million are independents, some of whom may be considered heterodox.[46] Importantly, however, the study points out that "owing to the difficulties of conducting such a [study] in China today – not the least of which is the sheer size of the country – there is [in the study's rough estimation] a margin of error of 20 percent." Thus, the study estimates that the number of Christians is between 83.4 million (6.1%) and 125.2 million (9.2%).

Asia Harvest's estimate of the number of Chinese Catholics is much higher than from other sources. Its study finds that China has about 20 million Catholics, or 1.5% of the population. This includes nearly 7.5 million people affiliated with the Chinese Patriotic Catholic Association and 13.4 million Catholics worshiping outside of officially recognized churches. In comparison, the Holy Spirit Study Centre in Hong Kong,[47] which monitors the number of Chinese Catholic priests, congregations and members, estimates that there are 12 million Catholics in both branches of the Catholic church – 6.3 million more than acknowledged by the government but far fewer than estimated by the Asia Harvest study. Asia Harvest's higher estimate could be due in part to double counting in some Catholic dioceses where churches and bishops are affiliated with both the official and unofficial churches.[48]

Independent survey estimates

While it did not cover the entire country, and thus is not a truly nationally representative survey, the 2007 Spiritual Life Study of Chinese Residents provides some valuable data on various levels of Christian identification in China.[49] The Spiritual Life Study was sponsored and independently carried out by the Horizon Research Consultancy Group, a Chinese public opinion polling firm, and the data are available through ARDA. Among the experts who consulted on the study were leading social science researchers both inside and outside China.[50] The survey covered three major municipalities and six provincial capitals and their surrounding areas, as well as some other regional cities and small towns. In all, about two thirds of all Chinese provinces were sampled to some extent. The Spiritual Life Study permitted respondents to indicate belief in more than one faith. In all, 3.2% – or the equivalent of about 44 million people if applied to China's 2010 population – self-identified as Christian (2.94% Protestant and 0.34% Catholic).[51]

But there are other indicators of possible Christian identity and/or contact with Christianity in the survey as well. For example, when belief in the existence of Jesus is considered, the portion of Chinese who indicate some connection to Christianity rises to as high as 5.9%. This is similar to the results of a slightly different question from a predominantly urban survey carried out by Horizon in 2005, which found that 6% of the Chinese respondents express belief in the existence of "God/Jesus" (in Chinese *Shangdi/Yesu*, a rough equivalent of the "Christian God") – more than 50% higher than the number of people who self-identified as a Christian in that earlier poll.[52] These figures, while not a direct indication of Christian identity, are important to note, given the problems associated with the ability of surveys to accurately and reliably measure Christian identity in a Communist country where atheism is the ideological norm.

In addition to the 5.9% of Chinese who either identified as Christian or expressed belief in the existence of Jesus in the Spiritual Life Study, an additional 1.4% reported having at least one Christian parent.[53] All things considered, the results of the Spiritual Life Study seem to suggest that a reasonable estimate for the share of Christians probably lies somewhere between the 3.2% who claimed Christianity as their religious identity and the 7.3% who expressed some loose connection to Christianity.[54]

Given the dual problems already discussed of higher refusal rates among Chinese Christians to participate in public opinion surveys (survey non-response) and/or reluctance to self-identify as a Christian when asked in the survey (item non-response), some of the primary investigators from the Spiritual Life Study, in collaboration with researchers at Peking University in Beijing, launched a follow-up study of non-response rates. Based on contacts in the Chinese Christian community, they acquired a listing of Chinese house church members from some of the same areas sampled in the Spiritual Life Study. Interviewers *unfamiliar* with the objectives of the follow-up study sought interviews with the house church members. The overall refusal rate in the Spiritual Life Study was 38%, but among the new sample of known house church members, 62% refused to be interviewed. When the investigators adjusted for this difference in survey response rates, they estimated that China has a total of 58.9 million Christians ages 16 and older.

To correct for the second problem, item non-response, the follow-up study also took into account the portion of Christians who agreed to be interviewed but did *not* identify as Christian (9%) when asked about their religion in the survey. The investigators concluded: "Correcting for that suppressor brings the number of Christian Chinese sixteen and older to 64.3 million. Of course, this total is for 2007. Obviously the total is higher now. It seems entirely credible to estimate that there are about 70 million Chinese Christians in 2011."[55] This figure is similar to other efforts that attempted to account for the number of Christians in both the state-approved denominations and unregistered churches summarized at the start of this methodology.

It is important to note that the researchers have not made the data or a detailed methodology from the follow-up study available. Therefore, as with the 2008–9 CASS survey, it is not possible to verify these findings. For instance, it is not possible to replicate the adjustment procedures used by the investigators because the overall impact of non-response not only depends on differences between the response rates of the original people sampled and house church Christians, but also on the actual number of house church members in the population, which is unknown.

Islam

China is home to a large Muslim population as well. The Horizon surveys found that some 1% or less of the adult population say they are Muslim. This falls short of the number suggested by government statistics, however. According to the 2000 census, for example, ethnic groups closely associated with Islam numbered 20.3 million, or approximately 1.5% of the total population.

The lower survey estimates likely are due in large part to the fact that the Horizon surveys were not conducted in autonomous regions with predominantly Muslim ethnic groups, such as the Ningxia Hui Autonomous Region, which has a large Hui Muslim population, and the Xinjiang Uyghur Autonomous Region, where most Uyghur Muslims live. According to the 2000 census, Hui, who live in many of China's provinces, number nearly 10 million, followed by the Uyghurs, who number more than 8 million.

In 2011, the Pew Forum, using the cohort component method, projected the Muslim population in the 2000 census forward and estimated that Muslims made up about 2% of the population in China.[56] However, because the country is so populous, its Muslim population was the eighteenth largest in the world in 2010. The Pew Forum projects the Muslim population in China will increase from more than 23 million in 2010 to nearly 30 million in 2030. Of all the countries in the world where Muslims live as religious minorities, only three others – India, Nigeria, and Ethiopia – have more than 20 million Muslims.[57]

In the Pew Forum projections, the number of Muslims in China is expected to grow at a slower rate in the period 2010–30 than it did in the previous two decades. From 1990 to 2010, the number of Muslims in China increased by 6.5 million, a 38.4% increase. The country is expected to add a similar number of Muslims from 2010 to 2030, but because the base number in 2010 is larger than it was in 1990, the projected percentage increase is smaller (28.5%).

The fertility rate for Muslims in China is higher than the fertility rate for non-Muslims. Muslim women in China have an average of 1.7 children, compared with a national average of 1.4 children.[58] This is one reason the Muslim share of China's total population is expected to increase slightly, from 1.8% in 2010 to 2.1% in 2030. Muslims in China are somewhat less urbanized and less educated than the general population. These characteristics often are associated with higher fertility rates. At the time of the 2000 census, 31.2% of Chinese Muslims lived in urban areas, compared with 36.9% of the country's population as a whole. In the same year, Muslims in China attended school an average of 6.8 years, compared with a national average of 7.6 years.

Muslims are not a new presence in China. Most of China's Muslim communities, including the Hui, Uyghurs, and Kazakhs, have lived in China for more than 1,000 years. The largest concentrations of Muslims today are in the Western provinces of Xinjiang, Ningxia, Qinghai, and Gansu. A substantial number of Muslims live in the cities of Beijing, Tianjin, and Shanghai.

Atheism

The secular, or the religiously unaffiliated, are the majority of the population in China. No reliable numbers for atheists in China are available. While government reports and sources do not provide estimates for the size of the atheist population, the majority of Chinese are widely reported as not belonging to any religious tradition. An analysis of the 2007 Horizon survey shows that 9% of Chinese (or about 120 million) are atheists. Since the survey does not ask respondents to self-identify as atheists (and lack of belief in the existence of God or supernatural spirits and forces are uniquely atheist characteristics), our estimate reflects, in part, answers to a question in the 2007 survey on belief in the supernatural. Respondents were told, "Here are some items I will ask you about one by one. Do you think any of them actually exists?" and were presented with 16 supernatural beings, gods, and spirits from virtually every religious tradition. We include, in constructing our estimate, only those who reported (1) having no religious affiliation and also no belief in the existence of *any* supernatural power, or (2) being an atheist.

A Comprehensive Estimate of Religious Affiliation in China

Taking into account multiple sources of data, this study estimates that while the majority (53%) of people in China have no religious attachments, only 9% of Chinese hold no beliefs in any god or spirit whatsoever, meaning that strict atheists make up only about 17% of the non-religious population. A substantial minority (44%) of Chinese, then, consider themselves non-religious while having some affiliation to religious faith or practice. The largest of the religious groups – traditional Chinese or folk-religionists – accounts for approximately one in five Chinese (23%). Buddhism is the largest organized religious group, accounting for more than one in six Chinese (18%). An estimated one in 20 Chinese adhere to one of the branches of Christianity (5%). While Muslims make up only 1.8% of the Chinese population, they are the eighteenth-largest Muslim population in the world. Daoists account for less than 1% of the overall population.

Table 12.7   Religious affiliation in China, 2010.*

	%	Estimated population
No religious attachments, including no belief in god(s) at all (9%)	**52.6%**	705,154,000
Some religious attachment	**47.4%**	636,181,000
Traditional/folk religion practitioners, including Confucianists (<0.2%)	22.0%	294,548,000
Buddhists	18.1%	242,103,000
Christians (Protestants, Catholics, Independents, and smaller groups)	5.0%	67,065,000
Muslims (by ethnicity)	1.8%	23,487,000
Other religious groups (Daoists, 0.65% other New Religionists)	0.7%	8,958,000
Hindus	<0.1%	18,000
Jews	<0.1%	3,000
Total	**100.00%**	**1,341,335,000**

*Estimates include all residents; they do not, however, include Hong Kong, Macau, or Taiwan. Figures might not add exactly due to rounding.

Sources: Total population – United Nations, Department of Economic and Social Affairs, Population Division, *World Population Prospects: The 2010 Revision* (New York: United Nations, 2011); Religious affiliation – this study's best estimates based on a review of multiple sources described in this chapter.

Hindus and Jews, as well as members of other smaller religious groups, tend to be expatriates more than local citizens, though some Chinese have adhered to Judaism for centuries.[59]

Government Officials Interested in Hearing about Religion

A final intriguing finding regarding religion in China today comes from an analysis by the Pew Forum of a 2005 survey[60] conducted by InterMedia, an international research and consulting organization specializing in media and communications. The Forum's analysis of this unprecedented survey, which included more than 10,000 adults across 21 of China's 31 mainland provinces, municipal districts, and autonomous regions, found that 33% of Communist Party officials and government employees are very or somewhat interested in having media access to information on the topic of religion. This makes them the most interested occupational group among the dozen or so groups reported.

There are other signs that the Communist Party is taking note of the growing interest in religion in the country. For instance, Hu Jintao, President and former General Secretary of the Communist Party of China, broke with former practice and included a formal discussion of religion at the National Congress in October 2007. In January 2008, Hu stated to the Chinese Politburo, "We must strive to closely unite religious

Table 12.8 Interest in the topic of religion by occupational group.

Occupational group	Very or somewhat interested	Not very interested	Not at all interested	Don't know	N
Government or Communist Party	33	37	22	8	241
Teacher or professor	24	44	23	8	313
Retired	24	39	30	7	699
Service worker	23	36	31	9	496
Full-time student	22	40	28	10	718
Business	22	40	28	10	1,776
Skilled labor	21	42	28	9	319
Unemployed	21	42	26	10	553
Labor	18	38	29	14	1,922
Housewife	17	38	34	11	287
Professional	16	43	32	9	345
Don't know or other					75
Total	**21**	**40**	**29**	**11**	**7,744**

Data source: InterMedia, "Survey on the Lifestyle of Chinese Residents," 2005. The religious interest question was only asked of those who had access to some form of media and who also expressed at least some interest in national or international events; 74% of the respondents fit these criteria. No question was asked about religious affiliation or the personal importance of religion in this 2005 InterMedia survey. Question wording: Please tell me how interested you would be in hearing the topic of ___ in reports/features/programs on radio, TV, the press, and the Internet? How interested are you in the topic of ___? Very interested, somewhat interested, not very interested, or not at all interested?

figures and believers ... to build an all-around ... prosperous society while quickening the pace toward the modernization of socialism."[61]

The relatively high level of interest by Communist Party and government employees in having reports/features/programs on radio, TV, the press, and the Internet about the topic of religion, in particular, might indicate that the government is seeking to come to terms with the interest in religion on the part of many people in China.

China, in less than four decades since the Cultural Revolution attempted to eradicate all religion, has become one of the world's most religiously diverse countries (see chapter 3). The future of religion in China, however, is likely one of the most difficult to project with accuracy. The evidence outlined in this chapter indicates that many people have become affiliated to some degree with religion in the past decades. Whether the trend will continue is unknown. Much more research and better sources of data are needed if we are to understand whether past trends are continuing, leveling off, or reversing.

There is some hope on the data horizon. Initiatives such as the Center on Religion and Chinese Society at Purdue University have been established to advance the social scientific study of religion in Chinese societies and among the Chinese in diasporas. The fruits of such initiatives will materialize in the years ahead.

Notes

1   This study by Brian J. Grim was initially presented under the title, "Counting Religion in China" at the Henry Kissinger Institute on China and the United States in the Woodrow Wilson International Center for Scholars, Washington, DC, October 2011. This chapter greatly updates and expands on Brian J. Grim and the Pew Forum on Religion and Public Life, *Religion in China on the Eve of the 2008 Beijing Olympics*, May 2, 2008, http://pewforum.org/docs/?DocID=301. It also includes material from the Pew Forum on Religion and Public Life, *The Future of the Global Muslim Population: Projections for 2010–2030*, January 27, 2011, http://pewresearch.org/pubs/1872/muslim-population-projections-worldwide-fast-growth. Portions are reprinted with permission of the Pew Research Center's Forum on Religion and Public Life. The research assistance of Noble Kuriakose and Anne Shi contributed greatly.

2   See http://en.beijing2008.cn/spectators/beijing/religion/.

3   The second author lived and taught in China at Hua Qiao University, Quanzhou, Fujian, from 1982–3.

4   Pew Research Center, "China's Optimism: Prosperity Brings Satisfaction – and Hope," Global Attitudes Project, November 16, 2005, http://www.pewglobal.org/2005/11/16/chinas-optimism/.

5   Pew Research Center, "Publics of Asian Powers Hold Negative Views of One Another: China's Neighbors Worry About Its Growing Military Strength," Global Attitudes Project, September 21, 2006, http://www.pewglobal.org/2006/09/21/publics-of-asian-powers-hold-negative-views-of-one-another/.

6   The Association of Religion Data Archives, "Spiritual Life Study of Chinese Residents," http://www.thearda.com/Archive/Files/Descriptions/SPRTCHNA.asp.

7   Committee of 100, "Hope and Fear: Full Report of C-100's Survey on American and Chinese Attitudes Toward Each Other," http://www.survey.committee100.org/2007/files/C100SurveyFullReport.pdf.

8 The Pew Forum on Religion and Public Life, *US Religious Landscape Survey*, 2007, http://religions.pewforum.org/.

9 Wu Jiao, "Religious Believers Thrice the Estimate," *China Daily*, February 7, 2007, http://www.chinadaily.com.cn/china/2007-02/07/content_802994.htm.

10 For a fuller discussion of Chinese folk-religion, see Wai Yip Wong, "Defining Chinese Folk Religion: A Methodological Interpretation," *Asian Philosophy* 21 (2007); Y. Y. Li, *Zong Jiao Yu Shen Hua Lun Ji* [A Treatise on Religion and Myth] (Taipei: New Century Publishing, 1998); Z. Z. Feng and F. H. Li, *History of Chinese Folk Religion* (Taipei: Wenchin, 1994).

11 "Govt Supports Buddhism in Building Harmonious World," *China View*, April 13, 2006, http://news.xinhuanet.com/english/2006-04/13/content_4417439.htm.

12 The last widespread popular demonstration of Tibetan Buddhists came in 2008, when Buddhist monks marched from monasteries in and around Lhasa on March 10 to mark the forty-ninth anniversary of a Tibetan uprising against Chinese rule. "Q&A: China and Tibet," *BBC*, June 19, 2008, http://news.bbc.co.uk/2/hi/asia-pacific/7299221.stm.

13 See Grim, *Religion in China*.

14 Venues include: "Religion and the Future of China Symposium," Council on Foreign Relations, New York (June 11, 2008); "Symposium on Religion and Spirituality in China Today," Center on Religion and Chinese Society at Purdue University (April 30, 2009); "Best Quantitative Estimate of Religion in China Today," Renmin University of China Beijing, immediately following and involving key researchers from the Seventh Symposium of the Social Scientific Study of Religion in China (July 28, 2010); "Religion in China Today," panel briefing provided to Assistant Secretary of State and US Special Representative to the Organization of Islamic Conference, Washington, DC (April 2011); "Religion in the Social Transition of Contemporary China," Kissinger Institute on China and the United States, Washington, DC (October 13, 2011); and "Religious Change and Conversion in China," Annual Meeting of the Society for the Scientific Study of Religion, Milwaukee, WI (October 29, 2011).

15 The Chinese Academy of Social Sciences (CASS), the highest academic research organization in the fields of philosophy and social sciences, is directly under the State Council of the People's Republic of China – the highest executive organ of state power as well as the highest organ of state administration.

16 The term "house church" is perhaps a misnomer, as is noted by Pace University Professor Joseph Tse-Hei Lee:

> The definitions of "open churches" (*dishang jiaohui*), "underground [Catholic] churches" (*dixia jiaohui*), and "[Protestant] house churches" (*jiating jiaohui*) prove ... problematic. Such terms do not accurately describe the reality of Chinese Catholicism and Protestantism. The contemporary Chinese government requires places of worship to register, whether they are churches, temples, monasteries or mosques. The "underground church" is not underground in a literal sense. Neither does the "house church" mean a religious meeting in a single household. Officially, the terms "underground church" and "house church" mean an unregistered religious body.

> See Joseph Tse-Hei Lee, "Christianity in Contemporary China: An Update," *Journal of Church and State* 49:2 (2007): 277–304.

17 An estimate of between 39–41 million Protestants was put forth in 2008 by Werner Bürklin, founder of China Partner, an international Christian organization. Bürklin's survey team interviewed 7,409 individuals in every province and municipality in China. His estimate, however, was based on a non-probability convenience sample survey of

Chinese citizens aged 15 and over. The survey team was asked to randomly ask people what religion, if any, they adhere to. The team interviewed them mainly on the streets and parks but also on trains, planes, subways, taxis, and buses, and in hotels, open-air markets, department stores, and mom-and-pop stores. See Werner Bürklin, "Facts About Number of Christians in China," *The Gospel Herald: Global Chinese Christian News Service*, December 9, 2008, http://www.gospelherald.net/article/opinion/44825/facts-about-numbers-of-christians-in-china.htm.

18 For an understanding of Chinese restrictions on religion in a global context, see Pew Forum on Religion and Public Life, *Rising Restrictions on Religion*, August 9, 2011, http://www.pewforum.org/Government/Rising-Restrictions-on-Religion(2).aspx. For a discussion of the historical and modern contexts of restrictions on religion in China, see Brian J. Grim and Roger Finke, *The Price of Freedom Denied: Religious Persecution and Conflict in the 21st Century* (Cambridge: Cambridge University Press, 2011), 120–40.

19 According to the Spiritual Life Study of Chinese Residents, a 2007 survey by the Chinese polling firm Horizon. The 2007 Spiritual Life Study of Chinese Residents (data archived at the Association of Religion Data Archives: http://www.thearda.com/Archive/Files/Descriptions/SPRTCHNA.asp) was a multi-stage random survey of mainland China administered in three municipalities (Beijing, Shanghai and Chongqing), six provincial capitals (Guangzhou, Nanjing, Wuhan, Hefei, Xi`an, and Chengdu), 11 regional cities, 16 small towns and 20 administrative villages. No major cities in the west, the far northeast or on the south-central coast were surveyed. The study was conducted with face-to-face interviews of 7,021 Chinese adults aged 16 and older and had an American Association of Public Opinion Researchers response rate of 28.1%.Interestingly, despite the requirement that Party members be atheist (see http://www.cfr.org/china/religion-china/p16272#p3), the survey found that more than 13% of Communist Party members expressed some religious affiliation, though none surveyed identified as Christian.

20 For an overview, see Yang Fenggang, *Religion in China: Survival and Revival under Communist Rule* (Oxford: Oxford University Press, 2011).

21 For an example, see Kenneth Dean, "Local Communal Religion in Contemporary South-East China," *The China Quarterly* 174 (2003): 338–58.

22 For an overview, see Yang Fenggang and Graeme Lang, eds., *Social Scientific Studies of Religion in China: Methodology, Theories, and Findings* (Leiden: Brill, 2011).

23 C. K. Yang, *Religion in Chinese Society: A Study of Contemporary Social Functions of Religion and Some of Their Historical Factors* (Berkeley: University of California Press, 1961). Sociologist C. K. Yang first introduced the term "diffused religion" to describe Chinese religious beliefs and practices expressed in family and community contexts rather than within an organized or institutional religion framework.

24 Among government scholars of Buddhism in China, for example, there is some disagreement on whether to define as adherents only those who have undergone official conversion ceremonies or to use the broader definition of anyone self-identifying as a Buddhist. (Less than one in 10 self-identified Buddhists in China underwent a conversion ceremony, compared with more than one in three Christians, according to an analysis of the 2007 Spiritual Life Study of Chinese Residents.) From the government perspective, counting the broader category involves the willingness to acknowledge that adherents of Buddhism can include those with no formal membership in a Buddhist organization or no definite conversion to the faith. For instance, Zheng Xiaoyun, the leading researcher on Buddhism at the Institute on World Religions at the Chinese Academy of Social Sciences (CASS), noted at a recent academic conference ("Religion in the Social Transition of Contemporary China," October 13, 2011, Kissinger Institute on China and the United States, Washington, DC) that CASS is debating whether to count only those Buddhists who have undergone a

formal conversion ceremony. Prior to the twentieth century, various Chinese dynastic policies counted as Buddhists only those who had undergone conversion ceremonies to become monks or nuns, in part because these people were no longer required to pay taxes to the government. A further complication in measuring Buddhism is that there exist a plethora of localized Chinese religious beliefs and practices expressed in family and community contexts rather than within an organized or institutional religious framework. Some of these incorporate elements of Buddhism, while others are closer to Daoism, and yet others blend animism. Most of these incorporate some form of ancestor veneration or worship. This diffused religious category is sometimes referred to as Chinese folk-religion. And finally, an added complication is that a number of Chinese, when given the option in the 2007 Spiritual Life Study of Chinese Residents identified as both Buddhist and Christian. For a fuller discussion of Chinese folk-religion, see Wong, "Defining Chinese Folk Religion"; Li, *Zong Jiao Yu Shen Hua Lun Ji*; Feng and Li, *History of Chinese Folk Religion*; and Jonathan Chamberlain, *Chinese Gods: An Introduction to Chinese Folk Religion* (Hong Kong: Blacksmith Books, 2011).

25   There are some localized forms of Christianity throughout China that sometimes blend local and Christian beliefs. For examples of these groups, see David Aikman, *Jesus in Beijing: How Christianity Is Changing the Global Balance of Power* (Washington, DC: Regnery Publishing, 2003). The intensely Chinese nature of Christianity existed prior to the establishment of the People's Republic of China in 1949. For instance, Professor Lian Xi demonstrates that indigenous Christianity in China was often localized, uniquely Chinese, millenarian and frequently anti-foreign. See Lian Xi, *Redeemed by Fire: The Rise of Popular Christianity in Modern China* (New Haven, CT: Yale University Press, 2010).

26   In an attempt to analyze the religious situation in contemporary China, a country with religious traditions and regulations drastically different from Europe and the Americas, Professor Yang describes a triple-market model: a red market (officially permitted religions), a black market (officially banned religions), and a gray market (religions with an ambiguous legal/illegal status). The gray market concept underscores the extent of non-institutionalized religiosity in China. See Yang Fenggang, "The Red, Black, and Gray Markets of Religion in China," *The Sociological Quarterly* 47 (2006): 93–122.

27   For a discussion of religion and law in China, see Liu Peng, "Religion in post-Hu China: What Changes are Probable?" paper presented at "Religion in the Social Transition of Contemporary China," Kissinger Institute on China and the United States, Washington, DC, October 13, 2011. Only since 2010 has there been a program to study religion and the rule of law at Peking University Law School. This is likely the only program on this topic being offered in China. See International Center for Law and Religion Studies, J. Reuben Clark Law School, "Second Summer Conference on Religion and the Rule of Law – Beijing, July 2011," http://iclrs.org/index.php?blurb_id=1335.

28   Reported in Rodney Stark, Byron Johnson, and Carson Mencken, "Counting China's Christians: There are as Many Christians in China as There are Members of the Communist Party," *First Things*, May 2011, http://www.firstthings.com/article/2011/05/counting-chinarsquos-christians.

29   As reported by Janice Wickeri, "Chinese Protestant Christians: Who, What, Where, Why – Findings of A Questionnaire Survey of Chinese Protestant Christian Households by the Institute of World Religions Research Group," *Amity News Service* 28 (2010): 8.

30   While an officially recognized institutional presence is only a rough indicator of religious concentrations, the most obvious result of this is the clear undercount of Muslims in numerous public opinion surveys, most of which report a 1% or lower share of Muslims. (See Grim, *Religion in China*, for a summary of recent survey findings.) Recognizing this bias, the Pew Forum's 2010 estimate of Chinese Muslims was based on a projection from

the 2000 Chinese Census, which does have a category for Muslim ethnic groups. Based on that information, that study concluded that approximately 1.8% of the population is Muslim (approximately 23.3 million Muslims). It is clear that the lower public opinion survey estimates for Muslims results from Western regions being largely excluded from the sampling frame of most such surveys.

31   The 2007 Spiritual Life Study of Chinese Residents.

32   "Freedom of Religious Belief in China (October 1997)," http://www.china.org.cn/e-white/Freedom/index.htm.

33   Natural population growth is not a likely reason for Christian growth given that there is no evidence that Chinese Christians have more children on average than the general population, which is below replacement level.

34   As mentioned by Wickeri, "Chinese Protestant Christians," the survey conducted by the Chinese Academy of Social Sciences might be the most comprehensive survey of Protestants in China to date.

35   http://www.bibleinchina.org/news/jiaohuishigong/2011/6/116231343566054.html

36   For instance, see "The 1-Million Catholic Bibles and NT Distribution" for a story of Catholics recently receiving their first Bible: http://www.ubscp.org/1-million-catholic-bibles/.

37   Certainly some Christians have multiple copies and replace worn-out copies; therefore, the quantity of Bibles produced is only a rough indicator of demand rather than the actual numbers of Christians. See "Sold a Buffalo to Pay for Bible School" for an example of the economic situation of a Bible student and her congregation in China: http://www.ubscp.org/sold-a-buffalo/.

38   http://www.ubscp.org/about/

39   http://www.ubscp.org/80-millionth-bible/

40   http://www.ubscp.org/about/

41   Prior to that, in the 1980s, Professor Liu Peng worked in the Communist Party of China Central Committee's united-front work department, where he helped draft numerous policy papers and became intimately familiar with China's administrative system on religious affairs.

42   Ku Ma, "Rule of Law Best Help to Freedom of Faith," *China Daily*, December 3, 2009, http://www.chinadaily.com.cn/opinion/2009-12/03/content_9106147.htm.

43   Todd M. Johnson, ed., *World Christian Database* (Leiden/Boston: Brill, accessed January 2012), http://www.worldchristiandatabase.org.

44   Carol Lee Hamrin, "China's Protestants: A Mustard Seed for Moral Renewal?" *AEI Online*, May 14, 2008, http://www.aei.org/paper/27992. In the same article, Hamrin also observes that

[i]t still is rare to observe public manifestations of Christianity in China other than crosses on church buildings symbolizing the presence of a registered congregation. Most Christian groups – like the majority of all nonprofit organizations in China – are not members of the government-sanctioned associations and thus are not registered with the relevant authorities. Nevertheless, most Christian groups no longer operate in strict secrecy. They meet in rural farmyards, urban apartments, factories, restaurants, or rented space in commercial or even state facilities. Church summer camps and weekend retreats are popular, too. A key result of this quasi religious freedom is that Christianity has begun to reach into different sectors and levels of society. The church has become a significant part of China's unofficial "second society," a concept introduced by sociologist Elemér Hankiss in the context of Communist Hungary to describe the social and economic activities thriving beyond the immediate control of the state and its

official organs. Indeed, the church's influence extends far beyond the visible religious activities and memberships within the officially sanctioned churches.

45 See Paul Hattaway, "How Many Christians are There in China?" Asia Harvest, 2010, http://www.asiaharvest.org/pages/Christians%20in%20China/How%20Many%20 Christians%20are%20There%20in%20China.pdf. The study includes figures that are provided by a documented source or where Christian leaders can make an "intelligent estimate" of their numbers. The study noted that while some house church networks do not keep statistics on their congregations, other large networks do keep detailed records about numbers of fellowships and believers. Hattaway's estimates are summarized in a series of national and province tables, many of which include links to sources used to makes the estimates. For instance, see sources for the estimates of Christians in Hunan at the bottom of the web page: http://www.asiaharvest.org/pages/Christians%20in%20 China/Provinces/Henan.htm.

46 See Yang, "Red, Black, and Grey," and Yang, *Religion in China* for a discussion of heterodox groups.

47 Holy Spirit Study Centre, "Estimated Statistics for Chinese Catholic 2009," http://www. hsstudyc.org.hk/en/china/en_cinfo_china_stat09.html.

48 For instance, Beijing Archbishop Joseph Li Shan, installed in September 2007, is openly recognized by both the Chinese Patriotic Catholic Church and the Vatican.

49 Another recent survey by researchers at Shanghai's East China Normal University reported in the state-approved *China Daily* found that "31.4% of Chinese aged 16 and above, or about 300 million, are religious." The survey also estimated that some 40 million Chinese adults are Christians. See Jiao, "Religious Believers Thrice The Estimate." The dataset for this survey has not been made publically available.

50 The principal investigators were Fenggang Yang (Purdue University), Victor Yuan (CEO-Horizon Key Research, Beijing), Anna Sun (Kenyon College/Princeton University), Lu Yengfang (Peking University), Rodney Stark (Baylor University), Byron Johnson (Baylor University), Eric Liu (Baylor University), Carson Mencken (Baylor University), and Chiu Heu-Yuan (Taiwan National University).

51 The data presented here are proportionately weighted based on population size: respondents from cities are proportionately weighted to reflect the distribution of cities in the analysis; respondents from the towns are proportionately weighted to reflect the distribution of towns in the analysis; respondents from rural villages are proportionately weighted to reflect the distribution of villages in the analysis. All respondents are assigned weights based on urban, town, or rural status in order to reflect the national distribution trends, based on the 5th Basic Statistics on National Population Census of China.

52 For more details on the 2005 survey, see Grim, *Religion in China*.

53 Though not normally considered an indicator of belief in the case of grown children, it is an interesting indication of additional people who have some connection to churches. This also may have measurement implications, since these people may be active in eventually bringing into the church their younger grandchildren – a demographic group not accounted for in the survey.

54 The 7.3% includes those who expressed either Christian affiliation, belief in the existence of Jesus, or having a Christian parent. Note that some self-identified Christians did not express belief in Jesus and many did not report having a Christian parent.

55 Stark, Johnson, and Mencken, "Counting China's Christians."

56 The Pew Forum on Religion and Public Life, *The Future of the Global Muslim Population*.

57   Ibid. The report estimates that Nigeria will become a Muslim-majority country by 2030.
58   There is some debate about the total fertility rate for China as a whole. The United Nations estimates that the rate is 1.8 children per woman. Others, however, including the Pew Forum's demographic consultants in China, put the figure between 1.4 and 1.5 children per woman. The Pew Forum's consultants also estimated that Muslim women in China have an average of 0.3 more children than the general population. For more information, see National Bureau of Statistics of China and the East–West Center, "Fertility Estimates for the Provinces of China, 1975–2000," July 2007, http://www.eastwestcenter.org/fileadmin/stored/pdfs/popfertilityestimateschina.pdf. Also see Baochang Gu and Yong Cai, "Fertility Prospects in China," United Nations Expert Group Meeting on Recent and Future Trends in Fertility, Population Division, United Nations Department of Social and Economic Affairs, November 17, 2009.
59   See Donald Leslie, *The Survival of the Chinese Jews: The Jewish Community of Kaifeng* (Leiden: Brill, 1972).
60   The Pew Forum purchased selected data from InterMedia's "Survey on the Lifestyle of Chinese Residents," which was conducted April–May 2005 (N = 10,451). Of the 31 provinces (including regions and municipalities) that constitute mainland China, the InterMedia survey covered 21, making it one of the most extensive surveys of China reported to date. Cities within the provinces and municipalities were selected via simple random selection. For rural areas, the survey selected counties (which include an urban center denoted as "county city" and rural areas). InterMedia randomly selected counties from the list of "county cities." Within these selected rural areas, villages were selected via simple random selection. Respondents were asked a battery of questions in the 2005 InterMedia survey, with the stem: "Please tell me how interested you would be in hearing the topic of ___ in reports/features/programs on radio, TV, the press, and the internet? How interested are you in the topic of ___? Very interested, somewhat interested, not very interested, or not at all interested?" The fourteenth item in that series is reported here: "Are you interested in the topic of religion?" Respondents qualified for the question if they had access to media and had an interest in national and international affairs; the total who qualified was 7,744. See http://www.intermedia.org/ for more information on the survey.
61   Edward Cody, "China's Leader Puts Faith in Religious," *The Washington Post*, January 20, 2008, http://www.washingtonpost.com/wp-dyn/content/article/2008/01/19/AR2008011902465.html.

References

Aikman, David. *Jesus in Beijing: How Christianity Is Changing the Global Balance of Power*. Washington, DC: Regnery Publishing, 2003.

Association of Religion Data Archives, The. "Spiritual Life Study of Chinese Residents." 2007. http://www.thearda.com/Archive/Files/Descriptions/SPRTCHNA.asp.

Bürklin, Werner. "Facts About Number of Christians in China." *The Gospel Herald: Global Chinese Christian News Service*. December 9, 2008. http://www.gospelherald.net/article/opinion/44825/facts-about-numbers-of-christians-in-china.htm.

Chamberlain, Jonathan. *Chinese Gods: An Introduction to Chinese Folk Religion*. Hong Kong: Blacksmith Books, 2011.

Cody, Edward. "China's Leader Puts Faith in Religious." *The Washington Post*, January 20, 2008. http://www.washingtonpost.com/wp-dyn/content/article/2008/01/19/AR2008011902465.html.

Committee of 100. "Hope and Fear: Full Report of C-100's Survey on American and Chinese Attitudes Toward Each Other." 2007. http://www.survey.committee100.org/2007/files/C100SurveyFullReport.pdf.

Dean, Kenneth. "Local Communal Religion in Contemporary South-East China." *The China Quarterly* 174 (2003): 338–58.

Feng, Z. Z., and F. H. Li. *History of Chinese Folk Religion*. Taipei: Wenchin, 1994.

Fenggang, Yang. *Religion in China: Survival and Revival under Communist Rule*. Oxford: Oxford University Press, 2011.

Fenggang, Yang. "The Red, Black, and Gray Markets of Religion in China." *The Sociological Quarterly* 47 (2006): 93–122.

Fenggang, Yang, and Graeme Lang, eds. *Social Scientific Studies of Religion in China: Methodology, Theories, and Findings*. Leiden: Brill, 2011.

"Govt Supports Buddhism in Building Harmonious World." *China View*, April 13, 2006. http://news.xinhuanet.com/english/2006-04/13/content_4417439.htm.

Grim, Brian J., and Roger Finke. *The Price of Freedom Denied: Religious Persecution and Violence in the 21st Century*. New York: Cambridge University Press, 2011.

Grim, Brian J., and Pew Forum on Religion and Public Life. *Religion in China on the Eve of the 2008 Beijing Olympics*. May 2, 2008. http://pewforum.org/docs/?DocID=301.

Gu, Baochang, and Yong Cai. "Fertility Prospects in China." United Nations Expert Group Meeting on Recent and Future Trends in Fertility, Population Division, United Nations Department of Social and Economic Affairs, November 17, 2009.

Hamrin, Carol Lee. "China's Protestants: A Mustard Seed for Moral Renewal?" *AEI Online*, May 14, 2008. http://www.aei.org/paper/27992.

Hattaway, Paul. "How Many Christians are There in China?" Asia Harvest, 2010. http://www.asiaharvest.org/pages/Christians%20in%20China/How%20Many%20Christians%20are%20There%20in%20China.pdf.

Information Office of the State Council of the People's Republic of China. "Freedom of Religious Belief in China." October 1997. http://www.china.org.cn/e-white/Freedom/index.htm.

InterMedia. "Survey on the Lifestyle of Chinese Residents." Conducted April–May 2005.

International Center for Law and Religion Studies, J. Reuben Clark Law School, "Second Summer Conference on Religion and the Rule of Law – Beijing, July 2011," http://iclrs.org/index.php?blurb_id=1335.

Jiao, Wu. "Religious Believers Thrice the Estimate." *China Daily*, February 7, 2007. http://www.chinadaily.com.cn/china/2007-02/07/content_802994.htm.

Johnson, Todd M., ed. *World Christian Database*. Leiden/Boston: Brill, 2007.

Lee, Joseph Tse-Hei. "Christianity in Contemporary China: An Update." *Journal of Church and State* 49:2 (2007): 277–304.

Leslie, Donald. *The Survival of the Chinese Jews: The Jewish Community of Kaifeng*. Leiden: Brill, 1972.

Li, Y. Y. *Zong Jiao Yu Shen Hua Lun Ji* [A Treatise on Religion and Myth]. Taipei: New Century Publishing, 1998.

Ma, Ku. "Rule of Law Best Help to Freedom of Faith." *China Daily*, December 3, 2009. http://www.chinadaily.com.cn/opinion/2009-12/03/content_9106147.htm

National Bureau of Statistics of China and the East–West Center. "Fertility Estimates for the Provinces of China, 1975–2000." July 2007.

Peng, Liu. "Religion in post-Hu China: What Changes are Probable?" Paper presented at "Religion in the Social Transition of Contemporary China," Kissinger Institute on China and the United States, Washington, D.C., October 13, 2011.

Pew Forum on Religion and Public Life. *The Future of the Global Muslim Population: Projections for 2010–2030.* January 27, 2011. http://pewresearch.org/pubs/1872/muslim-population-projections-worldwide-fast-growth.

Pew Forum on Religion and Public Life. *Rising Restrictions on Religion.* August 9, 2011. http://www.pewforum.org/Government/Rising-Restrictions-on-Religion(2).aspx.

Pew Forum on Religion and Public Life. *US Religious Landscape Survey.* 2007. http://religions.pewforum.org/.

Pew Research Center. "China's Optimism: Prosperity Brings Satisfaction – and Hope." Global Attitudes Project. November 16, 2005. http://www.pewglobal.org/2005/11/16/chinas-optimism/.

Pew Research Center. "Publics of Asian Powers Hold Negative Views of One Another: China's Neighbors Worry About Its Growing Military Strength." Global Attitudes Project. September 21, 2006. http://www.pewglobal.org/2006/09/21/publics-of-asian-powers-hold-negative-views-of-one-another/.

"Q&A: China and Tibet." *BBC*, June 19, 2008. http://news.bbc.co.uk/2/hi/asia-pacific/7299221.stm.

Stark, Rodney, Byron Johnson, and Carson Mencken. "Counting China's Christians: There are as Many Christians in China as There are Members of the Communist Party." *First Things*, May 2011. http://www.firstthings.com/article/2011/05/counting-chinarsquos-christians.

United Nations. *World Population Prospects: The 2010 Revision.* New York: United Nations, 2011.

Wickeri, Janice. "Chinese Protestant Christians: Who, What, Where, Why – Findings of A Questionnaire Survey of Chinese Protestant Christian Households by the Institute of World Religions Research Group." *Amity News Service* 28 (2010): 6–12.

Wong, Wai Yip. "Defining Chinese Folk Religion: A Methodological Interpretation." *Asian Philosophy* 21 (2007).

Xi, Lian. *Redeemed by Fire: The Rise of Popular Christianity in Modern China.* New Haven, CT: Yale University Press, 2010.

Yang, C. K. *Religion in Chinese Society: A Study of Contemporary Social Functions of Religion and Some of Their Historical Factors.* Berkeley: University of California Press, 1961.

Chapter 13

Assessing Religious Populations in the Sudans

The Sudans (Sudan and South Sudan) have suffered through two catastrophic civil wars since gaining independence (as the Republic of Sudan) from the United Kingdom in 1956.[1] The first Sudanese Civil War lasted from 1955–72 and the second from 1983–2005. Ethnic and religious clashes continued between the two wars, resulting in nearly 50 years of conflict. Millions of Sudanese died as a result of the violence and millions more have been displaced, both internally and across international borders.

The two civil wars in the Sudans were among 44 religious civil wars fought around the world between 1940 and 2010 (though religion had a more decisive role in the second).[2] Ethnicity and religion play an important part in the politics and daily lives of people in the Sudans; the primarily Arabic-speaking Muslim North and African, English-speaking, animist/Christian South have been at odds for decades. In fact, one of the predominant reasons for the Second Civil War was the North's desire to force their culture, religion, and language onto the South, which was overwhelmingly resistant to such efforts;[3] this also included a push for shari'a law. The end of this war was mediated under US President George W. Bush by former US Senator John Danforth (Special Envoy for Peace in Sudan, 2001), an ordained Episcopal priest and therefore respected as a "man of God" by Christian and Muslim leaders alike.[4] Danforth acutely understood the tensions surrounding the religious reality of the situation and thus was able to work for peace by bringing Muslim and Christian leaders together, utilizing the Sudanese Inter-Religious Council.[5]

In January 2011 a referendum on independence was held in Southern Sudan, a condition established in the 2005 peace agreement that ended the Second Sudanese Civil War. Voter turnout in Southern Sudan was 99%; only about 45,000 people voted to stay united with Northern Sudan and 3.8 million voted for secession (that is, 1.17% against and 98.83% in favor).[6] South Sudan officially became the world's newest country on July 9, 2011 (leaving a much-reduced Sudan or North Sudan as

The World's Religions in Figures: An Introduction to International Religious Demography,
First Edition. Todd M. Johnson and Brian J. Grim.
© 2013 John Wiley & Sons, Ltd. Published 2013 by John Wiley & Sons, Ltd.

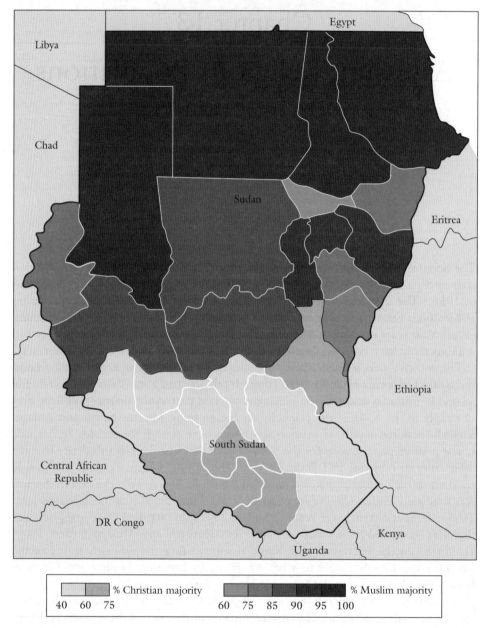

Figure 13.1 Majority religion in Sudan and South Sudan by province. Based on Todd M. Johnson and Kenneth R. Ross, eds., *Atlas of Global Christianity* (Edinburgh: Edinburgh University Press, 2009).

a second "new" country). Several key issues remain to be resolved, such as oil rights, border demarcation, and the status of Abyei.[7] Figure 13.1 illustrates the religious demography of Sudan and South Sudan, highlighting a clear North–South divide between Muslims and Christians.

Religious Demography of the North and South

David Barrett estimated the religious demographic profile of Sudan for the 1982 version of the *World Christian Encyclopedia*, which was updated for the second edition in 2001, drawing on the best sources of information available at the time. This profile was carried into the *World Christian Database* (2004) and later the *World Religion Database* (2008), and again compared with other best estimates. Unfortunately, one of the best surveys for the country – the 1990 Sudan Demographic and Health Survey – was only conducted in the North. The latest profile appears as table 13.1.

Assuming this religious profile is accurate, the question then becomes: where are these religious communities in relation to the new boundaries between North and South? This question can begin to be answered by examining the Sudans province by province. A provincial analysis utilizes information from churches (diocesan boundaries tend to match secular administrative ones) as well as a few surveys and interviews with informants in the Sudans. In addition, one can examine the religious composition of the two countries utilizing maps of the peoples of the Sudans. This helps to place the location of the largely Christian, Muslim, and ethnoreligionist peoples in one or other of the countries.[8] The results of that analysis are in table 13.2.

This analysis makes rough estimates of the placement of the four major religious categories (Christians, Muslims, non-religious [including agnostics and atheists], and ethnoreligionists). Summing the provincial results for North and South produces two new religious demographic profiles, shown in tables 13.3 and 13.4. The first thing to notice is that Sudan (North) has been at least 85% Muslim for the past 100 years. Over that same period, animists (or ethnoreligionists) have declined from almost 15% of the

Table 13.1   Religious adherents in Sudan before 2011 split.

Religion	1900 Adherents	%	1970 Adherents	%	2010 Adherents	%
Christians	2,475	0.0	1,176,000	8.0	8,289,000	19.0
Unaffiliated Christians	0	0.0	15,000	0.1	67,000	0.2
Affiliated Christians	2,475	0.0	1,161,000	7.9	8,222,000	18.9
Anglicans	30	0.0	300,000	2.0	2,074,000	4.8
Independents	0	0.0	4,000	0.0	68,000	0.2
Marginals	0	0.0	200	0.0	3,000	0.0
Orthodox	2,000	0.0	107,000	0.7	97,000	0.2
Protestants	0	0.0	60,000	0.4	1,401,000	3.2
Roman Catholics	445	0.0	690,000	4.7	6,382,000	14.7
Agnostics	0	0.0	102,000	0.7	337,000	0.8
Atheists	0	0.0	30,000	0.2	58,000	0.1
Ethnoreligionists	1,987,300	36.3	3,495,000	23.7	4,475,000	10.3
Muslims	3,480,000	63.6	9,962,000	67.5	30,385,000	69.8
Total population	**5,470,000**	**100.0**	**14,766,000**	**100.0**	**43,552,000**	**100.0**

Data source: Todd M. Johnson, ed., *World Christian Database* (Leiden/Boston: Brill, accessed May 2011). Numbers do not add up exactly because of rounding.

Table 13.2 Religion in Sudan (North) and South Sudan by province, 2011.

Province	Population	Christians	C %	Muslims	M %	Non-religious	N %	Ethnoreligionists	E %
North									
an-Nîl-al-Azraq	1,429,582	71,479	5.0	1,215,145	85.0	0	0	142,958	10.0
al-Qadârif	1,668,580	16,686	1.0	1,651,894	99.0	0	0	0	0
al-Jazîrah	3,433,116	20,599	0.6	3,412,517	99.4	0	0	0	0
Kassalâ	1,418,222	14,182	1.0	1,262,218	89.0	0	0	141,822	10.0
al-Kharṭûm	4,934,388	1,233,597	25.0	3,602,103	73.0	98,688	2.0	0	0
Shamâl Dârfûr	1,931,736	9,659	0.5	1,922,077	99.5	0	0	0	0
Shamâl Kurdufân	3,089,122	15,446	0.5	3,073,676	99.5	0	0	0	0
ash-Shamâlîyah	986,548	19,731	2.0	966,817	98.0	0	0	0	0
al-Bahr-al-Ahmar	1,376,754	1,377	0.1	1,375,377	99.9	0	0	0	0
Nahr-an-Nîl	1,263,267	1,263	0.1	1,262,004	99.9	0	0	0	0
Sinnâr	1,873,613	18,736	1.0	1,667,516	89.0	0	0	187,361	10.0
Janûb Dârfûr	3,426,499	17,132	0.5	3,238,042	94.5	0	0	171,325	5.0
Janûb Kurdufân	1,375,873	68,794	5.0	1,307,079	95.0	0	0	0	0
Gharb Dârfûr	1,231,391	2,463	0.2	1,105,789	89.8	0	0	123,139	10.0
Gharb Kurdufân	1,619,614	48,588	3.0	1,571,026	97.0	0	0	0	0
an-Nîl-al-Abyad	1,424,839	42,745	3.0	1,382,094	97.0	0	0	0	0
South									
Bahr-al-Jabal	402,778	253,750	63.0	20,139	5.0	8,056	2.0	120,833	30.0
Sharq-al-Istiwâ'îyah	286,976	172,186	60.0	14,349	5.0	0	0	100,442	35.0
Junqalî	1,479,101	739,551	50.0	73,955	5.0	0	0	665,595	45.0
al-Buhayrât	688,433	447,481	65.0	34,422	5.0	0	0	206,530	30.0
Shamâl Bahr-al-Ghazâl	1,022,389	613,433	60.0	102,239	10.0	0	0	306,717	30.0
al-Wahdah	326,350	195,810	60.0	32,635	10.0	0	0	97,905	30.0
A'âli-an-Nîl	1,433,888	932,027	65.0	71,694	5.0	0	0	430,166	30.0
Warab	1,143,819	629,100	55.0	57,191	5.0	0	0	457,528	40.0
Gharb Bahr-al-Ghazâl	1,814,496	1,088,698	60.0	181,450	10.0	0	0	544,349	30.0
Gharb-al-Istiwâ'îyah	2,110,625	1,266,375	60.0	105,531	5.0	0	0	738,719	35.0

Data source: Todd M. Johnson, ed., *World Christian Database* (Leiden/Boston: Brill, accessed May 2011). Numbers do not add up exactly because of rounding.

Table 13.3 Religion in Sudan (North), 1900–2010.

Religion	Adherents 1900	%	Adherents 1970	%	Adherents 2010	%
Christians	2,375	0.1	318,450	2.9	1,761,000	5.4
Unaffiliated Christians	0	0.0	4,600	0.0	31,000	0.1
Affiliated Christians	2,375	0.1	314,000	2.9	1,730,000	5.3
Anglicans	30	0.0	90,000	0.8	520,000	1.6
Independents	0	0.0	500	0.0	19,000	0.1
Orthodox	2,000	0.1	107,000	1.0	97,000	0.3
Protestants	0	0.0	53,000	0.5	238,000	0.7
Roman Catholics	345	0.0	62,900	0.6	1,081,000	3.3
Doubly affiliated	0	0.0	0	0.0	−225,000	−0.7
Agnostics	0	0.0	100,000	0.9	294,000	0.9
Atheists	0	0.0	30,000	0.3	50,000	0.2
Ethnoreligionists	594,400	14.9	800,000	7.3	925,000	2.8
Muslims	3,390,000	85.0	9,732,000	88.6	29,718,000	90.7
Total population	**3,987,000**	**100.0**	**10,981,000**	**100.0**	**32,754,000**	**100.0**

Data source: Todd M. Johnson, ed., *World Christian Database* (Leiden/Boston: Brill, accessed May 2011). Numbers do not add up exactly because of rounding.

Table 13.4 Religion in South Sudan, 1900–2010.

Religion	Adherents 1900	%	Adherents 1970	%	Adherents 2010	%
Christians	100	0.0	857,000	22.7	6,529,000	60.5
Unaffiliated Christians	0	0.0	10,000	0.3	36,000	0.3
Affiliated Christians	100	0.0	847,000	22.4	6,492,000	60.1
Anglicans	0	0.0	210,000	5.6	1,554,000	14.4
Independents	0	0.0	3,600	0.1	49,000	0.5
Marginals	0	0.0	200	0.0	3,000	0.0
Protestants	0	0.0	6,300	0.2	1,164,000	10.8
Roman Catholics	100	0.0	627,000	16.6	5,301,000	49.1
Doubly affiliated	0	0.0	0	0.0	−1,579,000	−14.6
Agnostics	0	0.0	2,000	0.1	43,000	0.4
Atheists	0	0.0	200	0.0	7,800	0.1
Ethnoreligionists	1,392,900	93.9	2,695,232	71.2	3,550,000	32.9
Muslims	90,000	6.1	230,000	6.1	667,000	6.2
Total population	**1,483,000**	**100.0**	**3,785,000**	**100.0**	**10,798,000**	**100.0**

Data source: Todd M. Johnson, ed., *World Christian Database* (Leiden/Boston: Brill, accessed May 2011). Numbers do not add up exactly because of rounding.

population to less than 3%, indicating a slow but steady stream of conversion to Islam. A significant Christian minority exists in the North, mostly in Khartoum, consisting mainly of Roman Catholics and Anglicans, many of them transplants from the South.

South Sudan, on the other hand, was largely animistic in 1900 but gradually became majority Christian, through the conversion of tribal groups, over the course of the century. The bulk of the growth has been since 1970, despite the civil wars and the death of as many as 2 million people in the South. Roman Catholic work in Sudan began in 1842, though much of it was focused on Khartoum. Anglicans started in 1899, also initially based in Khartoum. Each of these churches grew slowly throughout the twentieth century, picking up momentum when ethnoreligionists converted to Christianity in larger numbers after 1970.

Although the official split of South Sudan from Sudan was relatively peaceful, great possibility for tension and conflict remain. The return of refugees to an already-underdeveloped country will undoubtedly put strains on the nation's scant resources. Additionally, Dennis Blair (US Director of National Intelligence) warned the US Congress in 2010 that out of the countries he deemed most susceptible to "new outbreak[s] of mass killing … a new mass killing or genocide is most likely to occur in Southern Sudan."[9] It is clear that there is a need for a movement of ongoing inter-religious dialogue between Muslims and Christians, both within Sudan and South Sudan and between them, in order for the two communities to be able to live amicably together, despite their rough history.[10] In addition, the situation in South Sudan is arguably one of the worst health crises in the world. The new country has essentially no health-care system and is home to a combination of deadly, untreatable, and unique diseases.[11]

In examining changes in the religious demographic landscape of the Sudans over the past 100 years, it is readily apparent that both Muslims and Christians have grown at the expense of ethnoreligionists. For Christians, the work began during the nineteenth century, when European Christians, motivated by slave-trade guilt, came to Sudan but saw few converts. Christianity did not grow significantly before 1956, when missionaries were expelled at the start of the First Sudanese Civil War, which was followed by genocide and displacement. Ironically, it was under these unpromising conditions that both Roman Catholic and Anglican churches began to experience growth. The Episcopal Church of the Sudan (which includes both countries) is the fastest-growing church in the Anglican communion; this is apparent even in refugee camps scattered throughout South Sudan.[12]

The future growth or decline of religious communities in both Sudan and South Sudan is likely to depend on three factors: (1) government policies related to minority religious communities; (2) the continued conversion of ethnoreligionists to either Islam or Christianity; and (3) the emigration of religious communities to other countries. Regardless, the most likely scenarios still show the North will continue to be predominantly Muslim and the South predominantly Christian.

Notes

1   A preliminary version of this chapter was first published as Gina A. Bellofatto and Todd M. Johnson, "Southern Sudan," in *Lausanne Global Briefing: Furthering the Cape Town Commitment through Global Trends Analysis*, special report prepared for the Lausanne Biennial Leadership Meeting, June 20–24, 2011, Boston, MA. Available at http://www.lausanne.org/docs/LausanneGlobalBriefing-Boston.pdf.

2   Monica Duffy Toft, Daniel Philpott, Timothy Samuel Shah, *God's Century: Resurgent Religion and Global Politics* (New York: W. W. Norton & Company, Inc., 2011), 154, 162.

3   Francis M. Deng, "Sudan – Civil War and Genocide: Disappearing Christians of the Middle East," *Middle East Quarterly* 8:1 (Winter 2001): 13, cited in Toft, Philpott, and Shah, *God's Century*, 161.

4   Toft, Philpott, and Shah, *God's Century*, 192.

5   Ibid.

6   "South Sudan Backs Independence – Results," *BBC*, February 7, 2011, http://www.bbc.co.uk/news/world-africa-12379431.

7   As of May 22, 2011, the Sudanese Army occupied Abyei, claiming the town for North Sudan. See Jeffrey Gettleman and Josh Kron, "Warnings of All-Out War in Fight Over Sudan Town," *The New York Times*, May 22, 2011, http://www.nytimes.com/2011/05/23/world/africa/23sudan.html?_r=2&hp. This has great potential to cause continued conflict between the two countries.

8   People-group maps of the Sudans are found in Todd M. Johnson and Kenneth R. Ross, eds., *Atlas of Global Christianity* (Edinburgh: Edinburgh University Press, 2009), while the data on religious makeup of these peoples is found in Todd M. Johnson and Brian J. Grim, eds., *World Religion Database* (Leiden: Brill, 2012).

9   "Southern Sudan Votes to Split from the North," *CNN*, February 7, 2011, http://articles.cnn.com/2011-02-07/world/sudan.referendum.results_1_sudanese-president-omar-al-bashir-preliminary-results-comprehensive-peace-agreement/2?_s=PM:WORLD.

10 Grant LeMarquand, "Faith in Sudan: Recent Work on the History and Theology of Christianity in the Sudan," http://www.tsm.edu/sites/default/files/Faculty%20Writings/LeMarquand%20-%20Faith%20in%20Sudan.pdf, 2.

11 Emma Ross, "Southern Sudan has Unique Combination of Worst Diseases in the World," *Sudan Tribune*, January 28, 2004, http://www.sudantribune.com/Southern-Sudan-has-unique,1616.

12 LeMarquand, "Faith in Sudan," 1.

References

Bellofatto, Gina A., and Todd M. Johnson. "Southern Sudan." In *Lausanne Global Briefing: Furthering the Cape Town Commitment through Global Trends Analysis*. Special report prepared for the Lausanne Biennial Leadership Meeting, June 20–24, 2011, Boston, MA. Available at http://www.lausanne.org/docs/LausanneGlobalBriefing-Boston.pdf.

Deng, Francis M. "Sudan – Civil War and Genocide: Disappearing Christians of the Middle East." *Middle East Quarterly* 8:1 (Winter 2001).

Gettleman, Jeffrey, and Josh Kron. "Warnings of All-Out War in Fight Over Sudan Town." *The New York Times*, May 22, 2011. http://www.nytimes.com/2011/05/23/world/africa/23sudan.html?_r=2&hp.

Johnson, Todd M., ed. *World Christian Database*. Leiden/Boston: Brill, 2007.

Johnson, Todd M., and Brian J. Grim, eds. *World Religion Database*. Leiden/Boston: Brill, 2008.

Johnson, Todd M., and Kenneth R. Ross, eds. *Atlas of Global Christianity*. Edinburgh: Edinburgh University Press, 2009.

LeMarquand, Grant. "Faith in Sudan: Recent Work on the History and Theology of Christianity in the Sudan." http://www.tsm.edu/sites/default/files/Faculty%20Writings/LeMarquand%20-%20Faith%20in%20Sudan.pdf.

Ross, Emma. "Southern Sudan has Unique Combination of Worst Diseases in the World." *Sudan Tribune*, January 28, 2004. http://www.sudantribune.com/Southern-Sudan-has-unique,1616.

"South Sudan Backs Independence – results." *BBC*, February 7, 2011. http://www.bbc.co.uk/news/world-africa-12379431.

"Southern Sudan Votes to Split from the North." *CNN*, February 7, 2011. http://articles.cnn.com/2011-02-07/world/sudan.referendum.results_1_sudanese-president-omar-al-bashir-preliminary-results-comprehensive-peace-agreement/2?_s=PM:WORLD.

Toft, Monica Duffy, Daniel Philpott, and Timothy Samuel Shah. *God's Century: Resurgent Religion and Global Politics.* New York: W. W. Norton, 2011.

Chapter 14
Migration and Religious Diasporas

Migration has always been integral to the global human experience. Yet, there is little doubt that increased movement of peoples worldwide was a distinguishing characteristic of the twentieth century.[1] Both technology and transportation developed during this century, affording individuals more than just rudimentary knowledge about places all over the world and allowing them personal access to distant lands with relative ease.[2]

The movement of people has a direct impact on the religious composition of the lands in which they settle. In some cases, migrants bring an entirely new religion into a country or region; in other cases, they import a new form of an existing religion. Such movement creates what can be called "religionists in diaspora" or "religious diasporas."[3] Although some have had a lengthy history, some religious diasporas have grown around the world in recent decades, such as the growing Muslim populations in Western Europe. In light of current migration trends, religious diasporas will likely attract attention well into the twenty-first century. Diasporas also have an impact on religious diversity by introducing variety into the religious composition of countries and regions.

In order to attempt a quantitative study of religious diasporas, three things need to be in place: (1) a taxonomy of the world's peoples; (2) a taxonomy of the world's religions; and (3) a data collection mechanism by which information related to peoples and religions can be assessed. Taxonomies of the world's peoples and religions exist, and vast efforts are put into the collection of statistics relating to religions, languages, and peoples in today's world.[4] Utilizing the taxonomies of religions and peoples from the *World Christian Database* (*WCD*) and *World Religion Database* (*WRD*), a preliminary examination of the data shows 859 million people (12.5% of the world's population) from 327 peoples in diasporas around the world. Quantitative analysis of migration in the context of religious demography – births, deaths, conversions to, conversions from,

The World's Religions in Figures: An Introduction to International Religious Demography,
First Edition. Todd M. Johnson and Brian J. Grim.
© 2013 John Wiley & Sons, Ltd. Published 2013 by John Wiley & Sons, Ltd.

immigration, and emigration – provides a comprehensive view of changes in religious diasporas. The future of international relations will be greatly impacted by how diasporas are treated and understood by their host countries. See the end of this chapter for more information on the methodology for estimating religious diasporas.

Religious Diasporas

Nearly half (47.4%) of religionists living in diasporas are Christians; Christians also have the greatest proportion of adherents in diaspora (18.0%) of the larger world religions (Christianity, Islam, Hinduism, agnosticism, Chinese folk-religion, and Buddhism). Among smaller religions, Daoists, Jews, Spiritists, Baha'is, and Zoroastrians all have higher percentages in diasporas. One interesting observation is that Christians and Muslims make up 55.3% of the world's population, but represent 72.8% of all people in diaspora.

In 2012 the Pew Forum on Religion and Public Life released a report with similar findings for the religious makeup of migrants around the world.[5] The report states that about 214 million people (3% of the world's population) have migrated across international borders in 2010. Of these migrants, 49% were Christian and 27% Muslim (comparable to percentages in table 14.1, 47.4% for Christians and 25.4% for Muslims).

Table 14.1   Religionists in diaspora, mid-2010.

Religion	Global total	% of global pop.	# in diaspora	% in diaspora	% of all diasporas
Christians	2,260,440,000	32.8	407,548,000	18.0	47.4
Muslims	1,553,773,000	22.5	218,317,000	14.1	25.4
Hindus	948,575,000	13.8	81,429,000	8.6	9.5
Agnostics	676,944,000	9.8	57,379,000	8.5	6.7
Chinese folk-religionists	436,258,000	6.3	24,857,000	5.7	2.9
Buddhists	494,881,000	7.2	25,259,000	5.1	2.9
Ethnoreligionists	242,516,000	3.5	13,548,000	5.6	1.6
Atheists	136,652,000	2.0	10,060,000	7.4	1.2
New Religionists	63,004,000	0.9	7,431,000	11.8	0.9
Sikhs	23,927,000	0.3	1,642,000	6.9	0.2
Jews	14,761,000	0.2	3,249,000	22.0	0.4
Spiritists	13,700,000	0.2	2,749,000	20.1	0.3
Daoists	8,429,000	0.1	2,946,000	35.0	0.3
Baha'is	7,306,000	0.1	1,405,000	19.2	0.2
Confucianists	6,449,000	0.1	933,000	14.5	0.1
Jains	5,316,000	0.1	198,000	3.7	0.0
Shintoists	2,761,000	0.0	101,000	3.7	0.0
Zoroastrians	197,000	0.0	37,900	19.2	0.0
Global total	**6,895,889,000**	**100.0**	**859,088,900**	**12.5**	**100.0**

Data source: Todd M. Johnson and Brian J. Grim, eds., *World Religion Database* (Leiden/Boston: Brill, accessed February 2012).

Host and sending countries

Table 14.2 examines religious diasporas by the country in which they reside. The United States and India top the list, hosting nearly half of all religious diasporas worldwide (45.6%). Likewise, the Pew study cited the United States as the top destination for all migrants, and especially Christians, Buddhists, agnostics, and atheists.

Table 14.3 examines the countries that send out the largest diaspora communities. Apart from Mexico (which was cited as the top country of origin in the Pew report) and Argentina (and the Mestizo problem mentioned in note 20 of this chapter), Bangladesh emerges as a leading sending country of both Hindus (61 million) and Muslims (25 million). These are Bengalis found in over 20 countries around the world, though the vast majority are found just across the border in India.

Peoples in diaspora

Table 14.4 ranks the ethnolinguistic peoples in diaspora by the number of countries in which they are found. The top five peoples include several that reflect colonial and economic realities: English, French, USA White (Anglo-Americans), and German. Han Chinese (Mandarin) and Syrian-Arabian Arab (ranked 4 and 6, respectively), are largely spread out as foreign workers and refugees.

Table 14.5 ranks ethnolinguistic peoples in diaspora by the percentage in diaspora. This ranking reveals a different phenomenon, with 351,000 Assyrian Christians spread over 21 countries (80% in diaspora) and 2.9 million Kuwaiti Arabs (Muslims) in 10 countries (72% in diaspora).

Religionists in diaspora

Table 14.6 presents the largest ethnolinguistic diasporas for each of the four largest religious communities: Christians, Muslims, Hindus, and Buddhists. One can quickly see the origins of peoples representing the largest religious diasporas – Christians (Latin Americans and Europeans); Muslims (Asians and Africans); Hindus (South Asians) and Buddhists (East Asians). This is not surprising: the largest diaspora peoples come from the "traditional homelands" of each religion. The Pew study highlighted Jews (not listed in table 14.6) as having the highest level of international migration, with 25% of all Jews worldwide as migrants (currently living in another country than their birth country). This is significant for a religion that, on a global scale, is rather small (14 million adherents). Not surprisingly, the majority of Jewish migrants originate from Europe (56%, most notably Russia) and migrate primarily to the Middle East (76%, almost entirely to Israel).

Migration as One Component of Religious Change

As outlined in detail in chapter 9, the dynamics of change in religious communities over time can be limited to three sets of empirical population data: (1) births minus deaths; (2) converts to minus converts from; and (3) immigrants minus emigrants.

Table 14.2 Top 10 host countries of diasporas ranked by diaspora population, mid-2010.

Rank	Country	Pop 2010	Diaspora #	Diaspora %	Christians	Muslims	Hindus	Buddhists
1	United States	310,383,948	118,070,000	38.0	96,272,000	2,487,000	1,426,000	3,775,000
2	India	1,224,614,327	93,047,000	7.6	744,000	23,607,000	66,170,000	377,000
3	Colombia	46,294,841	34,203,000	73.9	33,048,000	22,800	9,300	1,800
4	Venezuela	28,979,857	25,608,000	88.4	24,123,000	95,300	0	35,400
5	North Korea*	24,346,229	24,298,000	99.8	388,000	0	0	362,000
6	Taiwan	23,216,236	22,780,000	98.1	1,055,000	80,700	0	6,122,000
7	Mexico	113,423,047	19,885,000	17.5	18,395,000	99,400	3,400	0
8	Pakistan	173,593,383	16,947,000	9.8	126,000	16,200,000	499,000	6,200
9	Chile	17,113,688	15,610,000	91.2	13,958,000	15,200	0	5,600
10	Afghanistan	31,411,743	15,539,000	49.5	29,500	15,468,000	10,700	0

*North Korea is considered a host country because the home country of Koreans was designated as South Korea. See additional methodological notes at the end of this chapter.

Data source: Todd M. Johnson and Brian J. Grim, eds., World Religion Database (Leiden/Boston: Brill, accessed February 2012).

Table 14.3 Top 10 "sending" countries, ranked by size of diaspora outside of host country, mid-2010.

Rank	Source country	Diaspora	Christians	Muslims	Hindus	Buddhists
1	Mexico	137,751,000	132,959,000	2,100	6,500	0
2	Bangladesh	87,873,000	446,000	24,728,000	60,785,000	0
3	Argentina	68,156,000	60,574,000	0	2,800	0
4	China	60,580,000	7,095,000	571,000	0	15,171,000
5	India	41,319,000	2,716,000	22,099,000	14,289,000	5
6	South Korea	30,453,000	3,245,000	310	0	1,867,000
7	Russia	24,063,000	15,646,000	2,618,000	0	0
8	Pakistan	22,055,000	52,200	19,026,000	2,909,000	0
9	United States	18,267,000	14,396,000	216,000	0	0
10	Syria	15,951,000	6,114,000	9,155,000	0	0

Data source: Todd M. Johnson and Brian J. Grim, eds., World Religion Database (Leiden/Boston: Brill, accessed February 2012).

Table 14.4 Top 10 peoples, ranked by number of countries in diaspora, mid-2010.

Rank	People name	Total population 2010	# of countries	Diaspora #	% in diaspora	Majority religion
1	English	52,486,000	171	8,304,000	15.82	Christians
2	French	32,281,000	138	6,333,000	19.62	Christians
3	USA White	121,096,000	118	3,310,000	2.73	Christians
4	Han Chinese (Mandarin)	857,342,000	116	12,293,000	1.43	Agnostics
5	German	65,125,000	90	14,504,000	22.27	Christians
6	Syrian-Arabian Arab	31,701,000	86	15,874,000	50.07	Muslims
7	Greek	13,721,000	85	4,308,000	31.40	Christians
8	Russian	133,886,000	75	21,064,000	15.73	Christians
9	Hindi	141,470,000	69	4,944,000	3.49	Hindus
10	Italian	33,415,000	64	13,039,000	39.02	Christians

Data source: Todd M. Johnson and Brian J. Grim, eds., *World Religion Database* (Leiden/Boston: Brill, accessed February 2012).

Table 14.5 Top 10 peoples, ranked by percentage in diaspora, mid-2010.

Rank	People name	Total population 2010	# of countries	Diaspora #	% in diaspora	Majority religion
1	Assyrian (Aisor, Chaldean)	439,000	21	351,000	79.9	Christians
2	Low German	543,000	11	427,000	78.6	Christians
3	Colored (Eurasian)	506,000	9	369,000	72.9	Christians
4	Syrian Aramaic (Eastern)	105,000	8	76,500	72.8	Christians
5	Kuwaiti Arab	4,034,000	10	2,906,000	72.0	Muslims
6	Euronesian (English)	65,800	9	47,300	71.9	Christians
7	Latin American Black	10,185,000	11	7,287,000	71.6	Christians
8	Jewish (Yiddish)	1,938,000	25	1,380,000	71.2	Jews
9	Hungarian Gypsy	1,710,000	16	1,191,000	69.7	Christians
10	Latin American White	97,528,000	37	67,598,000	69.3	Christians

Data source: Todd M. Johnson and Brian J. Grim, eds., *World Religion Database* (Leiden/Boston: Brill, accessed February 2012).

Table 14.6 Top 10 diaspora peoples by religion, mid-2010.

	Christians		Muslims		Hindus		Buddhists
People name	# in diaspora	People name	# in diaspora	People name	# in diaspora	People name	# in diaspora
Latin American Mestizo	132,959,000	Bengali	24,728,000	Bengali	60,785,000	Han Chinese (Min Nan)	6,658,000
Latin American White	60,326,000	Urdu	16,176,000	Tamil	5,140,000	Han Chinese (Yue)	3,792,000
Russian	15,395,000	Eastern Pathan	14,223,000	Hindi	3,493,000	Han Chinese (Mandarin)	3,308,000
German	11,496,000	Malay (Melaju, Melayu)	9,238,000	Nepalese	3,209,000	Japanese	2,036,000
Italian	10,826,000	Syrian-Arabian Arab	9,155,000	Sindhi	2,909,000	Vietnamese	1,962,000
Latin American Mulatto	9,496,000	Hausa	8,544,000	Bhojpuri Bihari	1,658,000	Korean	1,867,000
English	6,973,000	Tajik	7,339,000	Gujarati	1,561,000	Central Khmer	1,400,000
Latin American Black	6,336,000	Somali	7,302,000	Eastern Punjabi	803,000	Burmese	647,000
Filipino	6,335,000	Northern Kurd	6,799,000	Telugu	596,000	Central Thai	606,000
Syrian-Arabian Arab	6,040,000	Palestinian Arab	6,643,000	Malayali	504,000	Sinhalese	598,000

Data source: Todd M. Johnson and Brian J. Grim, eds., *World Religion Database* (Leiden/Boston: Brill, accessed February 2012).

Figure 14.1   Calculating net religious change. Based on Todd M. Johnson and Kenneth R. Ross, eds., *Atlas of Global Christianity* (Edinburgh: Edinburgh University Press, 2009).

These factors are explained in great detail in chapter 9 of this volume. Figure 14.1 shows how the six factors mentioned here can be expressed as a formula.

Births minus deaths

The primary mechanism of religious change globally is births minus deaths. Children are normally considered to have the religion of their parents (this is the law in Norway, for example, and many other countries). This means that a religious population has a close statistical relationship to the number of births into the community and the number of deaths out of it. Many religious communities around the world, in fact, experience little else in the dynamics of their growth or decline.

Converts to minus converts from

Nonetheless, individuals (or even whole villages or communities) often change allegiance from one religion to another (or to no religion at all). In the twentieth century, this change has been most pronounced in two general areas: (1) Tribal religionists (ethnoreligionists) have converted in large numbers to Christianity, Islam, Hinduism, and Buddhism; and (2) Christians in the Western world have left Christianity to become non-religious (agnostics) or atheists in large numbers. Both of these trends, however, had slowed considerably by the dawn of the twenty-first century.

Immigrants minus emigrants

It is equally important to consider the movement of people across national borders. During the colonial era in the nineteenth century, small groups of Europeans settled in Africa, Asia, and the Americas. In the late twentieth century, natives from these regions immigrated to the Western world. As a result, in the United States religions such as Islam, Hinduism, and Buddhism grew faster than either Christianity or the unaffiliated. This growth has been almost entirely due to the immigration of non-Christian Asians.[6] In Europe, massive immigration of Muslims has not only been transforming the spiritual landscape but has now become a major political issue, notably in France, Germany, Austria, and Italy, as well as in plans for European Union expansion.[7] In the Central Asian countries of the former Soviet Union, Christianity has declined significantly every year since 1990 due to the emigration of Russians, Germans, and Ukrainians.

The reasons underlying immigration and emigration include economic factors (such as seeking employment), social factors (desire for a better quality of life or family considerations), refugee status (escaping political or religious persecution), and environmental factors (such as natural disasters). These may be described in terms of push and pull factors: push factors are the reasons individuals or groups leave (are pushed out of) their home countries, including denial of needs or rights, while pull factors are the reasons people settle in (are pulled to) particular areas. Pull factors may include better economic opportunities, a preferred climate, lower crime rates, or general stability.[8] Thus, diasporas comprise both individuals who have chosen to leave and those who were forced to migrate. Such delineations, however, are not always clear-cut. A Syrian Orthodox Christian in the Middle East who loses his job, cannot find work in his Muslim-majority community, and feels there is no hope at home might migrate elsewhere in search of employment. Depending on the perspective, he could be considered either a political or an economic migrant.[9]

In the twenty-first century, migration trends are already altering the religious compositions of individual countries. By 2100 it might be difficult to find a country in which 90% or more of the population belong to any single world religion.

Civility

With the expected increase in the number of religious diasporas around the world, relations between religious majorities and minorities take on greater importance.[10] There are various models of collaboration among religionists that might address these challenges.[11] One example is found in medieval Spain. It was there that a Roman Catholic nun in the tenth century found herself overwhelmed with the surprisingly positive interactions among Christians, Muslims, and Jews in Cordoba.[12] She described Cordoba to her readers as "the ornament of the world."

A first step for cultivating better relationships and understanding[13] is more education on world religions. A 2010 survey by the Pew Forum on Religion and Public Life found that, on average, Americans correctly answered 16 out of 32 questions about several religious traditions. Atheists/agnostics, Jews, and Mormons scored the highest on the quiz, while the country's larger religious traditions – Evangelical Protestants, mainline Protestants, and Roman Catholics – scored, in some cases, significantly lower.[14] This implies that host countries have a significant task ahead of them in socially adjusting to the challenges that diasporas and migrant communities introduce.

Additional Methodological Notes

To enumerate religious diasporas, two taxonomies are needed: one for religions and one for peoples. The taxonomy for religions discussed throughout this book includes 18 standard categories for religion.[15] These categories can be applied directly to any people in the world. For example, Mandarin-speaking Han Chinese in China, numbering 841 million in 2010, are estimated to be 49% non-religious (agnostic and atheist), 22% Chinese folk-religionist, 18% Buddhist, and 10% Christian.[16]

A "peoples" taxonomy must take into account both ethnicity and language. The approach taken in "Ethnosphere" in Part 8 of the *World Christian Encyclopedia* was to match 432 ethnic codes with 13,500 different language codes to produce 12,600 distinct ethnolinguistic peoples.[17] Not all combinations of ethnicity and language are possible, but nevertheless every person in the world can be categorized as belonging to a (mutually exclusive) ethnolinguistic people. For example, there are ethnic Kazaks who speak Kazak as their mother tongue and ethnic Kazaks who speak Russian as their mother tongue. These are two separate ethnolinguistic peoples.

The next step was to determine the religious breakdown of the these 12,600 ethnolinguistic peoples. This work was begun in the 1970s in Africa, where many Christian churches reported the ethnic breakdown of their congregations. Utilizing data gathered by religions and in government censuses, estimates of religious affiliation for all peoples was completed in the mid-1990s and published in the *World Christian Encyclopedia*, second edition. These data continue to be updated and published in the *WCD* and *WRD*. The 2009 *Atlas of Global Christianity* also examined the more populous world religions in terms of their peoples and languages.[18]

In order to locate religious diasporas three steps were taken. First, the taxonomy of peoples developed for the *World Christian Encyclopedia* (now online at the *WCD* and *WRD*) was sorted by ethnic and linguistic codes in sequence. Second, a filter was added so that only unique codes that were present in more than three countries were counted.[19] Third, the largest population was designated as being in the home country and all others as diasporas. The results of this method produced the summary statistics found in table 14.1 – the religious affiliation of 859 million people living in diasporas (327 peoples), representing 12.5% of the global population. A more refined method would likely uncover more peoples, but the total number in diaspora would not likely rise substantially (this method captures the largest groupings).[20]

Notes

1   A preliminary version of this chapter was first published as Todd M. Johnson and Gina A. Bellofatto, "Immigration, Religious Diasporas, and Religious Diversity: A Global Survey," *Mission Studies* 29 (2012): 1–20, as well as "Immigration, Religious Diasporas, and Religious Diversity: A Global Survey," in *Global Diasporas and Mission*, ed. Chandler Im and Amos Yong (Regnum: forthcoming).

2   The United Nations estimates that the number of international migrants is now over 200 million, having doubled in the past 25 years, with 25 million added in the first five years of the twenty-first century. See United Nations, "Report to the Secretary-General, International Migration and Development, UN General Assembly, 60th Session," *UN Doc. A/60/871*, May 18, 2006 (New York: United Nations).

3   Robin Cohen, *Global Diasporas: An Introduction* (Seattle: University of Washington Press, 1997), 26. Cohen identifies nine common features of a diaspora which have particular relevance to this study on religious diasporas: (1) Dispersal from an original homeland, often traumatically, to two or more foreign regions; (2) alternatively, the expansion from a homeland in search of work, in pursuit of trade or to further colonial ambitions; (3) a collective memory and myth about the homeland, including its location, history, and achievements; (4) an idealization of the putative ancestral home and a collective commitment to its

maintenance, restoration, safety, and prosperity, even to its creation; (5) the development of a return movement that gains collective approbation; (6) a strong ethnic group consciousness sustained over a long time and based on a sense of distinctiveness, a common history, and the belief in a common fate; (7) a troubled relationship with host societies, suggesting a lack of acceptance at the least or the possibility that another calamity might befall the group; (8) a sense of empathy and solidarity with co-ethnic members in other countries of settlement; and (9) the possibility of a distinctive creative, enriching life in host countries with a tolerance for pluralism.

4   These data are updated quarterly in Todd M. Johnson, ed., *World Christian Database* (Leiden/Boston: Brill, 2007) and Todd M. Johnson and Brian J. Grim, eds., *World Religion Database* (Leiden/Boston: Brill, 2008).

5   Pew Forum on Religion and Public Life, *Faith on the Move: The Religious Affiliation of International Migrants*, March 8, 2012, http://pewresearch.org/pubs/2214/religion-religious-migrants-christians-muslims-jews.

6   In the case of Islam, conversions among African Americans to Islam also caused increased presence.

7   Turkey's desire for European Union membership has brought out the interesting contrast of a Union that is mainly "Christian" with one that could extend to countries not predominantly Christian.

8   Darrell Jackson and Alessia Passarelli, *Mapping Migration: Mapping Churches' Responses: Europe Study* (Brussels: Churches' Commission for Migrants in Europe, 2008), 5–6.

9   Ibid., 9.

10 Daniel C. Dennett's *Breaking the Spell: Religion as a Natural Phenomenon* (New York: Penguin Group, 2006) is one of many recent attempts to tame religion with Enlightenment assumptions.

11 Nancey Murphy's *Beyond Liberalism and Fundamentalism: How Modern and Postmodern Philosophy Set the Theological Agenda* (New York: Trinity Press International, 2007) offers clear evidence that Enlightenment foundationalism has a greatly diminished role to play in the future of humanity.

12 See María Rosa Menocal, *The Ornament of the World: How Muslims, Jews, and Christians Created a Culture of Tolerance in Medieval Spain* (New York: Little, Brown and Company, 2002).

13 For more on Christian civility, see Richard J. Mouw, *Uncommon Decency: Christian Civility in an Uncivil World* (Downers Grove, IL: InterVarsity Press, 2010).

14 Pew Forum on Religion and Public Life, "US Religious Knowledge Survey," September 28, 2010, http://pewresearch.org/pubs/1745/religious-knowledge-in-america-survey-atheists-agnostics-score-highest.

15 These 18 categories are agnostics, atheists, Baha'is, Buddhists, Chinese folk-religionists, Christians, Confucianists, Daoists, ethnoreligionists, Hindus, Jains, Jews, Muslims, New Religionists, Shintoists, Sikhs, Spiritists, and Zoroastrians.

16 This is by far the largest concentration of non-religious and atheists in the world. On the other hand, all major religious traditions are experiencing resurgence in China.

17 The construction of the taxonomy is explained in more detail in part 18, "Ethnolinguistics," in David B. Barrett, Todd M. Johnson, Christopher Guidry, and Peter Crossing, *World Christian Trends, AD 30–AD 2200: Interpreting the Annual Christian Megacensus* (Pasadena: William Carey Library, 2003). The ethnic or culture codes are outlined in Table 8-1 in *World Christian Encyclopedia* (*WCE*), vol. 2, *The World by Segments: Religions, Peoples, Languages, Cities, Topics* (Oxford: Oxford University Press, 2001). The languages are listed in *WCE*, Part 9 "Linguametrics" and are derived from David Dalby, David

18 Barrett, and Michael Mann, *The Linguasphere Register of the World's Languages and Speech Communities*, vol. 2 (Carmarthenshire, Wales: Linguasphere Press, 1999). All are available online at www.worldchristiandatabase.org.

18 See Todd M. Johnson and Kenneth R. Ross, eds., *Atlas of Global Christianity* (Edinburgh: Edinburgh University Press, 2009), part IV.

19 Practically speaking, our definition of "diaspora" includes both individuals who have moved overseas permanently (migrants) and individuals who are working overseas on a more temporary basis (expatriate residents). Diasporas can be one or the other of these. For example, Palestinians or Chinese are largely migrants whereas Americans or British tend to be expatriate residents.

20 One clear limitation of this method is how it treats Mestizos in Latin America. Because ethnolinguistic codes are not differentiated by dialect, Mestizos all across Latin America are treated as one people, even though they are clearly distinct from country to country. Because Mexico has the largest number of Mestizos, it is treated as the home country and all other Mestizos are considered diasporas. To fix this anomaly, one would have to utilize dialect codes to differentiate peoples. Unfortunately, this would artificially create new peoples where there are no significant differences.

References

Barrett, David B., Todd M. Johnson, Christopher Guidry, and Peter Crossing. *World Christian Trends, AD 30–AD 2200: Interpreting the Annual Christian Megacensus*. Pasadena, CA: William Carey Library Publication, 2003.

Cohen, Robin. *Global Diasporas: An Introduction*. Seattle: University of Washington Press, 1997.

Dalby, David, David Barrett, and Michael Mann. *The Linguasphere Register of the World's Languages and Speech Communities*. 2 vols. Carmarthenshire, Wales: Linguasphere Press, 1999.

Dennett, Daniel C. *Breaking the Spell: Religion as a Natural Phenomenon*. New York: Penguin Group, 2006.

Jackson, Darrell, and Alessia Passarelli. *Mapping Migration: Mapping Churches' Responses: Europe Study*. Brussels: Churches' Commission for Migrants in Europe, 2008.

Johnson, Todd M., ed. *World Christian Database*. Leiden/Boston: Brill, 2007.

Johnson, Todd M., and Gina A. Bellofatto. "Immigration, Religious Diasporas, and Religious Diversity: A Global Survey." *Mission Studies* 29 (2012): 1–20.

Johnson, Todd M., and Gina A. Bellofatto. "Immigration, Religious Diasporas, and Religious Diversity: A Global Survey." In *Global Diasporas and Mission*, edited by Chandler Im and Amos Yong (Regnum: forthcoming).

Johnson, Todd M., and Brian J. Grim, eds. *World Religion Database*. Leiden/Boston: Brill, 2008.

Johnson, Todd M., and Kenneth R. Ross, eds. *Atlas of Global Christianity*. Edinburgh: Edinburgh University Press, 2009.

Menocal, María Rosa. *The Ornament of the World: How Muslims, Jews, and Christians Created a Culture of Tolerance in Medieval Spain*. New York: Little, Brown and Company, 2002.

Mouw, Richard J. *Uncommon Decency: Christian Civility in an Uncivil World*. Downers Grove, IL: InterVarsity Press, 2010.

Murphy, Nancey. *Beyond Liberalism and Fundamentalism: How Modern and Postmodern Philosophy Set the Theological Agenda*. New York: Trinity Press International, 2007.

Pew Forum on Religion and Public Life. *Faith on the Move: The Religious Affiliation of International Migrants.* March 8, 2012. http://pewresearch.org/pubs/2214/religion-religious-migrants-christians-muslims-jews.

Pew Forum on Religion and Public Life. *US Religious Knowledge Survey.* September 28, 2010. http://pewresearch.org/pubs/1745/religious-knowledge-in-america-survey-atheists-agnostics-score-highest.

United Nations. "Report to the Secretary-General, International Migration and Development, UN General Assembly, 60th Session." *UN Doc. A/60/871.* May 18, 2006. New York: United Nations.

Conclusion

International religious demography is both expanding and maturing as an academic field of study. The previous chapters provide ample evidence that the discipline of counting religionists is at a critical stage in which more investment will yield rich dividends. More data are becoming available through censuses, polls, religious communities, and a host of other sources. These data are collated and analyzed by groups of scholars and researchers holding diverse viewpoints and using a variety of approaches. Indeed, reports on the growth and decline of religious communities around the world are gaining the attention of an ever-widening group of scholars, policy makers, analysts, government officials, and others. These are among numerous aspects contributing to the widening interest in international religious demography.

International religious demographic data are becoming increasingly available to scholars and the wider public as research teams publish their analyses. Throughout this book we have illustrated that these global analyses currently come from two major sources. First, the *World Religion Database* (WRD, www.worldreligiondatabase.org), edited by the authors of this book and published by Brill, presents data through a number of filters in an online, interactive format. Data in the *WRD* are also increasingly linked directly to source material, including census and poll data. Second, the Pew Forum on Religion and Public Life (www.pewforum.org), where Brian Grim works as Director of Cross-National Data, continues to examine religious trends worldwide, posting online a series of quantitative reports on Islam, Christianity, and other religions. In addition, demographic analyses of religion are increasingly done by professional research centers – for example, the Age and Cohort Change Project of the International Institute for Applied Systems Analysis (IIASA; www.iiasa.ac.at), which collaborates with the *WRD* and the Pew Forum. An increasing number of regional and national studies, many cited in previous chapters, also add to the amount of data available on religion around the world.

The World's Religions in Figures: An Introduction to International Religious Demography,
First Edition. Todd M. Johnson and Brian J. Grim.
© 2013 John Wiley & Sons, Ltd. Published 2013 by John Wiley & Sons, Ltd.

Nonetheless, the use of the most sophisticated statistical tools on a global scale is still limited by the paucity of data, especially on smaller religions. For instance, relatively little is known about fertility patterns among Daoists, the age structure of Baha'is, or the life expectancy of Jains. The most complete data sets are those that relate to homogeneous nation states (for example, where virtually everyone in a particular country belongs to the same religion). In these cases, national statistics apply directly to religious demography. Many nation states are becoming increasingly diverse in their religious composition, however, meaning that the demographics of minority religionists must be intentionally collected, analyzed, and reported. This is one of the greatest challenges facing religious demography. Indeed, a four-year study by the Pew Forum with assistance from demographers from IIASA (the *Global Religious Landscape* report; December 2012) was able to gather enough data to compare and contrast only eight religious groups.

The rise of the Internet and the resulting increase in data accessibility has both pros and cons for the study of international religious demography. It is beneficial because more information than ever before is available to the average user. If one wants to know how many Muslims are in France, the answer appears to be only a few keystrokes away. Unfortunately, simple queries like this, more often than not, produce a dizzying array of contradictory answers. There is apparently no simple way to judge between the accuracy of differing statistics.

The opportunities for further research in international religious demography are numerous. They range from the need for focused studies on minority religions to more robust examinations of cross-national data on larger religions. Advances made in data collection have yielded several pressing topics for future research. First, how will the global trend toward lower overall fertility affect the religious composition of nations and communities? For instance, as birthrates have plummeted in Western Europe, demand for laborers to fill the gaps has led in part to the immigration of large numbers of Muslims. Though fertility levels are dropping in most Muslim-majority countries, the effects of past high fertility have created youth bulges that potentially will result in Muslim youth continuing to look outside their home countries for employment. Will fertility levels among new Muslim immigrants quickly follow the generally lower fertility levels of their newfound homelands (the usual scenario), or will the new immigrants persist in having family sizes similar to those in their original homelands? More generally, will new Muslim immigrants successfully integrate with largely non-Muslim societies? Of course, not only Muslims immigrate to Western Europe – Hindus, Christians, and others of all faiths do so as well. How might immigrants to the more secularized lands of Europe from countries with high degrees of religiosity change the religious character of Europe?

Second, will the religious future of the world be determined by Asia and sub-Saharan Africa, where, combined, seven in 10 people live today? Global figures for all major religions – and those for agnostics and atheists – are all greatly impacted by trends in fertility, mortality, and conversion in countries such as China, India, Nigeria, and Indonesia.

Third, how can better religious demographic measures be developed – both for religions other than Christianity in general, and for difficult-to-estimate factors for all religions (such as conversion rates)? Particular gaps exist in estimating the sizes of subgroups of religions other than Christianity. Even basic religious traditions, such as

Sunni and Shi'a within Islam, are not estimated using census or survey data but rather primarily ethnographic and historical analyses. On the one hand, future surveys could develop better and more-layered religious affiliation questions. On the other hand, interdisciplinary work is needed, because, for instance, estimating how many people are associated with the four major schools of Islamic jurisprudence would require the cooperation of not only specialists in Islam but also historians, anthropologists, and ethnographers. Future work could also develop better estimations of how many people exit religious communities, convert to different religions, and revert to previous religious affiliations at later stages of life.

Fourth, does religious diversity lead to less social solidarity and more conflict, or to the opposite? To answer this, demographers need to better measure religious pluralities in ways that are concrete and sufficiently nuanced so that such a proposition can be tested. Some initial empirical tests have been done, but much more work remains before the full picture emerges of how religious diversity and different configurations of religious plurality relate to social solidarity and conflict.

Going forward, it is prudent to remember that the limits of traditional demographic projection methodologies are real. For instance, had traditional demographic analysis focusing on fertility, age structure, and life expectancy been done to project the religious composition of sub-Saharan Africa in the twentieth century, it never would have predicted the dramatic growth of Christianity from less than 10% in 1900 to approximately 60% today, because most of the growth was due to unanticipated conversion. Likewise, global migration patterns of today would have been difficult to predict during the time of the Cold War (and more broadly, between the 1960s and 1980s). Given such limits, in what way can future projections build in various scenarios that take into account religion-specific processes, as well as alternative scenarios of the future that consider economic and environmental impacts?

The most important challenge for international religious demography remains the development of better measures and analyses of both the present and the past, which form the basis of any future projections. Indeed, working on better measures means that many of the hotly debated issues of this generation of social scientists, such as the relationship between modernization and secularization, can be better answered. In addition, more resources need to be directed toward the study of religious data in Africa, Asia, and Latin America.

Finally, the application of religious demographic data to other disciplines is just beginning. While awareness of and interest in the significance of religion in sociology, international relations, and foreign policy seem to be growing (chapter 6), there is still a need for anthropologists, historians, and others to utilize quantitative analyses of religion. This will perhaps come about through increasing contact between scholars in previously isolated disciplines.

Despite predictions of its demise during the twentieth century, religion continues to play a significant role in human affairs. How we understand its quantitative dimensions and how these are applied to a myriad of interactions between human beings remains to be seen. What is certain is that religious dynamics – both positive and negative – will continue to be a central element in human society for years to come. International religious demography has much to offer in understanding religion's continuing impact in the world.

Appendix: World Religions by Country

The following table provides a quick-reference, country-by-country listing for many of the variables that appear in this volume. Except where noted, these statistics are found in the *World Religion Database* and are grouped by major subject areas. All figures are mid-2010. At the end of the list of countries we have included totals for the six continents and a global total. Chinese folk-religionists are listed as "Chinese FR." Exact numbers in smaller countries are unrounded to add up to the country population but do not represent precise estimates. Some country names have been abbreviated to fit in the alloted space. A fuller version of the table is also available on www.wiley.com/go/johnsongrim.

The headings are as follows (with short explanations where needed):

Geographic

Country, name of country in English
Population 2010, United Nations estimate, mid-2010

Religious adherents (chapters 1–2)

Agnostics
Agnostic %
Atheists
Atheist %
Baha'is
Baha'i %
Buddhists
Buddhist %
Chinese folk-religionists
Chinese folk-religionist %
Christians
Christian %

Confucianists
Confucianist %
Daoists
Daoist %
Ethnoreligionists
Ethnoreligionist %
Hindus
Hindu %
Jains
Jain %
Jews
Jew %

Muslims
Muslim %
New Religionists
New Religionist %
Shintoists
Shintoist %
Sikhs
Sikh %
Spiritists
Spiritist %
Zoroastrians
Zoroastrian %

The World's Religions in Figures: An Introduction to International Religious Demography,
First Edition. Todd M. Johnson and Brian J. Grim.
© 2013 John Wiley & Sons, Ltd. Published 2013 by John Wiley & Sons, Ltd.

Appendix: World Religions by Country

Country	Population 2010	Agnostics		Atheists		Baha'is		Buddhists		Chinese FR		Christians		Confucianists		Da
Afghanistan	31,412,000	6,900	0.0	710	0.0	16,500	0.1	6,300	0.0	0	0.0	32,400	0.1	0	0.0	0
Albania	3,204,000	160,000	5.0	16,800	0.5	7,100	0.2	0	0.0	0	0.0	1,011,000	31.6	0	0.0	0
Algeria	35,468,000	443,000	1.2	6,000	0.0	3,300	0.0	5,300	0.0	11,400	0.0	61,800	0.2	0	0.0	0
Am Samoa	68,400	480	0.7	7	0.0	200	0.3	200	0.3	250	0.4	67,300	98.3	0	0.0	0
Andorra	84,900	4,600	5.4	310	0.4	100	0.1	0	0.0	0	0.0	78,300	92.2	0	0.0	0
Angola	19,082,000	152,000	0.8	37,400	0.2	2,100	0.0	1,600	0.0	160	0.0	17,799,000	93.3	0	0.0	0
Anguilla	15,400	460	3.0	48	0.3	160	1.0	0	0.0	0	0.0	14,000	91.1	0	0.0	0
Antigua	88,700	1,400	1.6	110	0.1	860	1.0	0	0.0	0	0.0	82,500	93.0	0	0.0	0
Argentina	40,412,000	2,021,000	5.0	344,000	0.9	13,900	0.0	21,600	0.1	440	0.0	36,430,000	90.1	480	0.0	0
Armenia	3,092,000	117,000	3.8	31,700	1.0	1,200	0.0	310	0.0	0	0.0	2,891,000	93.5	0	0.0	0
Aruba	107,000	1,800	1.7	110	0.1	16	0.0	140	0.1	170	0.2	104,000	96.4	0	0.0	0
Australia	22,268,000	4,098,000	18.4	413,000	1.9	19,400	0.1	467,000	2.1	75,000	0.3	16,204,000	72.8	49,000	0.2	4,600
Austria	8,394,000	1,274,000	15.2	145,000	1.7	1,900	0.0	10,800	0.1	3,100	0.0	6,510,000	77.6	1,500	0.0	0
Azerbaijan	9,188,000	315,000	3.4	12,800	0.1	1,700	0.0	0	0.0	0	0.0	304,000	3.3	0	0.0	0
Bahamas	343,000	14,000	4.1	530	0.2	1,400	0.4	0	0.0	82	0.0	320,000	93.2	0	0.0	0
Bahrain	1,262,000	4,800	0.4	440	0.0	2,800	0.2	2,800	0.2	0	0.0	94,300	7.5	0	0.0	0
Bangladesh	148,692,000	106,000	0.1	11,500	0.0	9,600	0.0	921,000	0.6	3,200	0.0	739,000	0.5	0	0.0	0
Barbados	273,000	4,700	1.7	580	0.2	3,300	1.2	110	0.0	0	0.0	260,000	95.2	0	0.0	0
Belarus	9,595,000	2,131,000	22.2	330,000	3.4	100	0.0	1,200	0.0	0	0.0	7,082,000	73.8	0	0.0	0
Belgium	10,712,000	2,172,000	20.3	221,000	2.1	2,600	0.0	25,600	0.2	5,800	0.1	7,668,000	71.6	6,000	0.1	0
Belize	312,000	2,200	0.7	62	0.0	7,700	2.5	1,500	0.5	0	0.0	284,000	91.1	0	0.0	0
Benin	8,850,000	17,100	0.2	4,700	0.1	11,600	0.1	0	0.0	0	0.0	3,874,000	43.8	0	0.0	0
Bermuda	64,900	3,400	5.3	180	0.3	410	0.6	320	0.5	140	0.2	58,000	89.3	0	0.0	0
Bhutan	726,000	200	0.0	0	0.0	74	0.0	610,000	84.0	0	0.0	6,700	0.9	0	0.0	0
Bolivia	9,930,000	189,000	1.9	14,200	0.1	215,000	2.2	7,400	0.1	1,500	0.0	9,181,000	92.5	0	0.0	0
Bosnia	3,760,000	125,000	3.3	31,000	0.8	0	0.0	0	0.0	0	0.0	1,817,000	48.3	0	0.0	0
Botswana	2,007,000	3,100	0.2	130	0.0	16,500	0.8	1,100	0.1	110	0.0	1,378,000	68.7	0	0.0	0
Brazil	194,946,000	4,747,000	2.4	757,000	0.4	42,100	0.0	497,000	0.3	42,400	0.0	177,304,000	90.9	0	0.0	0
British Virgin Is	23,200	880	3.8	28	0.1	190	0.8	0	0.0	0	0.0	19,600	84.5	0	0.0	0
Brunei	399,000	4,600	1.1	140	0.0	1,200	0.3	38,600	9.7	20,900	5.2	54,800	13.7	7,500	1.9	0
Bulgaria	7,494,000	222,000	3.0	70,700	0.9	590	0.0	0	0.0	0	0.0	6,216,000	82.9	0	0.0	0
Burkina Faso	16,469,000	82,100	0.5	610	0.0	2,900	0.0	0	0.0	0	0.0	3,691,000	22.4	0	0.0	0
Burundi	8,383,000	5,000	0.1	130	0.0	6,800	0.1	0	0.0	0	0.0	7,725,000	92.2	0	0.0	0
Cambodia	14,138,000	321,000	2.3	35,100	0.2	16,700	0.1	12,007,000	84.9	417,000	2.9	343,000	2.4	0	0.0	0
Cameroon	19,599,000	110,000	0.6	33,200	0.2	49,900	0.3	350	0.0	750	0.0	11,381,000	58.1	0	0.0	0
Canada	34,017,000	6,192,000	18.2	846,000	2.5	46,800	0.1	499,000	1.5	672,000	2.0	23,515,000	69.1	0	0.0	0
Cape Verde	496,000	4,400	0.9	0	0.0	760	0.2	0	0.0	0	0.0	471,000	95.0	0	0.0	0
Cayman Is	56,200	3,000	5.4	220	0.4	430	0.8	0	0.0	0	0.0	45,600	81.1	0	0.0	0
CAR	4,401,000	30,000	0.7	590	0.0	10,900	0.2	0	0.0	0	0.0	3,139,000	71.3	0	0.0	0
Chad	11,227,000	10,600	0.1	1,700	0.0	94,500	0.8	1,700	0.0	3,600	0.0	3,905,000	34.8	0	0.0	0
Channel Is	153,000	20,100	13.1	1,600	1.1	520	0.3	5	0.0	0	0.0	131,000	85.2	0	0.0	0
Chile	17,114,000	1,323,000	7.7	409,000	2.4	26,400	0.2	10,800	0.1	2,300	0.0	15,168,000	88.6	0	0.0	0
China	1,341,335,000	437,155,000	32.6	97,643,000	7.3	6,000	0.0	206,898,000	15.4	408,959,000	30.5	106,035,000	7.9	0	0.0	5,483,000
Colombia	46,295,000	989,000	2.1	115,000	0.2	70,500	0.2	1,800	0.0	2,300	0.0	44,305,000	95.7	0	0.0	0
Comoros	735,000	900	0.1	73	0.0	650	0.1	0	0.0	0	0.0	3,500	0.5	0	0.0	0
Congo	4,043,000	120,000	3.0	2,000	0.1	25,900	0.6	170	0.0	280	0.0	3,629,000	89.8	0	0.0	0
DR Congo	65,966,000	260,000	0.4	14,300	0.0	283,000	0.4	3,700	0.0	0	0.0	62,673,000	95.0	0	0.0	0
Cook Islands	20,300	520	2.6	8	0.0	160	0.8	0	0.0	0	0.0	19,600	96.6	0	0.0	0
Costa Rica	4,659,000	129,000	2.8	11,200	0.2	13,500	0.3	1,200	0.0	24,200	0.5	4,464,000	95.8	0	0.0	0
Cote d'Ivoire	19,738,000	70,300	0.4	2,100	0.0	30,300	0.2	9,900	0.1	0	0.0	6,772,000	34.3	0	0.0	0
Croatia	4,403,000	138,000	3.1	64,700	1.5	0	0.0	0	0.0	0	0.0	4,117,000	93.5	0	0.0	0
Cuba	11,258,000	2,024,000	18.0	570,000	5.1	1,100	0.0	6,100	0.1	21,500	0.2	6,667,000	59.2	0	0.0	0
Cyprus	1,104,000	40,000	3.6	8,100	0.7	1,200	0.1	6,400	0.6	0	0.0	793,000	71.8	0	0.0	0
Czech Rep	10,493,000	4,139,000	39.4	515,000	4.9	970	0.0	11,100	0.1	3,400	0.0	5,811,000	55.4	0	0.0	0
Denmark	5,550,000	551,000	9.9	79,000	1.4	1,300	0.0	21,000	0.4	4,200	0.1	4,647,000	83.7	0	0.0	0
Djibouti	889,000	10,200	1.2	440	0.1	770	0.1	0	0.0	0	0.0	15,500	1.7	0	0.0	0
Dominica	67,800	330	0.5	30	0.0	1,200	1.7	88	0.1	41	0.1	64,000	94.4	0	0.0	0
Dominican Rep	9,927,000	213,000	2.1	46,600	0.5	6,900	0.1	1,800	0.0	7,700	0.1	9,429,000	95.0	0	0.0	0
Ecuador	14,465,000	206,000	1.4	21,300	0.1	17,800	0.1	15,200	0.1	14,000	0.1	14,042,000	97.1	0	0.0	0
Egypt	81,121,000	413,000	0.5	78,900	0.1	6,900	0.0	790	0.0	1,700	0.0	8,183,000	10.1	0	0.0	0
El Salvador	6,193,000	142,000	2.3	6,700	0.1	27,300	0.4	600	0.0	770	0.0	5,977,000	96.5	0	0.0	0
Eq Guinea	700,000	22,200	3.2	12,700	1.8	3,600	0.5	0	0.0	0	0.0	621,000	88.7	0	0.0	0
Eritrea	5,254,000	66,800	1.3	340	0.0	1,400	0.0	0	0.0	0	0.0	2,517,000	47.9	0	0.0	0
Estonia	1,341,000	683,000	50.9	62,500	4.7	500	0.0	710	0.1	0	0.0	589,000	43.9	0	0.0	0
Ethiopia	82,950,000	82,100	0.1	10,200	0.0	22,800	0.0	0	0.0	0	0.0	49,672,000	59.9	0	0.0	0
Faeroe Is	48,700	810	1.7	0	0.0	140	0.3	0	0.0	0	0.0	47,800	98.0	0	0.0	0
Falkland Is	3,000	340	11.1	29	1.0	89	3.0	6	0.2	0	0.0	2,500	83.0	0	0.0	0
Fiji	861,000	8,800	1.0	190	0.0	2,300	0.3	0	0.0	900	0.1	550,000	63.9	0	0.0	0
Finland	5,365,000	884,000	16.5	105,000	2.0	1,700	0.0	5,000	0.1	4,000	0.1	4,336,000	80.8	0	0.0	0
France	62,787,000	11,861,000	18.9	2,596,000	4.1	4,500	0.0	476,000	0.8	223,000	0.4	41,285,000	65.8	0	0.0	0
Fr Guiana	231,000	6,800	2.9	1,100	0.5	920	0.4	0	0.0	8,300	3.6	195,000	84.4	0	0.0	0
Fr Polynesia	271,000	11,900	4.4	1,500	0.6	670	0.2	260	0.1	1,200	0.4	254,000	94.0	0	0.0	0
FS Micronesia	111,000	830	0.7	50	0.0	570	0.5	470	0.4	330	0.3	105,000	94.8	0	0.0	0
Gabon	1,505,000	20,400	1.4	400	0.0	600	0.0	0	0.0	0	0.0	1,272,000	84.5	0	0.0	0
Gambia	1,728,000	10,400	0.6	78	0.0	14,200	0.8	0	0.0	0	0.0	75,200	4.3	0	0.0	0
Georgia	4,352,000	159,000	3.6	20,100	0.5	1,600	0.0	0	0.0	0	0.0	3,703,000	85.1	0	0.0	0
Germany	82,302,000	18,288,000	22.2	2,056,000	2.5	12,300	0.0	84,700	0.1	5,200	0.0	57,617,000	70.0	2,000	0.0	0

Ethnoreligionists		Hindus		Jains		Jews		Muslims		New Religionists		Shintoists		Sikhs		Spiritists		Zoroastrians	
4,300	0.0	10,700	0.0	0	0.0	2	0.0	31,326,000	99.7	0	0.0	0	0.0	3,500	0.0	0	0.0	4,300	0.0
0	0.0	0	0.0	0	0.0	310	0.0	2,008,000	62.7	0	0.0	0	0.0	0	0.0	0	0.0	0	0.0
0	0.0	0	0.0	0	0.0	570	0.0	34,937,000	98.5	0	0.0	0	0.0	0	0.0	0	0.0	0	0.0
0	0.0	0	0.0	0	0.0	0	0.0	0	0.0	0	0.0	0	0.0	0	0.0	0	0.0	0	0.0
0	0.0	420	0.5	0	0.0	290	0.3	870	1.0	0	0.0	0	0.0	0	0.0	0	0.0	0	0.0
881,000	4.6	0	0.0	0	0.0	0	0.0	208,000	1.1	0	0.0	0	0.0	0	0.0	0	0.0	0	0.0
0	0.0	61	0.4	0	0.0	23	0.2	88	0.6	0	0.0	0	0.0	0	0.0	520	3.4	0	0.0
0	0.0	140	0.2	0	0.0	0	0.0	490	0.6	0	0.0	0	0.0	0	0.0	3,200	3.6	0	0.0
90,400	0.2	5,900	0.0	0	0.0	501,000	1.2	787,000	1.9	102,000	0.3	0	0.0	1,200	0.0	93,300	0.2	0	0.0
0	0.0	0	0.0	0	0.0	540	0.0	6,700	0.2	44,100	1.4	0	0.0	0	0.0	0	0.0	0	0.0
0	0.0	0	0.0	0	0.0	150	0.1	220	0.2	100	0.1	0	0.0	0	0.0	1,200	1.1	0	0.0
61,700	0.3	185,000	0.8	1,600	0.0	111,000	0.5	439,000	2.0	95,000	0.4	0	0.0	36,500	0.2	6,600	0.0	2,600	0.0
300	0.0	7,100	0.1	0	0.0	8,300	0.1	426,000	5.1	5,000	0.1	0	0.0	1,200	0.0	0	0.0	0	0.0
0	0.0	0	0.0	0	0.0	29,500	0.3	8,523,000	92.8	1,500	0.0	0	0.0	0	0.0	0	0.0	0	0.0
0	0.0	100	0.0	0	0.0	340	0.1	310	0.1	0	0.0	0	0.0	0	0.0	6,500	1.9	0	0.0
320	0.0	81,600	6.5	0	0.0	63	0.0	1,074,000	85.1	320	0.0	0	0.0	0	0.0	0	0.0	0	0.0
669,000	0.5	14,096,000	9.5	0	0.0	180	0.0	132,112,000	88.8	0	0.0	0	0.0	24,500	0.0	0	0.0	340	0.0
28	0.0	1,100	0.4	0	0.0	33	0.0	2,600	1.0	440	0.2	0	0.0	0	0.0	55	0.0	0	0.0
480	0.0	0	0.0	0	0.0	25,500	0.3	25,300	0.3	0	0.0	0	0.0	0	0.0	0	0.0	0	0.0
2,100	0.0	3,200	0.0	840	0.0	28,500	0.3	565,000	5.3	1,400	0.0	0	0.0	5,400	0.1	3,800	0.0	11	0.0
2,000	0.6	6,200	2.0	0	0.0	3,400	1.1	1,600	0.5	0	0.0	0	0.0	0	0.0	3,000	1.0	0	0.0
2,689,000	30.4	0	0.0	0	0.0	0	0.0	2,253,000	25.5	1,300	0.0	0	0.0	0	0.0	0	0.0	0	0.0
0	0.0	0	0.0	0	0.0	19	0.0	570	0.9	58	0.1	0	0.0	0	0.0	1,800	2.7	0	0.0
24,500	3.4	82,700	11.4	0	0.0	0	0.0	1,600	0.2	0	0.0	0	0.0	0	0.0	0	0.0	0	0.0
312,000	3.1	0	0.0	0	0.0	3,700	0.0	2,000	0.0	1,700	0.0	0	0.0	0	0.0	1,900	0.0	0	0.0
0	0.0	0	0.0	0	0.0	380	0.0	1,786,000	47.5	0	0.0	0	0.0	0	0.0	0	0.0	0	0.0
599,000	29.8	2,800	0.1	0	0.0	420	0.0	5,500	0.3	0	0.0	0	0.0	240	0.0	0	0.0	0	0.0
324,000	0.2	9,700	0.0	0	0.0	147,000	0.1	192,000	0.1	1,456,000	0.7	7,800	0.0	0	0.0	9,421,000	4.8	0	0.0
0	0.0	280	1.2	0	0.0	0	0.0	270	1.2	0	0.0	0	0.0	0	0.0	2,000	8.4	0	0.0
40,200	10.1	3,400	0.9	0	0.0	0	0.0	228,000	57.0	90	0.0	0	0.0	0	0.0	0	0.0	0	0.0
0	0.0	0	0.0	0	0.0	3,600	0.0	981,000	13.1	0	0.0	0	0.0	0	0.0	0	0.0	0	0.0
3,850,000	23.4	0	0.0	0	0.0	0	0.0	8,842,000	53.7	570	0.0	0	0.0	0	0.0	0	0.0	0	0.0
462,000	5.5	7,000	0.1	0	0.0	0	0.0	177,000	2.1	0	0.0	0	0.0	0	0.0	0	0.0	0	0.0
648,000	4.6	30,400	0.2	0	0.0	0	0.0	276,000	1.9	43,800	0.3	0	0.0	0	0.0	0	0.0	0	0.0
4,089,000	20.9	0	0.0	0	0.0	0	0.0	3,927,000	20.0	7,700	0.0	0	0.0	0	0.0	0	0.0	0	0.0
136,000	0.4	390,000	1.1	14,300	0.0	480,000	1.4	795,000	2.3	84,500	0.2	0	0.0	328,000	1.0	15,200	0.0	3,400	0.0
5,600	1.1	0	0.0	0	0.0	63	0.0	13,700	2.8	0	0.0	0	0.0	0	0.0	0	0.0	0	0.0
0	0.0	140	0.3	0	0.0	1,000	1.8	110	0.2	0	0.0	0	0.0	0	0.0	5,700	10.1	0	0.0
618,000	14.0	0	0.0	0	0.0	0	0.0	602,000	13.7	0	0.0	0	0.0	0	0.0	0	0.0	0	0.0
932,000	8.3	0	0.0	0	0.0	0	0.0	6,278,000	55.9	0	0.0	0	0.0	0	0.0	0	0.0	0	0.0
0	0.0	120	0.1	0	0.0	100	0.1	120	0.1	0	0.0	0	0.0	0	0.0	0	0.0	0	0.0
131,000	0.8	0	0.0	0	0.0	20,600	0.1	16,300	0.1	6,900	0.0	0	0.0	0	0.0	0	0.0	0	0.0
7,890,000	4.3	18,100	0.0	0	0.0	2,700	0.0	21,012,000	1.6	215,000	0.0	0	0.0	19,100	0.0	0	0.0	67	0.0
302,000	0.7	11,200	0.0	0	0.0	11,300	0.0	22,800	0.0	3,100	0.0	0	0.0	0	0.0	461,000	1.0	0	0.0
7,100	1.0	0	0.0	0	0.0	0	0.0	723,000	98.3	0	0.0	0	0.0	0	0.0	0	0.0	0	0.0
193,000	4.8	0	0.0	0	0.0	0	0.0	56,200	1.4	16,700	0.4	0	0.0	0	0.0	0	0.0	0	0.0
1,655,000	2.5	98,900	0.2	0	0.0	400	0.0	972,000	1.5	5,600	0.0	0	0.0	0	0.0	0	0.0	0	0.0
0	0.0	0	0.0	0	0.0	0	0.0	0	0.0	0	0.0	0	0.0	0	0.0	0	0.0	0	0.0
8,300	0.2	560	0.0	0	0.0	2,900	0.1	0	0.0	0	0.0	0	0.0	0	0.0	3,800	0.1	0	0.0
4,838,000	24.5	1,600	0.0	0	0.0	0	0.0	8,009,000	40.6	4,800	0.0	0	0.0	0	0.0	0	0.0	0	0.0
0	0.0	0	0.0	0	0.0	790	0.0	83,000	1.9	0	0.0	0	0.0	0	0.0	0	0.0	0	0.0
0	0.0	23,300	0.2	0	0.0	830	0.0	9,100	0.1	810	0.0	0	0.0	0	0.0	1,934,000	17.2	0	0.0
0	0.0	3,300	0.3	0	0.0	200	0.0	242,000	21.9	0	0.0	0	0.0	9,800	0.9	0	0.0	0	0.0
0	0.0	9,500	0.2	0	0.0	7,300	0.1	1,300	0.0	4,500	0.0	0	0.0	0	0.0	0	0.0	0	0.0
0	0.0	360	0.0	0	0.0	7,100	0.1	225,000	4.1	5,200	0.1	0	0.0	0	0.0	0	0.0	0	0.0
0	0.0	0	0.0	0	0.0	0	0.0	861,000	96.9	0	0.0	0	0.0	0	0.0	0	0.0	0	0.0
170	0.3	68	0.1	0	0.0	0	0.0	95	0.1	17	0.0	0	0.0	0	0.0	1,800	2.6	0	0.0
0	0.0	0	0.0	0	0.0	720	0.0	2,200	0.0	3,300	0.0	0	0.0	0	0.0	217,000	2.2	0	0.0
139,000	1.0	0	0.0	0	0.0	4,400	0.0	2,000	0.0	3,200	0.0	0	0.0	0	0.0	0	0.0	0	0.0
0	0.0	810	0.0	0	0.0	95	0.0	72,436,000	89.3	0	0.0	0	0.0	0	0.0	0	0.0	0	0.0
35,200	0.6	0	0.0	0	0.0	560	0.0	1,700	0.0	1,900	0.0	0	0.0	0	0.0	0	0.0	0	0.0
12,100	1.7	350	0.1	0	0.0	0	0.0	28,400	4.0	0	0.0	0	0.0	0	0.0	0	0.0	0	0.0
32,500	0.6	1,100	0.0	0	0.0	0	0.0	2,635,000	50.1	0	0.0	0	0.0	0	0.0	0	0.0	0	0.0
0	0.0	710	0.1	0	0.0	1,500	0.1	3,700	0.3	0	0.0	0	0.0	0	0.0	0	0.0	0	0.0
5,017,000	6.0	6,200	0.0	0	0.0	15,800	0.0	28,123,000	33.9	0	0.0	0	0.0	0	0.0	0	0.0	0	0.0
0	0.0	0	0.0	0	0.0	0	0.0	0	0.0	55	1.8	0	0.0	0	0.0	0	0.0	0	0.0
320	0.0	239,000	27.7	1,400	0.2	110	0.0	53,400	6.2	0	0.0	0	0.0	4,400	0.5	0	0.0	0	0.0
0	0.0	0	0.0	0	0.0	1,300	0.0	24,300	0.5	2,700	0.1	0	0.0	0	0.0	0	0.0	0	0.0
116,000	0.2	47,400	0.1	0	0.0	628,000	1.0	5,367,000	8.5	157,000	0.3	0	0.0	0	0.0	25,100	0.0	630	0.0
5,200	2.2	3,700	1.6	0	0.0	120	0.1	2,100	0.9	260	0.1	0	0.0	0	0.0	7,600	3.3	0	0.0
260	0.1	0	0.0	0	0.0	160	0.1	0	0.0	450	0.2	0	0.0	0	0.0	0	0.0	0	0.0
3,100	2.8	0	0.0	0	0.0	0	0.0	0	0.0	400	0.4	0	0.0	0	0.0	0	0.0	0	0.0
48,600	3.2	0	0.0	0	0.0	0	0.0	154,000	10.2	9,200	0.6	0	0.0	0	0.0	0	0.0	0	0.0
95,500	5.5	280	0.0	0	0.0	0	0.0	1,533,000	88.7	0	0.0	0	0.0	0	0.0	0	0.0	0	0.0
0	0.0	0	0.0	0	0.0	11,800	0.3	457,000	10.5	270	0.0	0	0.0	0	0.0	0	0.0	0	0.0
3,600	0.0	93,400	0.1	0	0.0	224,000	0.3	3,838,000	4.7	53,300	0.1	0	0.0	24,700	0.0	0	0.0	0	0.0

(*continued*)

Country	Population 2010	Agnostics		Atheists		Baha'is		Buddhists		Chinese FR		Christians		Confucianists		D
Ghana	24,392,000	72,200	0.3	4,700	0.0	14,100	0.1	490	0.0	710	0.0	15,601,000	64.0	0	0.0	0
Gibraltar	29,200	720	2.5	75	0.3	100	0.3	0	0.0	0	0.0	25,800	88.3	0	0.0	0
Greece	11,359,000	368,000	3.2	34,700	0.3	190	0.0	5,300	0.0	10,200	0.1	10,430,000	91.8	0	0.0	0
Greenland	57,300	1,300	2.3	110	0.2	360	0.6	0	0.0	0	0.0	55,100	96.1	0	0.0	0
Grenada	104,000	980	0.9	14	0.0	150	0.1	0	0.0	0	0.0	101,000	96.6	0	0.0	0
Guadeloupe	461,000	8,600	1.9	2,900	0.6	1,600	0.4	0	0.0	0	0.0	442,000	95.9	0	0.0	0
Guam	180,000	2,900	1.6	130	0.1	2,100	1.2	1,900	1.1	1,900	1.1	169,000	94.2	180	0.1	0
Guatemala	14,389,000	134,000	0.9	62,200	0.4	19,900	0.1	2,500	0.0	4,700	0.0	14,010,000	97.4	0	0.0	0
Guinea	9,982,000	13,700	0.1	5,100	0.1	150	0.0	9,000	0.1	0	0.0	365,000	3.7	0	0.0	0
Guinea-Biss	1,515,000	18,400	1.2	1,400	0.1	270	0.0	0	0.0	0	0.0	185,000	12.2	0	0.0	0
Guyana	754,000	11,700	1.6	4,200	0.6	11,800	1.6	1,800	0.2	2,100	0.3	413,000	54.8	0	0.0	0
Haiti	9,993,000	260,000	2.6	4,900	0.0	22,600	0.2	0	0.0	260	0.0	9,429,000	94.3	0	0.0	0
Holy See	460	0	0.0	0	0.0	0	0.0	0	0.0	0	0.0	460	100.0	0	0.0	0
Honduras	7,601,000	140,000	1.8	15,800	0.2	37,600	0.5	4,300	0.1	540	0.0	7,278,000	95.8	0	0.0	0
Hong Kong	7,053,000	1,316,000	18.7	171,000	2.4	1,100	0.0	1,074,000	15.2	3,236,000	45.9	957,000	13.6	71	0.0	0
Hungary	9,984,000	765,000	7.7	440,000	4.4	290	0.0	4,300	0.0	5,000	0.1	8,653,000	86.7	0	0.0	0
Iceland	320,000	8,800	2.8	1,200	0.4	600	0.2	550	0.2	0	0.0	305,000	95.4	0	0.0	0
India	1,224,614,000	14,194,000	1.2	1,954,000	0.2	1,896,000	0.2	8,772,000	0.7	161,000	0.0	57,265,000	4.7	0	0.0	0
Indonesia	239,871,000	3,168,000	1.3	269,000	0.1	22,800	0.0	1,944,000	0.8	2,126,000	0.9	28,409,000	11.8	0	0.0	0
Iran	73,974,000	217,000	0.3	7,900	0.0	251,000	0.3	440	0.0	950	0.0	270,000	0.4	0	0.0	0
Iraq	31,672,000	160,000	0.5	56,400	0.2	3,800	0.0	280	0.0	610	0.0	489,000	1.5	0	0.0	0
Ireland	4,470,000	202,000	4.5	12,100	0.3	1,600	0.0	780	0.0	4,700	0.1	4,209,000	94.2	0	0.0	0
Isle of Man	82,900	11,000	13.2	1,800	2.2	0	0.0	0	0.0	0	0.0	69,700	84.1	0	0.0	0
Israel	7,418,000	317,000	4.3	36,900	0.5	12,000	0.2	28,500	0.4	27,600	0.4	180,000	2.4	0	0.0	0
Italy	60,551,000	7,808,000	12.9	2,178,000	3.6	5,100	0.0	8,800	0.0	46,300	0.1	48,927,000	80.8	0	0.0	0
Jamaica	2,741,000	113,000	4.1	1,400	0.1	5,200	0.2	330	0.0	3,600	0.1	2,318,000	84.5	0	0.0	0
Japan	126,536,000	12,873,000	10.2	3,630,000	2.9	15,600	0.0	71,307,000	56.4	286,000	0.2	2,601,000	2.1	121,000	0.1	0
Jordan	6,187,000	155,000	2.5	30,400	0.5	15,700	0.3	0	0.0	0	0.0	171,000	2.8	0	0.0	0
Kazakhstan	16,026,000	795,000	5.0	245,000	1.5	7,000	0.0	18,400	0.1	1,700	0.0	4,212,000	26.3	0	0.0	0
Kenya	40,513,000	31,900	0.1	1,700	0.0	423,000	1.0	1,300	0.0	1,900	0.0	32,923,000	81.3	0	0.0	0
Kiribati	99,500	600	0.6	3	0.0	2,500	2.5	13	0.0	0	0.0	96,500	96.9	0	0.0	0
Kosovo	2,084,000	17,900	0.9	4,000	0.2	0	0.0	0	0.0	0	0.0	122,000	5.9	0	0.0	0
Kuwait	2,737,000	19,000	0.7	480	0.0	9,000	0.3	0	0.0	0	0.0	241,000	8.8	0	0.0	0
Kyrgyzstan	5,334,000	432,000	8.1	91,700	1.7	1,400	0.0	24,800	0.5	0	0.0	412,000	7.7	0	0.0	0
Laos	6,201,000	53,200	0.9	18,000	0.3	13,400	0.2	3,236,000	52.2	22,200	0.4	181,000	2.9	0	0.0	280
Latvia	2,252,000	562,000	25.0	122,000	5.4	0	0.0	110	0.0	0	0.0	1,552,000	68.9	0	0.0	0
Lebanon	4,228,000	138,000	3.3	34,000	0.8	3,900	0.1	87,500	2.1	0	0.0	1,507,000	35.7	0	0.0	0
Lesotho	2,171,000	4,400	0.2	540	0.0	19,200	0.9	0	0.0	0	0.0	1,992,000	91.7	0	0.0	0
Liberia	3,994,000	60,500	1.5	510	0.0	11,200	0.3	0	0.0	0	0.0	1,619,000	40.5	0	0.0	0
Libya	6,355,000	10,700	0.2	820	0.0	640	0.0	20,200	0.3	1,800	0.0	172,000	2.7	0	0.0	0
Liechtenstein	36,000	1,500	4.1	28	0.1	11	0.0	0	0.0	0	0.0	32,200	89.4	0	0.0	0
Lithuania	3,324,000	336,000	10.1	24,400	0.7	270	0.0	660	0.0	0	0.0	2,950,000	88.8	0	0.0	0
Luxembourg	507,000	69,800	13.8	7,500	1.5	1,600	0.3	0	0.0	0	0.0	418,000	82.4	0	0.0	0
Macau	544,000	68,200	12.5	15,400	2.8	180	0.0	93,900	17.3	320,000	58.9	39,300	7.2	0	0.0	0
Macedonia	2,061,000	64,100	3.1	9,700	0.5	0	0.0	0	0.0	0	0.0	1,311,000	63.6	0	0.0	0
Madagascar	20,714,000	57,700	0.3	13,500	0.1	18,300	0.1	5,200	0.0	10,400	0.1	11,789,000	56.9	0	0.0	0
Malawi	14,901,000	39,400	0.3	250	0.0	34,300	0.2	0	0.0	0	0.0	11,885,000	79.8	0	0.0	0
Malaysia	28,401,000	105,000	0.4	31,500	0.1	67,500	0.2	1,502,000	5.3	5,220,000	18.4	2,527,000	8.9	0	0.0	0
Maldives	316,000	290	0.1	21	0.0	120	0.0	2,000	0.6	0	0.0	1,400	0.4	0	0.0	0
Mali	15,370,000	16,100	0.1	790	0.0	1,200	0.0	0	0.0	0	0.0	498,000	3.2	0	0.0	0
Malta	417,000	6,200	1.5	810	0.2	270	0.1	0	0.0	0	0.0	408,000	98.0	0	0.0	0
Marshall Is	54,000	740	1.4	35	0.1	1,400	2.7	0	0.0	0	0.0	51,600	95.5	0	0.0	0
Martinique	406,000	7,600	1.9	1,800	0.4	2,100	0.5	160	0.0	240	0.1	391,000	96.5	0	0.0	0
Mauritania	3,460,000	3,400	0.1	300	0.0	350	0.0	0	0.0	0	0.0	9,100	0.3	0	0.0	0
Mauritius	1,299,000	23,000	1.8	1,600	0.1	23,700	1.8	3,200	0.2	17,300	1.3	431,000	33.2	0	0.0	0
Mayotte	204,000	420	0.2	57	0.0	0	0.0	0	0.0	0	0.0	1,400	0.7	0	0.0	0
Mexico	113,423,000	2,952,000	2.6	121,000	0.1	38,900	0.0	26,300	0.0	11,600	0.0	108,721,000	95.9	0	0.0	0
Moldova	3,573,000	85,200	2.4	16,800	0.5	530	0.0	0	0.0	0	0.0	3,426,000	95.9	0	0.0	0
Monaco	35,400	3,400	9.5	750	2.1	67	0.2	0	0.0	0	0.0	30,500	86.0	0	0.0	0
Mongolia	2,756,000	475,000	17.2	76,700	2.8	55	0.0	1,493,000	54.2	16,500	0.6	46,000	1.7	0	0.0	0
Montenegro	631,000	29,200	4.6	5,400	0.8	0	0.0	0	0.0	0	0.0	488,000	77.3	0	0.0	0
Montserrat	5,900	260	4.3	28	0.5	86	1.4	0	0.0	0	0.0	5,500	93.5	0	0.0	0
Morocco	31,951,000	42,100	0.1	370	0.0	32,600	0.1	0	0.0	0	0.0	31,600	0.1	0	0.0	0
Mozambique	23,391,000	83,800	0.4	17,700	0.1	2,900	0.0	2,000	0.0	4,300	0.0	12,269,000	52.5	0	0.0	0
Myanmar	47,963,000	214,000	0.4	19,200	0.0	78,900	0.2	35,823,000	74.7	123,000	0.3	3,786,000	7.9	711,000	1.5	0
Namibia	2,283,000	43,600	1.9	510	0.0	11,000	0.5	0	0.0	0	0.0	2,082,000	91.2	0	0.0	0
Nauru	10,300	360	3.5	0	0.0	980	9.6	140	1.4	1,100	10.5	7,700	75.0	0	0.0	0
Nepal	29,959,000	78,000	0.3	17,300	0.1	4,400	0.0	3,441,000	11.5	20,900	0.1	908,000	3.0	0	0.0	0
Nether Ant	201,000	6,300	3.1	320	0.2	510	0.3	1,000	0.5	300	0.1	188,000	93.9	0	0.0	0
Netherlands	16,613,000	4,384,000	26.4	290,000	1.7	6,700	0.0	201,000	1.2	6,900	0.0	10,517,000	63.3	0	0.0	0
N Caledonia	251,000	23,400	9.3	2,700	1.1	940	0.4	1,600	0.6	0	0.0	214,000	85.2	0	0.0	0
New Zealand	4,368,000	1,335,000	30.6	57,000	1.3	7,500	0.2	95,200	2.2	14,000	0.3	2,666,000	61.0	0	0.0	0
Nicaragua	5,788,000	141,000	2.4	2,700	0.0	10,900	0.2	6,700	0.1	2,600	0.0	5,510,000	95.2	0	0.0	0
Niger	15,512,000	9,500	0.1	170	0.0	5,500	0.0	0	0.0	0	0.0	54,700	0.4	0	0.0	0
Nigeria	158,423,000	403,000	0.3	44,000	0.0	38,200	0.0	8,500	0.0	4,700	0.0	73,606,000	46.5	0	0.0	0
Niue	1,500	23	1.6	0	0.0	9	0.6	0	0.0	3	0.2	1,400	97.7	0	0.0	0

Ethnoreligionists		Hindus		Jains		Jews		Muslims		New Religionists		Shintoists		Sikhs		Spiritists		Zoroastrians	
3,824,000	15.7	4,900	0.0	0	0.0	0	0.0	4,843,000	19.9	26,700	0.1	0	0.0	0	0.0	0	0.0	0	0.0
0	0.0	530	1.8	0	0.0	580	2.0	1,400	4.9	0	0.0	0	0.0	0	0.0	0	0.0	0	0.0
0	0.0	15,000	0.1	0	0.0	5,700	0.1	481,000	4.2	2,200	0.0	0	0.0	5,700	0.1	940	0.0	0	0.0
450	0.8	0	0.0	0	0.0	0	0.0	10	0.0	0	0.0	0	0.0	0	0.0	0	0.0	0	0.0
0	0.0	710	0.7	0	0.0	0	0.0	340	0.3	49	0.0	0	0.0	0	0.0	1,300	1.3	0	0.0
0	0.0	2,300	0.5	0	0.0	0	0.0	1,700	0.4	200	0.0	0	0.0	0	0.0	1,800	0.4	0	0.0
650	0.4	0	0.0	0	0.0	0	0.0	54	0.0	730	0.4	0	0.0	0	0.0	0	0.0	0	0.0
120,000	0.8	0	0.0	0	0.0	1,300	0.0	1,200	0.0	2,600	0.0	0	0.0	0	0.0	30,100	0.2	0	0.0
1,124,000	11.3	0	0.0	0	0.0	0	0.0	8,465,000	84.8	0	0.0	0	0.0	0	0.0	0	0.0	0	0.0
636,000	42.0	0	0.0	0	0.0	0	0.0	674,000	44.5	0	0.0	0	0.0	0	0.0	0	0.0	0	0.0
18,000	2.4	227,000	30.1	0	0.0	57	0.0	56,800	7.5	0	0.0	0	0.0	0	0.0	7,800	1.0	0	0.0
0	0.0	0	0.0	0	0.0	240	0.0	2,400	0.0	3,600	0.0	0	0.0	0	0.0	271,000	2.7	0	0.0
0	0.0	0	0.0	0	0.0	0	0.0	0	0.0	0	0.0	0	0.0	0	0.0	0	0.0	0	0.0
42,800	0.6	0	0.0	0	0.0	400	0.0	11,100	0.1	2,400	0.0	0	0.0	0	0.0	67,500	0.9	0	0.0
480	0.0	17,400	0.2	0	0.0	700	0.0	93,800	1.3	183,000	2.6	0	0.0	850	0.0	2,100	0.0	71	0.0
0	0.0	0	0.0	0	0.0	91,800	0.9	23,600	0.2	0	0.0	0	0.0	0	0.0	0	0.0	0	0.0
300	0.1	830	0.3	0	0.0	0	0.0	560	0.2	300	0.1	0	0.0	0	0.0	1,500	0.5	0	0.0
5,891,000	3.7	893,642,000	73.0	5,085,000	0.4	11,000	0.0	173,367,000	14.2	0	0.0	0	0.0	22,303,000	1.8	0	0.0	73,400	0.0
5,521,000	2.3	3,891,000	1.6	0	0.0	190	0.0	190,521,000	79.4	3,993,000	1.7	0	0.0	6,000	0.0	0	0.0	0	0.0
4,400	0.0	33,900	0.0	0	0.0	19,100	0.0	73,079,000	98.8	12,600	0.0	0	0.0	8,900	0.0	0	0.0	68,400	0.1
0	0.0	3,800	0.0	0	0.0	22	0.0	30,886,000	97.5	65,600	0.2	0	0.0	6,300	0.0	0	0.0	0	0.0
1,900	0.0	4,700	0.1	0	0.0	2,000	0.0	30,700	0.7	0	0.0	0	0.0	0	0.0	680	0.0	0	0.0
0	0.0	170	0.2	0	0.0	60	0.1	170	0.2	0	0.0	0	0.0	0	0.0	0	0.0	0	0.0
0	0.0	300	0.0	0	0.0	5,379,000	72.5	1,434,000	19.3	2,000	0.0	0	0.0	0	0.0	0	0.0	0	0.0
2,100	0.0	7,900	0.0	0	0.0	40,000	0.1	1,485,000	2.5	18,600	0.0	0	0.0	24,200	0.0	0	0.0	0	0.0
0	0.0	16,300	0.6	0	0.0	540	0.0	2,400	0.1	2,800	0.1	0	0.0	0	0.0	278,000	10.1	0	0.0
9,900	0.0	24,200	0.0	1,500	0.0	1,500	0.0	194,000	0.2	32,809,000	25.9	2,660,000	2.1	2,000	0.0	0	0.0	0	0.0
0	0.0	0	0.0	0	0.0	0	0.0	5,812,000	93.9	3,100	0.1	0	0.0	0	0.0	0	0.0	0	0.0
26,300	0.2	0	0.0	0	0.0	5,800	0.0	10,705,000	66.8	7,100	0.0	0	0.0	800	0.0	0	0.0	2,400	0.0
3,588,000	8.9	204,000	0.5	78,400	0.2	2,400	0.0	3,219,000	7.9	0	0.0	0	0.0	37,100	0.1	0	0.0	810	0.0
0	0.0	0	0.0	0	0.0	0	0.0	1,940,000	93.1	0	0.0	0	0.0	0	0.0	0	0.0	0	0.0
0	0.0	98,100	3.6	0	0.0	0	0.0	2,365,000	86.4	0	0.0	0	0.0	4,100	0.2	0	0.0	0	0.0
22,400	0.4	0	0.0	0	0.0	1,900	0.0	4,345,000	81.5	2,600	0.0	0	0.0	0	0.0	0	0.0	800	0.0
2,654,000	42.8	5,000	0.1	0	0.0	0	0.0	7,300	0.1	10,500	0.2	0	0.0	0	0.0	0	0.0	0	0.0
270	0.0	840	0.0	0	0.0	9,200	0.4	5,700	0.3	0	0.0	0	0.0	0	0.0	0	0.0	0	0.0
0	0.0	0	0.0	0	0.0	2,400	0.1	2,454,000	58.1	0	0.0	0	0.0	0	0.0	0	0.0	0	0.0
153,000	7.0	1,300	0.1	0	0.0	0	0.0	1,000	0.0	0	0.0	0	0.0	0	0.0	0	0.0	0	0.0
1,663,000	41.6	0	0.0	0	0.0	0	0.0	641,000	16.0	0	0.0	0	0.0	0	0.0	0	0.0	0	0.0
490	0.0	5,700	0.1	0	0.0	130	0.0	6,141,000	96.6	0	0.0	0	0.0	2,300	0.0	0	0.0	0	0.0
0	0.0	0	0.0	0	0.0	47	0.1	2,300	6.3	0	0.0	0	0.0	0	0.0	0	0.0	0	0.0
120	0.0	530	0.0	0	0.0	4,800	0.1	6,400	0.2	0	0.0	0	0.0	0	0.0	0	0.0	0	0.0
0	0.0	0	0.0	0	0.0	820	0.2	9,600	1.9	0	0.0	0	0.0	0	0.0	0	0.0	0	0.0
0	0.0	0	0.0	0	0.0	29	0.0	1,100	0.2	5,100	0.9	0	0.0	0	0.0	0	0.0	12	0.0
0	0.0	0	0.0	0	0.0	980	0.0	675,000	32.7	0	0.0	0	0.0	0	0.0	0	0.0	0	0.0
8,370,000	40.4	12,000	0.1	0	0.0	310	0.0	437,000	2.1	0	0.0	0	0.0	0	0.0	0	0.0	0	0.0
942,000	6.3	31,900	0.2	0	0.0	270	0.0	1,966,000	13.2	570	0.0	0	0.0	740	0.0	0	0.0	0	0.0
982,000	3.5	1,780,000	6.3	2,300	0.0	0	0.0	16,076,000	56.6	60,400	0.2	0	0.0	47,100	0.2	0	0.0	0	0.0
0	0.0	1,100	0.3	0	0.0	0	0.0	311,000	98.4	0	0.0	0	0.0	0	0.0	0	0.0	0	0.0
1,460,000	9.5	0	0.0	0	0.0	0	0.0	13,393,000	87.1	830	0.0	0	0.0	0	0.0	0	0.0	0	0.0
0	0.0	44	0.0	0	0.0	61	0.0	1,000	0.2	0	0.0	0	0.0	0	0.0	0	0.0	0	0.0
240	0.4	0	0.0	0	0.0	0	0.0	0	0.0	0	0.0	0	0.0	0	0.0	0	0.0	0	0.0
0	0.0	960	0.2	0	0.0	0	0.0	880	0.2	210	0.1	0	0.0	0	0.0	430	0.1	0	0.0
18,000	0.5	0	0.0	0	0.0	0	0.0	3,429,000	99.1	0	0.0	0	0.0	0	0.0	0	0.0	0	0.0
2,600	0.2	574,000	44.2	0	0.0	0	0.0	219,000	16.8	740	0.1	0	0.0	2,900	0.2	0	0.0	0	0.0
940	0.5	0	0.0	0	0.0	0	0.0	201,000	98.6	0	0.0	0	0.0	0	0.0	0	0.0	0	0.0
1,275,000	1.1	10,300	0.0	0	0.0	140,000	0.1	106,000	0.1	15,200	0.0	0	0.0	5,700	0.0	0	0.0	0	0.0
220	0.0	0	0.0	0	0.0	27,300	0.8	16,400	0.5	0	0.0	0	0.0	0	0.0	0	0.0	0	0.0
0	0.0	0	0.0	0	0.0	600	1.7	160	0.4	0	0.0	0	0.0	0	0.0	0	0.0	0	0.0
512,000	18.6	0	0.0	0	0.0	0	0.0	137,000	5.0	0	0.0	0	0.0	0	0.0	0	0.0	0	0.0
0	0.0	0	0.0	0	0.0	0	0.0	109,000	17.2	0	0.0	0	0.0	0	0.0	0	0.0	0	0.0
0	0.0	6	0.1	0	0.0	0	0.0	0	0.0	0	0.0	0	0.0	0	0.0	9	0.2	0	0.0
0	0.0	0	0.0	0	0.0	4,800	0.0	31,840,000	99.7	0	0.0	0	0.0	0	0.0	0	0.0	0	0.0
6,887,000	29.4	37,700	0.2	0	0.0	230	0.0	4,086,000	17.5	0	0.0	0	0.0	0	0.0	0	0.0	0	0.0
4,575,000	9.5	818,000	1.7	2,400	0.0	24	0.0	1,809,000	3.8	0	0.0	0	0.0	1,400	0.0	0	0.0	700	0.0
136,000	5.9	0	0.0	0	0.0	2,600	0.1	7,900	0.3	0	0.0	0	0.0	0	0.0	0	0.0	0	0.0
3,922,000	13.1	20,282,000	67.7	7,500	0.0	0	0.0	1,268,000	4.2	0	0.0	0	0.0	10,500	0.0	0	0.0	0	0.0
0	0.0	420	0.2	0	0.0	650	0.3	390	0.2	150	0.1	0	0.0	0	0.0	2,200	1.1	0	0.0
660	0.0	107,000	0.6	0	0.0	26,200	0.2	1,023,000	6.2	12,000	0.1	0	0.0	13,300	0.1	24,400	0.1	300	0.0
440	0.2	0	0.0	0	0.0	110	0.0	6,900	2.8	1,000	0.4	0	0.0	0	0.0	0	0.0	0	0.0
41,000	0.9	88,900	2.0	0	0.0	4,900	0.1	44,900	1.0	4,100	0.1	0	0.0	8,700	0.2	1,200	0.0	0	0.0
27,500	0.5	0	0.0	0	0.0	230	0.0	980	0.0	1,100	0.0	0	0.0	0	0.0	84,000	1.5	0	0.0
638,000	4.1	0	0.0	0	0.0	0	0.0	14,800,000	95.4	0	0.0	0	0.0	3,700	0.0	0	0.0	0	0.0
2,152,000	7.7	0	0.0	0	0.0	1,100	0.0	72,149,000	45.5	16,500	0.0	0	0.0	0	0.0	0	0.0	0	0.0
0	0.0	0	0.0	0	0.0	0	0.0	0	0.0	0	0.0	0	0.0	0	0.0	0	0.0	0	0.0

(*continued*)

Country	Population 2010	Agnostics		Atheists		Baha'is		Buddhists		Chinese FR		Christians		Confucianists		D
North Korea	24,346,000	13,648,000	56.1	3,793,000	15.6	0	0.0	369,000	1.5	15,200	0.1	393,000	1.6	0	0.0	0
N Mariana Is	60,900	600	1.0	11	0.0	310	0.5	6,400	10.6	3,000	4.9	49,500	81.3	71	0.1	0
Norway	4,883,000	275,000	5.6	30,100	0.6	2,700	0.1	35,000	0.7	1,600	0.0	4,384,000	89.8	0	0.0	0
Oman	2,782,000	6,400	0.2	200	0.0	10,000	0.4	21,600	0.8	0	0.0	120,000	4.3	0	0.0	0
Pakistan	173,593,000	139,000	0.1	8,200	0.0	87,300	0.1	107,000	0.1	2,400	0.0	3,784,000	2.2	0	0.0	0
Palau	20,500	500	2.4	2	0.0	140	0.7	170	0.9	51	0.2	19,000	92.7	0	0.0	0
Palestine	4,039,000	224,000	5.6	4,200	0.1	2,000	0.1	0	0.0	0	0.0	75,100	1.9	0	0.0	0
Panama	3,517,000	132,000	3.8	20,100	0.6	41,200	1.2	26,900	0.8	5,100	0.1	3,182,000	90.5	0	0.0	0
PNG	6,858,000	40,200	0.6	1,800	0.0	59,900	0.9	11,200	0.2	5,100	0.1	6,503,000	94.8	0	0.0	0
Paraguay	6,455,000	115,000	1.8	14,600	0.2	10,600	0.2	14,800	0.2	0	0.0	6,159,000	95.4	0	0.0	0
Peru	29,077,000	350,000	1.2	51,800	0.2	41,300	0.1	65,400	0.2	19,100	0.1	28,045,000	96.5	0	0.0	0
Philippines	93,261,000	687,000	0.7	182,000	0.2	275,000	0.3	107,000	0.1	54,700	0.1	84,769,000	90.9	2,200	0.0	0
Poland	38,277,000	1,595,000	4.2	102,000	0.3	770	0.0	2,000	0.0	0	0.0	36,514,000	95.4	0	0.0	0
Portugal	10,676,000	635,000	5.9	149,000	1.4	2,000	0.0	59,800	0.6	22,100	0.2	9,752,000	91.4	0	0.0	0
Puerto Rico	3,749,000	104,000	2.8	14,600	0.4	2,700	0.1	490	0.0	680	0.0	3,591,000	95.8	0	0.0	0
Qatar	1,759,000	39,800	2.3	1,100	0.1	2,700	0.2	33,400	1.9	0	0.0	168,000	9.6	0	0.0	0
Reunion	846,000	16,100	1.9	1,200	0.1	7,300	0.9	1,600	0.2	0	0.0	741,000	87.6	0	0.0	0
Romania	21,486,000	188,000	0.9	33,200	0.2	1,900	0.0	470	0.0	940	0.0	21,161,000	98.5	0	0.0	0
Russia	142,958,000	8,653,000	6.1	1,512,000	1.1	19,300	0.0	540,000	0.4	910	0.0	116,147,000	81.2	0	0.0	0
Rwanda	10,624,000	21,400	0.2	29	0.0	19,600	0.2	0	0.0	0	0.0	9,722,000	91.5	0	0.0	0
St Helena	4,100	140	3.3	4	0.1	33	0.8	0	0.0	0	0.0	3,900	95.8	0	0.0	0
St Kitts	52,400	830	1.6	0	0.0	260	0.5	0	0.0	0	0.0	49,600	94.6	0	0.0	0
St Lucia	174,000	640	0.4	61	0.0	420	0.2	0	0.0	0	0.0	167,000	95.9	0	0.0	0
St Pierre	6,000	230	3.8	0	0.0	81	1.3	0	0.0	0	0.0	5,700	94.7	0	0.0	0
St Vincent	109,000	2,600	2.4	48	0.0	1,600	1.5	0	0.0	0	0.0	97,000	88.7	0	0.0	0
Samoa	183,000	1,100	0.6	20	0.0	970	0.5	18	0.0	18	0.0	181,000	98.8	0	0.0	0
San Marino	31,500	1,700	5.4	570	1.8	290	0.9	0	0.0	0	0.0	29,000	91.9	0	0.0	0
São Tomé	165,000	2,100	1.2	0	0.0	3,900	2.4	0	0.0	0	0.0	159,000	96.1	0	0.0	0
Saudi Arabia	27,448,000	176,000	0.6	8,500	0.0	5,100	0.0	89,600	0.3	24,600	0.1	1,196,000	4.4	0	0.0	0
Senegal	12,434,000	17,900	0.1	2,800	0.0	23,900	0.2	1,700	0.0	400	0.0	669,000	5.4	0	0.0	0
Serbia	7,772,000	244,000	3.1	45,300	0.6	1,300	0.0	0	0.0	0	0.0	6,933,000	89.2	0	0.0	0
Seychelles	86,500	1,900	2.2	120	0.1	350	0.4	0	0.0	46	0.1	82,900	95.8	0	0.0	0
Sierra Leone	5,868,000	71,800	1.2	180	0.0	13,800	0.2	0	0.0	0	0.0	778,000	13.3	0	0.0	0
Singapore	5,086,000	235,000	4.6	7,300	0.1	8,000	0.2	753,000	14.8	1,987,000	39.1	964,000	19.0	0	0.0	0
Slovakia	5,462,000	608,000	11.1	176,000	3.2	690	0.0	0	0.0	0	0.0	4,675,000	85.6	0	0.0	0
Slovenia	2,030,000	151,000	7.4	50,000	2.5	400	0.0	0	0.0	0	0.0	1,779,000	87.7	0	0.0	0
Solomon Is	538,000	1,400	0.3	250	0.0	3,300	0.6	1,700	0.3	0	0.0	513,000	95.3	0	0.0	0
Somalia	9,331,000	2,500	0.0	1,600	0.0	2,700	0.0	0	0.0	0	0.0	4,300	0.0	0	0.0	0
South Africa	50,133,000	2,700,000	5.4	139,000	0.3	239,000	0.5	159,000	0.3	33,600	0.1	41,106,000	82.0	20,100	0.0	0
South Korea	48,184,000	721,000	1.5	48,300	0.1	33,100	0.1	11,954,000	24.8	34,000	0.1	16,105,000	33.4	5,270,000	10.9	0
South Sudan	10,798,000	43,000	0.4	7,800	0.1	680	0.0	240	0.0	520	0.0	6,529,000	60.5	0	0.0	0
Spain	46,077,000	3,509,000	7.6	673,000	1.5	13,500	0.0	14,400	0.0	24,200	0.1	40,714,000	88.4	0	0.0	0
Sri Lanka	20,860,000	96,800	0.5	15,100	0.1	15,500	0.1	14,378,000	68.9	830	0.0	1,841,000	8.8	0	0.0	0
Sudan	32,754,000	294,000	0.9	49,800	0.2	2,000	0.0	740	0.0	1,600	0.0	1,761,000	5.4	0	0.0	0
Suriname	525,000	24,400	4.7	610	0.1	3,600	0.7	3,100	0.6	1,400	0.3	268,000	51.0	0	0.0	0
Swaziland	1,186,000	13,800	1.2	280	0.0	5,300	0.5	0	0.0	0	0.0	1,039,000	87.6	0	0.0	0
Sweden	9,380,000	1,865,000	19.9	1,099,000	11.7	7,100	0.1	39,000	0.4	4,700	0.1	5,963,000	63.6	6,100	0.1	0
Switzerland	7,664,000	828,000	10.8	101,000	1.3	3,900	0.1	24,800	0.3	0	0.0	6,317,000	82.4	0	0.0	0
Syria	20,411,000	391,000	1.9	23,800	0.1	430	0.0	0	0.0	0	0.0	1,061,000	5.2	0	0.0	0
Taiwan	23,216,000	975,000	4.2	43,400	0.2	16,300	0.1	6,145,000	26.5	9,995,000	43.1	1,397,000	6.0	0	0.0	2,929,000
Tajikistan	6,879,000	152,000	2.2	34,900	0.5	3,100	0.0	4,400	0.1	0	0.0	98,300	1.4	0	0.0	0
Tanzania	44,841,000	133,000	0.3	27,000	0.1	190,000	0.4	10,200	0.0	23,700	0.1	24,555,000	54.8	0	0.0	0
Thailand	69,122,000	1,224,000	1.8	35,200	0.1	65,100	0.1	60,298,000	87.2	644,000	0.9	845,000	1.2	251,000	0.4	0
Timor-Leste	1,124,000	4,400	0.4	0	0.0	1,000	0.1	2,100	0.2	1,800	0.2	961,000	85.5	0	0.0	0
Togo	6,028,000	13,200	0.2	1,700	0.0	30,400	0.5	0	0.0	0	0.0	2,831,000	47.0	0	0.0	0
Tokelau Is	1,100	11	1.0	0	0.0	50	4.4	0	0.0	0	0.0	1,100	94.7	0	0.0	0
Tonga	104,000	440	0.4	6	0.0	3,700	3.5	120	0.1	0	0.0	99,700	95.8	0	0.0	0
Trinidad	1,341,000	30,100	2.2	570	0.0	16,000	1.2	4,200	0.3	5,300	0.4	851,000	63.4	0	0.0	0
Tunisia	10,481,000	20,600	0.2	2,600	0.0	2,100	0.0	79	0.0	170	0.0	23,200	0.2	0	0.0	0
Turkey	72,752,000	746,000	1.0	61,000	0.1	21,300	0.0	35,400	0.0	12,700	0.0	198,000	0.3	0	0.0	0
Turkmenistan	5,042,000	151,000	3.0	33,300	0.7	1,100	0.0	710	0.0	0	0.0	77,400	1.5	0	0.0	0
Turks & Caicos	38,400	1,800	4.6	16	0.0	240	0.6	0	0.0	0	0.0	35,300	92.1	0	0.0	0
Tuvalu	9,800	290	2.9	38	0.4	200	2.0	12	0.1	0	0.0	9,300	94.4	0	0.0	0
Uganda	33,425,000	130,000	0.4	13,200	0.0	95,100	0.3	2,000	0.0	4,300	0.0	28,223,000	84.4	0	0.0	0
Ukraine	45,448,000	5,227,000	11.5	1,398,000	3.1	230	0.0	18,500	0.0	930	0.0	37,864,000	83.3	0	0.0	0
UAE	7,512,000	74,200	1.0	11,600	0.2	38,400	0.5	149,000	2.0	0	0.0	944,000	12.6	0	0.0	0
UK	62,036,000	12,169,000	19.6	885,000	1.4	47,600	0.1	197,000	0.3	61,500	0.1	45,044,000	72.6	0	0.0	0
United States	310,384,000	41,922,000	13.5	1,310,000	0.4	513,000	0.2	3,955,000	1.3	109,000	0.0	247,920,000	79.9	0	0.0	12,400
US Virgin Is	109,000	3,900	3.6	190	0.2	690	0.6	0	0.0	0	0.0	103,000	94.8	0	0.0	0
Uruguay	3,369,000	942,000	28.0	220,000	6.5	7,400	0.2	65	0.0	0	0.0	2,151,000	63.9	0	0.0	0
Uzbekistan	27,445,000	933,000	3.4	256,000	0.9	800	0.0	39,400	0.1	450	0.0	344,000	1.3	0	0.0	0
Vanuatu	240,000	850	0.4	140	0.1	3,300	1.4	470	0.2	0	0.0	224,000	93.5	0	0.0	0
Venezuela	28,980,000	1,211,000	4.2	62,400	0.2	170,000	0.6	35,400	0.1	6,100	0.0	26,823,000	92.6	0	0.0	0
Viet Nam	87,848,000	11,109,000	12.6	5,810,000	6.6	389,000	0.4	43,212,000	49.2	878,000	1.0	7,430,000	8.5	0	0.0	160
Wallis & Fut	13,600	73	0.5	6	0.0	110	0.8	0	0.0	0	0.0	13,200	97.4	0	0.0	0
W Sahara	530,000	1,700	0.3	480	0.1	220	0.0	0	0.0	0	0.0	820	0.2	0	0.0	0

Ethnoreligionists		Hindus		Jains		Jews		Muslims		New Religionists		Shintoists		Sikhs		Spiritists		Zoroastrians	
2,990,000	12.3	0	0.0	0	0.0	0	0.0	2,400	0.0	3,135,000	12.9	0	0.0	0	0.0	0	0.0	0	0.0
210	0.3	0	0.0	0	0.0	0	0.0	410	0.7	380	0.6	0	0.0	0	0.0	0	0.0	0	0.0
730	0.0	0	0.0	0	0.0	900	0.0	143,000	2.9	7,000	0.1	0	0.0	2,300	0.0	560	0.0	0	0.0
560	0.0	153,000	5.5	0	0.0	0	0.0	2,452,000	88.1	280	0.0	0	0.0	18,400	0.7	0	0.0	0	0.0
195,000	0.1	2,290,000	1.3	0	0.0	960	0.0	166,927,000	96.2	0	0.0	0	0.0	44,600	0.0	0	0.0	8,700	0.0
120	0.6	26	0.1	0	0.0	0	0.0	490	2.4	0	0.0	0	0.0	0	0.0	0	0.0	0	0.0
0	0.0	0	0.0	0	0.0	477,000	11.8	3,256,000	80.6	0	0.0	0	0.0	0	0.0	0	0.0	0	0.0
39,300	1.1	980	0.0	0	0.0	4,700	0.1	25,300	0.7	22,100	0.6	0	0.0	250	0.0	16,800	0.5	0	0.0
233,000	3.4	0	0.0	0	0.0	810	0.0	1,800	0.0	1,700	0.0	0	0.0	0	0.0	0	0.0	0	0.0
129,000	2.0	0	0.0	0	0.0	3,200	0.1	3,900	0.1	3,400	0.1	0	0.0	0	0.0	0	0.0	0	0.0
399,000	1.4	0	0.0	0	0.0	10,300	0.0	730	0.0	94,300	0.3	0	0.0	0	0.0	0	0.0	0	0.0
2,172,000	2.3	2,900	0.0	0	0.0	1,200	0.0	4,974,000	5.3	9,400	0.0	0	0.0	23,900	0.0	0	0.0	0	0.0
0	0.0	0	0.0	0	0.0	9,600	0.0	39,000	0.1	7,200	0.0	0	0.0	0	0.0	7,300	0.0	0	0.0
1,700	0.0	6,400	0.1	0	0.0	470	0.0	43,000	0.4	0	0.0	0	0.0	430	0.0	3,700	0.0	0	0.0
0	0.0	3,300	0.1	0	0.0	2,600	0.1	1,100	0.0	1,300	0.0	0	0.0	0	0.0	26,600	0.7	0	0.0
0	0.0	44,300	2.5	0	0.0	0	0.0	1,469,000	83.5	0	0.0	0	0.0	0	0.0	0	0.0	0	0.0
3,600	0.4	38,200	4.5	1,100	0.1	0	0.0	35,300	4.2	270	0.0	0	0.0	680	0.1	0	0.0	0	0.0
0	0.0	0	0.0	0	0.0	6,500	0.0	90,100	0.4	3,800	0.0	0	0.0	0	0.0	0	0.0	0	0.0
998,000	0.7	42,900	0.0	0	0.0	187,000	0.1	14,854,000	10.4	970	0.0	0	0.0	2,900	0.0	0	0.0	0	0.0
352,000	3.3	530	0.0	0	0.0	0	0.0	508,000	4.8	0	0.0	0	0.0	0	0.0	0	0.0	0	0.0
0	0.0	0	0.0	0	0.0	0	0.0	0	0.0	0	0.0	0	0.0	0	0.0	0	0.0	0	0.0
0	0.0	790	1.5	0	0.0	0	0.0	130	0.3	140	0.3	0	0.0	0	0.0	670	1.3	0	0.0
0	0.0	1,600	0.9	0	0.0	0	0.0	810	0.5	650	0.4	0	0.0	0	0.0	2,900	1.7	0	0.0
0	0.0	0	0.0	0	0.0	0	0.0	9	0.1	0	0.0	0	0.0	0	0.0	0	0.0	0	0.0
220	0.2	3,700	3.4	0	0.0	0	0.0	1,600	1.5	570	0.5	0	0.0	0	0.0	2,000	1.8	0	0.0
0	0.0	0	0.0	0	0.0	0	0.0	59	0.1	0	0.0	0	0.0	0	0.0	0	0.0	0	0.0
0	0.0	0	0.0	0	0.0	0	0.0	6	0.0	0	0.0	0	0.0	0	0.0	0	0.0	0	0.0
400	0.2	0	0.0	0	0.0	0	0.0	66	0.0	0	0.0	0	0.0	0	0.0	0	0.0	0	0.0
50,000	0.2	311,000	1.1	0	0.0	0	0.0	25,519,000	93.0	15,000	0.1	0	0.0	52,700	0.2	0	0.0	0	0.0
432,000	3.5	0	0.0	0	0.0	0	0.0	11,285,000	90.8	960	0.0	0	0.0	0	0.0	0	0.0	0	0.0
1,500	0.0	0	0.0	0	0.0	3,000	0.0	542,000	7.0	1,900	0.0	0	0.0	0	0.0	0	0.0	0	0.0
0	0.0	460	0.5	35	0.0	0	0.0	740	0.9	0	0.0	0	0.0	0	0.0	0	0.0	17	0.0
1,207,000	20.6	3,000	0.1	0	0.0	0	0.0	3,793,000	64.6	1,300	0.0	0	0.0	0	0.0	0	0.0	0	0.0
1,100	0.0	267,000	5.2	0	0.0	970	0.0	763,000	15.0	76,100	1.5	1,200	0.0	22,300	0.4	0	0.0	250	0.0
0	0.0	0	0.0	0	0.0	2,500	0.0	520	0.0	0	0.0	0	0.0	0	0.0	0	0.0	0	0.0
0	0.0	0	0.0	0	0.0	200	0.0	49,200	2.4	0	0.0	0	0.0	0	0.0	0	0.0	0	0.0
17,200	3.2	0	0.0	0	0.0	0	0.0	1,700	0.3	0	0.0	0	0.0	0	0.0	0	0.0	0	0.0
6,800	0.1	5,200	0.1	0	0.0	0	0.0	9,308,000	99.8	0	0.0	0	0.0	0	0.0	0	0.0	0	0.0
3,562,000	7.1	1,196,000	2.4	2,000	0.0	81,800	0.2	865,000	1.7	17,800	0.0	0	0.0	10,600	0.0	2,300	0.0	0	0.0
7,062,000	14.7	2,200	0.0	0	0.0	0	0.0	70,600	0.1	6,853,000	14.2	28,900	0.1	1,200	0.0	0	0.0	0	0.0
3,550,000	32.9	220	0.0	0	0.0	0	0.0	667,000	6.2	0	0.0	0	0.0	0	0.0	0	0.0	0	0.0
0	0.0	0	0.0	0	0.0	58,100	0.1	1,070,000	2.3	0	0.0	0	0.0	1,400	0.0	0	0.0	0	0.0
1,000	0.0	2,722,000	13.0	0	0.0	0	0.0	1,783,000	8.5	1,000	0.0	170	0.0	3,100	0.0	0	0.0	2,500	0.0
925,000	2.8	650	0.0	0	0.0	2,000	0.0	29,718,000	90.7	0	0.0	0	0.0	0	0.0	0	0.0	0	0.0
11,000	2.1	107,000	20.4	1,400	0.3	960	0.2	83,300	15.9	4,200	0.8	0	0.0	0	0.0	15,900	3.0	0	0.0
118,000	9.9	1,800	0.2	0	0.0	0	0.0	7,700	0.7	0	0.0	0	0.0	0	0.0	0	0.0	0	0.0
9,400	0.1	12,700	0.1	0	0.0	17,000	0.2	340,000	3.6	17,000	0.2	0	0.0	0	0.0	20	0.0	0	0.0
0	0.0	23,700	0.3	0	0.0	18,400	0.2	344,000	4.5	3,200	0.0	0	0.0	0	0.0	0	0.0	0	0.0
0	0.0	0	0.0	0	0.0	100	0.0	18,934,000	92.8	0	0.0	0	0.0	0	0.0	0	0.0	110	0.0
59,000	0.3	0	0.0	0	0.0	190	0.0	90,000	0.4	1,567,000	6.7	0	0.0	0	0.0	0	0.0	0	0.0
6,600	0.1	0	0.0	0	0.0	1,100	0.0	6,576,000	95.6	0	0.0	0	0.0	0	0.0	0	0.0	2,500	0.0
5,312,000	11.8	388,000	0.9	9,800	0.0	290	0.0	14,179,000	31.6	0	0.0	0	0.0	13,500	0.0	0	0.0	140	0.0
1,559,000	2.3	67,300	0.1	0	0.0	93	0.0	4,061,000	5.9	16,500	0.0	420	0.0	56,000	0.1	0	0.0	0	0.0
113,000	10.1	340	0.0	0	0.0	0	0.0	39,900	3.6	510	0.0	0	0.0	0	0.0	0	0.0	0	0.0
2,042,000	33.9	0	0.0	0	0.0	0	0.0	1,106,000	18.4	3,100	0.1	0	0.0	0	0.0	0	0.0	0	0.0
0	0.0	0	0.0	0	0.0	0	0.0	0	0.0	0	0.0	0	0.0	0	0.0	0	0.0	0	0.0
5	0.0	100	0.1	0	0.0	0	0.0	0	0.0	0	0.0	0	0.0	0	0.0	0	0.0	0	0.0
0	0.0	326,000	24.3	0	0.0	630	0.0	86,400	6.4	1,700	0.1	0	0.0	0	0.0	19,300	1.4	0	0.0
0	0.0	0	0.0	0	0.0	1,900	0.0	10,430,000	99.5	0	0.0	0	0.0	0	0.0	0	0.0	0	0.0
11,600	0.0	0	0.0	0	0.0	23,600	0.0	71,513,000	98.3	129,000	0.2	0	0.0	0	0.0	0	0.0	0	0.0
840	0.0	0	0.0	0	0.0	3,200	0.1	4,774,000	94.7	630	0.0	0	0.0	0	0.0	0	0.0	0	0.0
0	0.0	0	0.0	0	0.0	0	0.0	10	0.1	0	0.0	0	0.0	0	0.0	1,000	2.7	0	0.0
765,000	2.3	269,000	0.8	3,100	0.0	3,300	0.0	3,916,000	11.7	0	0.0	0	0.0	1,700	0.0	0	0.0	0	0.0
6,400	0.0	4,800	0.0	0	0.0	177,000	0.4	744,000	1.6	100	0.0	0	0.0	8,000	0.0	0	0.0	0	0.0
0	0.0	492,000	6.6	0	0.0	0	0.0	5,780,000	76.9	3,800	0.1	0	0.0	18,000	0.2	0	0.0	0	0.0
22,600	0.0	662,000	1.1	18,000	0.0	291,000	0.5	2,086,000	3.4	61,100	0.1	0	0.0	412,000	0.7	75,500	0.1	4,800	0.0
1,085,000	0.3	1,445,000	0.5	85,400	0.0	5,122,000	1.7	4,696,000	1.5	1,625,000	0.5	62,700	0.0	279,000	0.1	225,000	0.1	17,600	0.0
0	0.0	460	0.4	0	0.0	350	0.3	120	0.1	0	0.0	0	0.0	0	0.0	0	0.0	0	0.0
34	0.0	0	0.0	0	0.0	41,300	1.2	500	0.0	1,900	0.1	0	0.0	0	0.0	4,700	0.1	0	0.0
55,700	0.2	730	0.0	0	0.0	54,400	0.2	25,759,000	93.9	130	0.0	0	0.0	0	0.0	0	0.0	1,000	0.0
10,800	4.5	0	0.0	0	0.0	0	0.0	0	0.0	110	0.0	0	0.0	0	0.0	0	0.0	0	0.0
214,000	0.7	0	0.0	0	0.0	56,800	0.2	95,300	0.3	1,200	0.0	0	0.0	0	0.0	305,000	1.1	0	0.0
9,104,000	10.4	52,500	0.1	0	0.0	0	0.0	157,000	0.2	9,705,000	11.0	180	0.0	0	0.0	0	0.0	0	0.0
160	1.2	0	0.0	0	0.0	0	0.0	0	0.0	0	0.0	0	0.0	0	0.0	0	0.0	0	0.0
0	0.0	0	0.0	0	0.0	0	0.0	527,000	99.4	0	0.0	0	0.0	0	0.0	0	0.0	0	0.0

(*continued*)

Country	Population 2010	Agnostics		Atheists		Baha'is		Buddhists		Chinese FR		Christians		Confucianists		Da
Yemen	24,053,000	19,400	0.1	4,800	0.0	1,300	0.0	130	0.0	0	0.0	41,400	0.2	0	0.0	0
Zambia	13,089,000	20,100	0.2	3,900	0.0	241,000	1.8	3,900	0.0	8,400	0.1	11,187,000	85.5	0	0.0	0
Zimbabwe	12,571,000	128,000	1.0	19,700	0.2	39,900	0.3	190	0.0	400	0.0	10,265,000	81.7	0	0.0	0
Africa	1,022,236,000	6,499,000	0.6	571,000	0.1	2,143,000	0.2	254,000	0.0	132,000	0.0	494,052,000	48.3	20,000	0.0	0
Asia	4,164,252,000	504,759,000	12.1	114,850,000	2.8	3,439,000	0.1	487,037,000	11.7	434,613,000	10.4	342,011,000	8.2	6,363,000	0.2	8,412,000
Europe	738,197,000	93,325,000	12.6	15,698,000	2.1	153,000	0.0	1,789,000	0.2	439,000	0.1	580,114,000	78.6	16,000	0.0	0
L America	590,082,000	18,713,000	3.2	2,900,000	0.5	898,000	0.2	759,000	0.1	189,000	0.0	544,687,000	92.3	0	0.0	0
N America	344,529,000	48,119,000	14.0	2,156,000	0.6	561,000	0.2	4,454,000	1.3	781,000	0.2	271,554,000	78.8	0	0.0	12,000
Oceania	36,593,000	5,529,000	15.1	477,000	1.3	111,000	0.3	587,000	1.6	103,000	0.3	28,019,000	76.6	49,000	0.1	5,000
Global Total	**6,895,889,000**	**676,943,000**	**9.8**	**136,653,000**	**2.0**	**7,305,000**	**0.1**	**494,880,000**	**7.2**	**436,257,000**	**6.3**	**2,260,436,000**	**32.8**	**6,448,000**	**0.1**	**8,429,000**

Ethnoreligionists		Hindus		Jains		Jews		Muslims		New Religionists		Shintoists		Sikhs		Spiritists		Zoroastrians	
0	0.0	152,000	0.6	260	0.0	12	0.0	23,832,000	99.1	0	0.0	0	0.0	130	0.0	0	0.0	1,200	0.0
1,465,000	11.2	17,800	0.1	0	0.0	1,700	0.0	139,000	1.1	0	0.0	0	0.0	0	0.0	0	0.0	0	0.0
1,994,000	15.9	18,700	0.1	0	0.0	11,700	0.1	92,100	0.7	1,600	0.0	0	0.0	0	0.0	570	0.0	0	0.0
9,354,000	8.7	2,930,000	0.3	94,000	0.0	132,000	0.0	425,863,000	41.7	116,000	0.0	0	0.0	73,000	0.0	3,000	0.0	1,000	0.0
6,778,000	3.5	941,480,000	22.6	5,099,000	0.1	6,029,000	0.1	1,078,855,000	25.9	58,971,000	1.4	2,691,000	0.1	22,688,000	0.5	2,000	0.0	167,000	0.0
1,168,000	0.2	1,052,000	0.1	19,000	0.0	1,919,000	0.3	41,490,000	5.6	364,000	0.0	0	0.0	502,000	0.1	144,000	0.0	6,000	0.0
3,625,000	0.6	764,000	0.1	1,000	0.0	962,000	0.2	1,526,000	0.3	1,740,000	0.3	8,000	0.0	7,000	0.0	13,303,000	2.3	0	0.0
1,221,000	0.4	1,835,000	0.5	100,000	0.0	5,602,000	1.6	5,492,000	1.6	1,710,000	0.5	63,000	0.0	607,000	0.2	242,000	0.1	21,000	0.0
369,000	1.0	513,000	1.4	3,000	0.0	117,000	0.3	549,000	1.5	104,000	0.3	0	0.0	50,000	0.1	8,000	0.0	3,000	0.0
2,517,000	3.5	948,575,000	13.8	5,316,000	0.1	14,762,000	0.2	1,553,775,000	22.5	63,005,000	0.9	2,761,000	0.0	23,927,000	0.3	13,701,000	0.2	197,000	0.0

Glossary

This glossary contains terms that are unusual, technical, or related to the scientific study of religion and religious demography. It is designed to offer brief, definitive definitions of all such terms, especially of those that occur throughout this volume.

adherents   Followers, supporters, members, believers, devotees of a religion.

adult   A person who is 15 years old or above.

affiliated   Followers of a religion enrolled and known to its leadership, usually with names written on rolls.

age-sex structure   The composition of a population by age, usually in five-year age groups of males and females; used by demographers in projecting population growth or decline.

agnostics   Persons who lack a religion or profess unbelief in a religion. The term includes (1) "classical" agnostics (who hold that it is impossible to know for certain whether God – or deity of any kind – exists); (2) those who profess uncertainty as to the existence of God; (3) other non-religious persons such as secularists and materialists and; (4) people who do not claim any religious affiliation but do not self-identify as atheists.

annual net migration   The difference between emigration from and immigration to a geographic area (e.g., a country) in a given year. Sometimes expressed as annual net migration rate (e.g., as a percentage or per 1,000 population).

apostasy   The renunciation or abandonment of one's previous religious profession of faith.

The World's Religions in Figures: An Introduction to International Religious Demography,
First Edition. Todd M. Johnson and Brian J. Grim.
© 2013 John Wiley & Sons, Ltd. Published 2013 by John Wiley & Sons, Ltd.

apostates   Former members of a religion who have renounced or forsaken their faith; backsliders, lapsed, disaffiliated.

atheists   Persons professing atheism, the belief that there is no supernatural higher power; atheists might sometimes but not necessarily be hostile or militantly opposed to all religion (anti-religious).

average   An arithmetical term derived by dividing the sum of a group of numbers by their total number; arithmetic mean.

baseline population   (1) The number of individuals in a given population (i.e., the population size) at the beginning of a period of interest, to which subsequent change may be compared or from which such change may be projected. The number itself may be either known or estimated/calculated; (2) The individuals who constitute the population described in (1).

believer   One who adheres to or professes a religious faith; religionist.

billion   1,000 millions (American usage; typical British, French, and German usage is 1 million millions).

biological change   Demographic change in the population of a country or body due to natural causes properly so called, i.e. the annual net aggregate of births to members of the body minus deaths in it.

birthrate   The number of births per year in a population, expressed as a percentage or permillage of the total population.

census   A term used here solely for an official government population count or survey, usually with complete (100%) enumeration of the whole population.

census schedule   A form or questionnaire used for collection of information in a census.

children   Term describing all persons under 15 years old, though often a distinction is made between infants (0–4 years old) and children proper (5–14 years old).

church growth   The study of the growth of Christian churches is usually divided into (1) quantitative (numerical) growth; and (2) qualitative growth, the latter including organic and spiritual growth as well as other less tangible aspects.

church members   Affiliated Christians.

coding   Converting qualitative data into numeric data to facilitate analysis; for example, assigning survey answers values of 1 for "yes" and 0 for "no," or classifying age ranges as "0–14" = 1, "15–24" = 2, "25–34" = 3, etc.

cohort   A group having some statistical parameter(s) in common, especially a group defined by age and sex, such as males ages 15–19 or females ages 15–19.

cohort-component method   A method for projecting future population size by applying age- and sex-specific factors for fertility, mortality, and migration to each cohort in a baseline population.

compound annual growth rate Growth rate that takes into account that the population base for each year includes growth from the previous year.

confession (1) A creed, or statement of belief or doctrine; (2) in ecclesiastical demography, any large communion; (3) ecclesiastical tradition tracing its origins to a formal event, historic creed, or confession.

congregation (1) A local church or grouping of worshipers; (2) a religious order, society, or institute (mainly Roman Catholic usage).

continent Any of the United Nations major areas of Africa, Asia, Europe, Latin America, and Oceania, along with the United Nations region of Northern America.

conversion The change to or from one belief, faith, or religion to another (or to or from no religion).

conversion from Individuals who have left a religion or religious body either to other religions or religious bodies or to no religion (agnosticism, atheism).

conversion to Individuals who have joined a religion or religious body either from other religions or religious bodies or from no religion (agnosticism, atheism).

country of origin For both immigrant and native born, the country where individuals locate their family ancestry.

country population The total present-in-area resident population of a country at a given date.

cross-national survey A survey conducted in more than one country with the aim of having results that can be compared between countries.

crude birth rate The number of childbirths per year per 1,000 people.

crude death rate The total number of deaths per year per 1,000 people.

de facto population The actual population, enumerated population, or present-in-area population, i.e., physically present whether residents or non-residents, based on exactly where people have slept or spent the night; made up of all persons actually in the area on a particular day or census date, covering residents, non-residents, visitors, and transients, but excluding residents temporarily absent.

death rate The number of deaths per year in a population expressed as a percentage or per 1,000 of the total population.

demographic increase An increase in the size of a population when the sum of natural increase and migration balances is positive (e.g., births outnumber deaths and/or immigrants outnumber emigrants).

demographic time series The values of a demographic variable over a period of time.

demography The scientific and statistical study of human populations, primarily with respect to their size, age-sex structure, density, growth, distribution, development, migration, and vital statistics.

denomination An organized Christian church, tradition, religious group, community of believers, aggregate of worship centers or congregations, usually within a specific country, whose component congregations and members are called by the same name in different areas.

diaspora A people of one country dispersed into other countries; the migration, spread, scattering, exile of a people abroad.

disaffiliated One-time members of a religion who later repudiate that membership, and, in countries allowing it, obtain legal separation from their religion.

double-blind coding In this volume, the assignment of numeric values to a set of qualitative data by two or more individuals who work independently, without seeing each other's ratings. *See also* coding.

doubly affiliated Christians Persons affiliated to or claimed by two denominations at once.

emigrant A person who leaves a country or region to establish permanent residence elsewhere.

emigration The movement of emigrants *from* one country *to* another. *See also* immigration.

émigré A person forced to emigrate by political or other circumstances beyond his or her control.

ethnic Referring to a group distinguished by common cultural characteristics.

ethnolinguistic people A distinct homogeneous ethnic or racial group within a single country speaking its own language (one single mother tongue).

expatriate Strictly speaking, any person who has citizenship in one country but resides or lives in another country. In general usage, expatriate frequently connotes (1) temporary, often short-term, residence in the foreign country; and (2) higher socio-economic status, with those of lower socio-economic status being termed, e.g., "migrants."

family income, average The total income of an average family or household in an area, computed by multiplying per capita income by average household size.

fertility Capacity for reproducing, actual reproductive capacity, or birthrate of a population.

field survey An inquiry or survey in which information is obtained by personal interview. Field surveys include interviews of experts and individuals who may or may not be randomly selected, but chosen because of their knowledge of a more general situation or because they typify certain characteristics of interest.

future studies Research studies on the probable future development of a situation, involving the producing of alternative futures or possible scenarios.

general census A population census in which all inhabitants of a country are counted simultaneously.

general population survey   A type of survey or public opinion poll in which data are collected from a representative sample of a given population based on a probability sample. *See also* probability sampling.

geography of religion   The description and analysis of religious phenomena in terms of the science of geography (spatial variations in human and physical phenomena).

Government Restrictions Index (GRI)   A measure of the extent to which governments – including at the local or provincial level – attempt to restrict religious practices or beliefs. The GRI is based on 20 questions used by the Pew Forum on Religion and Public Life to gauge the extent to which governments try, both directly and indirectly, to control religious groups or individuals, prohibit conversions from one faith to another, limit preaching or proselytizing, or otherwise hinder religious affiliation by means such as registration requirements and fines.

government statistics of religion   Figures of adherents of religions promulgated by governments, usually derived from government censuses of population.

gross domestic product (GDP)   The total value of the finished goods and services produced *in a nation* – irrespective of the nationality of the entity (person, corporation, etc.) doing the producing – during a specific period (usually a year), and also comprising the total of expenditures by consumers and government; gross private investment; and exports from the country itself minus imports to the country itself.

gross national product (GNP)   For any given country, the total value of the goods and services produced by nationals (its citizens, corporations owned by its citizens, etc.) – irrespective of their physical location (i.e., both foreign and domestic) – during a specific period (usually a year), and also comprising the total of expenditures by national consumers and government plus gross national private investment. GNP is equal to Gross Domestic Product, plus any income earned by nationals from investments or production in other countries, minus income earned within the domestic economy by nationals of other countries.

gross national product per capita   National income per person.

growth rate   The annual increase in a population, measured as a percentage per year.

Herfindahl Index (Herfindahl-Hirschman Index, HHI)   A measure of the concentration of competitors within a market or industry, calculated as the sum of the square of the market share (expressed as a fraction) of each competitor; higher values reflect less competition. The maximum possible value of the HHI is 1 (when a monopoly exists). The minimum possible value for any given situation is $1/n$ (where n is the number of competitors) and occurs when each competitor has an equal market share.

household size, average   The average size of a household in a country or area, i.e., the number of persons sharing the same unit, whether private, collective, or institutional. Household size is slightly larger than average family size because it includes servants, maids, and lodgers, as well as nursing homes, dormitories, military barracks, and other institutions where people live.

immigrant   A person who enters a country or region from elsewhere in order to establish permanent residence there.

immigrant religion   A religion absent from a country until brought in by recent immigrants.

immigration   The movement of immigrants *to* one country *from* another. *See also* emigration.

income, average   National income per person.

index   An indicator, sign, or measure that indicates value or quantity. Good indexes must be valid representations of the concept being measured and be reliably replicated, i.e., different observers attempting to apply the set of indicators will obtain the same result.

indicator   A measure of a general concept. Multiple indicators are sometimes combined to obtain a single index.

indigenous   Originating or developing or produced naturally in a particular land or region or environment; not introduced directly or indirectly from the outside.

infants   Those under 5 years old, or the preschool population, including newborn babies (although the term is often restricted to children who have not reached their first birthday).

International Religious Demography Data Quality Index   A measure of the degree to which a source of religious demographic data for a country (such as a census or survey) accurately represents the country's religious composition; a higher score indicates greater accuracy. This index includes four components: geographic representation, response rate, sampling quality, and questionnaire design.

internationals   (1) Persons living abroad; workers, laborers, businessmen, entrepreneurs, students, and many other categories of persons who live, reside, and work in a foreign country; excluding tourists or other transients. *See also* expatriate; (2) professionals working for United Nations-related agencies or parallel global organizations (as contrasted with national or regional bodies).

inter-rater reliability   The degree to which coding done by multiple individuals agrees. A low degree of inter-rater reliability indicates that either (1) the coding scale is defective; or (2) the coders need additional training in how to apply it.

inter-religious   Existing between two or more religions; used of activities or relationships between two or more of the major world religions (Judaism, Islam, Hinduism, Christianity, Buddhism).

life expectancy   The expected number of years of life of individuals in a population, based on statistical probability. Life expectancy at birth is the average number of years a newborn would be expected to live if health and living conditions at the time of his/ her birth remained the same throughout his/her life.

literacy   The ability to read and write, as measured by the percentage of the adult population who can read and write their own names and a simple statement. A higher level of competence is required for functional literacy.

mail survey   A postal survey.

major area   United Nations term used in statistical enumerations instead of the looser "continent."

major civil division   United Nations term for the next level of administrative or political subdivision in a country immediately below the nationwide level.

margin of error   A measure of the uncertainty in a survey result due to random sampling errors. Larger sample sizes give rise to smaller margins of error.

maternal mortality rate   The annual number of deaths of women from pregnancy-related causes per 100,000 live births.

measure   (noun) A parameter; a means for quantifying, qualifying, or evaluating data. *See also* indicator.

members   Affiliated (which usually means enrolled with names recorded) adherents of a religion.

metadata   Information about data and how they were collected (such as the date, time, place, and method of collection).

migration   Geographical or spatial mobility; physical movement by humans from one area to another with the declared intention to reside in or leave a country for at least a year.

multivariate analysis   A statistical technique for analyzing the individual contributions that two or more related variables make simultaneously to a given outcome (e.g., the effect of age, gender, and nationality on religious adherence).

multiple religious belonging (double belonging)   Professed adherence to more than one religion (e.g., Judaism and Buddhism) simultaneously.

Muslim-majority country   A country in which the majority of the population (> 50%) are Muslims. This term can also be used to describe other religious populations, such as a Buddhist-majority country.

mutually exclusive categories   A typology or series of categories each not admitting of another in its coverage.

native   An individual born or raised in the territory in which he lives.

natural change   Demographic change as experienced by the whole population of a country or area including all its religious bodies, composed of biological change together with migration change.

natural growth rate   The net sum of crude birthrate in the population minus crude death rate, plus net immigration rate.

natural increase In United Nations usage, biological change or the excess of births over deaths in a population.

naturalization The process by which aliens acquire the nationality of their country of residence.

naturalized persons Former aliens who have now become citizens.

non-Muslim-majority country A country in which the majority of the population are non-Muslims. This term can also be used to describe other religious populations, such as a non-Buddhist-majority country.

non-religious (unaffiliated) Persons professing no religion, or professing unbelief or non-belief, non-believers, agnostics, freethinkers, liberal thinkers, non-religious humanists, indifference to both religion and atheism, opposed on principle neither to religion nor to atheism; sometimes termed secularists or materialists.

old-age population Persons over 65 years old.

organized religion A religion as formally organized by subdivisions, schools, sects, denominations, or other bodies or groupings requiring membership.

oversampling In surveying, selecting more members of a subgroup for participation than would be done if everyone in the sample population had an equal chance of being selected. Oversampling increases the reliability of data on small subgroups by decreasing the associated margins of sampling error (*see* margin of error) for the subgroups.

p.a. Per annum, per year, each year, every year, annual, yearly, over the previous 12 months.

p.d. Per diem, per day, daily.

people, people group A grouping of individuals who perceive themselves to have a common affinity for one another because of their shared language, religion, ethnicity, residence, occupation, class, or caste situation, or combination of these.

per capita Per head, per person usually used of some national attribute (GNP, etc.) divided by the total population (men, women, children, and infants).

poll An opinion inquiry taken at a single point in time, from a very small carefully constructed sample (usually around 1,500–2,500 adults) representative of the entire adult population, to solicit answers to carefully formulated questions, in order to derive information applicable to that entire population.

population For an area, the total of all inhabitants or residents of that area; or occasionally, the total number of persons who spend or spent the night in the area.

population census A government survey to obtain information about the state of the population at a given time.

population density The average population to 1 square mile or kilometer.

population parameter Any numerical value that characterizes an attribute of a population.

population projections Calculations showing the future development of a population based on certain assumptions and present trends.

postal survey An inquiry sending survey questionnaires by mail.

primary source A document, recording, or other source that presents the first-hand results of original observations, such as experiments, surveys, or eyewitness accounts of historical events. While sometimes present to a limited degree in primary sources, analysis, contextualization, and commentary are usually the province of secondary sources. Examples of primary sources include published results of research, government documents (such as censuses), surveys, correspondence, proceedings, and diaries.

probability sampling A method of sampling that utilizes some form of random selection in which the different units of the population being surveyed have equal probabilities of being chosen.

projection The carrying forward of a present trend into the future; an estimate of future possibilities based on the current situation and past trends.

pull factor A factor that attracts a person to a new place, such as increased economic opportunity; increased political or religious freedom; or availability of material resources.

purchasing power parity (PPP) The amount of money needed to purchase the same set of goods and services in two different countries. PPP is useful in comparing quantities such as Gross Domestic Product (GDP). For example, if the value of Country A's currency falls relative to that of Country B, Country A's GDP as measured in Country B's currency will fall as well, although Country A's GDP as measured in its own currency (as well as the standard of living of Country A's citizens) might remain relatively unchanged.

push factor An inducement to leave a particular place, such as decreased economic opportunity; decreased political or religious freedom; or lack of material resources.

qualitative analysis Analysis of (human) phenomena using non-statistical methods, such as case studies.

quality of life The effectiveness of social services in a country, measured by indexes such as the United Nations' Human Development Index (HDI).

quantification Measuring an item's quantity or number, or transforming qualitative data into quantitative through surveys or coding.

quantitative analysis Statistical analysis of (human) phenomena that can be counted or measured with numbers.

refugees Persons who have migrated due to strong pressures endangering their continued stay in their countries of origin, and who are unable or unwilling to return; excluding labor and other migrants and also returnees.

region In United Nations terminology, one of 21 areas into which the whole world is divided for purposes of analysis.

religion An organized group of committed individuals that adhere to and propagate a specific interpretation of explanations of existence based on supernatural assumptions through statements about the nature and workings of the supernatural and about ultimate meaning. In this volume, religion as used in a demographic sense includes the unaffiliated (i.e., agnostics and atheists).

religionists Persons professing adherence to any religion, as contrasted with the unaffiliated (i.e., agnostics or atheists).

religious change Changes from one religion or religious system to another within a certain time period, e.g., in the course of a year.

religious demography The scientific and statistical study of the demographic characteristics of religious populations, primarily with respect to their size, age–sex structure, density, growth, distribution, development, migration, and vital statistics, including the change of religious identity within human populations and how these characteristics relate to other social and economic indicators.

religious diversity The degree to which a population comprises individuals with differing religious adherences. Inter-religious diversity describes the degree of overall diversity of distinct religions (Islam, Hinduism, Judaism, and so on) within a population or geographic area, whereas intra-religious diversity encompasses the diversity found within a given world religion (for example, traditions such as Roman Catholicism, Orthodoxy, and Protestantism within Christianity).

Religious Diversity Index (RDI) A measure of the inter-religious diversity (*see also* religious diversity) of a particular country's or region's population using a scale from 0 (no diversity) to 1 (most diverse). The RDI is calculated as $1 - [(\rho - 1/N) / (1 - 1/N)]$, where $\rho = [(r_1/100)^2 + (r_2/100)^2 + ... + (r_N/100)^2]$ and $r_1, r_2, ... r_N$ represent the percentages of a country's total population that profess adherence to each of N different religions. Each r_i value is divided by 100 to change it from a percentage to a fraction. Thus, when a population exhibits the maximum possible religious diversity (each religion claims an equal percentage of adherents), then $r_i = 100/N$ for each religion, $\rho = 1/N$ and RDI = 1. Conversely, if there is no religious diversity (that is, 100% of a country's population adheres to a single religion), then $r_1 = 100$, all other r_i values = 0, $\rho = 1$, and RDI = 0.

religious liberty Freedom to practice one's religion with the full range of religious rights specified in the United Nations' 1948 Universal Declaration of Human Rights.

religious pluralism The peaceful co-existence of completely different religions or denominations within a particular community.

religious toleration The attitude of tolerance and acceptance, on the part of a state or a majority religion or religious tradition, toward religious minorities.

replacement fertility rate The number of children each woman in a specified area must bear in her lifetime to maintain the population of the area at its current level. Although theoretically this is approximately 2.0, the replacement level varies depending on mortality rates and sex ratios at birth. In countries with a normal sex ratio at birth and relatively low infant and child mortality, a fertility rate of about 2.1 children per woman is sufficient to replenish the population. In some developing countries with high infant and child mortality, the replacement fertility rate is substantially greater than 2.1 children per woman.

representative sample   A subset of a statistical population that accurately reflects the members of the entire population.

resident   One who lives in a certain place, sometimes temporarily or for a short duration. In some uses, it is distinguished from an inhabitant, which implies permanent or long-term habitation.

respondent   A person who answers questions in a survey or government census, in the latter case usually under a legal obligation to answer.

response rate   The number of eligible sample units that cooperate in a survey, often expressed as the ratio of the number of completed questionnaires, surveys, or interviews received or achieved to the total number of eligible participants contacted; generally expressed as a percentage.

returnee   An alien of long residence who is deported and forcibly repatriated to the country of his or her citizenship.

rolls   Written lists with names of members of religious groups of all varieties.

rural area   De facto areas classified as rural (that is, it is the difference between the total population of a country and its urban population); defined in many countries as an administrative district with a population of under 2,000.

sample, sampling   A small segment or quantity taken as evidence of the quality or character of the whole; a very small part of the population used for purposes of investigation and comparing properties.

scenario   A tool for studying the future: a series of events that we imagine happening in the future. For instance, population projections are what-if scenarios that aim to provide information about the likely future size and structure of the population.

schedule   *See* census schedule.

school-age children, school-age population   Those persons in the population who are 5–14 years old.

secondary source   A document, recording, or other source that does not present original data but rather reviews, discusses, analyzes, or interprets data obtained from a primary source. Examples of secondary sources include textbooks, encyclopedias, and review articles. Secondary survey data analysis is the statistical analysis of survey data collected by an organization or someone other than the analyst and his or her organization.

secular states   Nations and countries that regard themselves as secular, promoting neither religion nor irreligion, and maintaining strict separation between church and state.

secularism   A view of life or of any particular matter holding that religion and religious considerations should be ignored or purposely excluded.

secularization   The act or process of transferring matters under ecclesiastical or religious control to secular or civil or lay control; the process whereby religious thinking, practice, and institutions lose social significance.

self-enumeration   A census or survey method in which the questionnaire employed is completed by the respondents themselves.

sex structure   The composition of a population by gender, often measured using the sex ratio (the number of males per 100 females in a population). Sex structure is used by demographers in projecting population growth or decline.

Social Hostilities Index (SHI)   A measure of concrete, hostile actions that effectively hinder the religious activities of the targeted individuals or groups. The SHI is based on 13 questions used by the Pew Forum on Religion and Public Life to gauge hostilities both between and within religious groups, including mob or sectarian violence, crimes motivated by religious bias, physical conflict over conversions, harassment over attire for religious reasons, and other religion-related intimidation and violence, including terrorism and war.

socio-economic status (SES)   A measure of an individual's or group's position in society, based on factors including income, education, and occupation. Sometimes other factors – such as wealth, place of residence, race, ethnicity, and religion – are also used in determining SES.

sociology of religion   The study of religion from the standpoint of the science of society, social institutions, and social relationships.

SPSS   Computer software used for the analysis, management, and documentation of statistical data. Originally called Statistical Package for the Social Sciences; it is now a product of IBM.

standard deviation (σ)   A measure of how dispersed data are from their mean value. Standard deviation is the square root of the variance, where (1) variance for a population equals the sum of the differences between the mean and each value in the population divided by the number of values in the population; and (2) variance for a sample equals the sum of the differences between the mean and each value in the sample divided by one less than the number of values in the sample.

state religion   An established religion, national religion recognized in law as the official religion of a country.

structural equation modeling   A statistical technique for determining the degree of consistency between data on a set of variables and hypotheses that explain the interrelationships among the variables. It is used for testing and estimating causal relations using a combination of statistical data and qualitative causal assumptions.

survey   A systematic method for gathering information from (a sample of) entities for the purposes of constructing quantitative descriptors of the larger population of which the entities are members.

switching, religious   When individuals leave a religion or religious body either to other religions or religious bodies or to no religion (agnosticism, atheism).

time series   The values of a variable over a period of time.

total fertility rate (TFR)   For a specified geographical area (e.g., country) and time period (e.g., calendar year), the theoretical number of children a woman would bear during her complete reproductive lifetime (specified as, e.g., ages 15–44, 15–49, 10–44, or 10–49) if the exact age-specific fertility rates (ASFRs) for the specified time period applied to her throughout her reproductive lifetime. The TFR is obtained by summing the single-year ASFRs for the specified area and time period.

two-step question   A type of survey question consisting of two parts, in which the second part (or, sometimes, whether there is a second part) depends on the respondent's answer to the first part. "Are you religious? If yes, what is your religion?" is a two-part question (also called an indirect question). The analogous one-step (direct) question is "What is your religion?"

unaffiliated Christians   Persons identifying as Christians but who are not affiliated with a church.

urban areas   De facto population living in areas classified as urban according to the criteria used by each area or country; often these are agglomerations of 2,500 or more inhabitants, generally having population densities of 1,000 persons per square mile (391 persons per square kilometer).

urbanization   The state or extent of urban areas or the process of becoming urbanized, in a particular country.

variable   A quantity that changes or varies in size; dependent variable, independent variable, etc. In statistical analyses, measures such as indicators, indexes, and responses to survey and census questions can all be referred to as variables.

vital statistics   Registration statistics of births, deaths, marriages, divorces, etc.

weight   In statistics, (1) the relative importance of a value within the data set to which it belongs; (2) a factor assigned to a value in a data set to reflect that value's importance in the set (especially in a computation, such as counting more heavily people interviewed in a survey if they represent a certain demographic that is underrepresented in those who complete a survey according to census parameters); (3) to assign such factors to the values in a set. Data so manipulated, and computations performed on such data, are described as weighted (e.g., "weighted average" of a region is the average weighted by the population of each country in the region).

worldview   A general understanding of the nature of the universe and of one's place in it; outlook on the world, ideology, a cosmological conception of society and institutions.

yearbooks, denominational   Christian or church yearbooks, handbooks, directories, periodical lists, and other listings significant at national, international, denomination and confessional levels; number over 5,000.

youth bulge (1) A demographic state that is defined variously as (a) one in which the size of the population in prime childbearing years (typically ages 15–24 or 15–29) is increasing more rapidly than that of any other age range; (b) one in which the population in prime childbearing years is larger in size than that of any other age range; or (c) either of the preceding scenarios in which the "youth" age range includes everyone under a given age (e.g., ages 0–24 or 0–29). Strictly speaking, however, the youth "bulge" is apparent only under the first two scenarios; (2) the youth population itself according to any of the scenarios described in definition (1).

Index